Lecture Notes of the Institute for Computer Sciences, Social Informatics and Telecommunications Engineering 563

The LNICST series publishes ICST's conferences, symposia and workshops.

LNICST reports state-of-the-art results in areas related to the scope of the Institute. The type of material published includes

- Proceedings (published in time for the respective event)
- Other edited monographs (such as project reports or invited volumes)

LNICST topics span the following areas:

- General Computer Science
- E-Economy
- E-Medicine
- Knowledge Management
- Multimedia
- Operations, Management and Policy
- Social Informatics
- Systems

Honghao Gao · Xinheng Wang · Nikolaos Voros
Editors

Collaborative Computing: Networking, Applications and Worksharing

19th EAI International Conference, CollaborateCom 2023
Corfu Island, Greece, October 4–6, 2023
Proceedings, Part III

Springer

Editors
Honghao Gao
Shanghai University
Shanghai, China

Xinheng Wang
Xi'an Jiaotong-Liverpool
Suzhou, China

Nikolaos Voros
University of Peloponnese
Patra, Greece

ISSN 1867-8211 ISSN 1867-822X (electronic)
Lecture Notes of the Institute for Computer Sciences, Social Informatics
and Telecommunications Engineering
ISBN 978-3-031-54530-6 ISBN 978-3-031-54531-3 (eBook)
https://doi.org/10.1007/978-3-031-54531-3

This Springer imprint is published by the registered company Springer Nature Switzerland AG
The registered company address is: Gewerbestrasse 11, 6330 Cham, Switzerland

Paper in this product is recyclable.

Preface

We are delighted to introduce the proceedings of the 19th European Alliance for Innovation (EAI) International Conference on Collaborative Computing: Networking, Applications and Worksharing (CollaborateCom 2023). This conference brought together researchers, developers and practitioners around the world who are interested in fully realizing the promises of electronic collaboration from the aspects of networking, technology and systems, user interfaces and interaction paradigms, and interoperation with application-specific components and tools.

This year's conference accepted 72 submissions. Each submission was reviewed by an average of 3 reviewers. The conference sessions were: Day 1 Session 1 – Collaborative Computing; Session 2 – Edge Computing & Collaborative Working; Session 3 – Blockchain Application; Session 4 – Code Search and Completion; Session 5 – Edge Computing Scheduling and Offloading; Session 6 – Deep Learning and Application; Session 7 – Graph Computing; Session 8 – Security and Privacy Protection; Session 9 – Processing and Recognition; Session 10 – Deep Learning and Application; Session 11 – Onsite Session. Day 2 Session 12 – Federated Learning and Application; Session 13 – Collaborative Working; Session 14 – Edge Computing; Session 15 – Security and Privacy Protection; Session 16 – Prediction, Optimization and Applications. Apart from high-quality technical paper presentations, the technical program also featured two keynote speeches that were delivered by Christos Masouros from University College London and Michael Hübner from Brandenburgische Technische Universität (BTU).

Coordination with the steering chair, Xinheng Wang, and steering members Song Guo, Bo Li, Xiaofei Liao, Honghao Gao, and Ning Gu was essential for the success of the conference. We sincerely appreciate their constant support and guidance. It was also a great pleasure to work with such an excellent organizing committee team for their hard work in organizing and supporting the conference. In particular, the Technical Program Committee, led by our General Chairs Nikolaos Voros and General Co-Chairs Tasos Dagiuklas, Xinheng Wang, and Honghao Gao, TPC Chairs Christos Antonopoulos, and Eleni Christopoulou, and TPC Co-Chair Dimitrios Ringas completed the peer-review process of technical papers and made a high-quality technical program. We are also grateful to the Conference Manager, Karolina Marcinova, for her support and to all the authors who submitted their papers to the CollaborateCom 2023 conference.

We strongly believe that CollaborateCom provides a good forum for all researchers, developers and practitioners to discuss all science and technology aspects that are relevant to collaborative computing. We also expect that the future CollaborateCom conferences will be as successful and stimulating, as indicated by the contributions presented in this volume.

Honghao Gao

Xinheng Wang

Nikolaos Voros

Conference Organization

Steering Committee

Chair

Xinheng Wang   Xi'an Jiaotong-Liverpool University

Members

Bo Li   Hong Kong University of Science and
                                  Technology, China
Honghao Gao   Shanghai University, China
Ning Gu   Fudan University, China
Song Guo   University of Aizu, Japan
Xiaofei Liao   Huazhong University of Science and Technology,
                                  China

Organizing Committee

General Chair

Nikolaos Voros   University of the Peloponnese, Greece

General Co-chairs

Tasos Dagiuklas   London South Bank University, UK
Xinheng Wang   Xi'an Jiaotong-Liverpool University, China
Honghao Gao   Shanghai University, China

TPC Chair and Co-chairs

Christos Antonopoulos   University of the Peloponnese, Greece
Eleni Christopoulou   Ionian University, Greece
Dimitrios Ringas   Ionian University, Greece

Sponsorship and Exhibit Chair

Christina Politi   University of the Peloponnese, Greece

Local Chair

Eleni Christopoulou   Ionian University, Greece

Workshops Chair

Georgios Keramidas   Aristotle University of Thessaloniki, Greece

Publicity and Social Media Chair

Katerina Lamprakopoulou   University of the Peloponnese, Greece

Publications Chair

Christos Antonopoulos   University of the Peloponnese, Greece

Web Chair

Evi Faliagka   University of the Peloponnese, Greece

Technical Program Committee

Zhongqin Bi	Shanghai University of Electric Power, China
Shizhan Chen	Tianjing University, China
Lizhen Cui	Shandong University, China
Weilong Ding	North China University of Technology, China
Yucong Duan	Hainan University, China
Honghao Gao	Shanghai University, China
Fan Guisheng	East China University of Science and Technology, China
Haiping Huang	Nanjing University of Posts and Telecommunications, China
Li Kuang	Central South University, China
Youhuizi Li	Hangzhou Dianzi University, China
Rui Li	Xidian University, China
Xuan Liu	Yangzhou University, China

Tong Liu	Shanghai University, China
Xiaobing Sun	Yangzhou University, China
Haiyan Wang	Nanjing University of Posts & Telecommunications, China
Xinheng Wang	Xi'an Jiaotong-Liverpool University, China
Xiaoxian Yang	Shanghai Polytechnic University, China
Yuyu Yin	Hangzhou Dianzi University, China
Jun Zeng	Chongqing University, China
Zijian Zhang	Beijing Institute of Technology, China

Contents – Part III

Onsite Session Day 2

Multi-agent Reinforcement Learning Based Collaborative Multi-task
Scheduling for Vehicular Edge Computing 3
    Peisong Li, Ziren Xiao, Xinheng Wang, Kaizhu Huang, Yi Huang,
    and Andrei Tchernykh

A Novel Topology Metric for Indoor Point Cloud SLAM Based on Plane
Detection Optimization 23
    Zhenchao Ouyang, Jiahe Cui, Yunxiang He, Dongyu Li, Qinglei Hu,
    and Changjie Zhang

On the Performance of Federated Learning Network 41
    Godwin Idoje, Tasos Dagiuklas, and Muddesar Iqbal

Federated Learning and Application

FedECCR: Federated Learning Method with Encoding Comparison
and Classification Rectification 59
    Yan Zeng, Hui Zheng, Xin Wang, Beibei Zhang, Mingyao Zhou,
    Jilin Zhang, and YongJian Ren

CSA_FedVeh: Cluster-Based Semi-asynchronous Federated Learning
Framework for Internet of Vehicles 79
    Dun Cao, Jiasi Xiong, Nanfang Lei, Robert Simon Sherratt, and Jin Wang

Efficiently Detecting Anomalies in IoT: A Novel Multi-Task Federated
Learning Method 100
    Junfeng Hao, Juan Chen, Peng Chen, Yang Wang, Xianhua Niu, Lei Xu,
    and Yunni Xia

A Novel Deep Federated Learning-Based and Profit-Driven Service
Caching Method 118
    Zhaobin Ouyang, Yunni Xia, Qinglan Peng, Yin Li, Peng Chen,
    and Xu Wang

A Multi-behavior Recommendation Algorithm Based on Personalized
Federated Learning 134
    Zhongqin Bi, Yutang Duan, Weina Zhang, and Meijing Shan

FederatedMesh: Collaborative Federated Learning for Medical Data
Sharing in Mesh Networks 154
   Lamir Shkurti, Mennan Selimi, and Adrian Besimi

Collaborative Working

Enhance Broadcasting Throughput by Associating Network Coding
with UAVs Relays Deployment in Emergency Communications 173
   Chaonong Xu and Yujie Jiang

Dynamic Target User Selection Model for Market Promotion with Multiple
Stakeholders 191
   Linxin Guo, Shiqi Wang, Min Gao, and Chongming Gao

Collaborative Decision-Making Processes Analysis of Service Ecosystem:
A Case Study of Academic Ecosystem Involution 208
   Xiangpei Yan, Xiao Xue, Chao Peng, Donghua Liu, Zhiyong Feng,
   and Wang Xiao

Operationalizing the Use of Sensor Data in Mobile Crowdsensing:
A Systematic Review and Practical Guidelines 229
   Robin Kraft, Maximilian Blasi, Marc Schickler, Manfred Reichert,
   and Rüdiger Pryss

Enriching Process Models with Relevant Process Details for Flexible
Human-Robot Teaming 249
   Myriel Fichtner, Sascha Sucker, Dominik Riedelbauch,
   Stefan Jablonski, and Dominik Henrich

Edge Computing

Joint Optimization of PAoI and Queue Backlog with Energy Constraints
in LoRa Gateway Systems 273
   Lei Shi, Rui Ji, Zhen Wei, Shilong Feng, and Zhehao Li

Enhancing Session-Based Recommendation with Multi-granularity User
Interest-Aware Graph Neural Networks 291
   Cairong Yan, Yiwei Zhang, Xiangyang Feng, and Yanglan Gan

Delay-Constrained Multicast Throughput Maximization in MEC Networks
for High-Speed Railways 308
   Junyi Xu, Zhenchun Wei, Xiaohui Yuan, Zengwei Lyu, Lin Feng,
   and Jianghong Han

An Evolving Transformer Network Based on Hybrid Dilated Convolution
for Traffic Flow Prediction   329
    Qi Yu, Weilong Ding, Maoxiang Sun, and Jihai Huang

Prediction, Optimization and Applications

DualDNSMiner: A Dual-Stack Resolver Discovery Method Based
on Alias Resolution   347
    Dingkang Han, Yujia Zhu, Liang Jiao, Dikai Mo, Yong Sun,
    Yuedong Zhang, and Qingyun Liu

DT-MUSA: Dual Transfer Driven Multi-source Domain Adaptation
for WEEE Reverse Logistics Return Prediction   365
    Ruiqi Liu, Min Gao, Yujiang Wu, Jie Zeng, Jia Zhang, and Jinyong Gao

A Synchronous Parallel Method with Parameters Communication
Prediction for Distributed Machine Learning   385
    Yanguo Zeng, Meiting Xue, Peiran Xu, Yukun Shi, Kaisheng Zeng,
    Jilin Zhang, and Lupeng Yue

Author Index   405

Onsite Session Day 2

Multi-agent Reinforcement Learning Based Collaborative Multi-task Scheduling for Vehicular Edge Computing

Peisong Li[1], Ziren Xiao[1], Xinheng Wang[1]([✉]), Kaizhu Huang[2], Yi Huang[3], and Andrei Tchernykh[4]

[1] School of Advanced Technology, Xi'an Jiaotong-Liverpool University, Suzhou 215123, China
{peisong.li20,ziren.xiao20}@student.xjtlu.edu.cn,
xinheng.wang@xjtlu.edu.cn
[2] Data Science Research Center and Division of Natural and Applied Sciences, Duke Kunshan University, Suzhou 215316, China
kaizhu.huang@dukekunshan.edu.cn
[3] Department of Electrical Engineering and Electronics, University of Liverpool, Liverpool L69 3BX, UK
yi.huang@liverpool.ac.uk
[4] CICESE Research Center, carr. Tijuana-Ensenada 3918, 22860 Ensenada, BC, Mexico
chernykh@cicese.mx

Abstract. Nowadays, connected vehicles equipped with advanced computing and communication capabilities are increasingly viewed as mobile computing platforms capable of offering various in-vehicle services, including but not limited to autonomous driving, collision avoidance, and parking assistance. However, providing these time-sensitive services requires the fusion of multi-task processing results from multiple sensors in connected vehicles, which poses a significant challenge to designing an effective task scheduling strategy that can minimize service requests' completion time and reduce vehicles' energy consumption. In this paper, a multi-agent reinforcement learning-based collaborative multi-task scheduling method is proposed to achieve a joint optimization on completion time and energy consumption. Firstly, the reinforcement learning-based scheduling method can allocate multiple tasks dynamically according to the dynamic-changing environment. Then, a cloud-edge-end collaboration scheme is designed to complete the tasks efficiently. Furthermore, the transmission power can be adjusted based on the position and mobility of vehicles to reduce energy consumption. The experimental results demonstrate that the designed task scheduling method outperforms benchmark methods in terms of comprehensive performance.

Keywords: Multi-agent reinforcement learning · Vehicular edge computing · Multi-task scheduling · Cloud-edge-end collaboration

© ICST Institute for Computer Sciences, Social Informatics and Telecommunications Engineering 2024
Published by Springer Nature Switzerland AG 2024. All Rights Reserved
H. Gao et al. (Eds.): CollaborateCom 2023, LNICST 563, pp. 3–22, 2024.
https://doi.org/10.1007/978-3-031-54531-3_1

1 Introduction

Advancements in computing technologies and the widespread implementation of communication infrastructure have led to significant progress in the field of connected vehicles [1]. Connected vehicles are equipped with technology that enables communication with other vehicles, base stations, and the Internet, making them a rapidly evolving area. In addition to their traditional transportation role, connected vehicles are emerging as a mobile computing platform that offers a broad range of services to enhance safety, efficiency, and convenience for drivers and passengers. These services include navigation, entertainment, safety services, and so on [9].

The integration of task processing results from various onboard sensors is crucial for many in-vehicle services. Multi-task fusion, which involves combining data from cameras, Light Detection and Ranging (LiDAR), radar, ultrasonic sensors, and other sources, can provide a comprehensive understanding of the environment around the vehicle [7]. For instance, Advanced Driver Assistance Systems (ADAS) can utilize these sensors to enhance driver safety and offer additional assistance in driving, including adaptive cruise control, lane departure warning, and blind spot monitoring.

For these multiple sensors-supported services, completion time and energy consumption are both critical factors for guaranteeing the Quality of Service (QoS). Multi-task fusion requires processing large amounts of data from multiple sensors in real-time, and any delays in this process could lead to accidents or other safety issues. Additionally, energy consumption is an important consideration for autonomous vehicles, as they rely on a variety of sensors and computing systems that require significant amounts of energy. In this context, task scheduling is critical for connected vehicles. It involves allocating computing resources and offloading tasks. Effective task scheduling can help to improve the performance of connected vehicles by optimizing resource allocation and reducing latency. By prioritizing critical tasks and allocating computing resources based on their processing requirements, task scheduling can ensure that the services are delivered with minimal delay and maximum efficiency. However, task scheduling and resource allocation can be challenging due to the dynamic nature of vehicular environments.

In order to achieve an efficient task scheduling, vehicular edge computing (VEC) has been proposed and implemented [10]. VEC utilizes edge computing technology in connected vehicles to perform processing and storage closer to the data source, reducing latency and improving real-time response. Many task scheduling methods have been proposed for VEC in existing studies: In [16], a Genetic Algorithm-based collaborative task offloading model was formulated to offload the tasks to the base station. In [2], a Particle Swarm Optimization-based task scheduling method was proposed to address the problem of task offloading due to vehicle movements and limited edge coverage. These heuristic algorithms are rule-based and can be used to allocate tasks based on predefined rules, but they may not be able to handle complex and dynamic allocation problems that require more flexible and adaptive solutions. Recently, reinforcement learning was used to optimize the allocation of tasks by modeling the allocation problem as a Markov decision process (MDP) and training the agent to make optimal task scheduling decisions [6]. However, little research has focused on the simultaneous scheduling of multiple tasks generated from one vehicle and joint optimization of completion time and energy consumption.

In order to address the aforementioned issues, a collaborative multi-task scheduling method is proposed that employs a Multi-agent Reinforcement Learning method and cloud-edge-end collaboration architecture. Multi-agent reinforcement learning algorithms can learn from experience and adapt to changes in the environment or task requirements, providing a more flexible and adaptive solution. Among all the existing DRL algorithms, Proximal Policy Optimization (PPO) [14] is a new innovation known for being stable and scalable. Multi-Agent Proximal Policy Optimization (MAPPO) is a variant of the PPO algorithm designed for multi-agent reinforcement learning scenarios. In addition, cloud-edge-end collaboration provides a distributed computing architecture that leverages the strengths of each tier of computing resources to provide efficient task offloading and data processing in changing environmental conditions.

Specifically, the proposed multi-agent PPO algorithm-based task scheduling method is utilized to dynamically assign multiple computation tasks generated from one vehicle to other computing entities in real time. These entities include edge servers, idle vehicles, and the cloud server, and the allocation takes into account the tasks' characteristics, the current environmental state, and the workload of available computing entities. Additionally, the transmission power is adjusted according to the distances between vehicles and other computing entities to reduce the energy consumption for vehicles.

The main contributions are summarised as follows:

(1) A scheme for joint optimization with multiple objectives has been proposed, aiming to minimize both the completion time of service requests and the energy consumption of vehicles.
(2) A multi-agent PPO-based task scheduling and resource allocation method is proposed, which can dynamically allocate multiple tasks based on the changing environment and adjust transmission power according to the distance between the current vehicle and the computing entity. In addition, it allows vehicles to act independently and simultaneously in a decentralized manner, which reduces the need for centralized coordination and communication. This improves scalability and reduces the complexity of multi-agent systems.
(3) A cloud-edge-end collaboration scheme is designed, in which the vehicles can offload tasks to other vehicles, edge servers, and the cloud server in a collaborative way.

2   Related Work

In this section, the existing studies related to collaborative task scheduling and resource allocation in VEC are discussed.

In [3], a joint task offloading and resource allocation scheme for Multi-access Edge Computing scenarios was proposed. This scheme employs parked and moving vehicles as resources to enhance task processing performance and reduce the workload of edge servers. In [5], a joint secure offloading and resource allocation scheme was proposed for VEC networks, utilizing physical layer security and spectrum sharing architecture to improve secrecy performance and resource efficiency, with the aim of minimizing system processing delay. These studies commonly focused on transmission and computation resource allocation but little research focuses on the adjustment of transmission power. The power consumption of the wireless communication system is directly influenced by the transmission power, potentially affecting the battery life of connected vehicles [11].

In [18], a non-orthogonal multiple access based architecture for VEC was proposed, where various edge nodes cooperate to process tasks in real-time. In [4], a collaboration scheme between mobile edge computing and cloud computing is presented to process tasks in Internet of Vehicles (IoV), and a deep reinforcement learning technique is introduced to jointly optimize computation offloading and resource allocation for minimizing the system cost of processing tasks subject to constraints. These studies can effectively offload tasks to the edge server in a collaborative way. However, little research focuses on cooperative task processing among vehicles based on vehicle-to-vehicle (V2V) communications.

In [17], a mobile edge computing-enabled vehicular network with aerial-terrestrial connectivity for computation offloading and network access was designed, with the objective of minimizing the total computation and communication overhead, solved through a decentralized value-iteration based reinforcement learning approach. In [8], a collaborative computing framework for VEC was proposed to optimize task and resource scheduling for distributed resources in vehicles, edge servers, and the cloud, using an asynchronous deep reinforcement algorithm to maximize the system utility. These studies have focused on task scheduling in a dynamic environment but did not consider the simultaneous offloading of multiple tasks from one vehicle, which is a more complex issue that requires optimization in the current VEC scenario.

In order to address the above-mentioned problem, a multi-agent reinforcement learning-based multi-task simultaneous scheduling method is proposed in this paper. With the dynamic adjustment of transmission power and collaboration of computing entities, vehicular energy consumption and request completion time can be optimized jointly.

3   System Model and Problem Definition

In this section, the system model of VEC scenario is illustrated and then the optimization target is formulated.

3.1 Network Model

Figure 1 illustrates the VEC system. The three-tier VEC system is a hierarchical architecture comprising vehicles, edge servers, and a cloud server, each playing a distinct role in data processing and service delivery. At the bottom tier, vehicles act as the local computing nodes, equipped with onboard sensors and processing capabilities for immediate data analysis. The middle tier consists of edge servers strategically positioned within the vehicular network, serving as intermediate processing hubs. The top tier involves a central cloud server that acts as a centralized resource pool, offering extensive computational power and storage capacity. The cloud server supports complex and resource-intensive applications, allowing for scalable and efficient computing solutions across the entire vehicular network. This three-tier structure optimally balances computing resources and response times, ensuring a seamless and responsive VEC environment.

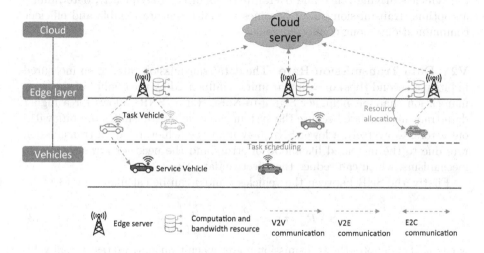

Fig. 1. System architecture

3.2 Mobility Model

Due to the perpetual movement and varying speeds, the positions of vehicles and the distances between them are in constant flux. This dynamic scenario affects the connectivity among vehicles and the choice of the computing entities to which tasks are offloaded [12]. Consequently, mobility emerges as a crucial factor that necessitates consideration in this investigation. In this study, it is assumed that vehicles are in motion on a highway, a standard two-way road.

For each vehicle, coordinate $(x(\tau), y(\tau))$ is used to denote the location at time τ on a 2D map. Thus, the distance between two vehicles i and j can be calculated by (1):

$$d_{i,j}(\tau) = \sqrt{(x_i(\tau) - x_j(\tau))^2 + ((y_i(\tau) - y_j(\tau))^2} \tag{1}$$

Similarly, the distance $d_{i,r}(\tau)$ between the vehicle i and the edge server r can be calculated by (2):

$$d_{i,r}(\tau) = \sqrt{(x_i(\tau) - x_r(\tau))^2 + ((y_i(\tau) - y_r(\tau))^2} \tag{2}$$

3.3   Communication Model

In this study, we dynamically adjust the transmission power over time, taking into account the distances between computing entities. This adjustment directly influences the power consumption of the wireless communication system, which, in turn, can impact the battery life of the connected vehicles. Increasing the transmission power extends the communication range, enabling vehicles to communicate over greater distances. However, this extension comes at a cost - higher power consumption, leading to faster battery drain and a reduction in the vehicle's driving range and overall performance. Consequently, determining an optimal transmission power becomes crucial to ensure reliable and efficient communication among connected vehicles.

V2V Data Transmission Rate. The data transmission rate, often measured in bits per second (bps) or a similar unit, is influenced by the quality of the communication channel. A higher Signal-to-Noise Ratio (SNR) allows for a higher data transmission rate because the system can reliably transmit more bits without errors. Conversely, a lower SNR may limit the achievable data transmission rate due to the increased likelihood of errors and the need for error-correction mechanisms, which can reduce the effective data rate.

Firstly, the SNR between the vehicles i and j can be calculated by (3):

$$SNR_{i,j}(\tau) = \frac{p_{i,j}(\tau) \cdot G_{i,j}(\tau)}{\xi_{i,j}(\tau) \cdot d_{i,j}(\tau) \cdot \sigma^2} \tag{3}$$

where $p_{i,j}(\tau)$ denotes the transmission power when transmitting tasks from vehicle i to vehicle j, $G_{i,j}(\tau)$ denotes the channel gain, $\xi_{i,j}(\tau)$ denotes the path loss, σ^2 denotes the white Gaussian noise, and $d_{i,j}(\tau)$ denotes the distance between two vehicles.

Therefore, the data transmission rate $R_{i,j}$ between vehicles i and j can be calculated by (4):

$$R_{i,j}(\tau) = b_{i,j}(\tau) \log_2 (1 + SNR_{i,j}(\tau)) \tag{4}$$

where $b_{i,j}(\tau)$ represents the allocated bandwidth resource between vehicle i and vehicle j.

V2E Data Transmission Rate. The V2E communication can be significantly influenced by interference. Interference refers to unwanted signals or noise that disrupt the intended transmission between communication devices. It can lead to degraded signal quality, increased error rates, and reduced data transmission rates. In wireless communication systems, interference from other devices, environmental factors, or overlapping signals can adversely affect the reliability and performance of the communication link. Managing and mitigating interference is crucial to maintaining clear and effective communication in vehicular networks. Thus, the interference noise $I_{i,r}(\tau)$ can be calculated by (5):

$$I_{i,r}(\tau) = (N_r(\tau) - 1) \cdot p_{i,r}(\tau) \cdot g_r \tag{5}$$

where $(N_r(\tau) - 1)$ denotes the number of vehicles connecting to the edge server r (except the vehicle i itself), $p_{i,r}(\tau)$ denotes the allocated transmission power to the vehicle i, and g_r denotes the channel gain.

Then, according to the calculated interference noise, the V2E data transmission rate can be calculated by (6):

$$R_{i,r}(\tau) = \eta_i \cdot B_r \cdot \log_2\left(1 + \frac{p_{i,r}(\tau)g_r}{I_{i,r}(\tau) + \sigma^2}\right) \tag{6}$$

where B_r denotes the total available bandwidth of edge server r, η_i denotes the proportion of the bandwidth allocated to vehicle i.

E2C Data Transmission Rate. Similarly, the interference noise $I_{r,cs}(\tau)$ can be calculated by (7):

$$I_{r,cs}(\tau) = \sum_{s \neq r, s \in S} p_s(\tau) \cdot g_r(\tau) \tag{7}$$

Then, according to the calculated interference noise, the E2C data transmission rate can be calculated by (8):

$$R_{r,cs}(\tau) = B_{r,cs} \cdot \log_2\left(1 + \frac{p_r(\tau)g_r(\tau)}{I_{r,cs}(\tau) + \sigma^2}\right) \tag{8}$$

3.4 Computation Model

Task Scheduling. Firstly, the computation tasks are generated by various sensors mounted on the vehicle. Then, the tasks are combined into a task processing request and forwarded to the *Runtime Optimizer*, which can generate task scheduling decisions based on the proposed scheduling method. Following that, the tasks are assigned to multiple computing entities according to the scheduling decision. Finally, the computation results are fused together and then fed back.

In this work, the number of vehicles and edge servers can be denoted by the set $\{1, 2, \cdots, v\}$ and set $\{1, 2, \cdots, s\}$, respectively. Each vehicle generates service requests continuously, with K computation tasks in each request. For each task, the scheduling direction can be denoted by α, where $\alpha \in \{0, 1, 2, 3\}$, $\alpha = 0$ denotes that the task is offloaded to the server, $\alpha = 1$ denotes that the task is allocated to another vehicle, $\alpha = 2$ denotes that the task is executed locally, $\alpha = 3$ denotes that the task is processed in the cloud. In addition, the property of each task can be donated by a tuple $\langle C, S, D \rangle$, where C represents the required CPU cycles to complete the task, S denotes the data size, and D represents the maximal processing time of the computing task.

After task scheduling, the tasks in the vehicle v at the moment can be represented by the set $L_v = \{l_1, l_2, \ldots, l_{ns}\}$, L_v involves the local tasks generated by the vehicle v itself and the scheduled tasks offloaded from other vehicles. Similarly, the tasks offloaded to the edge server s can be denoted by set $G_s = \{g_1, g_2, \ldots, g_{ms}\}$.

Local Computing. For local computing, The task completion time $T_{v,k}^L$ can be calculated according to (9):

$$T_{v,k}^L = T_{v,l_{ns}} + \frac{C_{v,k}}{f_v} \tag{9}$$

The energy consumption $E_{v,k}^L$ can be calculated according to (10):

$$E_{v,k}^L = \xi \cdot (f_v)^\gamma \cdot C_{v,k} \tag{10}$$

where $T_{v,l_{ns}}$ denotes the expected completion time of the tasks in the processing queue, l_{ns} denotes the ns^{th} task at vehicle v, f_v represents the computing power of the vehicle v, which is defined as the number of CPU cycles executed every second. $\xi = 10^{-11}$ and $\gamma = 2$ represent the power consumption coefficients, which are constants.

Edge Computing. Edge computing serves as an extension to local computing, allowing vehicles to offload and process data at edge servers, enhancing computational capabilities and enabling real-time, resource-efficient decision-making. For the offloaded task k, the execution time $T_{v,k}^O$ is comprised of task transmission time $T_{v,k}^{O,trans}$ and task execution time $T_{v,k}^{O,exe}$:

$$T_{v,k}^O = T_{v,k}^{O,trans} + T_{v,k}^{O,exe} \tag{11}$$

In (11), the task transmission time $T_{v,k}^{O,trans}$ can be calculated by:

$$T_{v,k}^{O,trans} = \begin{cases} T_{j,l_{ns}}^{V2V,trans} + \frac{S_{v,k}}{R_{v,j}}, & \alpha_{v,k} = 1 \\ T_{r,g_{ms}}^{V2E,trans} + \frac{S_{v,k}}{R_{v,s}}, & \alpha_{v,k} = 0 \end{cases} \tag{12}$$

where $T_{j,l_{ns}}^{V2V,trans}$ and $T_{s,g_{ms}}^{V2E,trans}$ represent the transmission completion time of the preceding task at vehicle j and edge server s, respectively. l_{ns} and g_{ms} represent the index of the preceding task at vehicle j and edge server s, respectively.

The task execution time $T_{v,k}^{V2E,exe}$ is defined by:

$$T_{v,k}^{O,exe} = \begin{cases} T_{j,l_{ns}}^{V2V,exe} + \frac{C_{v,k}}{f_j}, & \alpha_{v,k} = 1 \\ T_{s,g_{ms}}^{V2E,exe} + \frac{C_{v,k}}{f_s}, & \alpha_{v,k} = 0 \end{cases} \tag{13}$$

where $T_{j,l_{ns}}^{V2V,exe}$ and $T_{s,g_{ms}}^{V2E,exe}$ represent the completion time of the preceding task at vehicle j and edge server s, respectively, l_{ns} and g_{ms} represent the index of the preceding task.

In addition to the task completion time, the energy consumption of the task computation can be calculated by:

$$E_{v,k}^{O} = \begin{cases} p_v \cdot \frac{S_{v,k}}{R_{v,j}} + \xi \cdot (f_j)^{\gamma} \cdot C_{v,k}, & \alpha_{v,k} = 1 \\ p_v \cdot \frac{S_{v,k}}{R_{v,s}}, & \alpha_{v,k} = 0 \end{cases} \tag{14}$$

where p_v is the transmission power of vehicle v, representing the amount of data transmitted per second.

Cloud Computing. Cloud computing functions as an extension to edge computing, providing additional computational resources and storage capabilities for time-tolerant and computation-intensive tasks, enabling scalable processing and storage solutions for vehicular applications. This hierarchical architecture allows for a seamless integration of local, edge, and cloud resources to meet the diverse computing needs in vehicular environments. The total execution time of task k is expressed by:

$$T_{v,k}^{CS} = T_{v,k}^{V2E,trans} + T_{v,k}^{E2C,trans} + T_{v,k}^{CS,exe} \tag{15}$$

where $T_{v,k}^{V2E,trans}$ and $T_{v,k}^{E2C,trans}$ represent the task transmission time from vehicle v to the edge server and from the edge server to the cloud server, respectively, $T_{v,k}^{CS,exe}$ represents the task processing time on the cloud server.

In (15), the task transmission time $T_{v,k}^{E2C,trans}$ can be calculated by:

$$T_{v,k}^{E2C,trans} = T_{cs,h_{ls}}^{E2C,trans} + \frac{S_{v,k}}{R_{r,cs}} \tag{16}$$

where $T_{cs,h_{ls}}^{E2C,trans}$ represents the transmission completion time of the preceding task at cloud server cs.

The task execution time can be calculated by:

$$T_{v,k}^{E2C,exe} = T_{cs,h_{ls}}^{E2C,exe} + \frac{C_{v,k}}{f_s} \tag{17}$$

where $T_{cs,h_{ls}}^{E2C,exe}$ represents the completion time of the preceding task at the cloud server cs.

In the designed system model, the following assumptions were made to simplify the model: (1) The moving of vehicles is disregarded during the task offloading and results feedback. (2) The feedback time is neglected due to the small size of computed results [17].

3.5   Problem Formulation

The objective function serves as a quantifiable measure of performance for the proposed solution. The formulation of the objective function is a critical step in defining the problem and guiding the research towards finding a solution that aligns with the goals of the study. In this study, the primary objective of the designed task scheduling method is to jointly minimize the request completion time T and overall energy consumption E for multi-task allocation. Thus, the formulation of the objective function is expressed in (18):

$$
\begin{aligned}
obj :&min\left\{\omega_1 \cdot T + \omega_2 \cdot E\right\} \\
T =& max\left\{T_{L_1}, \ldots, T_{L_V}, \ldots, T_{E_1}, \ldots, T_{E_S}, \ldots, T_{CS}\right\} \\
E =& \sum_{v=1}^{V} \sum_{k=1}^{K} E_{v,k}
\end{aligned}
\tag{18}
$$

where ω_1 and ω_2 are weight factors, T_{L_V} and T_{E_S} denote the completion time of all tasks within the vehicle V and the edge server S, respectively. T_{CS} denotes the completion time of the tasks that are allocated to the cloud server. $E_{v,k}$ represents the consumed energy required to complete the task k generated by vehicle v.

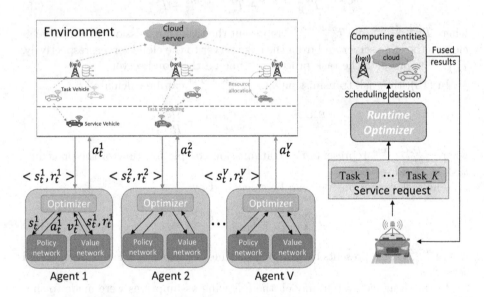

Fig. 2. Multi-agent reinforcement learning-based task scheduling procedure

4   System Design

In this section, the proposed PPO-based scheduling method is introduced.

4.1   Multi-agent Reinforcement Learning

Multi-agent reinforcement learning is a sub-field of reinforcement learning that involves multiple agents interacting with each other in a shared environment to achieve a common goal. In the context of VEC, multi-agent reinforcement learning can be used to coordinate the allocation of computing resources and the scheduling of tasks across multiple edge servers or vehicles.

In this work, as shown in Fig. 2, each vehicle can act as an agent v, which interacts with the environment and determines its task scheduling decisions, including offloading or local execution. Firstly, at each step t, the environment state s_t^v provides an observation to the policy (actor) network of each agent v. Secondly, the policy network generates the scheduling action a_t^v for v based on the observation, which is then executed in the environment. Thirdly, the environment provides reward r_{t+1}^v and new state s_{t+1}^v for each agent based on the actions taken by the agents. The value (critic) network of the agent v estimates the value of each state, which is used to calculate the advantages for policy updates. The *optimization* step updates the policy networks using backpropagation based on the advantages and the losses. The updated policies are then used to generate new trajectories, which are used for exploration and further training.

Overall, MAPPO involves multiple agents that interact with each other in a decentralized manner. The centralized training approach enables efficient learning from the collective experience of the agents, while the decentralized execution enables robust and scalable performance in complex multi-agent environments.

4.2   States, Actions, and Reward

States. The states are the present condition of the environment in which the agents operate. In our study, we depict states as a collection of observations received by vehicles from the environment. These observations encompass various aspects, such as the positions $P^e(t)$ of vehicles, the task-related information I^v from each vehicle, the transmission overhead $M^v(t)$ on each vehicle, and the computation overhead $C^e(t)$ on each computing entity. Consequently, the state space can be expressed as:

$$s_t = \{P^e(t), I^v, M^v(t), C^e(t)\} \tag{19}$$

Actions. The actions signify the choices made by agents based on the observed state of the environment. In this study, these actions encompass decisions related to offloading and the assigned transmission power for each vehicle.

$$A_t^v = \{a_1^1, \dots, a_1^K, \dots, a_i^k, \dots, a_V^K\},$$
$$a_i^k = \{\alpha_i^k, p_i^k\} \tag{20}$$
$$\forall i \in \{1, \dots, V\}, \forall k \in \{1, \dots, K\}, \alpha_{i,k} \in \{0, 1, 2, 3\}$$

where a_i^k represents the decisions made for task k generated by vehicle v, including the offloading decision α_i^k and the allocated transmission power p_i^k.

Reward. The rewards denote the responses that agents receive from the environment in accordance with their actions. They are generally crafted to incentivize agents toward actions that yield favorable outcomes, such as reducing request completion time and energy consumption.

According to the proposed objective function, the reward function is designed as:

$$r = \alpha \times \frac{exp_{time}}{max_{exp_{time}}} + \beta \times \frac{exp_{energy}}{max_{exp_{energy}}} \tag{21}$$

where exp_{time} and exp_{energy} represent the estimated completion time and energy consumption of the service request, respectively, $max_{exp_{time}}$ and $max_{exp_{energy}}$ represents the maximum exp_{time} and exp_{energy} the agent had reached. α and β are weight factors.

4.3   Deep Reinforcement Learning Algorithm

In this work, the Proximal Policy Optimisation (PPO) [14] is employed as the DRL agent training algorithm. It is a policy gradient-based actor-critic algorithm, which uses Stochastic Gradient Ascend (SGA) to update both actor (also namely policy) network π and critic (also namely value) network φ. The actor network predicts the next action and returns to the environment, while the critic network evaluates the performance of the actor network. Both networks are updated by the same loss function $L = L_{clip} + L_V + L_{entropy}$, which consists of three parts: the clipped surrogate loss L_{clip}, the value loss L_V and the entropy loss $L_{entropy}$.

In order to ensure that the policy changes are sufficiently conservative to maintain stability and avoid large deviations from the current policy, the surrogate objective function is utilized to limit the change in policy:

$$L_{clip} = \mathbb{E}[\min(\rho(s, a) A^{\pi_{\theta_{old}}}(s, a), \text{clip}(\rho(s, a), 1 - \epsilon, 1 + \epsilon) A^{\pi_{\theta_{old}}}(s, a))] \tag{22}$$

where the clip function clamps out-of-range values of $\rho(s, a)$ back to the constraint $(1 - \epsilon, 1 + \epsilon)$ instead of using KL divergence in TRPO, $\rho(s, a) = \frac{\pi_\theta(s,a)}{\pi_{\theta_{old}}(s,a)}$ is the importance sampling weight between the old $\pi_{\theta_{old}}(s, a)$ and new policy $\pi_\theta(s, a)$. Generalised Advantage Estimation (GAE) [13] is utilized to estimate the expectation of the advantage function $A^{\pi_{\theta_{old}}}(s, a))$:

$$\hat{A}_t(s, a) = \delta_t + (\gamma\lambda)\delta_{t+1} + \dots + (\gamma\lambda)^{N-t+1}\delta_{t+1}, \tag{23}$$

where δ_t is represented by $r_t + \gamma V_{\theta_v}(s_{t+1}) - V_{\theta_v}(s_t)$, $\gamma\lambda$ is the discount factor of future rewards to control the variance of the advantage function.

The prediction of values V indicates the ability to predict accumulated rewards. Therefore, it should be close to the advantage at a specific pair of the state s and action a, which formulates the equation of the value loss L_V:

$$L_V = \mathbb{E}_{s,a}[A^\varphi(s,a)] \tag{24}$$

where we use the Mean Squared Error (MSE) to estimate the expectation and minimise the loss.

Lastly, the entropy loss $L_{entropy}$ is introduced to encourage exploration during the learning process, which is added as a regularisation term. This is calculated by the negative entropy of the policy distribution, involving both continuous and discrete actions. As a result, the DRL agent may be less sensitive to local optimal solutions, which can lead to a more robust policy.

5   Experiment

5.1   Experimental Setting

Training and Test Environments. In the experimental phase, the multi-agent reinforcement learning-based task scheduling models are trained on a server equipped with an Intel Xeon W-22555 processor and an NVIDIA RTX 3070 GPU. Subsequently, the experiments are performed on a Windows 11 PC featuring an Intel i7-13700H processor and 16 GB DRAM. The detailed experimental parameters are outlined in Table 1.

Table 1. Experimental parameter setting

Parameters	Value	Parameters	Value
Number of vehicles	4–10	Data size	2–10 Mb
Number of edge servers	8	Bandwidth of edge server	100 MHz
Number of tasks	3–7	Speed of vehicles	≈ 15 m/s
Required CPU cycles of the tasks	10–20 cpu cycles	Transmission power of vehicles	1 dBm
Computation power of the cloud	4 cpu cycles/s	Execution power of vehicles	3-4 dBm
Computation power of edge servers	2 cpu cycles/s	Computation power of vehicles	1 cpu cycles/s

5.2   Benchmark Methods

In the experiments, the proposed PPO-based scheduling method is compared with the following methods:

(1) **Deep Deterministic Policy Gradient (DDPG)** [15] The task scheduling method based on DDPG designed in [15] primarily focuses on optimizing the request completion time. (2) **Random Scheduling (RS)** The RS

method makes task scheduling decisions randomly, by which the tasks are executed locally or distributed to edge servers and other vehicles randomly. (3) **Offloading-only Scheduling (OS)** The OS method allocates all tasks exclusively to edge servers or other vehicles. (4) **Local-only Scheduling (LS)** Different from the OS method, the LS method involves the execution of all tasks locally.

5.3   Performance Evaluation

Convergence. The convergence of the reward in multi-agent reinforcement learning refers to the process by which the rewards earned by the agents over time become more stable and consistent. Achieving convergence is an important goal in multi-agent reinforcement learning as it indicates that the agents have reached a level of performance that is close to optimal and can be used to make decisions in the real world. In this work, convergence is essential to ensure that the learning process terminates and the algorithm can produce a policy that performs well in making task scheduling decisions in the given environment.

The rewards are shown in Fig. 3a and Fig. 3b, where x coordinate denotes the current training episode and y coordinate denotes the reward obtained from the scheduling decision. As can be seen from the figures, the proposed PPO-based method converges fast under different numbers of vehicles and tasks.

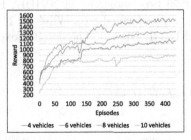

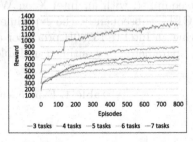

(a) Different number of vehicles   (b) Different number of tasks

Fig. 3. Convergence property

Request Completion Time. The service request completion time in vehicular edge computing refers to the time taken to complete a service request from the time it is generated by the vehicle until the result is feedback to the user. It is an important performance metric that determines the quality of service (QoS) in vehicular edge computing. The service request completion time can be influenced by several factors, mainly including the task processing time and the transmission delay between the vehicles and edge servers.

Figure 4a shows that the PPO method achieves shorter request completion times compared to other methods, for different numbers of vehicles. Figure 4b illustrates that as the number of tasks within a request increases, the completion

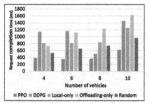 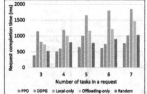 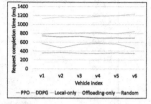

(a) Different number of ve- (b) Different number of (c) Completion time of each
hicles tasks vehicle

Fig. 4. Comparison of the request completion time

time also increases, however, the PPO-based scheduling method still achieves the shortest request completion time. In Fig. 4c, the request completion time for each vehicle is presented, and it can be observed that the PPO-based scheduling method results in similar completion times for requests generated from all vehicles.

Overall Energy Consumption. Overall energy consumption refers to the total electrical energy required to complete all the tasks in one request, including the energy consumption on task execution and data transmission involved in delivering service requests. Figure 5 compares the overall energy consumption under different conditions. As shown in Fig. 5a and Fig. 5b, vehicles have less energy consumption when all the tasks are offloaded based on the offloading-only method. The energy consumption based on the PPO method is similar to the DDPG method but lower than the local-only method and random-based method. Because all the tasks are executed locally based on a local-only scheduling method can result in significantly higher energy consumption compared to offloading them rationally.

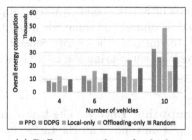 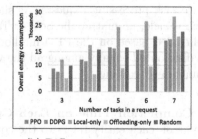

(a) Different number of vehicles   (b) Different number of tasks

Fig. 5. Comparison of the overall energy consumption

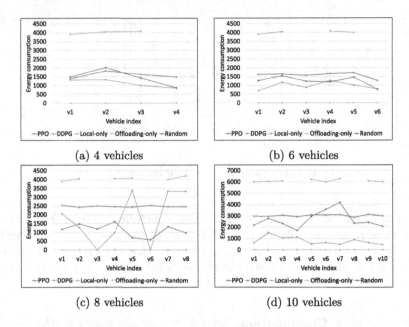

(a) 4 vehicles   (b) 6 vehicles

(c) 8 vehicles   (d) 10 vehicles

Fig. 6. Energy consumption on each vehicle

Energy Consumption on Each Vehicle. Balanced energy consumption can prevent overloading of a single vehicle. In a multi-vehicle system, if one vehicle consumes significantly more energy than others, it can become overloaded, causing delays in service delivery and reduced system performance. Figure 6 compares the energy consumed by each vehicle when processing tasks that are offloaded to it and generated by itself. When there are four vehicles, $v4$ served as the Service Vehicle (SeV), which does not generate task processing requests. Similarly, $v3$ and $v6$ are SeVs when there are six and eight vehicles. $v4$ and $v8$ are SeVs when there are ten vehicles. Other vehicles are called Task Vehicles, which can generate task processing requests. As shown in Fig. 6, the energy consumption on each vehicle, no matter the SeV or TaV, is almost the same when the tasks are scheduled based on the PPO method. In contrast, the energy consumption is not distributed equally among all the vehicles when using the DDPG method and random scheduling.

Task Completion Time on Each Computing Entity. The task completion time on each entity refers to the completion time of all the tasks that are allocated to the computing entity. Figure 7 illustrates a comparison of the task completion time among all computing entities, including vehicles, edge servers, and the cloud server. Based on the PPO scheduling method, the tasks allocated to all the entities are completed at almost the same time. However, based on the DDPG scheduling method, the completion time of the cloud server is much

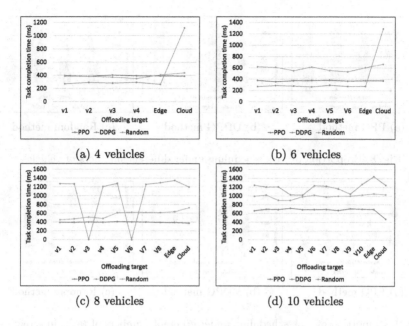

Fig. 7. Task completion time on each computing entity

higher than other computing entities when the number of vehicles is small, ultimately affecting the completion time of the vehicles' service requests.

Proportion of Task Scheduling. In Fig. 8 and Fig. 9, the proportion of the tasks that offloaded to vehicles, edge server, and the cloud server are compared.

As shown in Fig. 8a, with the number of vehicles increasing, more tasks are executed on vehicles and the proportion of tasks offloaded to edge servers or the cloud server decreases because the increasing number of vehicles can provide more computing resources, allowing more tasks to be executed on vehicles. However, in Fig. 8b, there is no clear trend in the change of proportion when scheduling tasks based on the DDPG method. In addition, the proportion of the offloaded tasks remains constant when using a random-based scheduling method, as shown in Fig. 8c.

As shown in Fig. 9a and Fig. 9c, the scheduling proportions of the tasks based on the PPO-based and random-based methods are not affected by the number of tasks in one service request. However, the PPO-based scheduling method offloads fewer tasks to the cloud server, which efficiently alleviates the bandwidth pressure for vehicles.

Quality of Method. As the goal of this study is to improve both the completion time and energy consumption of requests, a metric is needed to compare the overall performance of different methods in achieving these objectives. To this end, the Quality of Method (QoM) is defined and used to quantify and evaluate

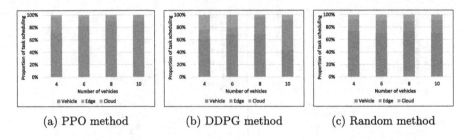

Fig. 8. Proportion of task scheduling under different numbers of vehicles

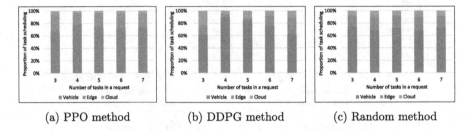

Fig. 9. Proportion of task scheduling under different numbers of tasks in a request

the performance of the method in a comprehensive manner. The QoM of each method can be calculated by:

$$QoM_i = \mu_1 \frac{T_{max} - T_i}{T_{max} - T_{min}} + \mu_2 \frac{E_{max} - E_i}{E_{max} - E_{min}} \tag{25}$$

where μ_1 and μ_2 represent the weight value of completion time and energy consumption, respectively. T_i and E_i represent the completion time and energy consumption of method i, respectively. In this work, we set $\mu_1 = 2$ and $\mu_2 = 1$. As shown in Fig. 10, the QoM of the PPO-based scheduling method is much higher than other methods no matter the number of vehicles and tasks. This means that the proposed PPO-based scheduling method can always have a better comprehensive performance in terms of shortening request completion time and reducing energy consumption.

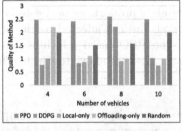 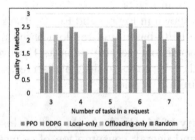

(a) Different number of vehicles   (b) Different number of tasks

Fig. 10. Comparison of the Quality of Method

6   Conclusion

In this work, a collaborative multi-task scheduling strategy is designed utilizing the multi-agent Proximal Policy Optimization algorithm and cloud-edge-end collaboration. The proposed method allows multiple computation tasks in one service request to be either executed locally or remotely by offloading to edge servers and the cloud server simultaneously, which helps to decrease request completion time. Moreover, the transmission power can be dynamically adjusted based on the distances between vehicles and other computing entities, which helps to reduce energy consumption. The experimental results demonstrate that the PPO-based scheduling method outperforms other methods in terms of reducing request completion time. Additionally, it achieves balanced energy consumption and task workload distribution among all computing entities, preventing overloading of a single entity. Furthermore, allocating tasks based on the PPO-based method results in fewer tasks being offloaded to the cloud server, alleviating the bandwidth pressure for vehicles. Finally, the comprehensive performance evaluation QoM results show that the proposed method outperforms other methods.

Acknowledgments. This research was funded by: Key Program Special Fund in XJTLU under project KSF-E-64; XJTLU Research Development Funding under projects RDF-19-01-14 and RDF-20-01-15; the National Natural Science Foundation of China (NSFC) under grant 52175030.

References

1. Abdelkader, G., Elgazzar, K., Khamis, A.: Connected vehicles: technology review, state of the art, challenges and opportunities. Sensors **21**(22), 7712 (2021)
2. Alqarni, M.A., Mousa, M.H., Hussein, M.K.: Task offloading using GPU-based particle swarm optimization for high-performance vehicular edge computing. J. King Saud Univ. Comput. Inf. Sci. **34**(10), 10356–10364 (2022)
3. Fan, W., Liu, J., Hua, M., Wu, F., Liu, Y.: Joint task offloading and resource allocation for multi-access edge computing assisted by parked and moving vehicles. IEEE Trans. Veh. Technol. **71**(5), 5314–5330 (2022)
4. Huang, J., Wan, J., Lv, B., Ye, Q., Chen, Y.: Joint computation offloading and resource allocation for edge-cloud collaboration in internet of vehicles via deep reinforcement learning. IEEE Syst. J. **17**, 2500–2511 (2023)
5. Ju, Y., et al.: Joint secure offloading and resource allocation for vehicular edge computing network: a multi-agent deep reinforcement learning approach. IEEE Trans. Intell. Transp. Syst. **24**, 5555–5569 (2023)
6. Kazmi, S.A., Otoum, S., Hussain, R., Mouftah, H.T.: A novel deep reinforcement learning-based approach for task-offloading in vehicular networks. In: 2021 IEEE Global Communications Conference (GLOBECOM), pp. 1–6. IEEE (2021)
7. Li, P., Wang, X., Huang, K., Huang, Y., Li, S., Iqbal, M.: Multi-model running latency optimization in an edge computing paradigm. Sensors **22**(16), 6097 (2022)
8. Liu, L., Feng, J., Mu, X., Pei, Q., Lan, D., Xiao, M.: Asynchronous deep reinforcement learning for collaborative task computing and on-demand resource allocation in vehicular edge computing. IEEE Trans. Intell. Transp. Syst. **24**, 15513–15526 (2023)

9. Lu, S., Shi, W.: Vehicle computing: vision and challenges. J. Inf. Intell. **1**, 23–35 (2022)
10. Raza, S., Wang, S., Ahmed, M., Anwar, M.R., et al.: A survey on vehicular edge computing: architecture, applications, technical issues, and future directions. Wirel. Commun. Mob. Comput. **2019**, 1–19 (2019)
11. Rubio-Loyola, J., et al.: Towards intelligent tuning of frequency and transmission power adjustment in beacon-based ad-hoc networks. In: VEHITS, pp. 648–656 (2018)
12. Saleem, U., Liu, Y., Jangsher, S., Li, Y., Jiang, T.: Mobility-aware joint task scheduling and resource allocation for cooperative mobile edge computing. IEEE Trans. Wireless Commun. **20**(1), 360–374 (2020)
13. Schulman, J., Moritz, P., Levine, S., Jordan, M., Abbeel, P.: High-dimensional continuous control using generalized advantage estimation. arXiv preprint arXiv:1506.02438 (2015)
14. Schulman, J., Wolski, F., Dhariwal, P., Radford, A., Klimov, O.: Proximal policy optimization algorithms. arXiv preprint arXiv:1707.06347 (2017)
15. Tian, H., et al.: CoPace: edge computation offloading and caching for self-driving with deep reinforcement learning. IEEE Trans. Veh. Technol. **70**(12), 13281–13293 (2021)
16. Wang, H.: Collaborative task offloading strategy of UAV cluster using improved genetic algorithm in mobile edge computing. J. Robot. **2021**, 1–9 (2021)
17. Waqar, N., Hassan, S.A., Mahmood, A., Dev, K., Do, D.T., Gidlund, M.: Computation offloading and resource allocation in MEC-enabled integrated aerial-terrestrial vehicular networks: a reinforcement learning approach. IEEE Trans. Intell. Transp. Syst. **23**(11), 21478–21491 (2022)
18. Xu, X., et al.: Joint task offloading and resource optimization in NOMA-based vehicular edge computing: a game-theoretic DRL approach. J. Syst. Architect. **134**, 102780 (2023)

A Novel Topology Metric for Indoor Point Cloud SLAM Based on Plane Detection Optimization

Zhenchao Ouyang[1,2](✉) 🆔, Jiahe Cui[1,3], Yunxiang He[4], Dongyu Li[1,2], Qinglei Hu[1,2], and Changjie Zhang[5]

[1] Zhongfa Aviation Institute, Beihang University, 166 Shuanghongqiao Street, Pingyao Town, Yuhang District, Hangzhou 311115, China
ouyangkid@buaa.edu.cn
[2] Tianmushan Laboratory, Hangzhou 310023, Zhejiang, China
[3] School of Computer Science and Engineering, Beihang University, Beijing 100191, China
[4] Zhejiang Leapmotor Technology CO., LTD., Hangzhou 31000, Zhejiang, China
[5] Wisedawn Auto Co., LTD., South Henglong Road, Jingzhou 434000, Hubei, China

Abstract. Accurate self-localization and navigation in complex indoor environments are essential functions for the intelligent robots. However, the existing SLAM algorithms rely heavily on differential GPS or additional measuring devices (such as expensive laser tracker), which not only increase research costs but also limit the deployment of algorithms in specific scenarios. In recent years, reference-free pose estimation methods based on the topological structure of point cloud maps have gained popularity, especially in indoor artificial scenes where rich planar information is available. Some existing algorithms suffer from inaccuracies in spatial point cloud plane segmentation and normal estimation, leading to the introduction of evaluation errors. This paper introduces the optimization of plane segmentation results by incorporating deep learning-based point cloud semantic segmentation and proposes measurement indicators based on the Plane Normals Entropy (PNE) and Co-Plane Variance (CPV) to estimate the rotation and translation components of SLAM poses. Furthermore, we introduce a ternary correlation measure to analyze the relationship between noise, relative pose estimation, and the two proposed measures, building upon the conventional binary correlation measure. Our proposed PNE and CPV metrics were quantitatively evaluated on two different scenarios of LiDAR point cloud data in Gazebo simulator, and the results demonstrate that these metrics exhibit superior binary and triple correlation and computational efficiency, making them a promising solution for accurate self-localization and navigation in complex indoor environments.

Keywords: Point Cloud · SLAM · Topology Entropy · Plane detection · Segmentation

H. Gao et al. (Eds.): CollaborateCom 2023, LNICST 563, pp. 23–40, 2024.
https://doi.org/10.1007/978-3-031-54531-3_2

1   Introduction

With the development of artificial intelligence technology, sensors, and computing hardware, intelligent mobile robots have the potential to assist or replace humans in performing repetitive and simple daily tasks, freeing people from heavy labor and providing significant commercial and social benefits. Environment understanding and autonomous localization are fundamental capabilities for mobile robots, and mainstream solutions often employ GPS [1], Ultra-Wideband (UWB) [2], or Simultaneous Localization And Mapping (SLAM) [3–5] techniques. However, GPS signals can be obstructed indoors, and the UWB approach requires modifications to the environment and additional costs. When a robot moves in a complex environment, it needs to have a global map and its current pose like a human. Therefore, to improve robot flexibility and autonomy, existing solutions often utilize environmental sensors (such as stereo cameras or LiDAR) mounted on the robot with SLAM-based solutions [3,6–8].

For the past two decades, the evaluation of SLAM has heavily relied on simulation data or expensive equipment such as laser trackers, motion capture devices, or total stations [9], due to its dependence on relative pose and absolute pose errors (RPE and APE) [10]. This has greatly hindered the development of SLAM, as the relative pose estimation and absolute pose estimation directly calculate the difference between the estimated robot coordinate and the true displacement, and require temporal and spatial synchronization of the data. Even with expensive measurement equipment, constructing corresponding SLAM datasets [11,12] for large-scale, non-line-of-sight covered environments remains challenging.

In contrast to complex natural environments, artificial indoor environments generally have relatively stable and regular topological structures. These features have been utilized to develop SLAM algorithms, and some studies [13–15] have attempted to indirectly evaluate the accuracy of pose estimation for feature maps constructed by SLAM based on topological analysis. In addition, as the cost of LiDAR continues to decrease, mobile robots can efficiently scan the environment structure, ensuring rich local map features. If there is an error in SLAM pose estimation, the local feature map overlaid based on the pose estimation will also become distorted and offset. By analyzing the consistency of the map features through topological measurements, it is possible to infer the pose estimation error [16].

The existing topological analysis-based optimization can be divided into the following two categories. 1) the graph optimization based on loop closure detection. This kind of method requires the robot to have the ability to discover revisited places while performing continuous pose estimation, and then construct a loop closure based on the features of revisited places (such as two frames of scans or local feature maps), followed by graph optimization. Loop closure can be detected based on heuristic methods [17], or through human assistance [18,19], and some solutions utilize neural network models [20] for detection. However, if the robot's trajectory cannot form a loop closure, graph optimization correction cannot be performed. 2) Estimation errors based on topological information from feature maps. The Mean Map Entropy (MME) and Mean Plane Variance (MPV) [13,14] estimate the consistency of the map by respectively estimating the entropy and planar variance of local point clusters in the map. However, both MME and MPV require traversing all the feature points of the map, resulting in low efficiency and an inability to provide specific error locations. Mutually Orthogonal Metric (MOM) [15] prunes the search space by selecting mutually orthogonal planar features, which greatly improves computational efficiency and makes the features more stable on mutually orthogonal planes. However, the deployment of MOM in real environments is affected by large errors in the plane detection algorithm as well as the introduction of normal estimation errors.

In order to provide a measure of pose estimation based on local topological features and overcome the problem of large errors in plane segmentation and numerous normal estimation errors in SLAM, this paper uses a neural network-based semantic segmentation method to improve the robustness and efficiency of plane segmentation. Furthermore, this paper analyzes the effects of rotation and translation components on different types of topological measurements in pose estimation and proposes a more comprehensive topological estimation method. Finally, we conduct a quantitative evaluation of our proposed method in an isometric simulation environment.

2   Basic Conception

2.1   Euclidean Transformation and RPE

The motion of the robot can be regarded as a coordinate transformation problem of a rigid body in Euclidean space, which consists of three mutually orthogonal axes. Rigid body motion can usually be split into two parts, rotation (R) and translation (t). The collection of three-dimensional rotation matrices based on a three-dimensional orthogonal basis is typically defined as Eq. 1, where $SO(3)$ is a special orthogonal group and I is the identity matrix, which is an orthogonal matrix with a determinant $(det(R))$ of 1.

$$SO(3) = \{R \in \mathbb{R}^{3*3} | RR^T = I, det(R) = 1\} \tag{1}$$

The Euclidean transformation of a robot from α to α' can be defined as Eq. 2, where the concepts of homogeneous coordinates and transformation matrices are introduced. The transformation matrix T forms a special Euclidean group, which is defined as Eq. 3.

$$\begin{bmatrix} \alpha' \\ 1 \end{bmatrix} = \begin{bmatrix} R & t \\ 0^T & 1 \end{bmatrix} \begin{bmatrix} \alpha \\ 1 \end{bmatrix} = T \begin{bmatrix} \alpha \\ 1 \end{bmatrix} \tag{2}$$

$$SE(3) = \left\{ T = \begin{bmatrix} R & t \\ 0^T & 1 \end{bmatrix} \in \mathbb{R}^{4*4} | R \in SO(3), t \in \mathbb{R}^3 \right\} \tag{3}$$

Usually, in order to simplify expression and calculation, the R component is expressed by the Rodrigues' Formula, which rotates around the unit vector by the rotation angle θ. The three-dimensional rotation R in real world is generally decomposed into the $[roll, pitch, yaw]$ rotation around the X-Y-Z axis with a fix order. The translation vector t is represented as $[x, y, z]^T$, and translation components T is called a pose of the robot.

$$RPE_{i,j} = ||E_{i,j} - I_{4*4}||$$
$$E_{i,j} = \Delta T_{i,j}^{gt}(\Delta T_{i,j}^{est})^{-1} \tag{4}$$

RPE compares the relative poses along the estimated $T^{est} = \{T_1^{est}, ..., T_N^{est}\}$ (from SLAM) and the reference $T^{gt} = \{T_1^{gt}, ..., T_N^{gt}\}$ (ground truth) trajectories as Eq. 4. This means that the calculation of RPE relies on GT ($\Delta T_{i,j}^{gt}$), but this value is difficult to obtain during actual robot deployment.

2.2 Topology-Based Metrics

During positioning, the robot continuously estimates its pose and integrates stable observation features into a local map. The topology-based metric algorithm indirectly evaluates the accuracy of pose estimation by assessing the consistency and stability of local map features.

MME. Mean map entropy (MME) calculates the mean value over all map points' entropy, and is defined as Eq. 5. Here, N represents the scale of the local map, which consists of a group of points. As point clouds are 3D data, in calculation, p_k represents the value of the determinant of the corresponding point cloud cluster covariance matrix of the k-th point.

$$MME = \frac{1}{N} \sum_{k=1}^{N} h(p_k)$$
$$h(p_k) = \frac{1}{2} ln|2\pi e \sum(p_k)| \tag{5}$$

MPV. The Mean Plane Variance (MPV) assumes that the space is mainly composed of planes and calculates the variance of points within a range to the plane. MPV also traverses all global points and fits a plane based on the points (N) within the KNN search, as Eq. 6. The variance of current plane is equal to the minimum eigenvalue λ_{min} of the corresponding covariance matrix of current point set of p_k.

$$MPV = \frac{1}{N} \sum_{k=1}^{N} v(p_k) = \frac{1}{N} \sum_{k=1}^{N} \lambda_{min} \tag{6}$$

MOM. Both MME and MPV suffer from measurement errors due to the inability to estimate the drift of plane feature points. Furthermore, these methods have low traversal efficiency when dealing with the global point cloud, particularly in spaces with many non-plane points, which can result in further measurement deviation.

Mutually Orthogonal Metric (MOM) improves the accuracy and efficiency of plane segmentation by introducing orthogonal plane detection and traversing the points belonging to the candidate orthogonal planes to compute the mean plane variance (according to Eq. 6) of the overall features. Orthogonal plane detection enables stable candidate point selection and filtering of non-planar features in complex scenes, resulting in a correlation metric with higher relevance compared to RPE. This, in turn, improves the accuracy and efficiency of plane segmentation.

2.3   Correlation Coefficient

Based on earlier studies, we introduce three binary correlation measures to analyze the correlation between different topology-based metrics and RPE. Furthermore, to consider the correlation between the rotation and translation components of the pose and the RPE, we introduce a new ternary correlation coefficient called the Multi-correlation coefficient.

Pearson Correlation Coefficient. Pearson product-moment correlation coefficient is defined as Eq. 7, where the numerator is the covariance of the two groups of variables X and Y, and the denominator is the power of the variance scores of the two groups of variables. Here, $\bar{(x)}$ represents the sample mean of the variable X.

$$Perason(x, y) = \frac{\sum_{i=1}^{n}(x_i - \bar{x})(y_i - \bar{y})}{\sqrt{\sum_{i=1}^{n}(x_i - \bar{x})^2}\sqrt{\sum_{i=1}^{n}(y_i - \bar{y})^2}} \tag{7}$$

Spearman Correlation Coefficient. The Spearman correlation coefficient is defined as the Pearson correlation coefficient between the ranked variables X and Y. The ranking operation affects the covariance, which is the numerator part of the correlation coefficient calculation.

Kendall Correlation Coefficient. Kendall correlation coefficient first forms a set $(x_1, y_1), ..., (x_n, y_n)$ based on the joint random variable X and Y. Kendall correlation coefficient evaluates the rank correlation between X and Y and is insensitive to the specific distribution of the variables. It first forms a set $(x_1, y_1), ..., (x_n, y_n)$ based on the joint random variable X and Y, and determines whether each pair of points is concordant or discordant based on their relative ranks. The number of discordant pairs is denoted by DP.

$$Kendall(x, y) = 1 - \frac{2 * DP}{\binom{n}{2}} \tag{8}$$

Multi-relation Coefficient. Multi-relation [21] extends the linear correlation between two variables to more variables, and defined the new metric based on orthogonal hyperplane. For k variables Y_i, with n observations each, we can form a kn matrix Y with kn total observations. Since each variable Y_i may be collected from a different background, we first normalize Y along each row to obtain a corresponding standardized matrix S. Using the standardized matrix S, we can calculate the sample correlation matrix R as $R = SS^T$. The Multi-relation coefficient is defined as Eq. 9, where $\lambda(R)$ represents the least eigenvalue of R, and $MR(Y_1, ..., Y_k) \in [0, 1]$ represents the strength of the multi-variable linear correlation.

$$MR(Y_1, ..., Y_k) = 1 - \lambda(R) = 1 - \lambda(SS^T) \tag{9}$$

3   The Proposed Topology Metric

3.1   Motivation

During our testing of the previous topology-based metrics in local simulation environments (Floor2 and Garage), we found that although MOM claims to improve the correlation of metrics with RPE through orthogonal plane detection, the algorithm's reliance on agglomerative clustering based on plane finding estimates suffers from the following drawbacks:

– As shown in the upper part of Fig. 1, agglomerative clustering based on normal can result in the loss of a significant number of critical plane features, which can have a significant impact on subsequent calculations.
– As shown in the bottom left of Fig. 1, clustering based on manual parameter tuning can significantly impact plane detection and generate a large number of incorrect plane results, which are represented by different colors.
– As shown in the bottom right of Fig. 1, plane detection errors can further impact normal estimation and result in multiple normal directions (represented by black lines) for the same plane.

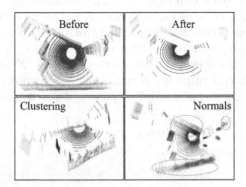

Fig. 1. Example of the drawbacks of orthogonal plane detection using a local point cloud map of five frames in Floor2.

We can see from the original point cloud (as shown in the top left of Fig. 1) that the topological structure of the point cloud map in the current area is relatively simple, and it does not contain any potential dynamic or semi-dynamic targets. However, heuristic algorithms that rely on manual parameter tuning have limited generalization abilities and are unable to understand the semantic information of the scene. As a result, when the topological information of the indoor scene is more complex and contains moving or potentially moving targets, MOM is likely to experience significant degradation.

3.2 The Workflow

We prefer to introduce the deep learning-based point cloud semantic segmentation to refine the plane detection, the whole workflow is as shown in Fig. 2.

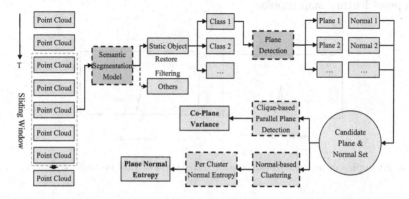

Fig. 2. The proposed workflow for calculating topology-based metrics involves a semantic segmentation model.

The algorithm first uses a sliding window to sample the continuous point cloud. In contrast to MOM, which only calculates orthogonal planes for the first frame of the point cloud, we segment each frame of the point cloud sequentially using a deep learning semantic segmentation model to obtain all semantic classes. This allows us to differentiate between static objects (such as walls, floors, and pillars) and other objects, and retain only the former after segmentation. Next, we apply robust statistical plane detection [22] to each class of static object points and estimate the corresponding plane normal. We store all candidate planes and normals for later topology metric calculation. Finally, we calculate the Co-Plane Variance (CPV) and Plane Normal Entropy (PNE) metrics based on all candidate planes and normals in the current window.

The selection of point cloud semantic segmentation models will be discussed in Sect. 4.2 of the experimental study, where we will comprehensively consider the segmentation accuracy, computational speed, and overall generalization ability of the models. Using semantic segmentation results of static targets in point clouds allows us to enhance the accuracy and completeness of plane detection, as demonstrated in the qualitative analysis shown in Fig. 7. As a result, even though we process all point cloud frames in the sliding window, the number of planes obtained is comparable to that obtained by MOM. Additionally, we update the normals of plane points based on the detected plane normal, which further improves the accuracy of normal estimation for later processes.

3.3   Calculation of CPV and PNE

As presented in Eq. 3, each pose consists of a rotation component and a translation component, and these components have differing effects on the plane topology when there is noise in the related parts. To address these varying effects, we propose the use of Co-Plane Variance (CPV) and Plane Normal Entropy (PNE) metrics to detect the two types of noise during SLAM pose estimation with a local point feature map topology.

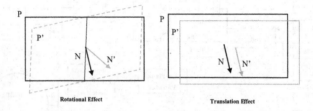

Fig. 3. Examples of how the rotation and translation of the pose affect plane changes.

Even slight translation noise can cause the same plane in two consecutive frames of point clouds to shift, as shown in Fig. 3 (right), leading to a larger variance of points on approximately co-planar planes. To mitigate this effect, we propose the use of a clique-based parallel plane detection algorithm. This algorithm identifies near co-planes based on the co-planar condition of Eq. 10 obtained from the parallel planes. This approach can be achieved through graph-based clique searching, which allows for efficient and accurate identification of near co-planes. Once the near co-planes have been identified, we calculate the point variance of all near co-planes as the final result of CPV. By using this approach, we can more accurately estimate the plane parameters and reduce the impact of translation noise on the topology of the point cloud.

$$Ax + By + Cz + D_1 = 0$$
$$Ax + By + Cz + D_2 = 0 \tag{10}$$
$$d = \frac{|D_2 - D1|}{\sqrt{A^2 + B^2 + C^2}} < \epsilon$$

Slight rotation noise can cause the same plane in two consecutive frames of point clouds to rotate, as shown in Fig. 3 (left). Although it also leads to an increase in the variance of the plane, the change in the normal direction is more significant. To detect the effect of rotation noise, we propose the use of Plane Normal Entropy (PNE), which is calculated based on clustering candidate normals and computing the entropy of all normals within each cluster. This approach is relatively simple and effective, as it allows us to accurately identify the change in the normal direction of the plane due to rotation noise.

4   Experimental Study

4.1   Data Introduction

To ensure the authenticity and reliability of the evaluation, we constructed a simulation environment in Gazebo [23] that was based on two local real scenes: Garage and Floor2. We deployed a Velodyne-32E (VLP-32) LiDAR with the same parameters as the actual robot configuration in the simulation environment, as shown in Fig. 4. By creating an equal-scale simulation environment, we were able to accurately evaluate the performance of our proposed method in a controlled and repeatable setting. Although both scenes contain a large number of orthogonal planes, the overall topological structures of the two local scenes are not highly regular. Moreover, Garage is a huge simulation scenario with a total area of up to 14,000 square meters. In addition, semi-dynamic objects such as tables and chairs are randomly added, which will also add certain interference to the robot's perception.

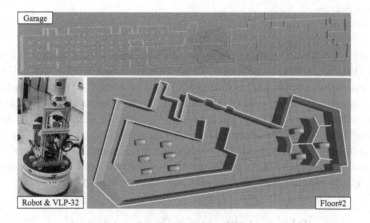

Fig. 4. Two public and real simulation scenes of local office and underground garage, and the robot equipped with VLP-32 LiDAR.

To collect the data for our evaluation, we controlled the robot to randomly move through each scene, collecting VLP-32 point cloud and the robot pose at a frequency of 5 Hz. To ensure comprehensive coverage of each scenario, we collected two sets of point cloud data with different trajectory sequences. We manually labeled the semantic information for each point cloud using the Point

Labeler tool [24], which allowed us to accurately evaluate the performance of our proposed method in detecting and classifying different objects in the point cloud data. We divided the labeled point cloud data into two non-overlapping sets, which were used for training and testing the semantic segmentation model, as well as for evaluating the topological metrics for SLAM. To illustrate the labeled point cloud data, we provide an example of the Garage scene in Fig. 5. The upper image shows the original point cloud, which is colored by height for the convenience of visualization. The bottom image shows the same point cloud data, but with colors assigned based on the manually labeled semantic information. This example illustrates the effectiveness of our labeling process in accurately identifying different objects and structures in the point cloud data.

Fig. 5. Visualization of Garage point cloud overlapped scene map before and after semantic annotation (bird's eye view): coloring by height (top) and coloring by semantic label (bottom).

Table 1 provides a summary of the point cloud frames that make up the Train Set and Test Set, which consist of 3779 and 3561 frames, respectively. To ensure the generalization and augmentation of our data, we combined data collected from different scenes for training and evaluation of the deep learning-based point cloud semantic segmentation models. We also added two public scenes (Office1 & 2) collected from the Gazebo community to further enhance the diversity of our dataset. The total indoor scene semantic targets include five categories, which are ground, wall, pillar, table, and chair. To ensure the validity of our segmentation model evaluation, the two datasets are disjoint and do not overlap.

Table 1. Details of the Train set and Test set.

Scenes	Train Set (frames)	Test Set (frames)	Classes
Office1	410	427	4
Office2	375	333	4
Floor2	678	577	3
Garage	2316	2224	3
Total	3779	3561	5

4.2 Point Cloud Segmentation Performance

We trained and tested all models on a GPU server with the following specifications: CPU@Intel i9-12900K, 128 GB Memory, NVIDIA RTX 3090@24 GB. The frame per second (FPS) was calculated based on the mean value of continuous segmentation processing of 1000 frames of point cloud data. We tested three different models in this study: MinkowskiNet [25], CylinderNet [26], and SPVCNN [27]. We used the data in Table 1 in Sect. 4.1 to train and test the three deep learning models, and the results are shown in Table 2. The three models shared the same training configurations, which included 36 epochs, Stochastic gradient descent (SGD) optimizer, 0.02 learning rate with 0.0001 weight decay and 0.9 momentum. However, the batch size was different due to the constraints of video memory and model parameter scale.

Table 2. Performances of the per frame point cloud semantic segmentation results.

Model	mIoU	Per Class IoU					FPS
		Floor	Wall	Pillar	Desk	Chair	
MinkowskiNet [25]	95.84676↑	98.8446	97.7756	92.656	93.4457	96.5119	347.28 ↑
CylinderNet [26]	89.8108	96.956	95.4882	86.6077	81.4631	88.539	309.47
SPVCNN [27]	91.09102	98.6575	96.4578	87.0115	84.241	89.0873	151.48

We consider both the per class intersection-over-union (IoU), mean Jaccard (mIoU), and frames per second (FPS) in our evaluation. The mIoU is defined as shown in Eq. 11, where TP_c, FP_c, and FN_c correspond to the number of True Positive (TP), False Positive (FP), and False Negative (FN) predictions for the points of class c in the current frame, and C is the number of classes (which is 5 in our case). A higher mIoU indicates better semantic segmentation accuracy.

$$mIoU = \frac{1}{C} \sum_{c=1}^{C} \frac{TP_c}{TP_c + FP_c + FN_c} * 100\% \tag{11}$$

Table 2 shows that all models converge very well, but MinkowskiNet achieves the highest mIoU of 95.84, which is also the highest for per class IoU. Additionally, it is the fastest model with 347.28 FPS for point cloud of VLP-32 ($\sim$57,600 points) on the GPU server. SPVCNN achieves the second highest mIoU, but its FPS is only about half of MinkowskiNet at around 151. CylinderNet has a slightly lower mIoU than SPVCNN at 89.8, but it achieves the second-fastest speed at 309 FPS. Figure 6 presents a detailed segmentation result (Confusion Matrix) of MinkowskiNet on the Test Set. In the confusion matrix, the values on the main diagonal represent the percentage of correctly segmented point clouds, while the remaining blocks indicate the specific category and percentage of wrongly segmented point clouds. The pillar and desk categories cause more incorrect segmentation, but the segmentation accuracy of the floor and wall categories, which contain planes, is both higher than 99%. This demonstrates that introducing a segmentation model can provide a guarantee for subsequent correct plane detection. Therefore, we prefer to choose MinkowskiNet as the semantic segmentation model in our system to obtain semantic labels for each frame of point cloud.

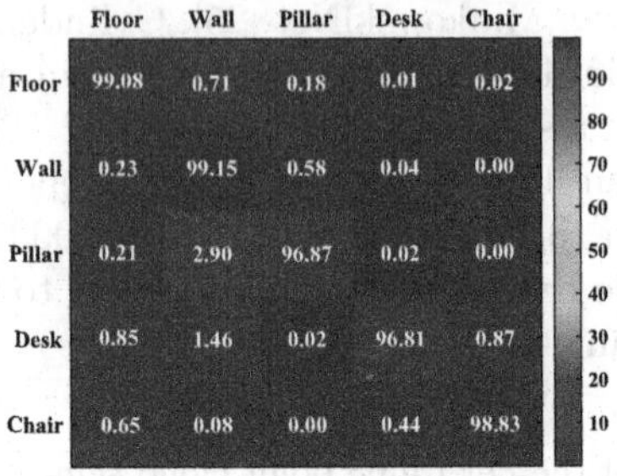

	Floor	Wall	Pillar	Desk	Chair
Floor	99.08	0.71	0.18	0.01	0.02
Wall	0.23	99.15	0.58	0.04	0.00
Pillar	0.21	2.90	96.87	0.02	0.00
Desk	0.85	1.46	0.02	96.81	0.87
Chair	0.65	0.08	0.00	0.44	98.83

Fig. 6. Confusion matrix of the semantic segmentation results of MinkowskiNet on Test Set.

4.3 Plane Detection

Since the dataset does not include labels for point cloud planes, we can only evaluate the effectiveness of plane detection and normal estimation qualitatively. Figure 7 shows the detected planes and estimated normals of the points on each plane. By comparing these results to those from MOM in Fig. 1 (bottom), it is evident that almost all planes are correctly detected, and the directions of the point normals are also consistent.

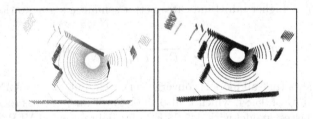

Fig. 7. The plane detection result based on semantic segmentation and robust statistic plane detection.

4.4 Binary Correlation Analysis

To analyze the correlation between RPE and different topology-based metrics, while considering the rotation and translation components of a pose, we added noise to the collected data's poses. Specifically, we added three types of noise patterns, namely $[r, t, rt]$, and three levels of noise magnitudes, namely $[1, 1.5, 2]$. Figure 8, Fig. 9, and Fig. 10 illustrate the binary correlations between RPE and rotation (r), translation (t), and transformation (rt) noise at different scales.

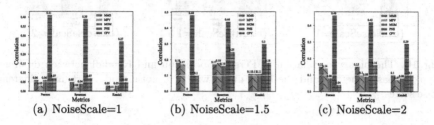

(a) NoiseScale=1   (b) NoiseScale=1.5   (c) NoiseScale=2

Fig. 8. The binary correlation of Person, Spearman and Kendall between different topology-based metrics and the RPE under win = 5, noise mode = r, and different noise scales.

By analyzing the correlation between RPE and different topology-based metrics with varying scales of rotation noise as shown in Fig. 8, we found that PNE exhibits the highest correlation with RPE compared to other topology-based metrics. This result confirms our hypothesis in Sect. 3.3, which suggests that noise in the rotation component significantly affects the normals of parallel planar points.

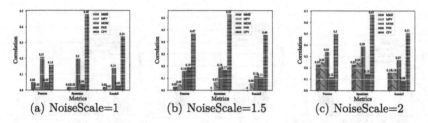

(a) NoiseScale=1   (b) NoiseScale=1.5   (c) NoiseScale=2

Fig. 9. The binary correlation of Person, Spearman and Kendall between different topology-based metrics and the RPE under win = 5, noise mode = t, and different noise scales.

By analyzing the correlation between RPE and different topology-based metrics with varying scales of translation noise as shown in Fig. 9, we found that CPV exhibits the highest correlation with RPE compared to other topology-based metrics, except for Pearson when NoiseScale = 1 (which is only slightly lower than MOM). This result confirms our hypothesis in Sect. 3.3 that noise in the translation component significantly affects the variance of points on nearby planes.

Simultaneously adding rotation and translation noise to the data poses resulted in various topology-based metrics showing no significantly strong correlation with RPE under different noise scales, as shown in Fig. 10. In some cases,

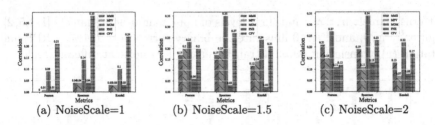

Fig. 10. The binary correlation of Person, Spearman and Kendall between different topology-based metrics and the RPE under win = 5, noise mode = rt, and different noise scales.

MOM showed the highest correlation, while in other cases, CPV showed the highest correlation. These results suggest that the combined effect of rotation and translation noise on pose estimation is complex, the current global topology metrics are difficult to evaluate and requires further investigation.

4.5   Triple Correlation Analysis

To evaluate the correlation between PNE, CPV, and RPE when both rotation and translation noise are added simultaneously, we used the Multi-relation of Eq. 9. As shown in Fig. 11, the Multi-relation (PNE, CPV, RPE) exhibited an extremely high correlation under different noise scales.

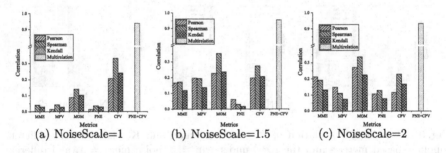

Fig. 11. The correlation of Person, Spearman, Kendall and Multi-relation between different topology-based metrics and the RPE under win = 5, noise mode = rt, and different noise scales.

Similar results were observed in the Garage scenario, as indicated by the correlation metrics. Considering redundancy, related results will not be presented here.

4.6   Time Complexity

Figure 12 presents a comparison of the time consumption of each topology-based metric under different sampling window sizes, namely 5, 10, and 15 frames. The test was conducted on a mobile edge device (AMD R9-5900HX@3.3 GHz) in a single-threaded manner to assess the algorithm's feasibility and real-time performance in actual mobile robot deployment. We evaluated the entire sequence of Floor2 TestSet using a sliding window to sample the collected point clouds during calculation. The window step was set equal to the window length (e.g., $winsize = winstep = 5$) to avoid repetition of sampling. Gaussian random noise was added to each frame point cloud to simulate the point cloud distortion caused by actual robot motion. Each box-plot displays the maximum, minimum, median, 1st, and 3rd quartiles of all computation time spent for each metric, and each sub-figure shows an enlarged result.

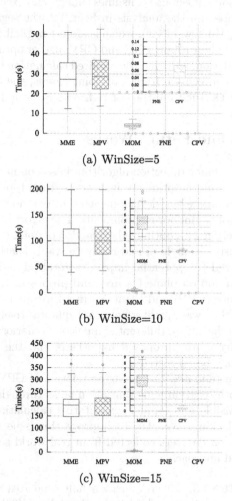

(a) WinSize=5

(b) WinSize=10

(c) WinSize=15

Fig. 12. Time complexity statistics of each metric calculation under different window sizes, i.e., 5, 10 and 15 frames are considered in this study.

The calculation of MME and MPV requires traversing the global point cloud, and the corresponding calculation time increases proportionally when the window size of the superimposed local map increases. MOM reduces computation time by checking candidate orthogonal planes only in the point cloud of the first frame and performing KNN search on a local map based on a small set of candidate points belonging to the orthogonal planes. However, MOM still needs to perform operations such as KD-Tree construction, search, and clustering based on large-scale point clouds, and the single calculation time consumption takes several seconds. By introducing deep learning-based point cloud semantic segmentation, the calculation of PNE and CPV can be greatly accelerated. Although the neural network model itself also consumes time, it can execute independently on the GPU, and based on the analysis in Sect. 4.2, the segmentation time is about 0.0028 s (using MinkowskiNet), which is almost negligible compared to the 5/10 Hz of low-speed indoor robot. PNE and CPV further optimize the follow-up topology metric calculation, reducing the required calculation time and volatility. When processing 15 consecutive frames of point clouds, the overall calculation time does not exceed 1 s (the total time of 15 frames is 3 s under 5 Hz sampling).

5   Conclusions and Future Works

This paper proposes a plane detection algorithm based on neural network point cloud semantic segmentation optimization, starting from topology-based SLAM pose estimation, to promote the development of autonomous localization techniques for mobile robots in indoor environments. The algorithm combines robust statistical plane detection with optimized extraction of point cloud plane features to ensure comprehensive, complete, and accurate stable spatial topological features. We also analyzed the potential impact of rotation and translation noise in SLAM pose estimation on plane features and proposed two evaluation metrics, Co-Plane Variance (CPV) and Plane Normal Entropy (PNE), respectively. The proposed algorithm was qualitatively and quantitatively evaluated using point cloud and pose data from different simulation scenarios in Gazebo, which confirmed the validity of the proposed hypothesis and the rationality of the corresponding topology-based metrics.

Although we have validated the strong correlation of CPV+PNE with RPE in the presence of both rotation and translation noise through triple correlation (Multirelation), a feasible and unified quantitative calculation method for the two metrics is still lacking. We plan to improve this issue in the future and conduct experiments on datasets collected from real-world scenarios to further validate our proposed approach.

ACKNOWLEDGMENTS. This research was fully supported by Zhejiang Provincial Natural Science Foundation of China under Grant No. LY23F020026, and partly supported by Tianmushan Laboratory Research Project TK-2023-B-010 and TK-2023-C-020.

References

1. Ohno, K., Tsubouchi, T., Shigematsu, B., Yuta, S.: Differential GPS and odometry-based outdoor navigation of a mobile robot. Adv. Robot. **18**(6), 611–635 (2004)
2. Xu, Y., Shmaliy, Y.S., Ahn, C.K., Tian, G., Chen, X.: Robust and accurate UWB-based indoor robot localisation using integrated EKF/EFIR filtering. IET Radar Sonar Navig. **12**(7), 750–756 (2018)
3. Zhang, J., Singh, S.: LOAM: lidar odometry and mapping in real-time. In: Robotics: Science and Systems, vol. 2, pp. 1–9. Berkeley, CA (2014)
4. Shan, T., Englot, B., Meyers, D., Wang, W., Ratti, C., Rus, D.: LIO-SAM: tightly-coupled lidar inertial odometry via smoothing and mapping. In: 2020 IEEE/RSJ International Conference on Intelligent Robots and Systems (IROS), pp. 5135–5142. IEEE (2020)
5. Shan, T., Englot, B.: LeGO-LOAM: lightweight and ground-optimized lidar odometry and mapping on variable terrain. In: 2018 IEEE/RSJ International Conference on Intelligent Robots and Systems (IROS), pp. 4758–4765. IEEE (2018)
6. Livingstone, D., Miranda, E.: Orb3: adaptive interface design for real time sound synthesis & diffusion within socially mediated spaces. In: Proceedings of the 2005 Conference on New Interfaces for Musical Expression, pp. 65–69 (2005)
7. Wang, Y., Tan, R., Xing, G., Wang, J., Tan, X., Liu, X.: Samba: a smartphone-based robot system for energy-efficient aquatic environment monitoring. In: Proceedings of the 14th International Conference on Information Processing in Sensor Networks, pp. 262–273 (2015)
8. Sumikura, S., Shibuya, M., Sakurada, K.: OpenVSLAM: a versatile visual slam framework. In: Proceedings of the 27th ACM International Conference on Multimedia, pp. 2292–2295 (2019)
9. Helmberger, M., Morin, K., Berner, B., Kumar, N., Cioffi, G., Scaramuzza, D.: The hilti SLAM challenge dataset. IEEE Robot. Autom. Lett. **7**(3), 7518–7525 (2022)
10. Michael Grupp. evo: Python package for the evaluation of odometry and slam (2017). github.com/MichaelGrupp/evo
11. Burri, M., et al.: The EuRoC micro aerial vehicle datasets. Int. J. Robot. Res. **35**(10), 1157–1163 (2016)
12. Sturm, J., Burgard, W., Cremers, D.: Evaluating egomotion and structure-from-motion approaches using the tum RGB-D benchmark. In: Proceedings of the Workshop on Color-Depth Camera Fusion in Robotics at the IEEE/RJS International Conference on Intelligent Robot Systems (IROS), vol. 13 (2012)
13. Droeschel, D., Stückler, J., Behnke, S.: Local multi-resolution representation for 6d motion estimation and mapping with a continuously rotating 3d laser scanner. In: 2014 IEEE International Conference on Robotics and Automation (ICRA), pp. 5221–5226. IEEE (2014)
14. Razlaw, J., Droeschel, D., Holz, D., Behnke, S.: Evaluation of registration methods for sparse 3d laser scans. In: 2015 European Conference on Mobile Robots (ECMR), pp. 1–7. IEEE (2015)
15. Kornilova, A., Ferrer, G.: Be your own benchmark: no-reference trajectory metric on registered point clouds. In: 2021 European Conference on Mobile Robots (ECMR), pp. 1–8. IEEE (2021)
16. Strasdat, H.: Local accuracy and global consistency for efficient visual SLAM. Ph.D. thesis, Department of Computing, Imperial College London (2012)
17. Guclu, O., Can, A.B.: Fast and effective loop closure detection to improve slam performance. J. Intell. Robot. Syst. **93**, 495–517 (2019)

18. Koide, K., Miura, J., Yokozuka, M., Oishi, S., Banno, A.: Interactive 3d graph slam for map correction. IEEE Robot. Autom. Lett. **6**(1), 40–47 (2020)

19. Ouyang, Z., Zhang, C., Cui, J.: Semantic SLAM for Mobile Robot with Human-in-the-Loop. In: Gao, H., Wang, X., Wei, W., Dagiuklas, T. (eds.) CollaborateCom 2022, Part II. LNICS, vol. 461, pp. 289–305. Springer, Cham (2022). https://doi.org/10.1007/978-3-031-24386-8_16

20. Chen, X., et al.: OverlapNet: loop closing for lidar-based slam. arXiv preprint arXiv:2105.11344 (2021)

21. Drezner, Z.: Multirelation–a correlation among more than two variables. Comput. Stat. Data Anal. **19**(3), 283–292 (1995)

22. Araújo, A.M.C., Oliveira, M.M.: A robust statistics approach for plane detection in unorganized point clouds. Pattern Recogn. **100**, 107115 (2020)

23. Koenig, N., Howard, A.: Design and use paradigms for gazebo, an open-source multi-robot simulator. In: 2004 IEEE/RSJ International Conference on Intelligent Robots and Systems (IROS) (IEEE Cat. No. 04CH37566), vol. 3, pp. 2149–2154. IEEE (2004)

24. Behley, J., et al.: SemanticKITTI: a dataset for semantic scene understanding of LiDAR sequences. In: Proceedings of the IEEE/CVF International Conference on Computer Vision (ICCV) (2019)

25. Choy, C., Gwak, J., Savarese, S.: 4d spatio-temporal convnets: Minkowski convolutional neural networks. In: Proceedings of the IEEE/CVF Conference on Computer Vision and Pattern Recognition, pp. 3075–3084 (2019)

26. Zhu, X., et al.: Cylindrical and asymmetrical 3d convolution networks for lidar segmentation. In: Proceedings of the IEEE/CVF Conference on Computer Vision and Pattern Recognition, pp. 9939–9948 (2021)

27. Tang, H., et al.: Searching efficient 3D architectures with sparse point-voxel convolution. In: Vedaldi, A., Bischof, H., Brox, T., Frahm, J.-M. (eds.) ECCV 2020, Part XXVIII. LNCS, vol. 12373, pp. 685–702. Springer, Cham (2020). https://doi.org/10.1007/978-3-030-58604-1_41

On the Performance of Federated Learning Network

Godwin Idoje[✉], Tasos Dagiuklas, and Muddesar Iqbal

Computer Science Department, London South Bank University,
London SE1 0AA, UK
idojeg2@lsbu.ac.uk
https://www.suitelab.org

Abstract. Federated Learning is a decentralised network platform where the edge nodes train their local models and send their updated weights to the server. The server combines all the various local weights received and sends the aggregated model back to the edge nodes for further training, and this process continues until convergence is achieved. This study models the Federated Learning (FL) network. The Traffic speed (TS), Round trip time (RTT), and Bandwidth delay-product (BDP) parameters have been considered for modelling the Federated Learning network. Through experimentation, it can be inferred that the TS has a high impact and high correlation on the BDP within the network, and the RTT has a low impact on the BDP. The decentralised and classical machine learning models' predictions have been compared. It has been observed that the decentralised machine learning model's prediction outperforms the classical machine learning model's prediction. The link experiences low latency because only the updated weights are transmitted within the link and not the raw data.

Keywords: Federated Learning · Bandwidth delay product ·
aggregate model · Round Trip time · Traffic speed

1 Introduction

Federated Learning is a decentralised Machine Learning framework where the edge nodes train their local models and send their updated weights to the server. The server combines all the various local updated weights received and sends the aggregated model back to the edge nodes for further training. This process continues until convergence is achieved [1]. The authors in [2] used the Network traffic Federated Learning extreme Learning machine models to analyse local network traffic data. Their model achieved a higher accuracy when compared with their benchmark models. The authors in [3] have used stochastic models, optimisation models and differential equations to model the optimisation of the federated Learning network. The stochastic models have been used to resolve uncertainty and variability data issues, while the convergence and stability challenges have been resolved using the deterministic models. This study discusses

© ICST Institute for Computer Sciences, Social Informatics and Telecommunications Engineering 2024
Published by Springer Nature Switzerland AG 2024. All Rights Reserved
H. Gao et al. (Eds.): CollaborateCom 2023, LNICST 563, pp. 41–56, 2024.
https://doi.org/10.1007/978-3-031-54531-3_3

the modelling of the network of queues of the federated Learning platform while considering the Bandwidth delay product (BDP) as a performance metric.

The authors in [4] discuss that Federated learning is a method in machine learning where a model is trained across numerous distributed edge devices or servers, each containing its own set of local data samples, without disclosing these data. This approach safeguards data privacy by storing it locally on a server or edge device during the model training process. Given legal constraints, this technique holds particular significance for hospitals, as it enables collaborative machine learning model development without transferring all the training data, such as patient records, to a centralised location. According to the authors in [5], Federated learning emerges as a privacy-centric approach to machine learning, which finds valuable application in intelligent healthcare. It involves orchestrating multiple hospitals to conduct deep learning training collaboratively without exchanging data. This federated learning technique standardises the individual training procedures by globally averaging feature vectors. Throughout the federated training process, the transmission of model parameters is unnecessary, and local clients merely upload the average feature vectors of each class. Clients can opt for distinct local models based on their computational capacities.

The authors in [6] discuss that Federated learning enables deep learning algorithms to gain insights from a wide range of data present in various databases. This innovative approach allows deep learning models to be trained using local patient data from different medical centres, with only model parameters shared among the facilities. The authors in [7] discuss that Federated Learning is the evaluation of models in a decentralised platform where the communication cost is reduced because only the updated weights of the local models are sent to the server. It can be inferred from their research that the Long short-term memory models considered for the federated Learning network have been five times faster in achieving prediction values than the centralised network. The authors in [8] discuss that the FL model has been used to aggregate the updated weights from health institutions (electronic records and primary & secondary health centres). The FL evaluation of the dataset has provided data privacy and security for health institutions.

It can be inferred from [1–8] that the FL technique enables data training while the dataset is domiciled at the local edge device. This method provides privacy for the data and reduces the communication cost of the network. Figure 1 and Fig. 2 depict the architecture of the decentralised and centralised network, respectively. The decentralised network only sends the updated weights to the server for aggregation, unlike the centralised network, where the raw datasets are sent to the server in the cloud for analysis. The decentralised network provides data privacy and security since the server in the cloud does not see the raw dataset for evaluation.

Our Contribution. Our paper models the FL network as a network of queues within a federated learning network, considering the network's Bandwidth delay product (BDP), Traffic speed and round trip time (RTT) as a performance metric. The convergence of decentralised and the classical centralised models has been compared. The decentralised model converged better than the classical centralised model. It has been observed that comparing the decentralised and centralised networks, the Bandwidth delay product of the decentralised network has been able to match a higher proportion of the predicted BDP with the original BDP values. Section 2 discusses the related works. Section 3 discusses the methodology adopted in conducting this research, while Sect. 4 discusses the results obtained from the experimentation. Section 5 narrates the conclusion and the Area of further work.

2   Related Work

The authors in [9] discuss that the congestion window within a network link, where the bandwidth capacity and the round-trip time (RTT) are considered, requires a maximum transmission rate and minimum delay scenario for optimal operation within the network. It can be inferred that the higher the transmission rate, the lower the delay within the network. The authors in [10] discuss the communication cost of the FL network reduction by introducing the federated sparse compression (FSC) algorithm. It can be inferred from their research that better generalisation and prediction have been achieved by using CapsNet to train data in edge devices. The authors in [11] have investigated bottleneck queue level (BQL) performance in a high bandwidth-delay product link. It has been observed that varying the RTT within the network has a very minimal effect on the link performance. They further iterate that the packet loss experienced within the network does not affect the congestion control performance.

The authors in [12] used the content popularity prediction of privacy-preserving (CPPPP) scheme based on federated learning and Wasserstein generative adversarial network (WGAN) to improve the cache hit ratio and resolve the data leakage during model training in an FL platform. It can be inferred that the transmission time using the FL scheme for caching has been reduced. [13] discuss that using Federated averaging + CNN + MobileNet models for the classification of breast cancer images has improved the classification accuracy of breast cancer detection using the federated averaging +CNN model. It can be inferred that their model classification results outperformed other centralised network models. According to [14], FL has been used to analyse chest X-ray images. The federated averaging models have been able to classify the infected lungs and healthy lungs from the image datasets. It can be inferred that their proposed model has reduced the bias in the prediction models because it combines all the updated weights and features of the various edge node models.

The authors in [15] discuss the slow convergence of Mobile edge nodes using Federated Learning for heterogeneous nodes. Their research results outperformed the existing centralised network in resource usage, accuracy, and convergence. [16] discuss that they analysed an Augmented Intelligence of Things (AIoT) network using BDP for a heterogeneous platform, and they affirmed that their solution improved the network's transmission rate by a factor of 3.72. The download rate has been boosted by 3.94 fold. Their solution improves the data transmission rate by reducing the round-trip time's impact and boosting the congestion window optimisation when data loss is experienced. It can be inferred that when the solution reduces the impact of the round-trip time within the network, the bandwidth-delay product is invariably affected positively. According to the authors in [17], many cache misses are experienced when the network's latency increases. Bandwidth and BDP capacities increase, which invariably results in about a 24% drop in throughput-per-core. [18] discuss that within a centralised network, when the RTT varies, as soon as the RTT drops below half of the average RTT, the bottleneck bandwidth round-trip propagation time (BBR) experiences payload collapse because of the congestion within the network.

3   Modelling of the FL Network

The BDP has been the performance metric for the accuracy of the federated Learning Network. The modelling has been achieved by making some assumptions to obtain the performance metric. The modelling Assumptions are the following;

The Arrival of the local model from the edge nodes is independent of each other and discrete events.

The Arrival rate of the local models follows Poisson distribution.

The inter-arrival rate time is independent, and we assume the service rate is said to be exponentially distributed. The edge nodes of the FL network link experience delay. This delay and bandwidth are represented as d_i and b_i, respectively, for the edge node.

Let b_i represent the effective bandwidth of the ith node.

Let d_i represent the effective delay of the ith node. The effective bandwidth of the server node of the Federated Learning network is represented as BW_eff and the delay at the server node is represented as DL_eff

Let BW_eff represent the effective bandwidth at the server.

Let DL_eff represent the effective delay at the server.

$$\sum_{j=1}^{k} b_i^j = b_i | min_j(d_i^j) d_i \tag{1}$$

$$(B_i, D_i) = (\sum_j b_i^j min_j(d_i^j)) \tag{2}$$

Equation 1 represents the summation of the bandwidth for the edge nodes that experience some delay. Equation 2 depicts the aggregate effective bandwidth and effective delay at the edge nodes. $BW_{eff} = min(B_s, B_i)$

$DL_{eff} = (D_s, D_i)$

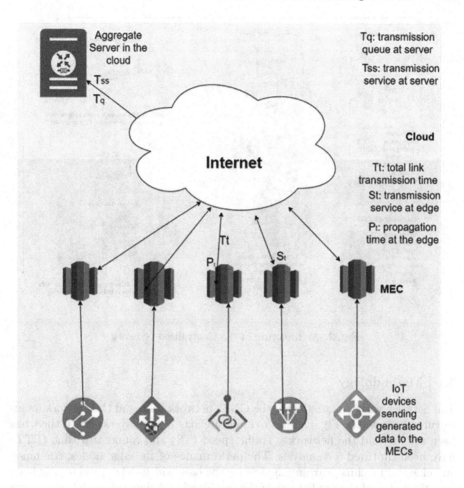

Fig. 1. Architecture of the Federated Learning Network

The Bandwidth Delay product can be calculated as

$$BW_{eff} \times DL_{eff} = \sum_{i=1}^{n} min\left(B_s, B_i\right) \times D_s \sum_{i=1}^{n} D_i$$

$$= \left(\sum_{i=1}^{n} min\left(B_s, \sum_{j=1}^{k} b_i^j\right) \times D_s \sum_{i=1}^{n} min\left(d_i^j\right) \right) \quad (3)$$

Equation 3 shows the product of the effective bandwidth and delay at the server node and the aggregate bandwidth and delay at the edge nodes. It can be inferred that the product of the bandwidth, measured in Megabits per second (Mb/s) and the delay, measured in seconds (s) within the federated learning network, produces the total packets transmitted within the network.

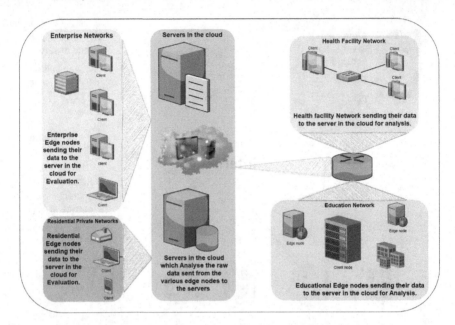

Fig. 2. Architecture of the Centralised Network

3.1   Methodology

The network was emulated using the GNS3 network tool, and the network architecture is shown in Fig. 1. The architecture has 3 tier layers. A Testbed has been set up, and the network's Traffic speed (TS) and round trip time (RTT) have been captured for analysis. The performance of the edge nodes, combined and classical machine learning models for the bandwidth-delay product has been investigated, and the predictions of the combined and classical models have been analysed. The generated data have been sent to the second tier layer containing the MEC nodes. The captured datasets are numerical. They were collected for a duration of Ninety days using the Paessler PRTG network monitor software installed on The database server within the network. The data has been pre-processed using the Python sci-kit library to remove Not A Number (NAN) values. These have been trained, and the local model updates have been sent to the server. The server aggregated all the various models from the respective edge nodes, creating a global model. The server sends the combined model to the edge nodes to train its local model with the new global model until it achieves convergence.

3.2   Time Complexity

The Big O notation is used to determine the time complexity of the Model mathematically.

The iteration

$$H = \frac{n}{2^H} \tag{4}$$

Taking the iteration to equal 100, which has been used for the training of the model during the training in the testbed,

$$n \div 2^H = 100$$

Therefore,

$$n = 100 * 2^H$$

taking the logarithm of both sides of the equation and note that 100 is a constant

$$log n = log 2^H$$

$$log \, n = H \times log_2 2, \quad where \quad log_2 2 = 1$$

$$log \, n = H$$

from the model developed the Big O notation for the FedAve algorithm is $O(log n)$.

It can be inferred that the time complexity for the model is in order of log n, O(log n). The Federated averaging time complexity from Eq. 4 above evaluation is time efficient. It can be inferred that the model will be less space-efficient since time and space complexity are always inversely proportional.

4   Results and Discussion

Figure 3 shows the univariate distribution of the TS, RTT and BDP from the emulated network. It can be inferred that there is a positive correlation between TS and the BDP. The RTT shows a bi-modal distribution having two peak values, and the RTT is skewed to the right, implying the RTT mean values are more than the median values in the dataset. The bi-modal peaks shown in Fig. 3 result from the mixture of the samples from the experimentation. Another reason is the errors within the dataset obtained from the experimentation of the network. The BDP and TS both show they have a single mode, indicating that a single sample of the dataset population represents the mean, and the probability density for the TS and BDP are skewed to the left, indicating the mean for TS and BDP are less than the median of the dataset.

From Fig. 3, it can be deduced that the correlation between the BDP and RTT, BDP and TS experience a lot of noise and has a positive correlation. The chart shows many outliers in the BDP and RTT, unlike the BDP and TS, which have fewer outliers. This indicates that round-trip time has a low influence on the BDP. Taking the TS and RTT from Fig. 3 indicates a positive correlation but a low influence on the BDP due to the high outlier, as shown in Fig. 2. The

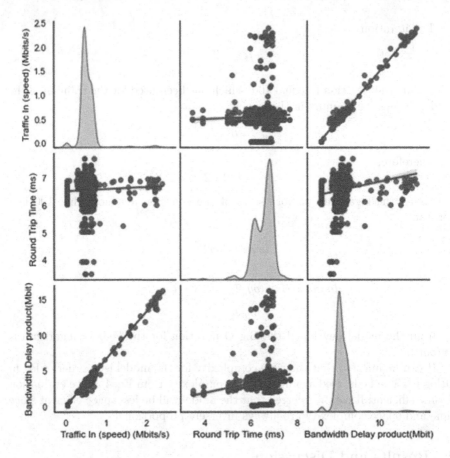

Fig. 3. Pairwise Plot of the Bandwidth Delay Product.

kernel density estimate indicates that the round-trip time is bi-modal while the traffic speed and BDP are unimodal. Figure 3 shows the pairwise plot to express the correlation between the variables, and it cannot be conclusive evidence of the relationship between the TS, RTT and BDP within the dataset. Further analysis is carried out on the BDP dataset using the federated and classical machine learning models. The positive correlation between the BDP and TS indicates a direct relationship. An increase in the TS will invariably increase the BDP. The outliers observed from the dataset captured from the experimentation are caused by the emulation tool used for the experiment. The tool inaccuracies and challenges caused the outliers.

To further substantiate our analysis of the BDP dataset, a heatmap has been developed, as shown in Fig. 4. The heatmap gives numerical values to the correlation between the variables in the BDP dataset. It can be inferred from Fig. 4 that the correlation value between TS and the RTT is 0.042, substantiating the findings in Fig. 3 that the correlation between the two variables is very weak. The correlation value between RTT and the BDP is 0.18, higher than that of

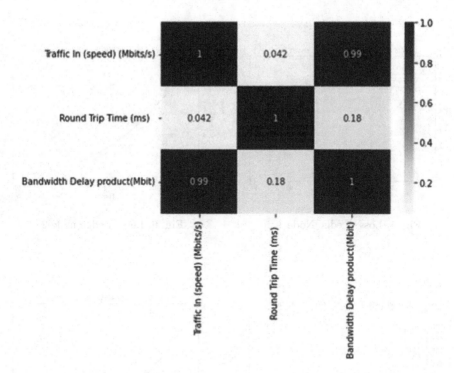

Fig. 4. Heat map correlation of the Bandwidth delay Product.

RTT and TS, but it also shows a weak correlation between the two variables. The correlation values between the BDP and TS have a correlation value of 0.99, which is extremely high, indicating the traffic speed within a federated learning network can influence the BDP values within the network. The diagonal values show the correlation of each to itself.

It can inferred from Figs. 5 to 28 that the convergence of each edge node varies for each node indicating the diversity of the traffic within the edge nodes. Figures 5 to 28 show the different epochs at which each edge node converges indicating the different patterns of the traffic within each edge node. The aggregate model predictions and the Original BDP values are shown in Fig. 29. It can be observed that a high portion of the predictions is very accurate with the original BDP value. This indicates that the aggregate model can combine the individual node models and produce an acceptable prediction of the BDP. This is shown in Fig. 29, where a plot of the predictions against the original BDP values is shown. It can be inferred that the Federated Learning model can predict a high proportion of the BDP original values. The research investigates the predictions of the classical machine learning model, as shown in Fig. 30, where a low proportion of the predicted BDP values accurately match the original BDP values. It can be observed from Figs. 29 and 30 that the aggregate model of the Federated Learning platform has been able to predict a high proportion of the original BDP values.

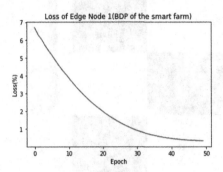

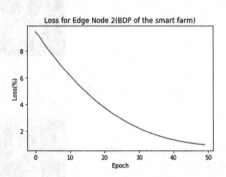

Fig. 5. Loss of edge Node 1

Fig. 6. Loss of edge node 2

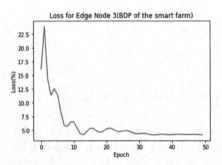

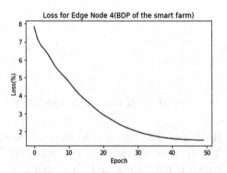

Fig. 7. Loss of edge Node 3

Fig. 8. Loss of edge node 4

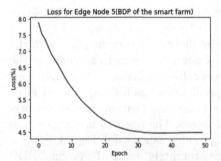

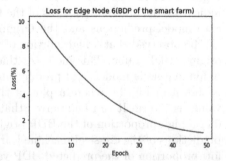

Fig. 9. Loss of edge Node 5

Fig. 10. Loss of edge node 6

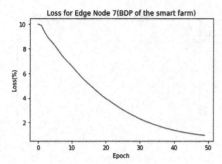

Fig. 11. Loss of edge Node 7

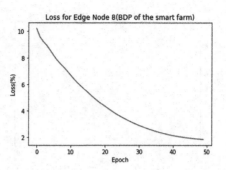

Fig. 12. Loss of edge node 8

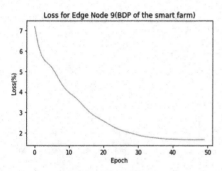

Fig. 13. Loss of edge Node 9

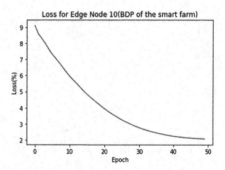

Fig. 14. Loss of edge node 10

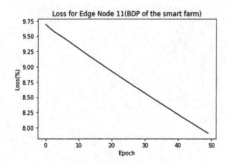

Fig. 15. Loss of edge Node 11

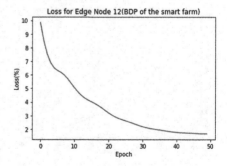

Fig. 16. Loss of edge node 12

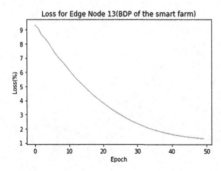

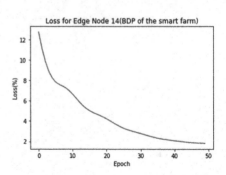

Fig. 17. Loss of edge Node 13

Fig. 18. Loss of edge node 14

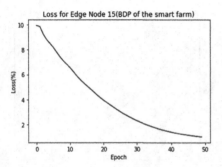

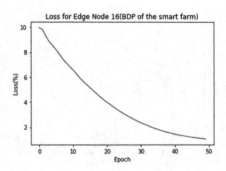

Fig. 19. Loss of edge Node 15

Fig. 20. Loss of edge node 16

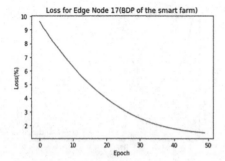

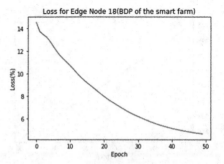

Fig. 21. Loss of edge Node 17

Fig. 22. Loss of edge node 18

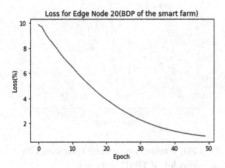

Fig. 23. Loss of edge Node 20

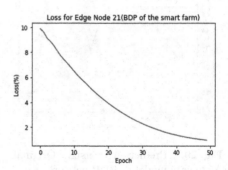

Fig. 24. Loss of edge node 21

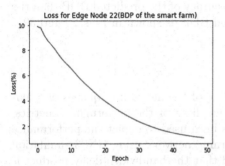

Fig. 25. Loss of edge Node 22

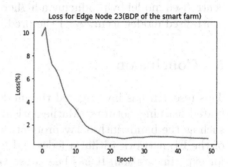

Fig. 26. Loss of edge node 23

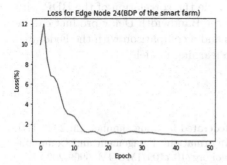

Fig. 27. Loss of edge Node 24

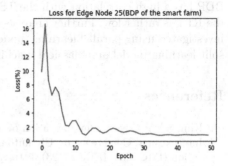

Fig. 28. Loss of edge node 25

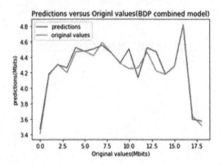
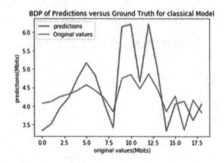

Fig. 29. Prediction versus Original Aggregate model of BDP network

Fig. 30. Prediction versus Original Classical model of BDP network

The Aggregate model of the decentralised network outperforms the centralised machine learning model in the accuracy of the predictions produced, which can be seen in Figs. 29 and 30. The decentralised model outperformed the centralised model by producing a higher accuracy of the predicted BDP than the centralised model accuracy of the predicted BDP as shown in Figs. 29 and 30.

5   Conclusion

This research has investigated the modelling of the network of queues of a federated learning network. Mathematical modelling of the performance metrics, such as the bandwidth-delay product, has been used to depict the performance of the FL network within a federated learning network using GNS3 simulation for experimentation. It has been observed that the bandwidth-delay product is an important parameter that affects the convergence of the federated Learning network. The FL network produced a higher accuracy of the predictions when compared with the centralised machine learning model using the BDP as a performance metric. The predictions of the decentralised machine learning model outperformed the classical machine learning model. It can be inferred that the BDP has a high correlation with the TS, while the correlation of the BDP with the RTT is rather low. Further analysis of the Bandwidth Delay product can be investigated using parallel learning models and a comparison with the Federated split learning model and classical machine learning model.

References

1. Kim, S.W.: Covert communication over federated learning channel. In: 2023 17th International Conference on Ubiquitous Information Management and Communication (IMCOM). IEEE (2023). https://doi.org/10.1109/IMCOM56909.2023
2. Qiu, C.: A network traffic classification method based on federated learning and extreme learning machine. In: 2023 IEEE International Conference on Control, Electronics and Computer Technology (ICCECT). IEEE (2023). https://doi.org/10.1109/ICCECT57938.2023.10140851

3. Kumar, B., Singh, S., Grover, R., Isabels, K.R., Garg, A., Dattatraya, B.C.: Analysis of mathematical modelling deterministic and stochastic problems in federated learning. In: 2023 3rd International Conference on Advance Computing and Innovative Technologies in Engineering (ICACITE), Greater Noida, India, 2023, pp. 1700–1704 (2023). https://doi.org/10.1109/ICACITE57410.2023.10183114

4. Korkmaz, A., Alhonainy, A., Rao, P.: An evaluation of federated learning techniques for secure and privacy-preserving machine learning on medical datasets. In: 2022 IEEE Applied Imagery Pattern Recognition Workshop (AIPR) (2022). https://doi.org/10.1109/AIPR57179.2022.10092212

5. Lai, W., Yan, Q.: Federated learning for detecting COVID-19 in chest CT images: a lightweight federated learning approach. In: 2022, 4th International Conference on Frontiers Technology of Information and Computer (ICFTIC), Qingdao, China, pp. 146–149 (2022). https://doi.org/10.1109/ICFTIC57696.2022.10075165

6. Abidin, N.Z., Ismail, A.R.: Federated deep learning for automated detection of diabetic retinopathy. In: 2022 IEEE 8th International Conference on Computing, Engineering and Design (ICCED), Sukabumi, Indonesia, pp. 1–5 (2022). https://doi.org/10.1109/ICCED56140.2022.10010636

7. Da Costa, L.F., Furtado, L.S., Rocha, P.H., Rego, P.A., Trinta, F.A.: Time series prediction in IoT: a comparative study of federated versus centralized learning. In: 2023 IEEE 20th Consumer Communications & Networking Conference (CCNC). IEEE (2023). https://doi.org/10.1109/CCNC51644.2023.10060467

8. Gupta, A., Maurya, C., Dhere, K., Chaurasiya, V.K.: Wellness detection using clustered federated learning. In: 2022, IEEE 6th Conference on Information and Communication Technology (CICT), Gwalior, India, pp. 1–5 (2022). https://doi.org/10.1109/CICT56698.2022.9997827

9. Bhanumathi, V., Dhanasekaran, R.: TCP variants - a comparative analysis for a high bandwidth-delay product in a mobile ad-hoc network. In: 2010, the 2nd International Conference on Computer and Automation Engineering (ICCAE) (2010). https://doi.org/10.1109/ICCAE.2010.5451683

10. Wang, A., Zhao, Y., Yang, L., Wu, H., Iwahori, Y.: Heterogeneous defect prediction algorithm combined with federated sparse compression. IEEE Access 11, 23739–23753 (2023). https://doi.org/10.1109/ACCESS.2023.3253765

11. Gupta, S., Singh, Y.: Comparative analysis of newer congestion control algorithms in high BDP networks (2022). https://doi.org/10.56726/IRJMETS30391

12. Wang, K., Deng, N., Li, X.: An efficient content popularity prediction of privacy preserving based on federated learning and Wasserstein GAN. IEEE Internet Things J. 10(5), 3786–3798 (2022). https://doi.org/10.1109/JIOT.2022.3176360

13. Nguyen Tan, Y., Tinh, Y.P., Lam, P.D., Nam, N.H., Khoa, T.A.: A transfer learning approach to breast cancer classification in a federated learning framework. IEEE Access 27462–27476 (2023). https://doi.org/10.1109/ACCESS.2023.3257562

14. Pereira, K., Parikh, A., Kumar, P., Devadkar, K.: Healthcare diagnostics service using federated learning. In: 2023 International Conference for Advancement in Technology (ICONAT). IEEE (2023). https://doi.org/10.1109/ICONAT57137.2023.10080053

15. Sun, W., Zhao, Y., Ma, W., Guo, B., Xu, L., Duong, T.Q.: Accelerating convergence of federated learning in MEC with dynamic community. IEEE Trans. Mob. Comput. (2023). https://doi.org/10.1109/TMC.2023.3241770

16. Zong, L., Qiao, D., Wang, H., Bai, Y.: Sustainable cross-regional transmission control for the industrial augmented intelligence of things. IEEE Trans. Industr. Inf. (2022). https://doi.org/10.1109/TII.2022.3230674

17. Cai, Q., Chaudhary, S., Vuppalapati, M., Hwang, J., Agarwal, R.: Understanding Host Network Stack Overheads. ACM (2021). ISBN 978-1-4503-8383-7/21/08. https://doi.org/10.1145/3452296.3472888
18. Kumar, R., et al.: TCP BBR for ultra-low latency networking: challenges, analysis, and solutions. In: 2019 IFIP Networking Conference (IFIP Networking), pp. 1–9. IEEE (2019). ISBN 978-3-903176-16-4

Federated Learning and Application

FedECCR: Federated Learning Method with Encoding Comparison and Classification Rectification

Yan Zeng[1,2,3], Hui Zheng[1] ⓘ, Xin Wang[1] ⓘ, Beibei Zhang[4] ⓘ,
Mingyao Zhou[5(✉)] ⓘ, Jilin Zhang[1,2,3] ⓘ, and YongJian Ren[1,2,3] ⓘ

[1] School of Computer Science and Technology, Hangzhou Dianzi University,
Hangzhou 310018, China
{yz,222050267,wangxin,jilin.zhang,yongjian.ren}@hdu.edu.cn
[2] Key Laboratory for Modeling and Simulation of Complex Systems,
Ministry of Education, Hangzhou 310018, China
[3] Data Security Governance Zhejiang Engineering Research Center,
Hangzhou 310018, China
[4] Zhejiang Lab, Hangzhou 311100, China
[5] Hangzhou Huawei Communication Technology Co., Ltd., Hangzhou 310052, China
zhoumingyao@huaewei.com

Abstract. Federated learning is a distributed training method that integrates multi-party data information using privacy-preserving technologies through dispersed client data sets to jointly construct a global model under the coordination of a central server. However, in practical applications, there is a high degree of data distribution skewness among clients, which causes the optimization direction of the client models to diverge, resulting in model bias and reducing the accuracy of the global model. Existing methods require the calculation and transmission of much information to correct the optimization direction of the client models, or only roughly limit the deviation of the client models end-to-end, ignoring targeted processing of the internal structure of the model, resulting in unclear improvement effects. To address these problems, we propose a federated optimization algorithm FedECCR based on encoding contrast and classification correction. This algorithm divides the model into an encoder and a classifier. It utilizes prototype contrastive training of the model encoder and unbiased classification correction of the classifier. This approach notably improves the accuracy of the global model while maintaining low communication costs. We conducted experiments on multiple data sets to evaluate the validity of our method, and the quantified results showed that FedECCR can improve the global model classification accuracy by approximately 1% to 6% compared to FedAvg, FedProx, and MOON.

Keywords: Federated Learning · Data Heterogeneity · Prototypical Learning · Contrastive Learning

ⓒ ICST Institute for Computer Sciences, Social Informatics and Telecommunications Engineering 2024
Published by Springer Nature Switzerland AG 2024. All Rights Reserved
H. Gao et al. (Eds.): CollaborateCom 2023, LNICST 563, pp. 59–78, 2024.
https://doi.org/10.1007/978-3-031-54531-3_4

1   Introduction

In recent years, 5G technology has experienced rapid development, digital trends have accelerated, and the significant increase in internet data transmission speed and massive growth of terminal devices have led to the generation and storage of vast amounts of data, providing tremendous opportunities for the development and utilization of big data. Intelligent collaborative computing technology has begun to combine with artificial intelligence, enabling it to have more extensive and in-depth application prospects in cross-domain and cross-organizational collaboration and innovation in areas such as healthcare, intelligent manufacturing, and intelligent logistics. This leads to more efficient and accurate decision-making and improved production efficiency. Intelligent collaborative computing [1] is a method achieving collaboration and interaction between multiple computer systems with artificial intelligence technology, to process data efficiently.

Federated Learning [2,3] is a kind of intelligent collaborative technology that enables training a global model with the cooperation of multiple computer systems, which can process data efficiently and in privacy. It is a client-server architecture machine learning technology. Where the server aggregates the local model updated by clients to generate a global model or update the global model, and sends the updated global model to clients, and each client trains a local model with the local dataset and the received global model. Benefiting from its excellent privacy protection capabilities, federated learning has been widely applied, such as Google's use of federated learning technology in the GB Board mobile keyboard [4]. Apple also used federated learning technology in the QuickType keyboard in iOS13 [5]. Even though federated learning has been widely used for large-scale user data analysis, it still faces many problems in practical scenarios, such as the decrease in the accuracy of global models caused by data heterogeneity.

In federated learning, the production and storage of user data occur on the client side, and their data distribution is largely influenced by factors such as client device type, user preference, and organization. As the client group in practical scenarios is usually large in size and structurally complex, these factors generally exhibit significant differences, causing the data distribution between each local data set to be uneven and deviate from the global data distribution, exhibiting non-independent and identical distribution (Non-IID) characteristics. This phenomenon is known as data heterogeneity. The heterogeneity of client data results in significant differences between local models. After aggregating these different local models, the obtained global model has a considerable discrepancy from the ideal model, and this discrepancy accumulates with an increase in aggregation rounds, resulting in a reduction in the accuracy of the global model.

Currently, research on solving data heterogeneity mainly focuses on optimizing local training on the client side, roughly divided into two directions: (1) data-based optimization methods, such as solving the data heterogeneity problem of different clients through data enhancement, so as to improve accuracy; (2) algorithm-based optimization methods, reconstructing the client's loss function by adding a regularization term to reduce the difference between the local model and global model. However, the former usually leads to training overfitting and poor prediction of new data samples; the regularization term in the latter is often an end-to-end limitation on model differences, providing limited precision improvement effects.

To address the above issues, we have proposed a federated optimization algorithm, FedECCR, based on encoding contrast and classification correction. FedECCR targets the optimization process through two stages: prototype contrastive training of the encoder and unbiased simulation correction of the classifier, which effectively suppresses the impact of heterogeneous data on the encoder and classifier. The main contributions of this paper are as follows.

- We classify all hidden layers of the model as encoders and the output layer as the classifier. By comparing the distribution differences between the global features extracted by the encoder in a data-heterogeneous environment and the client features, we found that there are significant differences in the distributions of client features and global features, and their discriminative power is poor.
- In response to differences in feature distribution, we designed a prototype comparison loss based on the prototype learning [6] and the feature similarity comparison of contrastive learning as a regularization term for local training. Then, we conducted an encoder prototype comparison training to align the feature mappings of the client encoder and improve the discriminability of the global encoder feature mappings.
- Based on high discriminability feature mappings, we estimated the statistical information of global features unbiasedly and used the corresponding Gaussian mixture model [7] to generate class-balanced simulated features for retraining the global classifier. This corrected the model parameters of the classifier and improved the classification accuracy of the global model on heterogeneous data.
- We conducted extensive experiments on datasets such as CIFAR-10 to evaluate the performance of TS-FedPC. The results indicate that compared to FedAvg, FedProx, and MOON, TS-FedPC can significantly improve the classification accuracy of the global model in heterogeneous data environments. Furthermore, it exhibits stability across different scenarios and possesses good scalability.

The arrangement of this article is as follows: first, we conducted related work in Sect. 2. Then, in Sect. 3, we introduced the FedECCR method. Experiments are presented in Sect. 4. Finally, in Sect. 5, we summarize the contents of this paper.

2   Related Work

There are two mainstream optimization methods for the problem of decreased overall model accuracy caused by data heterogeneity, including the optimization methods based on data and the optimization methods based on the algorithm of federated learning.

The Optimization Methods Based on Data. This method improves the model accuracy by resolving the data heterogeneity between different clients, including data sharing and data augmentation [8].

For the optimization method based on data sharing, Zhao et al. [9] proposed maintaining a globally shared data set on a central server. Clients would then randomly sample a portion of the data to mix with their local data set, reducing Non-IID. Similarly, [10, 11] have shared local data with the server to alleviate non-IID. While this method can improve global model performance, generating the shared data set is challenging because the server can't sense the local data set status. Additionally, downloading a portion of the shared data set violates privacy protection requirements.

Data augmentation is a technique to increase the diversity of training data by applying random transformations or knowledge transfer. It has been applied to federated learning in [12]. This method sends label distribution information of each client to the server, which calculates the sample number N_c and its mean value $\bar{N}$ for each category. If $N_c < \bar{N}$, the client needs to enhance the class data and use the locally augmented data set to train the model. Studies [13–15] have shown that data augmentation can improve the learning performance of the global model on non-IID data sets. However, most of these techniques require sharing label distribution information or some samples, which increases the risk of data privacy leakage.

The Optimization Methods Based on the Algorithm. The research on the algorithm level can be divided into three directions: gradient correction, regularization methods, and personalized federated learning.

The representative method of the optimization method based on the gradient correction direction is SCAFFOLD [16]. This method uses a control variable with the same size as the model gradient to predict the update direction of the global model and then uses this control variable in the local training to correct the client's gradient, adjusting the client's update direction to the update direction of the global model to alleviate the local model differences caused by Non-IID. [17, 18] also added control variables similar to SCAFFOLD to correct client gradients during the local training process. Li et al. proposed a method [19] to estimate the average update direction of the client and server-level classifiers (i.e., the last few fully connected layers), and use their differences as control variables to reduce the divergence of classifier update direction. It should be noted that the gradient correction method will lead to a significant increase in communication volume because an additional control variable containing multiple high-dimensional matrices needs to be transmitted between the server and clients in each aggregation round.

Regularization methods are commonly used in federated learning to suppress the divergence of local models caused by heterogeneous data. FedProx uses the squared Euclidean distance between the local model and the global model as the regularization term [20], while FedCurv and FedCL use Elastic Weight Consolidation (EWC) to prevent catastrophic forgetting [21, 22] based on the idea of life-long learning [23] and using EWC [24] regularization term to penalize significant updates to important parameters by local training, where important parameters refer to model parameters that have a greater impact on federated tasks. MOON applies contrastive learning to federated learning, adding the model contrastive loss between the global model and the local model as the regularization term [25] based on the contrastive learning technique [26], which significantly improves the accuracy of the global model under data heterogeneous environment. However, regularization methods may bring additional communication overhead or neglect the targeted handling of the internal structure of the model, resulting in an insignificant accuracy improvement.

Unlike the above two approaches, personalized federated learning aims to provide personalized solutions by adjusting the model according to the client's local task. Meta-learning and multi-task learning are the main types of person-alized methods [27,28]. G-FML [29] is a group-based federated meta-learning framework that adaptively divides clients into groups based on the similarity of data distribution. SpreadGNN [30] is a federated multi-task learning framework that uses a novel optimization algorithm with a convergence guarantee. Although personalized federated learning can solve the problem of data heterogeneity by building multiple personalized models, it does not consider the performance opti-mization of the global model, making it unsuitable for scenarios that require a powerful single global model.

Based on the research mentioned above, data augmentation and sharing methods pose privacy risks, gradient correction methods increase communication volume, and personalized federated learning isn't suitable for scenarios requiring a single global model. To train a powerful global model for practical applications, we propose a federated optimization method that uses encoding contrast and classification correction for non-IID optimization. This method aims to improve global model accuracy in a data heterogeneous environment by alleviating the impact of heterogeneous data on model encoders and classifiers without increas-ing communication costs.

3   Method

In this section, we will introduce the federated optimization algorithm FedECCR, which is based on encoding contrast and classification correction. First, we intro-duce the overall process and ideas of FedECCR, and then focus on introducing the two core steps of the algorithm, including encoder prototype contrastive training and classifier unbiased simulation correction.

3.1   Method Overview

FedECCR divides a model ω into two parts: the encoder ωe and the classifier ωc. The encoder is the collection of all hidden layers in the neural network, which is designed to encode the input data into features. The classifier is the output layer of the neural network, which is responsible for making classification decisions based on the features extracted by the encoder. The working principle of both is as follows: the encoder encodes data that is originally low-discriminatory to high-discriminatory features, and the classifier makes accurate classification decisions based on these high-discriminatory features.

Due to the heterogeneity of the data, both the encoder and classifier of the model have model biases. The model bias of the encoder can cause different clients to have different feature encoding methods (also known as feature mapping), which reduces the discriminatory power of the global model feature mapping and increases the difficulty of the classifier's decision-making. The model bias of the classifier can cause significant differences in the classification decisions of different clients for the same input data and decrease the overall classification accuracy. To address this issue, FedECCR first adopts encoder prototype comparison training to align the feature mapping of different client encoders, while improving the discriminatory power of the global encoder feature mapping. Then, through unbiased simulation correction of the classifier, the decision accuracy of the global classifier is improved. The overall architecture is shown in Fig. 1.

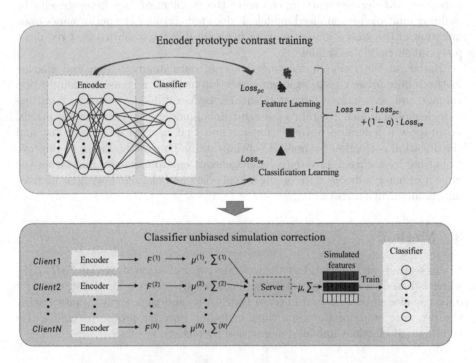

Fig. 1. FedECCR algorithm structure

As shown in Fig. 1, FedECCR mainly consists of the following two core stages:

(1) **Encoder prototype contrast training**: In order to align the feature mappings of different client encoders while improving their discriminability, FedECCR reconstructed the client loss function by adding the prototype contrast loss $Loss_{pc}$ on the basis of the original classification loss $Loss_{ce}$. The prototype refers to the center of each feature cluster. $Loss_{pc}$ can make the encoder extract feature vectors that aggregate towards the prototype of the corresponding category and away from the prototypes of other categories, thus supervising each client encoder to learn consistent and highly discriminative feature mappings. In the local training process, the client first calculates the prototype contrast loss $Loss_{pc}$ using the prototype and the features extracted by the encoder, then calculates the classification loss $Loss_{ce}$ based on the output of the classifier, and finally combines $Loss_{pc}$ and $Loss_{ce}$ as the final loss value for local model parameter optimization.

(2) **Classifier unbiased simulation correction**: In order to eliminate the model bias of the classifier and improve classification accuracy, FedECCR generates class-balanced simulation features based on a Gaussian mixture model and retrains the global classifier model parameters using the simulation features to correct classification decisions. Specifically, the client first extracts features on the local data set and calculates the mean $\mu^{(i)} = \{\mu_1^{(i)}, \mu_2^{(i)}, ..., \mu_C^{(i)}\}$ and covariance $\sum^{(i)} = \{\sum_1^{(i)}, \sum_2^{(i)}, ..., \sum_C^{(i)}\}$ of feature $F^{(i)}$. The server then aggregates the statistical information of the global features, i.e., the mean μ and covariance $\sum$. Based on the statistical information of the global features, the server uses a Gaussian distribution generator to generate an equal amount of simulation features for each data category and retrains the global classifier with these simulation features. As the classifier is the output layer of the model, the optimized output layer parameters obtained from the above steps can make more accurate classification decisions.

3.2   Encoder Prototype Comparison Training

The powerful data-fitting ability of deep learning models relies on the multi-level model structure and the discriminatory power of the encoder feature mapping directly affects the classification accuracy of the classifier. However, in federated learning, model bias caused by data heterogeneity causes different client encoders to learn inconsistent feature mappings. After model aggregation, the globally extracted features of the global encoder often do not have high discriminatory power, which in turn affects the classification accuracy of the model.

To address the above problems, we construct prototype contrast loss based on the feature similarity comparison of prototype learning and contrastive learning techniques, in order to supervise the learning of feature mapping for each client-side feature and enable the encoder of the client-side to learn consistent and highly separable feature mapping, thus reducing the model bias of the encoder.

According to reference [6], we refer to the prototype calculated based on client-side features as a local prototype, while the global prototype is obtained by averaging the local prototypes of each client side. The design idea of prototype contrast loss $Loss_{pc}$ is to move the features closer to the global prototype of the corresponding category while moving away from the global prototypes of other categories. The specific calculation method can be seen in Eq. (1).

$$Loss_{pc} = \log \frac{exp(sim(f_j^{(i)}, z_k)/\tau)}{\sum_{\tilde{k} \neq k} exp(sim(f_j^{(i)}, z_{\tilde{k}})/\tau)}, \tag{1}$$

$$where\ sim(f_j^{(i)}, z_k) = (\mathbf{f_j^{(i)}}^\top z_k)/(\| f_j^{(i)} \|_2 \cdot \| z_k \|_2)$$

Here, $f_j^{(i)}$ represents the features corresponding to the j input data of client i with category k, and z_k represents the global prototype of the k-th category features. sim represents the cosine similarity, and τ is the temperature parameter used to adjust the sensitivity of the $Loss_{pc}$ function to difficult-to-distinguish features. z_k can be calculated according to Eq. (2):

$$z_k = \frac{1}{N} \sum_{i=1}^{N} z_k^{(i)},$$

$$where\ z_k^{(i)} = \frac{1}{n_{i,k}} \sum_{(x_j, y_j) \in D_{i,k}} f_j^{(i)} \tag{2}$$

Here, $z_k^{(i)}$ represents the local prototype of the k-th category features of client i, $D_{i,k}$ is the collection of the k-th category data in the local data set of client i, and $n_{i,k}$ represents the amount of data in $D_{i,k}$.

In order to coordinate the feature mapping learning of the client's encoder and the classification learning, based on the research results of Mu et al. [31], we use a decay factor α to adjust the ratio between the client's prototype contrast $Loss_{pc}$ and classification $Loss_{ce}$. The final client loss function is represented by Eq. (3).

$$Loss = \alpha \cdot Loss_{pc} + (1 - \alpha) \cdot Loss_{ce} \tag{3}$$

Here, $\alpha = 1 - r/R$, r represents the current aggregation round of federated learning, and R represents the total aggregation rounds.

Based on the loss function, conducting prototype contrast training of the encoder can obtain a globally high feature-mapping discriminator encoder. The specific process is shown in Algorithm 1. In each round of aggregation, the server sends the global model and global prototype to the clients. After completing the local training, the clients upload the local models and local prototypes to the server, which aggregates them into new global models and global prototypes. Iterate this process until the round of aggregation is complete.

After the comparison training of the encoder prototype, the feature maps of each client encoder are supervised by the global prototype. The feature distribution shows the characteristics of intra-class cohesion and inter-class separation, which promotes the significant improvement of the feature mapping distinction of the global encoder aggregated by the client encoder.

Observing the algorithm process of the comparison training of the encoder prototype, it can be found that in each round of communication during the training process, in addition to transmitting the model, it is also necessary to transmit the prototype. However, the prototype is usually a collection of low-dimensional vectors, and its size can be ignored compared to the model parameters. Therefore, it will not increase too much communication cost.

3.3   Unbiased Simulation Correction of Classifier

The classifier takes the features extracted by the encoder as input, and the distribution of the features will directly affect the classification accuracy. In a data-heterogeneous environment, the heterogeneity of the input data is further amplified after passing through the layers inside the encoder and is ultimately manifested as a strong non-IID feature distribution. Therefore, heterogeneous data has a more serious model bias on the classifier than on the encoder.

We propose unbiased simulation correction of classifiers, which uses the generated simulation features with balanced categories to retrain the global classifier, eliminates the model bias of the classifier, and improves the global model classification accuracy.

Ideally, aggregating the data features of each client for retraining the global classifier is the best way to correct the model parameters of the classifier but it will cause a leakage of user privacy. Therefore, we assume that the values of each feature follow a Gaussian distribution [32], and simulated features are generated based on this distribution. Where each cluster of features follows a Gaussian distribution with corresponding mean and covariance, by aggregating the means and covariances of each cluster of features from all local data sets, we obtain an unbiased estimate of the mean and covariance of the global features and thus can generate simulated features that follow the Gaussian distribution of the global features.

Specifically, the server sends the globally trained encoder, which has been compared with the prototype encoder, to each client. Client i uses the global encoder to extract feature $F^{(i)} = \{f_1^{(i)}, f_2^{(i)}, ..., f_{n_i}^{(i)}\}$ from its local data set, where n_i is the local data set size of client i. After feature extraction, client i calculates the mean $\mu_k^{(i)}$ and covariance $\sum_k^{(i)}$ of each feature according to Eqs. (4) and (5).

$$\mu_k^{(i)} = \frac{1}{n_{i,k}} \sum_{(x_j, y_j) \in D_{i,k}} f_j^{(i)} \tag{4}$$

$$\sum_k^{(i)} = \frac{1}{n_{i,k} - 1} \sum_{(x_j, y_j) \in D_{i,k}} (f_j^{(i)} - \mu_k^{(i)})(\mathbf{f_j^{(i)}} - \mathbf{\mu_k^{(i)}})^\top \tag{5}$$

Then, clients upload statistical information of their own features, which includes the means $\mu^{(i)} = \{\mu_1^{(i)}, \mu_2^{(i)}, ..., \mu_C^{(i)}\}$ and covariances $\sum^{(i)} = \{\sum_1^{(i)}, \sum_2^{(i)}, ..., \sum_C^{(i)}\}$ of various features, to the server.

Next, the server aggregates the statistical information of all clients' features and estimates the mean and covariance of global features without bias. The aggregation method for feature mean is shown as Eq. (6), where N represents the total number of the k-th data class in the global data set.

$$\mu_k = \sum_{i=1}^{N} \frac{n_{i,k}}{n_k} \cdot \mu_k^{(i)} \tag{6}$$

Where n_k represents the total number of the k-th type of data in the global data set. The aggregation method of feature covariance $\sum_k$ is complex and can be calculated using the Eq. (7).

$$\sum_k = \sum_{i=1}^{N} \frac{n_{i,k}-1}{n_k-1} \sum_k^{(i)} + \sum_{i=1}^{N} \frac{n_{i,k}}{n_k-1} \mu_k^{(i)} \mu_\mathbf{k}^{(\mathbf{i})^\top} - \frac{n_k}{n_k-1} \mu_k \mu_\mathbf{k}^\top \tag{7}$$

After aggregation, the server obtains the means $\mu = \{\mu_1, \mu_2, ..., \mu_C\}$ and covariances $\sum = \{\sum_1, \sum_2, ..., \sum_C\}$ of various features. Then, according to the Gaussian distribution $\mathcal{N}(\mu, \sum)$, it generates M simulated features for each category.

Finally, after freezing the parameters of the global encoder, the server uses simulated features to retrain the global classifier, completes the correction of the classifier model parameters, and improves the classification accuracy of the global model. And the detail of this method is described as Algorithm 2.

It is worth noting that during the stage of unbiased simulation correction of classifiers, the client only exposes the statistical information of its own features to the server instead of the feature source, and, the server generates simulated features based solely on this statistical information instead of real features, which ensures the privacy and security of the client in the whole process. In addition, thanks to the high discriminative feature mapping that aggregates classes and separates them within the encoder, the simulation features generated by the server are closer to the real features. Therefore, a small number of simulation features can achieve a significant effect in correcting the classifier.

3.4   Algorithm Implementation

In this section, we provide detailed descriptions of the overall process of FedECCR, and the details are as follows:

(1) The server initializes the global model and global prototype, which are sent to the client during each round of aggregation (lines 1 to 5 of Algorithm 1).
(2) The client optimizes the local model during local training using classification loss and prototype comparison loss (lines 13 to 22 of Algorithm 1).
(3) After local training, the client uploads the local model and local prototypes to the server, which aggregates them to generate a new global prototype and global model (lines 23 to 28 of Algorithm 1).
(4) The client uses the global model to extract features from its local data set and uploads the mean and covariance of each feature to the server(lines 21 to 24 of Algorithm 2).

(5) The server aggregates the unbiased estimated values of the global feature mean and covariance (line 6 of Algorithm 2) and generates class-balanced simulated features to retrain the classifier of the global model (lines 7 to 17 of Algorithm 2).

Algorithm 1: Encoder prototype contrast training

Input: Total aggregation rounds R, local data set D_i, local training epochs E, number of data categories C, number of clients C, temperature parameter τ, and learning rate η

Output: Global model w_R

1 **Server:**

2 Initialize global model w_0 and global prototype z_0

3 **for** $r = 0, 1, ..., R - 1$ **do**

4   **for** $i = 1, 2, ..., N$ **do**

5   Send w_r and z_r to client i

6       $W_{r+1}^{(i)}, z_{r+1}^{(i)} = LocalTraining(i, r, w_r, z_r)$

7   **end**

8    $z_{r+1} = \frac{1}{N}\sum_{i=1}^{N} z_{r+1}^{(i)}$, $w_{r+1} = \sum_{i=1}^{N} \frac{n_i}{n} w_{r+1}^{(i)}$

9 **end**

10 **return** w_R

11 **Client:**

12 $LocalTraining(i, r, w_r, z_r)$:

13 **for** $epoch = 0, 1, 2..., E_l\text{-}1$ **do**

14   **foreach** $batch\{x_j, y_j\}$ in D_i **do**

15   Extracting Features from $w_{e,r}^i$ to f_j^i

16       $Loss_{pc} = -log\dfrac{exp(sim(f_j^{(i)}, z_{r,k})/\tau)}{\sum_{k'} exp(sim(f_j^{(i)}, z_{r,k'})/\tau)}$

17       $\alpha = 1 - r/R$

18       $Loss = \alpha \cdot Loss_{pc} + (1 - \alpha) \cdot Loss_{ce}$

19       $w_r^{(i)} = w_r^{(i)} - \eta\nabla Loss$

20   **end**

21 **end**

22 $w_{r+1}^{(i)} = w_r^{(i)}$

23 Encoder $w_{e,r+1}^{(i)}$ extracts feature $f_j^{(i)}$

24 **for** $k = 1, 2, ..., C$ **do**

25    $z_{r+1,k}^{(i)} = \frac{1}{n_{i,k}}\sum_{(x_j, y_j)\in D_{i,k}} f_j^{(i)}$

26 **end**

27 $z_{r+1}^{(i)} = \{z_{r+1,1}^{(i)}, z_{r+1,2}^{(i)}, ..., z_{r+1,C}^{(i)}\}$

28 **return** $w_{r+1}^{(i)}, z_{r+1}^{(i)}$

Algorithm 2: Classifier unbiased simulation correction

Input: Global model w_R, number of simulation features for each category M, epoch number of global classifier training E, learning rateη.

Output: Global model w_{R+1}

1 **Server:**
2 **for** $i = 1, 2..., N$ **do**
3   Send encoder $w_{e,R}$ to client i
4      $\mu^{(i)}, \sum^{(i)} = LocalFeatureStatistics(i, w_e, R)$
5 **end**
6 $\mu = \{\mu_1, \mu_2, ..., \mu_C\}$, $\sum = \{\sum_1, \sum_2, ..., \sum_C\}$
7 **for** $k = 1, 2..., C$ **do**
8      $F_k' = \{F_{1,k}', F_{2,k}', ..., F_{M,k}'\}$ based on Gaussian distribution $\mathcal{N}(\mu_k, \sum^k)$
9 **end**
10 **for** $epoch = 0, 1, 2..., E - 1$ **do**
11   **foreach** $batch\{f_j', y_j'\}$ in $F' = \{F_1', F_2', ..., F_C'\}$ **do**
12          $Loss_{ce} = CrossEntropyLoss(w_{c,R}; f_j', y_j')$
13          $w_{c,R} = w_{c,R} - \eta \nabla Loss_{ce}$
14   **end**
15 **end**
16 $w_{c,R+1} = w_{c,R}, w_{R+1} = (w_{e,R}, w_{c,R+1})$
17 **return** w_{R+1}
18 **Client:**
19 LocalFeatureStatistics(Encoder $w_{e,R}$, Server i):
20 **foreach** $batch\{x_j, y_j\}$ in D_i **do**
21   Extract feature $f_j^{(i)}$ from $w_{e,R}$
22 **end**
23 $\mu^{(i)} = \{\mu_1^{(i)}, \mu_2^{(i)}, ..., \mu_C^{(i)}\}$ for feature $\sum^{(i)} = \{\sum_1^{(i)}, \sum_2^{(i)}, ..., \sum_C^{(i)}\}$ by formulas (4) and (5).
24 **return** $\mu^{(i)}, \sum^{(i)}$

---

4 Experiment

In this section, we experimentally verify the federated optimization algorithm FedECCR based on encoder contrast and classifier correction. We conduct experiments to verify the accuracy and scalability of FedECCR with Non-IID data, compared with MOON, FedProx, and FedAvg algorithms. We also analyze the feature distribution of different algorithms to verify the high distinguishability of FedECCR features and conduct ablation experiments of classifier correction to demonstrate the accuracy improvement effect of FedECCR.

4.1 Experimental Setup

(1) Datasets and models: We used three popular datasets: EMNIST, CIFAR-10, and CIFAR-100. To introduce data heterogeneity, we partitioned non-IID datasets using the Dirichlet distribution [33]. We use a simple CNN model for EMNIST and CIFAR-10, which includes two convolutional layers, two pooling layers, and five fully connected layers, and a ResNet-50 for CIFAR-100.

(2) Parameter Setting: We used 10 clients, 100 aggregation rounds, 10 local epochs per client, a learning rate of 0.01, batch size of 64, and a Non-IID data set divided by 0.5. We adjusted the regularization coefficients for MOON and FedProx and set the temperature parameter to 0.5 in MOON and 0.5 or 1 in FedECCR, depending on the dataset. In the EMNIST dataset experiments, all algorithms converged after 30 rounds of aggregation, so the aggregation rounds were set to 30. For the unbiased classifier simulation correction phase, we generated 400 simulated features for each data class and set the number of epochs for service retraining classifiers to 20 based on multiple rounds of experimentation and testing.

(3) Environment: All experiments were conducted on Ubuntu using Python with the PyTorch framework. Data stream processing relied on the torchvision library, while Matplotlib was used for visualization. Other core libraries used include NumPy, Scikit-learn, and Wandb.

(4) Baseline: We used FedAvg, FedProx, and MOON as baselines. FedAvg is a classic and effective federated learning algorithm. FedProx introduces a regularization term to solve the heterogeneity problem of data, while MOON addresses the heterogeneity problem of data by introducing prototype features into federated learning.

4.2 Accuracy

We calculated the test accuracy of FedAvg, FedProx, MOON, and FedECCR algorithms on the EMNIST, CIFAR-10, and CIFAR-100 data sets respectively, and calculated the error range of the accuracy through multiple experiments, as shown in Table 1.

Table 1. Test accuracy of FedAvg, FedProx, MOON, and FedECCR on EMNIST, CIFAR-10, and CIFAR-100 data sets

	EMNIST	CIFAR-10	CIFAR-100
FedAvg	$84.77\% \pm 0.2\%$	$67.13\% \pm 0.2\%$	$66.85\% \pm 0.4\%$
FedProx	$85.33\% \pm 0.1\%$	$68.12\% \pm 0.3\%$	$67.27\% \pm 0.2\%$
MOON	$84.93\% \pm 0.1\%$	$69.18\% \pm 0.5\%$	$68.83\% \pm 0.4\%$
FedECCR	$\mathbf{85.66\% \pm 0.1\%}$	$\mathbf{70.89\% \pm 0.3\%}$	$\mathbf{74.32\% \pm 0.3\%}$

From the test accuracy results in Table 1, it can be seen that FedECCR has the highest test accuracy in different data set experiments, with test accuracies of

85.66%, 70.89%, and 74.32% on the EMNIST, CIFAR-10, and CIFAR-100 data sets respectively. The accuracy of FedProx is not significantly improved, compared with FedAvg, as it only uses end-to-end regularization to restrict model bias, and the regularization coefficient remains unchanged during training. On the EMNIST data set, it increases by about 0.56%, on CIFAR-10 it increases by about 0.99%, and on CIFAR-100 the accuracy decreases by 0.55%. MOON obtains a more significant improvement in accuracy by restricting the targeted bias of the encoder. Compared to FedAvg, it improves the model accuracy by about 2.05% and 0.96% on CIFAR-10 and CIFAR-100 respectively. However, in the experiments on EMNIST, the accuracy improvement of MOON is generally not significant, and the model accuracy is only about 0.16% higher than that of FedAvg. We believe this may be due to MOON's feature comparison technology being better suited for handling RGB image classification tasks.

The FedECCR algorithm benefits from the separate optimization of the model encoder and classifier, with the highest accuracy improvement. On EMNIST, it is approximately 0.89% higher than FedAvg, approximately 0.33% higher than FedProx, and approximately 0.73% higher than MOON. On CIFAR-10, it is approximately 3.76% higher than FedAvg, approximately 2.77% higher than FedProx, and approximately 1.71% higher than MOON. On CIFAR-100, it is approximately 5.13% higher than FedAvg, approximately 5.68% higher than FedProx, and approximately 4.17% higher than MOON.

In summary, compared to other algorithms, FedECCR can more effectively improve the accuracy of global models in federated learning in heterogeneous data environments.

4.3 Scalability

In order to verify the scalability of the FedECCR algorithm, we conducted experiments on different values of the Non-IID degree of the data set and the number of clients, and comprehensively compared the model accuracy of FedECCR with FedAvg, FedProx, and MOON in multiple scenarios.

(1) Degree of Non-IID of the data set:
We use prior distribution hyperparameters of the Dirichlet to control the degree of Non-IID of the data set. The smaller the value, the higher the degree of Non-IID of the data set. We set three different values of 0.1, 0.5, and 5, and compared

Table 2. Model accuracy of the algorithm under different degrees of Non-IID

	$\beta = 0.1$	$\beta = 0.5$	$\beta = 5$
FedAvg	61.86% ± 0.6%	67.13% ± 0.2%	73.34% ± 0.1%
FedProx	61.65% ± 0.4%	68.12% ± 0.3%	73.03% ± 0.1%
MOON	62.55% ± 0.1%	69.18% ± 0.5%	73.47% ± 0.1%
FedECCR	**65.49% ± 0.2%**	**70.89% ± 0.3%**	**73.80% ± 0.1%**

the model accuracy under these three values on the CIFAR-10 data set, as shown in Table 2.

The results show that when $\beta = 0.1$, the model accuracy of FedECCR is approximately 3.63% higher than FedAvg, approximately 3.84% higher than Fed-Prox, and approximately 2.94% higher than MOON. When $\beta = 0.5$, the model accuracy of FedECCR is approximately 3.76% higher than FedAvg, approximately 2.77% higher than FedProx, and approximately 1.71% higher than MOON. When $\beta = 5$, due to the low degree of Non-IID of the data set, we reduced the prototype contrastive loss of FedECCR by a factor of 10 to reduce the impact of feature mapping learning on classification learning, and the final model accuracy is approximately 0.46% higher than FedAvg, approximately 0.5% higher than FedProx, and approximately 0.33% higher than MOON.

From the above results, we can see that the FedECCR can maintain stable performance on data sets with different degrees of Non-IID, and the model accuracy is higher than FedAvg, FedProx, and MOON. In addition, it is worth noting that the model accuracy of FedProx decreases when the degree of Non-IID of the data set changes, which may be because its regularization term only considers end-to-end model differences and cannot control the penalty strength of internal structural differences in the model.

(2) Number of clients:

In order to test the performance of the algorithm under different client capacities, we expanded the number of clients from the default 10 to 50 and 100 respectively, and compared the model accuracy of all algorithms. The specific results are shown in Table 3. It should be noted that we used different client sampling rates for the setting of 50 clients and 100 clients. In the case of 50 clients, the client sampling rate is 1, and all clients participate in every round of model aggregation; in the case of 100 clients, we refer to MOON [27] and set the client sampling rate to 0.2, with only 20 clients participating in every round of model aggregation.

Table 3. Accuracy under different client numbers and aggregation rounds settings

	client $= 50$	client $= 100$
FedAvg	$66.42\% \pm 0.1\%$	$62.28\% \pm 0.4\%$
FedProx	$66.51\% \pm 0.2\%$	$62.22\% \pm 0.1\%$
MOON	$66.27\% \pm 0.3\%$	$62.99\% \pm 0.1\%$
FedECCR	$\mathbf{67.09\% \pm 0.2\%}(\tau = 0.5)$	$\mathbf{62.76\% \pm 0.2\%}(\tau = 0.5)$

The results showed that when Clients $= 50$, the model accuracy of FedECCR is higher than other algorithms, with an increase of approximately 0.67% over FedAvg, approximately 0.58% over FedProx, and approximately 0.82% over MOON. When Clients $= 100$, the model accuracy of FedECCR is better than FedAvg and FedProx, with approximately 0.48% higher than FedAvg and approximately 0.54% higher than FedProx.

It should be noted that when Clients = 100, the model accuracy of FedECCR is slightly lower than MOON, with a decrease of approximately 0.23%. At this time, we observed that the silhouette coefficient of the encoder feature distribution of FedECCR was highest only at 0.047, while it was highest at 0.092 when Clients = 50. This is because the sampling rate of 0.2 appears low when Clients = 100. A sampling rate that is too low will reduce the discrimination of the encoder feature map, resulting in a decrease in the effect of improving model accuracy.

4.4 Feature Discrimination

In order to verify that the prototype comparison training can promote the model encoder to learn high-discriminatory feature mapping, we compared the feature distributions of different algorithms on the EMNIST and CIFAR-10 data sets. From the result in Fig. 2, we can see that, compared with FedAvg, FedProx, and MOON, FedECCR has significantly higher cohesion and farther cluster distances for various feature clusters, and the feature distribution has higher discriminability.

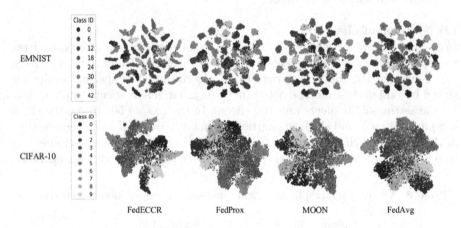

Fig. 2. Feature distribution of FedECCR, FedProx, MOON, and FedAvg

In order to observe the changes in feature mapping discriminability during the training process, we calculated the changes in silhouette coefficient of the feature distribution of each algorithm during the training process, and plotted the change curves, as shown in Fig. 3.

In Fig. 3, the final silhouette coefficients of FedECCR, FedProx, MOON, and FedAvg on the EMNIST data set are 0.3159, 0.1638, 0.1803, and 0.1633, respectively; on the CIFAR-10 data set, the final silhouette coefficients are 0.0809, 0.0366, 0.0343, and 0.0466, respectively. It can be seen that on these two data sets, the silhouette coefficients of FedECCR's feature distribution after training are the highest, and significantly higher than those of other algorithms.

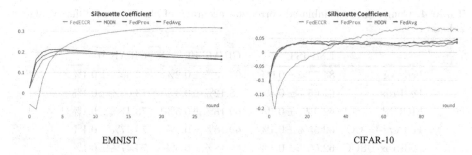

Fig. 3. The change curves of silhouette coefficients of the feature distribution of FedECCR, FedProx, MOON, and FedAvg.

This indicates that the feature mapping discriminability of the global encoder of FedECCR is higher than that of other algorithms.

The above results show that the prototype comparison training of FedECCR's encoder can indeed promote the characteristics of intra-cluster aggregation and inter-cluster separation of feature distribution, thus effectively improving the discrimination of the global encoder's feature mapping.

4.5   Classifier Correction Ablation Experiment

The higher the discriminability between features of different categories, the clearer the differences between the corresponding Gaussian distributions. At this time, the simulated features generated based on the mean and covariance of the features are closer to the real features, the correction effect on the classifier is better, and the model accuracy is significantly improved.

In this section, we performed unbiased simulation correction on FedAvg, Fed-Prox, and MOON, and analyzed the effect of feature mapping discriminability on classifier correction from the results of accuracy improvement, as shown in Table 4. We use USCC (Unbiased Simulation Correction of Classifier, the second stage of the FedECCR algorithm) to identify the classifier unbiased simulation correction operation, such as FedAvg-USCC, which represents the FedAvg algorithm after being corrected by the classifier unbiased simulation.

On the EMNIST data set, unbiased simulation correction brought about approximately 0.16%, 0.14%, and 0.21% accuracy improvement to FedAvg, Fed-Prox, and MOON, respectively; on the CIFAR-10 data set, it brought about approximately 1.05%, 1.58%, and 0.32% accuracy improvement, respectively; on the CIFAR-100 data set, it brought about approximately 0.23%, 0.09%, and 0.14% accuracy improvement, respectively.

From the results, even after adding unbiased simulation correction to other algorithms, FedECCR's accuracy improvement effect is still the best, which indicates that high-discriminatory feature mapping usually helps the classifier make more accurate classification decisions. And it mainly consists of two parts of calculation time for FedECCR. One is the encoder prototype comparison training phase, an additional 982.6 s of computation time was required to calculate

Table 4. Comparison of unbiased correction accuracy of classifiers of different algorithms

	EMNIST	CIFAR-10	CIFAR-100
FedAvg	84.77% ± 0.6%	67.13% ± 0.2%	73.34% ± 0.1%
FedProx	61.65% ± 0.4%	68.12% ± 0.3%	73.03% ± 0.1%
MOON	62.55% ± 0.1%	69.18% ± 0.5%	73.47% ± 0.1%
FedAvg-USCC	62.55% ± 0.1%	69.18% ± 0.5%	73.47% ± 0.1%
FedProx-USCC	62.55% ± 0.1%	69.18% ± 0.5%	73.47% ± 0.1%
MOON-USCC	62.55% ± 0.1%	69.18% ± 0.5%	73.47% ± 0.1%
FedECCR	**65.49% ± 0.2%**	**70.89% ± 0.3%**	**73.80% ± 0.1%**

prototype features for each epoch trained on local clients. The other is classifier stage, it was executed once at the end of training and only took 27 s. The total training time is about 25,000, so these two stages account for 4.03% of the overall computational cost.

5   Conclusion

The federated learning method is a popular distributed machine learning method, which cooperates with the clients and server to mine the large-scale data value while keeping data locally, which can protect the privacy of data. However, in practical applications, there is significant heterogeneity in the data on the federated learning client, which can cause divergence in the model update direction during local training, leading to local model bias. So the global model generated by aggregating biased models has significant differences from the ideal model, resulting in performance loss. To address the problem of poor accuracy of the global model due to local model bias in data heterogeneous environments, we propose a federated optimization algorithm FedECCR based on encoding contrast and classification correction. It specifically resolves model encoder and classifier bias, introducing prototype contrast loss as a regularization term in local training of the encoder, promoting consistent and separable feature maps to be learned by different clients, and then using simulated features generated from the statistical information of each client's features to retrain the classifier and correct its model parameters. Through experiments, we verified that compared with FedAvg, FedProx, and MOON, FedECCR can improve the accuracy of the global model by approximately 1% to 6% on multiple data sets such as CIFAR-10. In addition, FedECCR has good scalability and can maintain the high accuracy of the global model in situations where the Non-IID degree and the number of clients change. Since the classifier stage generates simulation features, which may cause overfitting during training, we will research the optimization for this problem in the future.

Acknowledgement. This work is supported by the Key Research and Development Program of Zhejiang Province 2023C03194; the National Natural Science Foundation of China under Grant No. 62072146; and the Natural Science Foundation of Zhejiang Province under Grant No. LQ23F020015.

References

1. Wang, X., Gao, H., Huang, K.: Artificial intelligence in collaborative computing. Mobile Netw. Appl. **26**, 2389–2391 (2021). https://doi.org/10.1007/s11036-021-01829-y
2. Yang, J., Zheng, J., Zhang, Z., Chen, Q.I., Wong, D.S., Li, Y.: Security of federated learning for cloud-edge intelligence collaborative computing. Int. J. Intell. Syst., 9290–9308 (2022). https://doi.org/10.1002/int.22992
3. McMahan, H.B., Moore, E., Ramage, D., Hampson, S., Arcas, B.: Communication-efficient learning of deep networks from decentralized data. arXiv: Learning (2016)
4. Hard, A., et al.: Federated learning for mobile keyboard prediction. arXiv: Computation and Language (2018)
5. Geyer, R.C., Klein, T., Nabi, M.: Differentially private federated learning: a client level perspective. Cornell University - arXiv (2017)
6. Tan, Y., Long, G., Liu, L., Zhou, T., Jiang, J.: FedProto: federated prototype learning over heterogeneous devices. arXiv: Learning (2021)
7. Reynolds, D.A.: Gaussian Mixture Models (2009)
8. Yan, Y., Zhu, L.: A Simple Data Augmentation for Feature Distribution Skewed Federated Learning (2023)
9. Zhao, Y., Li, M., Lai, L., Suda, N., Civin, D., Chandra, V.: Federated learning with non-IID data. Cornell University - arXiv (2018)
10. Tuor, T., Wang, S., Ko, B., Liu, C., Leung, K.K.: Overcoming noisy and irrelevant data in federated learning. arXiv: Learning (2020)
11. Yoshida, N., Nishio, T., Morikura, M., Yamamoto, K., Yonetani, R.: Hybrid-FL: Cooperative Learning Mechanism Using Non-IID Data in Wireless Networks (2019)
12. Wicaksana, J., et al.: FedMix: Mixed Supervised Federated Learning for Medical Image Segmentation (2022)
13. Seol, M., Kim, T.: Performance enhancement in federated learning by reducing class imbalance of non-IID data. Sensors, 1152 (2023)
14. Shin, M., Hwang, C., Kim, J., Park, J., Bennis, M., Kim, S.-L.: XOR mixup: privacy-preserving data augmentation for one-shot federated learning. Cornell University - arXiv (2020)
15. Jeong, E., Oh, S., Park, J., Kim, H., Bennis, M., Kim, S.-L.: Multi-hop federated private data augmentation with sample compression. arXiv: Learning (2019)
16. Karimireddy, S., Kale, S., Mohri, M., Reddi, S.J., Stich, S.U., Suresh, A.: SCAFFOLD: stochastic controlled averaging for federated learning. In: International Conference on Machine Learning (2020)
17. Gao, L., Fu, H., Li, L., Chen, Y., Xu, M., Xu, C.-Z.: FedDC: Federated Learning with Non-IID Data via Local Drift Decoupling and Correction
18. Liu, Y., Sun, Y., Ding, Z., Shen, L., Liu, B., Tao, D.: Enhance Local Consistency in Federated Learning: A Multi-Step Inertial Momentum Approach (2023)
19. Li, B., Schmidt, M.N., Alstrøm, T.S., Stich, S.U.: Partial Variance Reduction improves Non-Convex Federated learning on heterogeneous data (2022)
20. Li, T., Sahu, A., Zaheer, M., Sanjabi, M., Talwalkar, A., Smith, V.: Federated optimization in heterogeneous networks. arXiv: Learning (2018)

21. Shoham, N., et al.: Overcoming forgetting in federated learning on non-IID data. Cornell University - arXiv (2019)
22. Yao, X., Sun, L.: Continual local training for better initialization of federated models. In: 2020 IEEE International Conference on Image Processing (ICIP) (2020). https://doi.org/10.1109/icip40778.2020.9190968
23. Li, H., Krishnan, A., Wu, J., Kolouri, S., Pilly, P.K., Braverman, V.: Lifelong learning with sketched structural regularization. Cornell University - arXiv (2021)
24. Kirkpatrick, J., et al.: Overcoming catastrophic forgetting in neural networks. In: Proceedings of the National Academy of Sciences, pp. 3521–3526 (2017). https://doi.org/10.1073/pnas.1611835114
25. Li, Q., He, B., Song, D.: Model-contrastive federated learning. In: 2021 IEEE/CVF Conference on Computer Vision and Pattern Recognition (CVPR) (2021). https://doi.org/10.1109/cvpr46437.2021.01057
26. Chen, T., Kornblith, S., Norouzi, M., Hinton, G.E.: A simple framework for contrastive learning of visual representations. Cornell University - arXiv (2020)
27. Vanschoren, J.: Meta-learning: a survey. arXiv: Learning (2018)
28. Zhang, Y., Yang, Q.: An overview of multi-task learning. Natl. Sci. Rev., 30–43 (2018). https://doi.org/10.1093/nsr/nwx105
29. Yang, L., Huang, J., Lin, W., Cao, J.: Personalized federated learning on non-IID data via group-based meta-learning. ACM Trans. Knowl. Discov. Data., 1–20 (2023). https://doi.org/10.1145/3558005
30. He, C., Ceyani, E., Balasubramanian, K., Annavaram, M., Avestimehr, A.S.: SpreadGNN: serverless multi-task federated learning for graph neural networks. Cornell University - arXiv (2021)
31. Mu, X., et al.: FedProc: prototypical contrastive federated learning on non-IID data. arXiv: Learning (2021)
32. Miller, J.W., Harrison, M.T.: Mixture models with a prior on the number of components. arXiv: Methodology (2015)
33. Hsu, H., Qi, H., Brown, M.: Measuring the effects of non-identical data distribution for federated visual classification. arXiv: Learning (2019)

CSA_FedVeh: Cluster-Based Semi-asynchronous Federated Learning Framework for Internet of Vehicles

Dun Cao[1], Jiasi Xiong[1], Nanfang Lei[1], Robert Simon Sherratt[2], and Jin Wang[1(✉)]

[1] Changsha University of Science and Technology, Changsha 410114, China
jinwang@csust.edu.cn

[2] School of Biomedical Engineering, The University of Reading, Reading RG6 6AY, UK

Abstract. In Internet of Vehicles (IoV) system, Federated Learning (FL) is a novel distributed approach to processing real-time vehicle data that enables training of shared learning models while ensuring data privacy. However, existing FL still face numerous challenges in IoV. Firstly, the fast convergence with FL models is difficult to achieve due to the high mobility of vehicles and the non-independent identical distribution (Non-IID) among data collected by vehicles. Moreover, the parameter aggregation process of FL incurs significant communication overhead, and the varying computing power of vehicles results in the straggler. To address these issues, this paper proposes a Cluster-based Semi-Asynchronous Federated Learning framework for IoV (CSA_FedVeh). Specifically, we propose a Space-Time and Weight DBSCAN density clustering algorithm (STW-DBSCAN) that relies on both the space-time location and model weight similarities of vehicles. Clustering of vehicles can alleviate the impact of Non-IID data, and the joint training of data vehicles can reduce resource consumption and mitigate the straggler effect. In addition, we adopt a semi-asynchronous FL aggregation mechanism to reduce communication time and improve FL efficiency. Experimental results show that compared with baselines under Non-IID datasets, CSA_FedVeh can reduce the running time by about 24.6% to 60.2%, and reduce communication consumption by 3.4% to 62.07% on MNIST dataset and 1.01% to 68.6% on GTSRD dataset.

Keywords: Internet of vehicles · Federated learning · Cluster · Semi-asynchronous

1 Introduction

With the rapid development of wireless communication and Artificial Intelligence (AI) technologies, Internet of Vehicles (IoV) has emerged as a significant application scenario for 5G and beyond. It is playing a crucial role in the fields

H. Gao et al. (Eds.): CollaborateCom 2023, LNICST 563, pp. 79–99, 2024.
https://doi.org/10.1007/978-3-031-54531-3_5

of autonomous driving and Intelligent Transportation Systems (ITS) [1,2]. However, Intel estimates that each smart car will generate approximately 4000GB of data per day, which is equivalent to the data produced by nearly 3000 mobile phone users. The real-time processing of the data collected from the vehicles poses a thorny issue. Meanwhile, with the development of Mobile Edge Computing (MEC) and Federated Learning (FL) technologies, on the one hand, as the vehicle data is generated in IoV, MEC naturally combines with IoV, enabling data processing to be performed in the vicinity of the vehicles through the computing power and storage resources of edge server (ES) [3]. On the other hand, in 2016, Google proposed federated learning [4] as a distributed deep learning paradigm, which allows vehicles to train their local deep learning models independently using local data and aggregates them into a global model. Vehicles do not directly send local data and only share local model parameters, which to some extent, protects vehicle privacy [5]. As real-time computing services on the vehicular edge continue to grow, the combination of IoV and FL technology will become a research focus.

Although the existing FL clustering approaches and aggregation mechanisms have been effective in some IoV scenarios, several challenges persist in IoV, including: as a result of differences in sensors and processors of vehicles and devices, the data collected by vehicles is the non-independent identical distribution (Non-IID). When using such Non-IID data, FL model may significantly decrease in terms of convergence speed and accuracy [6,7]. Vehicles are typically in a state of high-speed mobility and their distance to ES varies over time, which can result in communication congestion and delays when participating vehicles of FL frequently update model parameters to ES. Additionally, the computational capabilities of some vehicles differ, resulting in slow-performing stragglers significantly prolonging the delay of each round FL aggregation and ultimately impacting the convergence speed of the global model.

To tackle the aforementioned three challenges, we acknowledge the significance of cooperation among vehicles and propose a novel vehicle clustering-based semi-asynchronous federated learning framework for IoV (CSA_FedVeh). Our contributions are summarized as follows:

- We establish a distributed training network for FL, which combines local training in vehicles and global aggregation in ES. To ensure the quality of FL model for vehicles and support the faster possible model convergence, we formulate a minimization problem for the convergence time of global model aggregation.
- Based on the CSA_FedVeh framework, we propose a Space-Time and Weight DBSCAN density clustering algorithm (STW-DBSCAN) that relies on both the space-time location similarities and model weight similarities of vehicles. This algorithm efficiently solves the straggler problem and accelerates local model training. Meanwhile, a semi-asynchronous federated aggregation mechanism is adopted to further reduce resource consumption and communication costs by adjusting server waiting time.

– We establish a simulation for vehicle-clustered FL network. Experimental results demonstrate that, under a fixed system operation time, our CSA_FedVeh framework outperforms four other benchmark frameworks by shortening the running time by approximately 24.6% to 60.2%, while achieving similar accuracy. Additionally, on MNIST dataset, the communication consumption is reduced by 3.4% to 62.07%, and on GTSRD dataset, the communication consumption is reduced by 1.01% to 68.6%, when compared to achieving similar accuracy.

2   Related Work

In recent years, an increasing number of scholarly investigations have endeavored to implement FL frameworks within IoV scenario [8–10]. Huang *et al.* [8] propose a novel FL framework called 'FedParking' that assists parked vehicles in providing computational offloading services and utilizes LSTM model for parking space estimation. Liang *et al.* [9] propose a semi-synchronous FL (Semi-SynFed) protocol and a dynamic aggregation scheme to asynchronously aggregate model parameters, in order to enhance the performance of FL in IoV scenario. Huang *et al.* [10] propose an asynchronous FL privacy-preserving computation model (AFLPC) for 5G-V2X, which aims to better utilize the low latency advantage of 5G networks, while also protecting data privacy in IoV. Similar to the aforementioned framework, we also considered the implementation of FL in IoV for real-time processing of data collected by vehicles.

Existing FL frameworks have been effective in addressing the impact of Non-IID data and resource constraints [11–13]. Ma *et al.* [11] propose a task offloading method based on data and resource heterogeneity in the HFEL environment, incorporating the statistical features of data through information entropy into the cost function to reshape the edge data. Briggs *et al.* [12] improve FL by introducing a hierarchical clustering step (FL+HC), which separates client clustering based on the similarity between clients' local updates and the global joint model. Tan *et al.* [13] propose a novel federated prototype learning (FedProto) framework, in which communication between devices and servers is done via class prototypes rather than gradients. Considering the presence of Non-IID data and resource constraints in IoV, we propose a clustering algorithm in this paper that alleviates the problem of Non-IID data and resource constraints in IoV, while effectively mitigating the impact caused by high vehicle mobility in IoV.

Since global aggregation is required for parameter uploading in FL, existing FL aggregation mechanisms can be classified into two types based on their aggregation mechanisms: synchronous [4] and asynchronous [14] mechanisms. For synchronous FL mechanisms, the ES needs to collect all the parameters obtained from the participating vehicles before executing the aggregation process. However, the impact of stragglers [15], caused by poor network or hardware resources of some vehicles, can lead to significant delays. As for asynchronous FL mechanisms, the ES can aggregate the parameters without waiting for all vehicles in a round FL aggregation, but this can result in gradient divergence,

further decreasing the performance of the FL model. In this work, we adopt
the semi-asynchronous mechanism [16–18], which further reduces resource consumption and communication costs by adjusting the server's waiting time. Sun
et al. [17] propose a semi-asynchronous FL framework for extremely heterogeneous devices. Ma *et al.* [18] propose a semi-asynchronous federated learning
mechanism called 'FedSA' and theoretically prove the convergence of FedSA. In
contrast to the aforementioned framework, we consider vehicles of high-speed
mobility and combine a semi-asynchronous mechanism with clusters of vehicles.

3 System Model and Problem Formulation

In this section, we firstly introduce the clustered federated learning process in
IoV scenario. Sequentially, we describe the cluster-based semi-asynchronous federated learning framework (CSA_FedVeh). Finally, we propose the problem of
minimizing the global model training time and formalize it for a better address
of the challenges in IoV federated learning.

3.1 Vehicle-Clustered Federated Learning Network

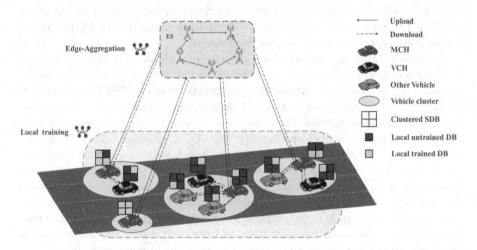

Fig. 1. Illustration of Cluster FL process in IoV.

As shown in the Fig. 1, we consider a vehicle-clustered FL network system,
consisting of vehicular users (VUs) and edge server (ES). Assuming N VUs randomly distributed in IoV system, forming a set of VUs $\mathcal{V} = \{1, ..., n, ..., N\}$,
these VUs are clustered into M vehicle clusters using the STW-DBSCAN algorithm that relies on both the space-time location similarities and model weight
similarities of vehicles (introduced in Sect. 4), forming a set of vehicle clusters

$\mathcal{C} = \{c_1, ..., c_m, ..., c_M\}$. Assuming convergence of FL model after K rounds of global aggregation, where $k \in \{1, 2, ..., K\}$.

In the vehicle-clustered FL network system, due to the close proximity of the VUs within a vehicle cluster, the collected information and the trained models also are highly similar, it can be assumed that the data of the VUs in the vehicle cluster are the same and can be partitioned into shared data blocks (SDBs). During the training process, VUs in the vehicle cluster only need to train their own models using their own historical experience data blocks (DBs), without the need to transmit local data, where DBs are partitioned according to the computing capabilities of VUs within each vehicle cluster. The main vehicle cluster head (MCH) is responsible for uploading and downloading and sending model weight parameters. If the MCH is offline, a vice vehicle cluster head (VCH) will be activated to take its place (Table 1).

Table 1. Notations and their meanings.

Notation	Meaning
$\mathcal{V}$	The set of vehicular users
$\mathcal{C}$	The set of vehicle clusters
K	The global model will converge after K rounds of global aggregation
$\mathcal{C}_k$	The vehicular users participating in the global updating in round k
q	The number of vehicle clusters participating in each round of global aggregation
$T_{v,n}^{soj}$	The sojourn time of vehicular user n at the current edge server
$T_{v,n}^{loc}$	The computation time of each round of local model training for vehicular user n
$T_{c,m}^{loc}$	The computation time of each round of local model training for vehicle cluster c_m
$T_{k,m}^{comm}$	The communication time for vehicle cluster c_m in the k-th round of global aggregation
$T_{k,m}^{comp}(s_k^m)$	The local computation time of vehicle cluster c_m between the start time of the k-th round of global aggregation and the end time of local training
$\mathcal{T}_k^{sort}$	Training time for all clusters sorted in the k-th round of global aggregation
$w_k^{v,n}$	The local model weight parameter derived by local updating on vehicular user n at the k-th round of global aggregation
$w_k^{c,m}$	The cluster model weight parameter derived by cluster updating on vehicle cluster c_m at the k-th round of global aggregation
w_k	The global model weight parameter in round k
$\nabla F_{v,n}(w_k)$	Gradient of vehicular user n at the k-th round of global aggregation
$\nabla F_{c,m}(w_k)$	Gradient of vehicle cluster c_m at the k-th round of global aggregation
$\nabla F(w_k)$	Global gradient of the k-th round of global aggregation
s_k^m	The number of global aggregation rounds that differ between the k-th round of global aggregation in which vehicle cluster c_m participated and the global aggregation in which this c_m participated last time
δ	The model weight parameter of similarity threshold
μ	The global aggregation stopping threshold
τ	The number of local model update rounds for all vehicle users when participating in a global aggregation
ε	The neighborhood threshold for clustering
$N_\varepsilon(n)$	The ε-neighborhood of vehicular user n
$N_\varepsilon^+(n)$	The ε+-neighborhood of vehicular user n

We consider an unidirectional, straight, multi-lane IoV scenario, where VUs travel along the X-axis in the direction of the arrow. At time t, assuming that VU n is traveling at a constant speed $\bar{v}_n$, its position can be denoted as $\{x_n(t), y_n(t)\}$. The associated ES e is located at a fixed position $\{x_e, y_e\}$ with a coverage radius of r. Therefore, the remaining distance of VU n within the coverage area of its ES can be defined as:

$$\Pi_i = \sqrt{r^2 - (y_e - y_n(t))^2} - (x_n(t) - x_e). \tag{1}$$

Only when VU n is within the coverage area of ES, the parameters can be uploaded to the current ES. Therefore, the sojourn time of VU n at the current ES is defined as:

$$T_{v,n}^{\text{soj}} = \frac{\Pi_n}{\bar{v}_n}, \tag{2}$$

where $\bar{v}_n$ is the speed of VU n.

In order to calculate the distance between arbitrary nodes i and j (including VUs and ES), the Euclidean distance formula is introduced:

$$dist(i, j) = \sqrt{(x_i - x_j)^2 + (y_i - y_j)^2}. \tag{3}$$

We resort to the Shannon capacity formula to compute the data rate of nodes i to j in FL the k-th round of global aggregation and denoted as:

$$R_{i,j}^k(dist(i, j)) = B_i \log_2(1 + \frac{P_i^{\text{tx}} \cdot h(dist(i, j))}{N_0}), \tag{4}$$

where N_0 represents the noise power, $h(dist(i, j))$ is the channel gain at the distance between node i and j, P_i^{tx} and B_i represent the transmission power and the communication bandwidth from node i to node j.

During the k-th round of global aggregation, the uplink transmission time for a vehicle cluster c_m to transmit its cluster model weight parameters to its corresponding ES can be expressed as:

$$T_{k,m}^{\text{tx}} = \frac{|w_m^k|}{R_{m,e}^k(dist(m, e))}. \tag{5}$$

The downlink transmission time for an ES to transmit global model weight parameters to the MCH of vehicle cluster c_m in its coverage area can be expressed as:

$$T_{k,m}^{\text{rx}} = \frac{|w_k|}{R_{e,m}^k(dist(e, m))}. \tag{6}$$

As the time for intra-cluster transmission of parameters from cluster member VUs to the MCH is short, this transmission time is neglected in this paper. Therefore, for the k-th round of global aggregation in ES, the communication time for a vehicle cluster c_m consists of the uplink transmission time and downlink transmission time of its MCH.

$$T_{k,m}^{\text{comm}} = T_{k,m}^{\text{tx}} + T_{k,m}^{\text{rx}}. \tag{7}$$

3.2 Cluster-Based Semi-asynchronous Federated Learning Framework for IoV (CSA_FedVeh)

In the CSA_FedVeh, assuming $\mathcal{C}_k$ represents the set of vehicle clusters participating in the k-th round of global aggregation, while semi-asynchronous aggregation quantity q is the number of vehicle clusters taking part in each round of global aggregation.

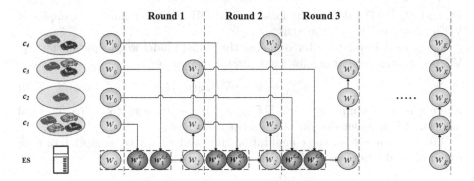

Fig. 2. Illustration of the CSA_FedVeh framework when $q=2$.

The vehicle cluster c_m that participate in global aggregation process download the global training model weight parameters w_k from the ES and distribute them to all VUs within the vehicle cluster. Each VU then updates its local model weight parameters based on its own historical data after uploads their new model weight parameters to the MCH, which synchronously aggregates vehicle cluster model weight parameters $w_{k+1}^{c,m}$ and sends them back to the ES. The ES collects q sequentially arrived cluster model weight parameters and performs global aggregation. Meanwhile, the vehicle clusters that did not participate in global aggregation continue their training. After the ES performs global aggregation, it generates the next round of global model weight parameters w_{k+1} and sends them to the MCHs that uploaded local weight parameters in the previous round, which then transmit them to the VUs within their respective vehicle clusters for the next round of training.

For instance, as shown in Fig. 2, The vehicle clusters participating in global aggregation in the first, second, and third rounds are $\mathcal{C}_1 = \{c_1, c_3\}$, $\mathcal{C}_2 = \{c_4, c_1\}$, and $\mathcal{C}_3 = \{c_2, c_3\}$, respectively.

To formalize the problem, we will introduce the CSA_FedVeh framework from three aspects: vehicle user model training, intra-cluster model aggregation, and semi-asynchronous global model aggregation, which is formally described in Algorithm 1.

Vehicle User Model Training. Local loss function: each VU trains a local model based on local DBs, where the loss function of the k-th round FL training model of VU n is defined as:

$$F_{v,n}(w_k^{v,n}) = \frac{1}{D_n} \sum_{(x_d,y_d) \in \mathcal{D}_n} f(w_k^{v,n}, x_d, y_d), \tag{8}$$

where $f(w_k^{v,n}, x_d, y_d)$ is the loss function of the model based on the training set samples x_d and their predicted labels y_d under the local weight parameter $w_k^{v,n}$, $\mathcal{D}_n$ and $D_n \triangleq |\mathcal{D}_n|$ denote the local trained DB and the number of samples of VU n after partitioning the SDB.

Local model update: after receiving the global model weight parameter w_k, VU n performs τ iterations for local parameter updates:

$$w_{k+1}^{v,n} \leftarrow w_k - \eta \nabla F_{v,n}(w_k), \tag{9}$$

where η is the learning rate and $\nabla F_{v,n}(w_k)$ is the gradient computed by local model of VU n under the global weight parameter w_k.

Local resource cost: the computation time and energy consumption of each round of local model training for VU n are denoted as:

$$T_{v,n}^{loc} = \frac{\sum_{d_n=1}^{D_n} \psi_{d_n}}{c_n^p \cdot f_n}, \ E_{v,n}^{loc} = p_n \cdot T_{v,n}^{loc}, \tag{10}$$

where ψ_{d_n} is the total number of Floating Point Operations per Second (FLOPS) required for sample d_n, VU is characterized by a processing capability equal to c_n^p (FLOPS) per CPU cycle, f_n is CPU frequency and p_n is the computational power of VU.

Intra-Cluster Model Aggregation. Cluster model aggregation: The VUs within vehicle cluster c_m pass the trained local model weight parameter $w_k^{v,n}$ to the MCH for intra-cluster aggregation, obtaining the cluster model weight parameter:

$$w_k^{c,m} \leftarrow \sum_{n \in c_m} D_n \cdot w_k^{v,n}, \tag{11}$$

Cluster gradient aggregation: in order to determine the convergence of the global model, it is necessary to upload the gradients from each vehicle cluster to ES. Therefore, the aggregation of gradients from vehicle cluster c_m is defined as:

$$\nabla F_{c,m}(w_k) \leftarrow \sum_{n \in c_m} \nabla F_{v,n}(w_k). \tag{12}$$

Cluster resource cost: the computation time and energy consumption for training each round of local model in vehicle cluster c_m is defined as:

$$T_{c,m}^{loc} = \max_{c \in c_m}\{T_{v,c}^{loc}\}, \ E_{c,m}^{loc} = \sum_{c \in c_m} E_{v,c}^{loc}. \tag{13}$$

Algorithm 1. CSA_FedVeh

Input: the set of vehicle clusters $\mathcal{C}$, semi - asynchronous aggregation parameters q, number of vehicle local iterations τ

Output: the final global model weight parameter $w*$

1: Initialize the cluster structure;
2: Initialize $w_0, k = 0, T = 0, E = 0$;
3: **while** $k \neq K$ and $\|\nabla F(w_k)\| > \mu \|\nabla F(w_{k-1})\|$ and $T < T_{\max}$ and $E < E_{\max}$ **do**
4:     **Global Aggregation at the Edge Server**
5:     set $k \leftarrow k + 1$, and $\mathcal{C}_k = \emptyset$;
6:     **while** $|\mathcal{C}_k| \neq q$ **do**
7:         Receive update c_m from $\mathcal{C}$;
8:         Compute $T_{k,m}^{\text{total}}$ according to Eq.(18);
9:         **if** $T_{k,m}^{\text{total}} \leq T_{c,m}^{\text{soj}}$ **then**
10:             update $\mathcal{C}_k \leftarrow \mathcal{C}_k + \{c_m\}, E \leftarrow E + E_{c,m}^{\text{loc}}$;
11:         **end if**
12:     **end while**
13:     Compute $w_k, \nabla F(w_k), T_k$ according to Eq.(14),Eq.(15),Eq.(16);
14:     Update $T \leftarrow T + T_k, w* \leftarrow w_k$;
15:     Send w_k back to $\mathcal{C}_k$;
16:     **Cluster Aggregation at c_m**
17:     Receive local updates from all VUs in vehicle cluster c_m;
18:     Update $T_{c,m}^{\text{soj}} \leftarrow \min_{n \in c_m} \{T_{v,n}^{\text{soj}}\}$;
19:     Compute $w_k^{c,m}, \nabla F_{c,m}(w_k), T_{c,m}^{\text{loc}}$ and $E_{c,m}^{\text{loc}}$ according to Eq.(11),Eq.(12),Eq.(13);
20:     Send $w_k^{c,m}, \nabla F_{c,m}(w_k), T_{c,m}^{\text{soj}}$ and resource consumption $T_{c,m}^{\text{loc}}, E_{c,m}^{\text{loc}}$ to ES;
21:     Receive w_k from ES and return it back to all VUs in vehicle cluster c_m;
22:     **Procedure at Vehicle User n in Cluster c_m**
23:     Receive w_k from c_m;
24:     Perform local updates;
25:     Compute $T_{v,n}^{\text{loc}}$ and $E_{v,n}^{\text{loc}}$, $T_{v,n}^{\text{soj}}$ according to Eq.(10),Eq.(2);
26:     Send $w_{k+1}^{v,n}, \nabla F_{v,n}(w_k), T_{v,n}^{\text{soj}}$ and resource consumption $T_{v,n}^{\text{loc}}, E_{v,n}^{\text{loc}}$ to MCH;
27: **end while**
28: **return** $w*$;

Semi-asynchronous Global Model Aggregation. Global model aggregation: during a round of global aggregation, when ES receives cluster model weight parameters transmitted by q vehicle clusters, ES performs global aggregation:

$$w_{k+1} \leftarrow \frac{1}{D\_k} \sum_{m \in \mathcal{C}_k} w_k^{c,m}, \tag{14}$$

where D_k is the total number of samples from all participating vehicle clusters in the k-th round of global aggregation.

Global Gradient aggregation: in order to determine the stopping criterion for the convergence of the global model [19], the global gradient is defined as:

$$\nabla F(w_{k+1}) \leftarrow \frac{1}{q} \sum_{m \in \mathcal{C}_k} \nabla F_{c,m}(w_k). \tag{15}$$

For the k-th round of FL aggregation in ES, the time taken for global aggregation is determined by the longest computation time of the participating vehicle cluster $\mathcal{C}_k$, denoted as:

$$T_k = T_k{}^{sort}[q], \tag{16}$$

where $T_k{}^{sort}[q]$ represents the q-th element in the set $T_k{}^{sort}$(defined in Eq.(20)).

Assuming that all VUs update their local weight parameters τ times during each cluster weight parameter upload, the local computation time of vehicle cluster c_m is the duration between the start time of the k-th round of global aggregation and the end time of local training, denoted as:

$$T_{k,m}^{comp}(s_k^m) = \begin{cases} T_{c,m}^{loc} \cdot \tau - \sum\limits_{k-s_k^m}^{k-1} T_k & , s_k^m > 0 \\ T_{c,m}^{loc} \cdot \tau & , s_k^m = 0 \end{cases}, \tag{17}$$

where s_k^m represents the number of global aggregation rounds that differ between the k-th round of global aggregation in which vehicle cluster c_m participated and the global aggregation in which this vehicle cluster c_m participated last time, for example in Fig. 2, where $s_1^3 = 0$, $T_{1,3}^{comp}(s_1^3) = T_3^{loc} \cdot \tau$; $s_2^1 = 0$, $T_{2,1}^{comp}(s_2^1) = T_1^{loc} \cdot \tau$; $s_3^2 = 2$, $T_{3,2}^{comp}(s_3^2) = T_2^{loc} \cdot \tau - \sum\limits_{3-2}^{3-1} T_k = T_2^{loc} \cdot \tau - T_2 - T_1$.

In the k-th round of ES global aggregation, the total time consumption of vehicle cluster c_m is the sum of local computation time and communication time, represented as:

$$T_{k,m}^{total} = T_{k,m}^{comp}(s_k^m) + T_{k,m}^{comm}. \tag{18}$$

Assuming that all vehicle clusters participate in the k-th round of global aggregation, and the set of training times for all vehicle clusters $\mathcal{C}$ in the k-th round of global aggregation is defined as:

$$T_k = \{T_{k,1}^{total}, ..., T_{k,m}^{total}, ..., T_{k,M}^{total}\}. \tag{19}$$

We sort the set of training times T_k in ascending order:

$$T_k{}^{sort} = sort(T_k). \tag{20}$$

We define the matrix of the number of times each vehicle cluster participates in the global aggregation of ES as:

$$G = (g_1 \cdots g_m \cdots g_M), \tag{21}$$

where g_m denotes the number of times that vehicle cluster c_m participates in the global aggregation of ES, $0 \leq g_m \leq K$.

We define the matrix of energy consumption of all vehicle cluster as follows:

$$E = (E_{c,1}^{loc} \cdots E_{c,m}^{loc} \cdots E_{c,M}^{loc}). \tag{22}$$

3.3   Problem Formulation

The optimization problem formulated by the vehicle-clustered federated learning network and the CSA_FedVe framework can be described as:

$$(P1): \min_{q,\mathcal{C}} \sum_{k=1}^{K} T_k$$

$$s.t. \begin{cases} C_1 : \left\| \nabla F(w_{k+1}) \right\| \leq \mu \left\| \nabla F(w_k) \right\| \\ C_2 : \sum_{k=1}^{K} T_k \leq T_{\max} \\ C_3 : \tau \cdot G \cdot E^T \leq E_{\max} \\ C_4 : T_{k,m}^{\text{total}} \leq \min_{c \in c_m} \{T_{v,c}^{\text{soj}}\} \\ C_5 : q \in \{1, 2, ..., M\}. \end{cases} \quad (23)$$

In problem P1, the objective function is to minimize the FL training time while satisfying the constraints under the semi-asynchronous aggregation quantity q and the vehicle network clustering strategy $\mathcal{C}$. Constraint C_1 corresponds to the global aggregation stopping condition [19], where $\mu(0 \leq \mu \leq 1)$. When $\mu = 0$, the global model achieves a precise solution, whereas $\mu = 1$ indicates that no progress has been made by the global model. Constraint C_2 represents the global training time constraint of FL, and constraint C_3 represents the global training energy constraint of FL. Here, $T_{\max}$ and $E_{\max}$ refer to the maximum acceptable global training time and energy consumption of FL, respectively. Constraint C_4 denotes the total time spent on the k-th round of global aggregation of vehicle cluster c_m must not exceed the minimum sojourn time of VUs in the vehicle cluster c_m.

As many machine learning models have complex intrinsic properties, it is difficult to find closed-form solutions for the objective function. Therefore, in Sect. 4, we designe some novel solutions that reduce the training time and resource costs of FL while maintaining learning accuracy.

4   Methodology

To solve the aforementioned problems, in this section, we propose the STW-DBSCAN clustering algorithm, which is designed to determine vehicle clustering strategies in dynamic IoV system. The algorithm decomposes the originally high-complex intrinsic properties problem into two sub-problems: the vehicle clustering problem and the semi-asynchronous aggregation mechanism problem, in order to approximate the solution to the original problem while mitigating the impact of Non-IID data on the FL process.

4.1   STW-DBSCAN Density Clustering Algorithm

In order to reduce the complexity of solving P1, we propose a density clustering algorithm (STW-DBSCAN) that relies on both the space-time location similarities and model weight similarities of vehicles to determine the clustering strategy

---

Algorithm 2. STW-DBSCAN

Input: the set of all VUs $\mathcal{V}$, neighborhood parameters $(\varepsilon, MinPts)$, similarity threshold $\delta(2\%$, default)

Output: $\mathcal{C} = \{c_1, ..., c_m, ..., c_M\}$

1: Initialize the vehicle structure;
2: Initialize candidate set $\Omega = \emptyset$, number of clusters m = 0, sets of unvisited vehicles $\Gamma = \mathcal{V}$, vehicle network clustering strategy $\mathcal{C} = \emptyset$;
3: **for** n in $\mathcal{V}$ **do**
4:    compute $N_\varepsilon(n)$ and $N_\varepsilon^+(n)$ according to Eq.(24) and (26);
5:    **if** $|N_\varepsilon^+(n) \cap N_\varepsilon(n)| \geq MinPts$ **then**
6:       $\Omega = \Omega \cup \{n\}$;
7:    **end if**
8: **end for**
9: **while** $\Omega = \emptyset$ **do**
10:    $\Gamma_{old} = \Gamma$;
11:    random selection of a candidate $o \in \Omega$, initializing queue $Q = <o>$;
12:    $\Gamma = \Gamma \backslash \{o\}$;
13:    **while** $Q \neq \emptyset$ **do**
14:       fetch the first sample q in the queue Q;
15:       **if** $|N_\varepsilon^+(q)| \geq MinPts$ **then**
16:          $\Delta = N_\varepsilon^+(q) \cap \Gamma$;
17:          add the samples in Δ to the queue Q;
18:          $\Gamma = \Gamma \backslash \Delta$;
19:       **end if**
20:    **end while**
21:    $m = m + 1$, generate clusters $c_m = \Gamma_{old} \backslash \Gamma$;
22:    select a random benchmark $\alpha \in c_m$;
23:    **for** β in c_m **do**
24:       **if** $\theta(w_1^{v,\alpha}, w_1^{v,\beta}) \leq \delta$ **then**
25:          $c_m \backslash \beta$;
26:       **end if**
27:    **end for**
28:    $\Omega = \Omega \backslash c_m$, $\mathcal{C} = \mathcal{C} \cup c_m$;
29: **end while**
30: **return** $\mathcal{C} = \{c_1, ..., c_m, ..., c_M\}$;

---

in problem P1. The algorithm integrates the space-time location constraints into the DBSCAN [20] clustering algorithm to guarantee that VUs within the ES region stay within the range of the vehicle cluster. Additionally, considering the Non-IID of data collected by vehicles, the cosine similarity between VU model weight parameters is calculated to ensure that the vehicle data within a cluster belongs to the same distribution [12]. Lastly, The MCH is chosen based on the latest sojourn time, while the VCH is chosen based on the second latest sojourn time. Based on the algorithm, we can acquire the set of vehicle clusters $\mathcal{C}$, and by combining $\mathcal{C}$ with Eq.(2), we can compute MCH and VCH.

The STW-DBSCAN algorithm is mainly determined by the parameters of neighborhood threshold ε, density threshold $MinPts$, vehicle sojourn time T_n^{soj}, vehicle speed $\bar{v}$, model weight parameter set of VU, and similarity threshold δ, where ε and $MinPts$ are system-determined hyperparameters. For a VU $n \in \mathcal{V}$, we select the set of VUs in the set $\mathcal{V}$ whose distance from VU n does not exceed ε, as the ε_neighborhood of the VU n $(N_\varepsilon(n))$, denoted as:

$$N_\varepsilon(n) = \{p \in \mathcal{V} | dist(n,p) \leq \varepsilon\}. \tag{24}$$

We determine the sojourn time among the VUs in the set $N_\varepsilon(n)$ by using Eq.(2) and compare it to determine the minimum sojourn time in $N_\varepsilon(n)$:

$$T_{N,n}^{soj} = \min_{p \in N_\varepsilon(n)+\{n\}} \{T_{v,p}^{soj}\}. \tag{25}$$

In IoV system, if the distance between the VU n and all other VUs in $N_\varepsilon(n)$ still satisfies within ε after the minimum sojourn time $T_{N,n}^{soj}$, then it is referred to as the ε+_neighborhood of the VU n $(N_\varepsilon^+(n))$ and denoted as:

$$N_\varepsilon^+(n) = \{p \in N_\varepsilon(n) | \sqrt{((x_n - \bar{v}_n \cdot T_{N,n}^{soj}) - (x_p - \bar{v}_p \cdot T_{N,n}^{soj}))^2 + (y_n - y_p)^2} \leq \varepsilon\}. \tag{26}$$

If $N_\varepsilon^+(n)$ has at least $MinPts$ other VUs and denoted as:

$$\left| N_\varepsilon^+(n) \right| \geq MinPts, \tag{27}$$

then vehicle cluster c_m is created, and VU n and all VUs in $N_\varepsilon^+(n)$ are added to the cluster, and all VUs in $N_\varepsilon^+(n)$ are added to the candidate set Ω. Each VU $o \in \Omega$ is checked in turn to see if $N_\varepsilon^+(o)$ contains at least $MinPts$ other VUs, if o has not been added to the vehicle cluster yet, it is added to vehicle cluster c_m, and o is removed from the candidate set Ω, and $N_\varepsilon^+(o)$ is added to the candidate set Ω. This process continues until $\Omega=\emptyset$. Additionally, if VUs that have not been clustered what contain at least $MinPts$ other VUs in their ε+_neighborhood, a new vehicle cluster and candidate set are created.

Randomly select a VU $\alpha \in c_m$ as a baseline, and calculate the cosine similarity of the model weight parameters between VU α and all other VUs $\beta \in c_m$,

$$\theta(w_1^{v,\alpha}, w_1^{v,\beta}) = \frac{(w_1^{v,\alpha})^T w_1^{v,\beta}}{\left\| w_1^{v,\alpha} \right\| \left\| w_1^{v,\beta} \right\|}, \alpha, \beta \in c_m, \tag{28}$$

judge whether the data distribution of VUs in vehicle cluster c_m is similar. If $\theta(w_1^{v,\alpha}, w_1^{v,\beta}) \leq \delta$, indicating low similarity, remove β from vehicle cluster c_m and re-cluster β, where $\delta(-1 \leq \delta \leq 1)$ is the similarity threshold, and the closer δ is to 1, the more similar the data distribution is, while the closer it is to - 1, the less similar it is. The STW-DBSCAN algorithm is formally described in Algorithm 2.

4.2 Semi-asynchronous

Once the clustering strategy $\mathcal{C}$ of STW-DBSCAN algorithm is fixed, P1 is redefined as a problem of solving a single variable q:

$$(P2) : \min_{q} \sum_{k=1}^{K} T_k \tag{29}$$
$$s.t.\, C_1, C_2, C_3, C_5.$$

We adopt a semi-asynchronous aggregation mechanism [16] to accelerate the global model training speed. Each time global aggregation selects q cluster model weight parameters that arrive in order for aggregation.

5 Performance Evaluation

5.1 Simulation Setting

Benchmarks. We utilize three classic FL frameworks and a semi-asynchronous framework with randomized clustering as benchmarks for performance comparison.

- FedAF: FedAF (FedAvgfull) is a synchronous FL framework, which is a variant of FedAvg [4]. In FedAF framework, all VUs participate in the global updating in each round.
- FedASY [14]: FedASY is an asynchronous FL framework, where ES immediately performs a global updating upon receiving local model weight parameters from any VU.
- SAFA [16]: SAFA is a semi-asynchronous FL framework. For simplicity, the client selection in SAFA is removed, and we naturally set it to half of the total number of VUs in our experiment, simulating the framework of semi-asynchronous aggregation under the condition of no clustering.
- R-SAFA: R-SAFA adopts the SAFA aggregation framework with K-means [21] random clustering, where K is set to be the same as the number of clusters in STW-DBSCAN, simulating the framework of semi-asynchronous aggregation under the condition of general clustering.

Models and Datasets. In order to ascertain the efficacy of CSA_FedVeh framework, we conducted experiments using two disparate training models (LR [22] and CNN [23]), and on two real-world datasets (MNIST [24] and German Traffic Sign Recognition Database (GTSRD) [25]). MNIST dataset comprises 60,000 training samples and 10,000 testing samples, each of which is a grayscale image of a handwritten digit measuring 28×28 pixels. GTSRD dataset includes 43 classes of RGB three-channel traffic sign images, divided into 39,209 training images and 12,630 testing images.

Performance Metrics. We have utilized four commonly-used performance metrics to evaluate the training performance, including:

1) Loss Function: used to measure the difference between predicted values and actual values.

2) Accuracy: indicates the proportion of correctly classified samples by the model among all samples in the dataset.

3) Runtime: indicates the time taken to complete the training process, used to measure the training speed of the model.

4) Communication Cost: represents the total communication time spent between all vehicles and the ES upon completion of the training process.

Data Distribution. Considering the heterogeneity of data distribution and the similarity of data collected from vehicles within a certain area among VUs in a real-world IoV scenarios, it is necessary to form a Non-IID dataset among VUs. To achieve data re-distribution, a mixed distribution based on Dirichlet distribution was applied [26], which highlights the similarity of data within the cluster and Non-IID among VUs. The parameters for the mixed distribution were set as $a = 1.0$ and $n = 3$.

Simulation Parameters. In the simulation of IoV scenarios for FL, we consider 50 VUs participating, with safe distances randomly scattered along the lane. The average vehicle speed is approximately 43.6km/h, and the vehicles are given random speeds. We set the neighborhood threshold ε=25m and the density threshold $MinPts$=1, with similarity threshold δ of 2%. We use the same $batchsize = 64$ for all VUs. The global learning rate is set to η=0.01 for both MNIST and GTSRD, and the number of local updates per epoch is set to H=30.

5.2 Simulation Results

In this section, we compared our CSA_FedVeh framework with the baseline by training models for 30000 s and 50000 s on Non-IID MNIST and GTSRD datasets, respectively. Finally, Table 2 lists more detailed training performance comparisons on MNIST and GTSRD datasets. The results show that CSA_FedVeh framework can work better even when the data distribution is Non-IID.

Table 2. Performance comparison of CSA_FedVeh with four benchmarks under two models.

Dataset-Model	Performance Metrics	FedAF	FedASY	SAFA	R-SAFA	CSA_FedVeh
MNIST-LR	Accuracy	91.8%	92.5%	92.2%	93.2%	**94.5%**
	Runtime for Loss=0.5	7381s	6060s	6458s	4857s	**3348s**
	Communication time for accuracy=90%	8.35s	18.352s	13.325s	7.04s	**6.96s**
MNIST-CNN	Average communication rounds	305	826.38	549	579	**501.76**
	Accuracy	97%	97.7%	97.6%	97.8%	**98.4%**
	Runtime for Loss=0.5	5412s	3230s	3785s	3276s	**2348s**
	Communication time for accuracy=90%	4.75s	7.55s	6.075s	3.9424s	**3.808s**
GTSRD-LR	Accuracy	76.4%	81.8%	79.9%	86%	**89.3%**
	Runtime for Loss=1	48027s	36749s	40852s	25689s	**19077s**
	Communication time for accuracy=75%	24.05s	49.375s	36.275s	15.76s	**15.6s**
GTSRD-CNN	Average communication rounds	509	1377.7	916	965.5	**838.4**
	Accuracy	88%	91.7%	90.3%	95.5%	**96.1%**
	Runtime for Loss=1	28934s	23014s	25318s	15751s	**11868s**
	Communication time for accuracy=75%	16.2s	33.476s	24.375s	11.352s	**10.496s**

Convergence Performance. In MNIST dataset, as shown in Fig. 3(e), when the global model training loss of LR model drops to 0.5, CSA_FedVeh reaches its fastest runtime of 3348 s, which is 44.7% faster than FedASY, 54.6% faster than FedAF, 48.1% faster than SAFA, and 31% faster than R-SAFA. In Fig. 3(f), when the global model training loss of CNN model drops to 0.5, CSA_FedVeh reaches its fastest runtime of 2348 s, which is 27.3% faster than FedASY, 56.6% faster than FedAF, 37.9% faster than SAFA, and 28.3% faster than R-SAFA. In GTSRD dataset, as shown in Fig. 3(g), when the global model training loss value reached 1.0, CSA_FedVeh reached the fastest running time at 19077 s, which was 48% faster than FedASY, 60.2% faster than FedAF, 53.3% faster than SAFA, and 25.7% faster than R-SAFA. As shown in Fig. 3(h), when CNN global model training loss value reached 1.0, CSA_FedVeh reached the fastest running time at 11868 s, which was 48.4% faster than FedASY, 58.9% faster than FedAF, 53.1% faster than SAFA, and 24.6% faster than R-SAFA. Results on different datasets and models indicate that CSA_FedVeh reduces the time required to reach the same loss value by about 24.6%-60.2%.

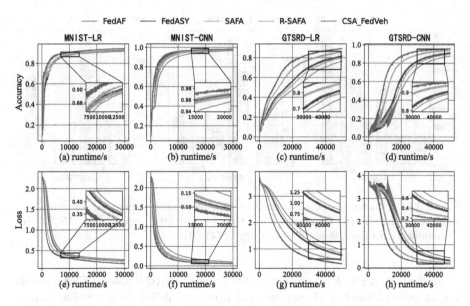

Fig. 3. Accuracy and Loss vs. Runtime with LR and CNN over MNIST and GTSRD.

Not only can CSA_FedVeh stabilize the convergence of the global model, but it also outperforms the four benchmarks in terms of accuracy and convergence speed. Additionally, when comparing Figs. 3(e) and 3(f), as well as Figs. 3(g) and 3(h), CSA_FedVeh exhibits faster convergence speed on CNN models compared to LR models.

Resource Constraints. In MNIST dataset, as shown in Fig. 3(a), when the running time constraint under LR model is set at 30,000 s, CSA_FedVeh achieved the highest accuracy of 94.5%. This is 2% higher compared to FedASY, 2.7% higher compared to FedAF, 2.2% higher compared to SAFA, and 1.3% higher compared to R-SAFA. As shown in Fig. 3(b), under CNN model with a running time constraint of 30,000 s, CSA_FedVeh achieved the highest accuracy of 98.4%. This is 0.7% higher compared to FedASY, 1.4% higher compared to FedAF, 0.8% higher compared to SAFA, and 0.6% higher compared to R-SAFA. In GTSRD dataset, as shown in Fig. 3(c), under a time constraint of 50000 s for LR model, CSA_FedVeh achieved the highest accuracy of 89.3%, which is 7.5% higher than FedASY, 12.9% higher than FedAF, 9.4% higher than SAFA, and 3.3% higher than R-SAFA. As shown in Fig. 3(d), under a time constraint of 50000 s for CNN model, CSA_FedVeh achieved the highest accuracy of 96.1%, which is 4.4% higher than FedASY, 8.1% higher than FedAF, 5.8% higher than SAFA, and 0.6% higher than R-SAFA. The results indicate that, under the same time budget, CSA_FedVeh achieved higher accuracy and lower loss than FedAF, FedASY, SAFA, and R-SAFA. This means that CSA_FedVeh can achieve good performance in terms of the balance between convergence speed and accuracy.

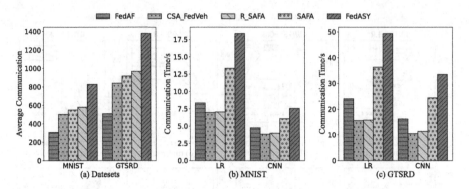

Fig. 4. The Comparison of Communication Resource Consumption. (a) Average Communication rounds. (b) Communication time cost at 90% accuracy of MNIST. (c) Communication time cost at 75% accuracy of GTSRD.

According to Fig. 4(a), on both MNIST and GTSRD datasets, CSA_FedVeh has an average number of communication rounds of 501.76 and 838.4, respectively. This is lower than FedASY by 324.62 and 539.3 rounds, lower than SAFA by 47.24 and 77.6 rounds, lower than R-SAFA by 77.24 and 127.1 rounds, and higher than FedAF by 196.76 and 329.4 rounds. These results indicate that CSA_FedVeh has a lower average number of communication rounds than FedASY, SAFA, and R-SAFA, and is second only to FedAF in this respect. Moreover, CSA_FedVeh achieves a higher accuracy than FedAF by 1.4%-12.9% and converges faster. According to Fig. 4(b), when LR and CNN models of MNIST dataset reach a training accuracy of 90%, the global communication time of CSA_FedVeh is 6.96 s and 3.808 s, respectively. This is a reduction of 16.6% and 19.83% compared to FedAF, a reduction of 62.07% and 49.56% compared to FedASY, a reduction of 47.76% and 37.31% compared to SAFA, and a reduction of 11.36% and 3.4% compared to R-SAFA. According to Fig. 4(c), when LR and CNN models of GTSRD dataset reach a training accuracy of 75%, the global communication time of CSA_FedVeh was 15.6 s and 10.496 s, respectively. This is a decrease of 35.13% and 35.21% compared to FedAF, a decrease of 68.4% and 68.6% compared to FedASY, a decrease of 56.99% and 56.93% compared to SAFA, and a decrease of 1.01% and 7.54% compared to R-SAFA. The results demonstrate that CSA_FedVeh achieves the optimal global communication time across all models. This implies that, with the same communication budget, CSA_FedVeh reduces communication costs between VUs and the ES by executing cluster-based semi-asynchronous aggregation.

In summary, our CSA_FedVeh framework has demonstrated superiority over four benchmarks in the following aspects. Firstly, as seen in Fig. 3, CSA_FedVeh consistently achieves better convergence than the benchmarks during training and reduces training time by approximately 24.6% to 60.2% to reach the same loss level. Secondly, as shown in Fig. 4(a), on both MNIST and GTSRD datasets, the average number of communication rounds for CSA_FedVeh is lower than

FedASY, SAFA, and R-SAFA, and only slightly more than FedAF. Additionally, CSA_FedVeh achieve the lowest total communication time, the highest accuracy and the fastest convergence speed. Finally, Figs. 4(b) and 4(c) demonstrate that, compared to the baselines, CSA_FedVeh reduces communication costs by 3.4% to 62.07% on MNIST dataset and by 1.01% to 68.6% on GTSRD dataset, while achieving similar accuracy.

6 Conclusion

In this paper, we propose CSA_FedVeh, a novel cluster-based semi-asynchronous FL framework for IoV. We aspire to enhance the effectiveness of FL in the dynamic and intricate scenarios of IoV. Under this guidance, We proposed the STW-DBSCAN clustering algorithm, which takes advantage of Non-IID of data collected by vehicles to cluster vehicles with similar vehicle space-time location and high model weights similarity, efficiently addressing the straggler problem and accelerating global model training. Meanwhile, we combine the semi-asynchronous federated aggregation mechanism to accelerate the speed of global aggregation. The experimental results indicate that our proposed framework can obtain excellent performance under resource constraints on the datasets of Non-IID compared with baselines. In the future, we will explore our CSA_FedVeh framework on vehicle tasks that require stable, low-latency, and highly reliable services in IoV, such as object tracking, high-definition (HD) map generation and augmented reality (AR) navigation.

Acknowledgment. This work was supported by the National Natural Science Foundation of China (No.62272063, No.62072056 and No.61902041), the Natural Science Foundation of Hunan Province (No.2022JJ30617 and No.2020JJ2029), open research fund of Key Lab of Broadband Wireless Communication and Sensor Network Technology, Nanjing University of Posts and Telecommunications (No.JZNY202102), Standardization Project of Transportation Department of Hunan Province (B202108), Hunan Provincial Key Research and Development Program (2022GK2019) and the Scientific Research Fund of Hunan Provincial Transportation Department (No.202143).

References

1. Banabilah, S., Aloqaily, M., Alsayed, E., Malik, N., Jararweh, Y.: Federated learning review: fundamentals, enabling technologies, and future applications. Inf. Process. Manage. **59**(6), 103061 (2022)
2. Chaudhry, S.A.: Designing an efficient and secure message exchange protocol for internet of vehicles. Secur. Commun. Netw. **2021**, 1–9 (2021). https://doi.org/10.1155/2021/5554318
3. Liu, S., Liu, L., Tang, J., Yu, B., Wang, Y., Shi, W.: Edge computing for autonomous driving: opportunities and challenges. Proc. IEEE **107**(8), 1697–1716 (2019). https://doi.org/10.1109/jproc.2019.2915983
4. McMahan, B., Moore, E., Ramage, D., Hampson, S., y Arcas, B.A.: Communication-efficient learning of deep networks from decentralized data. In: Artificial Intelligence and Statistics, pp. 1273–1282. PMLR (2017)

5. Cao, H., et al.: Prevention of GAN-based privacy inferring attacks towards federated learning. In: Gao, H., Wang, X., Wei, W., Dagiuklas, T. (eds.) Collaborative Computing: Networking, Applications and Worksharing. CollaborateCom 2022. LNICS, Social Informatics and Telecommunications Engineering, vol. 461, pp. 39–54. Springer, Cham (2022). https://doi.org/10.1007/978-3-031-24386-8_3

6. Pan, S.J., Yang, Q.: A survey on transfer learning. IEEE Trans. Knowl. Data Eng. **22**(10), 1345–1359 (2009). https://doi.org/10.1109/tkde.2009.191

7. Li, Q., Diao, Y., Chen, Q., He, B.: Federated learning on non-iid data silos: an experimental study. In: 2022 IEEE 38th International Conference on Data Engineering (ICDE), pp. 965–978. IEEE (2022). https://doi.org/10.1109/icde53745.2022.00077

8. Huang, X., Li, P., Yu, R., Wu, Y., Xie, K., Xie, S.: Fedparking: a federated learning based parking space estimation with parked vehicle assisted edge computing. IEEE Trans. Veh. Technol. **70**(9), 9355–9368 (2021). https://doi.org/10.1109/tvt.2021.3098170

9. Liang, F., Yang, Q., Liu, R., Wang, J., Sato, K., Guo, J.: Semi-synchronous federated learning protocol with dynamic aggregation in internet of vehicles. IEEE Trans. Veh. Technol. **71**(5), 4677–4691 (2022). https://doi.org/10.1109/tvt.2022.3148872

10. Huang, J., Xu, C., Ji, Z., Xiao, S., Liu, T., Ma, N., Zhou, Q., et al.: AFLPC: an asynchronous federated learning privacy-preserving computing model applied to 5g–v2x. Security and Communication Networks 2022 (2022). https://doi.org/10.1155/2022/9334943

11. Ma, M., Wu, L., Liu, W., Chen, N., Shao, Z., Yang, Y.: Data-aware hierarchical federated learning via task offloading. In: GLOBECOM 2022–2022 IEEE Global Communications Conference, pp. 1–6. IEEE (2022). https://doi.org/10.1109/globecom48099.2022.10000924

12. Briggs, C., Fan, Z., Andras, P.: Federated learning with hierarchical clustering of local updates to improve training on non-iid data. In: 2020 International Joint Conference on Neural Networks (IJCNN), pp. 1–9. IEEE (2020). https://doi.org/10.1109/ijcnn48605.2020.9207469

13. Tan, Y., Long, G., Liu, L., Zhou, T., Lu, Q., Jiang, J., Zhang, C.: FedProto: federated prototype learning across heterogeneous clients. In: Proceedings of the AAAI Conference on Artificial Intelligence, vol. 36, pp. 8432–8440 (2022). https://doi.org/10.1609/aaai.v36i8.20819

14. Xie, C., Koyejo, S., Gupta, I.: Asynchronous federated optimization. arXiv preprint arXiv:1903.03934 (2019)

15. Vu, T.T., Ngo, D.T., Ngo, H.Q., Dao, M.N., Tran, N.H., Middleton, R.H.: User selection approaches to mitigate the straggler effect for federated learning on cell-free massive MIMO networks. arXiv preprint arXiv:2009.02031 (2020)

16. Wu, W., He, L., Lin, W., Mao, R., Maple, C., Jarvis, S.: Safa: a semi-asynchronous protocol for fast federated learning with low overhead. IEEE Trans. Comput. **70**(5), 655–668 (2020). https://doi.org/10.1109/tc.2020.2994391

17. Sun, J., et al.: FedSEA: a semi-asynchronous federated learning framework for extremely heterogeneous devices. In: Proceedings of the 20th ACM Conference on Embedded Networked Sensor Systems, pp. 106–119 (2022). https://doi.org/10.1145/3560905.3568538

18. Ma, Q., Xu, Y., Xu, H., Jiang, Z., Huang, L., Huang, H.: FedSA: a semi-asynchronous federated learning mechanism in heterogeneous edge computing. IEEE J. Sel. Areas Commun. **39**(12), 3654–3672 (2021). https://doi.org/10.1109/jsac.2021.3118435

19. Xiao, H., Zhao, J., Pei, Q., Feng, J., Liu, L., Shi, W.: Vehicle selection and resource optimization for federated learning in vehicular edge computing. IEEE Trans. Intell. Transp. Syst. **23**(8), 11073–11087 (2021)
20. Ester, M., Kriegel, H.P., Sander, J., Xu, X., et al.: A density-based algorithm for discovering clusters in large spatial databases with noise. In: kdd. vol. 96, pp. 226–231 (1996)
21. MacQueen, J., et al.: Some methods for classification and analysis of multivariate observations. In: Proceedings of the Fifth Berkeley Symposium on Mathematical Statistics and Probability, vol. 1, pp. 281–297. Oakland, CA, USA (1967)
22. Hosmer Jr, D.W., Lemeshow, S., Sturdivant, R.X.: Applied Logistic Regression, vol. 398. Wiley, Hoboken (2013)
23. Shalev-Shwartz, S., Ben-David, S.: Understanding Machine Learning: From Theory to Algorithms. Cambridge University Press, Cambridge (2014)
24. LeCun, Y., Bottou, L., Bengio, Y., Haffner, P.: Gradient-based learning applied to document recognition. Proc. IEEE **86**(11), 2278–2324 (1998). https://doi.org/10.1109/5.726791
25. Stallkamp, J., Schlipsing, M., Salmen, J., Igel, C.: Man vs. computer: Benchmarking machine learning algorithms for traffic sign recognition. Neural Netw. **32**, 323–332 (2012). https://doi.org/10.1016/j.neunet.2012.02.016
26. Marfoq, O., Neglia, G., Bellet, A., Kameni, L., Vidal, R.: Federated multi-task learning under a mixture of distributions. Adv. Neural. Inf. Process. Syst. **34**, 15434–15447 (2021)

Efficiently Detecting Anomalies in IoT: A Novel Multi-Task Federated Learning Method

Junfeng Hao[1], Juan Chen[1], Peng Chen[1(✉)], Yang Wang[1], Xianhua Niu[1], Lei Xu[2], and Yunni Xia[3(✉)]

[1] School of Computer and Software Engineering, Xihua University, Chengdu, China
chenpeng@mail.xhu.edu.cn
[2] School of Emergency Management, Xihua University, Chengdu, China
[3] School of Computer Science, Chongqing University, Chongqing, China
xiayunni@hotmail.com

Abstract. With the development of IoT technology, a significant amount of time series data is continuously generated, and anomaly detection of this data is crucial. However, time series data in IoT is dynamic and heterogeneous, and most centralized learning also suffers from security and privacy issues. To address these issues, we propose a multi-task anomaly detection approach based on federated learning (MTAD-FL) to address these problems. First, we propose a distributed framework based on Multi-Task Federated Learning (MT-FL), which aims to solve multiple tasks simultaneously while exploiting similarities and differences between tasks; second, to identify complex anomaly patterns and features in the IoT environment, we construct a Squeeze Excitation (SE) based and External Attention (EA) based Enhance Dual Network (SE-EA-EDN) feature extractor to monitor real-time data features from IoT systems efficiently; finally, we design a Local-Global Feature-based Parallel Knowledge Transfer (LGF-PKT) to parallelize the updating of weights of local and global features. To validate the effectiveness of our approach, we conducted comparative experiments on three publicly available datasets, SMD, SWaT, and SKAB, and MTAD-FL improved F1 by 11%, 67.8%, and 27.5%, respectively, over the other methods.

Keywords: Internet of Things · Multi-Task Federated Learning · Anomaly Detection · Feature Extractor · Knowledge Transfer

1 Introduction

With the development of Internet of Things (IoT) technology, an increasing number of devices and sensors are being deployed, leading to a massive influx

This research is supported by the National Natural Science Foundation under Grant No. 62376043 and Science and Technology Program of Sichuan Province under Grant No. 2020JDRC0067, No. 2023JDRC0087, and No. 24NSFTD0025.

H. Gao et al. (Eds.): CollaborateCom 2023, LNICST 563, pp. 100–117, 2024.
https://doi.org/10.1007/978-3-031-54531-3_6

of heterogeneous time series data, and the urgency for extracting critical information from such data has become imperative [1]. Analyzing the quantitative performance plays an important role in understanding and improving the quality of cloud computing systems and cloud-based applications [2,7,9,10]. Anomaly Detection is a data analysis method used to identify behaviors or events that deviate from the expected pattern within the data. It has wide applications in many real-world domains, such as industrial manufacturing, network security, and financial fraud detection. Enhancing Quality of Service (QoS) in IoT cloud environments through anomaly detection techniques. However, the complexity and heterogeneity of multi-dimensional time series data pose challenges for traditional anomaly detection methods.

Federated Learning (FL) [3] effectively utilizes distributed resources to train machine learning models collaboratively. FL is a distributed machine learning approach where multiple edge devices co-train a model while keeping the original data dispersed and not moved to a single server or data center. FL efficiently trains a machine learning model using distributed resources and promises secure and privacy-preserving access to dispersed original data. In Federated Learning, the original data or data generated from the original data after secure handling is used as the training data. Federated Learning only allows intermediate data to be transmitted between distributed computing resources, avoiding data transmission of training data. Distributed computing resources refer to the mobile devices of terminal edge devices or servers of multiple organizations. Federated Learning brings the code to the data instead of bringing data to the code, resolving fundamental issues such as data privacy, ownership, and locality [4]. Therefore, Federated Learning allows multiple edge devices to train a model without leaking personal data.

Time series anomaly detection in IoT is to detect anomalies in the massive high-dimensional data collected, ensuring that the monitored objects are in a normal state and reducing unnecessary expenses in the future. Quantitative performance analysis is not easy because of the complexity of cloud provisioning control flows and the increasing scale and complexity of real-world cloud infrastructures [5]. There are many challenges in conducting time series anomaly detection in the IoT, one of which is how to jointly model data from different devices and locations. This has led to federated learning becoming a popular research direction to solve this problem [6]. Federated learning enables model training without exposing the raw data and can propagate updates from the global model to local models, thereby improving the accuracy and robustness of the model. Each time series dataset has specific characteristics, such as length and variance, which may be significantly different from other time series datasets, requiring multi-task anomaly detection methods [6]. Anomalous data in time series data is usually rare and overwhelmed by a large number of standard points. Therefore, in multi-task learning, it is generally believed that knowledge sharing between different tasks is helpful in improving the efficiency and accuracy of each task [8].

Therefore, we propose a multi-task anomaly detection method based on federated learning (MTAD-FL) to solve these problems. The approach consists of multiple edge nodes, each corresponding to an IoT edge device; the weight aggregation task is also a distributed node whose role is to process and compute the weights received from each node and then send them back to each edge node for the model update. Due to the highly heterogeneous nature of IoT time-series data, this poses a challenge for monitoring and performance modeling, so we first propose a distributed learning framework based on Multi-task Federated Learning to build anomaly detection models in different environments through the massive amount of data in the IoT environment; to identify complex anomaly patterns and features in the IoT environment To identify complex anomaly patterns and features in the IoT environment, we build a dual network feature extractor (SE-EA-EDN) based on Squeeze excitation (SE) and external attention (EA) to efficiently extract anomaly data features; anomalies in the IoT may have different definitions and diversity, different services may report different types of anomalies, and the definition of anomalies may vary depending on the business logic of the system. Therefore, designing a generic anomaly detection and diagnosis system becomes complex, and we design a parallel knowledge migration framework (LGF-PKT) based on local-global features to parallelize the weight update of local and global features.

Our main contributions are summarized as follows:

- To address the highly heterogeneous nature of time-series data in IoT systems, we propose a distributed learning framework based on Multi-task Federated Learning (MFL) to construct anomaly detection models in different environments through massive data in IoT environments;
- To identify complex anomaly patterns and features under IoT systems, we construct a dual network feature extractor (SE-EA-EDN) based on Squeeze Activation (SE) and External Attention (EA) to efficiently extract anomaly data features;
- To address the diversity of anomalies in the IoT environment. We designed a Local-Global Feature-based Parallel Knowledge Transfer Framework (LGF-PKT) parallelizing the implementation of local and global feature weight updates.

The rest of the paper is organized as follows. Section 2 briefly describes the algorithms related to time series anomaly detection; Sect. 3 describes our model architecture and the details of each component. Section 4 provides Sect. 4 provides detailed comparison results and experimental analysis. Section 5 summarises the main Sect. 5 summarises the main work of this paper and provides an outlook for future work.

2   Related Work

As mentioned earlier, the essence of anomaly detection in the IoT environment is to use time series anomaly detection techniques to analyze the time series data of individual system monitoring performance indicators collected by system monitoring. In this chapter, we first introduce classical methods for time series anomaly detection. We then give a brief overview of deep learning-based methods and models. Finally, we briefly describe federated learning-based methods.

2.1   Classical Methods

The general idea of the statistical-based anomaly detection algorithm is to determine a reasonable range of fluctuations in the current data from the data distribution over a historical period. The model assumes that the statistical model generates ordinary data objects and that data that do not fit the model are outliers. However, the validity of the statistical method is very dependent on the validity of the statistical model assumptions for the given data. The most common methods for detecting time series anomalies using statistical methods are based on the K-sigma algorithm and the ARIMA [11] moving average autoregressive data prediction model. The basic idea of clustering-based anomaly detection algorithms determines whether the current data is anomalous by classifying the data, such as OCSVM [12]. However, there is a significant difference between clustering and anomaly detection, as the goal of anomaly detection is to find abnormal data, while the goal of clustering is to determine the class to which the data belongs. PCA [13], or principal component analysis, is a technique that aims to use the idea of dimensionality reduction to eliminate redundant features from high-dimensional data and retain good features. The deviation of each data point from the rest of the data. In 2014, Twitter also released a seasonal anomaly detection method using a seasonal mixed extreme research bias test (S-H-ESD) [14]. This method is also a practical method based on a robust statistical method.

2.2   Deep Learning Methods

Classical methods cannot meet the requirements of complex, dynamic cloud computing systems, and deep learning approaches benefit from the powerful learning capabilities of neural networks. VAE [15] is an unsupervised anomaly detection algorithm where the algorithm determines anomalous data by reconstructing the error. DeepSVDD [16] learns a spherical boundary by mapping the data into a spherical hyperspace and using support vector machines to separate average data from anomalous data. CGNN-MHSA-AR [17] is a new method for detecting performance anomalies in fluctuating cloud environments that uses an interpretable approach based on neural graph networks (GNNs) and correlation analysis. HTA-GAN [18] is a predictive model based on generative adversarial networks (GANs) that can effectively detect operational anomalies in large-scale IoT. USAD [19] uses an auto-encoder with two decoders and an adversarial game-like training framework to classify normal and abnormal data. CausalRCA [20] enables fine-grained, automated, and real-time root cause localization. TranAD [21] is an anomaly detection and diagnosis model based on deep Transformer networks that use an attention-based sequence encoder to quickly infer information about temporal trends.GDN [22] combines structural learning methods with neural graph networks, using attention weights to explain detected anomalies. MSCRED [23] is a multi-scale convolutional recursive encoder-decoder for anomaly detection and diagnosis on multivariate time series data. ELBD [24] is a new framework based on integrated learning for robust and accurate performance anomaly detection and prediction. The framework combines machine learning algorithms and models to improve detection and prediction performance.

These detection algorithms implement multivariate anomaly detection through advanced deep-learning methods to improve detection accuracy. However, almost all of these algorithms are centralized single-task anomaly detection, and the training process for single-task centralized methods is bandwidth intensive and has significant privacy implications. The large amount of data generated in IoT systems at any given time would be catastrophic in the event of a data breach.

2.3 Federated Learning Methods

Recently, federated learning has emerged as a viable and compelling alternative to centralized learning methods. Rather than aggregating an increasing amount and type of data into a central location, federated learning distributes the global model training process so that the data from each participating distributed node can be used in situ to train local models [25]. DÏoT [26] is an anomaly detection system that uses federated learning to detect compromised IoT by aggregating anomaly detection profiles for intrusion detection devices. A self-encoder-based anomaly detection method is proposed on the server side [27] for detecting anomalous local weight updates from clients in federated learning systems. PFNM [28] is a probabilistic federated learning framework with a particular emphasis on training and aggregating neural network models by decoupling the learning of local models from their aggregation to global federated models. MT-DNN-FL [6] is a multi-task federated learning approach for anomaly detection in computer networks, traffic recognition, and classification tasks. FATHOM [29] is a federated multi-task hierarchical attention model for activity recognition and environmental monitoring using multiple sensors. Because detecting anomalies in centralized systems is often plagued by significant delays in response times, FSLSTM [25] is a novel privacy design federated learning model using stacked long short-term memory (LSTM) models, which is more than twice as fast during training convergence as centralized LSTMs. It is also essential for model updates in federated learning that FedAvg [30] calculates the average weights of all node models and shares the weights with each node in the federated learning system. The convergence of FedAvg on Non-IID Data (non-linear data) was analyzed by multiple nodes learning a model together [31]. FedTL introduces learning techniques to facilitate knowledge migration between nodes and improve system accuracy. Yang et al. [32] developed FedTL [33], a framework FedSteg for secure image privacy analysis. Unlike FedAvg and FedTL, FedKD takes the average of all node weights as the weights of all teachers and transfers each teacher's knowledge to the corresponding students through Knowledge Distillation (KD) [34]. A population knowledge migration training algorithm was used to train small convolutional neural networks (CNNs) and transfer their knowledge to a prominent server-side CNN [35]. By finding that existing federated learning methods typically employ a single global model to capture the shared knowledge of all users by aggregating their gradients, regardless of the differences between their data distributions. However, due to the diversity of user behavior, assigning users' gradients to different global models (i.e., centers) can better capture the heterogeneity of data distribution among users, and a multi-center federated learning FeSEM was proposed [36].

The more dynamic and volatile nature of the IoT environment poses challenges for monitoring and performance modeling; and the fact that anomalies in the IoT may have different definitions and diversity; as well as the need for efficient anomaly detection and diagnosis in the IoT environment, and the fact that rapid detection and response to anomalies is critical for system stability and reliability. The above federated learning approach brings us new ideas and directions. Therefore, we propose a Multi-Task Anomaly Detection Based on Federated Learning (MTAD-FL).

3   Method

This chapter first introduces the overall architecture of Multi-Task Anomaly Detection Based on Federated Learning (MTAD-FL), followed by a detailed description of each part.

3.1   Overview

In MTAD-FL, we assume there are t distributed nodes, where $t = 1, 2, ...,$ $I_{con}(I_{con}$ denotes the number of connected distributed nodes), each micro-distributed node has local system monitoring real-time data D_t, D_t is not shared with other nodes, the weight distance calculation is also a distributed node, the detailed system structure is shown in Fig. 1.

First, each running distributed node sends the local system monitoring real-time data as input to a dual network feature extractor (SE-EA-EDN) composed of Local and Transfer models based on Squeeze Excitation and External Attention, where the Local model starts the first round of training. The trained feature weights are sent to the distributed node for weight distance calculation. After all the nodes have After all connected nodes have uploaded the feature weights, the weight distance calculation decision is initiated for parallel knowledge migration based on local-global features; after all connected nodes receive the sent-back feature weights, they are loaded onto the Transfer model for the model update, local anomaly detection and diagnosis is performed, and then anomaly categories are output, after which a new round of training is initiated.

3.2   Multi-task Federated Learning Framework(MT-FL)

Suppose we have t tasks, where $t = 1, 2, ..., I_{con}(I_{con}$ denotes the number of connected distributed nodes), (X^t, y^t) denotes the training data for the task,

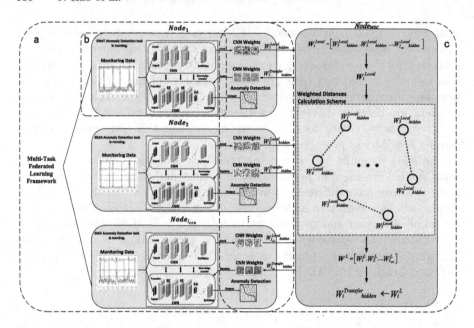

Fig. 1. MTAD-FL overall architecture. (a) denotes the Multi-Task Federated Learning framework; (b) denotes the Double Network Feature Extractor based on Squeeze Excitation and External Attention; (c) denotes the Local-Global Feature-based Parallel Knowledge Transfer.

the local system monitoring system generates X^t in real-time, and y^t denotes the truth label or output vector. Multi-task federated learning aims to minimize the objective function on all nodes to learn the feature weights.

Anomaly detection can be seen as a dichotomous task model where only "normal" and "abnormal" data are judged. For the anomaly detection task, we use the minimized cross-entropy as the loss function, which can be defined as:

$$L\left(y^t, \hat{y}^t\right) = -\frac{1}{m} \sum_{i=1}^{m} y^t log\left(\hat{y}^t\right) \tag{1}$$

where m is the number of input vectors, where are the truth labels and prediction probabilities for the t-th task.

3.3 Dual Network Feature Extractor Based on Equeeze Excitation and External Attention(SE-EA-EDN)

For complex system anomaly patterns and features under IoT, and the fast discovery and response of anomalies is crucial for the stability and reliability of the system, we, therefore, propose a dual network feature extractor. The dual network feature extractor consists of a Local model and a Transfer model deployed on each node; the model is shown in Fig. 2. Firstly, the Local model

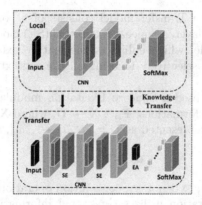

Fig. 2. Structure of a dual network feature extractor based on Squeeze Activation and External Attention.

trains the data of the current node, sends the weights with the characteristics of the node to the weight aggregation node to initiate weight distance calculation for weight update, and then performs parallel knowledge migration to send the matched feature weights back to the Transfer model for further training Squeeze Activation (SE) module and External Attention (EA) module are added to the Transfer model on top of the Local model.

Local Model. The Local model consists of a convolutional layer, an adaptive maximum pooling layer, and a fully connected layer. Each convolutional layer consists of a 1D-CNN module, a batch normalization module, and a ReLU activation function, defined as:

$$f_{conv}(x) = f_{relu}\left(f_{bn}\left(W_{conv} \otimes x + b_{conv}\right)\right) \tag{2}$$

In the formula, W_{conv} and b_{conv} are the weight and bias matrices of the CNN, respectively. $\otimes$ denote the convolution operation. f_{bn} and f_{relu} denote the batch normalization layer and the ReLU activation function, respectively.

Let $X_{bn} = x_1, x_2, ..., x_m$ be denoted as the input to the batch normalization layer, where x_i and m denote the i-th instance and batch size, respectively, defined as :

$$f_{bn}\left(X_{bn}\right) = f_{bn}\left(x_1, x_2, \ldots, x_m\right) = \left(\alpha \tfrac{x_1-\mu}{\delta-\varepsilon} + \beta, \alpha \tfrac{x_2-\mu}{\delta-\varepsilon} + \beta, \ldots, \alpha \tfrac{x_m-\mu}{\delta-\varepsilon} + \beta\right) \tag{3}$$

$$\mu = \frac{1}{m}\sum_{i=1}^{m} x_i \tag{4}$$

$$\delta = \sqrt{\sum_{i=1}^{m}\left(x_i - \mu\right)^2} \tag{5}$$

where $\alpha \in R+$ and $\beta \in R$ are the parameters to be learned in training.

Transfer Model. The Transfer model consists of a convolutional layer, an adaptive mean pooling layer, a Squeeze Excitation (SE) module, and an External Attention (EA) module, which enhances the feature extraction capability of the Transfer model by selectively focusing on the contextual features of other external nodes.

Hu et al. [37] proposed a Squeeze Excitation module as a computational unit for arbitrary transformations. $\mathbf{F}_{tr} : \mathbf{X} \to \mathbf{U}$, where $\mathbf{X} \in \mathcal{R}^{W' \times H' \times C'}$, $\mathbf{U} \in \mathcal{R}^{W \times H \times C}$, and $\mathbf{F}_{tr}$ is represented as $\mathbf{U} = [u_1, u_2, \cdots, u_c]$, where:

$$\mathbf{u}_c = \mathbf{V}_c \otimes \mathbf{X} \tag{6}$$

In the given expression, $\otimes$ denotes a convolution operation.

The squeezing operation utilizes contextual information beyond the local receptive field by using global average pooling to generate channel-wise statistical information. The transformed output $\mathbf{U}$ undergoes contraction along the spatial dimensions $\times H$ to compute the channel-wise statistics $z \in \mathbf{R}^C$. The c-th element of z is calculated by computing $\mathbf{F}_{sq}(\mathbf{u}_C)$, where $\mathbf{F}_{sq}(\mathbf{u}_C)$ is the channel-wise global average value over the spatial dimensions $W \times H$, defined as:

$$\mathbf{Z}_C = \mathbf{F}_{sq}(\mathbf{u}_C) = \frac{1}{W \times H} \sum_{i=1}^{W} \sum_{j=1}^{H} \mathbf{u}_C(i,j) \tag{7}$$

The excitation operation follows the aggregated information obtained from the squeeze operation, with the goal of capturing channel dependencies. To achieve this, a simple gating mechanism is applied with the Sigmoid activation, as shown below:

$$s = \mathbf{F}_{ex}(\mathbf{z}, \mathbf{W}) = \sigma(g(\mathbf{z}, \mathbf{W})) = \sigma(W_2 \delta(W_1 z)) \tag{8}$$

where $\mathbf{F}_{ex}$ is parameterized as a neural network, σ is the Sigmoid activation function, δ is the ReLU activation function, $W_1 \in \mathcal{R}^{\frac{C}{r} \times C}$ and $W_2 \in \mathcal{R}^{\frac{C}{r} \times C}$ are the learnable parameters of $\mathbf{F}_{ex}$, and r is the reduction ratio. W_1 and W_2 are used to constrain the complexity of the model and aid in generalization. W_1 is the parameter of the dimensionality reduction layer, while W_2 is the parameter of the dimensionality expansion layer.

Finally, the output of the Squeeze Excitation module is rescaled as follows:

$$\overline{X}_c = F_{scale}(u_c, s_c) = s_c \bullet u_c \tag{9}$$

In the equation, $\overline{X} = [\overline{x_1}, \overline{x_2}, \ldots, \overline{x_c}]$ and $F_{scale}(u_c, s_c)$ represents the multiplication operation of feature map $u_c \in \mathcal{R}^C$ and scale s_c across channels. That is, each channel in u_c is multiplied by the corresponding value in s_c to obtain a new feature map.

External Attention [38] is a mechanism in machine learning models that improves performance on a given task by selectively focusing on certain parts of the input data or features. This mechanism allows the model to focus on relevant information while ignoring irrelevant or redundant information. The formula for the external attention mechanism can be expressed as follows:

$$A = softmax\left(\frac{QK^T}{\sqrt{d_k}}\right) V \qquad (10)$$

In the formula, Q, K, and V respectively represent the Query, Key, and Value matrices, and d_k is the dimension size of the Key matrix.

3.4 Local-Global Feature-Based Parallel Knowledge Transfer(LGF-PKT)

Most existing approaches in federated learning frameworks [25–27,30,32,34] use average weight decisions to aggregate weights and thus update models without considering the differences between data distributions on nodes, which is more evident in the IoT environment, while anomalies in the IoT environment have different definitions and diversity. Therefore, we propose a parallel knowledge migration framework based on local-global features to perform local-to-global model updates using weight distance calculation decisions.

Weighted Distance Calculation Scheme. Let FL_{iter} denote the maximum number of cycles of federated learning. Let $W_i^{Local,k}$ and $W_i^{Transfer,k}$ be the k-th previously trained weight uploaded to the server and the weight sent from the server after weight matching, $k = 1, 2, \ldots, FL_{iter}$. The weights of their hidden layers are denoted by $W_i^{Local_{hidden},k} \subset W_i^{Local,k}$, $W_i^{Transfer_{hidden},k} \subset W_i^{Transfer,k}$ respectively.

Specifically, $W_i^{Local_{hidden},k}$ consists of Conv1, Conv2 and Conv3, i.e. $W_i^{Local_1,k}$, $W_i^{Local_2,k}$ and $W_i^{Local_3,k}$. Then we have $W_i^{Local_{hidden},k} = W_i^{Local_1,k}$, $W_i^{Local_2,k}, W_i^{Local_3,k}$. In the k-th federated learning phase, nodes $T_i, i = 1, 2, \ldots, I_{con}$ upload $W_i^{Local_{hidden},k}$ to the weight distance calculation node. The node then stores the uploaded weights in the set of weights defined in Eq. (11).

$$\mathbf{W} = \left[W_1^{Local_{hidden},k}, W_2^{Local_{hidden},k}, \ldots, W_{I_{con}}^{Local_{hidden},k}\right] \qquad (11)$$

The server then computes the set of weight distances d, d defined by $\mathbf{W}$:

$$d = \begin{bmatrix} d_1 \\ d_2 \\ \cdots \\ d_{I_{con}} \end{bmatrix} = \begin{bmatrix} d_{1,2} & \cdots & d_{1,I_{con}} \\ d_{2,1} & \cdots & d_{2,I_{con}} \\ \cdots & \cdots & \cdots \\ d_{I_{con},1} & \cdots & d_{I_{con},I_{con}-1} \end{bmatrix} \qquad (12)$$

where $d_{i,j}$ $(i, j \in 1, \ldots, I_{con}, i \neq j)$ is the weight distance between $W_i^{Local_{hidden},k}$ and $W_j^{Local_{hidden},k}$ obtained by the combination of Euclidean and Cosine distances, as defined in Eq. (15):

$$d_{i,j}^{eu} = \sqrt{\sum_{n=1}^{3} \left\| W_i^{Local_n,k} - W_j^{Local_n,k} \right\|^2} \qquad (13)$$

$$d_{i,j}^{cos} = \frac{\sum\limits_{n=1}^{3} W_i^{Local_{hidden},k} \bullet W_i^{Local_{hidden},k}}{\sqrt{\sum_{n=1}^{3} W_i^{Local_{hidden},k^2}} \bullet \sqrt{\sum_{n=1}^{3} W_i^{Local_{hidden},k^2}}} \tag{14}$$

$$d_{i,j} = \frac{d_{i,j}^{eu}}{d_{i,j}^{cos}} \tag{15}$$

Euclidean distances focus on the differences between feature vectors in each dimension. In contrast, Cosine distances focus on the angles between vectors, and we can better express the similarity between feature vectors by using the two together.

Parallelization of Knowledge Transfer. Parallelization of Knowledge Transfer aims to solve the problem of abnormal data scarcity. Through parallelized knowledge migration, data and knowledge accumulated can be used and migrated to other tasks where data is scarce, thus compensating for the lack of data and improving the model's learning efficiency and generalization ability.

We obtain the **ID** list by weight distance calculation. The **ID** is a ranked list of the most similar feature weights to the current node; the higher the similarity, the highest-ranked index is returned each time, and the most similar feature weights are returned through the index. **ID** is defined in Eq. (16).

$$\mathbf{ID} = [ID_1, ID_2, ..., ID_{I_{con}}] \tag{16}$$

where ID_i is the index of the T_i distance.

According to the ID, it is easy to obtain the set of weights based on the union equation $\mathbf{W}^L$ from $\mathbf{W}$, $\mathbf{W}^L$ is defined in Eq. (17):

$$\mathbf{W}^L = \left[W_1^{L,k}, W_2^{L,k}, ..., W_{I_{con}}^{L,k}\right] = [\mathbf{W}(ID_1), \mathbf{W}(ID_2), ..., \mathbf{W}(ID_{I_{con}})] \tag{17}$$

where $W_i^{L,k}$ are the weights matching T_i at the k-th federated learning cycle.

Once I_i has received $W_i^{L,k}$ from the server, T_i loads these weights into $W_i^{Transfer_{hidden},k}$ at the beginning of the following federated learning cycle. As defined in Eq. (18).

$$W_i^{Transfer_{hidden},k+1} \leftarrow W_i^{L,k} \tag{18}$$

The feature weights extracted from the Local model are migrated to the Transfer model to perform a local-global parallel weight update. Specifically, we first upload the feature weights from the Local model of all connected nodes to the node where the weight distance is calculated. After uploading the feature weights of all connected nodes, the Weight Distance Computation Scheme is launched, and the matching feature weights are passed back to the nodes for the Local-Global model update, which can be expressed as:

$$W_j^{Transfer} \leftarrow W_i^{Local} \tag{19}$$

4 Experiments and Analysis

Here is a description of three open experimental datasets, as shown in Table 1.

4.1 Dataset

Table 1. Settings and anomaly rates for the three datasets.

Dataset	SWaT	SMD	SKAB
Dimension	51	38	8
Train	7000	70843	12712
Test	3000	30361	5448
Abnormality Rate	29.2%	4.21%	35.1%

- SMD (Server Machine Dataset): It is a public data set for monitoring the performance and operation of servers in the data center. The SMD consists of data from 28 different machines.
- SWaT (Secure Water Treatment): It is a security testing platform for a simulated water treatment plant. Developed by the National University of Singapore, it is used to test and evaluate the network security performance of water treatment plants.
- SKAB (Skoltech Anomaly Benchmark): It consists of a water circulation system, its control system, and a data processing and storage system. The anomalies it generates include a partially closed valve, an unbalanced connecting shaft, re-duced motor power, cavitation, and flow disturbance.

4.2 Evaluation Metrics

For the anomaly detection experiments we used Precision(Pre), Recall(Rec), F1 Score(F1), and Matthews Correlation Coefficient (MCC) as the evaluation metrics.

Precision (Pre) indicates the proportion of samples that are actually abnormal to those that are detected as abnormal and is calculated as:

$$Pre = \frac{TP}{TP + FP} \times 100\% \tag{20}$$

Recall (Rec) represents the proportion of correctly detected anomalies to anomalous samples and is calculated as:

$$Rec = \frac{TP}{TP + FN} \times 100\% \tag{21}$$

F1 Score (F1) is the reconciled average of precision and recall, which is used to evaluate the overall performance of the model:

$$F1 = \frac{2 \times Pre \times Rec}{Pre + Rec} \tag{22}$$

Matthews Correlation Coefficient (MCC) [39] is a correlation coefficient that describes the correlation between the actual classification and the predicted classification, which can take values ranging from, a value of 1 indicates perfect prediction of the subject, a value of 0 indicates that the predicted result is not as good as the result of the random prediction, and −1 means that the predicted classification does not coincide at all with the actual classification:

$$MCC = \frac{TP \times TN - FP \times FN}{\sqrt{(TP + FP)(TP + FN)(TN + FP)(TN + FN)}} \tag{23}$$

Where: $TP + FP$ is the number of abnormal samples; $TN + FN$ is the number of normal samples; TP is the number of samples correctly detected as abnormal; TN indicates the number of samples correctly detected as normal; FP indicates the number of samples incorrectly detected as abnormal; FN indicates the number of samples incorrectly detected as normal.

4.3   Experiment Setup

Dataset Preprocessing: We performed MinMax normalization on each dataset and compressed it to [0,1].

Parameter Settings: We set the parameters for batch normalization layers and attention mechanisms to their default values and set the decay value of the Squeeze Excitation (SE) module to 16. At the same time, we used AdamW with PyTorch as the optimizer, with an initial learning rate of 0.02, a batch size of 128, and an epoch of 80. The simulation of multi-task learning is implemented on a virtual edge device based on Python3.9.

Baseline Methods: We modified the following three baseline federated learning frameworks to some extent for anomaly detection in the IoT environment. FedTL [33] used a multi-task federated learning framework with the Local model as a pre-trained model, modified to FedTL-AD for multi-task anomaly detection; FedAVG [30] used a multi-task federated learning framework with the Local model as the local model, weight aggregation using weight averaging decisions, modified to FedAVG-AD for multi-task anomaly detection; FedKD [32] used the Local model as the Student model and Teacher model, respectively, and updated the model using weight averaging decisions, modified to FedKD-AD for multi-task anomaly detection. The classical methods are PCA [13] and OCSVM [13] used as anomaly detection; the deep learning methods are VAE [15] and DeepSVDD [16] used as anomaly detection. The specific experimental groupings are as follows:

- Single-Task Anomaly Detection: Comparison of Local and Transfer, PCA, OC-SVM, VAE, DeepSVDD anomaly detection performance on SMD, SWaT, and SKAB using accuracy, recall, F1 score, and MCC as evaluation metrics.
- Multi-Task Anomaly Detection: Comparison of MTAD-FL and FedTL-AD, FedKD-AD, and FedAVG-AD methods for anomaly detection performance on SMD, SWaT, and SKAB using accuracy, recall, F1 score, and MCC as evaluation metrics.

We extracted 10,000 samples from SWaT; for SMD, we chose the first four subsets for the experiment; for SKAB, we used all data under the valve1 file. We took 70% of the samples from the three datasets as the training set and 30% as the test set. For multi-task, the simulation is based on virtual nodes implemented in Pytorch 1.13 and Python 3.9. All experiments were conducted on a PC with an NVIDIA 3070 (8G) graphics card, an Intel(R) Core(TM) i5-12600KF CPU @ 3.69 GHz, and 16 GB RAM.

4.4   Results

Table 2. SWaT, SMD, and SKAB results

Dataset	SWaT			SMD			SKAB		
Metric	Pre	Rec	F1	Pre	Rec	F1	Pre	Rec	F1
PCA	0.706	0.747	0.726	0.138	0.829	0.19	0.363	0.986	0.531
OCSVM	0.715	0.766	0.74	0.3	0.401	0.264	0.465	0.713	0.558
VAE	0.706	0.742	0.724	0.04	0.91	0.138	0.363	0.985	0.53
DeepSVDD	0.112	0.115	0.113	0.092	0.615	0.133	0.354	0.974	0.519
Local	0.992	0.59	0.74	0.943	0.73	0.815	0.906	0.787	0.842
Transfer	0.967	**0.864**	**0.913**	**0.999**	**0.997**	**0.998**	**0.923**	0.786	**0.849**
FedTL-AD	0.985	0.619	0.761	0.706	0.230	0.324	0.556	0.254	0.345
FedKD-AD	0.994	0.554	0.711	0.509	0.291	0.343	0.626	0.417	0.569
FedAVG-AD	0.994	0.554	0.711	0.491	0.191	0.238	0.738	0.39	0.454
MTAD-FL	0.902	**0.848**	**0.871**	**0.999**	**0.997**	**0.998**	**0.911**	**0.786**	**0.844**

Two experiments were conducted to demonstrate Single-Task and Multi-Task Anomaly Detection, respectively. We split the experiments into a Single-Task and Multi-Task to demonstrate the robustness and generalization of the two models in SE-AE-EDN for deployment in nodes and a Multi-Task to demonstrate that MTAD-FL is more suitable for deployment in IoT cloud environments than other baseline methods. The results of the anomaly detection experiments are shown in Table 2.

Single-Task Anomaly Detection. SWaT: The Transfer model is not as good as the other baseline models regarding the recall, but F1 is 17.3% higher than the best baseline model. Accuracy is slightly lower than the Local model but higher than the other baseline models.

SMD: The Transfer model outperformed the other three methods in all metrics overall, with an accuracy rate 5.6% higher than the best baseline method, a recall rate 16.8% higher than the best baseline task, and an F1 18.3% higher than the best baseline task.

The SKAB: Transfer model was inferior to the other baseline models (except the Local model) regarding the recall but was 1.7% and 0.7% higher than the best-performing baseline model in precision and F1, respectively.

Multi-Task Anomaly Detection. In the Multi-Task case, we all trained the experiments for four federated cycles, and the results were obtained as averages.

SWaT: Our method was inferior to the other three baseline tasks in terms of accuracy but was 22.9% better than the best baseline method in terms of recall and 11% better than the best baseline method in terms of F1.

SMD: Our method outperformed the other three methods in all metrics overall, with a 29.3% higher recall than the best baseline method, a 70.6% higher recall than the best baseline task, and a 65.5% higher F1 than the best baseline task.

SKAB: Our method was more consistent in overall performance than the best overall performance of all the baseline methods.

4.5   Matthews Correlation Coefficient(MCC)

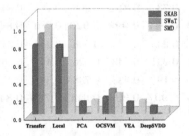 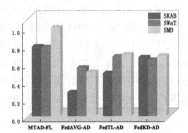

Fig. 3. The right panel shows the multitasking anomaly detection MCC results; the left panel shows the single-tasking anomaly detection MCC results. MTAD-FL and Transfer both outperform all the baseline methods.

When the MCC value is 1, the prediction of the test subject is perfect. When the MCC value is 0, the prediction is worse than the random prediction. -1 indicates that the predicted classification is entirely different from the actual classification.

The MCC values of four Multi-Task Federated Learning methods based on three different datasets are given in Fig. 3. Compared to the other three benchmark methods, our models achieve better performance, further demonstrating the effectiveness of our proposed models.

The Transfer model also performs optimally in the Single-Task Anomaly Detection experiments shown in Fig. 3, with PCA, VAE, and DeepSVDD achieving MCC results of 0 for the SWaT dataset indicating poorer prediction results than random predictions.

5   Conclusion and Future Work

In this article, we propose a multi-task anomaly detection approach based on federated learning (MTAD-FL). According to our experimental results, MTAD-FL outperforms all multi-task federated learning methods in anomaly detection of IoT cloud systems. In addition, we have also found that the model's performance is affected in the distributed case. The overall performance is better in the single-tasking case than in the multi-tasking case. The LGF-PKT framework in the experiments effectively improves specific models that perform poorly in the average weight updating. The average weight is better in an environment with fewer distributed nodes. The data variability is not too significant, yet the performance is still to be improved in the IoT-distributed cloud environment where the dynamics are high and the data variability is significant.

Future work can also be done in the following two areas. First, optimizing the performance of LGF-PKT and finding the commonality between edge nodes can improve the impact on model performance in a distributed environment. Second, our model can be improved to perform root cause localization when anomalies are detected, accurately and quickly locate anomalies in distributed IoT cloud environments, and generate responses immediately. In distributed cloud environments and generate immediate responses.

References

1. Cook, A.A., Mısırlı, G., Fan, Z.: Anomaly detection for IoT time-series data: a survey. IEEE Internet Things J. **7**(7), 6481–6494 (2019)
2. Peng, C., Yunni, X., Shanchen, P., et al.: A probabilistic model for performance analysis of cloud infrastructures. Concurrency Comput. Pract. Experience **27**(17), 4784–4796 (2015)
3. Bonawitz, K., Eichner, H., Grieskamp, W., et al.: Towards federated learning at scale: system design. Proc. Mach. Learn. Syst. **1**, 374–388 (2019)
4. McMahan, B., Moore, E., Ramage, D., et al.: Communication-efficient learning of deep networks from decentralized data. In: Artificial Intelligence and Statistics, PMLR, pp. 1273–1282 (2017)
5. Liu, Y., Garg, S., Nie, J., et al.: Deep anomaly detection for time-series data in industrial IoT: a communication-efficient on-device federated learning approach[J]. IEEE Internet Things J. **8**(8), 6348–6358 (2020)

6. Ying, Z., Junjun, C., Di, W., et al.: Multi-task network anomaly detection using federated learning. In: Proceedings of the 10th International Symposium on Information and Communication Technology, pp. 273–279 (2019)
7. Hongyun, L., Peng, C., Zhiming, Z., Towards a robust meta-reinforcement learning-based scheduling framework for time critical tasks in cloud environments. In: IEEE 14th CLOUD, vol. 2021, pp. 637–647. IEEE (2021)
8. Crawshaw M. Multi-task learning with deep neural networks: a survey. arXiv preprint arXiv:2009.09796 (2020)
9. Hongyun, L., Peng, C., Xue, O., et al.: Robustness challenges in reinforcement learning based time-critical cloud resource scheduling: a meta-learning based solution. Futur. Gener. Comput. Syst. **146**, 18–33 (2023)
10. Juan, C., Peng, C., Xianhua, N., et al.: Task offloading in hybrid-decision-based multi-cloud computing network: a cooperative multi-agent deep reinforcement learning. J. Cloud Comput. **11**, 90 (2022)
11. Box, G.E.P., Pierce, D.A.: Distribution of residual autocorrelations in autoregressive-integrated moving average time series models. J. Am. Stat. Assoc. **65**(332), 1509–1526 (1970)
12. Schölkopf, B., Platt, J.C., Shawe-Taylor, J., et al.: Estimating the support of a high-dimensional distribution. Neural Comput. **13**(7), 1443–1471 (2001)
13. Daffertshofer, A., Lamoth, C.J.C., Meijer, O.G., et al.: PCA in studying coordination and variability: a tutorial. Clin. Biomech. **19**(4), 415–428 (2004)
14. Vallis, O., Hochenbaum, J., Kejariwal, A.: A novel technique for long-term anomaly detection in the cloud. In: 6th USENIX Workshop on Hot Topics in Cloud Computing (HotCloud 14) (2014)
15. Haowen, X., Wenxiao, C., Nengwen, Z., et al.: Unsupervised anomaly detection via variational auto-encoder for seasonal kpis in web applications. In: Proceedings of the 2018 World Wide Web Conference, pp. 187–196 (2018)
16. Ruff, L., Vandermeulen, R., Goernitz, N., et al.: Deep one-class classification. In: International Conference on Machine Learning, PMLR, pp. 4393–4402 (2018)
17. Yujia, S., Ruyue, X., Peng, C., et al.: Identifying performance anomalies in fluctuating cloud environments: a robust correlative-GNN-based explainable approach. Futur. Gener. Comput. Syst. **145**, 77–86 (2023)
18. Peng, C., Hongyun, L., Ruyue, X., et al.: Effectively detecting operational anomalies in large-scale IoT data infrastructures by using a GAN-based predictive model. Comput. J. **65**(11), 2909–2925 (2022)
19. Audibert, J., Michiardi, P., Guyard, F., et al.: Usad: unsupervised anomaly detection on multivariate time series. In: 26th ACM SIGKDD, pp. 3395–3404 (2020)
20. Ruyue, X., Peng, C., Zhiming, Z.: Causalrca: causal inference based precise fine-grained root cause localization for microservice applications. J. Syst. Softw. **203**, 111724 (2023)
21. Tuli, S., Casale, G., Jennings, N.R.: Tranad: deep transformer networks for anomaly detection in multivariate time series data. arXiv preprint arXiv:2201.07284 (2022)
22. Deng, A., Hooi, B.: Graph neural network-based anomaly detection in multivariate time series. AAAI-21 **35**(5), 4027–4035 (2021)
23. Chuxu, Z., Dongjin, S., Yuncong, C., et al.: A deep neural network for unsupervised anomaly detection and diagnosis in multivariate time series data. AAAI-19. **33**(01), 1409–1416 (2019)
24. Ruyue, X., Peng, C., Zhiming, Z.: Robust and accurate performance anomaly detection and prediction for cloud applications: a novel ensemble learning-based framework. J. Cloud Comput. **12**(1), 1–16 (2023)

25. Sater, R.A., Hamza, A.B.: A federated learning approach to anomaly detection in smart buildings. ACM Trans. Internet Things **2**(4), 1–23 (2021)
26. Nguyen, T.D., Marchal, S., Miettinen, M., et al.: DĪoT: a federated self-learning anomaly detection system for IoT. In: 2019 39th ICDCS, pp. 756–767. IEEE (2019)
27. Suyi, L., Yong, C., Yang, L., et al.: Abnormal client behavior detection in federated learning. arXiv preprint arXiv:1910.09933 (2019)
28. Yurochkin, M., Agarwal, M., Ghosh, S., et al.: Bayesian nonparametric federated learning of neural networks. In: International Conference on Machine Learning, pp. 7252–7261. PMLR (2019)
29. Yujing, C., Yue, N., Zheng, C., et al.: Federated multi-task hierarchical attention model for sensor analytics. arXiv preprint arXiv:1905.05142 (2019)
30. Qu, Z., Lin, K., Li, Z., et al.: Federated learning's blessing: Fedavg has linear speedup. In: ICLR 2021 (2021)
31. Xiang, L., Kaixuan, H., Wenhao, Y., et al.: On the convergence of fedavg on non-iid data. arXiv preprint arXiv:1907.02189 (2019)
32. Yang, H., He, H., Zhang, W., et al.: FedSteg: a federated transfer learning framework for secure image steganalysis. IEEE Trans. Netw. Sci. Eng. **8**(2), 1084–1094 (2020)
33. Liu, Y., Kang, Y., Xing, C., et al.: A secure federated transfer learning framework. IEEE Intell. Syst. **35**(4), 70–82 (2020)
34. Seo, H., Park, J., Oh, S., et al.: 16 federated knowledge distillation. Mach. Learn. Wirel. Commun. **457** (2022)
35. He, C., Annavaram, M., Avestimehr, S.: Group knowledge transfer: Federated learning of large CNNs at the edge. Adv. Neural. Inf. Process. Syst. **33**, 14068–14080 (2020)
36. Guodong, L., Ming, X., Ming, X., et al.: Multi-center federated learning: clients clustering for better personalization. World Wide Web **26**(1), 481–500 (2023)
37. Hu, J., Shen, L., Sun, G.: Squeeze-and-excitation networks. In: Proceedings of the IEEE Conference on Computer Vision and Pattern Recognition, pp. 7132–7141 (2018)
38. Guo, M.H., Liu, Z.N., Mu, T.J., et al.: Beyond self-attention: external attention using two linear layers for visual tasks. IEEE Trans. Pattern Anal. Mach. Intell. **45**(5), 5436–5447 (2022)
39. Chicco, D., Jurman, G.: The advantages of the Matthews correlation coefficient (MCC) over F1 score and accuracy in binary classification evaluation. BMC Genomics **21**(1), 1–13 (2020)

A Novel Deep Federated Learning-Based and Profit-Driven Service Caching Method

Zhaobin Ouyang[1], Yunni Xia[1(✉)], Qinglan Peng[2], Yin Li[3], Peng Chen[4(✉)], and Xu Wang[5]

[1] College of Computer Science, Chongqing University, Chongqing, China
xiayunni@hotmail.com
[2] School of Artificial Intelligence, Henan University, Zhengzhou, China
[3] Guangzhou Institute of Software Application Technology, Guangzhou, China
[4] School of Computer and Software Engineering, Xihua University, Chengdu, China
chenpeng@mail.xhu.edu.cn
[5] College of Mechanical and Vehicle Engineering, Chongqing University, Chongqing, China

Abstract. Service caching is an emerging solution to addressing massive service request in a distributed environment for supporting rapidly growing services and applications. With the explosive increases in global mobile data traffic, service caching over the edge computing architecture, Mobile edge computing (MEC), emerges for alleviating traffic congestion as well as for optimizing the efficiency of task processing. In this manuscript, we propose a novel profit-driven service caching method based on a federated learning model for service prediction and a deep reinforcement learning mode for yielding caching decisions (FPDRD) in an edge environment. The proposed method is temporal service popularity and user preference-aware. It aims to ensure quality of service (QoS) of delivery of cached service while maximizing the profits of network service providers. Experimental results clearly demonstrate that the FPDRD method outperforms traditional methods in multiple aspects.

Keywords: service caching · profit maximization · popularity prediction · caching decisions · collaborative mechanism

1 Introduction

In recent years, the explosive growth of mobile applications and the growing need for low-latency and high-bandwidth services have placed significant strain on the traditional cloud-centric network infrastructure [1,2]. To tackle these challenges, edge computing has emerged as a promising paradigm that brings computing and storage capabilities closer to end-users. This proximity allows for Lower latency, minimized network congestion and enhanced quality of service (QoS) [3–5].

Edge service caching is a critical component of edge computing, which significantly contributes to the improvement of mobile application performance 3.

© ICST Institute for Computer Sciences, Social Informatics and Telecommunications Engineering 2024
Published by Springer Nature Switzerland AG 2024. All Rights Reserved
H. Gao et al. (Eds.): CollaborateCom 2023, LNICST 563, pp. 118–133, 2024.
https://doi.org/10.1007/978-3-031-54531-3_7

It involves the strategic storage of frequently accessed data and services on edge servers, referred to as Fog Access Points (FAPs). The purpose of this caching strategy is to reduce delay and alleviate the workload on central cloud data centers. By employing edge service caching, faster access to content and services is made possible, especially for latency-sensitive applications like augmented reality, video streaming and real-time data processing.

However, various challenges in this direction are yet to be properly addressed. Firstly, FAPs are with limited computational and storage resources, thus guaranteeing only a small amount of services is cachable and making hit rate low. Secondly, in a highly dynamic and volatile edge environment, static caching strategies are often inadequate in meeting the changing needs. Nevertheless, how to yield run-time caching decisions according to time-varying service popularity and user needs remains a difficulty. Finally, existing methods in this direction usually aim to optimize caching performance, in terms of hit rate and delivery latency. How to guarantee profit of service providers is less studied.

In this paper, we propose a novel caching method by leveraging a federated learning model for popularity prediction and a deep reinforcement learning model for yielding caching decisions (FPDRD). The FPDRD method takes both global service popularity and local user preferences as inputs and can achieve reasonable tradeoffs between caching performance and profit of providers. Extensive simulations are conducted based on a well-known dataset, Movielens. Numerical results clearly indicate that our proposed method outperform it peers.

The paper is organized as follows: Section 2 provides a literature review. Section 3 presents the system model and the problem formulation. Section 4 describes the proposed method. Section 5 presents the empirical analysis.

2   Related Work

Task offloading and caching in MEC have gained significant attention in recent years as a means to alleviate the resource constraints faced by FAPs. In their work, Gao et al. [7] presented a method that combines task offloading scheduling and resource allocation to minimize task delay and energy consumption. Liu et al. [8] proposed an approach that utilizes online computation offloading and resource scheduling to tackle the challenges arising from user mobility and network dynamics.

Due to resource and energy constraints, FAPs are usually allowed to cache limited services [9]. Thus, caching of highly popular services in FAPs has emerged as an effective solution when FAPs are limited in caching capacity. Zhong et al. [10] proposed the Cocktail Edge Caching method, which utilizes an ensemble learning algorithm to predict the popularity of services. However, this approach only takes into account the overall service popularity while neglecting the preferences of local users. In contrast, Li et al. [11] propose a service caching method that considers hit actions and user perception preferences. However, this approach raises concerns regarding user privacy and security, as it shares all users' personal information for prediction purposes.

Recently, the cooperative service caching mechanism was proposed as well for exploiting multiple cache nodes through making them working together [12–15]. The problem of cooperative service caching can be formulated as a Mixed-Integer Nonlinear Programming (MINLP) problem, which is known to be inherently NP-hard [16,17]. Wu *et al.* [18] and Xu *et al.* [19] propose a coalition formation algorithm that utilizes a hedonic game among cooperative service providers for optimizing both the overall profit of the coalition and the average profit of each individual participant. Li *et al.* [20] propose a DRL algorithm-based profit-driven cooperative service placement method in MEC.

3   System Models and Problem Formulation

Here, we consider a service caching system in MEC represented as $\mathcal{G} = (\mathcal{CCS} \cup \mathcal{N} \cup \mathcal{U} \cup \mathcal{L})$, as illustrated in Fig. 1. This system consists of a central cloud server (CCS), multiple fog access points (FAPs) denoted as $\mathcal{N} = \{\mathcal{N}_1, \mathcal{N}_2, ..., \mathcal{N}_n\}$, multiple users denoted as $\mathcal{U} = \{\mathcal{U}_1, \mathcal{U}_2, ..., \mathcal{U}_u\}$ and a set of service types denoted as $\mathcal{L} = \{\mathcal{L}_1, \mathcal{L}_2, ..., \mathcal{L}_l\}$. Network edge service providers operate each FAP, which is equipped with storage, computing and communication capabilities. Users are provided services by these FAPs by using a billing mechanism.

3.1   Caching Model

Due to capacity and storage limits, FAPs cache a subset of application services. These cached applications require periodic updates and replacement. The caching decisions is represented by a binary variable $x_{n,l}$, which can be expressed as:

$$x_{n,l} = \begin{cases} 1, & \text{if service } \mathcal{L}_l \text{ is cached in the FAP } \mathcal{N}_n, \\ 0, & \text{otherwise.} \end{cases} \tag{1}$$

The constraint on the storage space at the FAP $\mathcal{N}_n$ is:

$$\sum_{l \in \mathcal{L}} x_{n,l} \omega_l \leq \Omega_n \tag{2}$$

where ω_l represents the storage capacity required for service $\mathcal{L}_l$ and Ω_n the total cache capacity of FAP $\mathcal{N}_n$.

Users are charged for use of service $\mathcal{L}_l$. Such charge is proportional to use time:

$$F_l = t_l \cdot p_l \tag{3}$$

where p_l represent the price charged by the service provider for the execution of service $\mathcal{L}_l$ per unit of time.

Fig. 1. System model.

3.2   Computation and Communication Model

According to a collaborative service cache mechanism (CSCM) [21], where FAP $\mathcal{N}_n$ receives a service request from a user. Initially, FAP $\mathcal{N}_n$ checks its local cache to determine if service $\mathcal{L}_l$ is cached. If the service is cached locally, FAP $\mathcal{N}_n$ handles the user's service request directly. Otherwise, FAP $\mathcal{N}_n$ seeks cached services from neighboring FAPs. When multiple FAPs cache service $\mathcal{L}_l$, FAP $\mathcal{N}_n$ turns to FAP $\mathcal{N}_m$ with the lowest transmission cost. When none of the FAPs caches the required service $\mathcal{L}_l$, the user's service request is forwarded to the CCS. The cost $C_{n,l}^x$ represents the charge by FAP $\mathcal{N}_n$ when processing service $\mathcal{L}_l$ through server x:

$$C_{n,l}^x = \beta_1 \cdot L_{n,l}^x + \beta_2 \cdot E_{n,l}^x \tag{4}$$

where $L_{n,l}^x$ and $E_{n,l}^x$ denote the delay and energy consumption when FAP $\mathcal{N}_n$ processes service $\mathcal{L}_l$ through server x, respectively. β_1 and β_2 indicate the economic factors associated with the delay and energy consumption, respectively.

When FAP $\mathcal{N}_n$ receives a service request from a user, it first checks whether service $\mathcal{L}_l$ is cached locally. In this case, FAP $\mathcal{N}_n$ directly processes the user's service request. In such a scenario, FAP $\mathcal{N}_n$ places the service onto the thread of the queue with the shortest waiting time for processing. In this context, the local delay and energy consumption for service $\mathcal{L}_l$ are:

$$L_{n,l}^{local} = \left(\sum_{o \in q_n} \zeta_o + \zeta_l \right) \cdot t_c + L_{base} \tag{5a}$$

$$E_{n,l}^{local} = \zeta_l f_n^2 \epsilon_n + E_{base} \tag{5b}$$

where q_n represents the set of tasks in the queue with the shortest waiting time on FAP $\mathcal{N}_n$, ζ_l the computational workload, t_c the unit processing time for a task and f_n the computing capacity of FAP $\mathcal{N}_n$.

In case that service is not cached locally at FAP $\mathcal{N}_n$, the FAP $\mathcal{N}_n$ turns to other servers. According to Shannon's formula, the transmission rate between them is:

$$r_{i,j} = B_i \log_2 \left(1 + \frac{P_i |h_i|^2}{\sigma^2} \right) \tag{6}$$

where B_i represents the bandwidth rate, P_i the transmission energy consumption, $|h_i|^2$ the channel gain and σ^2 the variance of the additive white Gaussian noise (AWGN).

In case that FAP $\mathcal{N}_n$ finds one or more servers that cache service $\mathcal{L}_l$ among the neighboring FAPs, it chooses the FAP $\mathcal{N}_m$ with the lowest cost for processing the user's service request. In this case, the delay and energy consumption for executing service $\mathcal{L}_l$ are:

$$L_{n,l}^m = \left(\sum_{o \in q_m} \zeta_o + \zeta_l \right) \cdot t_c + \frac{d_{m,n}^l}{r_{m,n}} + L_{base} \tag{7a}$$

$$E_{n,l}^m = \zeta_l f_m^2 \epsilon_m + P_m \frac{d_{m,n}^l}{r_{m,n}} + E_{base} \tag{7b}$$

Where $d_{m,n}^l$ represents the bit size of the computed result of the service request l that is processed by FAP $\mathcal{N}_m$ and forwarded to FAP $\mathcal{N}_n$.

In case that neither FAP $\mathcal{N}_n$ nor its neighboring FAPs cache service $\mathcal{L}_l$, the service request is offloaded to the CCS. In this case, the delay and energy consumption for executing service $\mathcal{L}_l$ are:

$$L_{n,l}^{ccs} = \zeta_l \cdot t_c + \frac{d_{ccs,n}^l}{r_{ccs,n}} + L_{base} \tag{8a}$$

$$E_{n,l}^{ccs} = \zeta_l f_{ccs}^2 \epsilon_{ccs} + P_{ccs} \frac{d_{ccs,n}^l}{r_{ccs,n}} + E_{base} \tag{8b}$$

For each service request, the profit obtained by FAP $\mathcal{N}_n$ can be calculated as the gap between the service request's fee and the total cost incurred. The overall cost is comprised of the cost of caching service $C_{x,l}$ in the server x, the cost of collaboration $C_{n,l}^x$ with other servers x and the equipment-related baseline cost C_{base}. Thus, profit of service request is:

$$V_{n,l}^{local} = F_l - C_{n,l} - C_{n,l}^{\mathcal{N}_n} - C_{base} \tag{9a}$$

$$V_{n,l}^m = F_l - C_{m,l} - C_{n,l}^{\mathcal{N}_m} - C_{base} \tag{9b}$$

$$V_{n,l}^{ccs} = F_l - C_{ccs,l} - C_{n,l}^{CCS} - C_{base} \tag{9c}$$

Consequently, the total profit earned by FAP $\mathcal{N}_n$ is:

$$V_n = \sum_{l \in \mathcal{L}} \left(P_{n,l}^{local} \cdot V_{n,l}^{local} + P_{n,l}^{\mathcal{N}_m} \cdot V_{n,l}^m + P_{n,l}^{ccs} \cdot V_{n,l}^{ccs} \right) \tag{10}$$

where $P_{n,l}^{local}$, $P_{n,l}^{\mathcal{N}_m}$ and $P_{n,l}^{ccs}$ are binary variables represent the execution modes for FAP $\mathcal{N}_n$ to handle service request $\mathcal{L}_l$ as local execution, execution with assistance from FAP $\mathcal{N}_m$ and execution via the CCS, respectively.

Additionally, the QoS of users $\overline{U_l}$ is decided by the average delay $\overline{L_l}$ and average fee $\overline{F_l}$ of executing service $\mathcal{L}_l$:

$$\overline{U_l} = \eta_l \frac{\overline{L_l} - L_{min}}{L_{max} - L_{min}} + \eta_f \frac{\overline{F_l} - F_{min}}{F_{max} - F_{min}} \tag{11}$$

where η_l and η_f represent the impact factors of delay and price on the QoS of users, respectively. L_{max}, F_{max} and L_{min}, F_{min} represent the maximum and minimum of delay and fee for executing service $\mathcal{L}_l$, respectively.

3.3   Problem Formulation

Based on the system model given above we are interested in maximizing profits of service provider with the constraints of caching capacities. According to (10), the profit of FAP $\mathcal{N}_n$ is decide by the local cache hit rate $P_{n,l}^{local}$ and the collaborative cache hit rate $P_{n,l}^{\mathcal{N}_m}$. The resulting optimization formulation is thus:

$$\mathbf{P}: \quad \max \sum_{t \in T} \sum_{\mathcal{N}_n \in \mathcal{N}} V_n \tag{12}$$

s.t. $\mathbf{C1}: \overline{U_l} < U_{min}, \forall \mathcal{L}_l \in \mathcal{L}$ (13a)

$\mathbf{C2}: x_{n,l} \in \{0,1\}, \forall \mathcal{N}_n \in \mathcal{N}, \forall \mathcal{L}_l \in \mathcal{I}$ (13b)

$\mathbf{C3}: \sum_{l \in \mathcal{L}} x_{n,l} \omega_l \leq \Omega_n, \forall \mathcal{N}_n \in \mathcal{N}$ (13c)

$\mathbf{C4}: P_{n,l}^{local}, P_{n,l}^{\mathcal{N}_m}, P_{n,l}^{ccs} \in \{0,1\}, \forall \mathcal{N}_n, \mathcal{N}_m \in \mathcal{N}, \forall l \in \mathcal{L}$ (13d)

$\mathbf{C5}: P_{n,l}^{local}+, P_{n,l}^{\mathcal{N}_m} + P_{n,l}^{ccs} = 1$ (13e)

$\mathbf{C6}: V_n \geq 0, \forall \mathcal{N}_n \in \mathcal{N}$ (13f)

$\mathbf{C7}: Num_{n,l} \leq 1$ (13g)

Constraint (13a) ensures that the QoS of $\mathcal{L}_l$ is bounded. Constraints (13b) and (13c) indicate the limit of total storage capacity of cached services on FAP

$\mathcal{N}_n$. Constraint (13f) guarantees that the profit for each FAP $\mathcal{N}_n$ must be non-negative. Constraint (13g) indicates that each FAP $\mathcal{N}_n$ can cache service $\mathcal{L}_l$ at most once. The above optimization problem is clearly a Mixed-Integer Nonlinear Programming (MINLP) one, which is also NP-hard.

4   The Proposed Method

In this section, we present a detailed description of the FPDRD method. Firstly, we employ a Federated Learning model for accurate prediction of local popularity by taking the global popularity model and user perception preferences as inputs. We maintain a popularity priority queue $Q_c^{\mathcal{N}_n}$ of FAP $\mathcal{N}_N$ and feed the popularity priority queues Q_c for each FAPs as input of into a deep reinforcement learning model. The learning model yields collaborative service caching decisions according to the optimization objective and constraints.

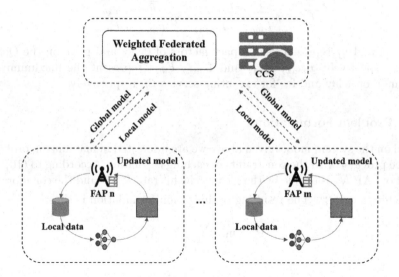

Fig. 2. Popularity prediction model.

4.1   Federated Learning for Popularity Prediction

As shown in Fig. 2, we implement the prediction of popular services based on FL algorithm. The popularity prediction includes the following three steps:

Download Global Model. At the start of each time slot t, every FAP retrieves the global model parameters $\mathbf{W}_t$ from the CCS (Lines 3). These model parameters facilitate the extraction of latent features to predict popular services. This enables each FAP to determine the overall popularity for services during the current time slot.

Local Model Training. Upon receiving the global model parameters $\mathbf{W}_t$, each FAP updates its local model through training iterations (Line 4–8). Subsequently, the updated local model $\mathbf{H}_t^{\mathcal{N}_n}$ is uploaded to the CCS (Line 9). This local model incorporates hidden features related to global service popularity as well as captures hidden features specific to the local users' service perception preferences. By utilizing FAP $\mathcal{N}_n$'s local model $\mathbf{H}_t^{\mathcal{N}_n}$, the local service popularity priority queue $Q_c^{\mathcal{N}_n}$ can be predicted (Line 10). The loss function employed is the categorical cross-entropy, a generalized version of binary cross-entropy, to determine the logarithmic loss for multi-class predictions. This loss function measures the misclassification between the true service $\mathcal{L}_l$ label $\boldsymbol{\pi}$ and the predicted service $\mathcal{L}_l$ label $\hat{\boldsymbol{\pi}}$ defined as cross-entropy:

$$L(\hat{\boldsymbol{\pi}}, \boldsymbol{\pi}) = -\sum_i \pi_i \log(\hat{\boldsymbol{\pi}}_i) \tag{14}$$

Then, we estimate the loss according to its Mean Squared Error (MSE):

$$L(\hat{\phi}, \phi) = \mathbb{E}[(\phi_i - \hat{\phi}_i)^2] \tag{15}$$

where ϕ_i is the real service request label and $\hat{\phi}_i$ the predicted one.

Algorithm 1. Federated Learning for Popularity Prediction

Input: A set of service requests.
Output: The predicted popularity priority queue Q_c.
1: **for** $t \in \mathcal{T}$ **do**
2:   **for** $\mathcal{N}_n \in \mathcal{N}$ **do**
3:     Download the global model $\mathbf{W}_t$.
4:     **for** the service requests received by $\mathcal{N}_n$ at time t **do**
5:       Calculate the loss of service $\mathcal{L}_l$ according to Eq.(14).
6:     **end for**
7:     Calculate the loss of FAP $\mathcal{N}_n$ according to Eq.(15).
8:     Update model parameters $\mathbf{H}_t^{\mathcal{N}_n}$.
9:     Upload $\mathbf{H}_t^{\mathcal{N}_n}$ to the CCS.
10:    Calculate the predicted queue $Q_c^{\mathcal{N}_n}$ of the FAP $\mathcal{N}_n$.
11: **end for**
12: The CCS update $\mathbf{W}_{t+1}$ according to Eq.(16).
13: **end for**
14: **return** The predicted popularity priority queue Q_c.

Federated Aggregation. After receiving the uploaded local models $\mathbf{H}_t$ from FAPs, the CCS updates the global model $\mathbf{W}_{t+1}$ (Line 12). To address the issue of imbalance in the local models across different FAPs, a weighted federated aggregation approach is employed by assigning different aggregation weights to the local models uploaded by different FAPs. In that case, the updated global model $\mathbf{W}_{t+1}$ is:

$$\mathbf{W}_{t+1} = \mathbf{W}_t + \sum_{\mathcal{N}_n \in \mathcal{N}} \nabla_t^{\mathcal{N}_n} \frac{M_t^{\mathcal{N}_n}}{\sum\limits_{\mathcal{N}_n \in \mathcal{N}} M_t^{\mathcal{N}_n}} (\mathbf{W}_t - \mathbf{H}_t^{\mathcal{N}_n}) \qquad (16)$$

where $\nabla_t^{\mathcal{N}_n}$ represents the gradient step size and $M_t^{\mathcal{N}_n}$ the number of service requests received by FAP $\mathcal{N}n$ at time t.

Algorithm 2. Cooperative Service Caching Mechanism

1: **for** $n = 1, 2, \ldots, N$ **do**
2:    **for** the service requests received by $\mathcal{N}_n$ at time t **do**
3:       Calculate the service fee F_l and caching cost $C_{n,l}^x$ for service l according to Eq.(3) and Eq.(4) respectively.
4:       **if** service l is cached in FAP $\mathcal{N}_n$ **then**
5:          Calculate $L_{n,l}^{local}$ and $E_{n,l}^{local}$ according to Eq.(5).
6:       **end if**
7:       **if** service l is cached in another FAP **then**
8:          Calculate $L_{n,l}^m$ and $E_{n,l}^m$ according to Eq.(7).
9:       **end if**
10:      **if** service l is not cached in any FAP **then**
11:         Calculate $L_{n,l}^{ccs}$ and $E_{n,l}^{ccs}$ according to Eq.(8).
12:      **end if**
13:      Calculate $\overline{U_l}$ of service l according to Eq.(11) and update t_l of service l according to Eq.(13a).
14:   **end for**
15:   Calculate the profit V_n for FAP-N according to Eq.(10).
16: **end for**
17: **return** Profits for each FAPs.

4.2   Deep Reinforcement Learning for Caching Decisions

Upon receiving the service popularity priority queue at each FAP for the current time slot, we utilize a deep Reinforcement learning model to determine the optimal cooperative caching decisions. The objective of this approach is to maximize the profits of FAPs while maintaining QoS for users.

State. We consider the services cached by FAP $\mathcal{N}_n$ as the current state $s^{\mathcal{N}_n}(t)$, where the cached services are primarily selected based on the predicted queue $Q_c^{\mathcal{N}_n}$ obtained from Algorithm 1. Therefore, the current state can be represented as $s(t)^{\mathcal{N}_n} = (s_1^{\mathcal{N}_n}, s_2^{\mathcal{N}_n}, ..., s_c^{\mathcal{N}_n})$, where $s_i^{\mathcal{N}_n}$ represents the ith popular service cached in FAP $\mathcal{N}_n$.

Algorithm 3. Deep Reinforcement Learning for Caching Decisions

---

Input: A set of service requests and the predicted popularity priority queue Q_c
Output: The caching decisions and profit of FAPs
1: **for** $t = 1, 2, \ldots, T$ **do**
2:   **for** $n = 1, 2, \ldots, N$ **do**
3:     Obtain the state $s(t)$
4:     Obtain the predicted popularity priority queue $Q_c^{\mathcal{N}_n}$.
5:     Calculate the action $a(t)$ according to Eq.(17).
6:     Obtain the next state $s(t+1)$ after executing $a(t)$.
7:     Obtain the profit according to Algorithm.(2).
8:     Obtain the reward $r(t)$.
9:     Store the tuple $(s(t), a(t), r(t), s(t+1))$ and randomly sample a minibatch
       from it.
10:     Calculate the loss function by Eq.(20).
11:     Calculate the gradient by Eq.(21).
12:     Update θ according to Eq.(22).
13:   **end for**
14:   Obtain the caching decisions according to θ.
15:   Each FAPs selects the services from the prediction queue $Q_c^{\mathcal{N}_N}$ for replacement.
16: **end for**
17: **return** The caching decisions and profit of FAPs.

Action. We define the action $a = (a^{\mathcal{N}_1}, a^{\mathcal{N}_2}, ..., a^{\mathcal{N}_n})$ to represent the set of actions for all FAPs.where $a^{\mathcal{N}_n} = (a_1^{\mathcal{N}_n}, a_2^{\mathcal{N}_n}, ..., a_c^{\mathcal{N}_n})$ represents whether it is necessary to replace the service in FAP $\mathcal{N}_n$. In this context, $a_i^{\mathcal{N}_n} = 0$ indicates that there is no need to replace the service stored in the ith position of FAP $\mathcal{N}_n$ cache, while $a_i^{\mathcal{N}_n} = 1$ indicates that it is necessary to replace the service stored in the ith position of the FAP $\mathcal{N}_n$. In case that the action function is implemented using the ε-greedy method:

$$a(t) = \operatorname{argmax}(Q(s(t), a; \theta)) \tag{17}$$

Reward. We define the reward function r(t) to maximize the profit obtained by FAPs. After taking action $a(t)$, the corresponding reward $r(t)$ is obtained and the transition from state $s(t)$ to $s(t+1)$ occurs. Consequently, we can construct a $(s(t), a(t), r(t), s(t+1))$ transition, which is stored in the replay buffer. Then, the action-value function is updated:

$$Q(s_{i+1}, a_{i+1}; \theta) = Q(s_i, a_i; \theta) + \alpha [y_i - Q(s_i, a_i; \theta)] \tag{18}$$

where α represents the learning rate and y_i the target Q-value of the target network of tuple i:

$$y_i = r_i + \gamma \max \hat{Q}(s_{i+1}, a_{i+1}; \theta) \tag{19}$$

where γ is the discount factor. The loss function $L(\theta_i^n)$ of network is:

$$L(\theta_i^n) = \mathbb{E}\left[(y_i - Q(s_j, a_j; \theta))^2\right] \tag{20}$$

The gradient calculation of the loss function $\nabla_\theta L(\theta)$ for all sampled tuples is:

$$\nabla_\theta L(\theta) = \mathbb{E}\left[(y_i - Q(s_i, a_i, \theta)) \nabla_{\theta^i} Q(s_i, a_i, \theta)\right] \tag{21}$$

At the end of time slot t, the parameters of the network θ are updated as:

$$\theta \leftarrow \theta - \eta_\theta \nabla_\theta L(\theta) \tag{22}$$

where η_θ is the learning rate of prediction network.

Firstly, at each time instant t, we take the predicted popularity priority queue Q_c that obtained in Algorithm (1) and the cache state $s(t)$ of the FAPs as input (Line 3–4). Secondly, we use a deep reinforcement learning model that combines the profit calculation model in Algorithm (2) as the model indicator for training to obtain the optimal caching decisions model (Line 5–12). Finally, each FAP $\mathcal{N}_N$ selects the services from the prediction queue $Q_c^{\mathcal{N}_N}$ for replacement according to the caching decisions model (Line 14–15).

5 Performance Evaluation

5.1 Simulation Configuration

In this paper, we developed a simulation environment based on the Movielens dataset (ml–25 m) [22], which consist of 25,000,095 ratings and 1,093,360 tags of 62,423 movies created by 162,541 users. The datasets also include the related information about the involved movies, such as titles and genres, as well as user attributes including ID number, gender, age and postcode. We assumed that user preferences are represented by movie ratings and the number of ratings corresponds to the number of user preferences. The publication time of ratings is considered as the request initiation time. All the experiments are conducted on the same computer with an AMD Ryzen7 4800H 2.90 GHz processor, 16.0 GB of RAM and using PyTorch 2.0.

5.2 Baselines

We compare our method against four baselines:

1) DRLVCC: The baseline initially employs a Convolutional Neural Network (CNN) model to assess the popularity of new requests at different locations. Subsequently, by a path-responsive vertical cooperative caching approach based on a deep reinforcement learning model to formulate caching decisions [23].

2) UPP-CL-CC: The baseline employs an LSTM model to dynamically capture user activities and preferences, thereby extracting local popularity information for FAPs which are subsequently subjected to clustering. Building upon this foundation, the author proposed a novel greedy approach to address the cache placement issue [24].

3) Random: Each FAP replaces unrequested services with a probability of ϵ. In our simulation, $\epsilon = 0.1$.
4) First-In-First-Out Scheme (FIFO): FAPs cache services based on the order of service requests and discard the oldest cached services when the cache space runs out.

5.3 Performance Analysis

We perform experiments under three scenarios:

1) We intercept different time spans of the datasets and increased them by one day at a time to observe how time spans impact service caching performance.
2) We study the impact of the number of service types on algorithm performance while fixing the time interval at 1 day and setting FAPs' cache capacity to 100.
3) We compare how FAPs' cache capacity influences algorithm performance while keeping the time interval fixed at 1 day and the number of service types fixed at 1000.

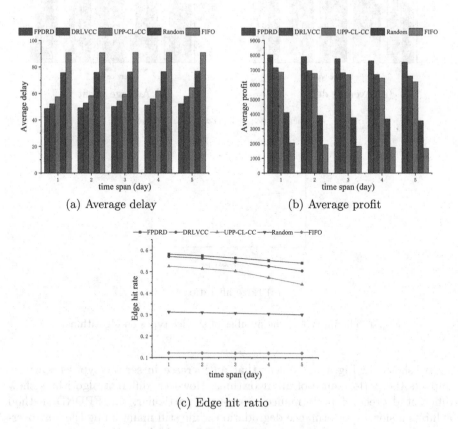

(a) Average delay

(b) Average profit

(c) Edge hit ratio

Fig. 3. The performance of algorithms in different time spans.

As shown in Fig. 3, the FPDRD method exhibits the best overall performance. Fig. 3(c) indicates that by considering the temporal variation of overall service popularity and the specific preferences of local users, our predictive queue aligns more closely with real-world scenarios, leading to significantly higher caching hit rates compared to the baseline algorithm. Figure 3(a) and Fig. 3(b) demonstrate that the FPDRD method achieves the lowest average delay and highest average profit on various time-span datasets. This achievement is attributed to the combination of a more accurate predictive model and the training of the decision-making network using DRL algorithms, resulting in a caching decisions model that can simultaneously safeguard the QoS of users and enhance providers' of network services' profit.

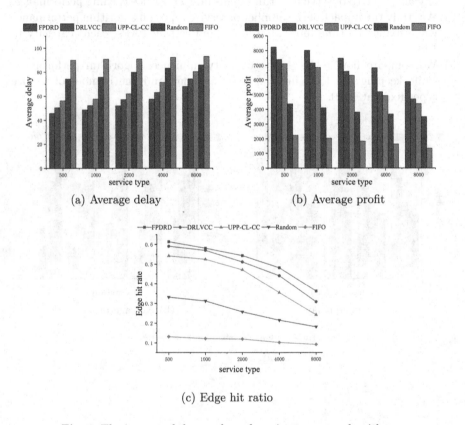

(a) Average delay   (b) Average profit

(c) Edge hit ratio

Fig. 4. The impact of the number of service types on algorithms.

As shown in Fig. 4, it is clear that an increase in service types negatively impacts the performance of all algorithms. However, different algorithms show different degrees of performance change. In particular, the FPDRD method exhibits a slower performance degradation while still maintaining the best overall performance. In contrast, the UPP-CL-CC method experiences a more rapid performance degradation. The observed trends suggest a trade-off between the algorithms' capacity to adapt and optimize caching decisions effectively as the number of service types rises. The ability of the FPDRD method to respond quickly to environmental changes enables it to maintain superior overall performance even when confronted with a progressively diverse range of service types.

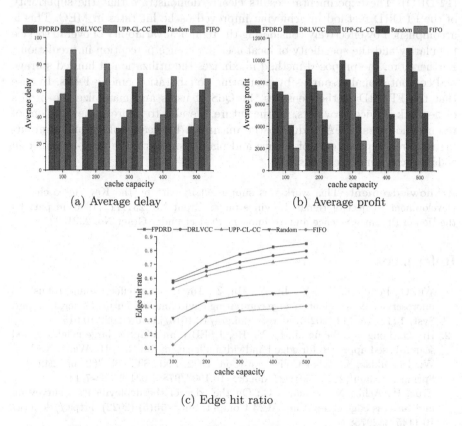

(a) Average delay   (b) Average profit

(c) Edge hit ratio

Fig. 5. The impact of the FAPs cache capacity on algorithms.

As shown in Fig. 5, the FPDRD algorithm achieves the highest performance for different FAPs cache capacities. Additionally, with increasing cache capacity of FAPs, the performance improvement of FPDRD method becomes more pronounced. The experimental results demonstrate the efficiency of the FPDRD method in popularity prediction and caching decisions, allowing for the efficient utilization of the available cache resources. As the cache capacity of FAPs increases, the algorithm can utilize this extra storage capacity to make more informed and optimized caching decisions. Therefore, the algorithm improves the cache hit rate and quality of service, ultimately enhancing network services and benefiting both end users and network service providers.

6   Conclusion

This paper investigates the service caching problem in MEC and proposes a novel caching method by leveraging a federated learning model for popularity prediction and a deep reinforcement learning model for yielding caching decisions (FPDRD). The experimental results clearly demonstrate that the superiority of the FPDRD method in achieving improved cache hit rates in MEC. This is accomplished by effectively considering the temporal variability of overall service popularity and the specificity of local user preference perception in predictions. Furthermore, the proposed method maximizes the utilization of limited storage and computational resources by promoting collaboration among FAPs. In case that the FPDRD method ensures the QoS of users and maximize the profits of network service providers. In the future, we aim to address the problem of resource idleness in FAPs due to the mismatch between storage and computing resource requirements of service and plan to optimize the fault-tolerance in collaborative service caching.

Acknowledgement. This work was supported in part by the Key Research and Development Project of Henan Province under Grant No. 231111211900, in part by the Henan Province Science and Technology Project under Grant No. 232102210024.

References

1. Wu, C., Peng, Q., Xia, Y., Jin, Y., Hu, Z.: Towards cost-effective and robust AI microservice deployment in edge computing environments. Futur. Gener. Comput. Syst. **141**, 129–142 (2023). https://doi.org/10.1016/j.future.2022.10.015
2. Hu, Q., Peng, Q., Shang, J., Li, Y., He, J.: EBA: an adaptive large neighborhood search-based approach for edge bandwidth allocation. In: Gao, H., Wang, X., Wei, W., Dagiuklas, T. (eds.) CollaborateCom 2022. LNICST, vol. 460, pp. 249–268. Springer, Cham (2022). https://doi.org/10.1007/978-3-031-24383-7-14
3. Cruz, P., Achir, N., Viana, A.C.: On the edge of the deployment: a survey on multi-access edge computing. ACM Comput. Surv. **55**(5) (2022). https://doi.org/10.1145/3529758
4. Liu, G., et al.: An adaptive DNN inference acceleration framework with end-edge-cloud collaborative computing. Futur. Gener. Comput. Syst. **140**, 422–435 (2023). https://doi.org/10.1016/j.future.2022.10.033
5. Sharghivand, N., Derakhshan, F., Mashayekhy, L., Mohammadkhanli, L.: An edge computing matching framework with guaranteed quality of service. IEEE Trans. Cloud Comput. **10**(3), 1557–1570 (2022). https://doi.org/10.1109/TCC.2020.3005539
6. Huang, C.K., Shen, S.H.: Enabling service cache in edge clouds. ACM Trans. Internet Things **2**(3) (2021). https://doi.org/10.1145/3456564
7. Gao, J., Kuang, Z., Gao, J., Zhao, L.: Joint offloading scheduling and resource allocation in vehicular edge computing: a two layer solution. IEEE Trans. Veh. Technol. **72**(3), 3999–4009 (2023). https://doi.org/10.1109/TVT.2022.3220571
8. Liu, T., Zhang, Y., Zhu, Y., Tong, W., Yang, Y.: Online computation offloading and resource scheduling in mobile-edge computing. IEEE Internet Things J. **8**(8), 6649–6664 (2021). https://doi.org/10.1109/JIOT.2021.3051427

9. Xue, Z., Liu, C., Liao, C., Han, G., Sheng, Z.: Joint service caching and computation offloading scheme based on deep reinforcement learning in vehicular edge computing systems. IEEE Trans. Veh. Technol. **72**(5), 6709–6722 (2023). https://doi.org/10.1109/TVT.2023.3234336

10. Zong, T., Li, C., Lei, Y., Li, G., Cao, H., Liu, Y.: Cocktail edge caching: ride dynamic trends of content popularity with ensemble learning. IEEE/ACM Trans. Networking **31**(1), 208–219 (2023). https://doi.org/10.1109/TNET.2022.3193680

11. Li, T., Li, D., Xu, Y., Wang, X., Zhang, G.: Temporal-spatial collaborative mobile edge caching with user satisfaction awareness. IEEE Trans. Netw. Sci. Eng. **9**(5), 3643–3658 (2022). https://doi.org/10.1109/TNSE.2022.3188658

12. Li, Y., et al.: Collaborative content caching and task offloading in multi-access edge computing. IEEE Trans. Veh. Technol. **72**(4), 5367–5372 (2023). https://doi.org/10.1109/TVT.2022.3222596

13. Li, Z., Yang, C., Huang, X., Zeng, W., Xie, S.: Coor: collaborative task offloading and service caching replacement for vehicular edge computing networks. IEEE Trans. Veh. Technol. **72**(7), 9676–9681 (2023). https://doi.org/10.1109/TVT.2023.3244966

14. Xu, Z., et al.: Energy-aware collaborative service caching in a 5g-enabled MEC with uncertain payoffs. IEEE Trans. Commun. **70**(2), 1058–1071 (2022). https://doi.org/10.1109/TCOMM.2021.3125034

15. Lin, C.C., Chiang, Y., Wei, H.Y.: Collaborative edge caching with multiple virtual reality service providers using coalition games. In: 2023 IEEE Wireless Communications and Networking Conference (WCNC), pp. 1–6 (2023). https://doi.org/10.1109/WCNC55385.2023.10118763

16. Zhou, H., Zhang, Z., Li, D., Su, Z.: Joint optimization of computing offloading and service caching in edge computing-based smart grid. IEEE Trans. Cloud Comput. **11**(2), 1122–1132 (2023). https://doi.org/10.1109/TCC.2022.3163750

17. Ma, X., Zhou, A., Zhang, S., Wang, S.: Cooperative service caching and workload scheduling in mobile edge computing. In: IEEE INFOCOM 2020 - IEEE Conference on Computer Communications, pp. 2076–2085 (2020). https://doi.org/10.1109/INFOCOM41043.2020.9155455

18. Wu, R., Tang, G., Chen, T., Guo, D., Luo, L., Kang, W.: A profit-aware coalition game for cooperative content caching at the network edge. IEEE Internet Things J. **9**(2), 1361–1373 (2022). https://doi.org/10.1109/JIOT.2021.3087719

19. Xu, Z., et al.: Near-optimal and collaborative service caching in mobile edge clouds. IEEE Trans. Mob. Comput. **22**(7), 4070–4085 (2023). https://doi.org/10.1109/TMC.2022.3144175

20. Li, Y., Liang, W., Li, J.: Profit driven service provisioning in edge computing via deep reinforcement learning. IEEE Trans. Netw. Serv. Manage. **19**(3), 3006–3019 (2022). https://doi.org/10.1109/TNSM.2022.3159744

21. Wang, Z., Du, H.: Collaborative coalitions-based joint service caching and task offloading for edge networks. Theoret. Comput. Sci. **940**, 52–65 (2023). https://doi.org/10.1016/j.tcs.2022.10.037

22. Harper, F.M., Konstan, J.A.: The movielens datasets: history and context. ACM Trans. Interact. Intell. Syst. **5**(4) (2015). https://doi.org/10.1145/2827872

23. Liu, Y., Jia, J., Cai, J., Huang, T.: Deep reinforcement learning for reactive content caching with predicted content popularity in three-tier wireless networks. IEEE Trans. Netw. Serv. Manage. **20**(1), 486–501 (2023). https://doi.org/10.1109/TNSM.2022.3207994

24. Somesula, M.K., Rout, R.R., Somayajulu, D.: Greedy cooperative cache placement for mobile edge networks with user preferences prediction and adaptive clustering. Ad Hoc Netw. **140**, 103051 (2023). https://doi.org/10.1016/j.adhoc.2022.103051

A Multi-behavior Recommendation Algorithm Based on Personalized Federated Learning

Zhongqin Bi[1], Yutang Duan[1], Weina Zhang[1($\boxtimes$)], and Meijing Shan[2]

[1] School of Computer Science and Technology, Shanghai University of Electric Power, Shanghai, People's Republic of China
mszhangwn@mail.shiep.edu.cn

[2] Institute of Information Science and Technology, East China University of Political Science and Law, Shanghai, People's Republic of China

Abstract. Multi-behavior recommendation algorithms comprehensively use various types of interaction behaviors between users and items, such as clicking, collecting, purchasing, and commenting, to model user preferences and item features. It captures high-level interactions between users and items, and effectively alleviates the data sparsity problem in recommendation algorithms. However, most existing multi-behavior recommendation algorithms are mainly centralized learning models. User behavior data is collected and uploaded to the server to train recommendation model parameters, which poses a risk of data leakage and compromises user privacy. To address this problem, a multi-behavior recommendation algorithm based on the federated learning paradigm (FedMB) is proposed. This approach uses the federated learning framework to establish a separate model for each end device and utilizes the data of the end device for user-end model training, which improves the privacy and security of user data. To enhance privacy and security during parameters uploaded, all uploaded parameters will be encrypted, At the same time, the precedence chart is used to optimize the model parameters distributed by the server, thereby improving the recommendation quality of the overall model. Compared with that of the latest methods, our federated model achieves good performance on the three datasets.

Keywords: Multi-behavior recommendation · Privacy security · Federated learning · Personalized model · Parameter encryption

1 Introduction

The purpose of a recommendation system is to analyze the user's personalized preferences and to recommend content to alleviate information overload. Personalized recommendation models acquire users' explicit or implicit information through the interaction between users and products. By doing so, they can obtain user preferences and more accurately learn the embedded expressions of nodes, thus improving the accuracy of recommendations [1].

This work was supported by Project of Shanghai Science and Technology Committee (No. 23010501500).

H. Gao et al. (Eds.): CollaborateCom 2023, LNICST 563, pp. 134–153, 2024.
https://doi.org/10.1007/978-3-031-54531-3_8

However, most traditional recommendation behaviors are based on a single behavior. For instance, in Fig. 1 (a), the recommendation system mainly relies on the user's purchase behavior to collect information and provide product recommendations. Users often generate more than one piece of interactive behavior data during the purchase process. In addition to purchase behavior, there are also actions such as adding items to the shopping cart and browsing, which can be considered interactive behaviors, such as Fig. 1 (b). The recommendation system can better discover user interests and preferences to assist the target behavior (such as purchasing) by using a variety of behavioral interactive information.

To fully extract the information from multi-behavior interactions, various multi-behavior recommendation models have appeared in recent years [2–6]. One approach is to directly build a variety of behaviors and to apply each behavior to a single line as a recommended model, without considering the differences between different behaviors. However, some models provide different learning rights to different behaviors to simulate the importance of various behaviors and to distinguish different behavioral semantics [3].

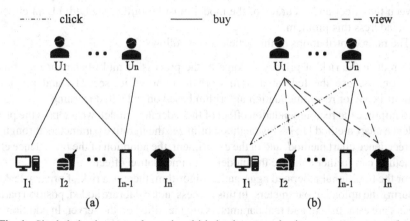

Fig. 1. Single behavior examples and multi-behavior examples in e-commerce scenarios.

Currently, effective integration of multiple types of behavior and capturing differences in multi-behavior are the main research methods recommended in many studies [7]. Commonalities between target and auxiliary behaviors must be identified to improve the target behavior and achieve higher recommendation effects. For example, commodities added to the shopping cart through purchasing behavior must have commonalities, such as the same style, category, or price. However, sparse supervision signals in traditional datasets do not guarantee the quality of graph learning, and buying behaviors are often the target behaviors in most multi-behavior recommendation models. GU S et al. proposed a method to address this issue by dividing different behaviors into two views for two or two comparison learning [2], but this method ignores the impact of auxiliary behavior on the target behavior.

Therefore, the use of user data for separate training models and independent recommendations is proposed to address the issue of personalization of behavior. Traditional multi-behavior recommendation models often focus on the data from the interaction of the overall user and ignore the differences between different users. By training the model continuously to allow it to learn the differences between different behaviors or the connection between users, the model can effectively improve recommendation accuracy. However, this paper highlights the need to balance the effect and accuracy of the model, which requires further study.

In traditional machine learning models, centralized learning is a mainstream method [8], where the provider of the service collects user data and trains the machine learning model by using interactive information from users and products. However, due to restrictions on regulations and laws such as the GDPR [9], data security and privacy protection have become increasingly important. To address this issue, federated learning (FL) was proposed in 2016 [10], allowing data collection and training to be completed on end devices without the need for transmission. FL greatly improves user data privacy protection performance and has much application space for privacy protection and multiparty computing [11]. Although various privacy protection algorithms and encryption algorithms have been proposed, such as encryption algorithms based on cryptography [12], blurred disturbance methods [13], and the differential privacy [14], the balance between the effect and accuracy of the model must be further studied. FL an effective way to address this problem.

The main contributions of this article are as follows:

- To reduce the risk of privacy leakage in the process of multi-behavior recommendation, we use the federated framework to improve its security, and propose a multi-behavior recommendation algorithm based on federated learning.
- To improve the recommendation effect of the federated model, we adopted the precedence chart method [15]. This method optimizes the iterative parameters through the precedence chart method, and in the experiment, the adoption of the precedence chart method can further enhance the model recommendation effect.
- For the traditional federated aggregation algorithm, there is a risk of privacy leakage during the upload of parameters. In this process, noise data are added, position parameters are established, and real parameters are identified on the server. In addition, the security during the upload of the parameters is improved.
- The effectiveness of our method is verified on three real-world datasets, which demonstrates that our method advances the recommendation performance compared with other baselines.

Organization. The remainder of this article is structured as follows: Sect. 2 describes related work, including introductions to multi-behavior recommendation, discussions on machine learning models of privacy recommendation methods, and introduction to the basic knowledge of federated learning. Section 3 introduces FedMB, which is a multi-behavior recommendation adaptation of FL settings. In Sect. 4, we present a hyperparameter study, an ablation study, and comparative experiments on FedMB. In Sect. 5, we summarize our work and draw conclusions.

2 Related Work

In the past three years, researchers' recommendations for multi-behavior have focused on the optimization of recommendation effects, but few people are paying attention to privacy protection in the process of multi-behavior recommendation.

2.1 Multi-behavior Recommendation Algorithm

In recent years, graph neural networks have been widely used in multi-behavior recommendation algorithms. For instance, Jin B et al. proposed a user-item communication layer to capture the behavior semantics and explore the intensity of behavior [3]. In 2021, Xiao L et al. integrated multi-behavior mode into the meta-learning paradigm and automatically extracted the heterogeneity and interaction of behavior [4], but they did not consider the impact of time on user behavior. Xiao L et al. proposed a time-coding strategy to incorporate time perception into the context and developed a multi-behavior mutual attention encoder to learn different types of behavioral structure dependencies [5]. However, they overlooked the complexity of user-item interactions. In 2022, Wei W et al. proposed a new comparison meta learning model that maintains dedicated cross-type behavior for different users [6]. It effectively learns the characteristics of users and items by using deep learning frameworks. These papers mainly focused on exploring behavior information and ignored the personalized perspective of user behavior. Wu Y et al. addressed this issue by using user personalized sequence information and global map information in the multi-view comparison learning [16]. However, these models have not considered the personalized training of the model at the data level.

2.2 Privacy Protection Recommendation Algorithm

In this section, we provide an overview of recommendation methods for privacy protection in both centralized and decentralized settings. Privacy protection recommendation systems must prevent the leakage of user personal privacy data, while also defending against attacks from various sources. Different types of attacks, such as user attribute attacks [8], reasoning attacks, and attack attacks, require different defense mechanisms. To effectively address these attacks, privacy protection algorithms were developed. There are three main ways to protect user data: cryptography-based privacy protection algorithms, data disturbance-based privacy protection algorithms, and federated learning-based privacy protection methods. These methods aim to achieve data privacy protection through algorithmic approaches. In this article, we focus on the use of federated learning architecture to achieve privacy protection. The data are encrypted during the transmission process. The privacy of user data can be better protected.

Federated learning is a distributed machine learning framework that is designed for privacy protection. FL stores the user's original data locally and uses the intermediate parameters of the client and server to optimize the system, resulting in improved forecasting performance. In this article, we combine the recommendation algorithm with federated learning, which allows us to shift the centralized learning framework to the federated learning paradigm. As a result, the federated recommendation algorithm based on privacy protection has garnered significant attention from researchers.

The traditional federated recommendation algorithms encrypt data based on the federated architecture, but there is still a risk of privacy leakage. Therefore, researchers focus on developing federated privacy recommendation algorithms. Early federated recommendation frameworks required users to upload only gradient information, but this information can still lead to privacy breaches. In 2020, Di Chai et al. proposed a distributed matrix decomposition framework by using homomorphic encryption [17], but this did not guarantee the security of the data source. To address this, Guanyu Lin et al. proposed a solution based on explicit feedback [19], which involved creating a collection of noninteracted items to predict user preferences. This approach improved privacy protection and ensured the security of terminal data processing. In 2021, Chuhan Wu et al. proposed using pseudo interacting data and anonymous neighbor methods to enhance privacy protection performance [20]. V Asileios Perifanis et al. proposed the FedNCF model [21], which uses SecAvg to resolve privacy issues in small-scale datasets. Jingwei Yi et al. developed the Efficient-FedRec model [22], which uses an effective security aggregation agreement to protect user privacy in training. Wei Yuan et al. proposed the FRU model, which enables the deletion of user contribution data to improve privacy protection [23]. These approaches aim to improve the privacy protection mechanisms of federated recommendation algorithms while ensuring high recommendation performance.

The use of a centralized learning model is common in multi-behavior recommendations because the use of global user data for training and can lead to more accurate recommendations. However, this approach has a significant risk of privacy leakage. Additionally, the recommendations provided are often more general and less personalized due to the use of models for the entire user base. To address these issues, we propose a personalized federated recommendation framework. This approach uses personalized models to provide more accurate recommendations for user data while ensuring privacy protection. The framework includes a privacy protection module during the parameter upload process, further improving the privacy performance and recommendation quality of the model.

Table 1. Comparison of different methods in privacy protection

	NMTR	EHCF	RGCN	MB-GMN	S-MBRec	FedMB
User data storge	Center	Center	Center	Center	Center	Local
Rec process protection	✔	✔	✔	✔	✔	✔
Rec result protection	✗	✗	✗	✗	✗	✔

To better demonstrate the advantage of our approach, we summarize the comparison between FedMB and existing methods on exploiting privacy protection in Table 1. "Rec" means recommendation, "Center" and "Local" represent centralized and decentralized data storage, respectively.

2.3 Federated Learning

Federated learning is a machine learning technology that enables the training of machine learning models in a decentralized and distributed manner. The core idea of this learning approach is that the training data on each device do not need to be sent to a central server for coordination among different entities. This approach is different from the traditional machine learning training method and provides a higher level of privacy protection.

Federated Learning Algorithm. The federated learning algorithm follows a specific process, which includes collecting data at the initial stage, establishing a client model, and training the client data on the client model. Each client trains its own client model, and after the training is complete, each client uploads the model parameters or gradient to the server. The server conducts overall training based on these parameters and does not collect any private data from the client, thus maintaining the privacy of the data. Essentially, the server acts as a learning resource for the terminal equipment. Once the server processes the parameters uploaded by the client, it distributes them back to the client for further training. The process is summarized as follows:

Step1: The server provides the global model to the clients. This global model can be either an initial randomized model or a pretrained model.
Step2: The client uses its own data to conduct local training and to update the model.
Step3: The client uploads the model parameters or intermediate parameters to be updated to the central server.
Step4: The server aggregates the model parameters or intermediate parameters from the local client and performs multiple rounds of repeated iteration updates.

The above steps are repeated multiple times until the model converges, and then local models are used for reasoning and prediction. Throughout the process, users' privacy data, such as browsing history, likes, and collection history, are preserved locally, ensuring the safety of user privacy data. This approach greatly improves the privacy protection level of the learning model, while also providing accurate recommendations and maintaining the confidentiality of user data. Therefore, it is a more effective and secure method for machine learning in sensitive environments.

Federated Aggregation Algorithm. The most common approach to general aggregation is the federated average aggregation algorithm (Fedavg) [10]. In a global iteration, each participating client completes a small number of local iterations, and then uploads the parameters or gradient of the training instance to the server.

The server aggregates the uploaded parameter set or gradient set by using an aggregator, which is updated globally in the following ways:

$$w_{t+1} = \sum\nolimits_{i=1}^{|c|} \frac{n_i}{n} w_t \tag{1}$$

where $|c|$ is the number of selected participants in a training round, w is a model parameter, n_i is the number of examples participating in this aggregation, n is the sum of the total number of participating instance training, w_t is the model parameter after the training of this participating instance, and t is the number of iterations.

3 Proposed Method

3.1 Problem Definition

We consider a scenario with multiple users (N > 2), each holding a private dataset. The goal is to build a federated learning system that can train models without compromising users' privacy. The datasets are generated locally by the users without any mutual transmission or interaction. We assume that the multi-behavior data generated by the users follow the principle of independence and distribution [21]. For a few users with less behavioral interaction, a pseudo interactive item is generated. Although this might have a negative impact on the recommendation results, this approach ensures the quality of the diagram learning, and the impact on the overall framework is small. This article is primarily focused on the stability of the overall framework.

The framework generates a list of previous recommendations for users using the local recommendation model. Training and recommendation are performed on the client side to ensure user privacy. For multi-behavior, the GCN [24] layer is used to extract user behavior characteristics.

3.2 FedMB Framework

The FedMB framework is illustrated in Fig. 2 and consists of four main parts: the client's training module, the server-side parameter selection module, the server-side parameter aggregation module, and the parameter encryption module. To enhance security during parameter transmission, noise data are added. To protect privacy, the model parameters after user-side model training are used. At the central server-side, the aggregated parameters are sent back to the client to complete each round of iteration training. The working principles of each module are explained in detail below.

Client Training. We adopt a self-supervised approach for multi-behavior recommendations, which is partitioned by user IDs in the dataset to allocate models for different users. The GCN layer is used to learn the embeddings of users and items, effectively extracting their personalized interaction characteristics (different users have different user-item interaction data, as shown in the Fig. 2). To differentiate between the importance of different behaviors, we propose a supervised task, and then use automatic learning to aggregate the embeddings of multi-behavior to distinguish between target behavior and auxiliary behavior. In each subgraph, the user and behavior embeddings are represented by R_k, where R_k denotes the k-th behavior graph, and the adjacent matrix A_k can be obtained from matrix R_k.

$$A_k = \begin{pmatrix} 0 & R_k \\ R_k^T & 0 \end{pmatrix} \tag{2}$$

Then, the GCN multilayer message communication formula is used to obtain the nodes of different behaviors embedded in the matrix. The formula is as follows:

$$X_k^{(l+1)} = \sigma\left(\widehat{A_k} X_k^{(l)} W_k\right) \tag{3}$$

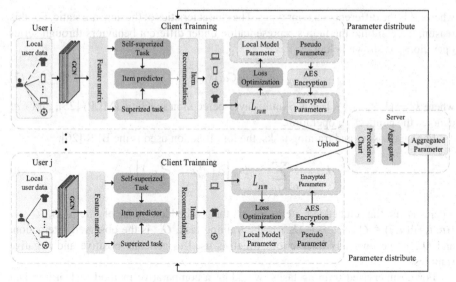

Fig. 2. The framework of FedMB

where $\widehat{A_k} = D_k^{-\frac{1}{2}}(A_k + I_k)D_k^{-\frac{1}{2}}$ is a self-connected normalized matrix. D_k is a $|V| * |V|$ dimension matrix under the k behavior. $|V|$ is the sum of the number of users and the number of items, $|V| = |U| + |I|$. I_k is the dimension matrix of $|V| * |V|$. $X_k^{(l)} \in R^{|V| * d}$ is the node embedded matrix in the node of the I_k behavior in the convolution layer. d is the dimension embedded. W_k and σ are model training parameters and non-linear activation functions. In order to ensure the embedding of the short connection node, the function of this article uses the function to merge all layers.

$$X_k = \int \left(X_k^{(l)}\right) \tag{4}$$

where $l = [0, 1 \ldots, L]$. X_k is composed of the user embedded matrix $X_{Uk} \in R^{|U| * d}$ and the item embedded matrix $X_{Ik} \in R^{|I| * d}$. $\int$ is the last layer of the connection operation.

First, a_{uk} is the semantic fusion coefficient of the user under the K behavior. Among them, we consider the proportion of the user's first behavior in all behaviors, and recognize the strength of different behaviors, as shown below:

$$a_{uk} = \frac{\exp(w_k * n_{uk})}{\exp(w_m * n_{um})} \tag{5}$$

where w_k said that under the behavior of the behavior k of all users, n_{uk} is the number of associations of user u under k.

X_{UK} and X_{IK} denote the embedded matrix of users and items under behavior k, while x_{uk} and x_{ik} denote the embedding of user u and item i under behavior k. Then the representation of all behaviors is merged. For user u, we merge all representations, as shown below.

$$e_u = \sigma \left\{ W \left(\sum_{m=1}^{K} a_{uk} * x_{uk}\right) \right\} \tag{6}$$

where W is the different behavior types. The characteristics of the item are static. For this reason, we combine the item's representation under different behaviors through series operations, as shown below.

$$e_i = g\{Cat(x_{ik})\} \tag{7}$$

where $k = [1, 2, \ldots, K]$, g is a multi-layer perception machine (MLP) [25], and Cat denotes the connection operation.

For supervision and training tasks, the loss function used is the BPR [26].

$$L_{st} = \sum_{(u,i,j)\in O} -log\left\{\sigma\left(e_u^T e_i - e_u^T e_j\right)\right\} \tag{8}$$

where e_i is the embedded item, e_u is the embedded item of the user, $O = \{(u, i, j)|(u, j) \in O_+, (u, j) \in O_-\}$ is the training task, O_+ is the observed interaction, and O_- is the unsteady interaction, which is used to generate positive and negative samples.

For unsupervised training tasks, we adopt a comparative method of learning and perform comparative learning between target behavior and auxiliary behavior subgraphs.

$$L_{sst_{k'}}^{user} = \sum_{u\in U} -log\frac{\sum_{u^+\in U} exp\left\{(x_{uK})^T x_u + \frac{k'}{\tau}\right\}}{\sum_{u^-\in U} exp\left\{(x_{uK})^T x_u - \frac{k'}{\tau}\right\}} \tag{9}$$

where $(x_{uK}, x_{u+k'})$ denotes the positive pair, and $(x_{uK}, x_{u-k'})$ denotes the negative pair. τ is a parameter, U is a user set, k' is auxiliary behavior, and K is target behavior. Similarly, we obtain a comparison loss $L_{sst_{k'}}^{item}$ through the loss function under the combination user and the item, and then, we add multiple comparison losses to obtain the total unsupervised loss, as shown below.

$$L_{sst} = \sum_{k'=2}^{K}\left(L_{sst_{k'}}^{user} + L_{sst}^{item}\right) \tag{10}$$

Parameter Selection on the Server. The main purpose of parameter aggregation is to select and weight the model parameters uploaded by clients. To achieve this, each uploaded parameter set is assigned a score based on the training loss reported by the client. This score reflects the quality of the client's model training, with higher scores indicating better performance. During each round of global iteration in federated Learning, the server aggregates the parameters of each client and computes a score value for each parameter. The parameters with high scores are then selected for aggregation to improve the overall model's recommendation quality.

To optimize the parameter selection process, we propose a method that uses pairwise comparison of precedence chart to assign weights to each factor. The use of precedence chart for weight assignments ensures fairness, avoids extreme score values, and reduces algorithmic complexity and training overhead compared to traditional machine learning methods. Applying this method to the federated Learning framework can shorten the global iteration time and can improve recommendation efficiency without compromising the results.

The weight assignment process involves evaluating the dataset, selecting the initial normal results, and assigning an initial weight score. Then, pairwise comparisons are performed to establish the corresponding mapping between the evaluation data and the weight value. Finally, the weight values are normalized and arranged to obtain different weights for different data.

Parameter Aggregation on the Server. The core engine of adaptive learning is personalized learning recommendation, which has greatly improved accuracy and diversity. Federated learning is a powerful data privacy protection machine learning solution that can safeguard data privacy and security while sharing data value. In this study, we combine federated learning with multi-behavior recommendation to create a federated personalized multi-behavior recommendation system and assess its feasibility and effectiveness.

Federated learning is comprised of two methods: global federated learning model training and training single models on clients. The global training method uses federated training plus local adaptation strategies and depends on the generalization performance of the global model for effective recommendations. The client training method focuses on personalized models that provide tailored solutions for each user. It modifies the aggregation process of the FL model to establish a personalized model and is advantageous for solving user preference drift. In this article, we use the client training method to train client models and to build a multi-behavior recommendation framework with strong generalization.

The client's training task is composed of self-supervised and unsupervised tasks. The total loss of the client's training is represented by the following formulas. L_{st} denotes unsupervised loss, while L_{sst} denotes the supervision loss.

$$L_{sum} = L_{st} + \lambda L_{sst} + \mu \|\Theta\|_2^2 \tag{11}$$

where Θ stands for training parameters, λ and μ indicate the control of self-supervision and $L2$ regularization proportional parameters, respectively.

$$S_n = PC(l_1, l_2 \ldots l_{n-1}, l_n) \tag{12}$$

On the server-side, the parameters are selected by the collected client model parameters and losses. Using precedence chart (PC) to give scores to different parameters, as shown in Formula (12), l_n denotes the n loss corresponding to the parameter, P_n is the n score, $S_n = (P_1, P_2 \ldots P_{n-1}, P_n)$, and the score set. We use the score set to give a native value to give power.

$$W_n = \frac{\gamma(P_1, P_2 \ldots P_{n-1}, P_n)}{\sum_{i=1}^{|n|} P_i} \tag{13}$$

where γ denotes the judgement function, which is used to remove extreme values. W_n denotes the weights allocated according to different scores. $W_n = (w_1, w_2 \ldots w_{n-1}, w_n)$,

W_n is the weight set corresponding to the n score of S_n. Perform parameter collection best according to different weights.

$$W_m = SelectN_\beta(w_1, w_2 \ldots w_{n-1}, w_n) \tag{14}$$

where $SelectN_\beta$ is the selection function, β is the proportion of the weight set to remove weights, $m = n * (1 - \beta)$, and $W_m = (w_1, w_2 \ldots w_{m-1}, w_m)$, which denotes the selected parameter weight collection. After obtaining the corresponding parameters, the parameters are averaged, and the aggregation formula is as follows.

$$p_{t+1} = \sum_{i=1}^{|m|} \frac{n_i}{n} p_t^i \tag{15}$$

where t is the current number of aggregation rounds, and the parameter p_{t+1} after the final aggregation is distributed down from the server-side, and participates in the next global iteration.

Parameter Encryption. Upon completing the training, the client uploads its parameters to the server, but this process is vulnerable to parameter interception and thus, can result in user privacy leakage.

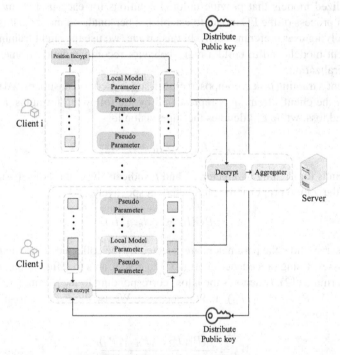

Fig. 3. Parameter encryption

To enhance the security, we increased the difficulty of identifying the real parameters, thereby reducing the risk of external malicious attacks. In accordance with the Fig. 3, the structure of the parameter encryption module is illustrated. In this article, noise data are added to the parameters uploaded from the client to increase the difficulty of identifying the real parameter. The noise data are derived from the pseudo parameters generated by the client itself. The formula is as shown below:

$$MI_{t+1}^i = Ip_{t+1}^i + \sum_{j \in c: j < k} IR_j \tag{16}$$

where IR_j denotes randomly generated parameters, Ip_{t+1}^i are real user parameters, and MI_{t+1}^i is the mask parameters. k is the number of pseudo ginseng generated by the client.

Adding noise to the parameters makes it more challenging to recognize the real parameters on the server. To address this issue, position parameters are generated on the client and uploaded to the server to identify the actual parameters. For position parameters, AES encryption is used, which is efficient and fast [27], and the server-distributed key is employed for encryption and decryption on the server. Compared to direct encryption of parameters, this proposed encryption method significantly reduces the encryption time overhead. The figure below illustrates the main process.

4 Experiments

In this experiment, we evaluate the recommendation quality of FedMB by using three datasets and introducing the experimental settings in detail. The evaluations are conducted through an ablation study and hyperparameter study to analyse the model and compare the effects of different modules and parameters on results. Finally, we compare the experimental results with other models to provide a comprehensive evaluation of FedMB.

4.1 Datasets and Evaluation Settings

To evaluate the performance of FedMB, we verify the model effect in 3 real-world datasets. The details are described as follows:

Table 2. Beibei, Taobao, Yelp dataset statistics

Dataset	User	Item	Interactions	Behavior Type
Beibei	21716	7977	3.36×10^6	{View, Cart, Purchase}
Taobao	48749	98249	2.40×10^6	{Click, Add to cart, Purchase}
Yelp	19800	22734	1.40×10^6	{Like, Neutral, Tip, Dislike}

The sparsity of data can be significantly reduced by setting both the target behavior and auxiliary behavior. Although the target behavior is typically considered the supervisory signal for training the model, it is often sparse, and sparse supervision cannot guarantee the training quality of the model. Even in multi-behavior recommendation, this phenomenon persists. To avoid this situation, we also regard auxiliary behavior as a supervisory signal for model training. When we cannot make recommendations based on user purchase behavior accurately, we can alternatively make recommendations based on user browsing or clicking behavior, which has been found to be effective.

To evaluate the model's recommendation effectiveness, we set up a corresponding test set for the client and utilize the user's target behavior as the test set. When the user has no target behavior interaction, the user's auxiliary behavior is used as the target behavior. In this paper, we utilize the NDCG and the Recall to better assess the model's recommendation effectiveness. NDCG accounts for the position of the recommendation ranking, while recall calculates the probability of the model recommending items that match the user's true interests. we report the Recall and NDCG values for k = 40 and k = 80, respectively, and the formulas for calculating NDCG and Recall are as follows:

$$DCG@k = \sum_{i=1}^{k} \frac{2^{rel_i} - 1}{log_2(i + 1)} \tag{17}$$

$$NDCG@k = \frac{DCG@k}{IDCG@k} \tag{18}$$

where rel_i denotes the relevance score of the ith recommended item, k is the length of the recommendation list, $DCG@K$ represents the discounted cumulative gain of the top k recommended items, and $IDCG@K$ represents the discounted cumulative gain of the top k relevant items.

$$Recall@k = \frac{TP@k}{TP@k + FN} \tag{19}$$

where the $TP@k$ metric represents the number of items that the user actually liked among the top k recommended items, while FN is defined as the difference between the total number of items that the user actually liked and the number of items that the user actually liked in the top k recommended items.

Experimental setup. The experiments in this paper are performed in an Ubuntu16.04 operating system. The hardware configuration used in the experiment is as follows: CPU: Intel Core i9-10900K; GPU: NVIDIA RTX 3080 TI. The programming language used is Python 3.7, and the deep learning development framework is PyTorch 1.7.

4.2 Experimental Settings

In this paper, we present a recommendation method that establishes end models and sets an aggregator on the server end. To optimize the aggregated parameter set, the federated weighted average algorithm is employed.

In terms of the setting of the federated framework, we divide users into different clients based on their IDs. By treating each ID as a different client, user data are read and the model is trained on the client side. As the number of clients is large, we set the number of client model trainings to 5, with a small number of iterations to avoid excessive time and space overhead. Due to the transitive nature of client parameters in the federated learning architecture, we focus more on the fitting of the overall global model on the server-side. An aggregate aggregator is established on the server-side, which aggregates the parameters and distributes them to the clients. To ensure that as many clients as possible participate in the global training, we set a large number of random extraction times. For example, on the Beibei dataset, which has a total of 21,716 users, we extract 70 clients each time for 430 global iterations, with a total of 30,100 random extractions, covering as many user IDs as possible.

4.3 Hyperparameter Study

Formula (14) introduces β as the proportion of deleted parameters in the parameter set, with its size determining the number of aggregated parameters. Notably, the final aggregated parameter set decreases as the β value increases. Nonetheless, both excessively large and small β values compromise the quality of the final model's recommendation results. Furthermore, the size of the aggregated parameter set directly impacts the aggregation time, which subsequently influences the model's training duration. In this study, we adopt varying β sizes to measure the model's training time and efficacy.

The Effect of Parameter β on Recommendation. During the execution of the weighted aggregation algorithm, the iterative transfer parameter's quality is optimized.

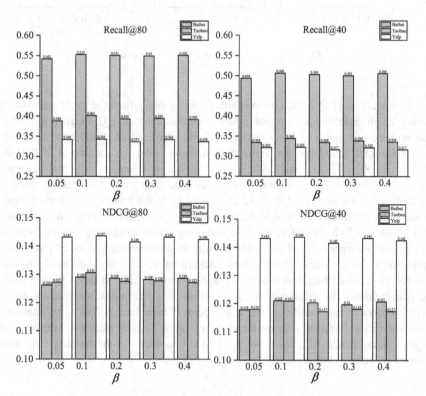

Fig. 4. Effects of different values of β on the results of FedMB

However, the final model results differ slightly under different optimal parameter β sizes. As illustrated in Fig. 4. From observation, a β value of 0.1 is optimal for the Beibei, Taobao, and Yelp datasets. Setting a larger β may remove too many well-trained parameters, resulting in a small parameter set that cannot achieve universal aggregation in training, hence reducing the quality of aggregated parameters and the recommendation effect. Conversely, a smaller β may select a smaller proportion of parameters, allowing client parameters with training disadvantages to participate in training, ultimately compromising the model training and results. Therefore, the experimental results show that setting β to less than 0.1 leads to a decrease in the results, validating the appropriateness of using a β value of 0.1.

The Effect of Parameter β on Training Time. While verifying the impact of parameter β on the results, we discovered its effect on the fitting time of the federated model training.

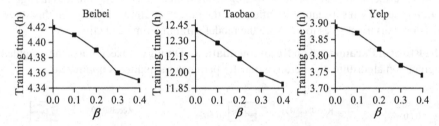

Fig. 5. Effect of parameter β on training time

Upon analyzing Fig. 5, we observed that the value of β affects the training time of the training client. Specifically, not using the precedence chart ($\beta = 0$) resulted in a longer training time compared to using the method. We also evaluated different values of β and set the total duration of the framework training under the training of 30,000 user instances to $\{0.1, 0.2, 0.3, 0.4\}$. We discovered that increasing the optimal parameter β led to a reduction in the overall framework's training time. The training time for the Taobao dataset decreased from 12.41 h to 11.89 h, the training time for the Beibei dataset reduced from 4.42 h to 4.35 h, and the training time for the yelp dataset reduced from 3.89 h to 3.74 h. Therefore, we concluded that when performing weighted optimal aggregation, a larger optimal parameter results in fewer server-processed parameters, leading to a shorter overall training time. Additionally, we observed that the training time for the Taobao dataset was longer compared to the training times for the Beibei and yelp datasets. The difference in training times was due to different datasets having varying orders of magnitude of interactive items. Since Taobao had more interactive items, the model required a larger interaction matrix, causing increased overhead and longer training times. Therefore, we set β to 0.1 to decrease the training time while ensuring recommendation quality.

4.4 Ablation Study

In federated aggregation, clients usually upload the gradient or parameters of the user model. However, this paper also includes the client training loss value to assess user training quality. The precedence chart plays a vital role in FedMB.

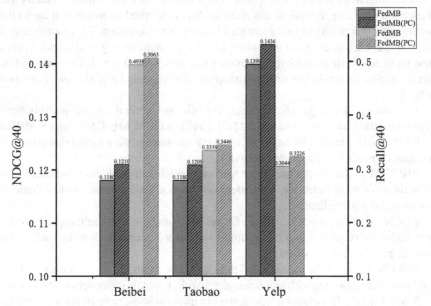

Fig. 6. Effect of precedence chart on the results of FedMB

In this paper, we conduct an experiment to demonstrate its effectiveness in improving the model's results under the influence of the precedence chart. We compare the results of our federated model, FedMB, with FedMB(PC), and observe an improvement in our model's performance. To investigate the impact of the precedence chart on the experimental results, we conducted an experiment and discussed its effect on the effectiveness of the federated recommendation model with and without PC. We refer to the "precedence chart" as PC for convenience. The results are shown in Fig. 6. The average quality of the recommended results on the Beibei dataset increased by 2.5%, while the improvement on the Taobao and Yelp datasets was 3% and 4.9%, respectively. These results indicate that using the precedence chart method to filter out the excellent training end model parameters and aggregate them has significant advantages over traditional federated aggregation methods. Furthermore, it improves the recommendation effect of the model. Therefore, we conclude that utilizing the precedence chart to optimize federated aggregation is crucial for enhancing the performance of the FedMB.

4.5 Comparative Experiments

In this paper, N GCN behavior user interaction views and N user behavior interaction views are set up, where N is the number of behaviors, N is set to 3. The weights are learned by optimizing supervised and unsupervised losses using the Adam [28] optimizer with a learning rate of 0.0001. In each experiment, 30,000 user rounds are trained on the Beibei and Taobao, Yelp datasets, with the number of client training rounds set to 5 rounds. The number of users participating in each round is set to 70. The difference in model quality in the global model with different numbers of users can be attributed to the heterogeneity among participants, which leads to variability in the overall effect. In each joint training, a random sampling method is adopted to ensure that each client has the same probability of being sampled in each global iteration. To comprehensively train the client, a higher sampling number and a larger number of global iteration rounds must be selected. Based on hyperparameter research, setting β to 0.1 ensures optimal efficiency with relatively low time consumption. The training batch size on clients is set to 1024.

We conduct a comparison between FedMB and several classic multi-behavior recommendation models, including NMTR, EHCF, RGCN, MB-GMN, and S-MBRec.

NMTR [29]: This is a hierarchical multitask recommendation model that effectively manages complex interconnected behaviors.

EHCF [30]: This model uses heterogeneous collaborative filtering and transferable predictions for multi-behavior. It transfers information across behaviors to enhance its precision and personalization.

RGCN [31]: This model improves factorization models with multistep information propagation in relational graphs, leading to enhanced accuracy in tasks such as link prediction and entity classification.

MB-GMN [4]: This model efficiently predicts multiple source-target tasks by combining meta learning with graph neural networks to obtain cross-behavior predictors.

S-MBRec [2]: The model adopts a star comparison strategy to create a comparison view of target and auxiliary behavior. It uses supervised and unsupervised tasks to recommend models, improving the accuracy and effectiveness of the recommendations.

Our goal is to emphasize the unique features and advantages of FedMB in comparison to these traditional models. Through this comparison, we provide a more comprehensive understanding of the strengths and limitations of each model. We also highlight the potential applications of FedMB in various real-world scenarios. According to Table 2, the proposed federated multi-behavior recommendation model outperforms the latest S-MBRec model on the Beibei dataset, with an average index increase of 12.6% points. While there are decreases in Recall@10 and NDCG@10 due to the larger number of interactions per user in the Beibei dataset, its performance also decreases in shorter recommendation lists when unable to obtain preferences from other users. However, the other two datasets exhibit some mitigation of this effect due to their smaller numbers of interaction items per user. Despite this, for other metrics such as Recall@40 and NDCG@40, they are both twice as high as the latest methods, and Recall@80 and NDCG@80 also experience significant improvement. On the Taobao dataset, all performance indicators show improvement, especially in Recall@40 and NDCG@40, resulting in an average indicator increase of 13.1% points. Similarly, the Yelp dataset also shows an average increase of 14.5% points. These results demonstrate the excellent recommendation performance of the proposed model, especially when recommending 40 items (Table 3).

Table 3. FedMB in Beibei,Taobao, and Yelp results comparison

Datatset	Metric	NMTR	EHCF	RGCN	MB-GMN	S-MBRec	FedMB
Beibei	Recall@10	0.0460	0.0456	0.0483	0.0496	**0.0529**	0.0443
	Recall@40	0.1370	0.1270	0.1262	0.1497	0.1647	**0.5063**
	Recall@80	0.1989	0.1923	0.1912	0.2018	0.2740	**0.5525**
	NDCG@10	0.0124	0.0131	0.0122	0.0134	**0.0148**	0.0137
	NDCG@40	0.0192	0.0217	0.0226	0.0395	0.0429	**0.1210**
	NDCG@80	0.0422	0.0435	0.0440	0.0465	0.0615	**0.1290**
Taobao	Recall@10	0.0367	0.0292	0.0370	0.0423	0.0608	**0.1764**
	Recall@40	0.0485	0.0594	0.0703	0.0873	0.1027	**0.3446**
	Recall@80	0.0982	0.1032	0.1525	0.1553	0.1647	**0.4011**
	NDCG@10	0.0237	0.0285	0.0213	0.0325	0.0391	**0.0819**
	NDCG@40	0.0404	0.0373	0.0314	0.0396	0.0464	**0.1209**
	NDCG@80	0.0329	0.0390	0.0443	0.0475	0.0583	**0.1306**
Yelp	Recall@10	0.0195	0.0172	0.0210	0.0230	0.0259	**0.1986**
	Recall@40	0.0697	0.0704	0.0844	0.0899	0.1135	**0.3226**
	Recall@80	0.0903	0.0873	0.1105	0.1350	0.1548	**0.3433**
	NDCG@10	0.0191	0.0166	0.0199	0.0275	0.0287	**0.1145**
	NDCG@40	0.0305	0.0298	0.0263	0.0220	0.0337	**0.1436**
	NDCG@80	0.0355	0.0330	0.0395	0.0430	0.0438	**0.1471**

The proposed federated multi-behavior recommendation model is different from the baseline model in that it trains a personalized model for each user and makes recommendations based on their interactions with personalized items. Unlike the comparative methods, this model explores the interaction of users' personalized items and trains a model for each user, and it does not weaken with the overall user preference. Additionally, a security encryption module is added to the parameter upload process to ensure user privacy and security while improving recommendation performance. Consequently, the model effectively explores users' personalized preferences and makes recommendations without revealing their private data.

5 Conclusion

In this paper, we present FedMB, a multi-behavior recommendation model that utilizes federated learning to preserve data privacy during the recommendation process. FedMB employs a personalized federated learning framework to address the challenge of user personalization in multi-behavior recommendation. Through personalized user models, the system can provide high-quality recommendations while still protecting the privacy of users' data. The effectiveness and efficiency of FedMB are evaluated in experiments, and we also discuss the impact of using a precedence chart on the performance of the federated model recommendation. The results show the feasibility of using federated learning in multi-behavior recommendation systems, with the proposed method performing well on three datasets.

In future research directions of multi-behavior recommendation under the federated learning paradigm, improving the security and efficiency of the system remains a top priority. Despite the higher privacy level provided by the decentralized data location and encrypted data transmission, there is still a risk of privacy leakage during parameter distribution. Additionally, enhancing the efficiency of client model training and compressing parameters to reduce communication overhead are crucial areas for further investigation.

References

1. Wang, L., Xiong, Y., Li, Y., Liu, et al.: A collaborative recommendation model based on enhanced graph convolutional neural network. J. Comput. Res. Dev. **58**(09), 1987–1996 (2021). (in Chinese)
2. Gu, S., Wang, X., Shi, C., et al.: Self-supervised graph neural networks for multi-behavior recommendation. In: International Joint Conference on Artificial Intelligence, Shenzhen (2022)
3. Jin, B., Gao, C., He, X., et al.: Multi-behavior recommendation with graph convolutional networks. In: Proceedings of the 43rd International ACM SIGIR Conference on Research and Development in Information Retrieval, Xian, pp. 659–668 (2020)
4. Xia, L., Xu, Y., Huang, C., et al.: Graph meta network for multi-behavior recommendation. In: Proceedings of the 44th International ACM SIGIR Conference on Research and Development in Information Retrieval, Montreal, pp. 757–766 (2021)
5. Xia, L., Huang, C., Xu, Y., et al.: Knowledge-enhanced hierarchical graph transformer network for multi-behavior recommendation. In: Proceedings of the AAAI Conference on Artificial Intelligence, vol. 35, no. 5, pp. 4486–4493 (2021)
6. Wei, W., Huang, C., Xia, L., et al.: Contrastive meta learning with behavior multiplicity for recommendation. In: Proceedings of the Fifteenth ACM International Conference on Web Search and Data Mining, New York, pp. 1120–1128 (2022)
7. Wu, J., Wang, X., Feng, F., et al.: Self-supervised graph learning for recommendation. In: Proceedings of the 44th International ACM SIGIR Conference on Research and Development in Information Retrieval, Montreal, pp. 726–735 (2021)
8. Zhang, H., Li, Y., Wu, J., et al.: A survey on privacy-preserving federated recommender systems. Acta Automatica Sinica **48**(09), 2142–2163. (in Chinese)
9. Voigt, P., Von dem Bussche, A.: The EU General Data Protection Regulation (GDPR). A Practical Guide, 1st edn. Springer, Cham (2017). https://doi.org/10.1007/978-3-319-57959-7
10. McMahan, B., Moore, E., Ramage, D., et al.: Communication-efficient learning of deep networks from decentralized data. In: Artificial Intelligence and Statistics, Fort Lauderdale, pp. 1273–1282. PMLR (2017)
11. Shmueli, E., Tassa, T.: Secure multi-party protocols for item-based collaborative filtering. In: Proceedings of the Eleventh ACM Conference on Recommender Systems, Como, pp. 89–97 (2017)
12. Kim, S., Kim, J., Koo, D., et al.: Efficient privacy-preserving matrix factorization via fully homomorphic encryption. In: Proceedings of the 11th ACM on Asia Conference on Computer and Communications Security, New York, pp. 617–628 (2016)

13. Berlioz, A., Friedman, A., Kaafar, M.A., et al.: Applying differential privacy to matrix factorization. In: Proceedings of the 9th ACM Conference on Recommender Systems, Vienna, pp. 107–114 (2015)
14. McSherry, F., Mironov, I.: Differentially private recommender systems: building privacy into the netflix prize contenders. In: Proceedings of the 15th ACM SIGKDD International Conference on Knowledge Discovery and Data Mining, New York, pp. 627–636 (2009)
15. Lu, K.P., Chang, S.T.: Detecting change-points for shifts in mean and variance using fuzzy classification maximum likelihood change-point algorithms. J. Comput. Appl. Math. **308**, 447–463 (2016)
16. Wu, Y., Xie, R., Zhu, Y., et al.: Multi-view multi-behavior contrastive learning in recommendation. In: International Conference on Database Systems for Advanced Applications, Hyderabad, pp. 166–182 (2022)
17. Chai, D., Wang, L., Chen, K., et al.: Secure federated matrix factorization. IEEE Intell. Syst. **36**(5), 11–20 (2020)
18. Zhang, S., Yin, H., Chen, T., et al.: Pipattack: poisoning federated recommender systems for manipulating item promotion. In: Proceedings of the Fifteenth ACM International Conference on Web Search and Data Mining, New York, pp. 1415–1423 (2022)
19. Lin, G., Liang, F., Pan, W., et al.: Fedrec: federated recommendation with explicit feedback. IEEE Intell. Syst. **36**(5), 21–30 (2020)
20. Wu, C., Wu, F., Cao, Y., et al.: Fedgnn: federated graph neural network for privacy-preserving recommendation. In: Proceedings of the Thirty-Eighth International Conference on Machine Learning (2021)
21. Perifanis, V., Efraimidis, P.S.: Federated neural collaborative filtering. Knowl.-Based Syst. **242**, 108441 (2022)
22. Yi, J., Wu, F., Wu, C., et al.: Efficient-FedRec: efficient federated learning framework for privacy-preserving news recommendation. In: Proceedings of the 2021 Conference on Empirical Methods in Natural Language Processing, Stroudsburg, pp. 2814–2824 (2021)
23. Yuan, W., Yin, H., Wu, F., et al.: Federated Unlearning for On-Device Recommendation. arXiv preprint arXiv:2210.10958 (2022)
24. Kipf, T.N., Welling, M.: Semi-supervised classification with graph convolutional networks. In: Proceedings of the 5th International Conference on Learning Representations. Palais des Congrès Neptune (2017)
25. Pinkus, A.: Approximation theory of the MLP model in neural networks. Acta Numer. **8**, 143–195 (1999)
26. Rendle, S., Freudenthaler, C., Gantner, Z., et al.: BPR: Bayesian personalized ranking from implicit feedback. In: Proceedings of the Twenty-Fifth Conference on Uncertainty in Artificial Intelligence, Montreal, pp. 452–461 (2009)
27. Lee, B.H., Dewi, E.K., Wajdi, M.F.: Data security in cloud computing using AES under HEROKU cloud. In: 27th Wireless and Optical Communication Conference (WOCC), Hualien, pp. 1–5 (2018)
28. KingaD, A.: A method for stochastic optimization. In: Anon. International Conference on Learning Representations. SanDego (2015)
29. Gao, C., He, X., Gan, D., et al.: Neural multi-task recommendation from multi-behavior data. In: 2019 IEEE 35th International Conference on Data Engineering, Macau, pp. 1554–1557 (2019)
30. Chen, C., Zhang, M., Zhang, Y., et al.: Efficient heterogeneous collaborative filtering without negative sampling for recommendation. In: Proceedings of the AAAI Conference on Artificial Intelligence, New York, vol. 34, no. 01, pp. 19–26 (2020)
31. Schlichtkrull, M., Kipf, T.N., Bloem, P., et al.: Modeling relational data with graph convolutional networks. In: European Semantic Web Conference, Heraklion, pp. 593–607 (2018)

FederatedMesh: Collaborative Federated Learning for Medical Data Sharing in Mesh Networks

Lamir Shkurti[1,2], Mennan Selimi[2(✉)], and Adrian Besimi[1]

[1] Faculty of Contemporary Sciences and Technologies, South East European University, Tetovo, North Macedonia
{ls29773,a.besimi}@seeu.edu.mk
[2] Max van der Stoel Institute, South East European University, Tetovo, North Macedonia
m.selimi@seeu.edu.mk

Abstract. Edge computing is a paradigm that involves performing local processing on lightweight devices at the edge of networks to improve response times and reduce bandwidth consumption. While machine learning (ML) models can run on smaller computing devices at the edge, training ML models presents challenges for low-capacity devices. This paper aimed to evaluate the performance of Federated Learning (FL) - a distributed ML framework, when training a medical dataset using Raspberry Pi devices as client nodes. The testing accuracy, CPU usage, RAM memory usage and network performance were measured for different number of clients and epochs. The results showed that increasing the number of devices generally improved the testing accuracy, with the greatest improvement observed in the earlier epochs. However, increasing the number of devices also increased the CPU usage, with a significant increase observed in the later epochs. Additionally, the RAM memory usage increased slightly as the number of clients and epochs increased. The findings suggest that FL can be an effective way to train medical models using distributed devices, but careful consideration must be given to the trade-off between accuracy and computational resources.

Keywords: edge computing · federated learning · mesh networks

1 Introduction

Edge computing complements cloud computing by utilizing local processing on lightweight computing devices, such as IoT gateways and wearable devices, at the edge of networks where data is produced. Local processing on these edge devices can improve response times of cloud services and reduce bandwidth consumption by transmitting less data to the cloud [1,2]. Edge computing is already operational in various industrial and consumer-oriented scenarios and some machine learning (ML) and artificial intelligence tasks can also be moved from the cloud to the edge.

© ICST Institute for Computer Sciences, Social Informatics and Telecommunications Engineering 2024
Published by Springer Nature Switzerland AG 2024. All Rights Reserved
H. Gao et al. (Eds.): CollaborateCom 2023, LNICST 563, pp. 154–169, 2024.
https://doi.org/10.1007/978-3-031-54531-3_9

Fig. 1. Resource-constrained devices: Raspberry Pi, Arduino - tinyML and some wearable and IoT devices.

Running ML models on smaller computing devices at the edge is becoming increasingly popular. Even tiny microcontroller boards are now capable of performing simple tasks with trained models [3]. However, training ML models is more computationally demanding and presents challenges for devices with low capacity. While using GPUs (Graphics Processing Units) instead of CPUs (Central Processing Units) can provide better performance, GPUs are not always available on devices like low capacity PCs (mini PCs) or single-board-computers (SBCs). As a result, CPUs have to handle a high load during training, which takes significantly more time compared to high-end devices. This means that training process takes significantly longer on low-capacity devices, making it unsuitable for applications with time constraints.

With the popularization of wearable and mobile devices, intelligent learning applications have been prominently used by many consumers. These devices collect user information about daily activities, providing valuable insights to enhance user lifestyle. The success of smart health applications largely relies on the ability to train ML models on large quantities of user data collected from wearables [4,5]. However, due privacy concerns, security issues, communication overhead, processing delay etc., traditional ML algorithms face challenges that work in a centralized fashion where all the available data is accumulated beforehand. For instance, in the case of wearable systems, privacy remains the key obstacle to implement data analytics algorithms. Most of the time users are sceptical in allowing their personal data to be analysed by the ML algorithms on cloud. Figure 1 depicts several low-constrained devices capable of performing ML functions including Raspberry Pi's, Arduino boards, tinyML devices etc.

Federated Learning (FL) is a paradigm for collaboratively training ML models on computation, storage, energy and bandwidth limited mobile devices in a distributed manner by addressing privacy concerns and reducing communication overhead and processing delay [6,7]. In FL, each node has its own training data to train a local model, and the subsequent aggregation of the local models leads to a new global model. Wireless mesh networks can be used to support FL on these edge devices, but this can be challenging due to several factors [8]. These challenges include limited resources on low-capacity devices, unreliable network connectivity, device heterogeneity and security and privacy concerns. These challenges can make it difficult to coordinate and aggregate model updates from devices in a FL setting, and to maintain consistent communication between devices [9,9].

The main contributions of the paper is *demonstration of FL in a real resource-constrained wireless mesh environment with dynamic, heterogeneous and intermittent resource availability.* To do this, we assess the possibility of implementing FL on *8* real IoT devices that have limited network and hardware resources and are connected in a wireless mesh network. Therefore, our goal with this contribution is to offer fresh insights that can help make the process of FL more doable on everyday devices that have limited resources. Our aim is to make FL work better on these devices that people commonly use. Further, we present practical observations on the use of resources (CPU, memory, network) and suggestions on the optimal training configurations that must be employed to ensure a satisfactory "training experience" on these low-capacity devices.

The rest of the paper is organized as follows. In Sect. 2 we describe the FL applications used and analyse the state-of-the-art work. Section 3 presents the FL model used. Section 4 provides details about how we set up our experiments, the specific experiments we conducted and the results we achieved. Moving on, Sect. 5 wraps up our findings and conclusions, also suggesting directions for potential future research.

2   Background and Related Work

In this section, initially we provide the background for our work and then present the related work.

2.1   FL Applications and Dataset

Federated Learning (FL) is predominantly utilized in situations that demand a significant emphasis on safeguarding privacy and optimizing resource allocation. The healthcare and medical sector is a major field where FL finds extensive applications. This section of the paper outlines the medical datasets used in the study. The dataset is selected from the healthcare applications mentioned below.

Healthcare Industry: Many hospitals, AI companies and regulatory agencies are responsible for protecting highly sensitive data of the users. In the health industry, many *wearable healthcare* devices are used to monitor patient's health, identify anomalies and treat health conditions. For instance, in each hospital a large amount of real electronic health records (EHR) are needed to train a powerful a medical model. However due to the sensitivity and privacy of medical data, the demand for a real dataset is hard to be satisfied. FL can solve this by maintaining data anonymity, thus removing many barriers to data sharing.

Dataset: For the FL experiments, we are using the Chest-X-Rays dataset provided in the following link [10]. The Chest-X-Rays dataset consists of 5,863 X-Ray images in JPEG format and 2 categories (Pneumonia/Normal). Chest-X-ray images (anterior-posterior) are selected from retrospective cohorts of pediatric patients of one to five years old from Guangzhou Women and Children's Medical Center, Guangzhou. The FL task to be executed in the experiments is to train a 6-layer Convolutional Neural Network (CNN) model with the Chest-X-Ray dataset. The CNN model has around 420, 000 parameters.

2.2 Related Work

This section describes a review of specific studies that focus on the implementation of FL on devices with limited capacity and research that examines techniques to maintain data privacy, a crucial consideration when training confidential personal health data.

Low-Constrained Devices and Federated Learning: Y. Gao and colleagues [11] conducted a practical assessment of two advanced ML methods - Federated Learning (FL) and split neural networks (SplitNN). The authors looked at different sets of data, tried various types of model designs, involved several users' devices and used different benchmarks to measure how well everything worked. Their study focused on learning, which depended on two types of data: one where the data balance was uneven and another where the data wasn't exactly the same across devices. The training of the model took place on Raspberry Pi devices, and they kept track of how much the CPU and memory was used, the extra communication needed, and how long the training took. Based on their results, FL outperformed SplitNN overall. This is mainly because FL involves less extra communication compared to SplitNN.

We have used some findings from the experiments carried out by Y. Goa on individual Raspberry Pi devices to establish the baseline system in our own research. In particular, we have employed their configuration of 1 and 5 epochs as reference epoch values.

FL for edge environments has been suggested in various studies as surveyed in [12]. Specific types of edge devices are investigated for instance in the Flower framework, where Raspberry Pi, Android phones and NVIDIA Jetson were used [13]. The work on Flower proposes a framework that first addresses the hardware heterogeneity of the clients by providing client-specific software implementations. For instance, the FL client for Android phones consists of a Java implementation applying a specific TensorFlow Lite Model Personalization support for Android Studio. The FL client for the Raspberry Pi and NVIDIA Jetson is implemented in Python.

After looking into similar research, it's clear that various methods have been suggested to make FL use up fewer computer resources. These methods include adjusting how ML models are trained and even shifting some tasks to other platforms. However, there's still a gap in our knowledge when it comes to how well FL actually works in real wireless mesh setups. Our study focuses on filling this gap. We're taking a hands-on approach by running FL on devices with limited power in mesh networks. This way, we're gathering important information on how to set up FL for different types of user situations.

In [14] study performs a multi-chest disease classification from the CXR images task using the proposed CNN architecture. Also, the authors introduce a new dataset consisting of 28833 CXR images, a mixture of COVID-19, non-covid viral or bacterial pneumonia, lung opacity, and normal cases by aggregating publicly available datasets to apply FL for the proposed models. Through experiments, they compared the results with central training, federated training, and communication-efficient federated training. Also, they have shown that federated training in chest disease classification is achieved with high percent accuracy and is an effective alternative to central training. This study's outcomes can inspire and encourage medical organizations to initiate or adopt their research and practices within the FL approach for chest disease classification.

The authors in the following paper [15] introduces a conceptual framework designed to harness edge computing for healthcare analytics, utilizing user-generated data. The intersection of technologies like cloud computing, edge computing, IoT, wearables, and FL is anticipated to encourage end-users to play a more participatory role in overseeing their health. The main objective is to strengthen patient empowerment and accountability in the domains of monitoring and preventing diseases. This stands as a crucial factor in ensuring the sustainability of contemporary healthcare systems. The proposed model offers the potential for seamless integration of user-generated wellness and behavioral data in an effective and scalable manner.

Privacy Through Federated Learning: Taking privacy as an important aspect while training medical data, the authors are proposing Dopamine [16], a system to train the medical data. This study investigates various ML and privacy-preserving methods. The approach involves using medical data to train Deep Neural Networks - DNNs for medical diagnoses. The training of these DNNs is carried out using distributed datasets through a combination of FL and Differentially-Private Stochastic Gradient Descent - DPSGD.

In a research study mentioned in [17], the authors of the paper combined blockchain technology and FL techniques to train ML models without exposing the actual data. This was particularly relevant for situations where lots of data comes in quickly from connected devices in a setting called the Industrial Internet of Things (IIoT). They pointed out that protecting this data from being leaked in industries is a big deal. To tackle this, they built a secure way of sharing data using blockchain and added privacy-preserving features to FL. They discovered that by using blockchain, they could share the model in the FL process while keeping data private.

Another paper, presented in [18], introduced the BlockFL system, which mixed blockchain with FL. Instead of having a central place (node) that collects updates from devices, the system used a distributed ledger to exchange these updates between mobile devices. They also studied how quickly learning was completed using this system. In their case, multiple mobile devices were used in order to train the model locally making use of the distributed ledger powered by blockchain technology.

In a different scenario, authors Passerat-Palmbach et al. discussed in [19] how blockchain could help to orchestrate FL for healthcare groups. They showed how data could be contributed to improve ML models while still ensuring privacy and accurate records. They set up a way to track events in the network without revealing who was involved.

Contrary, the work in [20] took a different approach. They proposed using IPFS[1] instead of a single central server for FL. This lets different nodes participate and lead the FL process. They also split the ML models into parts and shared the responsibility for each part among nodes. This was especially useful when dealing with devices that aren't very powerful.

The authors in this work [21] introduce Communication-Efficient Federated Averaging (CE-FedAvg), an adaptation of the Federated Averaging (FedAvg) algorithm FL in the context of IoT devices. The work addresses concerns about data privacy by allowing FL to be performed at the edge servers and gateways without sending data to a central server. CE-FedAvg uses an adapted form of the Adam optimization algorithm and novel compression techniques to reduce the number of communication rounds required for convergence, while also minimizing the data uploaded by clients. Extensive experiments with MNIST and CIFAR-10 datasets, both in IID and non-IID settings, demonstrate that CE-FedAvg achieves faster convergence and requires less total data uploaded compared to FedAvg. Additionally, experiments on a Raspberry Pi testbed confirm that CE-FedAvg can reach a target accuracy in less real time. This research contributes to the field of FL by improving the efficiency and robustness of FL algorithms in edge-computing scenarios.

In the [22] the authors use FL technology for Medical Image Classification to address the issues of medical data security. They present their algorithm FedSLD to utilize knowledge of label distributions to mitigate the challenges posed by data heterogeneity. FedSLD is designed to enhance the training of ML models for medical image classification in a FL setting by leveraging shared label distribution information, ultimately improving the model's accuracy and stability in the presence of data heterogeneity. They used datasets of MNIST, CIFAR10, Organ MNIST, and PathMNIST. This article is important for computer science researchers as it proposes a new method for training ML models in medicine using separated and privatized data. Additionally, the study primarily focuses on model performance without addressing all potential security and privacy challenges related to medical data, which are crucial in healthcare-based ML.

Looking at the reviewed papers in privacy, it's clear that there are various ways to keep data safe in FL. One popular method is called differential privacy and there are also ways to use external tools like blockchain to help. Also,

---

[1] Interplanetary File System. https://ipfs.io/.

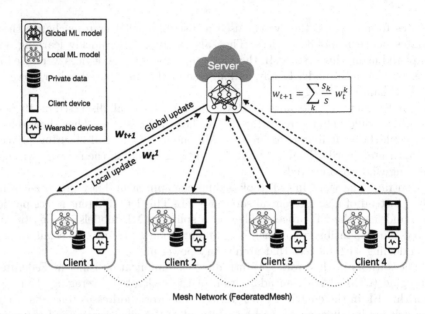

Fig. 2. FL architecture involving communication between the server and clients (such as mobile devices, wearables, etc.)

we noticed that ML applications that use personal information (medical data) and private data (sensor data from the Internet of Things) can gain significant advantages from FL.

3   System Model

3.1   Federated Learning

Federated Learning (FL) has gained significant interest in the research community as a model training technique that enables clients to train models collaboratively without the need to share their local data. FL has become a key area of interest in wearable systems and wireless communications, such as 5G, where edge nodes generate valuable data for applications while still maintaining data privacy [23,24]. FL is a distributed ML technique where numerous clients or workers, such as mobile or wearable devices, train a model in a collaborative manner guided by a central server located in the cloud, as shown in Fig. 2. The training data is stored directly on the devices.

The FL algorithm operates in the following way: the process starts with the server initializing a global model (w_t) and sending this model to all clients. Each of the clients k trains the global model on their own local data for several rounds of training called "epochs". One the local training is complete, the updated model is sent back to the server (w_t^k). The server receives the updated models from all the clients and combines (i.e., merges) them to update the global model (w_{t+1}).

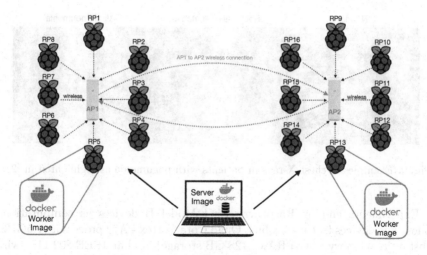

Fig. 3. Testbed used for the experiments

This process is repeated until the model converges or a maximum number of rounds (i.e., iteration of this process) is reached. Client k possesses a training dataset comprising s_k samples as depicted in Fig. 2.

In this section, we focus on a system made of Raspberry Pi edge devices that work together to train ML models using FL. We study *how much CPU and memory* the devices use when training FL models based on healthcare data. Further, we study the *accuracy of the model reached with different number of edge devices* and also *how long does it take to train the models* considering the impact of a real wireless mesh network.

Model: We use FL to train a 6-layer Convolutional Neural Network (CNN) model on the client nodes using the Chest X-Ray Images (Pneumonia) dataset of size 6.7 GB [10,25]. The CNN model has approximately 420,000 parameters.

By sharing our practical experiences, we hope to provide new information that can help improve ML training on edge devices in wireless mesh network.

4   Empirical Analysis and Findings

4.1   Experimental Setup

The setup used for the experiment has actual devices that are connected to each other through a wireless network. The setup consists of 8 Raspberry Pi (RPi) devices that are linked to a pair of wireless access points (4 by 4) as highlighted in Fig. 3. These access points are connected to each other through a wireless link using Ubiquiti Nanostation M5 devices[2]. These devices have a good performance in creating point-to-point links and can operate at a range of up to 15 km at 2.4 GHz and 5 GHz.

---

[2] https://store.ui.com/collections/operator-airmax-devices/products/nanostation-m5.

| Normal | Bacterial Pneumonia | Viral Pneumonia |

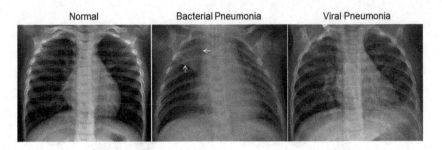

Fig. 4. Examples of chest X-rays in patients with pneumonia as highlighted in [25]

Experiments employ Raspberry Pi 4 Model B devices as computational nodes. The devices feature a robust Quad Core Cortex - A72 processor (1.5GHz), substantial memory (8 GB RAM, 128 GB storage), and an IEEE 802.11ac wireless connection. PyTorch version 1.8.0, OS Raspbian GNU/Linux 10 (buster) and Python version 3.7.3 are used as the software for the experiments. In total, 8 Raspberry Pi devices (4 connected to a single AP) act as workers (clients), and a laptop acts as a server. As highlighted in Fig. 3, as the central node (server) we use a laptop with CPU i5-8250U and 8 GB RAM with Windows 11 Operating System.

The experimental setup consists of two components: the worker and server parts. We developed Docker images for both parts, with the client image installed on Raspberry Pi devices and the server image on the laptop. To train ML models, we utilized the Keras API. During the model training, the data was divided into smaller groups called "batches", each with 10 samples. This allowed the model to be trained in smaller steps, which can improve memory usage and make the training process faster. The training was done for 100 rounds or iterations.

Dataset: Four our experiments the dataset obtained contains 5,863 X-Ray images in jPEG format categorized into two groups (Pneumonia/Normal). The images in this collection are chosen from past groups of young patients, aged one to five years old, at Guangzhou Women's and Children's Medical Center in Guangzhou [10]. Figure 4 highlights some of the examples from the dataset - chest X-rays in patients with different type of pneumonia [25].

4.2   Experimental Results

In the experiments, we aim to measure how accurate the FL model is when it is used with different numbers of clients in mesh networks. First we characterize the network used and also test how much stress the edge devices can handle and measure how much CPU and RAM they use.

Network Characterization. At first, our goal was to assess the performance of the mesh network we are currently utilizing. By utilizing the bandwidth and RTT (Round-trip time) ECDF graph, we can effectively visualize the distribution of our data from the wireless links and identify any irregularities or network issues

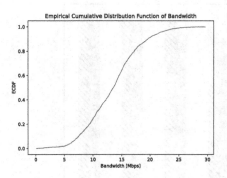

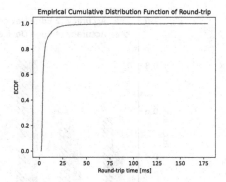

Fig. 5. ECDF - Network Bandwidth   **Fig. 6.** ECDF - Network RTT

that can make the FL impossible on this network. Figure 5 shows the ECDF (Empirical Cumulative Distribution Function) of the link bandwidth while the FL training experiments happen. The ECDF graph for bandwidth shows that the majority of the links (95%) has a bandwidth between 5 Mbps and 30 Mbps. The bandwidth increases as the ECDF value increases, indicating that higher percentages of the measured data have higher bandwidths. The results suggest that the bandwidth of the data varies widely, with some values as low as 5 Mbps and others as high as 30 Mbps. We can conclude that the *network has sufficient bandwidth to enable the exchange of model updates*, thus FL could be feasible on this network.

Figure 6 shows that the majority of the RTT values are relatively low, with most values falling between 3 ms and 6 ms. This suggests that the network is performing well, with relatively low latency. FL involves the exchange of model updates between client devices and the central server, and lower latency can help to reduce the time required for these exchanges and improve the overall efficiency of the process.

Testing Accuracy: Figure 7 depicts the testing accuracy when 2 and 4 edge devices are used for the training. Figure 7 demonstrates that the testing accuracy improves as the number of epochs increases for both 2 and 4 devices. However, the accuracy is generally higher for 4 devices as compared to 2 devices across all epochs. For the first few epochs (1 and 2, the difference in accuracy between 2 and 4 devices is significant. As the number of epochs increase (4–100), the difference in accuracy between 2 and 4 devices becomes smaller, but 4 devices consistently perform better. The results suggest that using more devices in FL can improve the testing accuracy of the model. However, the improvement *may not be significant after a certain number of epochs*, and other factors such as communication efficiency and device heterogeneity may also impact the performance.

CPU Usage: Figure 8 depicts the average CPU usage when training the model with different number of devices. Figure reveals that the CPU usage varies

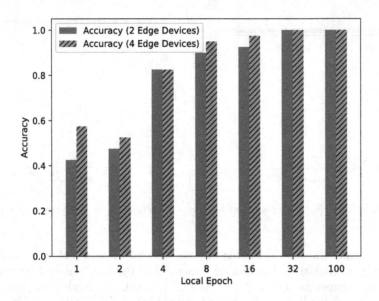

Fig. 7. Testing Accuracy vs Local Epoch (2 and 4 edge devices)

depending on the number of devices used for the training and the number of epoch completed. Additionally, we can see that the CPU usage increased as the number of epochs increased, regardless of the number of devices used. It is also worth noting that the highest CPU usage was observed for the epoch with the highest number of iterations, but even in that case, the CPU usage did not exceed 90% for any of the devices used. Overall, it seems that *training the model with more devices can lead to higher CPU usage*, but using a higher number of devices can also *potentially lead to faster training times*. Further, the peak CPU usage was observed during the model update communication with the client nodes.

Memory Usage: The memory usage during the training of the model with varying numbers of workers is depicted in Fig. 9. Based on the results, we see that the memory usage increased slightly as the number of devices increased for each epoch. However, the difference in memory usage between 2 and 4 devices was relatively small. Thinking about the memory capacity of the devices used in FL is crucial. This is because it might affect how well the training process works and how stable it is overall. In this case, the *Raspberry Pi devices with 8 GB of RAM appeared to handle the memory requirements well*, with relatively stable memory usage across different epochs and number of devices.

The **CPU temperatures** of the 4 Raspberry Pi devices were measured while training FL models. As highlighted in Fig. 10, training FL models requires a lot of computing power, which makes the CPU run at maximum capacity for long periods, reaching on average 80° CPU temperature. Based on the experiments performed, optimizing the training process and reducing the computational workload may help to prevent *overheating*. Overheating in Raspberry Pi

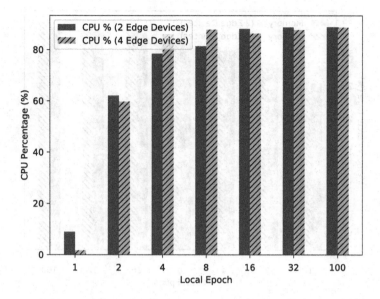

Fig. 8. CPU vs Local Epoch (2 and 4 edge devices)

devices can indeed be a significant concern, as it can lead to the shutdown and interruption of experiments or tasks being performed on the device.

4.3 Discussion

From the experiments performed, we observed that the using the FL in wireless mesh networks can effectively improve the accuracy of the model by increasing the number of devices and epochs. However, this comes at the cost of higher CPU and RAM usage, which needs to be considered when designing a FL system. In this particular study, the use of Raspberry Pi devices with 4 cores of CPU and 8 GB of RAM seems to be sufficient for the task.

It is interesting to note that the CPU usage is higher when communicating with client nodes, which suggests that optimizing the communication protocols can lead to more efficient FL systems. Optimizing the code, using pre-trained models, reducing the training data size or lowering the learning rate can improve the efficiency of the training process. Additionally, the fact that the RAM usage stabilizes after a certain number of epochs suggests that there may be an optimal number of epochs beyond which the model is no longer improving significantly.

Overall, the findings suggest that FL is a promising approach for improving ML models while preserving data privacy, but it requires careful consideration of hardware resources and communication protocols to ensure efficient and effective operation.

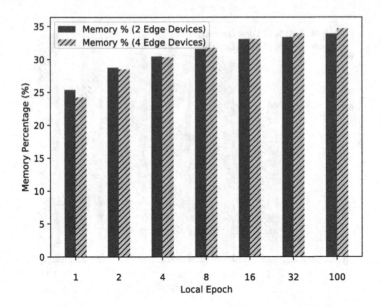

Fig. 9. RAM vs Local Epoch (2 and 4 edge devices)

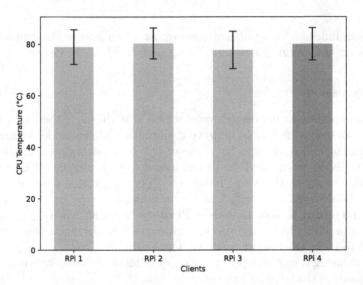

Fig. 10. CPU Temperature (°C) of Raspberry Pi devices

5   Conclusion

Based on the findings and results presented in this study, it can be concluded that FL is a promising technique for training ML models using decentralized data sources. The results showed that increasing the number of devices participating in the training process led to higher accuracy, especially after a certain number of epochs. However, this came at the cost of increased CPU and RAM usage, which should be considered when designing and implementing FL systems.

One of the major recommendations based on the findings is to carefully choose the number of devices and epochs for training. Finding the right balance between accuracy and how much resources are used is crucial, as training for too long or with too many devices can lead to diminishing returns and increased resource consumption. Additionally, it is recommended to monitor resource usage during training and optimize the system accordingly, for example by using more powerful devices or implementing resource-efficient algorithms.

In conclusion, FL is a powerful technique that can enable training of ML models on decentralized data sources. The findings from this study provide valuable insights into the trade-offs between accuracy and resource usage, and highlight the importance of careful system design and optimization. With further research and development, FL has the potential to revolutionize the field of ML by enabling secure and decentralized training of models on sensitive data. Further, the results obtained suggest that in order to achieve better performance in heterogeneous wireless environments where clients have varying bandwidth and hardware capabilities, it is recommended to develop *FL clients that can dynamically adjust the training parameters*. This will enable a context-aware FL approach, which can better accommodate the diversity of the participating clients and improve the overall efficiency and effectiveness of the training process. Further, the findings may hold potential applicability in various resource-limited edge scenarios. Our goal is to extend these results to embedded IoT devices, where the examined design could help tackle significant constraints in computing and communication resources.

Acknowledgment. This project has received funding from the European Union's Horizon 2020 research and innovation programme under grant agreement No 872614 - SMART4ALL. SMART4ALL is a four-year Innovation Action project funded under call DT-ICT-01-2019: Smart Anything Everywhere - Area 2: Customized low energy computing powering CPS and the IoT. The authors wish to express their gratitude to the SMART4All consortium partners for their valuable comments and feedback, which have contributed to the enhancement of this work.

References

1. Satyanarayanan, M.: The emergence of edge computing. Computer **50**(1), 30–39 (2017)
2. Selimi, M., Lertsinsrubtavee, A., Sathiaseelan, A., Cerdà-Alabern, L., Navarro, L.: Picasso: enabling information-centric multi-tenancy at the edge of community mesh networks. Comput. Netw. **164**, 106897 (2019)
3. Sakr, F., Bellotti, F., Berta, R., De Gloria, A.: Machine learning on mainstream microcontrollers. Sensors **20**(9), 2638 (2020)
4. Arikumar, K.S., et al.: FL-PMI: federated learning-based person movement identification through wearable devices in smart healthcare systems. Sensors **22**(4), 1377 (2022)

5. Farhad, A., Woolley, S., Andras, P.: Federated learning for AI to improve patient care using wearable and IoMT sensors. In: 2021 IEEE 9th International Conference on Healthcare Informatics (ICHI), p. 434 (2021)
6. Yang, Q., Liu, Y., Chen, T., Tong, Y.: Federated machine learning: concept and applications. ACM Trans. Intell. Syst. Technol. **10**(2), 1–19 (2019)
7. Yang, K., Jiang, T., Shi, Y., Ding, Z.: Federated learning via over-the-air computation. IEEE Trans. Wireless Commun. **19**(3), 2022–2035 (2020)
8. Pinyoanuntapong, P., Janakaraj, P., Wang, P., Lee, M., Chen, C.: Fedair: towards multi-hop federated learning over-the-air. In: 2020 IEEE 21st International Workshop on Signal Processing Advances in Wireless Communications (SPAWC), pp. 1–5 (2020)
9. Freitag, F., Vilchez, P., Wei, L., Liu, C.H., Selimi, M.: Performance evaluation of federated learning over wireless mesh networks with low-capacity devices. In: Rocha, Á., Ferrás, C., Méndez Porras, A., Jimenez Delgado, E. (eds.) ICITS 2022, pp. 635–645. Springer, Cham (2022). https://doi.org/10.1007/978-3-030-96293-7_53
10. Women, G., Center, C.M.: Chest X-ray images (pneumonia). https://www.kaggle.com/datasets/paultimothymooney/chest-xray-pneumonia. Accessed 28 Apr 2021
11. Gao, Y., et al.: End-to-end evaluation of federated learning and split learning for internet of things. In: 2020 International Symposium on Reliable Distributed Systems (SRDS), pp. 91–100 (2020)
12. Abreha, H.G., Hayajneh, M., Serhani, M.A.: Federated learning in edge computing: a systematic survey. Sensors **22**(2), 450 (2022)
13. Mathur, A., et al.: On-device federated learning with flower (2021)
14. Cetinkaya, A.E., Akin, M., Sagiroglu, S.: A communication efficient federated learning approach to multi chest diseases classification. In: 2021 6th International Conference on Computer Science and Engineering (UBMK), pp. 429–434 (2021)
15. Hakak, S., Ray, S., Khan, W.Z., Scheme, E.: A framework for edge-assisted healthcare data analytics using federated learning. In: 2020 IEEE International Conference on Big Data (Big Data), pp. 3423–3427 (2020)
16. Malekzadeh, M., Hasircioglu, B., Mital, N., Katarya, K., Ozfatura, M.E., Gunduz, D.: Dopamine: differentially private federated learning on medical data. arXiv abs/2101.11693 (2021)
17. Lu, Y., Huang, X., Dai, Y., Maharjan, S., Zhang, Y.: Blockchain and federated learning for privacy-preserved data sharing in industrial IoT. IEEE Trans. Industr. Inf. **16**(6), 4177–4186 (2020)
18. Kim, H., Park, J., Bennis, M., Kim, S.: On-device federated learning via blockchain and its latency analysis. CoRR abs/1808.03949 (2018)
19. Passerat-Palmbach, J., Farnan, T., Miller, R., Gross, M.S., Flannery, H.L., Gleim, B.: A blockchain-orchestrated federated learning architecture for healthcare consortia. CoRR abs/1910.12603 (2019)
20. Pappas, C., Chatzopoulos, D., Lalis, S., Vavalis, M.: IPLS: a framework for decentralized federated learning (2021)
21. Mills, J., Hu, J., Min, G.: Communication-efficient federated learning for wireless edge intelligence in IoT. IEEE Internet Things J. **7**(7), 5986–5994 (2020)
22. Luo, J., Wu, S.: FedSLD: federated learning with shared label distribution for medical image classification. In: 2022 IEEE 19th International Symposium on Biomedical Imaging (ISBI), pp. 1–5 (2022)
23. Niknam, S., Dhillon, H.S., Reed, J.H.: Federated learning for wireless communications: motivation, opportunities, and challenges. IEEE Commun. Mag. **58**(6), 46–51 (2020)

24. Ibraimi, L., Selimi, M., Freitag, F.: Bepoch: improving federated learning performance in resource-constrained computing devices. In: IEEE Global Communications Conference (GLOBECOM) (2021)
25. Kermany, D.S., et al.: Identifying medical diagnoses and treatable diseases by image-based deep learning. Cell **172**(5), 1122–1131.e9 (2018)

Collaborative Working

Enhance Broadcasting Throughput by Associating Network Coding with UAVs Relays Deployment in Emergency Communications

Chaonong Xu[✉] and Yujie Jiang

Beijing Key Lab of Petroleum Data Mining, China University of Petroleum-Beijing,
Beijing, China
chaonongxu@cup.edu.cn, 2021211271@student.cup.edu.cn

Abstract. During emergency scenarios, network access may be disrupted due to damaged Base Stations (BSs), and deploying Unmanned Aerial Vehicles (UAVs) as communication relays is common in rescue scenarios due to their convenience in ensuring network access. In such situations, the dissemination of rescue-related information messages is crucial, and broadcast messages are often prioritized. Thus, ensuring high broadcast throughput while guaranteeing accessibility for all victims and rescue teams is a significant challenge. Moreover, the broadcast burden is further aggravated by multiple rescue teams broadcasting messages simultaneously. To address this issue, Network Coding Based Cooperative (NCBC) broadcast scheme is a promising approach for enhancing broadcast throughput in emergency scenarios. By employing the NCBC broadcast scheme, we show that the broadcast throughput can be significantly improved. We propose a heuristic algorithm for generating optimal deployment of UAVs using network coding strategy and evaluate the broadcast throughput quantitatively. Simulation results show that our approach can ensure user accessibility and yield at least 26.69% throughput improvement compared to the traditional copy-and-forward relay protocol in a typical scenario.

Keywords: UAV deployment · Relay · Network coding based cooperation · Throughput · Broadcast

1 Introduction

After earthquakes, tsunamis, volcanoes, or other natural disasters, once Base Stations (BSs) in some disaster-stricken areas are damaged, those areas will be disconnected from the communication networks, as in Fig. 1. Since rescue and recovery rely heavily on communication systems nowadays, establishing a temporary communication network to support emergency communications is

Supported by National Key R&D Program of China (2022YFB4501600).

necessary. Due to their excellent mobility [17], Unmanned Aerial Vehicles (UAVs) acting as relays is a good way to provide network connections. Furthermore, to improve rescue efficiency, all kinds of information, such as disaster and aftershock information, rescue information, etc., have to be broadcast to victims and rescue teams, which brings a massive burden of broadcast communications. So, how to reasonably deploy UAVs to improve broadcast throughput with guaranteed access to all users is naturally a significant problem.

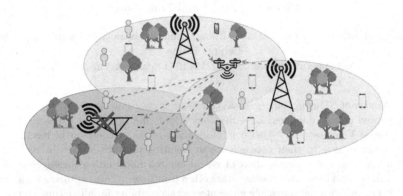

Fig. 1. UAV-assisted emergency network.

It is well-known that network coding can significantly enhance broadcast throughput. Ahlswede et al. [1] demonstrate how network coding improves throughput in wired network. In the wireless scenario illustrated in Fig. 2(a), two source nodes, S_1 and S_2, broadcast information to two destination nodes D_1 and D_2 through relay node R. Due to the long distance from S_1 to D_2, as well as S_2 to D_1, the relay node R needs to receive a from S_1 and b from S_2, and then broadcast them to D_1 and D_2. Traditional copy-and-forward relay requires four transmissions to accomplish this task. However, as shown in Fig. 2(b), the relay node R broadcasts network coding combined packet $a \oplus b$. Thus, the broadcast task can be accomplished with only three transmissions, resulting in a 25% reduction in transmissions compared to traditional copy-and-forward relay.

In emergency scenarios, the damaged BSs can result in communication disruptions that impede rescue and recovery efforts. To provide accessibility to every victim, UAVs can serve as relay nodes facilitating communication between the BSs and users, constituting an economical and effective solution. Additionally, when multiple rescue teams need to broadcast messages to all users, the primary transmissions become multiple-source broadcast transmissions, creating an opportunity to leverage the Network Coding Based Cooperative (NCBC) broadcast scheme for enhancing broadcast throughput. Consequently, a critical challenge lies in deploying UAV networks to maximize broadcast throughput using network coding, while simultaneously meeting access requirements.

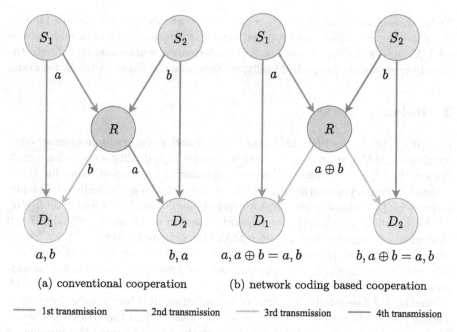

Fig. 2. Comparison of conventional cooperation and network coding based cooperation in broadcast.

To tackle this challenge, we present a three-stage heuristic algorithm. Firstly, we utilize a Depth-First Search (DFS) algorithm to identify potential areas for UAV deployment, ensuring uninterrupted user access to BSs. Subsequently, we introduce a Particle Swarm Optimization (PSO) algorithm to determine the optimal location for a UAV within each intersecting candidate area, maximizing the broadcast throughput. Lastly, we select the most favorable locations in the final step, aiming to achieve the highest cumulative broadcast throughput while maintaining user access to BSs. The primary contributions of our research are summarized as follows.

1. We point out the feature of multiple source broadcast transmissions in UAV-assisted emergency communications and introduce NCBC to deal with it effectively.
2. We present a quantitative formula of broadcast throughput for NCBC broadcast scheme, which we believe will serve as a solid theoretical foundation for future research in this area.
3. We propose a three-stage heuristic algorithm that provides a UAV deployment strategy that maximizes broadcast throughput while meeting users' access to BSs. We believe it can be utilized in practical emergency communication scenarios.

The structure of this paper is as follows. Section 2 provides a comprehensive review of related works. In Sect. 3, we introduce the network model and problem formulation. Section 4 presents an expression for the throughput for

NCBC broadcast scheme, which serves as the theoretical foundation for this study. Section 5 outlines our proposed algorithm for deploying optimal locations for UAV relays. In Sect. 6, we conduct performance evaluations to validate the effectiveness of our approach. Finally, we conclude the paper in the last section.

2   Related Works

Regarding the demand for the recovery of network coverage in emergency communication, UAVs are an efficient way to provide high-quality services for mobile devices. Erdelj and Natalizio [5] discuss applications and open issues for UAV-assisted emergency networks where UAV localization is one. To address this issue, Bupe et al. [2] propose a platform for quickly deploying UAVs and establishing a UAV backbone communication network based on an algorithm utilizing 7-cell clusters in a hexagonal pattern using MAVLink (Micro Air Vehicle Link). Meanwhile, Do-Duy et al. [4] propose a K-means clustering algorithm to deploy UAVs as a relay and an algorithm to optimize resource allocation in establishing a temporary emergency network. Liu et al. [11] propose a distributed SIC-free NOMA scheme for UAV-assisted emergency communication in heterogeneous Internet of Things (IoT), which yields a faster sum rate of users than the OFDMA scheme. The work of Tran et al. [15] proposes a method to maximize the number of served IoT devices by jointly optimizing bandwidth, power allocation, and the UAV trajectory while keeping the device's transmission requirement and the limited storage capacity of UAVs satisfied. Additionally, Feng et al. [7] consider power transfer by UAVs for IoT devices in emergency communications and analyze the problem of UAV trajectory and resource scheduling in three different scenarios.

To maximize the throughput of a UAV-based network in a territory affected by a disaster, Chiaraviglio et al. [3] propose an optimization framework called Maximum Throughput with Unmanned Aerial Vehicles (MT-UAV) to schedule the UAVs to maximize throughput while ensuring an acceptable UAV battery level. Similarly, Xu et al. [16] propose a UAVs deployment algorithm to maximize the sum of the data rates of users served by the UAVs subject to UAV service capacity and k UAVs connected. Our paper considers a similar problem aiming to maximize broadcast throughput and solve it using network coding technique.

Since the lack of reliability in broadcast transmissions, the network coding is naturally suitable for wireless networks. Therefore, many researchers have devoted themselves to applying network coding to wireless networks more than 20 years after the time Ahlswede et al. [1] proposed it. In 2007, Fragouli et al. [8] present the opportunities and challenges of wireless network coding research, highlighting its significant improvements in wireless network throughput, reliability, fairness, and management. Also, Ghaderi et al. [9] quantifies the reliability gain of network coding for reliable multicasting in a wireless network.

The combination of UAV and network coding is now on the rise [14] due to the excellent mobility characteristic of UAVs and the performance gained by network coding. We believe this research topic will have great potential for practical applications.

3   Network Models and Problem Formulation

3.1   Network Models

In emergency scenarios, users have no strong mobility in general. Thus, the location of UAVs is considered to be fixed in this paper. As shown in Fig. 1, there are n BSs $S_1, S_2, \ldots, S_n$ and m users $D_1, D_2, \ldots, D_m$ in the disaster area. A UAV relay-assisted emergency network consisting of q UAVs $R_1, R_2, \ldots, R_q$ is build to set up emergency network communications. The geographical locations of all users and BSs are known in advance and represented by a location function $\psi()$.

As to the communication model, all devices work in half-duplex mode. Besides, all channels are assumed to be mutually independent Rayleigh fading channels. The path loss from source S to destination D is modeled by

$$PL = 10\alpha \log_{10} \left(\frac{\|\psi(S) - \psi(D)\|}{d_0} \right) + PL_0 \tag{1}$$

where α is the path loss exponent whose value usually is in the range of 2 to 4, PL_0 is the reference path loss at a reference distance d_0, and $\|\psi(S) - \psi(D)\|$ is the Euclidean distance from S to D.

To compute outage probability, we think that only when the transmission rate is greater than γ the receiver receives one packet correctly. In that case, the outage probability of transmission [18] is

$$p = 1 - \exp \left(-\frac{2^{2\gamma} - 1}{\sigma^2} \times \frac{N_0}{P} \right) \tag{2}$$

where P is the transmit power, N_0 is background background noise, and $\sigma^2 = 10^{-0.1 \times PL}$.

Definition 1. *Communication range of a BS(UAV) is the maximal distance from a user to the BS(UAV). In other words, if the distance exceeds the communication range, the user cannot access the BS(UAV).*

Based on Definition 1, we get the communication range

$$d = d_0 \times 10^{\frac{-PL_0}{10\alpha}} \times \left(\frac{P}{N_0(2^{2\gamma} - 1)} \right)^{\frac{1}{\alpha}} \tag{3}$$

3.2   Problem Formulation

In emergency communication, users need to access specific BSs to receive broadcast messages. We define a BS-user pair set $\mathbb{V}$ to represent the access requirements, where each pair consists of a user located beyond the communication range of a corresponding BS. The problem can be formulated as follows.

$$\max_{\psi(R_1),\cdots,\psi(R_q)} \sum_{j=1}^{q} \Omega(\psi(R_j))$$

$$\text{s.t.} \quad \|\psi(S_i) - \psi(R_j)\| \leq d_S \tag{4}$$

$$\|\psi(R_j) - \psi(D_k)\| \leq d_R$$

$$\forall(S_i, D_k) \in \mathbb{V}, \exists R_j \in R_1, R_2, \cdots, R_q$$

where $\Omega(\psi(R_j))$ is the broadcast throughput of UAV R_j and expressed as a mathematical formula in Sect. 4. In this paper, we make the assumption that all BSs possess an equivalent communication range denoted as d_S, and similarly, all UAVs have an identical communication range denoted as d_R, which is derived from Formula (3). The objective of the problem is to maximize the cumulative broadcast throughput by strategically deploying UAVs while satisfying the access requirements.

4   Broadcast Throughput of Network Coding Based Cooperative Broadcast Scheme

4.1   Broadcast Protocol in Cooperative Broadcast

To present an expression for NCBC broadcast scheme, we take some assumptions and the throughput definition from [6].

Assumption 1. *Time is slotted.*

Assumption 2. *Average channel gain of each channel is only known to the receiver of the corresponding channel.*

Definition 2. *Throughput is defined as the average number of packets received correctly by all destinations per time slot in a saturated system.*

Based on Assumption 1, the time-division channel allocations for conventional cooperation and network coding based cooperation in the case shown in Fig. 2 is illustrated in Fig. 3.

The broadcast throughput is dependent on the chosen broadcast protocol. In paper [6], there are three protocols for single-source broadcast communications including Direct Broadcast (Protocol A), Relay-assisted Broadcast (Protocol B), and Relaying Broadcast with Network Coding (Protocol C). Our scenario is most closely related to Protocol C, and we extend it to multiple sources and destinations broadcast relay communications, which we refer to as Protocol D. The key differences between these protocols are:

1. Protocol D is designed for multiple sources, while Protocol C is intended for a single source.
2. Only the relay node can execute network coding in Protocol D, whereas both the source and relay nodes have network coding capabilities in Protocol C.

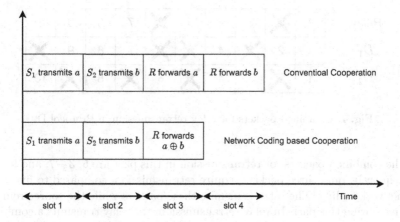

Fig. 3. Time-division channel allocations for conventional cooperation and network coding based cooperation in broadcast.

Next, we present a comprehensive explanation of how Protocol D achieves broadcast transmission through the utilization of relaying with network coding, which follows the same methodology as Protocol C [6]. Similar to Protocol C, Protocol D aims to enhance spectral efficiency by operating in iterations of X packets. Within each iteration, X new packets are successively transmitted by n sources during X transmission slots. It is important to note that these X packets originate from n sources, and we assume that each source has an equal probability of sending a packet over an extended period. After X transmission slots, the retransmission process commences.

During the packet retransmission phase, both n sources and the relay maintain a list of lost packets from their intended destinations, which is obtained through feedback from m destinations. The relay also provides feedback to n sources. To facilitate a clearer understanding of the retransmission procedure, we divide it into two distinct parts: relay retransmission and source retransmission. In relay retransmission, the relay transmits lost packets the lost packets that it has successfully received. Moreover, through XORing operations, the relay combines lost packets intended for different destinations, creating new packets for retransmission. This approach effectively reduces the number of packets requiring retransmission. Subsequently, any residual lost packets that were not successfully received by the relay undergo source retransmission, wherein they are retransmitted by the n sources.

In the relay retransmission, the protocol maximizes relay utilization by transmitting lost packets that the relay has successfully received. To employ network coding, the relay initially combines lost packets from different destinations that have been received successfully at the relay. For instance, consider Fig. 4, which depicts a 2-user broadcast network and the relay's feedback list (lost packets are indicated by a cross). The lost packets for destinations D_1 and D_2 are $(3, 5, 6, 10)$ and $(2, 5, 7, 9)$ respectively. Since the relay did not receive the 2nd and 6th pack-

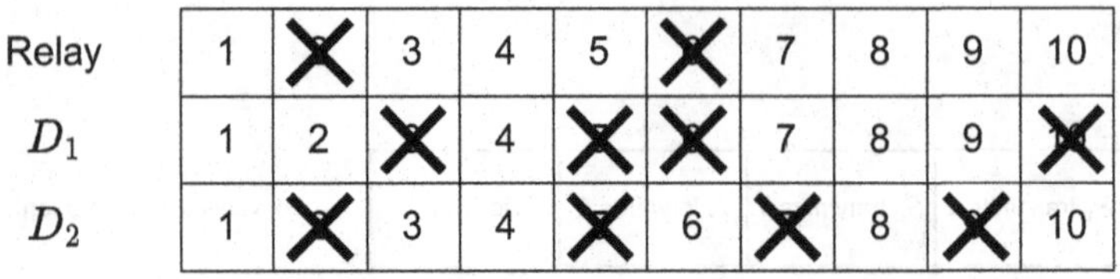

Relay	1	✗	3	4	5	✗	7	8	9	10
D_1	1	2	✗	4	✗	✗	7	8	9	✗
D_2	1	✗	3	4	✗	6	✗	8	✗	10

Fig. 4. Combined packets for relay retransmission in Protocol D.

ets, the combined packets for retransmission in this part are 5, $3 \oplus 7$, and $9 \oplus 10$. Consequently, only three packets require retransmission, compared to five without network coding. The relay transmits these packets while the source remains inactive during this part. In relay retransmission, the relay transmits a combined packet until it is successfully received by each intended destination. Subsequently, the relay transmits another combined packet or lost packet. Each destination can recover their lost packets from the combined packet since the destination already possesses knowledge of another packet included in the combined packet. Once this part is completed, the relay notifies n sources of the starting moment for source retransmission, if necessary.

In the source retransmission, the n sources successively retransmit the remaining lost packets to both the relay and the destinations. To illustrate this process, let us refer back to Fig. 4 as an example. The relay lost packets 2 and 6, D_1 only lost packet 6 and D_2 only lost packet 2. The sources transmit packets 2 and 6 once to both the relay and the destinations with lost packets record. Following this transmission, the relay retransmission recommences. The relay retransmission and source retransmission are performed alternately until X packets have been successfully transmitted.

From the above description, the implementation of this protocol can be divided into three steps for X-packet-delivery. Here, we just given a brief explanation of this protocol. A detailed flow chart to illustrate in Fig. 5.

Step 1 : n sources transmit X packets in X successive transmission time slots. In this step, by analyzing immediate feedback from m destinations, both the sources and the relay will construct a packet-loss table for the destinations. The table at the sources also includes the indices of the lost packets at the relay through feedback from the relay.

Step 2 : The relay node analyzes its table of received packets, assessing both the lost packets from the destinations and the packets it has successfully received. The relay combines the lost packets using the encoding technique as described above and successively transmits the combined packets. During this process, the relay repeatedly transmits a single combined packet until all intended destinations have successfully received it. At the end of Step 2, the relay node provides information to the source nodes regarding the successfully transmitted packets.

Step 3 : n sources check for residual packets that have not been successfully transmitted. These packets are retransmitted successively at once. Similar to Step

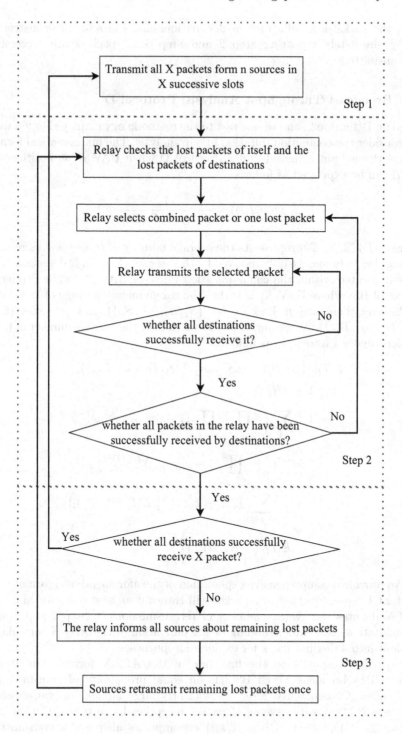

Fig. 5. Flowchart of Protocol D.

1, the packet-loss tables for m destinations and the relay are constructed. By alternately repeating Step 2 and Step 3, X packets are successfully transmitted.

4.2   Broadcast Throughput Analysis: Protocol D

Based on Definition 2, and in contrast to the methodology employed in [6], we do not consider the contention duration in our analysis. The mathematical formula for the throughput achieved under Protocol D when UAV R_j is positioned at $\psi(R_j)$ can be expressed as follows.

$$\Omega(\psi(R_j)) = \frac{1}{E[T_D\,(\mathbb{S}, R_j, \mathbb{D})]} \tag{5}$$

where $E[T_D\,(\mathbb{S}, R_j, \mathbb{D})]$ represents the average number of transmissions required for a packet to be successfully received by the user set $\mathbb{D}$. Here, $\mathbb{D}$ denotes a group of users located within the communication range of UAV R_j, while $\mathbb{S}$ refers to the set of BSs where UAV R_j is within the communication range of those BSs.

Assume there are n BSs ($\mathbb{S} = \{S_1, S_2, \cdots, S_n\}$) and m users ($\mathbb{D} = \{D_1, D_2, \cdots, D_m\}$). According to [6,13], we can get the average number of transmissions under Protocol D as follows.

$$\begin{aligned}
E[T_D\,(&\{S_1, S_2, \cdots, S_n\}, R_j, \{D_1, D_2, \cdots, D_m\})] \\
&= 1 + ARTN \\
&= 1 + \sum_{\Delta} \Bigg\{ \prod_{i \in [1,n]} \prod_{k \in [1,m]} (1 - p_{(S_i, D_k)})^{\delta_{ik}} p_{(S_i, D_k)}^{(1-\delta_{ik})} \\
&\quad \times \Bigg[\sum_{B} \Big(\prod_{x \in [1,n]} (1 - p_{(S_x, R_j)})^{\beta_x} p_{(S_x, R_j)}^{(1-\beta_x)} \\
&\quad \times \Big(\big(\sum_{z \in [1,|\mathbb{P}|]} (\mathbb{P}[z] - \mathbb{P}[z-1]) E[T_A(R_j, \mathbb{D}_z)] \big) \\
&\quad + E[T_D\,(\mathcal{S}, R_j, \mathcal{D})]\big) \Big) \Bigg] \Bigg\}
\end{aligned} \tag{6}$$

We provide a comprehensive explanation of the aforementioned formula. The constant 1 represents that any packet will transmit at least one time in Step 1. $ARTN$ denotes the average number of retransmissions in Step 2 and Step 3. To facilitate a clear understanding of the derivation of the $ARTN$ formula, we divide it into 4 distinct parts for explanation purposes.

Part 1 corresponds to the first line of the $ARTN$ formula. In Step 1, when n BSs broadcast, each BS has an equal probability of transmitting a new packet. Consequently, after a sufficiently large number of transmissions, there are $2^{n \times m}$ possible events of packet reception by m users. The set $\Delta = \{\delta_{ik} | \delta_{ik} \in (0,1), i \in [1,n], k \in [1,m]\}$ encompasses all possible transmitting-receiving events, where each δ_{ik} serves as an indicator function indicating whether D_k has successfully received the packet from S_i in Step 1. Specifically, $\delta_{ik} = 1$ denotes successful reception, while $\delta_{ik} = 0$ implies unsuccessful reception. The outage probability of the transmission from BS S_i to user D_k, denoted as $p_{(S_i,D_k)}$, can be computed using Formula (2). Notably, the expression $\prod_{i\in[1,n]} \prod_{k\in[1,m]} (1 - p_{(S_i,D_k)})^{\delta_{ik}} p_{(S_i,D_k)}^{(1-\delta_{ik})}$ represents the probability of a packet reception event by m users after Step 1.

Part 2 corresponds to the second line of the $ARTN$ formula. Similarly, there are 2^n possible packet reception events for UAV R_j in Step 1. The set $B = \{\beta_x | \beta_x \in (0,1), x \in [1,n]\}$ encompasses all possible transmitting-receiving events, where each β_x serves as an indicator function indicating whether R_j has successfully received the packet from S_x in Step 1. Specifically, $\beta_x = 1$ denotes successful reception, while $\beta_x = 0$ implies unsuccessful reception. The outage probability of the transmission from BS S_x to UAV R_j, denoted as $p_{(S_x,R_j)}$, can be computed using Formula (2). Notably, the expression $\prod_{x\in[1,n]} (1 - p_{(S_x,R_j)})^{\beta_x} p_{(S_x,R_j)}^{(1-\beta_x)}$ represents the probability of a packet reception event by UAV R_j after Step 1.

Part 3 corresponds to the third line of the $ARTN$ formula. It represents the average number of transmissions in Step 2. After Step 1, UAV R_j has received packets from $\{S_i | \beta_i = 1, \forall i \in [1,n]\}$, user D_k has not received packets from $\{S_i | \delta_{ik} = 0, \forall i \in [1,n]\}$. Therefore, the UAV needs to retransmit those lost packets. In Step 2, UAV R_j transmits a combination of packets or previously lost packets until all the lost packets that have been successfully received by the UAV are also successfully received by all the users. The proof of the average number of transmissions in Step 2 resembles proof of Theorem 2 in [13].

Proof. After a sufficiently large number of transmissions N from $\{S_1, S_2, \cdots, S_n\}$, where each BS has an equal probability of transmitting a new packet, the numbers of lost packets at users $\{D_1, D_2, \cdots, D_m\}$ are $Np_{(S_1,D_1)}, \cdots, Np_{(S_n,D_1)}$, $Np_{(S_1,D_2)}, \cdots, Np_{(S_n,D_2)}, \cdots, Np_{(S_1,D_m)}, \cdots, Np_{(S_n,D_m)}$, respectively (note that there are $n \times m$ BS-user paths). These outage probabilities can be sorted in ascending order, resulting in the set $\mathbb{P} = \{p_{(S_{x1},D_{y1})}, p_{(S_{x2},D_{y2})}, \cdots, p_{(S_{xn},D_{ym})}\}$. We can conceptually count the number of combinations for XORing the lost packets and transmit them in different rounds. In the first round, there are $N\mathbb{P}[1] = Np_{(S_{x1},D_{y1})}$ lost packets of S_{x1} to D_{y1} path that can be combined with the lost packets from other paths, except S_{x1} to D_{y1}. After these combinations, the numbers of remaining lost packets for each path are $0, N(\mathbb{P}[2]-\mathbb{P}[1]), N(\mathbb{P}[3]-\mathbb{P}[1]), \cdots, N(\mathbb{P}[|\mathbb{P}|] - \mathbb{P}[1])$ where $|\mathbb{P}|$ denotes the size of the set $\mathbb{P}$. In the subsequent rounds, the remaining $N(\mathbb{P}[2] - \mathbb{P}[1]) = N(p_{(S_{x2},D_{y2})} - p_{(S_{x1},D_{y1})})$ lost packets from S_{x2} to D_{y2} path are combined with the remaining lost packets from other paths, except S_{x1} to D_{y1} and S_{x2} to D_{y2}. Thus, the remaining lost packets for all paths are now $0, 0, N(\mathbb{P}[3] - \mathbb{P}[2]), \cdots, N(\mathbb{P}[|\mathbb{P}|] - \mathbb{P}[2])$. This process continues until there are no more lost packets. Therefore, the average number of transmissions that are required to successfully deliver all N packets to all the receivers is equal to

$$N + N\mathbb{P}[1]\phi_1 + N(\mathbb{P}[2] - \mathbb{P}[1])\phi_2 + N(\mathbb{P}[3] - \mathbb{P}[2])\phi_3$$
$$+ \cdots + N(\mathbb{P}[|\mathbb{P}|] - \mathbb{P}[|\mathbb{P}| - 1])\phi_{|\mathbb{P}|} \quad (7)$$

where ϕ_z denotes the average number of transmissions that are required to successfully transmit a combined packet in round z.

It is easy to know the average number of transmissions under Protocol A which is same as the Formula (7) in [6].

$$\phi_z = E[T_A(R_j, \mathbb{D}_z)] = \sum_\Delta \frac{(-1)^{1+\sum_{D_k \in \mathbb{D}_z} \delta_k}}{1 - \prod_{D_k \in \mathbb{D}_z} p^{\delta_k}_{(R_j, D_k)}} \quad (8)$$

where $\mathbb{D}_z = \{D_k | (\delta_{ik} = 0) \& (\beta_i = 1)\}$ represents the users where UAV R_j has successfully received a packet from S_i, but the corresponding user D_k has not received the same packet from S_i.

Part 4 corresponds to the fourth line of the $ARTN$ formula, which addresses the issue of lost packets requiring retransmission from the BSs. The retransmission method of BSs remains the same as in Step 1 where each lost packet is transmitted once. Following the source retransmission, UAV R_j will transmit lost packets according to Step 2. Hence, $E[T_D(\mathcal{S}, R_j, \mathcal{D})]$ represents a recursive formula. Here, $\mathcal{S} = \{S_i | \forall i \in [1, n], \exists k \in [1, m], (\delta_{ik} = 0) \& (\beta_i = 0)\}$ denotes a set of BSs for which there exists at least one user that has not successfully received a packet from this set after Step 2. Similarly, $\mathcal{D} = \{D_k | \forall k \in [1, m], \exists i \in [1, n], (\delta_{ik} = 0) \& (\beta_i = 0)\}$ represents a set of users that have not received a packet from at least one BS after Step 2.

5   Problem Solving

Our proposed algorithm is a three-stage heuristic approach to satisfy all access requirements. In the first stage, we determine the candidate areas for UAV deployment based on the BS-user pair set $\mathbb{V}$. By computing the intersection of these candidate areas, we obtain a set of basic cells, each of which can accommodate a UAV to satisfy a fixed number of BS-user pair access requirements. In the second stage, we identify the optimal location for the UAV by maximizing the broadcast throughput in each basic cell. The third stage is designed to ensure access requirements with a given number of UAVs, and the optimal deployment positions for the UAVs are selected from the second stage results to achieve the highest cumulative broadcast throughput.

5.1   Candidate Areas and Basic Cells

To ensure BS-user connection for all BS-user pairs in set $\mathbb{V}$, a UAV must be deployed in the corresponding candidate area of a BS-user pair. As shown in Fig. 6(a), the yellow area is the candidate area of pair (S_i, D_k).

We can identify the corresponding candidate area for each BS-user pair in the set $\mathbb{V}$. By computing the intersection of all candidate areas, we obtain a set

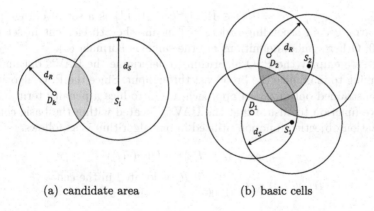

(a) candidate area   (b) basic cells

Fig. 6. Candidate area and Basic cells for BS-user pairs (Color figure online)

of basic cells, as illustrated in Fig. 6(b). This figure shows that three basic cells with different colors are obtained by intersecting the candidate areas of (S_1, D_2) and (S_2, D_1).

To identify all basic cells, we employ a Depth-First Search (DFS) algorithm with pruning, which is similar to generating all subsets of the set $\mathbb{V}$. For instance, given a pair list $(S_1, D_2), (S_2, D_1)$, we check if the candidate areas of all pairs in it intersect. If they do, we obtain one basic cell and add a new pair from $\mathbb{V}$ to the pair list. If they don't intersect, we backtrack to the pair list (S_1, D_2) and add a new pair from $\mathbb{V}$ to the pair list. Then we check if the candidate area of all pairs in the updated pair list intersect. Because intersection of candidate areas must be the intersection of multiple 3D spheres, we utilize the method described in reference [12] to determine if m 3D spheres intersect.

5.2 Finding the Optimal Location for UAV in Basic Cell

For each basic cell, we aim to find the optimal deployment location for the UAV R_j to maximize the broadcast throughput. However, since the Formula (6) is recursive and hard to use, we employ its lower bound instead. Meanwhile, we obtain the upper bound of the throughput by taking the inverse of this lower bound. By making the assumption that UAV R_j can successfully receive all packets transmitted by all BSs in Step 1, we can establish a lower bound for the average number of transmissions as follows.

$$E[T_D(\{S_1, S_2, \cdots, S_n\}, R_j, \{D_1, D_2, \cdots, D_m\})]^*$$

$$= 1 + \sum_{\Delta} \prod_{i \in [1,n]} \prod_{k \in [1,m]} \left\{ (1 - p_{(S_i, D_k)})^{\delta_{ik}} p_{(S_i, D_k)}^{(1 - \delta_{ik})} \right.$$

$$\left. \times \sum_{z \in [1, |\mathbb{P}|]} (\mathbb{P}[z] - \mathbb{P}[z - 1]) E[T_A(R_j, \mathbb{D}_z)] \right\} \tag{9}$$

where $\mathbb{P} = \{p_{(S_i,D_k)}|\delta_{ik} = 0, \forall i \in [1,n], \forall k \in [1,m]\}$ is a set of outage probabilities arranged in ascending order. $\mathbb{P}[z]$ means the zth element in set $\mathbb{P}$ and $\mathbb{P}[0] = 0$. Other symbol definitions are the same as Formula (6).

Next, we employ the PSO algorithm to determine the UAV's optimal location, aiming to maximize the broadcast throughput. Since the PSO algorithm is an unconstrained optimization approach, we introduce a penalty term into the objective function to ensure that the UAV is located within the basic cell. The optimization objective function utilized in our algorithm is as follows.

$$\max \quad \Omega(\psi(R_j)) + H(\psi(R_j))$$
$$H(\psi(R_j)) = \begin{cases} 0 & \text{if } R_j \text{ is located in the cell} \\ -1000 & \text{otherwise} \end{cases} \tag{10}$$

5.3   Choose Locations for UAVs

We need to choose UAV locations with the given number q from them to keep users accessible by BSs while maximizing cumulative broadcast throughput. This problem can be formulated as a zero-one linear optimization problem as follows.

$$\max_{\delta_1,\delta_2,\cdots,\delta_{|\mathbb{C}|}} \sum_{j\in[1,|\mathbb{C}|]} \delta_j \tilde{\Omega}(\psi(R_j))$$
$$\text{s.t.} \quad \sum_{j\in[1,|\mathbb{C}|]} \delta_j = q \tag{11}$$
$$\sum_{j\in[1,|\mathbb{C}|]} \delta_j v_{jk} = 1, \forall k \in [1,|\mathbb{V}|]$$

where $\mathbb{C}$ is basic cell set obtained by the algorithm in Sect. 5.1, $\tilde{\Omega}(\psi(R_j))$ is the maximal broadcast throughput when a UAV is deployed at the optimal location of the jth basic cell, which is the output of the algorithm in Sect. 5.2. $v_{jk} = 1$ means the jth basic cell is inside candidate area of the kth BS-user pair, otherwise $v_{jk} = 0$. $\delta_j = 1$ means we choose the location in the jth basic cell to deploy UAV, otherwise $\delta_j = 0$.

We utilize the Gurobi Optimizer [10] to solve the zero-one linear optimization problem.

6   Performance Evaluation

In this section, we evaluate the performance of deploying UAVs using Protocol D. We consider a downlink relay wireless network. The reference distance in the path loss formula is 0.1 km. The model of distance-dependent path loss is $86.429 + 36\log_{10}\frac{d}{0.1}$, where d is the distance between the transmitter and receiver in kilometers. Related simulation parameters are listed in Table 1.

In the first experiment, we focus on the throughput performance improvement by network coding technique. Specifically, we compare the performance of

Table 1. Simulation parameters setting

Parameter	Value	Meaning
γ	1 bit/s	minimum transmission rate
P_S	$500\,mW$	transmission power of BS
P_R	$300\,mW$	transmission power of UAV
N_0	$-65\,dBm$	background noise power
α	3.6	path loss exponent
z_S	$0.05\,km$	height of BS

Protocol D with extended Protocol B in [6]. For a fair comparison, we extend Protocol B into n-source m-destination broadcast transmissions by simply averaging the throughput of n BSs under Protocol B.

$$
E[T_B (\{S_1, S_2, \cdots, S_n\}, R_j, \{D_1, D_2, \cdots, D_m\})]
$$
$$
= \frac{1}{n} \sum_{i=1}^{n} E[T_B (S_i, R_j, \{D_1, D_2, \cdots, D_m\})]
\tag{12}
$$

where $E[T_B(S_i, R_j, \{D_1, D_2, \cdots, D_m\})]$ is the average number of transmissions under Protocol B.

The average number of transmissions under Protocol B is

$$
E[T_B (S_i, R_j, \{D_1, D_2, \cdots, D_m\})]
$$
$$
= 1 + \sum_{\Delta} \Bigg\{ \prod_{k \in [1,m]} (1 - p_{(S_i, D_k)})^{\delta_{ik}} p_{(S_i, D_k)}^{(1-\delta_{ik})}
$$
$$
\times \Big[(1 - p_{(S_i, R_j)}) \times E[T_A (R_j, \mathbb{D})]
$$
$$
+ p_{(S_i, R_j)} \times E[T_B (S_i, R_j, \mathbb{D})] \Big] \Bigg\}
\tag{13}
$$

Proof. The BS S_i broadcast packet, m users have 2^m possible packet reception events. Each δ_{ik} is an indication function denoting whether D_k has successfully received the packet from S_i or not. $\delta_{ik} = 1$ indicates that D_k has successfully received the packet from S_i. $\mathbb{D} = \{D_k | \delta_{ik} = 0, \forall k \in [1, m]\}$ represents a set of users that have not received the packet from BS S_i. $E[T_B (S_i, R_j, \mathbb{D})]$ is a recursive component that represents the number of retransmissions required in the next iteration of Protocol B.

For a fair comparison, we make the same assumption as Formula (9), assuming that the UAV can successfully receive all packets transmitted by all BSs. Then we get its lower bounds of the average number of transmissions under Protocol B.

$$E[T_B(\{S_1, S_2, \cdots, S_n\}, R_j, \{D_1, D_2, \cdots, D_m\})]^*$$

$$= 1 + \frac{1}{n} \sum_{i \in [1,n]} \left\{ \sum_{\Delta} \prod_{k \in [1,m]} \left[(1 - p_{(S_i, D_k)})^{\delta_{ik}} p_{(S_i, D_k)}^{(1-\delta_{ik})} \right. \right.$$

$$\left. \left. \times E[T_A(R_j, \mathbb{D})] \right] \right\} \tag{14}$$

We first consider the broadcast throughput in a basic cell, where there are one UAV, one or two BSs, and at most 20 users, and they are randomly deployed in the basic cell. 100 experiments are conducted for each parameter setting, and their average throughputs are illustrated in Fig. 7. It is obvious that the throughput of a UAV is higher using protocol D than protocol B, and it increases by at least 26.69% relative to the traditional copy-and-forward relay protocol. This improvement can be attributed to the fact that protocol D can combine two lost packets into one retransmitted packet using network coding technique. Additionally, the broadcast throughput exhibits a negative correlation with the number of users, as the probability of all users receiving packets correctly depends on the individual probability of each user receiving packets accurately. With the increase in the number of users, the probability of successful reception decreases, leading to an increase in transmission times and a decrease in broadcast throughput.

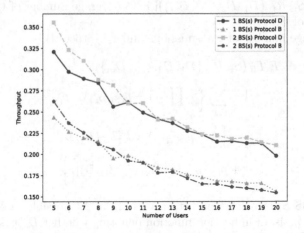

Fig. 7. Throughput performance improvement by network coding.

The second experiment focuses on the UAV deploying problem in a large area instead of a basic cell. 30 users and 3 BSs are randomly distributed within a square whose area is 1 km^2, as shown in Fig. 8(a), where users are represented by dots and BSs by triangles. There are 8 BS-user pairs, including (S_0, D_0), (S_0, D_1), (S_0, D_2), (S_1, D_3), (S_1, D_4), (S_2, D_5), (S_2, D_6) and (S_2, D_7), which can be verified easily in Fig. 8(a) since the communication ranges of the 3 BSs are intentionally labelled by dashed line circles. The users and their corresponding BS in the pair set are marked with the same color. We use 3 UAVs R_1, R_2, R_3 as

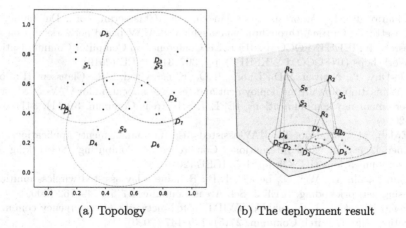

(a) Topology   (b) The deployment result

Fig. 8. Topology and Result of second experiment. (The dashed line represents the communication range of the BS, while the dotted line denotes the connection between the BS and the user established through an UAV.)

relays. Figure 8(b) illustrated the deployment of UAVs. Obviously, the deployment of the 3 UAVs makes the 8 users accessible by its corresponding BS which represented by dotted line with different colors in Fig. 8(b).

7   Conclusion

This paper focused on deploying UAVs to enhance information broadcasting using network coding technique. Initially, we considered a prototype topology consisting of two BSs, two users, and one UAV and presented an expression for the throughput of NCBC broadcast scheme. Based on this expression, we design a heuristic algorithm to generate optimal UAV deployment, achieving maximal broadcast throughput while ensuring access requirements within a given number of UAVs. Our experimental results demonstrate that network coding technique can significantly improve broadcast throughput. It increases the broadcast throughput by at least 26.69% relative to the traditional copy-and-forward relay protocol. We anticipate this scheme will gain widespread usage, particularly as the need for enhanced throughput in emergency communication scenarios expands.

References

1. Ahlswede, R., Cai, N., Li, S.Y., Yeung, R.W.: Network information flow. IEEE Trans. Inf. Theory **46**(4), 1204–1216 (2000)
2. Bupe, P., Haddad, R., Rios-Gutierrez, F.: Relief and emergency communication network based on an autonomous decentralized UAV clustering network. In: SoutheastCon 2015, pp. 1–8. IEEE (2015)

3. Chiaraviglio, L., Amorosi, L., Malandrino, F., Chiasserini, C.F., Dell'Olmo, P., Casetti, C.: Optimal throughput management in UAV-based networks during disasters. In: IEEE INFOCOM 2019-IEEE Conference on Computer Communications Workshops (INFOCOM WKSHPS), pp. 307–312. IEEE (2019)
4. Do-Duy, T., Nguyen, L.D., Duong, T.Q., Khosravirad, S.R., Claussen, H.: Joint optimisation of real-time deployment and resource allocation for UAV-aided disaster emergency communications. IEEE J. Sel. Areas Commun. **39**(11), 3411–3424 (2021)
5. Erdelj, M., Natalizio, E.: UAV-assisted disaster management: applications and open issues. In: 2016 International Conference on Computing, Networking and Communications (ICNC), pp. 1–5. IEEE (2016)
6. Fan, P., Zhi, C., Wei, C., Letaief, K.B.: Reliable relay assisted wireless multicast using network coding. IEEE J. Sel. Areas Commun. **27**(5), 749–762 (2009)
7. Feng, W., et al.: UAV-enabled SWIPT in IoT networks for emergency communications. IEEE Wirel. Commun. **27**(5), 140–147 (2020)
8. Fragouli, C., Katabi, D., Markopoulou, A., Medard, M., Rahul, H.: Wireless network coding: opportunities & challenges. In: MILCOM 2007-IEEE Military Communications Conference, pp. 1–8. IEEE (2007)
9. Ghaderi, M., Towsley, D., Kurose, J.: Network coding performance for reliable multicast. In: MILCOM 2007-IEEE Military Communications Conference, pp. 1–7. IEEE (2007)
10. Gurobi Optimization, LLC: Gurobi Optimizer Reference Manual (2023). https://www.gurobi.com
11. Liu, M., Yang, J., Gui, G.: DSF-NOMA: UAV-assisted emergency communication technology in a heterogeneous internet of things. IEEE Internet Things J. **6**(3), 5508–5519 (2019)
12. Maioli, D.S., Lavor, C., Gonçalves, D.S.: A note on computing the intersection of spheres in $\mathbb{R}^n$. ANZIAM J. **59**(2), 271–279 (2017)
13. Nguyen, D., Tran, T., Nguyen, T., Bose, B.: Wireless broadcast using network coding. IEEE Trans. Veh. Technol. **58**(2), 914–925 (2008)
14. Song, H., Liu, L., Shang, B., Pudlewski, S., Bentley, E.S.: Enhanced flooding-based routing protocol for swarm UAV networks: random network coding meets clustering. In: IEEE INFOCOM 2021-IEEE Conference on Computer Communications, pp. 1–10. IEEE (2021)
15. Tran, D.H., Nguyen, V.D., Chatzinotas, S., Vu, T.X., Ottersten, B.: UAV relay-assisted emergency communications in IoT networks: resource allocation and trajectory optimization. IEEE Trans. Wireless Commun. **21**(3), 1621–1637 (2021)
16. Xu, W., et al.: Throughput maximization of UAV networks. IEEE/ACM Trans. Networking **30**(2), 881–895 (2021)
17. Zeng, Y., Zhang, R., Lim, T.J.: Wireless communications with unmanned aerial vehicles: opportunities and challenges. IEEE Commun. Mag. **54**(5), 36–42 (2016)
18. Zhi, C., Wei, C., Fan, P., Letaief, K.B.: Relay aided wireless multicast utilizing network coding: outage behaviour and diversity gain. In: 2008 IFIP International Conference on Network and Parallel Computing, pp. 358–364. IEEE (2008)

Dynamic Target User Selection Model for Market Promotion with Multiple Stakeholders

Linxin Guo[1], Shiqi Wang[1], Min Gao[1(✉)], and Chongming Gao[2]

[1] Chongqing University, Chongqing, China
gaomin@cqu.edn.cn
[2] University of Science and Technology of China, Hefei, China

Abstract. While recommendation platforms present merchants with a vast and transparent sales avenue, they have inadvertently favored dominant merchants, often sidelining small-sized businesses. Addressing this challenge, platforms are deploying multifaceted market promotion strategies both to help merchants identify potential users and to spotlight emerging items for users. A crucial aspect of these strategies is the efficient selection of target users. By channeling resources towards the most responsive users, there's potential for a heightened return on marketing investments. In light of limited research in this domain, we put forth a tri-stakeholder considered user selection model with social networks (TriSUMS). This model recognizes the intertwined interests of three core stakeholders: merchants (items), platforms, and users. It harmonizes the objectives of these stakeholders through an integrated reward function and incorporates social networks to identify the prime target users for items of merchants adeptly. We validate TriSUMS using an exhaustive exposure user-item interaction dataset, assessed within a solid offline reinforcement learning framework.

Keywords: Market Promotion · Recommender System · Reinforcement Learning

1 Introduction

With the rapid development of information technology and the widespread application of big data technology, the Internet has penetrated into all aspects of human life. However, while technology enriches human life, it also brings out the problem of information overload. To solve the above problems, recommendation systems [2] have emerged. The recommendation systems use historical behavioral data to extract users' preferences and provide precise recommendations. It not only improves the accuracy of information propagation but also optimizes the user experience. Current mainstream personalized recommendation algorithms include content-based recommendations [8,14], collaborative filtering-based recommendations [16,17], and social network-based recommendations [3,21].

H. Gao et al. (Eds.): CollaborateCom 2023, LNICST 563, pp. 191–207, 2024.
https://doi.org/10.1007/978-3-031-54531-3_11

In the current competitive market environment, users are the core of marketing activities. Merchants pay special attention to target users to increase item sales, expand market share and enhance brand awareness. **Selecting appropriate target users for market promotion is the key link in the marketing process**. Nathan Fong et al. [4] found that targeted promotional activities based on personal purchase history can increase sales. Liu et al. [13] mentioned that the selection of target users in the advertising process usually takes into account the past behavior, identity, geographical location, and other attributes of consumers. Margaret et al. [1] found that brand familiarity will affect the effect of advertising repetition, so for brands familiar to users, the number of advertising repetitions can be higher.

The above research has shown that selecting appropriate target users for market promotion can benefit multiple stakeholders, i.e., merchants, platforms, and users. [19]. However, how to select appropriate users for market promotion is still under exploration. Most of these selection methods are based on heuristic rules and do not consider all stakeholders. Moreover, incompletely considering the interest of three stakeholders can lead to the collapse of the platform's entire business ecosystem. As the very core of market promotion, the interest of merchants is the exposure rate of their products. However, increasing the exposure of promoted products may harm the interest of users who require an accurate recommendation list to overcome the information overload problem. The platform needs to balance the demand of both merchants and users. While for the platform itself, improving the diversity of recommendation lists can also help discover potential new merchants and attract corresponding new users to help the further development of the platform.

To this end, we propose a dynamic target user selection model TriSUMS (Tri-Stakeholder User selection Model with Social networks), for all these stakeholders. For merchants, TriSUMS prioritizes the exposure of their products to ensure they receive the exposure increase they require. For users, the model emphasizes tailoring recommendations according to their interests, ensuring that they receive content relevant to their historical preferences, thus assisting them in navigating through the vast sea of information. As for the platform's longevity and growth, it places a strong emphasis on the diversity of the products showcased in the recommendation lists. Specifically, TriSUMS quantifies this balance through metrics like the frequency of an item's appearance in recommendation lists, the alignment of user recommendation lists with their historical interests, and the overall diversity of the recommendation list. In TriSUMS, three reward functions are designed for every kind of stakeholder. And these reward functions are combined into an integrated reward function to guild the training process. TriSUMS learns user-selecting policies in a dynamic environment, which can select optimal target users for market promotion to maximize the integrated reward function of multiple stakeholders. The contributions of this paper can be summarized as follow:

- We propose a target user selection model TriSUMS that considers multiple stakeholders. By comprehensively considering the interests of merchants, platforms, and users in marketing scenarios with users' social relationships, TriSUMS can increase the reward of the above-mentioned stakeholders.

- We construct a reliable simulation environment using a full exposure dataset and establish a robust offline reinforcement learning evaluation framework to assess user satisfaction when the user-selecting policy of TriSUMS is applied.
- We conduct extensive experiments to verify the effectiveness of the proposed model to validate the effectiveness of the model in improving the rewards of multiple stakeholders, demonstrating the model's superior performance in a reliable evaluation framework.

2 Preliminaries

To learn user-selecting policies in a dynamic environment, reinforcement learning technology [20] is a good way to achieve this. In this section, we introduce reinforcement learning and its variants, offline reinforcement learning. We also give the problem formulation of our work in this section.

2.1 Reinforcement Learning

The problem of reinforcement learning is how agents make decisions in complex and uncertain environments to maximize cumulative rewards. Different from supervised learning, agents explore the environment through trial and error and constantly seek better strategies to obtain the maximum cumulative rewards. The interaction process between intelligent agents and the environment can be formalized as a five-tuple $< A, S, P, R, \mu >$, including action space A, state space S, and state transition probability $P : S \times S \times A \rightarrow [0, 1]$, Reward Value $R : S \times A \rightarrow \mathcal{R}$ and the discounted factor $\mu \in [0, 1]$.

At the time t, the agent observes the environment state $s_t \in S$ and takes action $a_t \in A$ through the policy π. At the next time $t+1$, the environment feeds back a reward $r_t \in R$ and transports itself to a new state s_{t+1} through the state transition probability P. The agent constantly adjusts its policy π through the reward R, and steps into the next decision process. By repeating this process, the agent can get a trajectory $(s_0, a_0, r_0, s_1, a_1, r_1, ..., s_n, a_n, r_n)$. The target of reinforcement learning is to find out a policy π that can maximize the cumulative reward G_t:

$$G_t = r_0 + \mu r_1 + \mu^2 r_2 + ... + \mu^n r_n = \sum_{k=0}^{k=n} \mu^k r_k, \tag{1}$$

where μ is the discount factor that is used to weaken the future reward. Especially, if μ is close to 0, the agent focuses more on short-term reward, and if μ is close to 1, the agent tends to increase the long-term cumulative reward (Fig. 1).

2.2 Offline Reinforcement Learning

Conducting online reinforcement learning in real-life scenarios is significantly difficult, often facing high costs and risks. Plenty of application fields [6,9] have

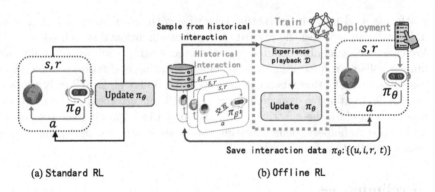

(a) Standard RL   (b) Offline RL

Fig. 1. The standard reinforcement learning and offline reinforcement learning

demonstrated its risk. In recommendation, users need to constantly interact with the agent. This process is unrealistic, as users do not have the patience to interact with an immature system.

To solve the above problems, a variant of reinforcement learning, i.e., offline reinforcement learning [10,11], came into being. It requires agents to learn from fixed batches of offline history data without any real-time interaction with the environment. The problem that offline reinforcement learning focuses on is how to effectively use the massive offline data to obtain a strategy that maximizes the cumulative reward. Offline reinforcement learning samples from the experience playback pool $\mathcal{D}$ and updates the strategy π_θ. After offline training, the model is deployed to the online environment to verify its effect. Compare to standard reinforcement learning, offline reinforcement learning is safer due to the removal of high-frequency real-time interaction with the environment.

2.3   Problem Formulation

Let U be the set of users and I be the set of items. $R \in \mathcal{R}^{|U| \times |I|}$ is the interaction where $R_{ui} = 1$ indicates user u has interacted with item i and $R_{ui} = 0$ indicates there is no interaction between u and i. $S \in \mathcal{R}^{|U| \times |U|}$ is the social relationship where $S_{uv} = 1$ indicates user u and v are friends and $S_{uv} = 0$ indicates user u and v do not know each other.

Our goal is to learn a user-selecting policy π that can maximize the reward of merchants, users, and the platform. The policy π selects optimal users to interact with merchants' promotional items to simulate the market promotion process. After the establishment of these interactions, the recommendation lists for users are changed. To ensure the overall reward of the three stakeholders at the same time, the designed integrated reward function R_s is maximized during the training process.

3   Methodology

In this section, we consider the interests of three stakeholders and propose a dynamic target user selection model TriSUMS (Tri-Stackholder User selection

Model with Social networks). TriSUMS considers not only the reward of merchants but also the reward of the platform and users. The framework introduces an offline reinforcement learning algorithm to train the interactive recommendation model and builds a reliable simulation environment based on the latest KuaiRec [5] dataset and the classic LastFM dataset to evaluate the effectiveness of the model.

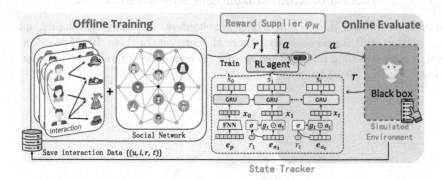

Fig. 2. The framework of TriSUMS

3.1   Overall Framework

TriSUMS mainly includes four key modules: a reward supplier, a reinforcement learning agent (RL Agent), a state tracker, and a simulated environment. As shown in Fig. 2, TriSUMS first utilizes offline interactive data $\{(u, i, r, t)\}$, a set of quadruples that contain user u interacted with item i at time t and user's social relationship r, to train the strategy. Then TriSUMS tests the impact of the model in a simulated environment. The details of the four modules are as follows:

The reward supplier is a recommendation model. Its recommendation performance can reflect the effect of market promotion. We use the interaction R and social relationship S to build the adjacent matrix, which is shown as follows:

$$A = \begin{pmatrix} S & R \\ R^T & 0 \end{pmatrix}, \tag{2}$$

and the LightGCN [7] with the above adjacent matrix is used as the reward supplier. The reward supplier provides reward signals in the dynamic interactive marketing process and evaluates the impact of user selection.

The state tracker is based on a GRU model, which can automatically extract the most relevant information for current market promotion from the vectors representing item attributes e_i and historical target user vectors $\{e_{a_1}, ..., e_{a_t}\}$.

The RL agent interacts with the reward supplier. During this interaction, the reward supplier is responsible for providing timely and accurate reward signals to the RL Agent. The RL Agent here can be any reinforcement learning algorithm, such as PPO [15], DDPG [12].

The simulated environment is used to simulate a real business environment, which is a black box that can return user feedback for model evaluation when the algorithm selects the target user.

3.2   Construction of Multi-stakeholder Reward Function

Market promotion involves multiple stakeholders, including merchants, users, and platforms. It is necessary to balance the interests of them. In this section, we design corresponding reward functions for each stakeholder and then synthesized them to form a reward function (Fig. 3):

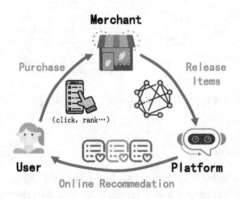

Fig. 3. The three stakeholders in market promotion

Reward Function for Merchants: Merchants are the very core of market promotion since the promotion is always launched by them. Merchants focus on the exposure of goods and expect to increase the exposure of goods through market promotion, thus increasing sales revenue. The direct way to measure the effect of market promotion is how many items of the merchants are recommended by the recommender system. Therefore, we set the reward function for the merchants as the change in the number of items displayed on the recommendation page:

$$\mathcal{R}_m(s_t, a_t) = \frac{Exp(I_p^t) - Exp(I_p^{t-1})}{Exp(I_p^{t-1})}, \tag{3}$$

where $Exp(I_p^t)$ indicates the number of promotional items displayed on the recommendation page at time t.

Reward Function for Users: Users are the receivers of market promotion. Moreover, it is evident that promoting appropriate items are acceptable for users, and users may feel unhappy when promoted improper items to them. Since recommendation metrics can effectively predict users' interests. Considering the change in recommendation loss can measure how users feel when the market promotion is adopted, we use the loss as the user reward function:

$$\mathcal{R}_u(s_t, a_t) = \frac{L_t - L_{t-1}}{L_{t-1}}, \tag{4}$$

where L_t is the loss of the LightGCN integrated with social networks when selecting the target users for the promotion.

Reward Function for Platform: The recommendation platform is the basis of online transactions, which connects users and merchants. The platform offers merchants a place where merchants can display their products to numerous users, and the platform also uses recommendation algorithms to filter appropriate products for users and reduce the information overload problem. Firstly, the platform needs to balance the interest of users and merchants, providing them with a good experience, this part is included in the reward function for merchants and users. However, traditional recommendation algorithms often focus on popular products, while long-tail items with relatively low sales but of a wide variety are ignored, leading to a monotonous recommended list, and finally result in damaging the overall ecology. Also, the recommendation platform has the following advantages in recommending long tail items: firstly, long tail items can meet users' diverse needs for products, thereby improving user stickiness and satisfaction. Secondly, although the sales of individual products are relatively low, long-tail items can bring more business opportunities. Finally, recommending long-tail items can also help the platform optimize product inventory and reduce warehousing costs. The long-tail item coverage is defined as the proportion of the long-tail items recommended to all items. Therefore, the change in long-tail item coverage is used as the reward function for the platform:

$$Diversity = \frac{\cup_{u \in U}(L_u)}{|V|}, \tag{5}$$

$$\mathcal{R}_p(s_t, a_t) = \frac{Diversity_t - Diversity_{t-1}}{Diversity_{t-1}}. \tag{6}$$

Integrated Reward Function for Multiple Stakeholders: In practical scenarios, there are often contradictions in the interests of these stakeholders. Merchants hope to maximize the exposure of their own products and attract more users to purchase, but this may lead to a waste of platform resources and user dissatisfaction; The platform hopes to enhance its uniqueness and diversity by increasing the exposure rate of long-tail products, but this may affect the exposure rate of mainstream products and the profits of corresponding merchants; Users hope to purchase their favorite products and enjoy discounts, but this may lead to waste of platform resources and reduced profits for merchants. To solve these contradictions, we integrate three rewards with a weighted summation, achieving balance and measurement of multi-party interests:

$$R_s(s_t, a_t) = \alpha R_m(s_t, a_t) + \beta R_u(s_t, a_t) + \gamma R_t(s_t, a_t). \tag{7}$$

The integrated reward function can balance the interests of merchants, platforms, and users during the optimizing process, improving the exposure of promoted items, coverage of long-tail items, user experience, and other indicators, thus achieving a win-win situation for multiple stakeholders. In addition, by adjusting the weight parameters α, β, and γ, the integrated reward function can also adjust to different market promotion scenarios with different benefit allocations, further improving promotion effectiveness.

3.3 Offline Reinforcement Learning-Driven Framework

In this section, we propose a dynamic target user selection model TriSUMS that takes multiple stakeholders into account. Figure 2 shows the process of selecting target users at different times in the model. The key variables involved in the model are as follows:

Action: a_t represents the action taken by the interactive strategy at the moment t. In this section, the action selects a user u, so the representation vector e_a of an action a and the standard vector of the user e_u selected by the action are equivalent, i.e., $e_a = e_u$.

Status: $s_t \in \mathbf{R}^{d_s}$ indicates the interaction state at t, which provide overall historical information for agent. s_t includes the representation vector e_i of the interactive information of the item and the user information that has been selected for the item in the whole interactive trajectory process $\{e_{a_1}, ..., e_{a_t}\}$. s_t.

Reward Signal: r_t represents the feedback signal provided by the reward provider φ_M after the policy selection action a_t at time t, which is calculated through the reward function of Eq. 7.

Policy Network: $\pi_\theta = \pi_\theta(a_t|s_t)$ selects actions a_t based on the current state s_t. It takes state s_t as input and outputs a probability distribution. The probability of action a_t being selected is as follows:

$$\pi_\theta(a_t|s_t) = ReLu(\sigma(W_s^T s_t + b_t), \tag{8}$$

where σ represents the nonlinear activation function, $W_s^T \in \mathcal{R}^{d_s \times d_a}$ and $b_t \in \mathcal{R}^{d_a}$ represent the weight matrix and bias, which are learned through the training process.

3.4 Proximal Policy Optimization

We use a variant of the PG algorithm - Proximal Policy Optimization (PPO) [15] to train the model. The PPO algorithm constrains the update amplitude by limiting the distance of new and old policies between each update step, solving the problem of the PG algorithm that may cause significant changes and unstable training in one step. The objective function of the PPO algorithm contains two parts, one is to improve the performance of the policy, other is to ensure the stability of the training process. The objective function of the PPO algorithm is defined as:

$$E_t[min(\frac{\pi_\theta(a_t|s_t)}{\pi_{\theta_{old}}(a_t|s_t)}\hat{A}_t, clip(\frac{\pi_\theta(a_t|s_t)}{\pi_{\theta_{old}}(a_t|s_t)}, 1-\epsilon, 1+\epsilon)\hat{A}_t], \tag{9}$$

where the first term in the objective function is to improve policy performance. The second term uses the pruning function $clip(\cdot)$ to limit the amplitude of policy updates. ϵ is a hyperparameter that limits the maximum update amplitude of the policy parameter θ in a single step. To achieve this, the $clip(x, a, b)$ function limits the value of x to the interval $[a, b]$. If x is smaller than a, then the output of $clip(x, a, b)$ is a, if x is bigger than b the output is b, and if x is between a and b the output is x. The θ_{old} represents the old version of the policy parameter θ. Thus, the update amplitude of θ is limited in ϵ. $\hat{A}_t$ is the function of cumulative reward:

$$\hat{A}_t = \hat{A}_t^{GAE(\mu,\lambda)} = \sum_{l=0}^{\infty}(\mu\lambda)^l \delta_{t+l}^V, \tag{10}$$

where λ is a hyperparameter that balances bias and variance. $\delta_t^V = r_t + \mu V(s_t + 1) - V(s_t)$ represents the residual of the value function V, μ is the discount factor. The value function V is as follows:

$$V(s_t) = V^{\pi_\theta,\mu}(s_t) = \mathbf{E}_{s_{t+1}:\infty,a_t:\infty}[\sum_{l=0}^{\infty}\mu^l r_{t+l}]. \tag{11}$$

3.5   Evaluation Framework

After the training process, we need to simulate the online evaluation. This process aims to analyze the impact on users in real scenarios. Therefore, it is necessary to develop a reliable and robust evaluation framework to accurately evaluate model performance. Figure 4 shows the evaluation methods of traditional static recommendation, sequential recommendation, and interactive recommendation.

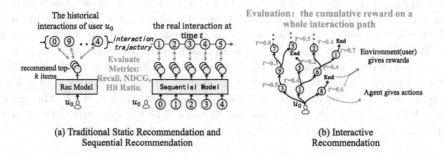

(a) Traditional Static Recommendation and Sequential Recommendation

(b) Interactive Recommendation

Fig. 4. Evaluation methods of traditional and interactive recommendation

Figure 4(a) shows the eval methods of traditional static recommendation and sequential recommendation. Among them, traditional static recommendation algorithms recommend a list of products that users may be interested in based on their interaction history. To evaluate the accuracy of recommendations, this product is generally compared with the real user interaction set in the test set, and evaluation indicators such as Recall, normalized discount cumulative gain (NDCG), and Hit Ratio are used to quantitatively analyze the recommendation effect. However, these evaluation methods that consider the products in the test set as standard answers do not conform to real recommendation scenarios. Because the interaction between users and products in the test set does not accurately reflect users' true preferences, it may only stem from curiosity or herd mentality. Meanwhile, the fact that one user has not interacted with a certain product does not mean that the user is uninterested in the product, it may be because the user has not yet discovered such a product. Also, in sequential recommendation methods, users' historical interactive products are typically modeled as sequences or trajectories with temporal characteristics. The goal is to predict the products that users may interact with at any given time. This method of using historical data as evaluation criteria is also not in line with actual recommendation scenarios, since fixed sequences or trajectories ignore the probability that users may interact with other items.

In actual recommendation scenarios, when users browse products on the recommendation platform, they may have no idea what they want. Meanwhile, they will provide feedback based on the platform's recommendation content and find the products they truly want to purchase through continuous interaction. If a good experience is obtained during this interaction process, users will continue to use the recommendation platform. Compared to static metrics such as accuracy and recall, recommendation platforms pay more attention to the long-term improvement of user experience satisfaction. These long-term metrics are often difficult to be covered and captured by traditional static and sequential recommendations modeling.

As shown in Fig. 4(b), in interactive recommendation scenarios, the interactions between users and agents are real-time rather than special history trajectories, presenting a divergent trend. Evaluation in interactive scenarios requires recording the cumulative reward of all these paths. This section uses the KuaiRec dataset [5] released by Kwai and the team of China University of Science and Technology to build a reliable evaluation framework and evaluate the impact of TriSUMS model on user satisfaction in real online recommendation scenarios. Compared with traditional highly sparse recommendation datasets, the KuaiRec dataset observation data contains a user-product interaction matrix with a density up to 99.6%, which can provide feedback for each action taken by the agent to calculate the cumulative satisfaction of users. The full exposure dataset as a simulation environment can provide strong support for the evaluation.

4   Experiments

This section introduces experimental design and analysis of experimental results to verify the effectiveness of the methods proposed in market promotion scenarios, as well as the effectiveness of social networks in improving recommendation performance. Specifically, we conduct experiments on two public datasets to analyze the following research questions (RQs):

- **RQ1:** How does the TriSUMS model improve the multi-stakeholder rewards compared with the static and collaborative filtering-based user selection strategy?
- **RQ2:** How does the TriSUMS model perform in the evaluation of the simulation environment compared with the static target user selection strategy and the user selection strategy based on collaborative filtering?
- **RQ3:** How do the user social relationships impact Precision, Recall, and NDCG in market promotion scenarios?

4.1 Datasets

We use two public datasets containing user social relationships, LastFM [18], and KuaiRec [5], for experiments. As shown in Table 1, the LastFM dataset is a commonly used dataset for music recommendation, containing interaction records of 1,892 users and 17,632 items. Since LastFM is highly sparse and cannot provide data support for the simulation environment in the model evaluation phase, matrix factorization is used to fill in the missing values.

Table 1. The statistics of the datasets

dataset	train/test	user	item	interaction	density	social relation
LastFM	train	1,892	4,489	42,135	0.62%	25,434
	test	1,858	3,285	78,286,830	100%	
KuaiRec	train	7,176	10,728	12,530,806	16.28%	670
	test	1,411	3,327	4,676,570	99.6%	

As shown in Fig. 5, the KuaiRec dataset consists of a sparse large matrix and a dense small matrix. The small matrix with red dashed lines contains almost no missing values for user video interactions, with a density of 99.6%. The missing 0.4% interactions are due to some users having blocklisted some video makers, and the platform cannot expose such videos to these users. We can treat these missing interactions as uninterest. This full exposure matrix can provide accurate and comprehensive feedback for the model evaluation stage. The blue dashed part is a large matrix with an interaction density of 16.3%, used for offline training of the model.

4.2 Baselines

The existing user-selecting policies are mainly based on historical behavior such as purchase [4] and brand familiarity [1], and there is no user selection algorithm for market promotion. To ensure the effectiveness of the experiment. Five static selection strategies are used, and two machine learning-based comparison methods are designed. Seven baselines include Random selection, Active first, Inactive first, High Rating first, Low Rating first, Item CF, and User CF. The details of the seven methods are shown as follows:

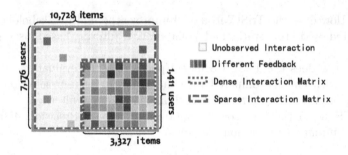

Fig. 5. The fully-observed dataset KuaiRec

Random Selection: Randomly select a target user and establish a connection with the promotional item set. The advantage of this method is that it is simple and easy to implement, but it may not be optimized for specific user groups, resulting in unstable promotion results.

Active First: This method sorts the user interaction volume (i.e. historical purchase data) and randomly selects target users from the top 30% of active users. Active users are more likely to notice promotional items, which may increase their exposure rate. However, this approach may overly focus on active users, leading to neglecting the needs of other user groups.

Inactive First: Contrary to the high activity priority selection method, this method randomly selects target users from the bottom 30% of non-active users. The purpose of this method is to avoid user churn and expand the audience for promoting the item. However, this method may result in less effective promotion, as inactive users may not be interested in new items.

High Rating First: This method calculates the average rating of users on all interactive items in the recommendation dataset and randomly selects target users from the top 30% of high-scoring users. High-scoring users may be more attracted to promotional items, increasing their exposure rate. However, this method may overlook the needs of low-scoring users and limit the scope of promotion effectiveness.

Low Rating First: Contrary to the high-scoring priority selection method, this method randomly selects target users from low-scoring users who rank in the bottom 30% of the score. This method attempts to expand the audience range of promotional items but may face the problem of low-rated users lacking interest in promoting the items.

Item CF: This method targets users who have purchased similar promotional items by analyzing and evaluating the similarity between items. This method helps find users interested in promoting the item, thereby increasing exposure. But this method may fail to identify potential new user groups.

User CF: By analyzing and evaluating the similarity between users, this method selects users similar to those who have already purchased promotional items as the target users. This method attempts to identify potentially interested users through user similarity, thereby increasing the exposure of promotional items. However, this method may be limited by the accuracy of calculating the similarity between users and may overlook potential user groups that have not yet been discovered.

4.3 Evaluation Metrics

Considering that the goal of TriSUMS is to balance the interests and needs of merchants, users, and platforms, we selected three evaluation metrics: **product exposure**, **recommendation accuracy**, and **recommendation coverage**. Product exposure reflects merchants' demand for product promotion, recommendation accuracy reflects users' demand for personalized recommendations, and recommendation coverage reflects the platform's demand for expanding recommendation scope.

In addition, we also use three common evaluation metrics for recommendation systems: $Precision@k$, $Recall@k$, and $NDCG@k$ to measure the impact of social networks on recommendation performance. $Precision@k$ is the ratio of the number of correctly predicted items in the recommendation results to the length of the recommendation list. It measures how many items on the recommendation list are truly of interest to users. $Recall@k$ refers to the ratio of the correct number of recommended items to the number of all items that should be recommended. It measures how many items that users are interested in are recommended. $NDCG@k$ considers the ranking of items and evaluates the accuracy of recommended item ranking.

4.4 Parameters Settings

The weights α, β, and γ of the reward function in Eq. 7 are set to 0.8, 0.1, and 0.1, respectively. Specifically, merchants are the direct beneficiaries and main supporters of market promotions, with the aim of increasing product exposure. Therefore, the interests of merchants should receive the greatest attention in the reward function, with a weight set at 0.8. As the strategy implementer of market promotions, the platform needs to ensure that the strategy implementation process does not affect the platform's own benefits. Therefore, the platform interests should be included in the weight setting, with a weight of 0.1. Users are also an essential part of market promotions, as they bring sales and profits by purchasing products. Therefore, during market promotions, it is necessary to ensure that users can obtain a diverse recommendation list with a weight of 0.1.

In the experiment, the model selects 100 target users (i.e. round length n) and establishes interaction with 1% of promotional items (i.e. the promotional item $|I_p|$). The length of the recommended list k is 10, and the discount factor μ is 0.9. The optimizer is Adam, and the initial learning rate is 0.005.

4.5 Overall Performance (RQ1)

Figure 6 shows the experimental results of eight methods on three evaluation metrics: product exposure, recommendation accuracy, and recommendation coverage. Observations can lead to the following conclusion:

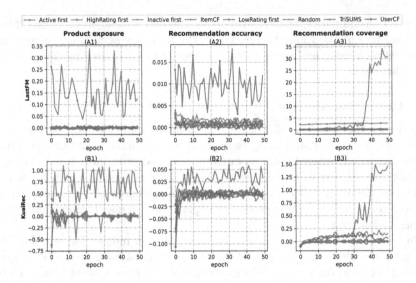

Fig. 6. Overall Performance

- TriSUMS outperformed the baseline model in all three evaluation metrics on two datasets, indicating that the TriSUMShas better overall performance in meeting user needs, improving platform revenue, and promoting the overall development of recommendation platforms.
- In terms of product exposure, the high activity priority selection method and the high score priority selection method perform relatively well. The performance of low activity priority selection and low rating priority selection methods is poor, mainly due to users with lower participation and low rating tendency, whose interest preferences are often vague and, therefore, not suitable as the target user group for promotional activities. The random selection method performs the worst because it does not utilize any information to optimize the selection strategy.
- In terms of recommendation accuracy, UserCF and ItemCF perform relatively well, due to the algorithm based on collaborative filtering fully mining the similarity information between users and products. At the same time, static strategies such as Active First, Inactive First, High Rating First, Low Rating First, and Random perform relatively poorly.
- In terms of recommendation coverage, the high activity priority selection method performs well, mainly due to frequent interaction between active users and recommendation platforms, as well as rich behavioral data. The interests and preferences of active users are more accurately captured, making them suitable target user groups for promotional activities.

In addition, it can be observed that the TriSUMS shows significant fluctuations in the result curves on all three metrics. There are two main reasons for this phenomenon: 1) Reinforcement learning needs to balance the exploration of unknown states and behaviors with the use of known information. 2) Reinforcement learning usually relies on delayed rewards. However, the TriSUMS algorithm achieved better performance in all three metrics in the later stage.

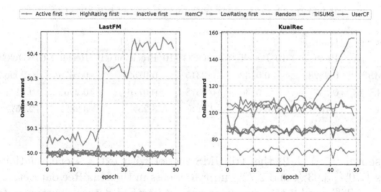

Fig. 7. Comparison of evaluation results in simulation environment

4.6   Online Reward Evaluation (RQ2)

Figure 7 shows the experimental results of the target user selection model TriSUMS and seven baseline models proposed in this section on the LastFM and KuaiRec datasets. The online reward (i.e., the values in the dense matrix) can reflect how satisfied users are. The horizontal axis epoch represents the number of test rounds, and the vertical axis represents online reward. We can find TriSUMS performs significantly better than the baseline model on both datasets, which means that TriSUMS can meet users' requirements in a dynamic environment.

In the LastFM dataset, the performance of the seven baseline models is relatively close. The online reward fluctuates between 49.98 and 50.01 because the baseline models cannot fully capture the dynamic interaction relationship between users and items. The online reward of our proposed TriSUMS fluctuates between 50.03 and 50.46.

In the KuaiRec dataset, Item CF performs well for its ability to effectively mine the similarity information between users and items. Meanwhile, the effect of the high rating first method (online reward fluctuates around 100) is significantly better than the low rating first method (online reward below 80) because users who tend to give high ratings to products are more likely to generate positive feedback. The performance of active first, inactive first, random, and user CF is similar. Their online reward value fluctuates between 81 and 90. It is worth noting that after training for a period of time, our TriSUMS model has an online reward above 140. This can be attributed to the advantages of reinforcement learning-based methods in capturing dynamic environmental changes more effectively and focusing on long-term benefits.

4.7   Ablation Study (RQ3)

To verify the role of user social relationships in improving the effectiveness of the model, this study designed an ablation experiment. The experiment compared the performance of the TriSUMS model and the model without social relationships, $TriSUMS^{w/oS}$, on the metrics of *Precision*@10, *Recall*@10, and *NDCG*@10.

Table 2. The comparison of two variants of TriSUMS

Dataset	KuaiRec			LastFM		
Metric	Precision@10	Recall@10	NDCG@10	Precision@10	Recall@10	NDCG@10
TriSUMS$^{w/oS}$	0.2528	0.0132	0.2315	0.0752	0.2679	0.2096
TriSuMS	0.2571	0.0136	0.2378	0.0776	0.2768	0.2141
improve	1.70%	3.03%	2.72%	3.25%	3.28%	2.15%

As shown in Table 2, the TriSUMS model with extra social relationships achieves 1.70%, 3.03%, and 2.72% improvements in the KuaiRec dataset, as well as 3.25%, 3.28%, and 2.15% improvements in LastFM dataset, compares to the TriSUMS$^{w/oS}$ model. This indicates that after adding user social relationships, the TriSUMS model can better capture user interests.

5   Conclusion

In this work, we introduce the dynamic selection model of TriSUMS. It considers the social relations of users and three major stakeholders in the market promotion process - merchants, platforms, and users, respectively. While improving the exposure of items, TriSUMS takes into account the accuracy and diversity of recommendations to meet the needs of different stakeholders. We utilize a full exposure dataset to construct a reliable simulation environment for evaluating the impact of the model on user satisfaction. The experimental results show that the TriSUMS performs better in improving user experience and other metrics compared to other models. This is mainly due to the following reasons: (1) Reinforcement learning usually focuses more on long-term rewards throughout the decision-making process. This section designs reward functions for multiple stakeholders to guide strategy updates to maximize cumulative benefits. (2) Reinforcement learning methods continuously explore the location environment during the learning process, which is more adaptable to changing new scenarios and adjust strategies adaptively compared to fixed selection strategies.

References

1. Campbell, M.C., Keller, K.L.: Brand familiarity and advertising repetition effects. J. Consum. Res. **30**(2), 292–304 (2003)
2. Covington, P., Adams, J., Sargin, E.: Deep neural networks for YouTube recommendations. In: Proceedings of the 10th ACM Conference on Recommender Systems, pp. 191–198 (2016)
3. Fan, W., et al.: Graph neural networks for social recommendation. In: The World Wide Web Conference, pp. 417–426 (2019)
4. Fong, N., Zhang, Y., Luo, X., Wang, X.: Targeted promotions on an E-book platform: crowding out, heterogeneity, and opportunity costs. J. Mark. Res. **56**(2), 310–323 (2019)

5. Gao, C., et al.: KuaiRec: a fully-observed dataset for recommender systems. arXiv preprint arXiv:2202.10842 (2022)
6. Gu, S., Holly, E., Lillicrap, T., Levine, S.: Deep reinforcement learning for robotic manipulation with asynchronous off-policy updates. In: 2017 IEEE International Conference on Robotics and Automation (ICRA), pp. 3389–3396. IEEE (2017)
7. He, X., Deng, K., Wang, X., Li, Y., Zhang, Y., Wang, M.: LightGCN: simplifying and powering graph convolution network for recommendation. In: Proceedings of the 43rd International ACM SIGIR Conference on Research and Development in Information Retrieval, pp. 639–648 (2020)
8. Javed, U., Shaukat, K., Hameed, I.A., Iqbal, F., Alam, T.M., Luo, S.: A review of content-based and context-based recommendation systems. Int. J. Emerg. Technol. Learn. (iJET) **16**(3), 274–306 (2021)
9. Kiran, B.R., et al.: Deep reinforcement learning for autonomous driving: a survey. IEEE Trans. Intell. Transp. Syst. **23**(6), 4909–4926 (2021)
10. Lange, S., Gabel, T., Riedmiller, M.: Batch reinforcement learning. In: Wiering, M., van Otterlo, M. (eds.) Reinforcement Learning: State-of-the-Art, vol. 12, pp. 45–73. Springer, Heidelberg (2012). https://doi.org/10.1007/978-3-642-27645-3_2
11. Levine, S., Kumar, A., Tucker, G., Fu, J.: Offline reinforcement learning: tutorial, review, and perspectives on open problems. arXiv preprint arXiv:2005.01643 (2020)
12. Lillicrap, T.P., et al.: Continuous control with deep reinforcement learning. arXiv preprint arXiv:1509.02971 (2015)
13. Liu-Thompkins, Y.: A decade of online advertising research: what we learned and what we need to know. J. Advert. **48**(1), 1–13 (2019)
14. Lops, P., de Gemmis, M., Semeraro, G.: Content-based recommender systems: state of the art and trends. In: Ricci, F., Rokach, L., Shapira, B., Kantor, P.B. (eds.) Recommender Systems Handbook, pp. 73–105. Springer, Boston, MA (2011). https://doi.org/10.1007/978-0-387-85820-3_3
15. Schulman, J., Wolski, F., Dhariwal, P., Radford, A., Klimov, O.: Proximal policy optimization algorithms. arXiv preprint arXiv:1707.06347 (2017)
16. Shen, J., Zhou, T., Chen, L.: Collaborative filtering-based recommendation system for big data. Int. J. Comput. Sci. Eng. **21**(2), 219–225 (2020)
17. Suganeshwari, G., Syed Ibrahim, S.P.: A survey on collaborative filtering based recommendation system. In: Vijayakumar, V., Neelanarayanan, V. (eds.) Proceedings of the 3rd International Symposium on Big Data and Cloud Computing Challenges (ISBCC – 16'). SIST, vol. 49, pp. 503–518. Springer, Cham (2016). https://doi.org/10.1007/978-3-319-30348-2_42
18. Tang, J., Gao, H., Liu, H.: mTrust: discerning multi-faceted trust in a connected world. In: Proceedings of the Fifth ACM International Conference on Web Search and Data Mining, pp. 93–102 (2012)
19. Wang, S., Gao, C., Gao, M., Yu, J., Wang, Z., Yin, H.: Who are the best adopters? User selection model for free trial item promotion. IEEE Trans. Big Data **9**(2), 746–757 (2023). https://doi.org/10.1109/TBDATA.2022.3205334
20. Wiering, M.A., Van Otterlo, M.: Reinforcement learning. Adapt. Learn. Optim. **12**(3), 729 (2012)
21. Zhao, T., McAuley, J., King, I.: Leveraging social connections to improve personalized ranking for collaborative filtering. In: Proceedings of the 23rd ACM International Conference on Conference on Information and Knowledge Management, pp. 261–270 (2014)

Collaborative Decision-Making Processes Analysis of Service Ecosystem: A Case Study of Academic Ecosystem Involution

Xiangpei Yan[1], Xiao Xue[1(✉)], Chao Peng[1], Donghua Liu[2], Zhiyong Feng[1], and Wang Xiao[3]

[1] School of Computer Software, College of Intelligence and Computing, Tianjin University, Tianjin, China
jzxuexiao@tju.edu.cn
[2] China Waterborne Transport Research Institute, Tianjin, China
[3] State Key Laboratory of Management and Control for Complex Systems, Institute of Automation, Chinese Academy of Sciences, Beijing, China

Abstract. With the collaboration of several intelligent services, a crowd intelligence service network has been formed, and a service ecosystem has gradually emerged. As a novel service organization model, the Service Ecosystem (SE) can provide more sophisticated, precise, and thorough services and has attracted widespread attention. However, it also brings negative effects such as involution, and information cocoon room. Thus, how to analyze the collaborative decision-making mechanism between the SE regulation algorithm and the crowd intelligence group, exploring the reasons behind the negative effects, and finding effective intervention strategies have become problems in this field. To solve the challenges, we propose a Computational Experiments-based method Decision-making processes Analysis model in SE, namely CEDA. The proposed CEDA model consists of three modules: the autonomous evolution mechanism module, the learning evolution mechanism module, and the collaborative decision-making analysis module. Among them, the computational experiments can provide a customized test environment for the analysis of collaborative decision-making processes and find out the appropriate intervention strategy. Finally, the validity of the CEDA model is verified through the case of academic ecosystem involution. The results show that computational experiments can provide new ideas and paths for collaborative decision-making processes analysis.

Keywords: Collaborative Decision-making Processes · Case Studies of Collaborative Application · Performance Evaluation · Service Ecosystem · Interaction Mechanism · Computational Experiments

1 Introduction

With the era of the intelligent interconnection of all things, new technologies and products such as big data, cloud computing, and artificial intelligence continue to pour into the modern service industry, which can be combined and integrated to meet complex

H. Gao et al. (Eds.): CollaborateCom 2023, LNICST 563, pp. 208–228, 2024.
https://doi.org/10.1007/978-3-031-54531-3_12

application scenarios [1, 2]. "Data + computing power + AI algorithm = intelligent service" is forming a new type of social infrastructure. In this technical architecture, "Everything as a Service", the service gradually endows everything in society with a unified logic, including applications, platforms, data, algorithms, and resources, and the entire social landscape is redefined under the service logic [3]. By focusing on the structure of the process and neglecting the exchange of data and resources between collaborators traditional service systems gradually turn into Service Ecosystems (SE) where many agents (people, companies, governments, intelligent machines, etc.) work together and operate together [1], as shown in Fig. 1.

As a complex service system that is influenced by many factors, the efficient operation of the service ecosystem requires collaboration between the supply and demand sides. The supply side constantly pursues high efficiency (Efficiency = output/time), while the demand side continuously provides valuable output (Effectiveness = valuable output/time). This collaboration is crucial to prevent the whole system from falling into a loop of ineffective output. In this context, intelligent regulation algorithms play an increasingly important role in helping individuals, businesses, and governments make decisions and deal with everyday matters. These algorithms provide a more granular, precise, and thorough model of service operation in a more intelligent way than traditional service. For example, recommendation algorithms can influence the speed of enhancing people's access to information [2] and service platform algorithms can perform route planning [4]. Intelligent regulation algorithms are playing an increasingly important role in the collaborative decision-making and processing of everyday affairs, enabling significant changes in how services are organized and operated. They are also having a growing impact on shaping the processes of human interaction with politics, economics, and society [3]. However, the complexity, opacity, and lack of interpretability of intelligent moderation algorithms themselves [3]. Have led to a rise in the risks associated with their use. For example, algorithms for ranking scientific results have led the academic ecosystem into a state of involution with diminishing marginal effects [5]. In addition, problems such as complex network wind [4], and "information cocoon room" [6]. Caused by intelligent regulation algorithms pose new challenges to the service efficiency of the public intelligence service system. To ensure the effective and efficient operation of the service ecosystem, it is crucial to address the risks and challenges associated with the use of intelligent regulation algorithms.

Therefore, exploring the reasons for the negative effects and interaction processes between the regulation algorithm and the crowd intelligence group becomes the key to research. For example, Shi et al. used a simulation system to simulate the real world and effectively assess the impact of the interaction between algorithms and people [8, 9]. Kang et al. use quantitative methods to analyze interaction data and conclude that algorithm-human interaction exacerbates algorithm discrimination [2, 10]. However, the inherent complexity, opacity, and lack of interpretability of intelligent regulation algorithms have increased the risks of SE. Existing analysis methods ignore the complexity and dynamics of the interaction between algorithms and agents, making it difficult to reveal the underlying mechanisms of system evolution and to give effective regulation strategies. In this context, this paper investigates the mechanism of interaction between the regulation algorithm and the intelligent behavior of the crowd intelligence group in SE and explores the reasons for the negative effects of the interaction between the regulation algorithm and the crowd intelligence group.

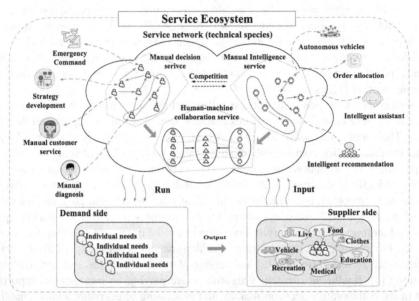

Fig. 1. The SE consists of several agents such as people, enterprises, intelligent machines, and regulation algorithms, which are self-learning and capable of self-evolution, as well as interacting with other agents to accelerate their evolution and facilitate the evolution of SE.

Computational experiments are based on the underlying agents to simulate real-world microscopic behavior and have the advantage of being accurate, controllable, and repeatable. This paper combines the characteristics of computational experiments to connect the micro and macro and proposes a Computational Experiments-based Decision-making processes Analysis model in SE, referred to as the CEBA model. The CEBA model describes the cyclic mechanism of positive and negative feedback between the intelligent regulation algorithm and the crowd intelligence group in SE from a macroscopic perspective and analyses the state properties, behavior changes, and correlations between the two from a microscopic perspective. Finally, the case of scientific academic ecosystem involution using the CEBA model is analyzed to explore the internal mechanism of the creation, exacerbation, and mitigation of scientific academic ecosystem involution.

2   Background and Motivation

The SE is a complex service system that facilitates the service effectiveness of the service system under limited resources through the centralized provision of infrastructure and public services. The operation logic of the SE consists of three parts: crowd intelligence group, service network, and value network [11, 12].

In recent years, the SE has become the most important organizational form of the service system [13, 14]. In a SE, agents autonomously adjust their behaviors and decisions according to their value output to improve their effectiveness, while the regulation algorithm regulates the behavior and habits of the intelligence to improve the service effectiveness of the whole service system. With the increasing complexity of the coupling between intelligent regulation algorithms and crowd intelligence group, it is becoming more important to analyze the interaction processes between the two [14]. A review of the literature reveals that current research approaches to algorithm-human interaction fall into three main categories.

The first category is to evaluate the impact of the interaction between algorithms and humans based on real systems or simulated systems using A/B tests or combinations of multiple variables. Miikkulainen et al. [5] proposed to use of an evolutionary algorithm to select the A/B test feature space; Shi et al. [8] proposed to use reinforcement learning to establish a virtual Taobao for A/B testing; Koster et al. [10] proposed a virtual environment to explore the influence of people on algorithm-making policy.

The second category is qualitative analysis from psychology, causality, and influencing factors. Bucher et al. [15] investigated the emotional dimension and perception of algorithms and people; Alvarado et al. [16] proposed an algorithmic experience (analytical framework for analyzing the experience of algorithm-human interaction; Shin et al. [17] proposed the models to influence users' perceptions of algorithmic systems in the context of algorithmic ecology.

The third category is to collect interactive data based on questionnaires, interviews, and web crawlers for quantitative analysis. Li et al. [19] proposed a psychological perspective on the positive impact of anthropomorphism in the interaction of AI assistants; Kang et al. [2] investigated the impact of AI features embedded in core aspects of social media; Vlasceanu et al. [9] verified that non-human factors induce lasting social influence outside the group environment.

Currently, all existing methods of interaction analyses have certain limitations. For online systems, too much analysis can put pressure on the system and degrade the user experience. Simulation systems focus on top-down modeling, and the simulation process requires human participation, which does not allow for large-scale, long-term simulation. Qualitative analysis methods cannot quantify the interactions between factors, and can only provide a rough analysis from a macro perspective, which is insufficient to explain the decision-making and interaction processes. Quantitative analysis methods cannot effectively analyze the decision-making and interaction processes since a large number of assumptions and a large amount of data are required when building the model.

To solve the problems in the interaction analysis methods for the SE regulation algorithm and crowd intelligence groups, this paper proposes a Computational Experiments-based Decision-making processes Analysis model in SE. The model separates the crowd intelligence group and the regulation algorithm in the hybrid system and then abstracts them into an artificial society agent and the SE regulation algorithm respectively. It can simulate the interaction processes between the SE regulation algorithm and the artificial society agent, and analyze the circular feedback logic and inner mechanism of the interaction between the SE regulation algorithm and the artificial society agent. Finally, the proposed model is validated by setting up different types of intervention strategies and different types of artificial society agents to analyze the generation, exacerbation, and mitigation of the phenomenon of involution in the academic ecology.

3 Computational Experiments-Based on Collaborative Decision-Making Processes Model in SE

This section first introduces the proposed CEBA model, followed by a detailed description of the autonomous evolution mechanism of the regulation algorithm and the learning evolution mechanism of the artificial society agent model, and then describes the cyclical mechanism and dynamic evolution process between the two. Finally, individual effectiveness, system effectiveness, and other analysis indicators are given.

3.1 Computational Experimental Analysis Model of SE

The CEBA model uses computational experiments to model the whole process of interaction between the SE regulation algorithm and the artificial society agent, focusing on the analysis of the changes in the artificial society agent. Additionally, exploring the internal mechanism of the interaction between the SE regulation algorithm and the artificial society agent can help to mitigate the negative effect of the regulation algorithm on the artificial society. As shown in Fig. 2, the first is to introduce the SE regulation algorithm, and the agents perceive and make corresponding feedback. Secondly, the introduction of the SE regulation algorithm will accelerate the evolution process of artificial society learning, thus affecting the interaction between the SE regulation algorithm and the artificial society agent. Finally, after a period of operation, the artificial society produces certain negative phenomena of the algorithm. To mitigate or avoid the negative phenomenon of the SE regulation algorithm, the SE regulation algorithm will be modified or replaced. Therefore, the CEDA model will analyze the collaborative decision-making and interaction processes between the SE regulation algorithm and artificial society from the following three aspects, and explain the internal mechanism of the generation, exacerbation, and mitigation of social phenomena caused by the interaction between the two.

(1) **The changes in the artificial society agent before and after the regulation**

The SE regulation algorithm has changed the organizational norms and management measures of the service system, which makes the evaluation, allocation, and recommendation more rational, automatic, and standardized. However, agents need to learn the best strategy to improve competitiveness and rewards in the process of interaction between the regulation algorithm and other agents, due to the limitation of resources and the pursuit of reward maximization. The agent strategy is gradually homogenized and biased, forming a negative effect, with a certain social phenomenon emerging, such as ①, ②, ③, ④, ⑤, ⑥ processes in Fig. 2. Therefore, we set up an artificial society agent experiment after regulation, and analyze the performance differences of the crowd intelligence group after the regulation algorithm is applied, meanwhile explore the impact of the regulation algorithm on the effectiveness and negative effects of SE.

(2) **Artificial society agent changes, while the regulation algorithm remains unchanged**

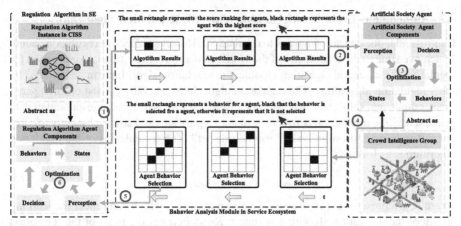

Fig. 2. The framework of the proposed CEDA model, consists of three modules: the SE regulation algorithm module, the collaborative decision-making processes analysis module, and the artificial society agent module. The left side represents the SE regulation algorithm module abstracted from different SE regulation algorithm instances, the right side represents the artificial society agent abstracted from different crow intelligence group instances modules, and the middle represents the abstracted collaborative decision-making processes analyses module.

From the interaction processes in Fig. 2 ③, ④, ⑤, ⑥, ①, ②, we can see that: Many factors affect SE regulation algorithms, different artificial society agents have different influences on the SE regulation algorithm, such as the organizational structure of the agent, the intelligence degree of the agent, and individual differences. We need to determine and analyze the factors, so we set different values for the influencing factors of different artificial society agents and then design a group of controlled experiments to analyze the performance differences between the same regulation algorithm and the crowd intelligence groups with different settings. Besides, we can explore how the influence factors of the artificial society agent shape the behavior mode and evolution of the agent process and also evaluate the impact of negative effects on the regulation algorithm.

(3) **The regulation algorithm changes, but the artificial society agent remains unchanged**

The original intention of introducing the management and regulation algorithm into the SE is further improving service efficiency through refined management. However, the regulation algorithm affects the job evaluation and income distribution of the agent, so there could be a negative impact on the direction and speed of the artificial society learning evolution. It is necessary to update the regulation algorithm, migrate or avoid the negative impact as much as possible meanwhile ensuring the goal of the regulation algorithm, as shown in the process of ⑥, ①, ②, ③, ④, ⑤ in Fig. 2. Therefore, we set up controlled experiments to analyze the attributes and state changes of the agent under the regulation algorithm of different intervention strategies and explore the mitigation effect of the regulation algorithm on the negative impact of the algorithm under different intervention strategies.

3.2 Autonomous Evolution Mechanism of the SE Regulation Algorithm

Control and induction are two ways to regulate SE. However, effective regulation cannot be achieved due to the complexity of the system. Therefore, induction is usually used for regulation. As a general algorithm module, the regulation algorithm can be replaced by other regulation algorithms. The regulation algorithms generally consist of three parts: input, output, and self-learning capabilities. Self-learning is using a large amount of data generated by the interaction between regulatory algorithms and artificial society to carry out self-training and evolution to form a "rule set". The formulation of the regulation algorithm is as follows:

$$RA_{out,t} = RA_t \odot RA_{in,t} \quad t \geq 0 \tag{1}$$

where RA_t represents the regulation algorithm at time t, which can reflect the learning ability of the regulation algorithm at time t. $RA_{in,t}$ denotes the input of the regulation algorithm at time t, and its input is the comprehensive output of factors such as the state of the regulation algorithm and the emergence of social phenomena from artificial society agents. $RA_{out,t}$ represents the output of the regulation algorithm at time t after evolution. $\odot$ represents the update of the regulation algorithm RA_t based on the comprehensive output of the artificial society at time t.

The characteristic index space $\{q_{j,t}\}$ of the SE regulation algorithm RA_t is defined as follows:

$$\{q_{j,t}\} = \left\{q_{j,t}^1, q_{j,t}^2, q_{j,t}^3, \ldots, q_{j,t}^N\right\} \tag{2}$$

where $\{q_{j,t}\}$ is the set of all agent index j feature values, and N is the number of all agents in the artificial society agent model. The average reward index of the agent is defined as:

$$\text{Income}_{agent_T} = \frac{\sum_{i=0}^{i=N} \sum_{t=0}^{t=T} Reward_{t,i}}{N} \quad t \geq 1 \tag{3}$$

where $Reward_{t,i}$ indicates the income of the agent i from $t-1$ to t and Income_{agent_T} indicates the average income of the agent in the artificial society at time T.

The input of the regulation algorithm $RA_{in,t}$, that is, the index system $Qos(i, t)$ value of agent i at time t is defined as follows:

$$Qos(i, t) = \sum_{j=0}^{j=M} w_{j,t} q_{j,t}^i \tag{4}$$

where M represents the number of characteristic indicators of the SE regulation algorithm RA, $q_{j,t}^x$ represents the feature value of the index j of the agent x at time t, and w_j represents the preference weight of the index system at time t.

The index discrimination degree $D_{j,t}$ of SE regulation algorithm RA_t is defined as follows:

$$D_{j,t} = \frac{H_{j,t} - L_{j,t}}{Max_{j,t}} \quad t \geq 0 \tag{5}$$

Here, the discrimination calculation method adopts the two-end grouping method: first, the values of $\{q_{j,t}\}$ at time t are arranged in descending order, and the first $\alpha\%$ entities are listed as high-scoring entities, and the latter $\alpha\%$ entities are listed as low-scoring entities group, then the discrimination degree of index j is $D_{j,t}$. Among them, $H_{j,t}$ is the average score of the high group in index j, $L_{j,t}$ is the average score of the low group in index j, $Max_{j,t}$ is the highest score value of index j.

The index system discrimination degree D_t of SE regulation algorithm RA_t is defined as follows:

$$D_t = max(D_{0,t}, \ldots D_{j,t}, D_{m,t})\ t \geq 0 \tag{6}$$

where D_t represents the maximum value of discrimination in all index systems. m represents the number of indicators under the indicator system.

The fitness function of the SE regulation algorithm RA at time t is as follows:

$$Fit_{RA,t} = \alpha * \text{Income}_{agent_t} + (1 - \alpha) * D_t\quad 0 \leq \alpha \leq 1 \tag{7}$$

where $Fit_{RA,t}$ represents the fitness function of the regulation algorithm at time t, which is not only related to the interaction of the artificial society but also affected by the regulation algorithm itself. α is a proportional coefficient, which is used to indicate the average income of an artificial society occupies the size of the fitness function value. When α is larger, it means that the average income of the artificial society occupies a larger fitness function value and vice versa.

3.3   The Learning Evolution Mechanism of the Artificial Society Agent Model

The artificial society agent is a complex system composed of a large number of agents that follow certain rules, interact with each other, and have certain autonomous capabilities, which can simulate the structure, function, and evolution mechanism of SE. The artificial society agent is regarded as an alternative version of the crowd intelligence group to study various phenomena in reality. Artificial society is divided into three parts: input, output, and self-learning ability. The learning evolution process of the artificial society agent model can be modeled using the SLE framework [19]. SLE is a customized evolution model that includes three evolution modules: individuals, organizations, and society. The evolution of the three models can be specifically expressed as:

(1) **Individual evolution mechanism**

An individual refers to a single agent in different types of artificial societies, a genetic component. The agent has the characteristics of autonomy, responsiveness, initiative, and sociality, and it perceives, makes decisions, acts, and optimizes through the propagation of information flows, forming an evolutionary mechanism with the following behavioral rules expressed as follows:

$$\forall v_t \in V_t, \varepsilon(\alpha, v_t, E_t, Y_t) \Rightarrow \langle S, D_t, N, max(Value_{t+1})\rangle \tag{8}$$

$\varepsilon(\alpha, v_t, E_t, Y_t)$ represents the evaluation of the result of the agent α completing the behavior v_t in the environment E_t and the decision Y_t, $\Rightarrow$ means "satisfied", N represents the constraints on the agent, S represents static attributes, D_t represents dynamic attributes at time t, $max(Value_{t+1})$ indicates the task standard.

In an artificial society, the agent is not unconscious or does not lack initiative, and its learning process is an important dynamic mechanism for system evolution. During this operation, the agent updates its rule by interacting with the environment, which can affect its decision-making mechanism. Generally speaking, the agent will adopt the feedback learning principle of "increasing rewards" to gradually optimize its decision-making mechanism, so that it can take actions that are closer to the accomplishment of the goal. The formula is expressed as follows:

$$Y_{t+1} = Y_t \oplus Fit_{AS,t}(E_t) \quad t \geq 0 \tag{9}$$

$Fit_{AS,t}(.)$ represents the fitness function at time t, which is used to describe the survivability of the agent and can be regarded as the mapping relationship between strategy and fitness. $\oplus$ indicates that the decision mechanism Y_t is based on the update of the environment state E_t.

(2) **Organizational learning evolution mechanism**

In the real world, the agent can adapt to the external environment through individual learning, and it also learns to evolve by observing and imitating the corresponding organization where the organization is composed of agents with the same activity scope and behavior set.

Organizational learning is to transform different small organizations formed in the process of neighbor learning into smaller and higher-level organizations. In the same learning organization, there is not only competition but also a certain degree of collaboration among agents within the organization due to the principle of knowledge sharing within the learning organization. Different organizations will compete with each other to obtain favorable positions based on the organization as a unit, and the competitiveness is reflected in the income and vision of the leaders within the organization. The competitiveness of agents can be improved continuously by learning from excellent partners. Whether the agent wants to learn from the organization depends on the following formula:

$$O(org_j, v_{i,t}, v_{org_j,t}) > 1?Evo(yes) : Evo(no) \tag{10}$$

$$O(org_j, v_{i,t}, v_{org_j,t}) = \frac{\left| Income_{(org_j,v_{org_j,t})} - Income_{v_{i,t}} \right|}{Distance}$$

where $Income_{(org_j,v_{org_j,t})}$ represents the income of the agent i in the organization j at the time t of behavior $v_{org_j,t}$, $Income_{v_{i,t}}$ represents the reward of agent i making behavior $v_{i,t}$ at time t, and $Distance$ represents the cost of learning organization j for agent i. If $O(org_j, v_{i,t}, v_{org_j,t})$ is greater than 1, the agent i will learn the excellent strategy of the organization to improve its ability. Otherwise, the agent will continue to take action according to its original strategy.

(3) **Social learning evolution mechanism**

According to the principle of survival of the fittest, the artificial society selects the most adaptive agent as the elite, and its excellent knowledge will be passed on to the top.

It builds a culture through knowledge accumulation and also spreads the culture to other agents for learning. The specific policy rules of the social learning layer are as follows:

1) **The policy of probability principle:** the agents can choose different rewards to achieve strategy selection. For example, some agents will pursue the maximum income so that they will learn from low-income individuals with a small probability.

2) **The principle of income comparison:** an agent with a small income will imitate the behavior and strategy of an agent with a large income, while the agent with a larger income maintains its original behavior and strategy.

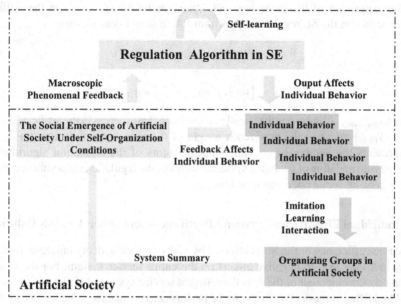

Fig. 3. The cyclic mechanism and dynamic evolution process, the output of the SE regulation algorithm acts on artificial society agents, and the artificial society agents learn, imitate and interact with themselves to form a certain organizational group in the artificial society. After a period of learning and the evolution of different organizational groups, a macroscopic social phenomenon will emerge. The macro-phenomenon influences the direction of the regulation algorithm's learning evolution. The organizational groups and the output of the regulation algorithm in turn change the cognition of the artificial society agents, resulting in different agents behaving differently, thus forming a circular process of action.

3.4 The Cyclic Mechanism and Dynamic Evolution Process Between Regulation Algorithm and Artificial Society

The learning evolution of the SE regulation algorithm and artificial society is the process of interaction between artificial society and the SE regulation algorithm, as shown in Fig. 3.

The SE regulation algorithm acting on the artificial society is expressed as follows:

$$Fit_{AS,t+1} = Fit_{AS,t} \otimes R_t \quad t \geq 1 \tag{11}$$

$$R_t = \{Reward_{t,0}, Reward_{t,1} \ldots Reward_{t,N}\}$$

where R_t represents the set of gains for all agents from $t-1$ to time t, and N is the number of all agents in the artificial society. $\otimes$ represents the update of the fitness function $Fit_{AS,t+1}$ of the artificial society agent at time $t+1$ based on the fitness function $Fit_{AS,t}$ of the artificial society agent at time t and R_t.

The expression of the emerging social phenomena $AS_{phenomenal,t}$ in the artificial society acting on the SE regulation algorithm RA_t at time t is as follows:

$$W_{t+1} = RA_t \odot AS_{phenomenal,t} \quad t \geq 0 \tag{12}$$

$$W_{t+1} = \{w_{0,t+1}, w_{1,t+1} \ldots, w_{M,t+1}\}$$

where $AS_{phenomenal,t}$ indicates the social phenomenon that emerges in the artificial society time t. W_{t+1} represents the preference weight of the index system at time $t+1$, and M represents the number of characteristic indicators of the regulation algorithm. $\odot$ represents the updating of the index system weights of the regulation algorithm according to the emerging social phenomena at time t.

3.5 Individual Effectiveness, System Effectiveness, and Other Analysis Indicators

The service efficiency of the SE is affected by many factors, and any failure or problem in any link may lead to negative effects on the entire service system. For the healthy and orderly development of the crowd intelligent service system, this paper proposes an Individual Effectiveness IE to evaluate the performance of agents in the service system. In particular, the IE is a concave function, which is increasing the agent's income and linearly decreasing in the cost. The Individual Effectiveness $IE_{T,i}$ is a function of the change in reward $\sum_{t=0}^{t=T} Reward_{t,i}$ and cost $\sum_{t=0}^{t=T} Cost_{t,i}$ for agent i from time 0 to T, the formula looks like this:

$$IE_{T,i} = crra\left(\sum_{t=0}^{t=T} Reward_{t,i}\right) - \sum_{t=0}^{t=T} Cost_{t,i} \tag{13}$$

$$Cost_{agent_T} = \frac{\sum_{i=0}^{i=N} \sum_{t=0}^{t=T} Cost_{t,i}}{N} t \geq 0$$

$$crra(z) = \frac{z^{1-\eta} - 1}{1 - \eta} \eta > 0$$

where $Cost_{t,i}$ denotes the cost of agent i from time $t-1$ to t and $Cost_{agent_T}$ denotes the average cost of all agents in the artificial society at moment T. The $crra$ function is marginal in effect, and its magnitude may decrease as the reward increases. The parameter η controls the degree of non-linearity: higher η indicates more non-linear behavior.

To balance the healthy development of the SE and the number of output results, the system effectiveness of the SE is defined below. A new indicator for judging the healthy development of the SE, namely the System Effectiveness SE_T at time T, is synthesized here and defined as follows:

$$SE_T = \frac{\sum_{i=0}^{i=N} \sum_{t=0}^{t=T} IE_{t,i}}{N} * \frac{\sum_{i=0}^{i=N} \sum_{t=0}^{t=T} Task_{t,i}}{N} \tag{14}$$

where $\frac{\sum_{i=0}^{i=N} \sum_{t=0}^{t=T} IE_{t,i}}{N}$ is the average of the individual effectiveness of all agents at time T. When this value is less than or equal to 0, it indicates that there is involution in the SE at this time. $Task_{t,i}$ denotes the number of tasks completed by agent i from time $t-1$ to t, $\frac{\sum_{i=0}^{i=N} \sum_{t=0}^{t=T} Task_{t,i}}{N}$ denotes the average number of tasks completed by all agents at time T.

Here are some other analytical metrics that use the number of agents that occurs across space to reflect the state of competition within a disciplinary area, with the following formula:

$$Cross_T = \sum_{i=0}^{i=P} \sum_{t=0}^{t=T} Cross_{field_i,t} \quad t \geq 0 \tag{15}$$

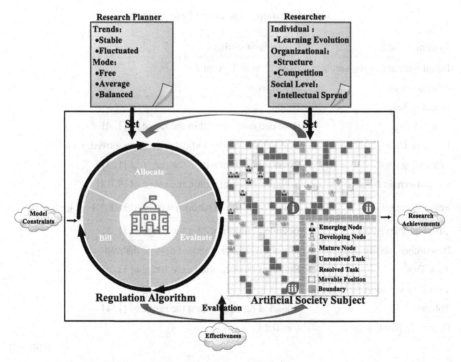

Fig. 4. Design of Computational Experiment System.

where $Cross_{field_i,t}$ denotes the number of domains crossed by field i from time $t-1$ to t, and P represents the number of fields.

4 A Case Study of the Academic Ecosystem

To verify the validity of the model, this paper uses the CEBA model to simulate and analyze the involution of the academic ecosystem. The involution of the academic ecosystem is mainly due to the shortcomings of the research regulation algorithm itself. For example, ignoring the correlation between the difficulty of a research project and the amount of funding support for the project leads to more difficult projects and less support funding for unpopular fields of research. Many researchers in unpopular fields will turn to research in popular fields, leading to a dramatic increase in the number of researchers in popular fields. Researchers in popular fields who engage in some low-value research need to maintain their competitive edge by guaranteeing their number of research outputs, which leads to involution. At the same time, the formation process of involution is influenced by a variety of factors, but the current research on the mechanism of the trend of involution mainly adopts a qualitative analysis method, and it is difficult to fully and dynamically reflect the inner operating mechanism of the involution of the academic ecosystem. Therefore, this paper constructs an experimental system of academic ecology based on the proposed CEBA model for analysis.

Table 1. Parameter settings of experiments

System variable	Experiment setting
Initial Number of Researchers	Area 1: Area 2: Area 3 = 6: 6: 6
Fund for a Tick	$Revenue_t = 20$
Running Time	1000
Vision Range	Bounded random within the range of $[1, 4]$
Distance Cost	$Y = k * x$ ($x > 0$, x indicates distance moved. $k = 1$)
Processing Cost	Bounded random within the range of $[1, 3]$
Cross-Domain Cost	Bounded random within the range of $[9, 14]$
Solve Payment	$Y = \frac{km^k}{x^{k+1}}, * 3$ (x is random within $[0,1000]$, $k = 4$, $m = 18$)
Task Complexity	Bounded random within the range of $[1, 3]$
Researcher Ability	The ability obeys standard normal distribution
Task Type	Bounded random within the range of $[1, 3]$
Task Regeneration probability	0.1
Tolerance	Bounded random within the range of $[1, 4]$
Degree of Nonlinearity	$\eta = 0.23$

(continued)

Table 1. (*continued*)

System variable	Experiment setting
Task Generation Rules	$Y = N + M * \sin(T)$. N represents the task and M represents the fluctuation range. Area 1, N = 40, M = 5 Area 2, N = 30, M = 3 Area 3, N = 20, M = 2
Distribution of Task	Tasks are distributed randomly in three areas with centers of (6, 6) (Area 1), (18, 6) (Area 2), and (6, 18) (Area 3) respectively

This section first proposes the general framework of the experimental system, then introduces how to design and construct an academic ecology computing experimental system based on the CEBA model, and finally presents a statistical analysis of the obtained experimental results.

4.1 The Framework of the Experimental System

The experimental system has two roles: the researcher and the research planner. Disciplinary tasks are assigned to various disciplinary areas according to certain rules. Researchers take the initiative to explore and tackle disciplinary tasks, generating some cost. New disciplinary tasks are automatically generated when they are tackled. The research planner evaluates the work of the researchers and distributes the incomes according to a regulation algorithm.

The framework of the CEBA model-based academic ecosystem shown in Fig. 4 is constructed, where the entire academic ecosystem is divided into four regions.

Different numbers of disciplinary tasks and researchers are scattered across the three disciplinary regions: i, ii, and iii (emerging, developing, and mature disciplinary nodes). And various experimentation scenarios can be customized by setting different SE moderation algorithms and parameters of the academic ecosystem. In addition, the involution pattern of the academic ecosystem is analyzed by observing the evolutionary phenomena in the experimental system.

4.2 Experimental System Design

The CEBA model proposed in this paper focuses on three aspects of the interaction processes between the regulation algorithm and the academic ecosystem: before and after the regulation, changes in the artificial society agent, and changes in the regulation algorithm. Specifically, this paper sets up two sets of controlled experiments using the same initialization conditions and a fixed total amount of money for the researcher and disciplinary tasks, as well as different learning mechanisms and regulation algorithms for different artificial society agents.

Experiment 1 used the free model regulation algorithm, with funding allocated according to the ratio of the number of disciplinary tasks tackled by the researcher to the number of all disciplinary tasks tackled in the system. Then we can reveal the process of involution generation and exacerbation by exploring the impact of the academic ecosystem with different learning mechanisms (individual, organizational, and social learning) on the individual effectiveness of the system. The different learning mechanisms represent different capabilities of information dissemination.

Experiment 2 is carried out based on the social learning used in Experiment 1. The impact of regulation algorithms on system effectiveness is explored by setting up the regulation algorithm with different intervention strategies (free mode, average mode, and balanced mode), which in turn enables the mitigation of involution in the academic ecosystem through adjusting the intervention strategies. The income of researchers under different intervention strategies is as follows.

$$Reward_{t,i} = \frac{\beta * Revenue_t}{N} + (1 - \beta) * Revenue_t * Proportion_{t,i} \tag{16}$$

where $Proportion_{t,i}$ represents the number of disciplinary tasks that researcher i has tackled in time $t - 1$ to t as a proportion of the number of all disciplinary tasks in the system. N is the number of all agents in the academic ecosystem. $Revenue_t$ indicates the total amount of allocated funds in a cycle. Three different intervention models were set up based on the ratio of basic income to performance incentives: Free mode parameter: $\beta = 0$ (Liberal Distribution); Average mode parameter: (Strict Egalitarian Redistribution); Balanced mode parameter: $\beta = 0.5$ (Liberal Egalitarian Redistribution).

The length of the experimental environment is 25 cells and the width is 25 cells, with different types of nodes randomly distributed in their respective areas. The experimental parameters are mainly set at the same scale scaled according to the global scientific community surveyed in Nature [20]. The experimental parameters are set as shown in Table 1. In this paper, the average income to researchers, average cost consumed, the average number of disciplinary tasks tackled, individual effectiveness, and system effectiveness are used to assess the impact of different models of the SE regulation algorithms and different learning capabilities of the academic ecosystem on the generation, exacerbation and mitigation of academic ecosystem involution.

4.3 Experimental System Analysis

a) **Experiment 1:** Classified academic ecosystems into three categories based on the speed of information dissemination: those with different learning mechanisms. It helps us explore the impact of academic ecosystems with different learning mechanisms on individual effectiveness.

Figure 5 compares and analyses the changes in the average income, the average cost of consumption, the average number of disciplinary tasks tackled, and the mean individual effectiveness of researchers during the evolution of learning in the academic ecosystem under three different learning mechanisms. The results of the experiment are as follows.

(1) By analyzing the income and individual effectiveness under the three types of learning in Fig. 5(a)–(c), it is concluded that: 1) With individual learning, the gap in income between researchers is larger, but those with individual effectiveness greater

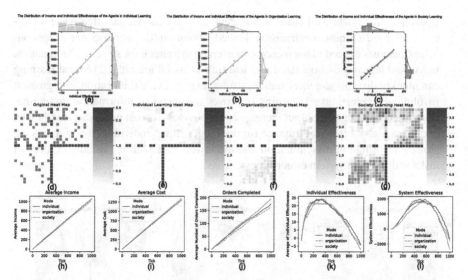

Fig. 5. Comparative analysis of the characteristic index of academic ecosystems under three different learning mechanisms

than zero occupy the majority, and the degree of involution is not serious. 2) With organizational learning, researchers' incomes are normally distributed, and the gap in the overall average level of incomes narrows; those with individual effectiveness less than zero occupy the majority, and involution deepens. 3) With social learning, the returns increase, and the gap between the researchers' incomes is further reduced; the majority of those with individual effectiveness less than zero are more severely involuted.

(2) By analyzing the heat maps of the initialized disciplinary task distribution under the three learning mechanisms in Fig. 5(d)–(g) and the heat maps of the researchers' trajectory run, it can be summarized that 1) the heat maps of the researchers' trajectories under individual learning are lighter in except for a few darker squares, which indicates a certain randomness of movement focusing on free exploration and no aggregation effect. 2) under organizational learning and social learning, the aggregation effect is obvious in the heat map of the researcher's trajectory, with social learning being the most evident. This suggests that the researchers learn through interaction and follow those with higher gains to explore less randomly. Moreover, the movement trajectories can appear highly overlapping.

(3) By analyzing the average income, the average cost of consumption, the average number of disciplinary tasks tackled, the average individual effectiveness, and the system effectiveness of the researchers under the three learning mechanisms shown in Fig. 5 (h)–(l), it can be obtained that 1) for the average income and cost of consumption, social learning > organizational learning > individual learning; for the number of tasks tackled, social learning > organizational learning > individual learning; indicating that the researcher's learning ability and the ability to disseminate information

is stronger, meanwhile all indicators increase. For the individual effectiveness indicator, all three learning mechanisms showed involution (the increase in average consumption costs exceeded the increase in average incomes); for system effectiveness, individual learning > organizational learning > social learning. 2) Social learning can quickly disseminate information, strong inter-individual imitation, and greatest involution; organizational learning improves the speed of information dissemination, where although its output increase is not obvious, its cost is not increased much and it maintains high performance for the longest time; individual learning has the slowest information dissemination and the lowest cost with the middle number of tasks and the best system effectiveness.

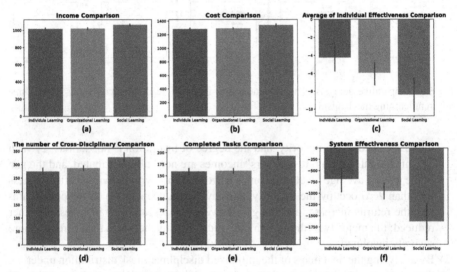

Fig. 6. The average value is calculated in the case of 10 groups of random numbers, and the comparison chart of each index.

The results of a single run in Fig. 5 show that the distribution of incomes according to the number of tasks completed in the discipline creates an involution as the system is run. Since individual mechanisms, organizational mechanisms, and social learning mechanisms are more utilized, the ability of the academic ecosystem to learn and evolve (the ability to disseminate information) increases, accelerating the rate of learning and evolution of the academic ecosystem and deepening the degree of involution.

To further verify the validity of the model and also avoid the possible randomness in a single experiment, 10 random groups are randomly selected for the experiment and results are averaged to obtain the following experimental results, as shown in Fig. 6(a)–(f). The analysis shows that individual learning, organizational learning, and social learning lead to increasing information dissemination among researchers, decreasing mean individual effectiveness, accelerating the rate of evolution of the academic ecosystem, and deepening the degree of involution.

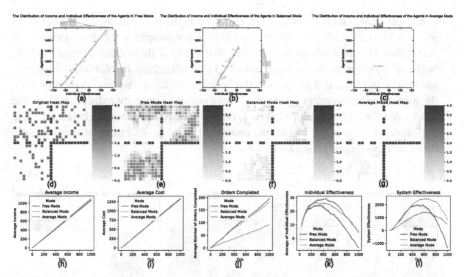

Fig. 7. Comparative analysis of the characteristic index of academic ecosystems under three different learning mechanisms.

b) **Experiment 2:** Improving or updating the regulation algorithm through three different intervention strategies to observe the mitigation effect of different intervention strategies of the regulation algorithm on the involution of the academic ecosystems.

Figure 7 compares and analyses the different characteristic indicators of the learning evolution of the academic ecosystem under the three different intervention modes.

(1) Figure 7 (a)–(c) shows the distribution of researchers' incomes and individual effectiveness under the free, balanced, and average modes, yielding that: 1) under the free mode, the majority of effectiveness values are less than 0 and the degree of involution is severe; there is a large gap in researchers' incomes; 2) under the balanced mode, the proportion of effectiveness values greater than 0 increases and the degree of involution decreases; the gap in researchers' incomes decreases; 3) under the average mode, most of the effectiveness values are greater than 0 with the mean value of effectiveness greater than that of the balanced mode; the incomes of different researchers are equal, and there is no gap in researchers' incomes.

(2) Figure 7 (d)–(g) represents the heat map of the disciplinary task distribution and the heat map of the researcher's trajectory for the three intervention modes, yielding: 1) the aggregation effect and the overlap between the researcher's trajectory and the disciplinary task are both highest in the free mode; 2) the aggregation effect occurs in the balanced mode and there is a degree of overlap between the researcher's trajectory and the location of the disciplinary task distribution; 3) the colors are lighter in the average mode, and the researcher's movement is somewhat exploratory and random, meanwhile, there is no overlap in the movement trajectory.

(3) By analyzing the average income, the average cost of consumption, the average number of disciplinary tasks tackled, the average individual effectiveness, and system effectiveness for the researchers in the three intervention modes in Fig. 7 (h)–(l), it

can be concluded that: 1) For the average income, the average mode > the balanced mode > the free mode. For the average cost of consumption, the three are close to each other. For the number of tasks, the free mode > the balanced mode, and the balanced mode is > the average mode. 2) For mitigating involution, the average mode is > the balanced mode, and the balanced mode > the free mode; however, the number of tasks completed by the average mode is severely reduced, making the academic ecosystem develop slowly. 3) For system effectiveness, the balanced mode performs best and it can ensure the continued rapid development of the academic ecosystem while mitigating involution.

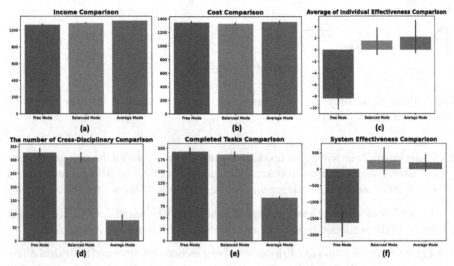

Fig. 8. The average value is calculated in the case of 10 groups of random numbers, and the comparison chart of each.

Figure 7 analyzes the results of a single run of the experiment and shows that the degree of involution is continually mitigated as the proportion of the researcher's basic income to the total income of the researchers rises, but the total number of disciplinary tasks tackled in the whole academic ecosystem is constantly decreasing. Considering the specificity of involution and disciplinary areas in the academic ecosystem, we chose a balanced mode. We cannot choose the average mode that is most effective in mitigating involution, nor the free mode that is most effective in accelerating the development of the discipline of studying ecosystems. The advantage of the balanced mode is that it reduces involution while rapidly developing each disciplinary area.

To verify the validity of the results of a single experiment, 10 random sets of random numbers are randomly selected for the experiment, and the results are averaged as shown in Fig. 8 (a)–(f). The analysis shows that: 1) in the average mode, there is randomness in the researcher's behavior to get more disciplinary tasks; 2) in the free mode, the academic ecosystem has the most serious involution, which is mitigated in the balanced model and the average mode; 3) the balanced mode can mitigate involution based on ensuring rapid disciplinary development of the academic ecosystem and the highest system effectiveness.

5 Conclusion

To better analyze the decision-making processes between the regulation algorithm and the crowd intelligence group in the SE, the CEBA model is proposed in this paper. The above work can provide new research ideas and tools for decision-making processes analysis of SE. For example, in the delivery industry, the delivery time of takeaway riders is getting shorter and shorter under the intelligent regulation algorithm, while more and more effort cannot produce any increase in income, showing an overall state of decreasing marginal effect of involution, etc.

In future work, the CEBA will be further refined and the research will focus on two aspects: 1) comparing artificial society agents with real crowd intelligence groups; 2) replacing the algorithms in the analysis model with the current widely used recommendation algorithms, etc.

Acknowledgment. This work has been supported in part by National Key Research and Development Program of China (No. 2021YFF0900800), National Natural Science Foundation of China (No. 61972276, No. 62206116, No. 62032016), New Liberal Arts Reform and Practice Project of National Ministry of Education (No. 2021170002), Open Research Fund of The State Key Laboratory for Management and Control of Complex Systems (No. 20210101), Tianjin University Talent Innovation Reward Program for Literature & Science Graduate Student (C1-2022-010).

References

1. Xue, X., et al.: Research roadmap of service ecosystems: a crowd intelligence perspective. Int. J. Crowd Sci. **6**, 28 (2022)
2. Kang, H., Lou, C.: AI agency vs. human agency: understanding human–AI interactions on Tik-Tok and their implications for user engagement. J. Comput.-Mediated Commun. **27**, zmac014 (2022)
3. Gal, U., Jensen, T.B., Stein, M.-K.: Breaking the vicious cycle of algorithmic management: a virtue ethics approach to people analytics. Inf. Organ. **30**(2), 100301 (2020)
4. Chen, J., Wang, L., Wang, S., Wang, X., Ren, H.: An effective matching algorithm with adaptive tie-breaking strategy for online food delivery problem. Complex Intell. Syst., 107–128 (2022)
5. Geertz, C.: Agricultural Involution. University of California Press (2020)
6. Bruns, A.: Filter bubble. Internet Policy Rev. (2019)
7. Miikkulainen, R., et al.: Sentient ascend: AI-based massively multivariate conversion rate optimization. In: AAAI, vol. 32 (2018)
8. Shi, J.-C., Yu, Y., Da, Q., Chen, S.-Y., Zeng, A.-X.: Virtual-Taobao: virtualizing real-world online retail environment for reinforcement learning. In: AAAI, vol. 33, pp. 4902–4909 (2019)
9. Duderstadt, V.H., Mojzisch, A., Germar, M.: Social norm learning from non-human agents can induce a persistent perceptual bias: a diffusion model approach. Acta Physiol. **229**, 103691 (2022)

10. Koster, R., et al.: Human-centered mechanism design with democratic AI. Nat. Hum. Behav. **6**(10), 1398–1407 (2022)
11. Xue, X., Chen, F.Y., Zhou, D., Wang, X., Lu, M., Wang, F.Y.: Computational experiments for complex social systems Part I: the customization of computational model. IEEE Trans. Comput. Soc. Syst. **9**(5), 1330–1344 (2022)
12. Lu, M., Chen, S., Xue, X., Wang, X., Zhang, Y., Wang, F.Y.: Computational experiments for complex social system Part II: the evaluation of computational model. IEEE Trans. Comput. Soc. Syst. **9**(4), 1224–1236 (2022)
13. Xue, X., Yu, X.N., Zhou, D.Y., Peng, C., Wang, X., Wang, F.Y.: Computational experiments for complex social systems, Part III: the docking of domain models. IEEE Trans. Comput. Soc. Syst. (2023)
14. Xue, X., Yu, X.N., Zhou, D.Y., Peng, C., Wang, X., Wang, F.Y.: Computational experiments: past, present and perspective. Acta Automatica Sinica **49**(2), 1–26 (2023)
15. Bucher, T.: The algorithmic imaginary: exploring the ordinary affects of Facebook algorithms. Inf. Commun. Soc. **20**, 30–44 (2017)
16. Alvarado, O., Waern, A.: Towards algorithmic experience: initial efforts for social media contexts. In: Proceedings of the 2018 CHI Conference on Human Factors in Computing Systems, pp. 1–12. ACM, Montreal, QC, Canada (2018)
17. Shin, D., Zhong, B., Biocca, F.A.: Beyond user experience: what constitutes algorithmic experiences? Int. J. Inf. Manage. **52**, 102061 (2020)
18. Li, X., Sung, Y.: Anthropomorphism brings us closer: the mediating role of psychological distance in user–AI assistant interactions. Comput. Hum. Behav. **118**, 106680 (2021)
19. Xue, X., Wang, S., Zhang, L., Feng, Z., Guo, Y.: Social learning evolution (SLE): computational experiment-based modeling framework of social manufacturing. IEEE Trans. Ind. Inf. **15**, 3343–3355 (2019)
20. Woolston, C.: Satisfaction in science. Nature, 611–615 (2018)

Operationalizing the Use of Sensor Data in Mobile Crowdsensing: A Systematic Review and Practical Guidelines

Robin Kraft[1,2] , Maximilian Blasi[1], Marc Schickler[1] , Manfred Reichert[1] ,
and Rüdiger Pryss[3(✉)]

[1] Institute of Databases and Information Systems, Ulm University, Ulm, Germany
robin.kraft@uni-ulm.de
[2] Department of Clinical Psychology and Psychotherapy, Ulm University, Ulm,
Germany
[3] Institute of Clinical Epidemiology and Biometry, University of Würzburg,
Würzburg, Germany
ruediger.pryss@uni-wuerzburg.de

Abstract. Smartphones have found their way into many domains because they can be used to measure phenomena of common interest. The Global Overview Report Digital 2022 states that two-thirds of the world's population uses a smartphone. This creates a power for measurements that many researchers would like to leverage. However, this in turn requires standardized approaches to collaborative data collection. Mobile crowdsensing (MCS) is a paradigm that pursues collaborative measurements with smartphones and the available sensor technology. Although literature on MCS has existed since 2006, there is still little work that has systematically studied existing systems. Especially when developing technical systems based on MCS, design decisions must be made that affect the subsequent operation. In this paper, we therefore conducted a PRISMA-based literature review on MCS, considering two aspects: First, we wanted to be able to better categorize existing systems, and second, we wanted to derive guidelines for developers that can support design decisions. Out of a total of 661 identified publications, we were able to include 117 papers in the analysis. Based on five main criteria (application area, goals, sensor utilization, time constraints, processing device), we show which goals the research area is currently pursuing and which approaches are being used to achieve these goals. Following this, we derive practical guidelines to support researchers and developers in making design decisions.

Keywords: Mobile crowdsensing · Mobile sensing · Systematic review

1 Introduction

Mobile crowdsensing (MCS) is a mobile sensing paradigm coined by Ganti et al. [19] where, on the one hand, the sensory capabilities of smartphones are exploited and, on the other hand, the crowd is placed in the foreground.

© ICST Institute for Computer Sciences, Social Informatics and Telecommunications Engineering 2024
Published by Springer Nature Switzerland AG 2024. All Rights Reserved
H. Gao et al. (Eds.): CollaborateCom 2023, LNICST 563, pp. 229–248, 2024.
https://doi.org/10.1007/978-3-031-54531-3_13

This concept is promoted by the fact that two-thirds of the world's population own a smartphone [29], and is particularly suitable for measuring phenomena of common interest. MCS applications can be further distinguished between *participatory* [6] and *opportunistic sensing* [7] applications. Participatory sensing applications require active user involvement in the sensing process (e.g., the user has to actively trigger a sound measurement), while opportunistic sensing applications perform sensor measurements and data transmission automatically (e.g., the sound measurement happens in the background) [32]. MCS is used, for example, in the automotive [50] or medical [42] domain to capture large amounts of real-world data in a rather short time. However, the use of the paradigm is also accompanied by many challenges [31,34]. For example, data quality of the measurements must be ensured, incentives for contributing data must be provided, and the privacy of the users must be protected. The concept has existed for some time and can look back on more than 20 years of development [30]. However, it is still not widely used, and there are still too few studies [19] that systematically examine MCS and derive general development recommendations. In addition, such studies should be regularly updated and there are many pitfalls to consider. Therefore, this paper conducts a systematic literature review that addresses the following research questions (RQ):

- **RQ1**: What are the main goals of MCS applications?
- **RQ2**: Which sensors are MCS applications using to achieve these goals and how are they used?
- **RQ3**: What time constraints do MCS applications have?
- **RQ4**: On which processing device are MCS applications performing their computations (i.e., smartphone or server)?

Another goal of this literature review is to derive practical development guidelines that incorporate the aforementioned research questions. We conducted the analysis of the above research questions and the derivation of the guidelines based on the PRISMA guidelines [38]. 661 papers resulted from our search in the following databases used: ACM Digital Library, IEEE Xplore, PubMed, and Google Scholar. In the end, 117 papers could be included in the analysis. Despite the long history of the field of MCS, this shows that the number of papers presented should be considered rather small. In the following, we present the results of the review and show which general statements and practical guidelines can be derived to support MCS system design and development, for example, how the selection of the processing device can be systematically addressed.

The paper is organized as follows: In Sect. 2, related work is discussed. Material and methods are presented in Sect. 3, and the results are discussed in Sect. 4. Practical guidelines are derived in Sect. 5. The findings are discussed in 6, and the paper concludes in Sect. 7.

2   Related Work

Overall, there is an abundance of literature on MCS. As such, several general reviews and surveys related to MCS have already been conducted over the years.

In 2010, Lane et al. [32] present a survey on mobile phone sensing by reviewing existing applications and systems in this context. The authors describe the sensors available on smartphones at the time and discuss their capabilities. Furthermore, different application areas and sensing paradigms—including participatory and opportunistic sensing—are extracted and a general architectural framework is proposed. In their initial work on MCS in 2011, Ganti et al. [19] survey existing crowdsensing applications and classify them—similar to our work—into environmental, infrastructural, and social applications. Moreover, the authors discuss unique characteristics and respective research challenges of MCS applications. Similarly, in 2015, Guo et al. [23] review existing MCS applications and techniques along a number of categories. In addition, the authors highlight the unique characteristics of MCS applications and propose a conceptual framework based on the reviewed literature. Furthermore, the work considers MCS as human-in-the-loop systems and discusses the findings in terms of combining human and machine intelligence. More recently, in 2019, the survey of Liu et al. [34] aims to provide a comprehensive overview of recent advances in MCS research. The authors review the literature with respect to incentive mechanisms, security and privacy, resource optimization, data quality, and data analysis, with a particular focus on the data flow within MCS systems. Moreover, similar to our work, the findings and MCS applications are presented along four categories: indoor localization, urban sensing, environmental monitoring, and social management. Also, in 2019, Capponi et al. [8] present a comprehensive survey that considers MCS as a four-layered architecture consisting of an application, a data, a communication, and a sensing layer. In addition, the authors propose a number of taxonomies based on this architecture, classify existing MCS publications and systems according to these taxonomies, and discuss various conceptual and technical aspects of MCS systems. In addition to these more general and comprehensive reviews, there is also related work that focuses on specific aspects of MCS, such as incentives mechanisms [28,61], task allocation [52], data quality [25,33,46], resource limitations [53,54], security and privacy [13,25,41], or software architectures [35,57].

Overall, in the literature, either a rather general overview on MCS is provided or details on very specific aspects are discussed. However, there is a lack of practical guidance for researchers and system operators seeking to use MCS to achieve a specific goal, especially if they are new to this area of research. In this work, we aim to provide such guidance by reviewing the existing literature and identifying best practices for operationalizing MCS and the decisions to be made during system design. Furthermore, none of the above reviews include a review protocol that would make the review process transparent, traceable, and reproducible by other researchers. In particular, we were unable to find any reviews on MCS that use the PRISMA guidelines.

3   Materials and Methods

To produce transparent and reproducible results, we established a review protocol guided by the *Preferred Reporting Items for Systematic Reviews and Meta-
Analyses* (PRISMA) statement. PRISMA is a collection of items designed to
promote a transparent approach for systematic reviews and meta-analyses [38].
In the following, the defined eligibility criteria (see Sect. 3.1), the search strategy used (see Sect. 3.2), as well as the selection and data collection process (see
Sect. 3.3) are described.

3.1   Eligibility Criteria

We established criteria that we used to decide on the eligibility of publications,
i.e., whether a particular publication should be included or excluded. In this process, the following inclusion criteria (IC) were defined: **IC1:** The paper describes
an MCS application; **IC2:** The paper describes a system using one or more
mobile devices (e.g., smartphone or wearable) as sensors. In addition, we defined
following exclusion criteria (EC) for the systematic review at hand: **EC1:** The
system described in the paper does not use any mobile sensors; **EC2:** The paper
does not describe how the data is sensed; **EC3:** The publication is older than
2007; **EC4:** The full text of the paper is not available or not available in English;
EC5: The publication is not peer-reviewed. The search was limited to papers
published from 2007 onwards. This year was chosen because it was the year
Apple Inc. introduced its iPhone [14], which can be considered the beginning of
the smartphone era [21].

3.2   Search Strategy

We used the scientific databases ACM Digital Library, IEEE Xplore, and
PubMed as information sources for the review. In addition, a manual search via
Google Scholar was performed. To identify relevant publications that met the
eligibility criteria, the following search query was issued to the three databases
on August 4, 2022:

```
Abstract :( crowdsens ^*) AND ( AllField :( application ) OR
   AllField :( app ))
```

Listing 1.1. Search query used for the databases.

As shown in Listing 1.1, the abstract or title had to contain a word beginning
with *crowdsens* and somewhere in the paper the word *application* or *app* had
to occur. In addition, a filter was applied limiting the search to only papers
published from 2007 onwards to address exclusion criterion EC3.

3.3   Selection and Data Collection Process

The results of the queries to the chosen scientific database and the manual search
were combined and duplicate records were removed. For the selection process,

these papers were then screened based on their abstract and title to eliminate papers that are not relevant for this review. After screening, the full text of the remaining papers was examined, and further papers were excluded based on the defined inclusion and exclusion criteria. Furthermore, we extracted the following data from the included papers and used Microsoft Excel to record the results:

- Application area: Each paper is assigned to one of the four categories based on its application area (1) *urban sensing*, (2) *indoor localization*, (3) *environmental monitoring*, and (4) *social management, public safety, & healthcare*.
- Goals: The goals and subgoals pursued by the paper. Subgoals are smaller goals that the paper pursues (e.g., map matching or location matching), while goals are used as a broader term that encompasses multiple subgoals (e.g., localization). Each paper can be associated with any number of goals and subgoals.
- Sensor utilization: The sensors that are utilized by the MCS system and in what way or to achieve which of the identified goals and subgoals they are used (e.g., GPS used for localization or to measure the electron density in the atmosphere).
- Time constraint: The time constraints on the processing of the data (i.e., were the results needed in (near) real-time).
- Processing device: Which parts of the data processing were performed on which component of the system (e.g., smartphone or server).

4   Results

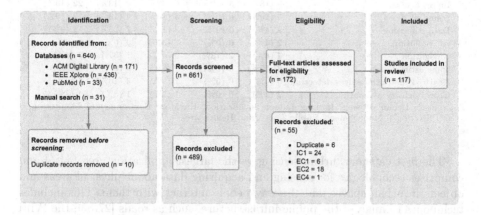

Fig. 1. PRISMA 2020 [38] flow diagram of the publication selection and screening process.

The publication selection and screening process is illustrated in Fig. 1. The database search returned a total of 640 publications. After adding 31 additional records through manual search and removing all duplicate results, 661 papers remained. The abstracts and titles of these publications were then screened, of which 489 papers were excluded. The full texts of the remaining 172 records were then assessed for eligibility and 55 records were excluded based on the defined inclusion and exclusion criteria. This process resulted in 117 publications included for the analysis at hand.

In the following, the results of the extracted data are presented. Note that for reasons of readability and space limitations, only a limited number of representative references are provided in the text for each category and aspect.

4.1 Application Areas

First, we analyzed the publications that were assigned to each category of application area. The number of publications per category is shown in Table 1.

Table 1. Number of publications per category ($n = 117$) and number of publications in each category that share a specific goal, in descending order by number of total occurrences. Each publication has been assigned to a single category, but may have multiple goals.

Category	UrbSens	IndLoc	EnvMon	SMPSH	All
Total	51 (44%)	16 (14%)	19 (16%)	31 (26%)	117 (100%)
Goal					
Localization	49 (96%)	16 (100%)	15 (79%)	22 (71%)	102 (87%)
Activity recognition	16 (31%)	4 (25%)	1 (5%)	6 (19%)	27 (23%)
Map generation	14 (27%)	7 (43%)	4 (21%)	1 (3%)	26 (22%)
Street observation	22 (43%)	0 (0%)	1 (5%)	0 (0%)	23 (20%)
Image analysis	9 (18%)	3 (19%)	6 (32%)	4 (13%)	22 (19%)
Sound analysis	5 (10%)	0 (0%)	3 (16%)	4 (13%)	12 (10%)
Data collection	2 (4%)	0 (0%)	3 (16%)	7 (23%)	11 (9%)
Air pollution	2 (4%)	0 (0%)	7 (37%)	0 (0%)	9 (8%)
Navigation	4 (8%)	2 (13%)	0 (0%)	1 (3%)	7 (6%)
Time estimation	6 (12%)	0 (0%)	0 (0%)	0 (0%)	6 (5%)
Nearby Bluetooth devices detection	0 (0%)	0 (0%)	1 (5%)	3 (10%)	4 (3%)
Crowd density estimation	2 (4%)	0 (0%)	1 (5%)	1 (3%)	4 (3%)

UrbSens: Urban Sensing, IndLoc: Indoor Localization, EnvMon: Environmental Monitoring, SMPSH: Social Management, Public Safety, and Healthcare.

The first category, urban sensing, is the largest application area (44%) and comprises technologies for sensing and acquiring data about physical areas and objects in urban spaces and the way people interact with them. This includes techniques to analyze the public infrastructure, such as roads [27,55], the WiFi density of a city [18], the waiting time for specific services [60,62], or other specific applications such as an online reposting system for fliers [22]. The second application area, indoor localization, comprises 14% of the included publications and focuses on localization techniques for indoor environments. This is a nontrivial problem, as conventional localization methods have many problems due to sensor inaccuracies within buildings, resulting in inaccurate data. Indoor localization techniques include localization on an indoor map [45, 59], the reconstruction of indoor maps [11, 59], or other applications such as generating a map of the WiFi coverage of a floor [44] and collecting fingerprints of a specific location [58]. The third application area, environmental monitoring, encompasses 16% of the publications. Environmental monitoring is conventionally implemented with wireless sensor networks (WSN). However, the installation and maintenance of WSNs are expensive, which is why MCS is often used to circumvent these costs. These applications include analyzing nightlife behavior of participants [48], detecting beautiful places in the city [36], or measuring electron counts in the ionosphere [40]. The last and second largest application area (26%) is social management, public safety, and healthcare. This category includes all applications that concern the physical and mental well-being of participants [26, 43], as well as applications for disaster relief [49], disease detection [17], observation of large crowds [9, 56], letting people report events they witness [37], or determining the relationship between two people [16].

4.2 Goals

Second, we analyzed the included publications in each category in terms of the goals they pursue and how these goals are achieved. The number of publications in each category that share a specific goal is shown in Table 1. Note that each publication may have multiple goals and corresponding subgoals.

For urban sensing, the most common goal is localization. In this context, map matching [27, 39, 55] matches the current position to a road on existing maps. In some cases, the number of possible routes can be restricted in order to have more options to reach this goal. One specific example case is route matching [62], where a list of possible routes is known. Another subgoal is simply to determine the position of the user, which is referred to as location matching [18, 60]. This knowledge can, in turn, be used to extract features at a particular location [27], or to determine the time spent at a location [60]. Another prevalent goal in urban sensing is street observation. This goal includes application areas related to roads, such as inferring new roads [55], classifying intersections [27], detecting traffic anomalies [39], determining parking spaces [15], and monitoring road surfaces [2]. Activity recognition is another goal that can be used to reduce the amount of false data (i.e., sensing data at the wrong time) [5, 62], sometimes aided by the use of sound recognition [62]. Activity recognition is often performed to help achieve other subgoals, such as road surface monitoring [2] or turn detection [10]. Another common goal is time estimation, which is often used to give an estimated time to enhance the user experience. This can be achieved in the form of predicting the arrival time, i.e., arrival time prediction [62], or the waiting time, i.e., waiting time prediction [5, 60], of certain services to improve the user experience. Furthermore, many urban sensing applications aim to achieve map generation. These maps to be generated range from WiFi coverage maps [18] to cellular coverage maps [51], to maps highlighting road surface conditions [2], or free parking spaces on streets [15]. Other less common subgoals of urban sensing include photo quality determination [22], photo tagging [22], and photo grouping [22]. A common type of data collected is GPS traces, which are sometimes split to analyze the data for specific information [27, 39].

Inherently, for indoor localization, the most prevalent goal is also localization. As the usage of GPS in indoor environments is highly error-prone, this goal is often achieved through the use of fingerprinting. With fingerprinting, the user's current location is determined by comparing the current sensor readings to previously recorded sensor readings with a corresponding location. This can be achieved either by WiFi fingerprinting [44, 45], where a list of wireless access points (WAP) and their location is stored, or by magnetic fingerprinting [59], where the user needs to walk a bit to get the location, since the magnetic fingerprints a 3D vector and thus requires a temporal dimension. Another option to achieve this goal is tracking [20, 44, 45], using the accelerometer, gyroscope, and sometimes magnetometer to track the user's movement patterns. One of these tracking techniques is pedestrian dead reckoning (PDR) [44, 45]. In PDR, the user's movement is tracked by knowing the starting location and estimating the distance and direction travelled. Since PDR makes estimates continuously, the estimation error accumulates over time, so a combination of PDR and another indoor localization technique has proven to be very beneficial. Furthermore, simple location matching [11] can also be used to detect the rough location in indoor environments. Map generation is another common goal of indoor localization. An application example is the reconstruction of a floor plan [11, 20, 59], which is implemented by using a PDR-similar approach [59], estimating the travelled distance and direction, or by letting participants record videos or photos of the environment [11, 20]. These pictures are used for information extraction [11, 20], picture concatenation [20], and connecting adjacent wall segments on photos to continuous boundaries to obtain hallway connectivity, orientation, and room sizes. Some MCS-applications also aim to map WiFi coverage of an indoor floor [44]. Other indoor localization subgoals are the navigation in an indoor environment [59], activity recognition [44, 45], fingerprint collection [58], and QR code forgery detection [58].

Localization is also the most common goal in environmental monitoring, but most localization tasks in this area are fairly simple, such as location matching [4], as only the location of the user is needed for these applications, or detecting the location of a physical event (e.g., flowering cherries) [36]. Air pollution detection is one of the biggest challenges in environmental monitoring with MCS, as conventional smartphones usually lack the required sensors to address this problem. Therefore, most applications in this context use an external connected mobile sensor to measure the required data [4], but some applications attempt to detect air pollution by analyzing images captured by the mobile phone camera [24]. Image analysis is also used for other purposes, such as analyzing the brightness level of a video [48], analyzing the loudness level of a video [48], or simply extracting information from a picture [24, 36] to detect a specific feature in the photos. Other subgoals of environmental monitoring include conducting a questionnaire [48], detecting points of interest [36], expanding areas of interest [36], and measuring electron counts in the ionosphere [40].

As in all other areas, localization is the most common goal for applications in the social management, public safety, and healthcare category. Location matching [16, 26, 37] is often required to simply determine the participant's current location. In some cases, an exact location is not required, but information about whether the participant is in a certain area is sufficient, which is referred to as geofencing [9]. Other event detection methods, such as swipe localization [37], where multiple participants indicate a direction in which an event is occurring, are also commonly performed. The second most frequent goal in this category is data collection [43, 47]. This goal can be achieved through many different methods, such as conducting a questionnaire [43, 47]. Other subgoals of this area include activity recognition [9, 26], nearby people detection [16], relationship inference [16], determining swipe direction [37], detecting nearby Bluetooth devices [56], and crowd density estimation [56].

4.3 Sensor Utilization

Furthermore, we analyzed which sensors are used by the included applications and how they are used to achieve the goals and subgoals identified in Sect. 4.2.

The GPS sensor can be used for map matching [27, 55] and location matching [11, 60]. However, simply using GPS can lead to errors when the exact location is relevant, and therefore [60] proposed a possible solution by using the center of consecutive GPS readings. To measure electron counts in the ionosphere [40], dual-frequency GPS can be used. To do this, GPS signals are sent to the receiver at two different frequencies, and the delay between the arrival of these two signals can be used to calculate the electron count. Another option used for location matching is the usage of WiFi to detect WAP locations or to directly detect a specific WAP [5]. The WiFi sensor can also be used for WiFi density detection [18], route matching [62], which fingerprints cell tower IDs, and WiFi fingerprinting [44, 45], where a list of WAPs is associated with a specific location and used for localization. GPS and WiFi can also be used together for location matching [16] or geofencing [9] to achieve even more accurate results. The magnetometer can be used for magnetic fingerprinting [59], which works much like the WiFi equivalent, with the only exception that a temporal dimension is required (i.e., the participant must walk the path for a while to determine the location). WiFi and the magnetometer can also be used in combination to produce a combined fingerprint for fingerprint collection [58].

Activity recognition is most often implemented by using the accelerometer [5, 44, 62]. This can be supported by utilizing the microphone for sound recognition [62]. Another way to use the accelerometer is to determine the tilt angle of the phone. This information can be used together with the magnetometer for swipe localization [37]. A variety of sensors can be used for movement tracking. Using solely the gyroscope, it is possible to detect whether the participant is making a turn [59]. Accelerometer and gyroscope can be used together to measure distances and orientation between start and finish [20]. Accelerometer, magnetometer and optionally gyroscope can be used together for PDR [44,45].

Other sensors used include the power sensor, the camera, the microphone, the Bluetooth sensor, and the ambient light sensor. The power sensor can be used, for example, to detect whether a phone is charging [27]. The camera can be used to take photos [20,22] and videos [11,36,48]. The microphone can record ambient sound [43], while Bluetooth can be used to detect nearby Bluetooth devices [56]. Finally, a combination of accelerometer, magnetometer and ambient light sensor can be used to determine photo quality [22].

4.4   Time Constraints

The time constraints per category of application areas are shown in Table 2. It can be seen that most applications either have no time constraints at all (51%), or only some of their components are time-relevant (27%). Only 21% of all considered publications state that their MCS application is completely real-time dependent.

Table 2. Number of publications with real-time constraints, without time constraint, and with a mixed approach. Per category of application areas and in total ($n = 117$).

Category	UrbSens	IndLoc	EnvMon	SMPSH	All
Total	$n = 51$	$n = 16$	$n = 19$	$n = 31$	$n = 117$
Real-time	10 (20%)	1 (6%)	4 (21%)	10 (32%)	25 (21%)
No time constraint	25 (49%)	10 (62%)	10 (53%)	15 (48%)	60 (51%)
Mixed	16 (31%)	5 (31%)	5 (26%)	6 (19%)	32 (27%)

UrbSens: Urban Sensing, IndLoc: Indoor Localization, EnvMon: Environmental Monitoring, SMPSH: Social Management, Public Safety, and Healthcare.

Most MCS applications do not have time constraints [20,27,48] because they are used to collect information that is not time-sensitive, for example, to update maps or obtain information only for eventual data analysis. As shown in Table 2, the highest percentage of application without time constraints can be found in the category of indoor localization, with many non-time-sensitive applications such as the reconstruction of indoor floor plans [11,20]. Other MCS applications aim to relay the gathered information to participants as quickly as possible, i.e., in real-time [26,36,62]. The highest proportion of applications with a real-time constraint is found in the area of social management, public safety, and healthcare. This category includes comparatively many time-sensitive applications such as healthcare monitoring [1], fall detection [26], disaster management during earthquakes [49], and crowd-management in mass gatherings [9]. Many MCS applications use a combination of real-time components and non-time-sensitive components [39,45,55]. The reason for the time constraints of these individual components is in most cases the same as mentioned above: a non-time-sensitive information is needed to further process the time-sensitive information. For example, the typical routing behavior of drivers is calculated without time constraint in order to detect traffic anomalies in real time [39].

4.5   Processing Device

In all the applications studied, data collection is always done via the smartphone or via external sensors connected to the phone. However, there are differences in the devices used to process the sensed data. The distribution of processing devices used per category of application areas is shown in Table 3.

Table 3. Number of publications that use local pre-processing or upload the data directly to a server where it is then processed. Per category of application areas and in total ($n = 117$).

Category	UrbSens	IndLoc	EnvMon	SMPSH	All
Total	$n = 51$	$n = 16$	$n = 19$	$n = 31$	$n = 117$
Local pre-processing	28 (55%)	7 (44%)	8 (42%)	15 (48%)	58 (50%)
Direct upload	23 (45%)	9 (56%)	11 (58%)	16 (52%)	59 (50%)

UrbSens: Urban Sensing, IndLoc: Indoor Localization, EnvMon: Environmental Monitoring, SMPSH: Social Management, Public Safety, and Healthcare.

Interestingly, about 50% of the analyzed MCS applications across all categories did not perform any local pre-processing before uploading the data to the server. This is often the case when the main purpose of the application is data collection [3], since no processing is required for this purpose, or when the application is not intended to interfere with the normal use of the phone and therefore does not require many computing resources [20,44]. The processing and computations performed by the server are usually more expensive calculations and include, for example, detecting traffic anomalies [39], arrival time prediction [62], waiting time prediction [5,60], or reconstructing a floor plan [11,20,59]. Many applications pre-process the data locally on the smartphone to reduce the amount of data to be uploaded and the burden on the participant devices [43,45,55]. In cases where avoiding data transfer is a higher priority than avoiding computations, these computations can be performed locally on the smartphone. These pre-processing and computation subgoals include route matching [62], splitting GPS traces [27,39], sound recognition [62], conducting questionnaires [43,48], recording ambient sound [43], determining swipe direction [37], and detecting nearby Bluetooth devices [56]. Finally, the processing of various subgoals is often executed either on the phone or the server. These include map matching [27,39,55], location matching [11,18,36], inferring new roads [55], extracting features at a given location [27], extracting information from a picture [11,20,36], intersection classification [27], activity recognition [5,26,45], fingerprinting [45,58,59], PDR [44,45], and geofencing [9]. In particular, activity recognition [5,44,45] is usually performed to verify the prerequisites for sensing data (e.g., the user is standing in a queue) and is therefore often performed locally on the smartphone.

5   Practical Guidelines

Based on the literature presented in the previous sections, best practices for operationalizing MCS are identified, including the decisions that must be made during the design and development of an MCS system. These decisions include the goals to be achieved by the system as well as the choice of sensors and the processing device to achieve these goals.

5.1   Goals, Subgoals, and Sensors

The first step in an MCS project is to consider what goals and subgoals the application should fulfill and how they should be achieved. Many goals require other goals or subgoals to achieve them. In addition, different sensors are required to achieve these goals and subgoals. Some common connections between goals, subgoals, and sensors are illustrated in Fig. 2 and are described in the following.

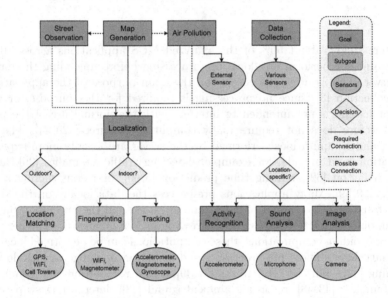

Fig. 2. Typical goals, subgoals, and sensors of MCS applications and their connections. Note that only common connections and not all possible connections are displayed.

If the location of the user is required for the application, localization must be performed. This goal can be achieved in different ways. The standard approach in large and open areas (e.g., a city) is location matching using GPS and, in some cases, WiFi or cell tower signals. If the application is intended to work in indoor environments, fingerprinting and tracking methods are preferable. In some cases, the user's location cannot be identified by coordinates, but by another concept, for example, if the user is on a train. This is a very application-specific problem, but the most commonly used techniques to address this problem are activity recognition (e.g., detecting the movement patterns of a particular vehicle) and sound analysis (e.g., detecting the sound of the IC card reader when boarding a bus [62]). Since street observation attempts to determine different road conditions, the participant's current location is always relevant for this purpose. Thus, some form of localization is always required, and depending on the specific subgoals (e.g., road surface monitoring), activity recognition is often additionally required to identify the specific road condition being monitored. Measuring air pollution with MCS can be performed only with smartphone-internal sensors using image analysis, but the more accurate solution is to use an external sensor connected to the smartphone (e.g., via Bluetooth). In this way, even more detailed information about air pollution can be collected, such as what types of substances pollute the air and to what extent. This measurement is usually always coupled with the location of the sensed air pollution, so in addition localization is required. Map generation also requires some form of localization to infer the coordinates of the objects or events being mapped. Typical applications are WiFi/cellular coverage maps of cities, maps containing information generated through street observation, air pollution, or reconstructing a floor plan. Activity recognition, image analysis, and sound analysis are most often used as utility functions to support another goal or subgoal of the application. Finally, if the main purpose of the application is data collection, the methods to achieve this goal depend on the data to be collected. For example, any combination of sensors can be recorded or a questionnaire can be conducted.

5.2 Processing Device

Another important consideration when designing an MCS application is the choice of the processing device. In other words, it must be decided whether the application will perform computations locally (i.e., on the smartphone) or on the server. This decision can be made for the entire application as a whole, but in most cases, it makes more sense to make this decision for each component of the application separately. The reason for this is that some components may have, for example, less security-relevant data or only some components have to deliver their results in real time. The most common aspects that are crucial for this decision are illustrated in Fig. 3 and explained in more detail in the following.

For each component of the MCS application, the first and probably most important aspect to consider is whether the component is intended to operate in (near) real time or whether it is not subject to any time constraints. If the results of the component are not time-sensitive, this aspect can be ignored. However, if the component is to evaluate and/or present the results to the user in (near) real time, the data must either be processed locally on the smartphone or a constant network connection is required (i.e., no opportunistic upload when connected to hotspots is possible). Most MCS applications are not time-sensitive or have only some time-sensitive parts, which means that only these parts of the application need special consideration when specifying the processing device. The second aspect to consider is whether it is feasible to run the components of the application locally at all. Components that only use the local data can easily run locally.

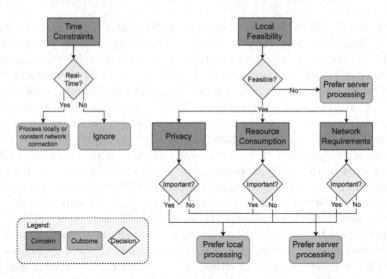

Fig. 3. Decision diagram for deciding on the processing device of a component of an MCS application.

However, components that require data from multiple devices/users (e.g., clustering GPS locations of multiple users) would need to download the remaining data from the server, while still uploading their own data for the other users to use. In most cases, it makes more sense to let the server perform this type of processing and download only the processing results from the server. If the local feasibility is generally given, privacy, resource consumption, and network requirements of the component should be considered. With respect to privacy, the more data a user uploads to the servers, the more privacy issues may arise. By performing as many computations as possible locally on the smartphone, the amount of potentially sensitive raw data uploaded can be reduced, thus avoiding privacy issues. For example, aggregations of raw data per time period can be performed directly on the smartphone, and only the aggregated data can be uploaded. Resource and power consumption are another aspect worth considering, also in terms of usability. Users will not be content with the application if the entire computational resources of their mobile device are occupied by the application and the battery life of their device is noticeably shortened by using the application. Since time-consuming computations can noticeably affect the battery life [12], it is preferable for such components to upload the data to the server and perform these computations there. Another aspect to consider is the network requirements. Due to the variable network coverage and mobility of users in MCS, a stable Internet connection cannot be guaranteed. In addition, most users will not have an unlimited amount of mobile network data. If the data should be able to be uploaded from anywhere possible, it is preferable to compress the data locally for further computations. For example, classification tasks where multiple data types are used as input and the result is only a class label can be performed locally to reduce the transferred data. Another option is to cache the collected data on the mobile device and opportunistically upload it when the device is connected to a WiFi hotspot. This approach circumvents the problem of mobile data usage and network connectivity for the participant, but does not allow real-time results.

6   Discussion

Overall, according to our analysis, urban sensing is the largest (44%) application area of MCS. The second largest area is social management, public safety, and healthcare (26%), followed by environmental monitoring (16%) and indoor localization (14%). In terms of the goals that MCS application pursue, localization is by far the most common (87%) goal. Activity recognition (23%), map generation (22%), street observation (20%), and image analysis (19%) are other commonly used goals in MCS. Depending on the specific application scenario, different sensors are used to achieve these goals. For example, GPS, WiFi, and cell towers are commonly used for outdoor localization, while WiFi, magnetometer, accelerometer, magnetometer, and gyroscope can be used for indoor localization. We propose that system designers of MCS applications explicitly define the goals and subgoals that the application should pursue and select the sensors and approaches that are best suited for these purposes and, in the optimal case, have been proven in the literature. The practical guidelines in Sect. 5.1 can be used to support this process. Only half (50%) of the analyzed MCS applications perform pre-processing locally on the mobile device (e.g., smartphone) before uploading the collected data to a server. We argue that for each component of the MCS application, separate consideration should be given to whether local pre-processing is feasible and reasonable, carefully balancing time constraints and resource consumption on the one hand, and privacy and network requirements on the other. This should be considered especially in light of the fact that most MCS applications have no time constraints (51%) or only some time-sensitive components (21%). However, some application scenarios, such as health monitoring and disaster management, are time-sensitive and therefore need to relay the collected information as quickly as possible, avoiding additional processing steps and prioritizing timeliness over resource consumption or network requirements. The decision diagram in Sect. 5.2 can be used to support the decision on the processing device for a particular component of an MCS application.

7   Conclusion

Mobile crowdsensing is a strategy that capitalizes on the current capabilities and prevalence of smartphones. From a technical point of view, many challenges have been identified and solutions presented that are promising so far. For example, incentive mechanisms and data quality are identified as challenges in the literature. Although the research field is not young, there are still too few fundamental considerations (e.g., in the form of literature reviews) or guidelines on how MCS systems can be designed. Therefore, using the existing literature, we examined what the goals of current approaches are, how these goals are achieved, and what guidelines for developers and researchers can be derived based on the widely used PRISMA guidelines. We have shown that localization is the most important goal of current approaches, followed by activity recognition and map generation. Nevertheless, we see the opportunities, for example in healthcare, much broader than MCS is operationalized so far. Despite the very focused goals currently being pursued with MCS, we were able to gain new insights for the work at hand based on the defined research questions. On the one hand, we were able to derive technical results, such as guidelines for decisions on sensors, processing devices, and time constraints. On the other hand, it should be noted that this systematic literature review using major academic databases resulted in only 117 papers that provided enough technical details to be included, despite the long history since the introduction of the technology. The presumption is, and the COVID-19 pandemic has made it clear, that we need the wisdom of the crowd. Technical operationalization certainly lags behind the opportunities, as the present study shows. With the extracted practical guidelines, we hope to have taken another step towards dissemination of MCS and its potential.

References

1. Abdo, M.A., Abdel-Hamid, A.A., Elzouka, H.A.: A cloud-based mobile healthcare monitoring framework with location privacy preservation. In: 2020 International Conference on Innovation and Intelligence for Informatics, Computing and Technologies (3ICT), pp. 1–8 (2020). https://doi.org/10.1109/3ICT51146.2020.9311999
2. Aly, H., Basalamah, A., Youssef, M.: Map++: a crowd-sensing system for automatic map semantics identification. In: 2014 Eleventh Annual IEEE International Conference on Sensing, Communication, and Networking (SECON), pp. 546–554 (2014). https://doi.org/10.1109/SAHCN.2014.6990394
3. Beierle, F., et al.: Corona health-a study- and sensor-based mobile app platform exploring aspects of the COVID-19 pandemic. Int. J. Environ. Res. Public Health 18(14) (2021). https://doi.org/10.3390/ijerph18147395
4. Bosello, M., Delnevo, G., Mirri, S.: On exploiting gamification for the crowdsensing of air pollution: a case study on a bicycle-based system. In: Proceedings of the 6th EAI International Conference on Smart Objects and Technologies for Social Good, GoodTechs 2020, pp. 205–210. Association for Computing Machinery, New York, NY, USA (2020). https://doi.org/10.1145/3411170.3411256
5. Bulut, M.F., Demirbas, M., Ferhatosmanoglu, H.: LineKing: coffee shop wait-time monitoring using smartphones. IEEE Trans. Mob. Comput. 14(10), 2045–2058 (2015). https://doi.org/10.1109/TMC.2014.2384032
6. Burke, J.A., et al.: Participatory sensing. In: First Workshop on World-Sensor-Web: Mobile Device Centric Sensory Networks and Applications (WSW 2006) at the 4th ACM Conference on Embedded Networked Sensor Systems (SenSys) (2006)

7. Campbell, A.T., Eisenman, S.B., Lane, N.D., Miluzzo, E., Peterson, R.A.: People-centric urban sensing. In: Proceedings of the 2nd Annual International Workshop on Wireless Internet, p. 18-es (2006)
8. Capponi, A., Fiandrino, C., Kantarci, B., Foschini, L., Kliazovich, D., Bouvry, P.: A survey on mobile crowdsensing systems: challenges, solutions, and opportunities. IEEE Commun. Surv. Tutorials **21**(3), 2419–2465 (2019)
9. Cardone, G., Cirri, A., Corradi, A., Foschini, L., Ianniello, R., Montanari, R.: Crowdsensing in urban areas for city-scale mass gathering management: geofencing and activity recognition. IEEE Sens. J. **14**(12), 4185–4195 (2014). https://doi.org/10.1109/JSEN.2014.2344023
10. Chen, D., Shin, K.G.: TurnsMap: enhancing driving safety at intersections with mobile crowdsensing and deep learning. Proc. ACM Interact. Mob. Wearable Ubiquitous Technol. **3**(3) (2019). https://doi.org/10.1145/3351236
11. Chen, S., Li, M., Ren, K., Qiao, C.: Crowd map: accurate reconstruction of indoor floor plans from crowdsourced sensor-rich videos. In: 2015 IEEE 35th International Conference on Distributed Computing Systems, pp. 1–10 (2015). https://doi.org/10.1109/ICDCS.2015.9
12. Chon, Y., Lee, G., Ha, R., Cha, H.: Crowdsensing-based smartphone use guide for battery life extension. In: Proceedings of the 2016 ACM International Joint Conference on Pervasive and Ubiquitous Computing, UbiComp 2016, pp. 958–969. Association for Computing Machinery, New York, NY, USA (2016). https://doi.org/10.1145/2971648.2971728
13. Christin, D., Reinhardt, A., Kanhere, S.S., Hollick, M.: A survey on privacy in mobile participatory sensing applications. J. Syst. Softw. **84**(11), 1928–1946 (2011)
14. Cohen, P.: Macworld expo keynote live update: introducing the iPhone. Macworld (2007). https://www.macworld.com/article/183052/liveupdate-15.html. Accessed 7 Feb 2023
15. Coric, V., Gruteser, M.: Crowdsensing maps of on-street parking spaces. In: 2013 IEEE International Conference on Distributed Computing in Sensor Systems, pp. 115–122 (2013). https://doi.org/10.1109/DCOSS.2013.15
16. Cranshaw, J., Toch, E., Hong, J., Kittur, A., Sadeh, N.: Bridging the gap between physical location and online social networks. In: Proceedings of the 12th ACM International Conference on Ubiquitous Computing, UbiComp 2010, pp. 119–128. Association for Computing Machinery, New York, NY, USA (2010). https://doi.org/10.1145/1864349.1864380
17. Edoh, T.: Risk prevention of spreading emerging infectious diseases using a Hybrid-Crowdsensing paradigm, optical sensors, and smartphone. J. Med. Syst. **42**(5), 91 (2018). https://doi.org/10.1007/s10916-018-0937-2
18. Farshad, A., Marina, M.K., Garcia, F.: Urban WiFi characterization via mobile crowdsensing. In: 2014 IEEE Network Operations and Management Symposium (NOMS), pp. 1–9 (2014). https://doi.org/10.1109/NOMS.2014.6838233
19. Ganti, R.K., Ye, F., Lei, H.: Mobile crowdsensing: current state and future challenges. IEEE Commun. Mag. **49**(11), 32–39 (2011)
20. Gao, R., et al.: Jigsaw: indoor floor plan reconstruction via mobile crowdsensing. In: Proceedings of the 20th Annual International Conference on Mobile Computing and Networking, MobiCom 2014, pp. 249–260. Association for Computing Machinery, New York, NY, USA (2014). https://doi.org/10.1145/2639108.2639134
21. Gartner: Number of smartphones sold to end users worldwide from 2007 to 2021 (in million units) (2022). https://www.statista.com/statistics/263437/global-smartphone-sales-to-end-users-since-2007/. Accessed 7 Feb 2023

22. Guo, B., Chen, H., Yu, Z., Xie, X., Huangfu, S., Zhang, D.: FlierMeet: a mobile crowdsensing system for cross-space public information reposting, tagging, and sharing. IEEE Trans. Mob. Comput. **14**(10), 2020–2033 (2015). https://doi.org/10.1109/TMC.2014.2385097
23. Guo, B., et al.: Mobile crowd sensing and computing: the review of an emerging human-powered sensing paradigm. ACM Comput. Surv. (CSUR) **48**(1), 1–31 (2015)
24. Hao, P., Yang, M., Gao, S., Sun, K., Tao, D.: Fine-grained PM2.5 detection method based on crowdsensing. In: 2020 IEEE International Conference on Consumer Electronics - Taiwan (ICCE-Taiwan), pp. 1–2 (2020). https://doi.org/10.1109/ICCE-Taiwan49838.2020.9258279
25. He, D., Chan, S., Guizani, M.: User privacy and data trustworthiness in mobile crowd sensing. IEEE Wirel. Commun. **22**(1), 28–34 (2015)
26. He, Y., Li, Y., Bao, S.D.: Fall detection by built-in tri-accelerometer of smartphone. In: Proceedings of 2012 IEEE-EMBS International Conference on Biomedical and Health Informatics, pp. 184–187 (2012). https://doi.org/10.1109/BHI.2012.6211540
27. Hu, S., Su, L., Liu, H., Wang, H., Abdelzaher, T.F.: SmartRoad: smartphone-based crowd sensing for traffic regulator detection and identification. ACM Trans. Sen. Netw. **11**(4) (2015). https://doi.org/10.1145/2770876
28. Jaimes, L.G., Vergara-Laurens, I.J., Raij, A.: A survey of incentive techniques for mobile crowd sensing. IEEE Internet Things J. **2**(5), 370–380 (2015)
29. Kepios: Digital 2022: Global Overview Report (2022). https://datareportal.com/reports/digital-2022-global-overview-report. Accessed 04 Mar 2023
30. Koh, J.Y., Peters, G., Nevat, I., Leong, D.: Spatial Stackelberg incentive mechanism for privacy-aware mobile crowd sensing. J. Mach. Learn. Res. **1**, 1–48 (2000)
31. Kraft, R., et al.: Combining mobile crowdsensing and ecological momentary assessments in the healthcare domain. Front. Neurosci. **14**, 164 (2020)
32. Lane, N.D., Miluzzo, E., Lu, H., Peebles, D., Choudhury, T., Campbell, A.T.: A survey of mobile phone sensing. IEEE Commun. Mag. **48**(9), 140–150 (2010)
33. Liu, J., Shen, H., Narman, H.S., Chung, W., Lin, Z.: A survey of mobile crowdsensing techniques: a critical component for the internet of things. ACM Trans. Cyber-Phys. Syst. **2**(3), 1–26 (2018)
34. Liu, Y., Kong, L., Chen, G.: Data-oriented mobile crowdsensing: a comprehensive survey. IEEE Commun. Surv. Tutorials **21**(3), 2849–2885 (2019)
35. Marjanović, M., Antonić, A., Žarko, I.P.: Edge computing architecture for mobile crowdsensing. IEEE Access **6**, 10662–10674 (2018)
36. Morishita, S., et al.: SakuraSensor: quasi-realtime cherry-lined roads detection through participatory video sensing by cars. In: Proceedings of the 2015 ACM International Joint Conference on Pervasive and Ubiquitous Computing, UbiComp 2015, pp. 695–705. Association for Computing Machinery, New York, NY, USA (2015). https://doi.org/10.1145/2750858.2804273
37. Ouyang, R.W., Srivastava, A., Prabahar, P., Roy Choudhury, R., Addicott, M., McClernon, F.J.: If you see something, swipe towards it: crowdsourced event localization using smartphones. In: Proceedings of the 2013 ACM International Joint Conference on Pervasive and Ubiquitous Computing, UbiComp 2013, pp. 23–32. Association for Computing Machinery, New York, NY, USA (2013). https://doi.org/10.1145/2493432.2493455
38. Page, M.J., et al.: The Prisma 2020 statement: an updated guideline for reporting systematic reviews. Syst. Control Found. Appl. **10**(1), 1–11 (2021)

39. Pan, B., Zheng, Y., Wilkie, D., Shahabi, C.: Crowd sensing of traffic anomalies based on human mobility and social media. In: Proceedings of the 21st ACM SIGSPATIAL International Conference on Advances in Geographic Information Systems, SIGSPATIAL 2013, pp. 344–353. Association for Computing Machinery, New York, NY, USA (2013). https://doi.org/10.1145/2525314.2525343

40. Pankratius, V., Lind, F., Coster, A., Erickson, P., Semeter, J.: Mobile crowd sensing in space weather monitoring: the Mahali project. IEEE Commun. Mag. **52**(8), 22–28 (2014). https://doi.org/10.1109/MCOM.2014.6871665

41. Pournajaf, L., Garcia-Ulloa, D.A., Xiong, L., Sunderam, V.: Participant privacy in mobile crowd sensing task management: a survey of methods and challenges. ACM SIGMOD Rec. **44**(4), 23–34 (2016)

42. Pryss, R., Schlee, W., Langguth, B., Reichert, M.: Mobile crowdsensing services for tinnitus assessment and patient feedback. In: 2017 IEEE International Conference on AI & Mobile Services (AIMS), pp. 22–29. IEEE (2017)

43. Pryss, R., Reichert, M., Herrmann, J., Langguth, B., Schlee, W.: Mobile crowd sensing in clinical and psychological trials - a case study. In: 2015 IEEE 28th International Symposium on Computer-Based Medical Systems, pp. 23–24 (2015). https://doi.org/10.1109/CBMS.2015.26

44. Radu, V., Kriara, L., Marina, M.K.: Pazl: a mobile crowdsensing based indoor WiFi monitoring system. In: Proceedings of the 9th International Conference on Network and Service Management (CNSM 2013), pp. 75–83 (2013). https://doi.org/10.1109/CNSM.2013.6727812

45. Rai, A., Chintalapudi, K.K., Padmanabhan, V.N., Sen, R.: Zee: zero-effort crowdsourcing for indoor localization. In: Proceedings of the 18th Annual International Conference on Mobile Computing and Networking, Mobicom 2012, pp. 293–304. Association for Computing Machinery, New York, NY, USA (2012). https://doi.org/10.1145/2348543.2348580

46. Restuccia, F., Ghosh, N., Bhattacharjee, S., Das, S.K., Melodia, T.: Quality of information in mobile crowdsensing: survey and research challenges. ACM Trans. Sens. Netw. (TOSN) **13**(4), 1–43 (2017)

47. Rivron, V., Khan, M.I., Charneau, S., Chrisment, I.: Refining smartphone usage analysis by combining crowdsensing and survey. In: 2015 IEEE International Conference on Pervasive Computing and Communication Workshops (PerCom Workshops), pp. 366–371 (2015). https://doi.org/10.1109/PERCOMW.2015.7134065

48. Santani, D., et al.: The night is young: Urban crowdsourcing of nightlife patterns. In: Proceedings of the 2016 ACM International Joint Conference on Pervasive and Ubiquitous Computing, UbiComp 2016, pp. 427–438. Association for Computing Machinery, New York, NY, USA (2016). https://doi.org/10.1145/2971648.2971713

49. Visuri, A., Zhu, Z., Ferreira, D., Konomi, S., Kostakos, V.: Smartphone detection of collapsed buildings during earthquakes. In: Proceedings of the 2017 ACM International Joint Conference on Pervasive and Ubiquitous Computing and Proceedings of the 2017 ACM International Symposium on Wearable Computers, UbiComp 2017, pp. 557–562. Association for Computing Machinery, New York, NY, USA (2017). https://doi.org/10.1145/3123024.3124402

50. Wan, J., Liu, J., Shao, Z., Vasilakos, A.V., Imran, M., Zhou, K.: Mobile crowd sensing for traffic prediction in internet of vehicles. Sensors **16**(1), 88 (2016)

51. Wang, H., Guo, B., Wang, S., He, T., Zhang, D.: CSMC: cellular signal map construction via mobile crowdsensing. Proc. ACM Interact. Mob. Wearable Ubiquitous Technol. **5**(4) (2022). https://doi.org/10.1145/3494959

52. Wang, J., Wang, L., Wang, Y., Zhang, D., Kong, L.: Task allocation in mobile crowd sensing: state-of-the-art and future opportunities. IEEE Internet Things J. **5**(5), 3747–3757 (2018)
53. Wang, J., Wang, Y., Zhang, D., Helal, S.: Energy saving techniques in mobile crowd sensing: current state and future opportunities. IEEE Commun. Mag. **56**(5), 164–169 (2018)
54. Wang, L., Zhang, D., Wang, Y., Chen, C., Han, X., M'hamed, A.: Sparse mobile crowdsensing: challenges and opportunities. IEEE Commun. Mag. **54**(7), 161–167 (2016)
55. Wang, Y., Liu, X., Wei, H., Forman, G., Chen, C., Zhu, Y.: CrowdAtlas: self-updating maps for cloud and personal use. In: Proceeding of the 11th Annual International Conference on Mobile Systems, Applications, and Services, MobiSys 2013, pp. 27–40. Association for Computing Machinery, New York, NY, USA (2013). https://doi.org/10.1145/2462456.2464441
56. Weppner, J., Lukowicz, P.: Bluetooth based collaborative crowd density estimation with mobile phones. In: 2013 IEEE International Conference on Pervasive Computing and Communications (PerCom), pp. 193–200 (2013). https://doi.org/10.1109/PerCom.2013.6526732
57. Xiao, Y., Simoens, P., Pillai, P., Ha, K., Satyanarayanan, M.: Lowering the barriers to large-scale mobile crowdsensing. In: Proceedings of the 14th Workshop on Mobile Computing Systems and Applications, pp. 1–6 (2013)
58. Xu, Q., Zheng, R.: MobiBee: a mobile treasure hunt game for location-dependent fingerprint collection. In: Proceedings of the 2016 ACM International Joint Conference on Pervasive and Ubiquitous Computing: Adjunct, UbiComp 2016, pp. 1472–1477. Association for Computing Machinery, New York, NY, USA (2016). https://doi.org/10.1145/2968219.2968590
59. Zhang, C., Subbu, K.P., Luo, J., Wu, J.: GROPING: geomagnetism and cROwdsensing powered indoor navigation. IEEE Trans. Mob. Comput. **14**(2), 387–400 (2015). https://doi.org/10.1109/TMC.2014.2319824
60. Zhang, F., Wilkie, D., Zheng, Y., Xie, X.: Sensing the pulse of urban refueling behavior. In: Proceedings of the 2013 ACM International Joint Conference on Pervasive and Ubiquitous Computing, UbiComp 2013, pp. 13–22. Association for Computing Machinery, New York, NY, USA (2013). https://doi.org/10.1145/2493432.2493448
61. Zhang, X., et al.: Incentives for mobile crowd sensing: a survey. IEEE Commun. Surv. Tutorials **18**(1), 54–67 (2015)
62. Zhou, P., Zheng, Y., Li, M.: How long to wait? Predicting bus arrival time with mobile phone based participatory sensing. IEEE Trans. Mob. Comput. **13**(6), 1228–1241 (2014). https://doi.org/10.1109/TMC.2013.136

Enriching Process Models with Relevant Process Details for Flexible Human-Robot Teaming

Myriel Fichtner[(✉)] , Sascha Sucker , Dominik Riedelbauch ,
Stefan Jablonski, and Dominik Henrich

University of Bayreuth, Universitätsstrasse 30, 95447 Bayreuth, Germany
{myriel.fichtner,sascha.sucker,dominik.riedelbauch,stefan.jablonski,
dominik.henrich}@uni-bayreuth.de

Abstract. Human-robot teaming is crucial for future automation in small and medium enterprises. In that context, domain-specific process models are used as an intuitive description of work to share between two agents. Process designers usually introduce a certain degree of abstraction into the models. This way, models are better to trace for humans, and a single model can moreover enable flexibility by capturing several process variations. However, abstraction can lead to unintentional omission of information (e.g., experience of skilled workers). This may impair the quality of process results. To balance the trade-off between model readability and flexibility, we contribute a novel human-robot teaming approach with incremental learning of relevant process details (RPDs). RPDs are extracted from imagery during process execution and used to enrich an integrated process model which unifies human worker instruction and robot programming. Experiments based on two use cases demonstrate the practical feasibility and scalability of our approach.

Keywords: Process Model Optimization · Task Annotation ·
Explanation Models · Intelligent Robots · Process Variety · Product
Variety

1 Introduction

The demographic change and a trend towards small-batch production of goods with high variability pose new challenges to the future of manufacturing systems. Particularly when using domain-specific process models to describe workflows in manufacturing settings, highly varying processes require the inclusion of many specific alternatives. This can lead to large and hardly traceable process models, which can only be created with high effort. Since human-robot collaboration is considered a key enabler of partial automation in small and medium enterprises, this issue relates to process models for instructing robots and humans alike [15]. It is usually solved through abstraction: (i) In the context of robotics, we have proposed a *graphical robot programming* method based on *precedence graphs* with

© ICST Institute for Computer Sciences, Social Informatics and Telecommunications Engineering 2024
Published by Springer Nature Switzerland AG 2024. All Rights Reserved
H. Gao et al. (Eds.): CollaborateCom 2023, LNICST 563, pp. 249–269, 2024.
https://doi.org/10.1007/978-3-031-54531-3_14

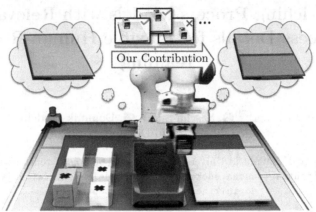

Fig. 1. The robot execution with varieties [28] is susceptible to overly coarse task modeling (upper left: no restrictions on the goal location (green)). We present an approach to specify these tasks with RPDs based on image extraction [11] resulting in increased process quality (upper right: the goal location is restricted, i.e., locations that lead to reduced process success are excluded (red)). (Color figure online)

generalized skill templates [28]. Contrasting to traditional robot programming, our precedence graph-based approach enables quick task specification and online adaptation to concrete situations in the robot workspace rather than requiring manual re-programming after each change to a new task variant. (ii) For manual labor tasks to be done by humans, several execution variants of a single process step are often aggregated into one abstract sub-task of a *business process model*. This abstraction maintains the readability of business process models by partly discarding information on process details (e.g., [5,22,23]). In both robot and human task modeling, the success of the process (e.g., in terms of product quality) can be degraded if models are designed too coarsely – this happens whenever *relevant process details* (RPDs) are omitted or inaccessible to the modeler (e.g., experience and best-practices of skilled workers). RPDs carry hidden information, significantly affecting the overall success of a process. This process knowledge must be revealed and incorporated into a model to ensure the accurate execution of a task. Thereby, RPDs can be used as task specifications for a given process model to further refine existing task instructions. For example, one RPD may prescribe a concrete position on a workbench where an object has to be placed for successful task execution. Our approach [11] therefore shows how RPDs can automatically be extracted from image data to enrich process models with task annotations, hence balancing the trade-off between model readability and preservation of necessary details.

In this paper, we bridge the gap between process model-based human-to-human and precedence graph-based human-to-robot knowledge transfer: We contribute a novel approach to human-robot collaboration with intrinsically legible task representations enriched by RPDs. This way, humans and robots can rely on domain expert knowledge encoded in RPDs for increased process quality (Fig. 1). The practical feasibility of the approach is demonstrated in two use cases.

2   Background and Related Work

Process models give an overview of the work steps to be done during the execution of a process. They serve as the basis for process execution by human and robot agents. Hence, process modeling is an essential basis of knowledge transfer in production contexts with a broad range of established techniques.

In **Business Process Management (BPM)** [34], process models are primarily intended for human workers. The focus lies on presenting process descriptions in a clear and easy-to-understand manner. To this end, *process modeling languages* as the Business Process Model and Notation (BPMN) [6], the Unified Modeling Language (UML) [30], Event-Driven Process Chains [29], etc., have been proposed. They typically define a set of *modeling elements* to map different aspects of a process. *Modeling guidelines* (e.g., [3,16]) are intended to establish standardized ways for manually composing complex processes from modeling elements. Despite these efforts to structure the model design process, mapping concrete tasks to informative but lean process models for human readers is still challenging. The trade-off between the level of detail and model complexity strongly relies on human intelligence to complete missing information omitted at model design time. Research related to automatic model optimization and improvement addresses this issue. Established approaches support model designers from *representation-related* (e.g., [5,22,23]) and *content-related* (e.g., [1,12,18]) perspectives. Representation-related techniques seek to improve the readability of process models in various ways. This involves accepting the loss of information in favor of model traceability, which is a common reason for the lack of process details. In contrast, content-related techniques refer to the modeled quantity, accuracy, relevance, and order of information. Analysis of RPDs is part of the latter category, which has hardly been addressed in research. Therefore, we have previously introduced a novel approach by employing the *Local Interpretable Model-Agnostic Explanations* method to extract the RPDs essential for process success from labeled imagery of correct/erroneous execution results [11]. The RPDs are then used to enrich process models with human-legible hints without compromising the overall model readability. Thus, process models are optimized from a content- and representation-related perspective.

In the field of **Collaborative Robotics**, process models (often also referred to as *task models*) enable robots to participate in a task. Similar to the BPM domain, complex tasks are composed of robot-executable building blocks following a pre-defined structure, e.g., UML/P state charts [33], precedence graphs [26], or AND/OR trees [8,19]. The work steps are then dispatched to human and robot agents. This leads to a collaborative process by task-sharing (e.g., [8,25]). Robot-readable task models are predominantly created manually by domain experts with *visual programming* techniques [9] (e.g., [20,26,28,31,32]) based on *robot skills* [2]. To keep the task model manageable during programming and to keep the process flexible concerning product and process variety, recent visual programming [20,31] and task sharing approaches [8] including our work [28] mimic the abstraction process as used in business process modeling: work steps are intentionally left partly under-specified by omitting information in gener-

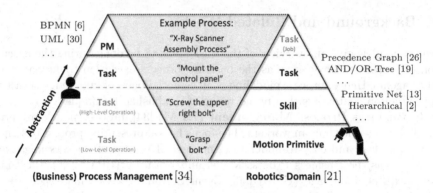

Fig. 2. Mapping of terms stemming from the domains of BPM and robotics.

alized skills (e.g., *"Put the part into the bin"* rather than *"Put the part with id 1 to cartesian position* $(0.4, 0.6, 0.01)$*"*), and the robot system resolves missing information online by reasoning on the scene perceived with cameras just as humans would do with a BPMN model. Yet the decision on how to generalize task models is left to the programmer, thus yielding a potential loss of RPDs.

In conclusion, there is a strong analogy between abstract process models and related challenges in BPM and Collaborative Robotics. We therefore hypothesize that human-robot collaboration approaches would benefit from an analogous enrichment of process models with learnt RPDs as previously enabled by our method to improve business process models [11]. In this paper, we contribute (i) a unified terminology of task modeling in the BPM and Collaborative Robotics domains, (ii) a novel approach to human-robot collaboration based on a single, hierarchical human-robot process model with RPD annotations, and (iii) an incremental learning approach which renders RPDs machine-readable for robots.

3   Terms and Definitions

Connecting the fields of robotics and (Business) Process Management requires the alignment of terminologies and the understanding of how processes and activities are defined and executed in both domains. In the robotics domain (Fig. 2; right), tasks describe actions a robot should perform. A task either refers to a single abstract activity as e.g., *"mount the control panel"*, or to a more complex job that has to be done (e.g., *"X-Ray Scanner Assembly Process"*). Tasks for robots are usually represented by task models as outlined in Sect. 2, with a clearly defined entry and exit point. Since robots require concrete program code to accomplish a task, tasks are decomposed into *skills*, which specify necessary actions on a more fine-grained level [21]. For example, *"screw the upper right bolt"* could be a skill that contributes to the task *"mount the control panel"*. Skills are further decomposed in hierarchies [2] or net structures [13] until ultimately reaching primitives. These *primitives* define the most specific set of actions that correspond e.g., to a single motion command to the robot. They include the specification of points in the environment that the robot needs to reach as well as gripper actions (e.g., *"grasp bolt"*) [13].

In the BPM domain (Fig. 2; left), process models (PM) describe workflows or processes (e.g., "X-Ray Scanner Assembly Process") to achieve a certain goal [34]. Process models typically consist of an entry point (e.g., a start event in BPMN) defining the beginning, and an exit point (e.g., an end event in BPMN) demarcating the end of the process flow. In between, a series of tasks can be modeled, connected through directional edges to define the control flow. Tasks can be assigned to process participants such as employees or customers (e.g., through pools and swimlanes in BPMN). Furthermore, tasks contain descriptions of activities needed to complete the process. The level of detail in task descriptions is not predetermined and must be decided by the model designer. The designer also has the choice of breaking down a task into smaller sub-tasks. For instance, *"mount the control panel"* can be modeled as a single task or be divided into several sub-tasks describing the task at an operational level. An example high-level operational task is *"screw the upper right bolt"* – a low-level operational task is *"grasp bolt"*. Hence, contrasting to the skill and primitive notions in robotics, the term *"task"* is used independently of the level of detail and type of instruction.

The mapping depicted in Fig. 2 shows that, depending on whether a human or robot performs an activity, a task must be defined in more or less detail for proper execution. Humans apply context knowledge and experience subconsciously. Thus, implicitly necessary substeps of a task are automatically done, and the matching of objects mentioned in the task description with those available in the environment is done intuitively. In contrast, such reasoning cannot be assumed when assigning tasks to a robot but must be considered explicitly during task modeling. This is achieved by the aforementioned division of tasks into skills and primitives. The second aspect, the anchoring [7] of parts, is contained in the skill definition and deals with the mapping of object specifications (describing fictitious objects) to physical objects acquired by the sensors of a robot. In this paper, we call such object specifications *part templates* and physical objects *part states*.

Based on the mapping, we propose a consolidated process model to support collaborations between humans and robots effectively. To this end, *human-readable process models* (HPM) are first created by process experts with according process modeling languages from the BPM domain (e.g., BPMN). In this model, all workers (humans and robots) are considered participants of the process. They are each assigned a swimlane with a pool of tasks to work off (Fig. 3), i.e., task allocation to human or robot resources is achieved by a modeler's decision to assign process steps to swimlanes. This decision is supported by structured criteria from the field of capability-aligned process planning (e.g., [4]). At this stage of the model, tasks assigned to the robot are presented similarly to those assigned to humans. Yet, as previously explained, this description level is insufficient for a robot to perform the task. Therefore, all robot tasks are further enriched with skill- and primitive-based descriptions using visual programming

(Sect. 4.1). This leads to a unified process model composed of dedicated human and robot tasks, each being represented in a manner suitable for the corresponding agent according to Fig. 2 (see PM in Fig. 3 for a visualization). Hereinafter, we will use the term "process model" to refer to this type of unified process model which contains task descriptions for humans, skills for execution by a robot, and the allocation of tasks to humans and robots.

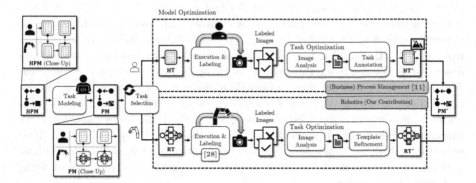

Fig. 3. Adaption of our previous concept [11] to the robotic domain.

4   Extending Unspecified Process Models

Our approach is summarized in Fig. 3. In our previous work [11], the input is a BPMN diagram designed for human workers. In contrast, our new approach additionally allows the input of joint human-robot process models according to Sect. 3. In the *Task Selection* stage, a single task is selected from the input process model. This task is the entry point to *Model Optimization*. Tasks to be executed by humans (HT) trigger the optimization procedure from our previous work [11] (top of Fig. 3). Similarly, for robot tasks (RT) that are expressed as task models, we can utilize our previous procedure by making minor adjustments to accommodate a robotic agent (bottom of Fig. 3). The input process model is executed, and after the execution of the selected task, an image of the workspace is captured. Thereby, in contrast to HTs, RTs are executed as further described in Sect. 4.2. At the end of the process model execution, the recorded image is labeled regarding process success. This is repeated several times until sufficient labeled data is collected. Then, the task is analyzed for relevant process details in the *Task Optimization* step (Sect. 4.3). The output is either a human (HT*) or robot task (RT*) enriched with relevant process details, resulting in an optimized process model (PM*). The cycle can be repeated for further optimizations by returning to the *Task Selection* step.

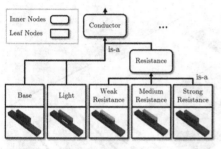

(a) Excerpt from the part type taxonomy.

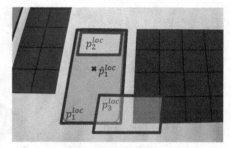

(b) Location examples.

Fig. 4. Part types and locations contain varying degrees of ambiguity. The part type taxonomy (a) includes generic inner nodes ('conductor' and 'resistance') that comprise specific types in the leafs (e.g.,'base' or 'light'). Locations (b) encompass generic area descriptions (p_1^{loc} - p_3^{loc}) or specific poses ($\hat{p}_1^{\mathrm{loc}}$).

4.1   Robot Task Modeling

For robot execution, steps in the process model must be mirrored in the robotics domain. We achieve this by visual robot programming of robot-executable precedence graphs with varieties following our previous work [28]. In this approach, *part states* encode physical objects in the workspace, whereas *part templates* describe partially ambiguous requirements to objects (cf. Sect. 3). Both part states and templates have the same features depending on the domain. In this paper, the features are the part type and its location. A *part type* is an entry in a tree-shaped taxonomy with 'is-a'-relations between its set P^{type} of nodes (Fig. 4a). Leaf nodes denominate *specific part types* $\hat{P}^{\mathrm{type}} \subset P^{\mathrm{type}}$ which parts in the physical world can be classified as. When ascending from a leaf towards the root node, inner nodes encode *generic part types*, i.e., fictitious type concepts, which enable variety in the part description. We use the predicate is_a($p_i^{\mathrm{type}}, p_j^{\mathrm{type}}$) to state whether $p_i^{\mathrm{type}} = p_j^{\mathrm{type}}$ or p_i^{type} is a child of p_j^{type}.

  Part locations P^{loc} describe the rigid body pose of parts. We distinguish two cases: (i) A *specific location* $\hat{p}^{\mathrm{loc}} \in \hat{P}^{\mathrm{loc}}$ is a rigid body transform $^wT_{\mathrm{part}} \in \mathbb{R}^{4\times4}$ indicating the part translation and rotation concerning some world frame w (with $\hat{P}^{\mathrm{loc}} \subset P^{\mathrm{loc}}$). (ii) An ambiguous *generic location* $p^{\mathrm{loc}} \in P^{\mathrm{loc}}$ specifies the 3D volume in which a part is expected. Similarly to part types, we use the predicate is_in($p_i^{\mathrm{loc}}, p_j^{\mathrm{loc}}$) to state whether p_i^{loc} is part of the volume p_j^{loc}. This predicate can be applied between specific-specific ($\hat{p}_i^{\mathrm{loc}} \approx \hat{p}_j^{\mathrm{loc}}$); specific-generic ($\hat{p}_i^{\mathrm{loc}} \in p_j^{\mathrm{loc}}$); and generic-generic location pairs ($p_i^{\mathrm{loc}} \subseteq p_j^{\mathrm{loc}}$). For example, p_2^{loc} and $\hat{p}_1^{\mathrm{loc}}$ are in p_1^{loc}, whereas p_3^{loc} has no relation to any other location in Fig. 4b.

  The *world state* is represented by a set $\hat{P} = \{\hat{p}_1, \hat{p}_2, ...\}$ of part states. Each *part state* $\hat{p}_i = (\hat{p}_i^{\mathrm{type}}, \hat{p}_i^{\mathrm{loc}})$ is an entity with specific part type $\hat{p}_i^{\mathrm{type}}$ at specific location $\hat{p}_i^{\mathrm{loc}}$. Thus, part states contain only well-defined parameters. By contrast, *part templates* $p_i = (p_i^{\mathrm{type}}, p_i^{\mathrm{loc}})$ are generic in their type p_i^{type} and location p_i^{loc}.

  A *robot task* is a precedence graph $T = (S, \prec_S, P)$ composed of partially ordered skills $S = \{s_1, s_2, ...\}$ to manipulate a set P of part templates. The

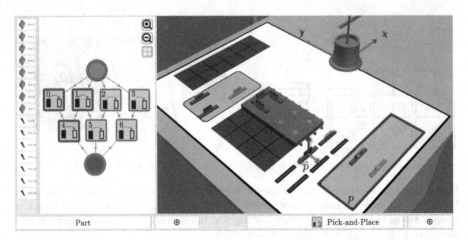

Fig. 5. Our task editor enables icon-based precedence graph modeling (left) with scene creation in a virtual workspace (right). The modeling outputs precedence graphs with inherent ambiguities (e.g., the specific $\hat{p}$ and generic p location).

partial order $\prec_S$ defines "earlier-later" relations between skills. Skills represent any operation to change a part feature (e.g., moving a part to a new location). Thus, we define *generic skills* as a tuple $s = (p, \psi)$ of a part template $p \in P$ and a prediction function ψ. The part template p represents the skill's *precondition*, i.e., the required features of a part to be utilized. Given p, the *prediction* ψ states the required features of the part after a successful execution. Thus, ψ maps a precondition p to another part template p^* – i.e., the *postcondition* of the skill. Given the set S of skills, we call the *predicted templates*

$$P^* = \{p^* \mid \forall (p, \psi) \in S : p^* = \psi(p)\}. \tag{1}$$

Our skill definition differs from the traditional approach of fully specific skills [21] since skills may involve ambiguous part types and locations. A skill $s \in S$ may only be applied to a part $\hat{p}_j$ iff $\hat{p}_j$ *satisfies* the part template $p_i \in s$, i.e., if it matches the precondition encoded by the input part template:

$$\text{satisfies}(\hat{p}, p) = \text{is\_a}(\hat{p}^{\text{type}}, p^{\text{type}}) \wedge \text{is\_at}(\hat{p}^{\text{loc}}, p^{\text{loc}}). \tag{2}$$

In practice, precedence graphs, as introduced above, are created by domain experts using the intuitive graphical editor shown in Fig. 5. Parts can be placed within a virtual workspace to be used as input parameters to skills, which can then be connected to precedence graphs. Please refer to our previous publications for details on this visual programming process [26, 28].

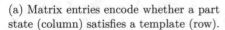

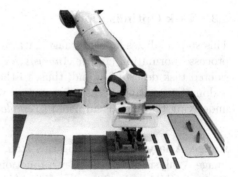

(a) Matrix entries encode whether a part state (column) satisfies a template (row).

(b) The robot executes a fully specified pick-and-place skill.

Fig. 6. The underspecified part templates are anchored to the part states by solving the assignment problem utilizing a satisfaction matrix (a). Given an admissible assignment (green entries), robot skills can be executed (b). (Color figure online)

4.2 Robot Task Execution

For robots to cope with ambiguity, the underspecified skills are anchored using the approach from our prior work [28]: Initially, the robot detects all parts in the workspace with object recognition techniques and builds up a world state $\hat{P}$. The anchoring process matches each part template $p \in P$ with a part state $\hat{p} \in \hat{P}$ that satisfies p (Eq. 2). To find an admissible assignment, at least one part state must be provided per template ($|\hat{P}| \geq |P|$), yielding $\mathcal{O}(|\hat{P}|!)$ possible assignments. Even for few part states ($|\hat{P}| \leq 10$), testing each assignment is infeasible. However, we can solve this assignment problem with efficient algorithms, e.g., the Kuhn-Munkres algorithm [17] with $\mathcal{O}(|\hat{P}|^3)$ runtime complexity:

Let $\mathbf{A} = (a_{i,j})$ denote a $|P| \times |\hat{P}|$ cost matrix with a row for each part template and a column for each part state (Fig. 6a). Any correct assignment of $\hat{p}_j$ to p_i has no cost, whereas false assignments have infinite costs, i.e.,

$$a_{i,j} = \begin{cases} 0 & \text{if satisfies}(\hat{p}_j, p_i) \\ \infty & \text{otherwise} \end{cases}, i \in \{1, ..., |P|\}, j \in \{1, ..., |\hat{P}|\}. \tag{3}$$

The Kuhn-Munkres algorithm outputs an injective mapping $f : \{1, ..., |P|\} \rightarrow \{1, ..., |\hat{P}|\}$ which minimizes the cost term $\sum_i a_{i,f(i)}$ ($i \in \{1, ..., |P|\}$). By construction of $\mathbf{A}$, an admissible assignment f has 0 cost, and any solution involving a wrong assignment has an infinite overall cost. This occurs if necessary parts are missing in the current world state. In other words, f says that part template p_i must be associated with part state $\hat{p}_{f(i)}$ to incur an overall correct assignment.

Given this assignment, the precedence graph can be scheduled into a skill sequence. In addition, generic skill parameters must be specified. For example, a grid-based placement planner determines specific transformations from generic goal locations. A fully specified skill can then be executed by a typical state-of-the-art skill architecture (e.g., [2, 21]) as shown in Fig. 6b.

4.3   Task Optimization

This step analyzes labeled image data by applying techniques to extract hidden process information (*Image Analysis*). This gives us RPDs attached to the considered task description and, thus, to the process model. For human tasks, this is done by creating a *Task Annotation* resulting in HT*, whereas, for RTs, the underlying template is adjusted (*Template Refinement*) resulting in RT*.

Image Analysis. Regarding this step, we follow our previous work [11]. The Image Analysis is described by a function ϕ mapping labeled images V to RPDs D, i.e., $\phi(V) = D$. Thereby, $V = \{(v_1, l_1), (v_2, l_2), ...\}$ is a set of images v_i recorded after execution of a task T and labeled as $l_i \in \{0, 1\}$. The label indicates whether the process was successful ($l_i = 1$) or failed ($l_i = 0$). The Image Analysis step has three phases: (i) A *convolutional neural network* (CNN) is trained with the labeled image data to predict whether an image shows a successful or failed execution. (ii) We employ *Local Interpretable Model-Agnostic Explanations* (LIME) [24] to generate an explanation for each positively labeled input image $\{(i, l) \in V \mid l = 1\}$. LIME highlights image regions relevant for predicting the positive class, i.e., features decisive for process success. (iii) We derive D from these local explanations in a generalization step. Thereby, we focus on image content semantically representing the same object or part across all images to derive global insights. Initially, we search for parts within the highlighted regions of each local explanation. We then analyze each identified part for further information based on a selected set of features. Thereby, the set of features is domain-specific and exchangeable. For instance, the color, shape, or position can be determined of each part identified in a local explanation. Across all local explanations, we receive a set of features and values for each part, representing relevant process details. Formally, the output of this step is a set of RPDs D. Each $d \in D$ refers to exactly one part for which relevant details were found. Thus, d comprises a set of analyzed features and values for that object. Given the features of our part templates, we define a RPD $d = (d^{\text{type}}, d^{\text{loc}})$ as a tuple of a generic type $d^{\text{type}} \in P^{\text{type}}$ and a generic location $d^{\text{loc}} \in P^{\text{loc}}$. Furthermore, D always details the task instruction of T. How T is to be adapted varies depending on the agent, as described in the subsequent sections.

Task Annotation for Human Workers. The discovered RPDs have to be integrated into the process model while preserving model readability for human workers. Therefore, intuitive *task annotations* (e.g., texts, diagrams, images) are created [10]. The task annotations are then attached to the original process model as proposed by [35]. This gives us an improved task HT*, which enriches the input process model PM by RPDs.

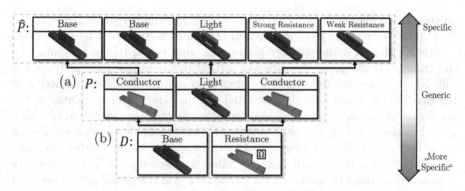

Fig. 7. For a successful execution of tasks with varieties, every part template $p \in P$ must be correctly mapped to one part state $\hat{p} \in \hat{P}$ (a). If the tasks with varieties are modeled too coarsely, the part templates must be specified by the RPDs by mapping every detail $d \in D$ to one template $p \in P$.

Template Refinement for Robot Tasks. In contrast to task annotations for humans, robots require explicit adjustments to the task description. Therefore, the skills and part templates in the task must be identified and adjusted corresponding to the RPDs. This problem is analogous to the mapping from part templates to part states (Fig. 7): RPDs D and templates P constitute generic features of parts and, therefore, are modeled equally (cf. Image Analysis). However, RPDs D refer to the world state *after* execution, whereas part templates P specify requirements of the initial world state *before* execution. We can bridge this gap due to our skill modeling, which allows us to predict expected part templates P^* after execution (Eq. 1). These predicted templates may be too generic and must, therefore, be restricted by the RPDs. To this end, a mapping from each detail $d \in D$ to exactly one template $p \in P^*$ is required. The RPDs can only arise from the execution of overly coarse skills – in consequence, (i) there are fewer RPDs than templates, and (ii) the RPDs must be equally or more specific an the part templates. For that, we define the predicate specifies: $D \times P \rightarrow \{\text{TRUE}, \text{FALSE}\}$ that returns whether a RPD d_i is at least as specific as the template p_j. This means that d_i^{type} is equal to, or a child of p_j^{type}, and that d_i^{loc} is equal to or lies in p_j^{loc}. Due to the general definitions of our part types and locations, the specifies function is defined analogously to satisfies:

$$\text{specifies}(d, p) = \text{is\_a}(d^{\text{type}}, p^{\text{type}}) \land \text{is\_at}(d^{\text{loc}}, p^{\text{loc}}). \quad (4)$$

Again, a brute force mapping between RPDs D and templates P is infeasible due to the number of feasible combinations but can be achieved with the Kuhn-Munkres algorithm (Sect. 4.2): Let $\mathbf{B} = (b_{i,j})$ denote a $|D| \times |P|$ cost matrix with a row for each RPD and a column for each part template. We model wrong assignments with the *specifies*-function:

$$b_{i,j} = \begin{cases} 0 & \text{if specifies}(d_i, p_j) \\ \infty & \text{otherwise} \end{cases}, i \in \{1, ..., |D|\}, j \in \{1, ..., |P|\}. \quad (5)$$

Solving the assignment problem gives us the minimum cost assignment g : $\{1, ..., |D|\} \rightarrow \{1, ..., |P|\}$ stating that RPD d_i must restrict part template $p_{g(i)}$.

Having identified the part templates belonging to the RPDs, they must be constrained. Transferring the values of a RPD to the assigned templates is not sufficient because the templates are already transformed by the prediction of the task. Thus, it must be differentiated whether the initial templates or the prediction of the skills must be adjusted. To this end, the prediction of a skill must be considered: If the skill adjusts the feature to be constrained during execution, the prediction must be adjusted (e.g., the target location in Pick-and-Place-Skills). If the skill does not affect the feature, the initial template (precondition) must be adjusted. For example, this is the case if part types need to be restricted and only Pick-and-Place-Skills are used.

5   Evaluation

We have evaluated our approach and prototypical implementation in two experiments motivated by possible use cases from the manufacturing sector (Sect. 5.1). The results and optimization steps to improve the knowledge extraction are elaborated in Sect. 5.2. In Sect. 5.3, we finally discuss the results from different perspectives and provide recommendations for similar setups.

5.1   Experimental Validation

We designed two use cases built upon benchmark tasks of [27] and previous real-world process use cases of [11]. Both use cases address process steps that involve a robot to place a set of work pieces (conductors) in a given working environment (Fig. 8). Use Case 1 (UC1) describes an assembly and Use Case 2 (UC2) a kitting task. For our experiments, we assumed that the use cases are designed as task models with the purpose of being executed by a robot agent and that they are part of a given process model (Sect. 4). Furthermore, we made the following assumptions:

1. Labeled images are given. The data stems from executions of the respective task model, i.e., UC1 or UC2. After execution, an image of the workspace is captured and labeled according to the success of process outcomes.
2. The task models for both use cases are too generic and lead to deviating process outcomes.
3. We precisely know the missing process detail causing process failure. This allows us to validate that our approach succeeds in finding the missing RPD.

In order to have sufficient and qualitatively adequate data we used synthetically generated images corresponding to the scenes in Fig. 8. We generated and labeled images for each use case based on known, predefined rules that distinguish a successful execution from an unsuccessful one. The process domain remains consistent across both experiments and all task executions, resulting in an unchanged background image.

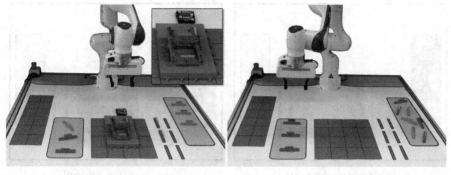

(a) Use Case 1: Assembly   (b) Use Case 2: Kitting

Fig. 8. We evaluate our approach with use cases from real-world process environments. Figures (a) and (b) show the world states before (semi-transparent) and after task execution for each use case respectively.

Use Cases. The first use case (UC1) is an assembly scenario. The task is to mount conductors on a circuit board in a specific arrangement. Six conductors must be placed, each being identified by its color: base conductors are blue, resistance conductors are green, yellow, or pink, and light conductors are orange. Different colors of resistance conductors indicate different resistance values (weak = yellow, medium = green, strong = pink). The board is positioned in the scene at a fixed location. The conductors are initially located in two areas (Fig. 8a). Precise positions within the grey regions can vary. As commonly observed in practice (e.g., [14,18]), we assume that the task model was created by a non-expert who is familiar with the process flow but who does not know further details about the process. Consequently, the task model contains information that the circuit board needs to be populated by three base conductors, two light conductors, and one resistance conductor at specific positions. However, it is not specified which resistance conductor (which strength) should be placed. If a low-value resistance (yellow) is attached, the light conductor will burn out, thus rendering the process unsuccessful. On the other hand, if the resistance is too strong (pink), the light conductor glows too weakly. Therefore, placing a medium resistance (green) at the given position on the circuit board is crucial for process success. Since the task model has no further specifications, the robot picks a resistance conductor of any type that is available in the workspace during task execution. Deviating process outcomes are observed from which labels are derived for the captured images. We validate if the RPD, i.e., the right type of resistance, can be extracted from a labeled image data set. This means that the association of the feature "color" with process success has to be identified.

The second use case (UC2) covers a kitting scenario, i.e., the delivery of all components required for the assembly of a product. In the initial situation of UC2, all available conductors are located within the right region of the workspace (Fig. 8b). The final state requires three conductors (a base, light, and resistance each) to be positioned in the left region. In this scenario, we assume that a

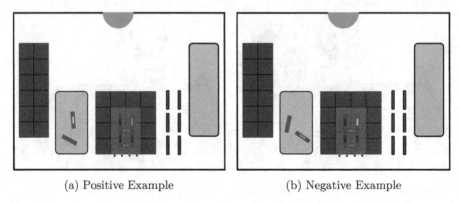

(a) Positive Example   (b) Negative Example

Fig. 9. Example input data for Use Case 1.

process expert created a generic task model to move one conductor of each type from the right to arbitrary, varying positions in the left region. This generic task model was sufficient as long as the subsequent process of assembling the parts was performed by human workers who were able to deal with varying part-feeding locations. Over time, the assembly line was restructured, and the subsequent assembly process was assigned to a robot that expects parts in a specific order for grasping: The base conductor must be placed in the top, the light conductor in the middle, and the resistance conductor in the bottom third of the left region. The initial kitting task model does not contain these new RPDs regarding more specific part goal locations. Executing this model yields the observation that the process occasionally fails. With UC2, we show that the location-related RPDs can be extracted with our approach. This involves a more complex association between two features (color and position) and process outcomes.

Implementation. We trained a classification model using TensorFlow[1] for both use cases. Regarding the CNN, we followed a standard model architecture which comprised three convolution layers followed by corresponding pooling layers. Subsequently, the output was flattened and fed into a fully-connected dense layer to derive the final classification outcome. As training data, we generated image data per use case representing the respective setups. For UC1, we generated 1000 images, of which 500 showed positive (Fig. 9a) and 500 negative states (Fig. 9b) of the workspace after task execution from a top-down view. The positions of the six conductors on the circuit board were fixed across all images since they were defined precisely in the task model. The position and orientation of the two remaining conductors were determined at random – this reflects the variability of the process concerning initial part locations. For UC2, we generated 10000 images comprising 5000 positive (cf. Fig. 10a) and 5000 negative samples (cf. Fig. 10b). The position and orientation of each conductor was again determined randomly within the respective rectangular regions. The training of the CNN

---

[1] https://www.tensorflow.org/ (Accessed: 02 May 2023).

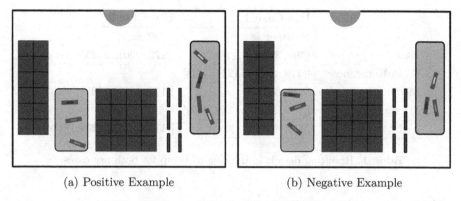

(a) Positive Example   (b) Negative Example

Fig. 10. Example input data for Use Case 2.

per use case was performed until a sufficient high accuracy rate (> 0.95) and low loss (< 0.1) were achieved.

The first experiments were conducted with the basic version of LIME as provided in the official python package[2]. We defined important input parameters according to the process domain and experimental setup: the parameter $n_{features}$ describes the maximum number of image segments to be considered in the explanation. This parameter is crucial for useful and interpretable results since consideration of too many features would lead to uncertainty in which segments are of real importance for the classification. In contrast, not all important segments are highlighted by selecting a too-low value. We know that, in our domain, the reason for process success or failure is always related to the parts since the image background is fixed across task executions. The number of parts is, hence, a good guide in choosing $n_{features}$. However, since we do not know which object or object feature is relevant, all possible occurring objects must be considered. In UC1, a maximum of 8 and UC2, a maximum of 7 conductors may occur in the scene. Therefore, we set $n_{features}$ accordingly. The number of sample instances used by LIME to generate a local explanation is defined by $n_{samples}$. Higher values produce more samples and more accurate explanation at the cost of computation time. Inspired by existing code examples and experience from prior experiments, the value for both use cases was set to 1000.

We implemented the generalization step using an object recognition procedure based on color. For each local explanation, we extracted the color information from all highlighted segments and identified the parts in individual segments this way. We then identified all regions of the segment that correspond to an object, i.e., regions that differ in color from the background. We calculated the centroid of each object region, which is used to determine the object's position. The object information identified in this way is collected across all local explanations, and a list of positions is output at the end for each object type.

---

[2] https://github.com/marcotcr/lime (Accessed: 30 April 2023).

	Use Case 1	Use Case 2
Type	*Position*	*Position*
Base	(390, 382)	[(172, 290),...,(258, 341)]
Weak Resistance	[(179, 316),...,(247, 471)]	-
Medium Resistance	(434, 382)	[(176, 429),...,(258, 480)]
Strong Resistance	[(179, 302),...,(258, 458)]	-
Light	(410, 463)	[(171, 359),...,(259, 409)]

Table 1. Resulting details in the default setup for both use cases.

5.2   Results and Optimizations

The output of the generalization step, i.e., the derived RPDs, for each use case is summarized in Table 1. For UC2, the default setup provides correct results since the analyzed RPDs align with the anticipated specifications: for each of the three conductors (base, light, and medium resistance), a region for the parts to be placed was extracted. The regions are represented by a bounding box for each RPD, referring to the top, middle, and bottom third of the left area, as expected in this use case. In UC1, five RPDs were detected. They indicate that five conductors (base, light, weak resistance, medium resistance, strong resistance) must be present at the computed positions during the execution of the task for process success – this does not match our expectations since only a single conductor (a medium resistance) at a specific position is relevant for success in this case. To get to the root cause of this result, we examined the partial results of each step of our analysis process. Examples of the results of the explanation step, i.e., the local explanations, for each use case are shown in Fig. 11. The images provide evidence that the error occurred during this step. In UC1 (Fig. 11; left), eight image segments (as determined by n_{features}) are highlighted, meaning that they were essential for the image to be classified as a successful process execution. Across all explanations for UC1, the segment containing the base (blue rectangle) and medium resistance (green rectangle) conductor is always highlighted. While this

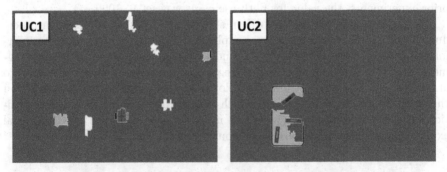

Fig. 11. Exemplary local explanations in the default setup.

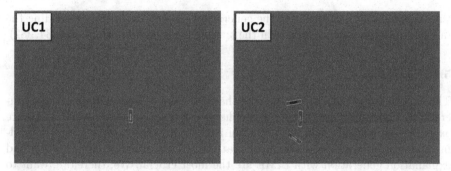

Fig. 12. Exemplary local explanations in the optimized setup.

partially aligns with the expected outcome, it is inaccurate due to the highlighting of the base conductor. This is the result of the segmentation sub-step of LIME, where both conductors are assigned to the same segment. Consequently, either both conductors or none of them can be marked relevant in the explanation. Furthermore, in a few cases (18%), some highlighted segments contain small parts of the other resistance conductors placed in the left area of the scene. Since the generalization step considers all highlighted segments in all explanations, these parts are also analyzed, and identified conductors are erroneously declared as RPDs (Table 1). The inaccurate outcomes can thus be attributed to a sub-optimal execution of intermediate steps. Therefore, we applied optimizations to enhance the knowledge extraction:

1. The segmentation process of LIME was adapted to ensure that each object is assigned to a single segment. Additionally, we replaced the quick shift algorithm, which is by default used in the LIME implementation, with the SLIC algorithm. SLIC is better suited for the shape of parts in our domain.[3]
2. Based on a segmentation that assigns an individual segment to each conductor, the optimal value for the LIME parameter $n_{features} = 1$ in UC1 (3 in UC2). This value can be obtained by determining a cut-off based on the weight-ordered sorting of segments for classification purposes. If the distance between the values exceeds a certain threshold, the segments should not be merged while we define the cut-off at this point.

These optimizations enable the adaptation of the LIME implementation to our domain. They result in a tendency to highlight fewer patches and increase the robustness of the generalization step, in turn reducing requirements for this step. The local explanations resulting from the optimized setup are shown in Fig. 12. For UC2, the results of the generalization remain unchanged in the optimized setup compared to the default version. However, the local explanations are more precise, thereby rendering them more reliable. For UC1, we are able to achieve

---

[3] https://scikit-image.org/docs/dev/api/skimage.segmentation.html
(Accessed: 08 May 2023).

the expected RPD, resulting in the generalization step exclusively providing the medium resistance conductor with the specific positional information $(434, 382)$.

5.3 Discussion

The experimental results demonstrate the efficacy of our novel approach for concretizing underspecified task models. The processing pipeline in which steps are executed sequentially leads to potential issues with error propagation. Regarding this aspect, we have determined that the results of image classification and explanation generation with LIME are the most crucial. We, therefore, want to discuss these two steps regarding their scalability to other process environments:

(i) In the initial step of training a CNN predictor for process outcomes, we particularly encountered the challenge of acquiring a sufficient amount of training data. In our experiments, we found that a data set with at least 10000 images was indispensable for favorable outcomes in UC2 – insufficient sample size or imbalanced distribution of positive and negative samples led to inadequate outcomes in the explanation step. Small and medium-sized enterprises may have difficulties with obtaining this amount of data since manufacturing processes may here not occur sufficiently frequently. Therefore, alternative strategies for the training process in real-world settings are needed. Data augmentation approaches that generate additional samples from a smaller data set might mitigate this issue. Additionally, pre-trained CNNs from similar domains in which large-scale data sets are available could be a viable alternative.

(ii) Our results regarding the local explanation generation step have shown that LIME requires modifications to ensure efficacy for our objectives. Despite a well-trained CNN, an appropriate value of the parameter n_{features} had to be tuned meticulously, and the segmentation approach had to be adapted for more precise outcomes. However, we do not consider this a major issue. On the one hand, the results of UC2 demonstrate that satisfactory outcomes can be obtained in principle with the default settings of LIME in some scenarios. On the other hand, domain knowledge, such as the number and features of parts, is usually available for individual process environments. Our experiments show that knowing the number of parts in the process provides guidance for an initial estimate and consecutive improvement of n_{features}. Furthermore, due to other methods employed during the design, engineering, and production stages of manufacturing environments (e.g., quality control processes), appropriate segmentation techniques adapted to the process might be readily available. Based on the low level of effort required and the significant results optimization, we highly recommend adapting the LIME segmentation step to increase the probability of successfully identifying RPDs.

6   Conclusion and Future Work

We presented a novel approach to improve human and robot process models by deriving specifications from relevant process details. Our approach unlocks new potentials regarding human-robot collaboration through enriching process models for both agents. It extends previous work in the context of BPM and proves its applicability for further domains. We evaluated our work with two use cases inspired by the manufacturing industry. The experimental results provide strong evidence of its effectiveness in identifying relevant process details.

Future research should focus on the improvement of the robustness of the approach. This includes examining data augmentation techniques to enable more straightforward applicability in real process environments that come with limitations in execution data quantity and quality. Furthermore, we aim to conduct experiments with more complex parts and settings to explore opportunities for enhancement and provide recommendations for implementing the approach in sophisticated process settings.

Acknowledgements. We thank Philipp Jahn and Carsten Scholle for their valuable work supporting the implementation and evaluation of our approach.

References

1. Ahmadikatouli, A., Aboutalebi, M.: New evolutionary approach to business process model optimization. In: Proceedings of the International MultiConference of Engineers and Computer Scientists, vol. 2 (2011)
2. Andersen, R.H., Solund, T., Hallam, J.: Definition and initial case-based evaluation of hardware-independent robot skills for industrial robotic co-workers. In: 41st International Symposium on Robotics (ISR), pp. 1–7. VDE (2014)
3. Becker, J., Rosemann, M., Von Uthmann, C.: Guidelines of business process modeling. In: BPM: Models, Techniques, and Empirical Studies, pp. 30–49 (2002)
4. Beumelburg, K.: Fähigkeitsorientierte Montageablaufplanung in der direkten Mensch-Roboter-Kooperation (2005)
5. Bobrik, R., Reichert, M., Bauer, T.: View-based process visualization. In: Alonso, G., Dadam, P., Rosemann, M. (eds.) BPM 2007. LNCS, vol. 4714, pp. 88–95. Springer, Heidelberg (2007). https://doi.org/10.1007/978-3-540-75183-0_7
6. Chinosi, M., Trombetta, A.: BPMN: an introduction to the standard. Comput. Stand. Interfaces **34**(1), 124–134 (2012)
7. Coradeschi, S., Saffiotti, A.: An introduction to the anchoring problem. Robot. Auton. Syst. **43**(2–3), 85–96 (2003)
8. Darvish, K., et al.: A hierarchical architecture for human-robot cooperation processes. IEEE Trans. Rob. **37**(2), 567–586 (2021)
9. Dietz, T., et al.: Programming system for efficient use of industrial robots for deburring in SME environments. In: 7th German Conference on Robotics, pp. 1–6 (2012)
10. Fichtner, M., Fichtner, U.A., Jablonski, S.: An experimental study of intuitive representations of process task annotations. In: Sellami, M., Ceravolo, P., Reijers, H.A., Gaaloul, W., Panetto, H. (eds.) CoopIS 2022. LNCS, vol. 13591, pp. 311–321. Springer, Cham (2022). https://doi.org/10.1007/978-3-031-17834-4_19

11. Fichtner., M., Schönig., S., Jablonski., S.: How lime explanation models can be used to extend business process models by relevant process details. In: Proceedings of the 24th International Conference on Enterprise Information Systems. vol. 2, pp. 527–534 (2022)

12. Gounaris, A.: Towards automated performance optimization of BPMN business processes. In: New Trends in Database and Information Systems (ADBIS), pp. 19–28 (2016)

13. Hasegawa, T., Suehiro, T., Takase, K.: A model-based manipulation system with skill-based execution. IEEE Trans. Robot. Autom. **8**(5), 535–544 (1992)

14. Koschmider, A., et al.: Business process modeling support by depictive and descriptive diagrams. In: Enterprise Modelling and Information Systems Architectures, pp. 31–44 (2015)

15. Matheson, E., Minto, R., Zampieri, E.G., Faccio, M., Rosati, G.: Human-robot collaboration in manufacturing applications: a review. Robotics **8**(4), 100 (2019)

16. Mendling, J., Reijers, H.A., van der Aalst, W.M.: Seven process modeling guidelines (7pmg). Inf. Softw. Technol. **52**(2), 127–136 (2010)

17. Munkres, J.: Algorithms for the assignment and transportation problems. J. Soc. Ind. Appl. Math. **5**(1), 32–38 (1957)

18. Niedermann, F., Radeschütz, S., Mitschang, B.: Deep business optimization: a platform for automated process optimization. INFORMATIK - Business Process and Service Science - Proceedings of ISSS and BPSC (2010)

19. Nottensteiner, K., et al.: A complete automated chain for flexible assembly using recognition, planning and sensor-based execution. In: Proceedings of 47st International Symposium on Robotics (ISR), pp. 1–8 (2016)

20. Paxton, C., et al.: Costar: instructing collaborative robots with behavior trees and vision. In: IEEE International Conference on Robotics and Automation (ICRA), pp. 564–571 (2017)

21. Pedersen, M.R., et al.: Robot skills for manufacturing: from concept to industrial deployment. Robot. Comput. Integr. Manuf. **37**, 282–291 (2016)

22. Polyvyanyy, A., Smirnov, S., Weske, M.: Process model abstraction: a slider approach. In: 12th International IEEE Enterprise Distributed Object Computing Conference (2008)

23. Reichert, M., et al.: Enabling personalized visualization of large business processes through parameterizable views. In: Proceedings of the 27th Annual ACM Symposium on Applied Computing, pp. 1653–1660 (2012)

24. Ribeiro, M.T., Singh, S., Guestrin, C.: "why should i trust you?" explaining the predictions of any classifier. In: Proceedings of 22nd ACM SIGKDD, pp. 1135–1144 (2016)

25. Riedelbauch, D.: Dynamic Task Sharing for Flexible Human-Robot Teaming under Partial Workspace Observability. Ph.D. thesis, University of Bayreuth (2020)

26. Riedelbauch, D., Henrich, D.: Fast graphical task modelling for flexible human-robot teaming. In: 50th International Symposium on Robotics (ISR), pp. 1–6. VDE (2018)

27. Riedelbauch, D., Hümmer, J.: A benchmark toolkit for collaborative human-robot interaction. In: 31st IEEE International Conference on Robot and Human Interactive Communication (RO-MAN), pp. 806–813. IEEE (2022)

28. Riedelbauch, D., Sucker., S.: Visual programming of robot tasks with product and process variety. In: Annals of Scientific Society for Assembly, Handling and Industrial Robotics (to appear) (2022)

29. Scheer, A.W., Thomas, O., Adam, O.: Process modeling using event-driven process chains. In: Process-Aware Information Systems: Bridging People and Software through Process Technology, pp. 119–145 (2005)
30. Selic, B., et al.: Omg unified modeling language (version 2.5). Technical Report (2015)
31. Senft, E., et al.: Situated live programming for human-robot collaboration. In: ACM Symposium on User Interface Software and Technology, pp. 613–625 (2021)
32. Steinmetz, F., Wollschläger, A., Weitschat, R.: Razer - a HRI for visual task-level programming and intuitive skill parameterization. IEEE Robot. Autom. Lett. **3**(3), 1362–1369 (2018)
33. Thomas, U., et al.: A new skill based robot programming language using UML/P statecharts. In: IEEE International Conference on Robotics and Automation (2013)
34. Van Der Aalst, W.M., Ter Hofstede, A.H., Weske, M.: Business process management: a survey. Bus. Process Manage. **2678**(1019), 1–12 (2003)
35. Wiedmann, P.C.K.: Agiles Geschäftsprozessmanagement auf Basis gebrauchssprachlicher Modellierung. Universitaet Bayreuth (Germany) (2017)

Edge Computing

Joint Optimization of PAoI and Queue Backlog with Energy Constraints in LoRa Gateway Systems

Lei Shi[1,2], Rui Ji[1,2]([✉]), Zhen Wei[1,2], Shilong Feng[1,2], and Zhehao Li[1,2]

[1] School of Computer Science and Information Engineering,
Hefei University of Technology, Hefei 230009, China
`jirui@mail.hfut.edu.cn`
[2] Engineering Research Center of Safety Critical Industrial Measurement
and Control Technology, Ministry of Education, Hefei 230009, China

Abstract. Peak Age of Information(PAoI), as a performance indicator representing the freshness of information, has attracted the attention of researchers in recent years. The data packet transmission rate in the LoRa network determines the information freshness level for system packets. In order to study the optimal scheduling of data packets, we try to use the PAoI to describe the real-time level of the end devices(*EDs*) and reduce it. We use edge servers to process monitoring data packets at the edge of the network to improve the efficiency of *EDs* and the information freshness level of data. Since packet transmission will be constrained by *EDs* battery queue energy and gateway queue backlog, we propose an optimization problem that aims to minimize the long-term average PAoI of *EDs* while ensuring network stability. With the Lyapunov optimization framework, the long-term stochastic optimization problem is transformed into a single-slot optimization problem. Furthermore, to avoid the problem of too large search space, we propose a dynamic strategy space reduction algorithm (SSDR) to shrink the strategy space. The simulation experiments show that our SSDR algorithm can optimize the PAoI index of *EDs* in various situations and satisfy the constraints of long-term optimization.

Keywords: PAoI · LoRa · Lyapunov optimization · scheduling algorithms

1 Introduction

In monitoring scenarios such as outdoor fire warning and dam water level monitoring, the traditional wireless communication network deployed by existing base stations is greatly limited. Moreover, whether the monitoring data can be processed by the server in time is also one of the key factors. LoRa is a self-deployed

The work is supported by the Key Technology Research and Development Project of Hefei, NO. 2021GJ029.

wireless network that does not rely on existing base stations. *EDs* can be self-charged by solar energy and other means without connecting to the power grid, which can adapt well to special scenarios where base stations are scarce and power grid coverage is not comprehensive [1]. LoRa technology modulates the baseband signal using a Chirp Spreading Spectrum, based on carrier frequency (CF), spreading factor (SF), bandwidth (BW) and coding rate (CR) [2,3]. Due to the orthogonality of the transmission sub-bands and quasi-orthogonality of the spreading factors, gateway can simultaneously receive signals from multiple end devices.

The Age of Information (AoI) is an emerging data freshness metric in wireless networks. It is defined as the time elapsed since the last data packet was generated at the source and received at the destination [4,5]. Another age-related metric is the Peak Age of Information (PAoI), which characterizes the staleness of the last received packet at the time of updating the AoI value, i.e., when a transmitter sends a data packet to the receiver [6]. PAoI focuses more on the worst-case scenario during the scheduling process, which can be used to monitor scheduling events that occur less frequently but have a severe impact on the real-time performance of the system [7,8]. With the help of PAoI indicators, the occurrence of special events can be better monitored and reduced, thereby improving the response speed of the system.

Deploying edge servers at the network edge allows monitoring devices to send data to the edge server through a gateway, instead of sending data packets to the cloud center, which can accelerate the decision-making and processing of monitoring information [9,10]. The generation of data packets from end devices and battery queue charging process are random. The traditional LoRa monitoring network has in-depth research on the energy consumption of *EDs*, but there is insufficient research on the timeliness of data packet transmission. Using AoI/PAoI can better evaluate the data freshness level of *EDs*, and design an appropriate data packet scheduling strategy based on the backlog of buffer queues of the gateway and the energy consumption of *EDs*. Based on the AoI buffer queue model of *EDs*, we derive the peak AoI of the *EDs* and attempt to minimize the expected long-term PAoI to improve the data freshness level performance of the wireless network system. In summary, the main contributions are summarized as follows:

1) According to the characteristics of LoRa wireless network, the PAoI performance index of end device is derived, and the long-term PAoI optimization problem of end device is given under the condition of queue backlog constraint and battery queue energy constraint.
2) Using the Lyapunov optimization framework, we have localized the solution to stochastic optimization problems, previously evaluated over the long term, to each time slot. To address the impact of a large search space on algorithm efficiency, we introduce the SSDR algorithm, which dynamically reduces the strategy space. This enables fast identification of the optimal scheduling strategy.

3) The simulation experiments conducted under various parameter settings validated the reliability of the SSDR algorithm and included comparative experiments with three other commonly used scheduling algorithms. The simulation results demonstrate that our SSDR algorithm reduces the PAoI for end devices while ensuring overall system stability, and outperforms the compared algorithms in terms of performance.

The rest of the paper is organized as follows: In Sect. 2, we introduce the related work. In Sect. 3, we introduce the system model of LoRa wireless dispatching network, and give our optimization problems. In Sect. 4, we use the Lyapunov optimization framework to transform the problem into a single-time-slot optimization problem. In Sect. 5, we design a strategy space dynamic reduction algorithm to search for the optimal scheduling strategy in the strategy space as soon as possible. We present the simulation results and analysis in Sect. 6. Finally, in Sect. 7, we summarize this paper.

2   Related Work

In recent years, many literature has considered the use of AoI and PAoI indicators to improve data freshness and improve the real-time level of the system when integrating different scenarios. In [6], the author derived the distribution of PAoI for systems in series, including M/M/1 and M/D/1 systems, and analyzed the possible optimization of these two systems, which may be a complex operation that needs to be performed in real-time. In [11], the author investigated the age-optimal scheduling in a multiple access channel with stability constraints, where two heterogeneous source nodes transmit to a common receiver. In [12], the author utilized a probabilistic scheduling method to minimize the AoI metric for the entire wireless transmission system.

As an alternative to cloud computing, edge computing has been studied to improve the real-time level of data by using edge servers deployed at the edge of the network to provide computing resources. In [13], Tang et al. analyzed the AoI performance metrics of a multi-user mobile edge computing (MEC) system, where the base station generates and sends compute-intensive packets to the user device for computation. The processing of real-time information is critical for many applications. In [14], Lv et al. used edge computing resources to reduce AoI levels and devised a pricing mechanism to determine the allocation decisions of real-time computing tasks. In [15], Liu et al. consider a unicast network scenario where the sender periodically sends data to the receiver over a multihop network. AoI/PAoI indicators have also been studied in the Internet of Things, and in [16], Hu et al. studied the optimal arrival rate of packets under AoI and PAoI constraints. Based on the violation probability of AoI and PAoI, the optimal arrival rate of receiver status update is analyzed from the perspective of asymptotic optimality. In [17], Wang et al. investigated the design of an optimal strategy to minimize the long-term mean information age in a cognitive radio-based IoT monitoring system.

In real-time status update systems, energy consumption is an important factor that cannot be ignored in packet transmission scheduling. In [18], the authors performed an analysis of AoI based on queuing theory, in which transmitter nodes powered by energy harvesting systems frequently send status update packets to destinations. The SHS method was used to derive MGF closed expressions for AoI under several queuing rules of transmitters, including non-preemption (LCFS-NP) and service/waiting preemption (LCFS-PS/LCFS-PW) strategies, and similar related work was done [19,20]. In order to save energy consumption, in [21], the authors designed a trade-off between sensor transmission data and energy consumption, and after the service is completed, the sensor can go into a sleep state, thus saving energy. In [22], the authors examine the energy-saving scheduling problem for AoI minimization in opportunistic NOMA/OMA downlink broadcast wireless networks, where user devices operate with different QoS requirements. The Lyapunov framework is used to convert the original long-term time mean into a single-slot multi-objective optimization problem. Zhou et al. [23] investigated how to optimize the freshness of real-time data from energy-harvesting (EH)-based networked embedded systems in energy-constrained situations. The proposed solution can reduce the average AoI by an average of 47.2% and 69.1% with a low harvest rate. In [24], Fang et al. studied the Age of Peak Information (PAoI) in underwater wireless sensor networks (UWSN), as well as the energy cost of transmitting packets. Active and idle modes are designed to reduce energy consumption. The closed expressions of average PAoI and energy cost under AQM and non-AQM strategies are derived, and the results are verified by simulation experiments. In general, the work on AoI and PAoI focuses on ensuring the real-time level of the entire system, while considering constraints such as throughput, energy consumption, transmit power, etc. or joint optimization.

As a long-distance low-power radio communication technology, LoRa wireless network has good anti-interference and sensitivity, and has a wide range of application scenarios in wireless monitoring and power supply, and has many related papers [2,25–27]. In [28], the authors investigated resource management in a LoRa wireless network based on instantaneous channel coefficient and energy availability when LDs are powered by energy harvesting sources. They developed an optimal SF allocation, device scheduling, and power allocation algorithm that maximizes the number of scheduled LDs. In [29], two offline scheduling algorithms for LoRa-based data transmission were proposed. The algorithms allocate time slots and assign SF to nodes to minimize the overall data collection time. In [9], Liu et al. propose a new design of a LoRa system that uses edge computing on a LoRa gateway. This design enables some of the time-computing tasks of latency-sensitive applications to be processed in a timely manner. In [30], the authors assumed that in a house, all smart appliances are connected to a smart meter with edge devices and LoRa nodes. An energy-efficient smart metering system using remote edge computing is proposed to solve the problem of latency and energy consumption.

3 System Model

In this section, we introduce the system model, as shown in Fig. 1. In the LoRa network, *EDs* are deployed in an energy-constrained environment and need to obtain energy from the environment for self-charging. When *EDs* transmit data to the gateway, their AoI decreases. If the gateway receives too much data, the queue backlog will increase. Therefore, it is necessary to design a suitable scheduling algorithm. Our goal is to minimize the information age of *EDs* while ensuring energy constraints and gateway backlog constraints. Next, we will sequentially introduce the network and energy models, the peak information age formula, and the derivation of the gateway queue backlog model.

3.1 LoRa Network Model and Battery Status

In a single-server monitoring network,consider $\mathbb{N} = \{1, 2, ..., N\}$ as *EDs*. When there are no packets on the *EDs*, it monitor the nearby environmental conditions and generate packets based on a random process. If the packet already exists on the *EDs*, the packet is no longer obtained according to the random process. The packet is time-stamped to record the current age of information(AoI) changes. AoI is an indicator for expressing the freshness of information, which will be explained in detail in Sects. 3.2. We discretize time into intervals of the same length.

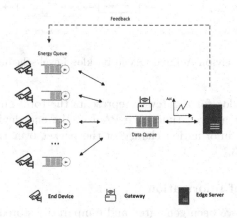

Fig. 1. Lora Network Organization

Suppose that the unit energy consumption for transmitting a data packet is E^{trans}. Assuming that the charging process follows the Bernoulli process with probability λ, the charging probability of each device follows $\lambda \in (0, 1)$. $E(t)$ represents the battery status of the end device. Battery status can be expressed as

$$E_i(t + 1) = \min\{E_i(t) - \mu_i(t) \cdot (E_c + E^{trans}) + \lambda(t) \cdot E, E_{max}\}, \quad (1)$$

where E_{max} indicates the maximum capacity of the battery queue, E_c represents a fixed energy consumed by the circuit, E represents the unit of energy for charging, and the greater the probability of charging $\lambda_i(t)$, the more energy the battery charges. $\mu_i(t)$ indicates whether end device i successfully transmits packets in time slot t, $\mu_i(t) = 1$ when it is successfully transmitted to the gateway, otherwise $\mu_i(t) = 0$. The battery queue status of all EDs at t time slot is represented by the set $E(t) = \{E_0(t), E_1(t), ..., E_i(t), ..., E_N(t)\}, i \in \mathbb{N}$.

The gateway maintains an AoI cache queue and does not discard any data packets transmitted by EDs. The gateway can connect to the power grid, so energy is not a concern. The EDs are guided by a scheduling controller that considers the current network status. This controller provides a strategy π to determine if EDs should send data packets in the next time slot. The controller is deployed in the edge server. After the gateway receives packets from the EDs at time slot t, these packets are stored in the gateway's cache queue and processed sequentially according to the gateway's packet service rate. The packet transmission process is shown in Fig. 2 below.

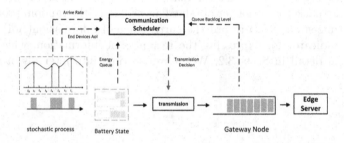

Fig. 2. EDs rely on AoI and Queue Backlog Level scheduling strategy

The queue backlog for a gateway represents the total number of packets in the cache queue at a given time. The PAoI of the end device is derived from the average age of information change of the packet over time, which we will describe in Sect. 3.3.

3.2   Peak Age of Information

For packets that have been generated and temporarily stored in the end device, the age of the information will increase when it is not their turn to transmit the time slot. When it is the turn of the appropriate transmission time slot, the packet is transmitted to the gateway and the information age drops to 1. Its packets are cached in the gateway's AoI cache queue along with packets transmitted by other EDs. When it is the appropriate transmission time slot, packets are in turn transmitted to the Edge Server for processing, with a service rate μ_{gw} affected by the hardware performance of the gateway. The status update process of information age is shown in Fig. 3, where the information age corresponds to the change of the data packets information age of ED_i

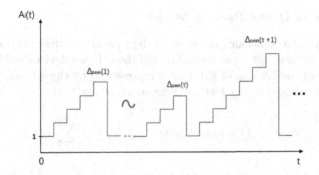

Fig. 3. AoI status update process

As we can see from the figure above, the AoI of the data packet decreases after transmission to the Edge Server. At the time slot t, the AoI of the *EDs* is defined as the difference between the current time t and the timestamp Δt of the outgoing packet [4]. Then the AoI of the *EDs* at the time slot t is defined as

$$A(t) = t - \Delta t. \tag{2}$$

Suppose that in each discrete time slot, AoI takes an integer value, i.e., $A(t) \in \{1, 2, 3, ...\}$. We suppose that the *EDs* sending a packet can be completed before the end of the previous time slot. In this paper, the AoI of all data packets on all *EDs* is constructed into a set $\mathbb{A}(t) = \{A_0(t), A_1(t), ..., A_i(t), ..., A_N(t)\}, i \in \mathbb{N}$, and $\mathbb{A}(t)$ represents the AoI of all *EDs* under t time slot. $\mu_i(t)$ indicates whether to transmit data packets in the current time slot. Then the AoI variation formula for two consecutive time slots can be updated to

$$A_i(t + 1) = A_i(t) + 1 - \mu_i(t)A_i(t). \tag{3}$$

It can be seen from the AoI change plot that when $\mu_i(t) = 1$, the AoI of the t time slot is the PAoI. Average PAoI is defined as

$$\overline{A_i^{peak}} = \lim_{t \to +\infty} \frac{\mathbb{E}[\sum_{\tau=0}^{t-1} \mu_i(\tau)A_i(\tau)]}{\mathbb{E}[\sum_{\tau=0}^{t-1} \mu_i(\tau)]}. \tag{4}$$

Our goal is to optimize the PAoI of the *EDs*. However, reducing the PAoI may have a certain impact on the queue backlog of gateway, so we propose a queue backlog model of gateway below to analyze the impact of packet transmission on gateway.

3.3 Gateway Queue Backlog Model

The gateway's queue backlog depends on data packets arrival rate and gateway service rate. In time slot t, the service rate of the i-th end device can be expressed as $\mu_i(t)$, the queue backlog of gateway is represented by the symbol $S_{gw}(t)$. The queue backlog model in $t + 1$ at the next moment, we have

$$S_{gw}(t + 1) = max[S_{gw}(t) - \mu_{gw}(t), 0] + \sum_{i=0}^{N} \mu_i(t), \tag{5}$$

where $\mu_{gw}(t)$ is the service rate of the gateway at time t, and $\sum_{i=0}^{N} \mu_i(t)$ is the sum of all packets transmitted to the gateway by all *EDs* at time slot t.

Since queue models are affected by stochastic processes, we need to consider the long-term stability of the queue. When the time t tends to infinity, the total number of packets enqueued should be less than or equal to the total number of packets out of the queue, i.e., $\lim_{t \to +\infty} \frac{1}{T} \sum_{\tau=0}^{t-1} \mathbb{E}[\sum_{i=0}^{N} \mu_i(\tau) - \mu_{gw}(\tau)] \leq 0$. We convert the queue model into an inequality constraint, we have

$$S_{gw}(t + 1) \geq S_{gw}(t) + \sum_{i=0}^{N} \mu_i(t) - \mu_{gw}(t). \tag{6}$$

The inequality transformation yields $\sum_{i=0}^{N} \mu_i(t) - \mu_{gw}(t) \leq S_{gw}(t) - S_{gw}(t + 1)$. When $S_{gw}(0) = 0$, combining the first *EDs* time slots to the above equation-accumulate transformation, we have

$$\sum_{\tau=0}^{t-1} [\sum_{i=0}^{N} \mu_i(\tau) - \mu_{gw}(\tau)] \leq S_{gw}(t) - S_{gw}(0) = S_{gw}(t) - 0 = S_{gw}(t). \tag{7}$$

Then we expect both sides of the inequality to be at the same time, we have

$$\frac{1}{t} \sum_{\tau=0}^{t-1} \mathbb{E}[\sum_{i=0}^{N} \mu_i(t) - \mu_{gw}(t)] \leq \frac{\mathbb{E}[S_{gw}(t)]}{t}. \tag{8}$$

Observing the above equation, in order to meet the stability constraint of the left equation, we can ensure that the queue achieves long-term stability through $\lim_{t \to \infty} \frac{\mathbb{E}[S_{gw}(t)]}{t} = 0$, i.e., the queue can achieve mean rate stable. Based on the above considerations, the optimization problems of this article are given below.

3.4 Problem Formulation

The optimization goal of this paper is to select a suitable scheduling strategy for each time slot that helps to keep the gateway's queue stable while minimizing the average PAoI.

Firstly, we provide the definition of packet arrival probability. The data arrival probability refers to the probability that the *EDs* obtains the monitoring data in the random process, and different data arrival probabilities will affect the data packet generation rate of *EDs*. We define the data arrival probability as θ, and $\theta \in (0,1)$.

We define the scheduling strategy π as a row vector composed of the dequeue rates of all *EDs* at a certain moment. It is expressed as $\pi = (\mu_0, \mu_1, ..., \mu_i, ..., \mu_N), i \in \mathbb{N}$, where μ_i represents whether the i-th end device transmits data packets to the gateway. Define scheduling strategy space: $\Pi = (\pi_0^T(t), \pi_1^T(t), ..., \pi_m^T(t), ...)$, where $\pi_m^T(t)$ represents the scheduling strategy for all *EDs* in the time slot t. Our goal is to find the best scheduling strategy to minimize average system PAoI. *EDs* energy and gateway queue backlog serve as optimization constraints. The optimization problem in this article is defined as

$$\text{P1}: \quad \min_{\pi \in \Pi} \mathbb{E}[\overline{A_i^{peak}}] \tag{9}$$

$$\text{s.t.} \quad \lim_{t \to \infty} \frac{\mathbb{E}[S_{gw}(t)]}{t} = 0 \tag{9a}$$

$$\overline{A_i^{peak}} = \lim_{t \to +\infty} \frac{\mathbb{E}[\sum_{\tau=0}^{t-1} \mu_i(\tau) A_i(t)]}{\mathbb{E}[\sum_{\tau=0}^{t-1} \mu_i(\tau)]} \tag{9b}$$

$$\mu_i \in (0,1), \quad \forall i \in \mathbb{N}, \tag{9c}$$

$$E_i \le E_{max}, \quad \forall i \in \mathbb{N}, \tag{9d}$$

$$\lambda \in (0,1), \tag{9e}$$

$$\theta \in (0,1). \tag{9f}$$

This optimization problem is a stochastic optimization problem. A random number of packets are generated in each time slice. The objective function will be influenced by random events and the chosen scheduling strategy. Long-term averaging involving objective functions and constraints cannot be directly solved by traditional optimization techniques. This paper adopts the Lyapunov optimization framework. It convert a stochastic optimization problem measured from a long-term perspective into a single time slice.

4   PAoI-Queue-Aware Scheduling Using Lyapunov Framework

For the above optimization problem, our goal is to transform the long-term optimization problem into single-slot online optimization, and find the appropriate scheduling strategy from the scheduling strategy space Π. Suppose that the network state at time t is $\Omega(t) = [S_{gw}(t), \mathbb{A}(t), E(t)]$. We define the quadratic Lyapunov function $L(t) = \frac{S_{gw}^2(t)}{2}$ [23,31]. The Lyapunov drift $\triangle L(t)$ is defined as

$$\triangle L(t) = L(t+1) - L(t). \tag{10}$$

For the objective function, we use a penalty function $p = P(\Omega(t), \pi_m^T(t))$ to represent the impact of the current AoI and the scheduling decision taken on the objective function. We define a non-negative weight coefficient V as the balance factor between the penalty function and Lyapunov drift. We aim to continuously solve for the minimum of the Lyapunov drift combined with the penalty function in each time slot. Then our optimization problem **P1** can be rewritten as

$$P2: \quad \min_{\pi \in \Pi} \mathbb{E}[\triangle L(t) + Vp(t)], \tag{11}$$

$$\text{s.t.} \quad (9c), (9d), (9e), (9f),$$

$$\triangle L(t) = L(t+1) - L(t), \tag{11a}$$

$$p = P(\Omega(t), \pi_m^T(t)). \tag{11b}$$

Optimization problem **P2** converts the original long-term optimization function into the optimization objective function in a single time slot. But the Lyapunov drift here is by definition known to know $L(t+1)$ in the next time slice. It goes against our goal of single-slot online optimization. In order to solve this problem, $\triangle L(t) + Vp(t)$ can be scaled to a certain extent [32]. $\triangle L(t)$ has an upper bound, i.e. $\triangle L(t) \le B + S_{gw}(t) \sum_{i=0}^{N} \mu_i(t)$, where B is a normal number. Because both the arrival rate and service rate of the gateway cache queue are bounded, therefore there must be a bounded constant $B > 0$ that ensures $\mathbb{E}[B(t) \mid \Omega(t)] \le B$ in each time slot, i.e. $\triangle L(t) \le B + S_{gw}(t) \sum_{i=0}^{N} \mu_i(t)$.

In a single time slot, observe the cache queue status of the gateway and give a Drift-Plus-Penalty function about PAoI, we have

$$\triangle L(t) + Vp(t) \le B + S_{gw}(t) \sum_{i=0}^{N} \mu_i(t) + Vp(t), \tag{12}$$

where $p(t)$ is the penalty function associated with the PAoI state, battery queue state and action strategy of the *EDs*. We can solve the optimization problem **P2** by solving the minimum value to the right of the above inequality. At this point, the optimization problem **P2** can be transformed into problem P3

$$P3: \quad \min_{\pi \in \Pi} \mathbb{E}[B + S_{gw}(t) \sum_{i=0}^{N} \mu_i(t) + Vp(t)] \tag{13}$$

$$\text{s.t.} \quad (9c), (9d), (9e), (9f), (11a), (11b),$$

$$B > 0. \tag{13a}$$

Based on the optimization problem **P3**, we can finally give a single-slot optimization algorithm, as shown in Algorithm 1.

Algorithm 1. DPP Algorithm for PAoI and Queue Backlog

1: Initialization:$S_{gw}(0) \leftarrow 0, \mathbb{A}(0) \leftarrow 0, E(0) \leftarrow 0, p_i(t) = 14dBm$. Select $BW, \alpha_i(t), PL, H, DE, CR$ according to the LoRa network architecture. Choose appropriate V and E_{max}. Set $t = 1$.

2: Under the t time slot, observe the network state $\Omega(t) = [S_{gw}(t), A(t), E(t)]$ and select the appropriate scheduling strategy $\pi \in \Pi$ so that it satisfies the Lyapunov drift-plus-penalty function:

$$\min_{\pi \in \Pi} \mathbb{E}[B + S_{gw}(t) \sum_{i=0}^{N} \mu_i(t) + Vp(t)]$$

where the Lyapunov drift-plus-penalty function satisfies the following constraints: (9c),(9d),(9e), (9f), (11a),(11b).

3: Update the LoRa network architecture:

$$E_i(t+1) = \min\{E_i(t) - \mu_i(t) \cdot (E_c + E_i^{trans}(t)) + \lambda_i(t) \cdot E, E_{max})\},$$

$$A_i(t+1) = A_i(t) + 1 - \gamma_i(t)B_i(t)A_i(t),$$

$$S_{gw}(t+1) = max[S_{gw}(t) - \mu_{gw}(t), 0] + \sum_{i=0}^{N} \mu_i(t).$$

4: In the next time slot t + 1, repeat the previous steps.

5 Strategy Space Dynamic Reduction Algorithm

In LoRa network, the LoRa gateway can support a large number of *EDs*. The increase in the number of *EDs* will cause the strategy space to increase exponentially. It is obviously inappropriate to traverse the entire strategy space to obtain the optimal solution for the Lyapunov drift-plus-penalty function in a single time slot. In order to solve this problem, this paper proposes a Strategy Space Dynamic Reduction (SSDR) algorithm. It reduces the dimension of the action strategy space through further analysis of the LoRa network structure. It finds an approximate optimal solution that satisfies the constraints of the optimization problem in the strategy space more quickly.

5.1 Battery Queue State and AoI Constraints

As can be seen from the LoRa network system model, the battery queue status in the end device will determine whether the packet can be successfully transmitted to the gateway. If at one moment, the end device does not acquire enough energy to store in the battery queue, the decision to transmit packets at the next moment will be invalidated. Assuming that there are N end devices in the current LoRa network, the action strategy space Π_1 is represented as

$$\Pi_1 = \begin{bmatrix} \mu_{0,0} & \mu_{0,1} & \cdots & \mu_{0,2^N} \\ \mu_{1,0} & \mu_{1,1} & \cdots & \mu_{1,2^N} \\ \vdots & \vdots & & \vdots \\ \mu_{N,0} & \mu_{N,1} & \cdots & \mu_{N,2^N} \end{bmatrix}. \tag{14}$$

It can be seen that the size of the current strategy space is $N \times 2^N$, and the increase in the number of *EDs* represents that the strategy space rises according to the exponential trend. It is not appropriate to take an exhaustive method to traverse the entire search space. We base constraints on the battery queue status of the *EDs* when the battery status of the device does not meet the constraints, we have

$$E_i(t) \geq E_c + E_i^{trans}(t). \tag{15}$$

Assuming that the number of *EDs* that do not meet the above constraints is β_1, remove these *EDs* from the strategy space and rebuild the strategy space Π_2

$$\Pi_2 = \begin{bmatrix} \mu_{0,0} & \mu_{0,1} & \cdots & \mu_{0,2^{N-\beta_1}} \\ \mu_{1,0} & \mu_{1,1} & \cdots & \mu_{1,2^{N-\beta_1}} \\ \vdots & \vdots & & \vdots \\ \mu_{N-\beta_1,0} & \mu_{N-\beta_1,1} & \cdots & \mu_{N-\beta_1,2^{N-\beta_1}} \end{bmatrix}. \tag{16}$$

At this point, the size of the strategy space Π_2 is $(N - \beta_1) \times 2^{(N-\beta_1)}$ and the dimension drops to $N - \beta_1$.

Observing the strategy space, it is not difficult to find that when the packet AoI of the end device is 1, it means that the packet has been successfully transmitted to the gateway, or no packet is generated or store in the end device at the current moment. We remove the *EDs* with an AoI of 1 from the strategy space because the transmission decision will be meaningless when there is no packet in the end device. Assuming that the number of *EDs* with AoI=1 is β_2, rebuild the strategy space Π_3

$$\Pi_3 = \begin{bmatrix} \mu_{0,0} & \mu_{0,1} & \cdots & \mu_{0,2^{N-\beta_1-\beta_2}} \\ \mu_{1,0} & \mu_{1,1} & \cdots & \mu_{1,2^{N-\beta_1-\beta_2}} \\ \vdots & \vdots & & \vdots \\ \mu_{N-\beta_1-\beta_2,0} & \mu_{N-\beta_1-\beta_2,1} & \cdots & \mu_{N-\beta_1-\beta_2,2^{N-\beta_1-\beta_2}} \end{bmatrix}. \tag{17}$$

After analyzing the battery status and the AoI state of the *EDs*, the strategy space size at this time is reduced to $(N - \beta_1 - \beta_2) \times 2^{(N-\beta_1-\beta_2)}$ and the dimension is $N - \beta_1 - \beta_2$.

5.2   Further Analysis of AoI

Through the above analysis, the dimension of the strategy space has been reduced to a certain extent. We further analyze that the AoI of each end device and the queue backlog of the gateway will determine whether to transmit packets. All *EDs* with the same AoI are essentially the same in our transmission decisions. Therefore, the action behavior of these end devices with the same AoI is somewhat repeated in the strategy space.

Suppose that the number of *EDs* with the same AoI is η. For example, when $\eta = 5$, we number the five *EDs* as 1, 2, 3, 4, 5. Through the permutation analysis, we can obtain a total of 32 possibilities for the transmission decision of 5 end devices. There are six effective decisions in these decisions. So when $\eta = 5$, the original 32 strategies can be reduced to 6. That is, the original 2^N action decisions now only need $\eta + 1$ decisions. We set up a hash table, when there are η end devices with the same AoI, store $\eta + 1$ decisions in this table. When the decision scheduling of a specific number of *EDs* is searched, the specific action decision can be taken out from the hash table.

Based on the above analysis, for a certain time, when there are β_1 end devices with insufficient battery energy and β_2 end devices with 0 AoI in the LoRa network, and the number of end devices with the same AoI (excluding 1) is η, our SSDR algorithm can reduce the total number of policies from 2^N to $(\eta + 1) \times 2^{(N-\beta_1-\beta_2-\eta)}$. If more than one AoI indicator is the same, that is, there are $\phi = (\eta_0, \eta_1, \cdots, \eta_\kappa)$ duplicates, then the total number of strategies that can be implemented by the SSDR algorithm is $(\eta_0+1)(\eta_1+1)\cdots(\eta_\kappa+1) \times 2^{(N-\beta_1-\beta_2-\eta_0-\eta_1-\cdots-\eta_\kappa)}$. The specific SSDR algorithm is shown below.

Algorithm 2. SSDR Algorithm

Input: Initialize the parameter environment of the LoRa wireless network: Select $BW, \alpha_i(t), PL, H, DE, CR$ according to the LoRa network architecture. Choose appropriate V, LoopTime and E_{max}. Set $t = 1$.

1: $S_{gw}(0) = 0, \mathbb{A}(0) = 0, E(0) = 0, p_i(t) = 14dBm$.
2: **for** each $i \in Looptime$ **do**
3:     Update the AoI of all end devices.
4:     Update the battery queue for all end devices.
5:     **if** $E_i(t) < E_c + E_i^{trans}(t)$ **then**
6:         Remove devices that do not meet energy constraints from the scheduling strategy.
7:     **else**
8:         Add end devices to the scheduling strategy space.
9:     **end if**
10:    **if** Traverse to the end device that has duplicate AoI **then**
11:       Store the duplicate AoI end device in a hash table.
12:    **end if**
13:    Execute the DPP algorithm, search the dynamically reduced strategy space, and find the most suitable scheduling strategy π.
14:    According to the obtained scheduling strategy, update the AoI index, gateway backlog level, and battery queue energy level of the end device.
15: **end for**

---

6   Simulation Results

In this section, we evaluated the performance of the SSDR algorithm through simulation experiments and conducted controlled experiments using other commonly used algorithms for comparison to compare the average PAoI performance under different algorithm strategies. Our simulation experiment results are shown below.

6.1   Parametric Analysis Under SSDR Algorithm

The calculation of the preamble and payload duration can be obtained through the LoRa chip calculation tool officially provided by Semtech [3]. Suppose that the initial network environment is: data arrival probability is $\theta = 0.4$, the number of EDs is $N = 10$, and the spreading factor is $SF = 8$. By setting different energy arrival probabilities, the simulation results obtained are shown in Fig. 4. As the energy arrival probability increases, the energy in the battery queue of EDs is no longer in a state of shortage. Moreover, due to the long-term scheduling of SSDR, the overall stability of the system is improved. So the energy state of the battery will maintain at a steady level after a period of time.

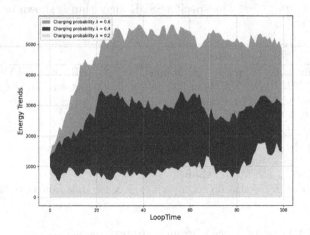

Fig. 4. Trend of Battery Energy with Varying Charging Probabilities.

In order to better observe the trend of queue backlog status and the average PAoI variation under the SSDR algorithm, we set the energy arrival probability to $\lambda = 0.4$ based on the above parameter environment. The queue backlog status of the gateway and the average PAoI change trend of the system are shown in Fig. 5 and Fig. 6.

As shown in Fig. 5, it can be seen that the queue backlog of the gateway has a significant initial decrease, followed by fluctuations at a lower level. It indicating that our SSDR algorithm does not fully sacrifice the queue backlog

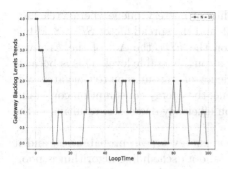

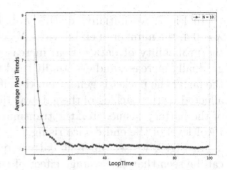

Fig. 5. Gateway Backlog.

Fig. 6. Average PAoI Level.

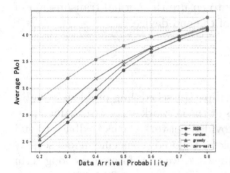

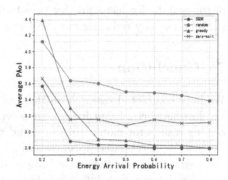

Fig. 7. Different Data Arrival Probabilities.

Fig. 8. Different Battery Energy Arrival Probabilities.

of the gateway to minimize the system average PAoI. Figure 6 shows that the system's average PAoI can rapidly decrease at the initial stage under the SSDR algorithm, and then stabilize at a very low level. It is in line with our expectations for the LoRa wireless monitoring network.

6.2 Compare with Other Algorithms

We have chosen three common wireless network scheduling algorithms to compare the performance of the SSDR algorithm. The random scheduling algorithm randomly selects a specific number of *EDs* for transmission in each time slot while satisfying the queue backlog constraint. The greedy scheduling algorithm searches for the *EDs* with the highest AoI in each time slot and selects a specific number of *EDs* for data transmission. The zero-wait scheduling strategy is a common AoI scheduling strategy that maximizes system resource utilization to avoid any task waiting or suspension. In each time slot, once a qualifying data packet is generated, it is immediately transmitted, thereby reducing the PAoI level of *EDs*.

In Fig. 7, we initially set the probability of battery queue energy reaching $\lambda = 0.4$, the number of end devices $N = 10$, and the spread factor $SF = 8$. While the probability of data arrival increases on the *EDs*, the AoI of the *EDs* will gradually increase, and eventually tend to a roughly stable level. This is because the faster the packet is generated, the efficiency of transmission to the gateway is affected by the backlog of the gateway queue, the energy consumption constraint of the battery queue, etc., the transmission efficiency decreases, resulting in the PAoI level of the end device rising.

In Fig. 8, we set different battery queue energy arrival probabilities, and it can be seen that the average effect of the random scheduling algorithm is poor, the greedy scheduling algorithm converges quickly and eventually tends to the effect of our SSDR algorithm, while the zero-wait strategy decreases moderately. This is because when the probability of energy reaching increases, the battery of the end device has a greater possibility to ensure the normal transmission of packets, thereby reducing the PAoI level of the end device.

7   Conclusion

We have conducted research on the optimal packet scheduling problem in LoRa wireless networks. By utilizing edge servers at the network edge, we obtained processing results for monitoring data and provided network status feedback to end devices. We formulated optimization problems tailored to specific model scenarios. Using the Lyapunov optimization framework, we transformed the long-term optimization problem into a single time slot optimization problem for selecting the best scheduling strategy. To address the challenge of a large search space, we introduced the SSDR algorithm, which dynamically reduces the strategy space to quickly identify the optimal scheduling strategy. Through simulation experiments, we analyzed the performance of the SSDR algorithm under varying network conditions and compared it with three other commonly used scheduling algorithms. The simulation results demonstrate that our SSDR algorithm consistently achieves favorable optimization outcomes across different parameter settings, significantly reducing the age of information for *EDs*.

References

1. Liya, M., Aswathy, M.: Lora technology for internet of things(IoT):a brief survey. In: 2020 Fourth International Conference on I-SMAC (IoT in Social, Mobile, Analytics and Cloud) (I-SMAC), pp. 8–13 (2020). https://doi.org/10.1109/I-SMAC49090.2020.9243449
2. Shanmuga Sundaram, J.P., Du, W., Zhao, Z.: A survey on Lora networking: research problems, current solutions, and open issues. IEEE Commun. Surv. Tutor. **22**(1), 371–388 (2020). https://doi.org/10.1109/COMST.2019.2949598
3. Gkotsiopoulos, P., Zorbas, D., Douligeris, C.: Performance determinants in Lora networks: a literature review. IEEE Commun. Surv. Tutor. **23**(3), 1721–1758 (2021). https://doi.org/10.1109/COMST.2021.3090409

4. Kaul, S., Yates, R., Gruteser, M.: Real-time status: how often should one update? In: 2012 Proceedings IEEE INFOCOM, pp. 2731–2735 (2012). https://doi.org/10.1109/INFCOM.2012.6195689

5. Yates, R.D., Sun, Y., Brown, D.R., Kaul, S.K., Modiano, E., Ulukus, S.: Age of information: an introduction and survey. IEEE J. Sel. Areas Commun. **39**(5), 1183–1210 (2021). https://doi.org/10.1109/JSAC.2021.3065072

6. Chiariotti, F., Vikhrova, O., Soret, B., Popovski, P.: Peak age of information distribution for edge computing with wireless links. IEEE Trans. Commun. **69**(5), 3176–3191 (2021). https://doi.org/10.1109/TCOMM.2021.3053038

7. Wu, D., Zhan, W., Sun, X., Zhou, B., Liu, J.: Peak age of information optimization of slotted aloha. In: 2022 IEEE 96th Vehicular Technology Conference (VTC2022-Fall), pp. 1–7 (2022). https://doi.org/10.1109/VTC2022-Fall57202.2022.10012799

8. Bingöl, E., Yener, A.: Peak age of information with receiver induced service interruptions. In: MILCOM 2022–2022 IEEE Military Communications Conference (MILCOM), pp. 229–234 (2022). https://doi.org/10.1109/MILCOM55135.2022.10017555

9. Liu, Z., Zhou, Q., Hou, L., Xu, R., Zheng, K.: Design and implementation on a Lora system with edge computing. In: 2020 IEEE Wireless Communications and Networking Conference (WCNC), pp. 1–6 (2020). https://doi.org/10.1109/WCNC45663.2020.9120572

10. Sarker, V.K., Queralta, J.P., Gia, T.N., Tenhunen, H., Westerlund, T.: A survey on Lora for IoT: integrating edge computing. In: 2019 Fourth International Conference on Fog and Mobile Edge Computing (FMEC), pp. 295–300 (2019). https://doi.org/10.1109/FMEC.2019.8795313

11. Chen, Z., Pappas, N., Björnson, E., Larsson, E.G.: Optimizing information freshness in a multiple access channel with heterogeneous devices. IEEE Open J. Commun. Soc. **2**, 456–470 (2021). https://doi.org/10.1109/OJCOMS.2021.3062678

12. Wang, Y., Chen, W.: Adaptive power and rate control for real-time status updating over fading channels. IEEE Trans. Wireless Commun. **20**(5), 3095–3106 (2021). https://doi.org/10.1109/TWC.2020.3047426

13. Tang, Z., Sun, Z., Yang, N., Zhou, X.: Age of information analysis of multi-user mobile edge computing systems. In: 2021 IEEE Global Communications Conference (GLOBECOM), pp. 1–6 (2021). https://doi.org/10.1109/GLOBECOM46510.2021.9685769

14. Lv, H., Zheng, Z., Wu, F., Chen, G.: Strategy-proof online mechanisms for weighted AoI minimization in edge computing. IEEE J. Sel. Areas Commun. **39**(5), 1277–1292 (2021). https://doi.org/10.1109/JSAC.2021.3065078

15. Liu, Q., Zeng, H., Chen, M.: Minimizing AoI with throughput requirements in multi-path network communication. IEEE/ACM Trans. Netw. **30**(3), 1203–1216 (2022). https://doi.org/10.1109/TNET.2021.3135494

16. Hu, L., Chen, Z., Jia, Y., Wang, M., Quek, T.Q.S.: Asymptotically optimal arrival rate for IoT networks with AoI and peak AoI constraints. IEEE Commun. Lett. **25**(12), 3853–3857 (2021). https://doi.org/10.1109/LCOMM.2021.3119350

17. Wang, Q., Chen, H., Gu, Y., Li, Y., Vucetic, B.: Minimizing the age of information of cognitive radio-based iot systems under a collision constraint. IEEE Trans. Wireless Commun. **19**(12), 8054–8067 (2020). https://doi.org/10.1109/TWC.2020.3019056

18. Abd-Elmagid, M.A., Dhillon, H.S.: Closed-form characterization of the MGF of AoI in energy harvesting status update systems. IEEE Trans. Inf. Theory **68**(6), 3896–3919 (2022). https://doi.org/10.1109/TIT.2022.3149450

19. Abd-Elmagid, M.A., Dhillon, H.S.: Distributional properties of age of information in energy harvesting status update systems. In: 2021 19th International Symposium on Modeling and Optimization in Mobile, Ad hoc, and Wireless Networks (WiOpt), pp. 1–8 (2021). https://doi.org/10.23919/WiOpt52861.2021.9589825

20. Abd-Elmagid, M.A., Dhillon, H.S.: Age of information in multi-source updating systems powered by energy harvesting. IEEE J. Sel. Areas Inf. Theory 3(1), 98–112 (2022). https://doi.org/10.1109/JSAIT.2022.3158421

21. Yates, R.D.: Lazy is timely: Status updates by an energy harvesting source. In: 2015 IEEE International Symposium on Information Theory (ISIT), pp. 3008–3012 (2015). https://doi.org/10.1109/ISIT.2015.7283009

22. Sharan, B.A.G.R., Deshmukh, S., B. Pillai, S.R., Beferull-Lozano, B.: Energy efficient AoI minimization in opportunistic NOMA/OMA broadcast wireless networks. IEEE Trans. Green Commun. Netw. 6(2), 1009–1022 (2022). https://doi.org/10.1109/TGCN.2021.3135351

23. Zhou, Z., Fu, C., Xue, C.J., Han, S.: Energy-constrained data freshness optimization in self-powered networked embedded systems. IEEE Trans. Comput. Aided Des. Integr. Circuits Syst. 39(10), 2293–2306 (2020). https://doi.org/10.1109/TCAD.2019.2948905

24. Fang, Z., Wang, J., Jiang, C., Wang, X., Ren, Y.: Average peak age of information in underwater information collection with sleep-scheduling. IEEE Trans. Veh. Technol. 71(9), 10132–10136 (2022). https://doi.org/10.1109/TVT.2022.3176819

25. Lavric, A., Popa, V.: Internet of things and Lora^{TM} low-power wide-area networks: a survey. In: 2017 International Symposium on Signals, Circuits and Systems (ISSCS), pp. 1–5 (2017). https://doi.org/10.1109/ISSCS.2017.8034915

26. Saari, M., bin Baharudin, A.M., Sillberg, P., Hyrynsalmi, S., Yan, W.: Lora - a survey of recent research trends. In: 2018 41st International Convention on Information and Communication Technology, Electronics and Microelectronics (MIPRO), pp. 0872–0877 (2018). https://doi.org/10.23919/MIPRO.2018.8400161

27. Pagano, A., Croce, D., Tinnirello, I., Vitale, G.: A survey on Lora for smart agriculture: current trends and future perspectives. IEEE Internet Things J. 10(4), 3664–3679 (2023). https://doi.org/10.1109/JIOT.2022.3230505

28. Hamdi, R., Qaraqe, M.: Resource management in energy harvesting powered Lora wireless networks. In: ICC 2021 - IEEE International Conference on Communications, pp. 1–6 (2021). https://doi.org/10.1109/ICC42927.2021.9500638

29. Zorbas, D., Abdelfadeel, K.Q., Cionca, V., Pesch, D., O'Flynn, B.: Offline scheduling algorithms for time-slotted lora-based bulk data transmission. In: 2019 IEEE 5th World Forum on Internet of Things (WF-IoT), pp. 949–954 (2019). https://doi.org/10.1109/WF-IoT.2019.8767277

30. Kumari, P., Mishra, R., Gupta, H.P., Dutta, T., Das, S.K.: An energy efficient smart metering system using edge computing in Lora network. IEEE Trans. Sustain. Comput. 7(4), 786–798 (2022). https://doi.org/10.1109/TSUSC.2021.3049705

31. Hadi, M., Pakravan, M.R., Agrell, E.: Dynamic resource allocation in metro elastic optical networks using Lyapunov drift optimization. J. Opt. Commun. Netw. 11(6), 250–259 (2019). https://doi.org/10.1364/JOCN.11.000250

32. Xu, J., Chen, L., Zhou, P.: Joint service caching and task offloading for mobile edge computing in dense networks. In: IEEE INFOCOM 2018 - IEEE Conference on Computer Communications, pp. 207–215 (2018). https://doi.org/10.1109/INFOCOM.2018.8485977

Enhancing Session-Based Recommendation with Multi-granularity User Interest-Aware Graph Neural Networks

Cairong Yan[✉][iD], Yiwei Zhang, Xiangyang Feng, and Yanglan Gan

School of Computer Science and Technology, Donghua University, Shanghai, China
{cryan,fengxy,ylgan}@dhu.edu.cn, ywzhang@mail.dhu.edu.cn

Abstract. Session-based recommendation aims at predicting the next interaction based on short-term behaviors within an anonymous session. Conventional session-based recommendation methods primarily focus on studying the sequential relationships of items in a session while often failing to adequately consider the impact of user interest on the next interaction item. This paper proposes the **M**ulti-granularity **U**ser **I**nterest-aware **G**raph **N**eural **N**etworks (MUI-GNN) model, which leverages item attributes and global context information to capture users' multi-granularity interest. Specifically, in addition to capturing the sequential information within sessions, our model incorporates individual and group interest of users at item and global granularity, respectively, enabling more accurate item representations. In MUI-GNN, a session graph utilizes the sequential relationships between different interactions to infer the scenario of the session. An item graph explores individual user interest by searching items with similar attributes, while a global graph mines similar behavior patterns between different sessions to uncover group interest among users. We apply contrastive learning to reduce noise interference during the graph construction process and help the model obtain more contextual information. Extensive experiments conducted on three real-world datasets have demonstrated that the proposed MUI-GNN outperforms state-of-the-art session-based recommendation models.

Keywords: Recommender system · Session-based recommendation · Graph neural network · Self-supervised learning

1 Introduction

Recommender systems can effectively alleviate the issue of information overload encountered in the digital age. They are widely used in domains such as online shopping, social applications, and news media. Traditional recommendation methods [1,7,23] predict items or services based on the interaction history of a specific user over a long period. However, in some real-world scenarios, user information may be anonymous, while platforms can record only short-term

© ICST Institute for Computer Sciences, Social Informatics and Telecommunications Engineering 2024
Published by Springer Nature Switzerland AG 2024. All Rights Reserved
H. Gao et al. (Eds.): CollaborateCom 2023, LNICST 563, pp. 291–307, 2024.
https://doi.org/10.1007/978-3-031-54531-3_16

interactions of a user within a session. The research on session-based recommendation has consequently emerged, which employs interactions logged in the session to predict the next item or service, without relying on the user identity [22].

Early researchers use Markov chains (MCs) to capture short-term transition relationships between items in a session [6,18], which assume that the next item is only related to the most recent one or a few preceding items. Recurrent Neural Networks (RNNs) are then utilized to solve sequence-related problems. RNN-based approaches [8,19] consider each session as a sequential sequence and have shown fine results. However, RNNs heavily rely on the temporal order of items in a session, limiting the accuracy of item predictions. In recent years, Graph Neural Networks (GNNs) [27] have become popular in session-based recommendation tasks [16,17,25,26,30]. GNN methods employ graph structures to transfer information between items in a session. These methods have demonstrated superior performance compared to previous models.

Despite achieving remarkable results, most previous methods primarily focus on analyzing the sequential patterns of items in sessions without exploring the multi-granularity user interest adequately. As a result, the potential wealth of auxiliary information can be untapped during calculation. While session-based recommendation mainly addresses short and anonymous sequences, it is possible to incorporate individual and global user interest by combining item attribute information and global contextual information, respectively. For instance, Fig. 1 illustrates an example of a session-based recommendation task, demonstrating the collective utilization of sequential relationships with individual and group user interest contributes to more comprehensive and enriched recommendation outcomes.

From the granularity of a session, we can infer the session scenario and user demands by the sequential relationships among different items within the session. As in Fig. 1, we recommend items such as a mouse and a USB drive based on the presence of a keyboard and a computer in the session. At the item granularity, we explore individual user interest by identifying items with similar attributes to those already recorded in the session. As can be seen, we may recommend a black phone (in the same category as iPhone) or an iPad (in the same brand as iPhone). In terms of global granularity, we measure the similarity between different sessions by comparing the frequency of occurrences of the same item. Then we are able to understand the group interest of multiple users with similar behavior patterns. In the figure, a data cable and Airpods are recommended based on the contextual information derived from other sessions. Therefore, by analyzing user interest at different levels of granularity, the comprehensiveness and diversity of recommendation results can be further improved.

Self-supervised learning(SSL) [9,14] has recently gained significant attention recommender systems. In our case, we employ self-supervised learning to facilitate the model in studying global representation information. Additionally, given the large number of items with similar attributes, contrastive learning methods

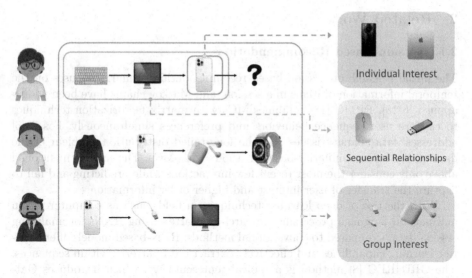

Fig. 1. An example of session-based recommendation incorporating multi-granularity user interest. The gray box recommends items by sequential relationships in the session. The blue and red boxes capture the users' multi-granularity interest and offer richer options to enhance recommendation performance. (Color figure online)

can also be used to reduce noise interference during the initial construction process of the item graph.

Overall, the main contributions of this paper are summarized as follows:

- We propose a model structure which captures sequential relationships, individual interest, and group interest of users from three different levels of granularity: session, item, and global, respectively. Multi-granularity user interest is used to enhance the result of the model prediction.
- We apply contrastive learning to fuse global representations and reduce noise interference during model construction, thereby enabling the model to obtain more contextual information and improve recommendation effectiveness.
- Extensive experiments on three real-world datasets have shown that our model achieves greater performance compared to the state-of-the-art methods in session-based recommendation tasks.

The remainder of this paper is organized as follows. Section 2 briefly discusses related work. Section 3 presents the methodology. In Sect. 4, we demonstrate the effectiveness of this method through experiments. Section 5 gives a conclusion.

2   Related Work

2.1   Session-Based Recommendation

The initial research on session-based recommendation primarily focuses on the temporal information of items in a session, and Markov chains have been widely applied [6,18]. FPMC [18] combines MCs with matrix factorization techniques to capture user sequence behaviors and preferences simultaneously. Fossil [6] addresses data sparsity issues and the long-tailed distribution problem in the datasets by fusing similarity-based methods with MCs. The models mentioned above only consider the most recent few interactions while predicting and fail to capture the transfer of user interest and higher-order information.

With the rise of deep learning techniques in fields such as computer vision and natural language processing, researchers started using RNNs for analyzing session data. Compared to conventional methods, RNN-based models offer superior learning capabilities and effectively extract data patterns within sequences. The GRU4REC [8] method is a typical representative, which introduces Gating Recurrent Units (GRUs) to session-based recommendation and yields good results. Later, data augmentation techniques [19] are used to further improve the recommendation performance by RNN-based models. NARM [12] proposes a hybrid encoder with an attention mechanism, which allows the model to focus on the most relevant items during the recommendation process. STAMP [13] employs simple multi-layer perception and attention networks to capture user interest and explicitly accounts for users' current behavior on their next action.

GNNs have recently gained significant attention in session-based recommendation tasks. Compared to previous methods, GNNs capture complex item transition relationships by the graph structure and offer improved accuracy in calculating item and session representations. SR-GNN [26] is a pioneering work in this area, employing Gated Graph Neural Networks (GGNNs) to learn the transition relationships of items in the session, and achieves promising results. GC-SAN [30] obtains local dependencies and long-range dependencies through GNNs and multi-layer self-attention networks, respectively. FGNN [17] uses a multi-head attention layer to help aggregate neighbor information by nodes with different weights. TAGNN [31] takes into account the diverse interest of users towards target items, thereby personalizing the recommendation task. GCE-GNN [24] utilizes a subtle approach to exploit the item transition relationships across all sessions to better infer the user preferences in the current session. SHARE [21] employs hypergraph attention networks to exploit item correlations within various contextual windows.

Most existing works analyze sessions primarily based on the sequential information of items in the session and do not comprehensively consider user interest from multi-granularity, which impedes the model performance.

2.2 Self-supervised Learning

Self-supervised learning is a type of unsupervised learning method where the label of positive and negative samples is marked through the inherent properties of the data itself, without manual intervention. Self-supervised learning can mainly be categorized into contrastive learning [4;9] and generative learning [3,15]. Generative learning, represented by auto-encoding [10], transforms the original data into vector representations using an encoder and then reconstructs it by a decoder. Contrastive learning usually consists of the paradigm of agent tasks combined with an objective function. Positive and negative sample pairs are automatically generated by agent tasks, and the Noise Contrastive Estimation (NCE) is used for the loss function. Notable examples of contrastive learning methods include SimCLR [2] and MoCo [5].

Self-supervised learning has also been introduced into sequence-related recommendation tasks. S^3-Rec [32] employs Mutual Information Maximization (MIM) principle to establish correlations among attributes, items, subsequences, and sequences. S^2-DHCN [29] first introduces self-supervised learning to session-based recommendation and applies contrastive learning on two hypergraph channels to improve recommendation performance. COTREC [28] explores the internal and external connectivity of sessions from two different perspectives. MGS [11] utilizes attribute information in sessions and adopts a contrastive learning strategy to reduce noise generated by neighboring items with similar attributes. Self-supervised learning can effectively alleviate the data sparsity issue that appeared in session-based recommendation.

3 The Proposed Method

In this section, we first formalize the definition of session-based recommendation. Then we present a detailed introduction to the proposed model. Figure 2 gives a graphic illustration of the problem definition. Figure 3 demonstrates the overall structure of the MUI-GNN model.

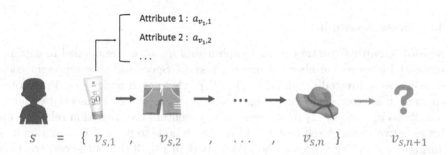

Fig. 2. A graphic illustration of a session-based recommendation task.

3.1   Problem Definition

Session-based recommendation tasks aim to predict the next item based on a user's limited historical interaction sequence. Here, we use $V = \{v_1, v_2, \ldots, v_{|V|}\}$ to represent the item set, where $|V|$ is the total number of the items. Each session is composed of several chronological items, denoted as $s = \{v_{s,1}, v_{s,2}, \ldots, v_{s,n}\}$, where $v_{s,i} \in V (1 \leq i \leq n)$ denotes the i-th item in session s, and n is the length of the session s. The embedding vector for each item v_i is represented as x_i. The ultimate goal of the recommendation model is to predict the next item $v_{s,n+1}$ by recommending top-K items under the given session s.

For each item v_i in the session, we label its attribute values as $\mathcal{A}_{v_i} = \{a_{v_i,1}, a_{v_i,2}, \ldots, a_{v_i,o}\}$, where $a_{v_i,j} (1 \leq j \leq o)$ denotes the value of item v_i under the j-th attribute. The number of attribute types o varies from different datasets. By utilizing item attributes, we can find k neighbors which share the same attribute value with v_i. We formalize this item set as $\mathcal{N}_{v_i}$ for each attribute, $|\mathcal{N}_{v_i}| = k$.

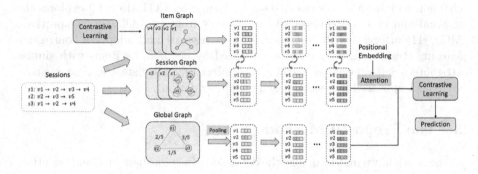

Fig. 3. The overall structure of MUI-GNN.

3.2   Session Graph

Session Graph Construction. Graph neural networks are applied to capture sequential information about items in a session. Specifically, we represent each session s as a directed graph $G_s = \{\mathcal{V}_s, \mathcal{E}_s\}$, where each node $v_{s,i} \in \mathcal{V}_s$ denotes an item in session s and each edge $e = (v_{s,i}, v_{s,i+1}) \in \mathcal{E}_s$ connects two adjacent items $v_{s,i}$ and $v_{s,i+1}$ in the session, representing the transition relationship between two items. A self-loop is added to each node to prevent information loss during the iterative process. The middle part in Fig. 3 shows the construction process of the session graph for session $s1$.

Session Graph Convolution. Graph convolution is operated to learn the transition relationships of adjacent items in the session. We use Graph Attention Networks(GAT) [20] to help each node learn the representation of the neighboring nodes. Specifically, for each item v_i in the session, the attention coefficients of each neighboring node are computed:

$$\alpha_{ij} = \frac{exp\left(LeakyReLU\left(e_{ij}^T\left(x_i^{(l-1)} \odot x_j^{(l-1)}\right)\right)\right)}{\sum_{v_k \in N_{v_i}} exp\left(LeakyReLU\left(e_{ij}^T\left(x_i^{(l-1)} \odot x_k^{(l-1)}\right)\right)\right)}, \tag{1}$$

where e_{ij} is the embedding of the relation between x_i and x_j, and l denotes the layer of graph convolution. $x_i^{(l-1)}$ is the embedding vector of item v_i in the previous layer. The representation $x_i^{(l)}$ in the l-th layer is then summed:

$$x_i^{(l)} = \sum_{x_j \in N_{x_i}} \alpha_{ij} x_j^{(l-1)}, \tag{2}$$

where $x_i^{(0)} = x_i$ in the first layer.

3.3   Item Graph

Item Graph Construction. Collecting items with similar attributes helps us better explore the individual interest of users at the item granularity. Thus we construct an item graph. To initialize the representations in the item graph, an attention mechanism is utilized to aggregate attribute information from the neighbors of item v_i:

$$\alpha_{ij} = \frac{exp\left(LeakyReLU\left(q_j^T\left(x_i\|x_j\right)\right)\right)}{\sum_{x_k \in N_{v_i}} exp\left(LeakyReLU\left(q_j^T\left(x_i\|x_k\right)\right)\right)}, \tag{3}$$

$$m_i = \sum_{x_j \in N_{x_i}} \alpha_{ij} v_j, \tag{4}$$

where m_i is the initial representation of the item v_i in the item graph. $\|$ is the concatenation operator, and q_j is the embedding vector of the j-th attribute.

Item Graph Convolution. We update representations in item and session graphs together by a dual refinement method. First, we update x_i with m_i:

$$\beta_i = \frac{\left(W_1^s x_i^{(l)}\right)^T W_2^s m_i^{(l-1)}}{\sqrt{d}}, \tag{5}$$

$$x_i^{(l)} = x_i^{(l)} + \beta_i\left(m_i^{(l-1)} - x_i^{(l)}\right), \tag{6}$$

where d is the size of the embedding vector, $W_1^s, W_2^s \in \mathbb{R}^{d \times d}$ are learnable parameters, and l denotes the number of layers in the item graph convolution, $m_i^{(0)} = m_i$ in the first layer.

Then we use the updated $x_i^{(l)}$ to adjust $m_i^{(l)}$ by following attention mechanism,

$$\alpha_{ij} = \frac{exp\left(\left(W_1^m m_i^{(l-1)}\right)^T W_2^m x_j^{(l)}\right)}{\sum\limits_{k=1}^{n} exp\left(\left(W_1^m m_i^{(l-1)}\right)^T W_2^m x_k^{(l)}\right)}, \tag{7}$$

$$m_i^{(l)} = \sum_{j=1}^{N} \alpha_{ij} m_j^{(l-1)}, \tag{8}$$

where $W_1^m, W_2^m \in \mathbb{R}^{d \times d}$ are also learnable parameters. Note that they are different from previous W_1^s and W_2^s. Finally, after the convolution of L layers, we get the final representation of the session items:

$$\pi_i = sigmoid\left(W_h\left[x_i^{(0)} || x_i^{(L)}\right]\right), \tag{9}$$

$$x_i^{(L)} = \pi_i x_i^{(0)} + (1 - \pi)x_i^{(L)}, \tag{10}$$

where $W_h \in \mathbb{R}^{d \times 2d}$ is a learnable parameter.

3.4   Global Graph

Global Graph Construction. The group interest of users can be captured by mining similar behavior patterns across sessions. Specifically, we treat each session as a node in the global graph. Sessions are connected if there is at least one common item appears.

The weight of the edge is set to $W_{i,j}$, whose value is the size of the intersection set of items in the two sessions divided by the size of the union set. For example, in Fig. 3, the edge weight between session $s1$ and session $s2$ is $2/5$, as the intersection set is $\{v2, v3\}$, and the union set is $\{v1, v2, v3, v4, v5\}$.

Global Graph Convolution. The initial embedding $\theta^{(0)}$ of each session is the average of all item embedding x_i in the session, and then a convolution process is operated.

$$\theta^{(l+1)} = \hat{D}^{-1} \hat{A} \theta^{(l)}, \tag{11}$$

where $\hat{D}^{-1}$ is the inverse matrix of the degree matrix. At each convolution layer, $\theta^{(l)}$ learns different levels of cross-session information. Thus we average the embedding of each layer to obtain the final session representation.

$$\theta_f = \frac{1}{L+1} \sum_{l=0}^{L} \theta^{(l)}. \tag{12}$$

3.5 Prediction Layers

Session Representation. Intuitively, items at different positions in the session contain different semantic information, so we impose a positional encoding p_i on each item in the session:

$$h_i = x_i^{(L)} + p_i . \tag{13}$$

We use a soft attention mechanism to obtain the session representations fusing the user's individual interest and the last item.

$$\beta_i = g^T sigmoid \left(W_1 h_i + W_2 m_i^{(L)} + W_3 x_n^{(L)} + b \right) , \tag{14}$$

$$z_s = \sum_{i=1}^{n} \beta_i h i , \tag{15}$$

where $W_1, W_2, W_3 \in \mathbb{R}^{d \times d}$ and $g, b \in \mathbb{R}^d$ are all learnable parameters. $m_i^{(L)}$ and $x_n^{(L)}$ denote the final result in the item graph and session graph convolution, respectively.

Finally, a gated mechanism is employed to reinforce the last behavior $x_n^{(L)}$ to the importance of the session representation explicitly.

$$\theta = sigmoid \left(W_4 \left[z_s || x_n^{(L)} \right] \right) , \tag{16}$$

$$s_f = (1 - \mu\theta) \odot z_s + \mu\theta \odot x_n^{(L)}, \tag{17}$$

where $W_4 \in \mathbb{R}^{d \times 2d}$ is the learnable parameter. μ controls the weight of the gating unit. s_f is the session representation we eventually gain.

Prediction. We implement the inner product of the embedding x_i of the item and the final representation s_f of the session to get a score $\hat{z}_i$ for each item.

$$\hat{z}_i = s_f^T x_i . \tag{18}$$

A softmax function is used to calculate the probability $\hat{y}$ that the item will be recommended.

$$\hat{y} = softmax (\hat{z}_i) . \tag{19}$$

The model is optimized by a cross-entropy loss function, which is also commonly used in recommender systems.

$$\mathcal{L}_r (\hat{y}) = -\sum_{i=1}^{N} y_i log (\hat{y}_i) + (1 - y_i) log (1 - \hat{y}_i) , \tag{20}$$

where y_i is the one-hot representation of the item x_i being recommended ground truth.

Self-supervised Learning. To further enhance the feature representation, we also set up self-supervised auxiliary tasks to optimize the model, which is primarily used to learn feature information across sessions. We use InfoNCE [5] with a standard binary cross-entropy loss function on positive and negative samples.

$$\mathcal{L}_{SSL} = -\log\sigma\left(f_D\left(\theta_i^h, \ \theta_i^l\right)\right) - \log\sigma\left(1 - f_D\left(\widetilde{\theta}_i^h, \ \theta_i^l\right)\right). \tag{21}$$

The final loss function of the model is:

$$\mathcal{L} = \mathcal{L}_r + \phi\mathcal{L}_{SSL_1} + \beta\mathcal{L}_{SSL_2}, \tag{22}$$

where ϕ and β are hyper-parameters controlling the weights of $\mathcal{L}_{SSL_1}$ and $\mathcal{L}_{SSL_2}$, respectively, which are shown as contrastive learning modules in Fig. 3.

4   Experiments

In this section, we first describe the experimental settings. Then a series of evaluations of model performance are conducted by answering the following questions:

RQ1: Does the MUI-GNN model surpass state-of-the-art session-based recommendation baseline models on several real-world datasets?

RQ2: Does capturing user interest from item and global granularity effectively enhance the performance of our model?

RQ3: How do key parameters, such as GNN layer number and embedding size, affect model performance?

4.1   Experimental Settings

Datasets. We conduct experiments on three real-world datasets, namely Diginetica, 30music, and Tmall, from different fields and with different data sparsity. All datasets contain session sequences and attribute information of items. Diginetica is a personalized e-commerce search challenge dataset in the CIKM Cup 2016 competition. Here, referring to [17,26,30], we only use its transaction data. 30music is a dataset collected and extracted through the Last. fm API, which contains user music playback data and divides playback events into different sessions. Tmall records the purchase logs of anonymous users on the Tmall website during the first six months of "Double Eleven" and the day of "Double Eleven" from the IJACI-15 competition.

We process the datasets in the same way as [26,29]. We remove sessions of length 1 and items that appear less than 5 times in the dataset. To enrich the training and testing data, we subdivide each session into several sub-sessions. Specifically, on each dataset, from a session $s = \{v_1, \ v_2, \ v_3, \ \ldots, \ v_n\}$, we generate new sequences $([v_1], \ v_2)$, $([v_1, \ v_2], \ v_3)$, $\ldots$, $([v_1, \ v_2, \ \ldots, \ v_{n-1}], \ v_n)$ for both training and testing sets. Similar to [26,29], sessions with interactions in the past week are used as the testing data, while other sessions are used as the training data. Table 1 shows the statistical information of three datasets after preprocessing.

Table 1. Statistical details of datasets.

Datasets	Diginetica	30music	Tmall
train sessions	719,470	1,153,622	351,268
test sessions	60,858	122,517	25,898
clicks	982,961	1,429,251	443,479
items	43,097	132,647	40,727
average length	4.85	9.33	6.69

Baseline Methods. We compare our model with the following classical and state-of-the-art models:

FPMC [18]: It includes Markov Chains and Matrix Factorization models to capture user interest and interaction sequence.

GRU4REC [8]: It utilizes session parallel mini-batches and a ranking loss function to enable GRUs to study sequence behaviors.

NARM [12]: It combines RNNs with an attention mechanism to understand interactions in a session.

SR-GNN [26]: It is the first model to apply GNNs to session-based recommendation, utilizing GGNNs and a soft attention mechanism to learn the representation of items.

GCE-GNN [24]: It uses a subtle approach to combine local and global item transition relationships.

S^2-DHCN [29]: It devises two different hypergraph channels to study inter-session and cross-session information, applying self-supervised learning to enhance recommendation.

MGS [11]: It constructs a mirror graph based on item attribute information and employs an iterative dual refinement mechanism to transfer data.

Evaluation Metrics. Similar to previous works [11,29], we measure model performance through two widely used metrics in session-based recommendation tasks: P@K and MRR@K.

P@K (Precision) indicates whether ground truth is at the top-K position of the prediction list:

$$P@K = \frac{1}{|U|} \sum_{v \in U} \prod (R_v < K), \tag{23}$$

where $|U|$ is the size of testing set, R_v represents the position of ground truth item v in the top K of the prediction list.

MRR@K (Mean Reciprocal Rank) measures the position of ground truth in the top-K recommendation list. Compared to P@K, MRR@K considers the impact of the result order.

$$MRR@K = \frac{1}{|U|} \sum_{v \in U} \frac{1}{R_v}. \tag{24}$$

Hyper-parameters Settings. According to [26,30], the size of each mini-batch is selected based on the size of the hidden vectors. To ensure a fair comparison, we quote the experimental results of baseline models reported in the original paper as possible, which is in their best hyper-parameter settings. All parameters follow a Gaussian distribution with an average value of 0 and a standard deviation of 1. The L2 norm value of the model is set to 10^{-5} and uses the Adam optimizer. The initial learning rate is 0.001, and there is a decay rate of 0.1 after the first three epochs.

Table 2. Performance Comparison of Different Methods on Diginetica dataset.

Method	Diginetica			
	P@10	MRR@10	P@20	MRR@20
FPMC	15.43	6.20	26.53	6.95
GRU4REC	17.93	7.33	29.45	8.33
NARM	35.44	15.13	49.70	16.17
SR-GNN	36.86	15.52	50.73	17.59
GCE-GNN	41.54	<u>18.29</u>	54.64	<u>19.20</u>
S^2-DHCN	41.16	18.15	53.18	18.44
MGS	<u>41.80</u>	18.20	<u>55.05</u>	19.13
Ours	**42.17**	**18.29**	**55.67**	**19.23**

Table 3. Performance Comparison of Different Methods on 30music dataset.

Method	30music			
	P@10	MRR@10	P@20	MRR@20
FPMC	1.51	0.55	2.40	0.61
GRU4REC	15.91	10.46	18.28	10.95
NARM	37.81	25.95	39.40	26.55
SR-GNN	36.49	26.71	39.93	26.94
GCE-GNN	39.93	21.21	44.71	21.55
S^2-DHCN	40.05	17.58	45.49	17.79
MGS	<u>41.51</u>	<u>27.67</u>	<u>46.46</u>	<u>28.01</u>
Ours	**42.04**	**28.58**	**47.26**	**28.89**

Table 4. Performance Comparison of Different Methods on Tmall dataset.

Method	Tmall			
	P@10	MRR@10	P@20	MRR@20
FPMC	13.10	7.12	16.06	7.32
GRU4REC	9.47	5.78	10.93	5.89
NARM	19.17	10.42	23.30	10.70
SR-GNN	23.41	13.45	27.57	13.72
GCE-GNN	29.19	15.55	34.35	15.91
S^2-DHCN	26.22	14.60	31.42	15.05
MGS	_35.39_	_18.15_	_42.12_	_18.62_
Ours	**36.33**	**18.42**	**42.69**	**18.85**

4.2 Experimental Results (RQ1)

Tables 2 to 4 show the performance of our model and baselines on three real-world datasets. The best and second-best results are highlighted in boldface and underlined, respectively. From the above tables, we can obtain the following observations:

RNN-based models (e.g. GRU4REC, NARM) utilize deep learning methods to capture item transition relationships in sessions, significantly improving model performance compared to earlier methods (e.g. FPMC), indicating the importance of utilizing sequential information in sessions. Among them, NARM performs better than GRU4REC because it uses an attention mechanism to model user interaction and purpose distinctively.

GNN-based methods demonstrate superior performance compared to RNN-based models, reflecting GNNs' ability to model sequential information and understand complex item transition relationships. The SR-GNN model, as it does not use any information out of session sequence, has a relatively lower performance than GCE-GNN, which combines global information to model user interest. S^2-DHCN uses the strategy of self-supervised learning combined with the hypergraph structure of multiple channels. MGS uses the attributes of items to build mirror graphs to help learn the representation information of items. Their improvement in model results supports that the application of auxiliary information plays an important role in session-based recommendation.

Our proposed MUI-GNN shows superior results on all three datasets compared to these traditional and deep learning approaches mentioned above, suggesting that considering multi-granularity user interest with sequential relationships in sessions can effectively enhance the model performance in session-based recommendation tasks.

4.3   Model Analysis and Discussion (RQ2 and RQ3)

Impact of Item/Global Graph. To explore the distinctive influence of multi-granularity user interest on prediction results, we adjust the MUI-GNN model to verify the effectiveness of the item graph and global graph respectively. Ablation experiments are conducted on Diginetica and 30music datasets. Table 5 demonstrates the results of the experiments, with the best performance highlighted in boldface.

Table 5. Impact of item/global graph

Method	Diginetica		30music	
	P@20	MRR@20	P@20	MRR@20
MUI-GNN	**55.78**	**19.21**	**47.26**	**28.89**
MUI-GNN w/o global	54.97	19.06	46.49	28.69
MUI-GNN w/o item	55.32	18.73	44.38	**28.89**

In the table, MUI-GNN w/o global and MUI-GNN w/o item indicates the MUI-GNN model without global graph/ item graph, respectively. We find that model's performance is optimal when the MUI-GNN model contains both the item and global graph modules, which captures the individual and group interest of users simultaneously. In general, the absence of either module will cut down the performance in recommendation results.

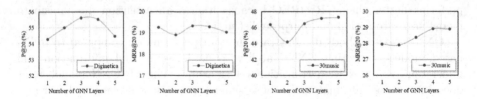

Fig. 4. Impact of depths in GNNs.

Impact of Depths in GNNs. We set the item graph and global graph into the same layer number and tested the performance of models with different depths over two datasets. The layer number of the graph neural networks in our model is set to {1, 2, 3, 4, 5}.

As can be seen from Fig. 4, in the Diginetica dataset, it is reasonable to set the depth of the graph neural networks to 3 or 4, as an over-smoothing problem will arise when the networks get too deep. While in the 30music dataset, increasing layers of graph neural networks can further improve the performance of the model. A possible reason is the average length of the 30music dataset is nearly as double as of Diginetica, which shows that the data pattern in the 30music dataset is more complex and requires deeper networks to mine the users' individual and global interest.

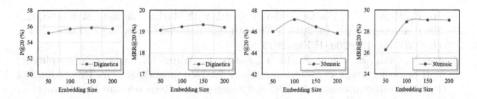

Fig. 5. Impact of embedding size.

Impact of Embedding Size. We test the embedding size in {50, 100, 150, 200} of the MUI-GNN model. Results are shown in Fig. 5. When the embedding vectors rise to the size of 100, our model achieves considerable performance. However, the continuous increase of embedding size will not always lead to better results, as an overly large embedding size may cause massive computation and overfitting problems.

5   Conclusion

The short and anonymous nature of sessions brings great challenges to session-based recommendation tasks. In this paper, we propose the MUI-GNN model, which not only incorporates the sequential relationships in a session but also explores users' interest at the item and global granularity to enhance model performance. Existing models often fail to capture this valuable auxiliary information comprehensively. Contrastive learning methods are used to reduce the noise during the graph construction and help the model learn the contextual information of the session better. Extensive experiments conducted on three real-world datasets exhibit the effectiveness and superiority of our model considering multi-granularity user interest.

References

1. Chang, J., Gao, C., He, X., Jin, D., Li, Y.: Bundle recommendation with graph convolutional networks. In: Proceedings of the 43rd International ACM SIGIR Conference on Research and Development in Information Retrieval, pp. 1673–1676 (2020)
2. Chen, T., Kornblith, S., Norouzi, M., Hinton, G.: A simple framework for contrastive learning of visual representations. In: International Conference on Machine Learning, pp. 1597–1607. PMLR (2020)
3. Devlin, J., Chang, M.W., Lee, K., Toutanova, K.: BERT: pre-training of deep bidirectional transformers for language understanding. arXiv preprint arXiv:1810.04805 (2018)
4. Gidaris, S., Singh, P., Komodakis, N.: Unsupervised representation learning by predicting image rotations. In: International Conference on Learning Representations (2018)
5. He, K., Fan, H., Wu, Y., Xie, S., Girshick, R.: Momentum contrast for unsupervised visual representation learning. In: Proceedings of the IEEE/CVF Conference on Computer Vision and Pattern Recognition, pp. 9729–9738 (2020)

6. He, R., McAuley, J.: Fusing similarity models with Markov chains for sparse sequential recommendation. In: 2016 IEEE 16th International Conference on Data Mining (ICDM), pp. 191–200. IEEE (2016)

7. He, X., Deng, K., Wang, X., Li, Y., Zhang, Y., Wang, M.: LightGCN: simplifying and powering graph convolution network for recommendation. In: Proceedings of the 43rd International ACM SIGIR Conference on Research and Development in Information Retrieval, pp. 639–648 (2020)

8. Hidasi, B., Karatzoglou, A., Baltrunas, L., Tikk, D.: Session-based recommendations with recurrent neural networks. arXiv preprint arXiv:1511.06939 (2015)

9. Jaiswal, A., Babu, A.R., Zadeh, M.Z., Banerjee, D., Makedon, F.: A survey on contrastive self-supervised learning. Technologies 9(1), 2 (2020)

10. Kingma, D.P., Welling, M.: Auto-encoding variational Bayes. arXiv preprint arXiv:1312.6114 (2013)

11. Lai, S., Meng, E., Zhang, F., Li, C., Wang, B., Sun, A.: An attribute-driven mirror graph network for session-based recommendation. In: Proceedings of the 45th International ACM SIGIR Conference on Research and Development in Information Retrieval, pp. 1674–1683 (2022)

12. Li, J., Ren, P., Chen, Z., Ren, Z., Lian, T., Ma, J.: Neural attentive session-based recommendation. In: Proceedings of the 2017 ACM on Conference on Information and Knowledge Management, pp. 1419–1428 (2017)

13. Liu, Q., Zeng, Y., Mokhosi, R., Zhang, H.: Stamp: short-term attention/memory priority model for session-based recommendation. In: Proceedings of the 24th ACM SIGKDD International Conference on Knowledge Discovery & Data Mining, pp. 1831–1839 (2018)

14. Liu, X., et al.: Self-supervised learning: generative or contrastive. IEEE Trans. Knowl. Data Eng. 35(1), 857–876 (2021)

15. Van den Oord, A., Kalchbrenner, N., Espeholt, L., Vinyals, O., Graves, A., et al.: Conditional image generation with PixelCNN decoders. In: Advances in Neural Information Processing Systems, vol. 29 (2016)

16. Pan, Z., Cai, F., Chen, W., Chen, H., De Rijke, M.: Star graph neural networks for session-based recommendation. In: Proceedings of the 29th ACM International Conference on Information & Knowledge Management, pp. 1195–1204 (2020)

17. Qiu, R., Li, J., Huang, Z., Yin, H.: Rethinking the item order in session-based recommendation with graph neural networks. In: Proceedings of the 28th ACM International Conference on Information and Knowledge Management, pp. 579–588 (2019)

18. Rendle, S., Freudenthaler, C., Schmidt-Thieme, L.: Factorizing personalized Markov chains for next-basket recommendation. In: Proceedings of the 19th International Conference on World Wide Web, pp. 811–820 (2010)

19. Tan, Y.K., Xu, X., Liu, Y.: Improved recurrent neural networks for session-based recommendations. In: Proceedings of the 1st Workshop on Deep Learning for Recommender Systems, pp. 17–22 (2016)

20. Velickovic, P., Cucurull, G., Casanova, A., Romero, A., Lio, P., Bengio, Y., et al.: Graph attention networks. Stat 1050(20), 10–48550 (2017)

21. Wang, J., Ding, K., Zhu, Z., Caverlee, J.: Session-based recommendation with hypergraph attention networks. In: Proceedings of the 2021 SIAM International Conference on Data Mining (SDM), pp. 82–90. SIAM (2021)

22. Wang, S., Cao, L., Wang, Y., Sheng, Q.Z., Orgun, M.A., Lian, D.: A survey on session-based recommender systems. ACM Comput. Surv. (CSUR) 54(7), 1–38 (2021)

23. Wang, X., Wang, R., Shi, C., Song, G., Li, Q.: Multi-component graph convolutional collaborative filtering. In: Proceedings of the AAAI Conference on Artificial Intelligence, vol. 34, pp. 6267–6274 (2020)
24. Wang, Z., Wei, W., Cong, G., Li, X.L., Mao, X.L., Qiu, M.: Global context enhanced graph neural networks for session-based recommendation. In: Proceedings of the 43rd International ACM SIGIR Conference on Research and Development in Information Retrieval, pp. 169–178 (2020)
25. Wu, S., Sun, F., Zhang, W., Xie, X., Cui, B.: Graph neural networks in recommender systems: a survey. ACM Comput. Surv. **55**(5), 1–37 (2022)
26. Wu, S., Tang, Y., Zhu, Y., Wang, L., Xie, X., Tan, T.: Session-based recommendation with graph neural networks. In: Proceedings of the AAAI Conference on Artificial Intelligence, vol. 33, pp. 346–353 (2019)
27. Wu, Z., Pan, S., Chen, F., Long, G., Zhang, C., Philip, S.Y.: A comprehensive survey on graph neural networks. IEEE Trans. Neural Netw. Learn. Syst. **32**(1), 4–24 (2020)
28. Xia, X., Yin, H., Yu, J., Shao, Y., Cui, L.: Self-supervised graph co-training for session-based recommendation. In: Proceedings of the 30th ACM International Conference on Information & Knowledge Management, pp. 2180–2190 (2021)
29. Xia, X., Yin, H., Yu, J., Wang, Q., Cui, L., Zhang, X.: Self-supervised hypergraph convolutional networks for session-based recommendation. In: Proceedings of the AAAI Conference on Artificial Intelligence, vol. 35, pp. 4503–4511 (2021)
30. Xu, C., et al.: Graph contextualized self-attention network for session-based recommendation. In: IJCAI, vol. 19, pp. 3940–3946 (2019)
31. Yu, F., Zhu, Y., Liu, Q., Wu, S., Wang, L., Tan, T.: Tagnn: target attentive graph neural networks for session-based recommendation. In: Proceedings of the 43rd International ACM SIGIR Conference on Research and Development in Information Retrieval, pp. 1921–1924 (2020)
32. Zhou, K., et al.: S3-rec: Self-supervised learning for sequential recommendation with mutual information maximization. In: Proceedings of the 29th ACM International Conference On Information & Knowledge Management, pp. 1893–1902 (2020)

Delay-Constrained Multicast Throughput Maximization in MEC Networks for High-Speed Railways

Junyi Xu[1], Zhenchun Wei[1(✉)], Xiaohui Yuan[2], Zengwei Lyu[1], Lin Feng[1], and Jianghong Han[1]

[1] School of Computer Science and Information Technology,
Hefei University of Technology, Hefei, China
`weizc@hfut.edu.cn`

[2] Department of Computer Science and Engineering, University of North Texus,
Denton, TX, USA
`xiaohui.yuan@unt.edu`

Abstract. Multi-access Edge Computing presents a compelling solution for delivering seamless connectivity to computing services. In this study, we aim to optimize multicast throughput to ensure high-quality experiences for passengers engaged in inter-train interactions within dedicated MEC networks designed for high-speed railways. Considering the unique challenges associated with high-speed railways, we model multicast routing paths as group Steiner trees. Subsequently, we devise a rapid tree construction method by converting the root search into the Generalized Assignment Problem (GAP). This innovative approach skillfully balances accuracy and computational efficiency. We demonstrate that this problem can be effectively reduced to the bounded knapsack problem with setups. In addition, we recognize the presence of precedence constraints between tasks and their respective outcomes. Consequently, we introduce a new variant of the knapsack problem, which we refer to as the Precedence-constrained Bounded Knapsack Problem with Setups. Our approach, termed the GAP-and knapsack-based Group Steiner Tree (GKGST), offers a relative performance guarantee of 1/2. We evaluate the GKGST algorithm against three baseline algorithms, which are adapted and extended from existing literature. Simulation results indicate that our proposed algorithm exhibits considerable potential for enhanced performance.

Keywords: Edge Computing · High-Speed Railways · Multicast Throughput · Generalized Assignment Problem · Knapsack Problem

1 Introduction

Mobile devices are an integral part of our daily life and taking high-speed railways (HSRs) is a popular mode of transportation for long- and short-distance commuters. Improving the quality of experience (QoE) for the commuters on board of HSRs is imperative. Multi-access Edge Computing (MEC) presents

H. Gao et al. (Eds.): CollaborateCom 2023, LNICST 563, pp. 308–328, 2024.
https://doi.org/10.1007/978-3-031-54531-3_17

a compelling approach to delivering seamless connectivity to computing services. Figure 1 illustrates a scenario of trains accessing a dedicated MEC network through trackside base stations (BSs). By offloading computation-intensive, time-sensitive tasks, MEC-based interactions among passengers can be realized.

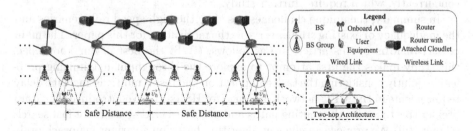

Fig. 1. A scenario of MEC-based computing services among passengers on trains.

Achieving a high QoE for passengers faces great challenges when taking into account the speed of HSRs. To facilitate the computing service on HSRs requires frequent handovers between trackside BSs, which leads to interruptions in data transmissions. The long distances between HSR trains require multicast solutions to deliver contents across expansive geographic areas and maintain low latency. In addition, the limited resources, e.g., computational capacity, storage, and bandwidth, pose additional constraints to a solution.

Multicast, a communication mode that transmits the same computation results to a group of nearby destinations, is essential to provide such services, which has been studied in the context of the Internet of Vehicles (IoV) or Vehicular Ad-hoc Networks(VANETs). Babu et al. [1] proposed a distributed tree-based multicast routing algorithm to reduce tree fragmentation and rejoining delay in VANETs. Kadhim et al. [8] proposed a delay-efficient approach that utilizes parked vehicles, fog computing, and software-defined network (SDN) to discover the optimal multicast route. Keshavamurthy et al. [10] explored the multicast group-based vehicle-to-vehicle communications by allocating the sidelink resources subject to the reliability requirements and half-duplex limitation. However, these techniques are inapplicable to HSR due to the safe distance of tens of kilometers between neighboring trains [13], while IoV multicast grouping schemes rely on clustering adjacent vehicles.

As edge-enabled applications for HSRs constitute crucial use cases for 5G networks, extensive research has been conducted to explore edge caching, content delivery, and data offloading strategies within MEC environments for HSR scenarios. Xiong et al. [21] proposed a strategy to facilitate collaboration between user terminals in HSRs and advocated wireless caching of services on the routing relay to enhance connectivity and performance. Li et al. [11] addressed task offloading and scheduling problems in high mobility scenarios and designed a genetic algorithm-based scheme for offloading and task scheduling of predictive computations with mobility. Li et al. [12] studied a mmWave-based train-ground communication system for HSRs, which minimizes the average task process-ing latency for all users subject to the local device and onboard mobile relay energy consumption. However, the multi-user, real-time applications on HSR, e.g., video conferencing, multimedia pushing, and multiplayer gaming, demand high throughput communication with minimum delays to support multiple users concurrently, which requires further study.

In summary, the unique challenges posed by the high-speed rail scenarios and the inadequacy of existing studies serve as the motivation for this paper. The main **contributions** of this article are as follows. (i) To the best of our knowledge, this study makes the first attempt to explore the throughput maximizing prob-lem by jointly considering the task computation and result multicasting with delay requirements in the MEC network designed for HSRs. (ii) We introduce the group Steiner tree to model the routing paths and propose a GAP-based root fast search scheme. (iii) We propose an efficient algorithm based on a variant knapsack prob-lem for one-shot optimization, as long as dividing the time into equal time slots and periodically invoking the proposed algorithm in each slot.

The rest of the paper is organized as follows. Section 2 introduces system models and basic concepts. Section 3 gives the definition of various delays and costs in the MEC network. Section 4 defines our problem and formulates the defined problem as an integer linear programming (ILP). Section 5 divides the ILP into independent phases to facilitate a step-by-step algorithm. Section 6 shows the experimental results of the performance of the proposed algorithm. Section 7 concludes this work.

2   System Model

Let H denote a set of moving trains h at a steady speed. Each train may operate at a different speed. A MEC network, denoted with an undirected graph $G = (V, E)$, provides communication and computing services to the trains, where V is the set of routers and E is the set of wired links. A subset of routers $V_c \subset V$ is connected to cloudlets with a computing capacity of C_v. These cloudlets utilize container-based virtualization technology, where the computing capacity refers to the maximum number of containers available within each cloudlet. Let F_v denote the number of CPU cycles per second in each container of a cloudlet v. Data transmission through routers and links introduces communication latency: $d(e)$ and $d(v)$ denote the delay on link $e \in E$ and router $v \in V$, respectively, in the transmission of a unit of data traffic. A centralized controller based on software-defined networks (SDN) [6,18] is used to facilitate global network management. A set of BSs with routing capabilities, denoted as $B \subset V$, is uniformly deployed along the tracks and $B \cap V_c = \emptyset$.

Each train offloads tasks to the MEC network, which processes these tasks into the computation results. Subsequently, these computation results are trans-mitted to the designated trains. Specifically, let $K_H(t)$ denote the task set and $k_{i,h} \in K_h$ is the ith task from train h, $k_{i,h} = \langle H_{i,h}^{des}; z_{i,h}, o_{i,h}, f_{i,h}, d_{i,h} \rangle$, where $H_{i,h}^{des} \subseteq H$ is the set of *destination trains* to which the computation results are sent, $z_{i,h}$ is the task volume, $o_{i,h}$ is the volume of the result, $f_{i,h}$ is the CPU cycles for computing the task, and $d_{i,h}$ is the end-to-end delay requirement of the task. Task $k_{i,h}$ is processed in a cloudlet $v_{i,h} \in V_c$, called the *comput-ing cloudlet*. A cloudlet can compute a task if there is an idle container. Each task is computed exclusively by a container, consuming one unit of computing capacity. Otherwise, a new container will be initialized. Let $r_{i,h,h'}$ be the com-putation result of $k_{i,h}$ sent to train h', where $h' \in H_{i,h}^{des}$. Note that during the multicasting process, the computation results of task $k_{i,h}$ are sent to different destinations as identical copies, i.e., $r_{i,h,1} = \dots = r_{i,h,h'} = \dots = r_{i,h,|H_{i,h}^{des}|}$. Let $R_{i,h}$ denote the results of task $k_{i,h}$, such that $R_{i,h} = \bigcup_{h' \in H_{i,h}^{des}} r_{i,h,h'}$. The set of computation results associated with task set $K_H(t)$ is denoted as R_H, where $R_H = \bigcup_{h=1}^{|H|} \bigcup_{i=1}^{|K_h|} \bigcup_{h' \in H_{i,h}^{des}} r_{i,h,h'}$. The network throughput is measured by the total data volume of the tasks and their computation results that can be routed in the MEC network.

Given that the data volume of any task $k_{i,h}$ is arbitrary, a train is required to traverse multiple BSs to upload the task. Similarly, the data volume of the results of task $k_{i,h}$ can also be arbitrary, necessitating the use of multiple BSs to transmit the result to trains. The BSs that receive the task data are designated as the source BS group, while the BSs that receive the results are referred to as the destination BS groups. These BS groups can be subsequently considered as multicast groups for multicast routing, with the routing paths of a task and its results constituting a multicast tree. The construction of the tree requires ascertaining the minimum number of paths needed to connect each multicast group with the tree's root. To tackle the challenge, we model the multicasting path as a group Steiner tree (GST) [7], defined as follows. Let $\{g_i\}$ be a collection of vertex subsets in $G = (V, E)$, where each subset g_i is designated as a group. The objective is to identify the minimum-cost tree T, which includes at least one vertex of each group g_i. The tree T is referred to as a Steiner group tree. In the practical implementation, let $T_{i,h}$ be a group Steiner tree used to route task $k_{i,h}$ and its results $R_{i,h}$. The tree $T_{i,h}$ has its root at vertex $v_{i,h}$, which

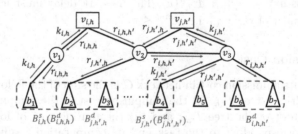

Fig. 2. An example of the GSTs, where $v_{i,h}$ and $v_{j,h'}$ are computing cloudlets, v_1, v_2 and v_3 are regular routers, $\{b_1, ..., b_7\}$ are BSs, $B_{i,h}^s(B_{i,h,h}^d)$ means that such a group is both a source group and a destination group for task $k_{i,h}$ and its result copy $r_{i,h,h'}$. The same applies to $B_{j,h'}^s(B_{j,h',h'}^d)$.

connects to all BS groups in $B_{i,h}$. A simple path $\pi_{i,h}$ connects the source BS group $B_{i,h}^s \subset B_{i,h}$ and the root vertex $v_{i,h}$. Similarly, let $\pi_{i,h,h'}$ represent the simple path that connects the destination BS group $B_{i,h,h'}^d \subset B_{i,h}$ with the root vertex $v_{i,h}$. Figure 2 presents a representative example of GSTs. In this instance, tree $T_{i,h}$ is used to route task $k_{i,h}$ and its corresponding results, $r_{i,h,h}$ and $r_{i,h,h'}$. Tree $T_{i,h}$ connects the BS groups $B_{i,h}^s$ and $B_{i,h,h'}^d$ to the root $v_{i,h}$ through paths $\pi_{i,h} = \langle b_1, v_1, v_{i,h} \rangle$ and $\pi_{i,h,h'} = \langle v_{i,h} v_2, v_3, b_7 \rangle$, respectively. The BS group $B_{i,h}^s$ is comprised of BSs b_1 and b_2, while $B_{i,h,h'}^d$ consists of BSs b_6 and b_7. Similarly, tree $T_{j,h'}$ functions as the GST for task $k_{j,h'}$ along with its respective results $r_{j,h',h}$ and $r_{j,h',h'}$. A detailed description of tree $T_{j,h'}$ is omitted here due to the limited space.

3 Delays and Costs in MEC Networks

3.1 Experienced Delay

Theoretically, passengers achieve the optimal QoE when the delay of task $k_{i,h}$ and result set $R_{i,h}$ on multicast tree $T_{i,h}$ satisfies the end-to-end delay requirement $d_{i,h}$. The delay of each task $k_{i,h}$ and its result set $R_{i,h}$ in G comprises (i) the *computation delay* in the cloudlet and (ii) the *routing delay*.

Computation Delay: Let $d_{i,h}^{cmp}(v)$ denote the delay of task $k_{i,h}$ when calculated in cloudlet $v \in V_c$. $d_{i,h}^{cmp}(v)$ can be expressed as $d_{i,h}^{cmp}(v) = f_{i,h}/F_v$. where $f_{i,h}$ denotes the required CPU cycles for task $k_{i,h}$ and F_v signifies the CPU cycles per second available in each container within cloudlet v.

Routing Delay: Let $d_{i,h}^{rou}$ be the routing delay of task $k_{i,h}$ and its results in $T_{i,h}$, which includes the delay of routing the task $k_{i,h}$ on path $\pi_{i,h} \subseteq T_{i,h}$ and the delay of routing result $r_{i,h,h'}$ on each path $\pi_{i,h,h'} \subseteq T_{i,h}$, where $h' \in H_{i,h}^{des}$. $d_{i,h}^{rou}$ can be calculated as $d_{i,h}^{rou} = \left(\sum_{e \in \pi_{i,h}} d(e) + \sum_{e \in \pi_{i,h}} d(v) \right) \cdot z_{i,h}$ $+ \max_{h' \in H_{i,h}^{des}} \left\{ \left(\sum_{e \in \pi_{i,h,h'}} d(e) + \sum_{e \in \pi_{i,h,h'}} d(v) \right) \cdot o_{i,h} \right\}$. The total delay $d_{i,h}^{net}$ for task $k_{i,h}$ is $d_{i,h}^{net} = d_{i,h}^{rou} + d_{i,h}^{com}(v)$, The network delay must not exceed the delay requirement of task $k_{i,h}$ i.e., $d_{i,h}^{net} \le d_{i,h}$.

3.2 Admission Cost

For task $k_{i,h}$, its admission cost in network G is the sum of the following costs on a feasible multicast tree $T_{i,h}$: (i) the computing cost in the computing cloudlet, which is the root of the tree $T_{i,h}$; and (ii) the routing cost of forwarding the data traffic corresponding to the task and its computation results along links and routers on the multicast tree. Denote $c(v)$ and $c(e)$ as the costs of one unit of data traffic consuming resources at router $v \in V$ and link $e \in E$, respectively. Additionally, denote $c^{cmp}(v)$ as the computing cost for using one unit of CPU frequency to process one unit of data in one container of cloudlet $v \in V_c$.

First, let $c_{i,h}^{cmp}(v)$ denote the computing cost of task $k_{i,h}$ in cloudlet $v \in V_c$, which can be calculated as $c_{i,h}^{cmp}(v) = c^{cmp}(v) \cdot z_{i,h} \cdot f_{i,h}$. Next, denote $c_{i,h}^{rou}$ as the routing cost of transferring task $k_{i,h}$ along path $\pi_{i,h} \subseteq T_{i,h}$ to computing cloudlet v, i.e., $c_{i,h}^{rou} = \left(\sum_{v \in \pi_{i,h}} c(v) + \sum_{e \in \pi_{i,h}} c(e)\right) \cdot z_{i,h}$, and let $c_{i,h,h'}^{rou}$ represent the cost of routing result $r_{i,h,h'}$ on multicast tree $T_{i,h}$. $c_{i,h,h'}^{rou}$ can be obtained by $c_{i,h,h'}^{rou} = \left(\sum_{v \in \pi_{i,h,h'}} c(v) + \sum_{e \in \pi_{i,h,h'}} c(e)\right) \cdot o_{i,h,h'}$, where $\pi_{i,h,h'} \subseteq T_{i,h}$.

Let $C(T_{i,h})$ be the cost of admitting task $k_{i,h}$ on tree $T_{i,h}$, which can be expressed as $C(T_{i,h}) = c_{i,h}^{pro} + c_{i,h}^{rou} + \sum_{h' \in H_{i,h}^{des}} c_{i,h,h'}^{rou}$. Denote C_H as the total cost of admitting task set $K_H(t)$, and C_H can be expressed by $C_H = \sum_{h=1}^{|H|} \sum_{i=1}^{|K_h|} C_{i,h}$. In practice, MEC service providers must establish budgets to generate profits. Let β be the budget allocated for admitting tasks and multicasting results within the MEC network. The total cost C_H must meet the constraint $C_H \leq \beta$.

4   Problem Definition and an ILP Formulation

Given a trackside MEC network $G = (V, E)$, tasks from the trains are offloaded to the BSs, each task having the same delay requirements. The results are then multicast to the designated trains. The *delay-constrained multicast throughput maximization problem* aims to maximize the total data volume of the admitted tasks and their results. This is achieved by identifying a group Steiner tree rooted at a suitable computing cloudlet, meeting the following criteria: (i) task data traffic is routed from the source BS group to the root for computing, (ii) the computation result is routed to the destination BS groups, and (iii) the costs, including routing, transmission, and computing, are minimized and comply with the delay and resource requirements of each task.

In the following, we formulate the defined problem into an ILP. To simplify the description, we transform the undirected graph $G = (V, E)$ into a directed graph $G_d = (V_d, E_d)$. Specifically, for each node $v \in V$, we include node v in V_d. For each link $e \in E$, we add directed edges $\langle u, v \rangle$ and $\langle v, u \rangle$ to E_d, where $u, v \in V$. The weights of edges $\langle u, v \rangle$ and $\langle v, u \rangle$ are equal to the weight of link $e \in E$, i.e., $V_d = \{v \mid v \in V\}$, $E_d = \{\langle u, v \rangle \mid u, v \in V\}$.

The decision variables of the ILP are as follows. $\mathbf{n}_{i,h,v}$ takes a value of 1 if task $k_{i,h}$ is computed in cloudlet $v \in V_d$ and value 0 otherwise. $\mathbf{n}_v$ is 1 if cloudlet v is chosen as a computing cloudlet and value 0 otherwise. $\mathbf{x}_{i,h}$ is 1 if task $k_{i,h}$ is admitted or 0 otherwise. $\mathbf{y}_{i,h,h'}$ is 1 if result $r_{i,h,h'}$ is multicast or 0 otherwise. $\mathbf{m}_{i,h,v}$ takes a value of 1 if node v is used to transport the traffic of task $k_{i,h}$ or its result set $R_{i,h}$; otherwise, the value is 0. Decision variable $\mathbf{m}_{i,h}^{u,v}$ holds the value of 1 if the edge $\langle u, v \rangle$ is used for the transportation of task $k_{i,h}$ or its corresponding result set $R_{i,h}$. Otherwise, the value is 0.

Our objective function is

$$\max \sum_{h=1}^{|H|} \sum_{i=1}^{|K_h|} \left(z_{i,h} \cdot \mathbf{x}_{i,h} + \sum_{h' \in H_{i,h}^{des}} o_{i,h} \cdot \mathbf{y}_{i,h,h'} \right). \tag{1}$$

To guarantee the fulfillment of the following requirements: (i) a task is processed exclusively within a single cloudlet; (ii) the total number of nodes designated as computing cloudlets does not exceed the aggregate count of incoming tasks; and (iii) node v is capable of executing a task only if $v \in V_c$, it is necessary to adhere to the ensuring constraints.

$$\sum_{v \in V_c} \mathbf{n}_{i,h,v} = \mathbf{x}_{i,h}, \ i \in K_h, \ h \in H. \tag{1a}$$

$$\sum_{v \in V_c} \mathbf{n}_v \leq |K_H(t)|, \ i \in K_h, \ h \in H. \tag{1b}$$

$$\mathbf{n}_{i,h,v} = \mathbf{n}_v = 0, \ \forall v \in V_d \setminus V_c. \tag{1c}$$

Constraint (1d) enforces the capacity constraint for each cloudlet $v \in V_c$.

$$\sum_{h=1}^{|H|} \sum_{i=1}^{|K_h|} \mathbf{x}_{i,h} \leq C_v, \ \forall v \in V_d, \ \mathbf{n}_v \geq 1. \tag{1d}$$

The data traffic associated with an accepted task, as well as its resulting output, will be routed on a GST. A GST can be expressed as the constraint [7], in which $\varpi(V')$ denotes the set of edges that possess exactly one endpoint in V'.

$$\sum_{\langle u,v \rangle \in \varpi(V')} \mathbf{m}_{i,h}^{u,v} \geq 1, \forall V' \subseteq V, \text{such that} \begin{cases} \mathbf{n}_{i,h,v} \in V' \text{ and } \mathbf{n}_{i,h,v} = 1, \\ \text{and } V' \cap B_{i,h} = \emptyset \text{ for some } i \text{ or } h. \end{cases} \tag{1e}$$

Constraint (1f) enforces the total cost for routing the tasks and the results on GST $T_{i,h}$ will not exceed the budget, where $T_{i,h}$ needs to satisfy the constraint (1e).

$$\sum_{h=1}^{|H|} \sum_{i=1}^{|K_h|} \left(\begin{array}{l} z_{i,h} \mathbf{x}_{i,h} \left(\sum_{\langle u,v \rangle \in T_{i,h}} c(\langle u,v \rangle) + \sum_{v \in T_{i,h}} c(v) \right) + \mathbf{x}_{i,h} \cdot c_{i,h}^{cmp}(v') \\ + \sum_{h' \in H_{i,h}^{des}} \left(o_{i,h} \mathbf{y}_{i,h,h'} \sum_{\langle u,v \rangle \in T_{i,h}} c(\langle u,v \rangle) \right) \end{array} \right) \leq \beta,$$

$$\forall \mathbf{m}_{i,h}^{u,v} = 1, \ \forall \mathbf{m}_{i,h,u}, \mathbf{m}_{i,h,v} = 1, \ \mathbf{m}_{i,h,v'} = \mathbf{n}_{i,h,v'} = 1. \tag{1f}$$

The total delay of an admitted task and its results on GST $T_{i,h}$ must meet the delay requirement of task $k_{i,h}$, as stipulated by the subsequent constraint.

$$\max_{h' \in H_{i,h}^{des}} \left\{ \left(\sum_{v \neq u} \mathbf{m}_{i,h}^{u,v} d(e) + \sum_{v \in V_d} \mathbf{m}_{i,h,v} d(e) \right) \mathbf{y}_{i,h,h'} \right\} + \mathbf{n}_{i,h,v} \cdot d_{i,h}^{cmp}(v) \leq d_{i,h}$$

$$+ \left(\sum_{v \neq u} \mathbf{m}_{i,h}^{u,v} d(e) + \sum_{v \in V_d} \mathbf{m}_{i,h,v} d(e) \right) \mathbf{x}_{i,h}, \ \forall \mathbf{m}_{i,h}^{u,v} = 1, \ \forall \mathbf{m}_{i,h,u}, \mathbf{m}_{i,h,v} = 1. \tag{1g}$$

Drawing inspiration from the network flow model [14] for multicasting routing in the directed Steiner tree, we propose our flow model (Constraints (1h)-(1o)) to capture the traffic changes in GST $T_{i,h}$. We call a node *consumes* a task/result if the node removes one task/result from the passing data flow. Such a node can be a computing cloudlet or a BS in the BS group, while other nodes do not consume tasks or results. Let $K_{i,h}^{u,v}$ and $R_{i,h}^{u,v}$ be the aggregate number of tasks and results going from vertex u to v, respectively. Constraint (1h) enforces that the number of results routing on the path of GST $T_{i,h}$ is less than the number of the results multicast by the root. Constraint (1i) ensures that no result can be returned to the root. Constraints (1j) and (1k) address four cases of results consumed by BS groups, where node v will not consume any result if (i) $v \notin B_{i,h}$ or (ii) v is in a specific BS group and v connects to other nodes in the same group. Otherwise, node v will consume $\sum_{h=1}^{|H|} \sum_{i=1}^{|K_h|} y_{i,h,h'}$ amount of results if (iii) v is in a specific BS group, and v connects to a node $u \notin B_{i,h}$ or (iv) v is in a specific BS group, and v connects to a node $u \in B_{i,h}$ belonging to another BS group. Constraint (1l) ensures that no unprocessed task can leave the root of GST $T_{i,h}$. Constraint (1m) and constraint (1n) ensure that only the root can consume tasks and that no other nodes will consume tasks. Constraint (1o) ensures that only when an edge between vertex u and vertex v is included in the GST is it possible that $K_{u,v} > 0$.

$$\sum_{u \neq v} \mathbf{m}_{i,h}^{v,u} \cdot R_{i,h}^{v,u} \leq \sum_{h=1}^{|H|} \sum_{i=1}^{|K_h|} \sum_{h' \in H_{i,h}^{des}} y_{i,h,h'}, \forall u, v \in V_d, \ \mathbf{n}_{i,h,v} = 1. \tag{1h}$$

$$\sum_{u \in V, u \neq v} R_{i,h}^{u,v} = 0, \ \mathbf{n}_{i,h,v} = 1. \tag{1i}$$

$$\sum_{v \neq u} \mathbf{m}_{i,h}^{u,v} \cdot R_{u,v} - \sum_{v \neq w} \mathbf{m}_{i,h}^{v,w} \cdot R_{v,w} = 0,$$
$$\forall \mathbf{n}_{i,h,v}, \mathbf{n}_{i,h,u}, \mathbf{n}_{i,h,w} \neq 1, \begin{cases} \text{Case 1:} \forall v \notin B_{i,h}; \\ \text{Case 2:} v \in B_{i,h,h'}, \ \forall u, w \in B_{i,h,h'}. \end{cases} \tag{1j}$$

$$\sum_{v \neq u} \mathbf{m}_{i,h}^{u,v} R_{u,v} - \sum_{v \neq w} \mathbf{m}_{i,h}^{v,w} R_{v,w} = \sum_{h=1}^{|H|} \sum_{i=1}^{|K_h|} y_{i,h,h'},$$
$$\forall \mathbf{n}_{i,h,v}, \mathbf{n}_{i,h,u}, \mathbf{n}_{i,h,w} \neq 1, \begin{cases} \text{Case3} : v \in B_{i,h,h'}, \exists u \notin B_{i,h}; \\ \text{Case4} : v \in B_{i,h,h'}, \forall u \in B_{i,h,h''}. \end{cases} \tag{1k}$$

$$\sum_{u \neq v} K_{v,u} = 0, \ \forall u, v \in V_d, \ \mathbf{n}_{i,h,v} = 1. \tag{1l}$$

$$\sum_{v \neq u} \mathbf{m}_{i,h}^{u,v} K_{u,v} - \sum_{v \neq w} \mathbf{m}_{i,h}^{v,w} K_{v,w} = 0, \begin{cases} \forall u, v, w \in V_d, \\ \forall \mathbf{n}_{i,h,v}, \mathbf{n}_{i,h,u}, \mathbf{n}_{i,h,w} \neq 1. \end{cases} \quad (1m)$$

$$\sum_{v \neq u} \mathbf{m}_{i,h}^{u,v} K_{u,v} - \sum_{v \neq w} \mathbf{m}_{i,h}^{v,w} K_{v,w} = \sum_{h=1}^{|H|} \sum_{i=1}^{|K_h|} \mathbf{x}_{i,h}, \begin{cases} \forall u, v, w \in V_d, \\ \mathbf{n}_{i,h,v} = 1, \forall \mathbf{n}_{i,h,u}, \mathbf{n}_{i,h,w} \neq 1. \end{cases}$$
$$(1n)$$

$$\sum_{h=1}^{|H|} \sum_{i=1}^{|K_h|} \mathbf{x}_{i,h} \cdot \sum_{\langle u,v \rangle \in E_d} \mathbf{m}_{i,h}^{u,v} \geq K_{u,v}, \quad \forall u, v \in V_d. \quad (1o)$$

Constraints (1p), (1q), (1r) are employed to confine the decision variables within the binary range of 0 and 1. Constraints (1s) and (1t) describe the priority relationships between tasks and their results. These constraints indicate that the number of results is greater than that of the corresponding tasks, and a result can be multicast if and only if its corresponding task has been admitted.

$$\mathbf{n}_{i,h,v}, \mathbf{n}_v \in \{0, 1\}, \quad \forall v \in V_c, \forall i \in K_h, \forall h \in H. \quad (1p)$$

$$\mathbf{m}_{i,h}^{u,v}, \mathbf{m}_{i,h,v} \in \{0, 1\}, \quad \forall u, v \in V_d. \quad (1q)$$

$$\mathbf{x}_{i,h}, \mathbf{y}_{i,h,h'} \in \{0, 1\}, \quad \forall i \in K_h, \forall h \in H. \quad (1r)$$

$$\mathbf{x}_{i,h} \geq \mathbf{y}_{i,h,h'}, \quad \forall i \in K_h, \forall h, h' \in H. \quad (1s)$$

$$\mathbf{x}_{i,h} \leq \sum_{h' \in H_h^{des}} \mathbf{y}_{i,h,h'} \leq \mathbf{x}_{i,h} \cdot |R_{i,h}|, \forall i \in K_h, \forall h, h' \in H. \quad (1t)$$

Solving the formulated ILP directly can be time-consuming for large problem instances, due to the substantial number of variables and the potential inter-dependence between them. Achieving the optimal solution remains a feasible endeavor in instances where the problem size is comparatively modest. Consequently, we will focus on simplifying certain variables within the ILP and dividing it into independent phases to facilitate a more manageable step-by-step approach in the remainder of this paper. This approach skillfully balances accuracy and computational efficiency.

5   Proposed Method

5.1   Delay-Constrained Minimum-Cost GST Construction

Taking into account the computational constraints of cloudlets within network G, and considering a given cloudlet $v \in V_c$, a delay-constrained minimum-cost group Steiner tree $T_{i,h}(v)$ rooted at v can be identified in G by employing the $|H|$-approximate algorithm [19]. In particular, this optimization is conducted without considering the delay requirement of task $k_{i,h}$. Duin et al. [5] proposed a procedure to transform a GST instance into a Steiner tree. Consequently, an iterative algorithm to find the minimum-cost Steiner tree with delay constraints [17] can be applied directly to the transformed GST. In the end, $T_{i,h}(v)$ is derived from the transformed Steiner tree and $T_{i,h}(v)$ can satisfy the delay requirement of task $k_{i,h}$. The mentioned transformation and application are easily implemented, thus we omit details due to the limited space. To this end, we refer to the tree $T_{i,h}(v)$ as a candidate tree for task $k_{i,h}$. Disregarding the limitations of the cloud computing capacity of cloudlets in network G, our aim is to identify a set of candidate GSTs, denoted as $T_{i,h}^{can}$, for each task $k_{i,h} \in K_H(t)$:

$$T_{i,h}^{can} = \bigcup_{v \in V_c} T_{i,h}(v). \tag{2}$$

5.2   GST Root Fast Search Scheme

Identifying a suitable computing cloudlet $v_{i,h}$ for each task $k_{i,h} \in K_H(t)$, to serve as the root of GST $T_{i,h}$, presents a significant challenge. Xu et al. [22] discovered that the most time-consuming aspect of their research is the allocation of appropriate computing cloudlets to each task. In the worst-case scenario, the algorithm necessitates traversing all cloudlets within network G. Consequently, the responsiveness of the algorithm may be adversely affected by potential delays in execution. The efficacy of this search scheme is mainly attributable to the identification of a candidate solution that admits a subset of $K_H(t)$, dependent on the residual computing capacities of the cloudlets in network G when $K_H(t)$ arrives at G. Significantly, these residual computing capacities are not subject to updates when evaluating all tasks within $K_H(t)$. The process initiates by determining a candidate solution, which subsequently undergoes iterative refinement until all computing capacity violations are resolved, thus ensuring a robust and efficient approach.

Essentially, selecting an optimal GST $T_{i,h}(v)$ involves identifying the task $k_{i,h}$ with the lowest admission cost from the candidate GST set $T_{i,h}^{can}$. This process must also ensure that the constraint of computing capacity in cloudlet $v \in V_c$, which serves as the root of $T_{i,h}(v)$, is satisfied. Consequently, this is equivalent to selecting an appropriate cloudlet v within network G to serve as the computing resource for task $k_{i,h}$.

Given that various cloudlets may have different residual computing capacities and CPU cycles per second, this indicates that processing $k_{i,h}$ on different cloudlets will lead to different levels of resource consumption costs. Therefore, this problem can be reformulated as the Generalized Assignment Problem (GAP) [16], which aims to optimize the assignment profit associated with each task. In this context, we treat each cloudlet $v \in V_c$ as an agent and the capacity of agent v is equal to the residual computing capacity C_v^{res} of v. When assigning a task $k_{i,h}$ to agent v, the size of $k_{i,h}$ is represented by the demanded CPU cycles, $f_{i,h}$. The profit derived from placing task $k_{i,h}$ into agent v is the inverse of the admission cost of task $k_{i,h}$ on tree $T_{i,h}(v)$, i.e., $1/C(T_{i,h}(v))$. To this end, we have reformulated the problem of determining the optimal computing cloudlet for each task within the set $K_H(t)$ as a GAP. Cohen's $(2 - \zeta)$-approximation algorithm [3] is adopted to address the GAP, where ζ satisfies $0 < \zeta \leq 1$.

5.3   Knapsack-Based Throughput Maximization

In this paper, we establish that problem $\mathbf{P}$ can be effectively reduced to the bounded knapsack problem with setups (BKPS) [2]. This approach incorporates a *setup* cost and a nonnegative *setup* value for each item within the capacity constraint and the objective function, respectively. Initially, we consider either the budget $\beta \in \mathbb{R}^+$ or the cloudlet computing capacity $C_v \in \mathbb{Z}^+$ as the capacity constraint of the knapsack problem (KP). The items in question consist of tasks from set $K_H(t)$, along with their corresponding result copies in R_H. The weights of the items represent the costs associated with routing data across the edges and vertices of a GST, while the profit of each item contributes to the network throughput. Variable $\mathbf{x}_{i,h}$ is considered a setup operation for task $k_{i,h}$, and $z_{i,h} \left(\sum_{\langle u,v \rangle \in T_{i,h}} c(\langle u,v \rangle) + \sum_{v \in T_{i,h}} c(v) \right) + c_{i,h}^{cmp}(v_{i,h})$ constitutes the setup cost. Similarly, $\mathbf{y}_{i,h,h'}$ and $o_{i,h} \sum_{\langle u,v \rangle \in T_{i,h}} c(\langle u,v \rangle)$ serve as the setup operation and cost for result $r_{i,h,h'}$, respectively. Moreover, we identify the existence of precedence constraints between tasks and their corresponding results, i.e., a result copy can only be multicast if and only if its associated task has been admitted. Consequently, we introduce a new variant of the knapsack problem, which we refer to as the Precedence-constrained Bounded Knapsack Problem with Setups (PCBKPS). To efficiently address the PCBKPS, we subsequently propose an efficient algorithm with a relative performance guarantee of $1/2$.

Let $c_{i,h}^k$ and $c_{i,h,h'}^r$ be the values of $z_{i,h} \left(\sum_{\langle u,v \rangle \in T_{i,h}} c(\langle u,v \rangle) + \sum_{v \in T_{i,h}} c(v) \right)$ $+ c_{i,h}^{cmp}(v_{i,h})$ and $o_{i,h} \sum_{\langle u,v \rangle \in T_{i,h}} c(\langle u,v \rangle)$, respectively. Define the *routing efficiency* as the cost of transmitting or processing one unit of data on a GST. Consequently, the routing efficiency of task $k_{i,h}$ is denoted by $z_{i,h}/c_{i,h}^k$, while the routing efficiency of the result set $r_{i,h,h'}$ is given by $o_{i,h}/c_{i,h,h'}^r$.

We define the task priority set, denoted as K_k, as follows: a task $k_{i,h}$ and its corresponding results are included in K_k if they satisfy the condition $z_{i,h}/c_{i,h}^k > \left(o_{i,h} |R_{i,h}| / \sum_{h' \in H_{i,h}^{des}} c_{i,h,h'}^r \right)$. Similarly, we define the result priority set, denoted as K_r, so that a task $k_{i,h}$ and its corresponding results are included in K_r if they meet the condition $z_{i,h}/c_{i,h}^k \leq \left(o_{i,h} |R_{i,h}| / \sum_{h' \in H_{i,h}^{des}} c_{i,h,h'}^r \right)$. It is crucial to note that the task set $K_H(t)$ is partitioned by the sets K_k and K_r.

Without considering the precedence constraint, we focus only on the BKPS component of problem $\mathbf{P}$, denoted as problem $\mathbf{P}_{BKS}$. We perform a continuous relaxation for $\mathbf{P}_{BKS}$, and the continuous linear constraint is

$$\mathbf{x}_{i,h}, \mathbf{y}_{i,h,h'} \in [0,1]. \tag{3}$$

The fundamental concept is to consolidate the decision variables $\mathbf{x}_{i,h}$ and $\sum_{h' \in H_{i,h}^{des}} \mathbf{y}_{i,h,h'}$ in the objective function of the BKPS into a single decision variable. If task $k_{i,h} \in K_r$, it implies that transferring the results of $k_{i,h}$ consumes more resources than transferring task $k_{i,h}$, i.e., $\mathbf{x}_{i,h} \leftarrow \sum_{h' \in H_{i,h}^{des}} \mathbf{y}_{i,h,h'} / |R_{i,h}|$. We evenly distribute the values of $z_{i,h}$ and $c_{i,h}^k$ to each result $r_{i,h,h'}$, transforming the routing efficiency of $r_{i,h,h'}$ to $\frac{z_{i,h}/|R_{i,h}|+o_{i,h}}{c_{i,h}^k/|R_{i,h}|+c_{i,h,h'}^r}$.

If task $k_{i,h} \in K_k$, it indicates that transferring task $k_{i,h}$ consumes more resources than transferring the results of $k_{i,h}$. In this situation, two cases arise.

Case 1: If $\sum_{h' \in H_{i,h}^{des}} \mathbf{y}_{i,h,h'} \geq 1$, then $\mathbf{x}_{i,h} \leftarrow 1$, and we distribute the values of $z_{i,h}$ and $c_{i,h}^k$ to result r_{i,h,h^*}, where r_{i,h,h^*} has the smallest routing efficiency among the result set $R_{i,h}$. Consequently, the routing efficiency of r_{i,h,h^*} becomes $(z_{i,h} + o_{i,h}) \big/ \left(c_{i,h}^k + c_{i,h,h^*}^r \right)$.

Case 2: If $\sum_{h' \in H_{i,h}^{des}} \mathbf{y}_{i,h,h'} < 1$, then $\mathbf{x}_{i,h} \leftarrow \mathbf{y}_{i,h,h'}$, and the routing efficiency of each result $r_{i,h,h'}$ remains unchanged.

Ultimately, the constraint of $\mathbf{x}_{i,h}$ is transformed as follows.

$$\mathbf{x}_{i,h} = \begin{cases} 1, & k_{i,h} \in K_k, \; \sum_{h' \in H_{i,h}^{des}} \mathbf{y}_{i,h,h'} \geq 1, \\ \sum_{h' \in H_{i,h}^{des}} \mathbf{y}_{i,h,h'}, & k_{i,h} \in K_k, \; \sum_{h' \in H_{i,h}^{des}} \mathbf{y}_{i,h,h'} < 1, \\ \sum_{h' \in H_{i,h}^{des}} \mathbf{y}_{i,h,h'} \big/ |R_{i,h}|, & k_{i,h} \in K_r. \end{cases} \tag{4}$$

The objective function of problem $\mathbf{P}$ is as follows.

$$\begin{aligned} \text{maximize} \quad & \sum_{k_{i,h} \in K_r} \sum_{h' \in H_{i,h}^{des}} \left(\frac{z_{i,h}}{|R_{i,h}|} + o_{i,h} \right) \mathbf{y}_{i,h,h'} \\ & + \sum_{k_{i,h} \in K_k} (z_{i,h} + o_{i,h}) \mathbf{y}_{i,h,h^*} + \sum_{k_{i,h} \in K_k} \sum_{h' \in H_{i,h}^{des}} o_{i,h} \mathbf{y}_{i,h,h'}. \end{aligned} \tag{5}$$

Additionally, Constraint(1f) of problem $\mathbf{P}$ is rewritten accordingly.

$$\begin{aligned} & \sum_{k_{i,h} \in K_k} \sum_{h' \in H_{i,h}^{des}, h' \neq h^*} c_{i,h,h'}^r \mathbf{y}_{i,h,h'} + \sum_{k_{i,h} \in K_k} \frac{z_{i,h} + o_{i,h}}{c_{i,h}^k + c_{i,h,h^*}^r} \mathbf{y}_{i,h,h^*} \\ & + \sum_{k_{i,h} \in K_r} \sum_{h' \in H_{i,h}^{des}} \frac{z_{i,h} + o_{i,h}|R_{i,h}|}{c_{i,h}^k + c_{i,h,h'}^r |R_{i,h}|} \mathbf{y}_{i,h,h'} \leq \beta. \end{aligned} \tag{6}$$

By incorporating Constraints (4) and (6), problem $\mathbf{P}_{BKS}$ is transformed into an instance of the classic bounded knapsack problem (BKP) [9] by relaxing the relevant constraints. Consequently, the variable $\mathbf{x}_{i,h}$ is eliminated, leaving only the variables associated with $\mathbf{y}_{i,h,h'}$ in the equation.

Let $\mathcal{Y}_j$ represent item type j in BKP, with p_j^{BKP} and c_j^{BKP} denoting the profit and cost of item type j in BKP, respectively. The upper bound of the copies of item type j in BKP is indicated by b_j^{BKP}.

By examining the objective function (5) and constraint (6), we can map the variables and parameters of problem $\mathbf{P}_{BKS}$ to the variables and parameters of BKP as follows: (i) Map each task $k_{i,h} \in K_r$ in problem $\mathbf{P}_{BKS}$ to item type $\mathcal{Y}_j$ in BKP, where $j := \{1, ..., |K_r|\}$. Profit p_j^{BKP} and cost c_j^{BKP} of item type $\mathcal{Y}_j$ are $\frac{z_{i,h}}{|R_{i,h}|} + o_{i,h}$ and $\frac{z_{i,h}+o_{i,h}|R_{i,h}|}{c_{i,h}^k+c_{i,h,h'}^r|R_{i,h}|} \cdot \sum_{h' \in H_{i,h}^{des}} y_{i,h,h'}$, respectively. The bound b_j^{BKP} is $|R_{i,h}|$. (ii) Map each task $k_{i,h} \in K_k$ with case 1 in problem $\mathbf{P}_{BKS}$ to item type $\mathcal{Y}_j$ in BKP, where $j := \{|K_r|+1, ..., |K_r|+|K_k|\}$. Profit p_j^{BKP} and cost c_j^{BKP} of item type $\mathcal{Y}_j$ are $z_{i,h}+o_{i,h}$ and $\frac{z_{i,h}+o_{i,h}}{c_{i,h}^k+c_{i,h,h'}^r}$, respectively. The bound b_j^{BKP} is 1. (iii) Map each task $k_{i,h} \in K_k$ with case 2 in problem $\mathbf{P}_{BKS}$ to item type $\mathcal{Y}_j$ in BKP, where $j := \{|K_r|+|K_k|+1, ..., |K_r|+2|K_k|\}$. Profit p_j^{BKP} and cost c_j^{BKP} of item type $\mathcal{Y}_j$ are $o_{i,h}$ and $c_{i,h,h'}^r$, respectively. The bound b_j^{BKP} is $|R_{i,h}| - 1$.

As a result, the total number of item types in BKP is $|K_r|+2|K_k|$. The BKP can be represented as follows.

$$\mathbf{BKP}: \text{ maximize} \quad \sum_{j=1}^{|K_r|+2|K_k|} p_j^{BKP}\mathcal{Y}_j \tag{7}$$

$$\text{s.t.} \quad \sum_{j=1}^{|K_r|+2|K_k|} c_j^{BKP}\mathcal{Y}_j \leq \beta, \tag{7a}$$

$$0 \leq \mathcal{Y}_j \leq b_j^{BKP}, \ \mathcal{Y}_j \in \mathbb{Z}^+, j = 1,..., |K_r|+2|K_k|. \tag{7b}$$

Arrange each item type $\mathcal{Y}_j$ in BKP according to the following order:

$$\frac{p_1^{BKP}}{c_1^{BKP}} \geq \frac{p_2^{BKP}}{c_2^{BKP}} \geq \cdots \geq \frac{p_j^{BKP}}{c_j^{BKP}} \geq \cdots \geq \frac{p_{|K_r|+2|K_k|}^{BKP}}{c_{|K_r|+2|K_k|}^{BKP}}. \tag{8}$$

Following the order of p_j^{BKP}/c_j^{BKP} in Eq. (8), item type $\mathcal{Y}_j$ is added to the knapsack until the cumulative cost of the first entry exceeds the capacity of the knapsack. The first item type that causes the capacity to be exceeded is called the *split item type*, denoted as $\mathcal{Y}_l$. The expression for $\mathcal{Y}_l$ is:

$$\mathcal{Y}_l = \arg\min_l \left\{ \sum_{j=1}^l c_j^{BKP}b_j^{BKP} > \beta \right\}, 1 < l \leq |K_r|+2|K_k|. \tag{9}$$

The split item type, $\mathcal{Y}_l$, can be identified in $O(|K_r|+2|K_k|)$ time without sorting the items in BKP using the well-known linear median algorithm [9,

Section 3.1]. The optimal solution vector $\mathbf{Y} = (\mathcal{Y}_1, ..., \mathcal{Y}_{|K_r|+2|K_k|})$ is determined by:

$$
\begin{cases}
\mathcal{Y}_j = b_j^{BKP} \text{ for } j = 1, ..., l-1, \\
\mathcal{Y}_l = \frac{1}{c_l^{BKP}} \left(\beta - \sum_{j=1}^{l-1} c_j^{BKP} b_j^{BKP} \right), \\
\mathcal{Y}_j = 0 \text{ for } j = l, ..., |K_r| + 2|K_k|.
\end{cases}
\tag{10}
$$

An integer solution without considering the precedence constraint for problem $\mathbf{P}$ can be constructed from the optimal solution vector of BKP as follows. In BKP, apart from the split item type, the number of result copies for tasks belonging to set K_r is either zero or equal to the upper bound. Consequently, the same number of result copies for tasks within K_r is added to the knapsack in the $\mathbf{P}_{BKS}$ instance. Furthermore, the number of result copies for tasks belonging to set K_k that can be multicast is either zero, one, or equal to the upper bound. Therefore, the same number of result copies for tasks within K_k is added to the knapsack in the $\mathbf{P}_{BKS}$ instance. Moreover, as many result copies corresponding to the split item type are added to the knapsack such that the remaining capacity satisfies $\beta - \sum_{j=1}^{l-1} c_j^{BKP} b_j^{BKP} \geq 0$. Finally, the constructed solution must be scrutinized as follows. For all $\mathbf{x}_{i,h}$ and $\sum_{h' \in H_{i,h}^{des}} \mathbf{y}_{i,h,h'}$, if the corresponding $\mathbf{x}_{i,h}$ for task $k_{i,h}$ is zero, then the value of $\sum_{h' \in H_{i,h}^{des}} \mathbf{y}_{i,h,h'}$ should also be set to zero. This procedure enforces the precedence constraint between $\mathbf{x}_{i,h}$ and $\sum_{h' \in H_{i,h}^{des}} \mathbf{y}_{i,h,h'}$, ensuring that a result can only be multicast if its corresponding task has been admitted.

Theorem 1. *The proposed algorithm has a relative performance guarantee of* $1/2$.

Proof. First, let $q_{\max}$ be a feasible solution of the ILP, where we admit the task with the largest data volume of $z_{i,h} + \sum_{h' \in H_{i,h}^{des}} o_{i,h}$ and the results are also multicast, i.e. $q_{\max} = \max_{i,h} \left\{ z_{i,h} \mathbf{x}_{i,h} + \sum_{h' \in H_{i,h}^{des}} o_{i,h} \mathbf{y}_{i,h,h'} \right\}$. Then, denote p^{LP} as the optimal solution of linear relaxation of $\mathbf{P}$, where p^{LP} is an upper bound of the optimal solution. Furthermore, denote by p^G the objective function value obtained by the proposed algorithm. p^G takes the best solution among p^{LP} and $q_{\max}$, and p^G can be expressed as follows $p^G = \max \{ p^{LP}, q_{\max} \}$. Considering the optimal solution of $\mathbf{P}$, which is denoted as p^*, it can be seen that the following inequality for p^* holds: $p^* < p^{LP} + q_{\max}$. Let $\rho = \frac{p^G}{p^*}$ be the approximation ratio and we can get with $\rho = \frac{p^G}{p^*} = \frac{\max\{p^{LP}, q_{\max}\}}{p^*} > \frac{\max\{p^{LP}, q_{\max}\}}{p^{LP} + q_{\max}}$. Clearly, $p^{LP} + q_{\max} \leq 2 \cdot \max \{ p^{LP}, q_{\max} \}$, thus $\rho > \frac{\max\{p^{LP}, q_{\max}\}}{2 \cdot \max\{p^{LP}, q_{\max}\}} = \frac{1}{2}$.

6   Results and Discussion

6.1   Simulation Settings

The track length is set at 80 km, with four trains initially located at 1, 20, 40, and 60 km. The velocity of each train is set at 90 m/s. GT-ITM tool [20] is used to generate the network topologies. We set the number of BSs in network G as 40. The parameter settings follow the descriptions in [11,12,21,22]. Each cloudlet's computing capacity varies from 100 to 500, and the CPU cycles in a cloudlet are 1.5 GHz. The cost of routing per task/result on a link is randomly set between 0.01 and 0.1, while the cost for a router to route a task/result varies from 0.05 to 0.1. The processing cost of a cloudlet to compute a task is randomly drawn from 0.5 to 2. The delay on a link or at a router ranges from 1 to 10 ms. Each multicast group size is selected from a range of 1 to 5. Each task $k_{i,h}$, and its result set, $R_{i,h}$, are generated as follows: a task randomly chooses its destination set, $H_{i,h}^{des}$, from train set H. Volumes $z_{i,h}$ and $o_{i,h}$ are uniformly distributed within the range of [0.01MB, 30MB]. The demanded CPU cycles, $f_{i,h}$, vary from 500 to 2000 MHz, and the delay requirement, $d_{i,h}$, is randomly chosen from 100 to 1000 ms. The network size $|V|$ is set to 100. The computational performance was evaluated using a system equipped with a 3.2 GHz AMD Ryzen-7 8-core processor and 32 GB of RAM. Each value displayed in the figures was derived by averaging the results of 50 trials.

To our knowledge, this study represents the first attempt to maximize multicast throughput in MEC networks for HSRs. We have developed an innovative method, which we refer to as the GAP- and knapsack-based group Steiner tree (GKGST). Our approach is compared with three baseline algorithms, namely TradeoffSPT, MinDelaySteiner, and MinCostSteiner, which have been adapted and extended from [15,23].

To compare the performance of these algorithms within the same network, we introduce a tuning parameter, λ, and normalize the weights of the edge and nodes in the network accordingly. The normalized weight $w_\lambda(e)$ of edge $e \in E$ is determined by: $w_\lambda(e) = \lambda \cdot c(e) + (1 - \lambda) \cdot d(e)$, and the normalized weight $w_\lambda(v)$ of node $v \in V$ is calculated by $w_\lambda(v) = \lambda \cdot c(v) + (1 - \lambda) \cdot d(v)$. All baseline algorithms consistently select the cloudlet with adequate capacity and minimum cost, wherein the aforementioned formula computes the cost with the adjusted turning parameter. The routing trees generated by the baseline algorithms include the source BSs and all destination BSs within the given multicast groups for each task and its corresponding results. These trees are rooted at the cloudlet with the lowest computing normalized weight. To organize the task and result sets $K_H(t)$ and R_H, the baseline algorithms sort them in ascending order according to the data volume of each task and result. Subsequently, the task-result pair with the smallest data volume from sets $K_H(t)$ and R_H is chosen until both sets have been completely traversed. We specifically classify GKGST, MinDelaySteiner, and MinCostSteiner as multicast algorithms, while TradeoffSPT is considered a unicast algorithm. The baseline algorithms are described below.

- TradeoffSPT: The value of λ for TradeoffSPT is set to 0.5, which means that the TradeoffSPT pathfinding strategy makes a trade-off between costs and delays. It is a greedy-based algorithm for unicast paths that requires finding the shortest path trees (SPTs) using Dijkstra's algorithm [4].

• MinDelayStenier: The value of λ is set to 0, which means that the Min-DelayStenier algorithm always routes tasks and results along the path with the minimum delay. In a multicast group, it is possible for multiple multicast trees to co-exist. To maximize network resource utilization and prevent link congestion, these multicast trees are coordinated through a global operation known as packing. MinDelayStenier serves as an extension of the method described in [23], adapted to the specific context of this study.

• MinCostSteiner: We set the value of λ to 1 in the MinCostSteiner algorithm. As a result, the algorithm aims to identify the optimal routing path for each task, minimizing the aggregate weight of both edges and nodes. This approach does not account for delay requirements and focuses solely on cost efficiency. The MinCostSteiner algorithm is an extension of the work presented in [15].

6.2 Performance Evaluation of Different Algorithms

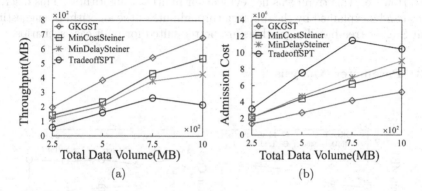

Fig. 3. Throughput and admission cost with respect to the total data volume.

We evaluate the performance of the GKGST algorithm compared to the Min-CostSPT, MinDelaySPT, and TradeoffSteiner algorithms, focusing on throughput and admission cost. The total data volume of $K_H(t)$ and R_H ranges from 250 MB to 1000 MB, while maintaining a constant cloudlet-to-router ratio $|V_c|/|V|$ of 1/5, and the average size of the multicast group is 5. The results are illustrated in Fig. 3. As depicted in Fig. 3(a), the GKGST algorithm outperforms all baseline algorithms, consistently achieving the highest throughput among the evaluated methods. When the data volume is small (less than 250MB), the performance disparities between GKGST, MinDelayStenier, and MinCostSteiner are relatively insignificant. This occurs because, with a limited data volume of $K_H(t)$ and R_H, the network resources are sufficient and the required resources are minimal. Consequently, the impact of computing capacity is less pronounced when there are fewer tasks, enabling the baseline algorithms to efficiently plan paths that satisfy delay requirements. Nevertheless, as the total data volume increases, the performance gap between the multicast algorithms and the unicast becomes more pronounced. In particular, the unicast algorithm shows a drop in throughput when the data volume exceeds 750MB. Eventually, when the total data volume reaches 1000 MB, GKGST's throughput exceeds that of the MinCostStenier, MinDelayStenier, and TradeoffSPT algorithms by 26.5%, 59.3% and 214.9%, respectively. Figure 3(b) demonstrates that the total cost of task admission increases as the total data volume expands, while GKGST consistently achieves a lower admission cost compared to the three baseline algorithms. This can be attributed to GKGST's construction of GAP instances to effectively search computing cloudlets, thereby the computing costs of various task admission options can be captured, and the network resources can be efficiently utilized. Moreover, GKGST plans GSTs to route tasks and results concurrently. A GST connects at least one BS within a multicast group, resulting in fewer edges and vertices compared to SPTs and Steiner trees, significantly reducing routing costs. Furthermore, we observed that as the throughput of TradeoffSPT decreases, the cost of this algorithm also shows a decrease when the data volume exceeds 750 MB. However, this trend was not evident for multicast algorithms. This discrepancy can be explained by the differing throughputs of the algorithms, suggesting that Steiner tree-based algorithms are better suited for multicast scenarios.

6.3 Parameter Analysis

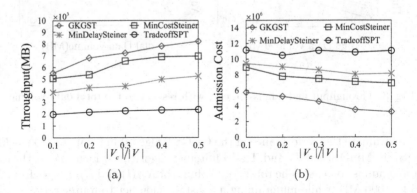

(a)   (b)

Fig. 4. Throughput and admission cost with respect to the ratio $|V_c|/|V|$.

We assess the performance of the GKGST algorithm by comparing it with the MinDelaySteiner, MinCostSteiner, and TradeoffSPT algorithms. The evaluation metrics used are throughput and total admission cost. To perform this analysis, we varied the ratio of the number of cloudlets ($|V_c|$) to the number of routers ($|V|$) in the range of 0.1 to 0.5. Additionally, the data volume for $K_H(t)$ and R_H was set at 1000 MB. The average size of the multicast group is 5. The outcomes of this comparison are illustrated in Fig. 4. The ratio $|V_c|/|V|$

represents the difficulty in identifying suitable computational cloudlets within a network for a specific task. A higher ratio indicates a larger number of potentially suitable computational cloudlets, thus increasing the likelihood that the algorithm converges to an improved result within a limited time period.

Figure 4(a) clearly illustrates that the GKGST algorithm consistently outperforms all baseline algorithms in terms of throughput. Moreover, the throughput of all algorithms generally increases as the ratio $|V_c|/|V|$ increases. The throughput of the unicast algorithm, TradeoffSPT, is less influenced by the ratio $|V_c|/|V|$ than that of the Steiner-based algorithm. Specifically, when the ratio $|V_c|/|V|$ increases from 0.1 to 0.5, the throughput of TradeoffSPT merely increases by 19.9%, while the performance of MinDelaySteiner, MinCostSteiner, and GKGST increase by 36.2%, 37.4%, and 49.1%, respectively. This phenomenon can be attributed to GKGST's utilization of a rapid search scheme based on the GAP problem for locating computing cloudlets, whereas all other baseline algorithms employ a greedy strategy to select the lowest turning cost cloudlets after sorting them in ascending order of reconciliation cost. As shown in Fig. 4 (b), the total admission cost tends to decrease with increasing ratio $|V_c|/|V|$. Compared to the three baseline algorithms, GKGST consistently achieves a lower admission cost. This can be explained by the fact that, given a constant number of nodes within the network, the number of cloudlets possessing idle computing power increases as the cloudlet ratio increases. When the ratio $|V_c|/|V|$ is low, tasks either fail to find available computational cloudlets or are forced to utilize cloudlets near their compute the capacity limit. For example, at a ratio $|V_c|/|V|$ of 0.1, the availability of cloudlets is limited, resulting in GKGST saving 36.2%, 39.7%, and 48.5% of admission costs compared to the MinCostSteiner, MinDelaySteiner, and TradeoffSPT algorithms, respectively. As GKGST consistently demonstrates the ability to identify cloudlets with lower computational costs, it can significantly reduce network operating expenses.

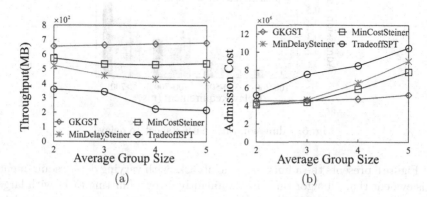

Fig. 5. Throughput and admission cost with respect to the size of the multicast group.

We examine the influence of the multicast group size by systematically altering its average size within a range of 2 to 5. The data volume for both $K_H(t)$ and

R_H was set at 1000 MB, while the ratio of $|V_c|/|V|$ was set at 0.2. We compared the performance of the proposed GKGST algorithm with MinDelaySteiner, Min-CostSteiner, and TradeoffSPT. The evaluation metrics employed were throughput and admission cost. The comparative analysis of these algorithms is depicted in Fig. 5. The average group size is indicative of the data volume for tasks and results that need to be transmitted; a larger data volume requires more BSs, resulting in a larger average group size. As illustrated in Fig. 5(a), the throughput of GKGST remains relatively unaffected by the average group size, while the three baseline algorithms exhibit a greater degree of sensitivity. Specifically, both MinCostSteiner and MinDelaySteiner demonstrate a decreasing trend as the average group size increases. TradeoffSPT experiences a significant drop in throughput when the group size exceeds three, maintaining a low value even as the group size continues to increase. Figure 5(b) presents the admission cost of GKGST compared to the three baseline algorithms, influenced by the average group size. Reflecting the findings in Fig. 5(a), the admission cost of GKGST is largely unimpacted by the average group size. In contrast, the admission cost for the three baseline algorithms shows an increasing trend along with the growth in the average group size. The observations in Fig. 5 can be attributed to the inherent properties of the GKGST, which is a GST characterized by at least one path between its root node and each member of the group. Consequently, GST can be constructed as long as there is a feasible path, irrespective of group size variations. On the other hand, all three baseline algorithms essentially construct a separate routing tree for each BS in the group. As the group size expands, more leaf nodes must be constructed for the routing tree, leading to an increase in the admission cost. This elevated admission cost consequently results in a decrease in throughput when operating costs are constrained.

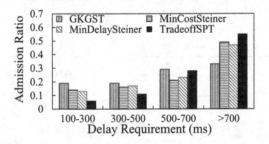

Fig. 6. Admission ratio with respect to delay.

Figure 6 presents the admission ratio of tasks with varying delay requirements. It is evident that all algorithms predominantly favor admitting tasks with larger delay requirements ($\geq$ 500 ms). In particular, we first examine two extreme delay requirement categories: greater than 700 ms and less than 300 ms. We observe that the proportions of tasks with delay requirements exceeding 700 ms among those admitted by GKGST, MinCostSteiner, MinDelaySteiner, and Tradeoff-SPT are 33.4%, 49.2%, 37.3% and 55.6% of the total number of admitted tasks, respectively. On the contrary, the ratios of tasks with delay requirements between 100–300 ms to the total number of admitted tasks are 19.5%, 14.3%, 13.4% and 6.8%, respectively. To assess the preferences of GKGST and the three baseline algorithms (MinCostSteiner, MinDelaySteiner, and TradeoffSPT) in terms of task admission with distinct delay requirements, we use the standard deviation as an evaluation metric. Standard deviations of the percentage of total admitted tasks for the four groups with different delay requirements were calculated for GKGST, MinCostSteiner, MinDelaySteiner, and TradeoffSPT, yielding 6.7%, 14.3%, 13.8%, and 19.4%, respectively. These results indicate that GKGST tends to admit tasks with diverse latency requirements in a more balanced manner. This can potentially be attributed to the fact that GKGST's ranking of item importance is based on the routing efficiency defined in this study, which enables the algorithm to minimize the preference for a single dimension when considering the delay demands and resource consumption of tasks during the routing tree planning process. On the contrary, the three baseline algorithms employ a greed-based selection approach, which may inadvertently amplify the influence of delay on path planning.

7   Conclusion

This paper examines the multicast throughput maximization problem in a trackside MEC network within a snapshot scenario. The original problem is formulated into an ILP formulation. Subsequently, we introduce a GAP-based cloudlet search strategy, along with a 1/2-approximate multicast throughput maximization algorithm based on a novel variant knapsack problem, achieved by simplifying and partitioning the ILP into independent stages. Simulation results demonstrate that the proposed algorithm effectively achieves high throughput by accommodating tasks and multicasting results with diverse data volumes and varying delay requirements for passengers aboard trains.

Acknowledgement. This work was supported in part by the Natural Science Foundation of Anhui Province, China under Grant 2108085MF202, in part by the National Natural Science Foundation of China under Grant 62002097, and in part by the Fundamental Research Funds for the Central Universities of China under Grant PA2023GDGP0044.

References

1. Babu, S., Parthiban, A.R.K.: DTMR: an adaptive distributed tree-based multicast routing protocol for vehicular networks. Comput. Stand. Interfaces **79**, 103551 (2022)
2. Cacchiani, V., Iori, M., Locatelli, A., Martello, S.: Knapsack problems-an overview of recent advances. Part II: multiple, multidimensional, and quadratic knapsack problems. Comput. Oper. Res. **143**, 105693 (2022)
3. Cohen, R., Katzir, L., Raz, D.: An efficient approximation for the generalized assignment problem. Inf. Process. Lett. **100**(4), 162–166 (2006)

4. Dijkstra, E.W.: A note on two problems in connexion with graphs. In: Edsger Wybe Dijkstra: His Life, Work, and Legacy, pp. 287–290 (2022)
5. Duin, C., Volgenant, A., Voß, S.: Solving group Steiner problems as Steiner problems. Eur. J. Oper. Res. **154**(1), 323–329 (2004)
6. Gao, M., et al.: Efficient hybrid beamforming with anti-blockage design for high-speed railway communications. IEEE Trans. Veh. Technol. **69**(9), 9643–9655 (2020)
7. Garg, N., Konjevod, G., Ravi, R.: A polylogarithmic approximation algorithm for the group Steiner tree problem. J. Algorithms **37**(1), 66–84 (2000)
8. Kadhim, A.J., Seno, S.A.H., Naser, J.I., Hajipour, J.: DMPFS: delay-efficient multicasting based on parked vehicles, fog computing and SDN in vehicular networks. Veh. Commun. **36**, 100488 (2022)
9. Kellerer, H., Pferschy, U., Pisinger, D.: Knapsack Problems. Springer, Berlin, Heidelberg (2004)
10. Keshavamurthy, P., Pateromichelakis, E., Dahlhaus, D., Zhou, C.: Resource scheduling for V2V communications in co-operative automated driving. In: 2020 IEEE Wireless Communications and Networking Conference (WCNC), pp. 1–6. IEEE (2020)
11. Li, H., et al.: Mobility-aware predictive computation offloading and task scheduling for mobile edge computing networks. In: 2021 7th International Conference on Computer and Communications (ICCC), pp. 1349–1354. IEEE (2021)
12. Li, L., et al.: Resource allocation and computation offloading in a millimeter-wave train-ground network (early access). IEEE Trans. Veh. Technol. **71**, 1–16 (2022)
13. Li, S., Yang, L., Gao, Z.: Distributed optimal control for multiple high-speed train movement: an alternating direction method of multipliers. Automatica **112**, 108646 (2020)
14. Liu, T., Liao, W.: Multicast routing in multi-radio multi-channel wireless mesh networks. IEEE Trans. Wireless Commun. **9**(10), 3031–3039 (2010)
15. Ma, Y., Liang, W., Wu, J., Xu, Z.: Throughput maximization of NFV-enabled multicasting in mobile edge cloud networks. IEEE Trans. Parallel Distrib. Syst. **31**(2), 393–407 (2019)
16. Nutov, Z., Beniaminy, I., Yuster, R.: A $(1-1/e)$-approximation algorithm for the generalized assignment problem. Oper. Res. Lett. **34**(3), 283–288 (2006)
17. Parsa, M., Zhu, Q., Garcia-Luna-Aceves, J.: An iterative algorithm for delay-constrained minimum-cost multicasting. IEEE/ACM Trans. Networking **6**(4), 461–474 (1998)
18. Ren, H., et al.: Efficient algorithms for delay-aware NFV-enabled multicasting in mobile edge clouds with resource sharing. IEEE Trans. Parallel Distrib. Syst. **31**(9), 2050–2066 (2020)
19. Sun, Y., Xiao, X., Cui, B., Halgamuge, S., Lappas, T., Luo, J.: Finding group Steiner trees in graphs with both vertex and edge weights. Proc. VLDB Endowment **14**(7), 1137–1149 (2021)
20. Institute of Technology, G.: Georgia tech internetwork topology models (GT-ITM) is a network topology generate tool (2023). https://www.cc.gatech.edu/projects/gtitm/
21. Xiong, J., Xie, H., Liu, B., Li, B., Gui, L.: Cooperative caching services on high-speed train by reverse auction. IEEE Trans. Veh. Technol. **70**(9), 9437–9449 (2021)
22. Xu, J., Wei, Z., Lyu, Z., Shi, L., Han, J.: Throughput maximization of offloading tasks in multi-access edge computing networks for high-speed railways. IEEE Trans. Veh. Technol. **70**(9), 9525–9539 (2021)
23. Zhang, X., Wang, Y., Geng, G., Yu, J.: Delay-optimized multicast tree packing in software-defined networks. IEEE Trans. Serv. Comput. **16**(1), 261–275 (2021)

An Evolving Transformer Network Based on Hybrid Dilated Convolution for Traffic Flow Prediction

Qi Yu[1,2] , Weilong Ding[1,2(✉)] , Maoxiang Sun[1,2], and Jihai Huang[3]

[1] School of Information Science and Technology, Beijing 100144, China
dingweilong@ncut.edu.cn
[2] Beijing Key Laboratory on Integration and Analysis of Large-Scale Stream Data,
Beijing 100144, China
[3] Zhengzhou University of Technology, Zhengzhou 450044, China

Abstract. Decision making based on predictive traffic flow is one of effective solutions to relieve road congestion. Capturing and modeling the dynamic temporal relationships in global data is an important part of the traffic flow prediction problem. Transformer network has been proven to have powerful capabilities in capturing long-range dependencies and interactions in sequences, making it widely used in traffic flow prediction tasks. However, existing transformer-based models still have limitations. On the one hand, they ignore the dynamism and local relevance of traffic flow time series due to static embedding of input data. On the other hand, they do not take into account the inheritance of attention patterns due to the attention scores of each layer's are learned separately. To address these two issues, we propose an evolving transformer network based on hybrid dilated convolution, namely HDCformer. First, a novel sequence embedding layer based on dilated convolution can dynamically learn the local relevance of traffic flow time series. Secondly, we add residual connections between attention modules of adjacent layers to fully capture the evolution trend of attention patterns between layers. Our HDCformer is evaluated on two real-world datasets and the results show that our model outperforms state-of-the-art baselines in terms of MAE, RMSE, and MAPE.

Keywords: Traffic flow prediction · Transformer · Hybrid dilated convolution · Time series · Attention mechanism

1 Introduction

Traffic congestion on highways has always been a major issue in large cities. With the rapid growth of urbanization and car ownership, the volume and complexity of traffic travel data have become increasingly large [14]. Accurate predictive traffic flow guides cost-effective traffic decisions to alleviate road congestion and enhance the efficiency of highway operations [25].

Supported by the Key-Area Research and Development Program of Guangzhou City.

The traffic flow prediction task refers to extracting useful information from historical data through technical means and then outputting the most likely future traffic flow. Capturing and modeling the dynamic temporal relationships in traffic flow data is an important part of this task. The current traffic flow prediction task has the following characteristics. First, the complexity of the relationships between data increases due to the massive amount of traffic data, so it is difficult to efficiently extract the relevance between key data. Second, in addition to being influenced by historical traffic flow, the traffic flow data on roads is also closely related to the surrounding context of the data points. Third, traffic flow data time series usually exhibit obvious periodicity (hourly, daily, weekly), which is also a problem that researchers need to consider. In recent years, the vanilla transformer networks [26] has demonstrated powerful capabilities in capturing long-range dependencies and interactions in sequences. Compared with traditional deep learning networks such as convolutional neural networks (CNNs) or recurrent neural networks (RNNs), the original transformer (i.e., vanilla transformer) replaces the most commonly used recurrent layer in the encoder-decoder architecture with multi-head self-attention and models sequences entirely based on attention mechanisms, allowing the network to process all input data in parallel to ensure that the model learns the global relevance of time series. In addition, it also proposes a position encoding mechanism to preserve the order of elements in a sequence. Traffic transformer [5] captures the continuity and periodicity of traffic flow time series using a transformer framework. RPConvformer [29] uses one-dimensional convolution to embed traffic flow time series data as a replacement for the word embedding method of the original transformer.

However, existing transformer network-based traffic flow prediction models still have limitations. On the one hand, the static data embedding method cannot enable the model to learn the dynamic relevance of time series well. The increase in convolution operations that can learn the local correlation of sequences is limited by the size of the convolution kernel. On the other hand, most existing attention-based models do not take into account the inheritance of attention patterns between layers. They simply stack encoding modules repeatedly and learn the attention scores of each layer separately.

To address the aforementioned issues, we propose an Evolving Transformer Network based on Hybrid Dilation Convolution, called HDCformer, for traffic flow prediction. First, in order to capture the dynamic relevance of time series while paying attention to the relevance of local areas, we use a hybrid dilated convolution layer to embed the original time series data. Dilated convolution can increase the receptive field on the basis of standard one-dimensional convolution while also solving the problem of reduced accuracy caused by max pooling operations. Second, in order to capture the dependency relationship between attention scores of different layers, we directly connect attention modules from adjacent layers so that attention calculation can depend on the results of the previous layer and promote information sharing between different layers. In summary, the main contributions of this paper are as follows.

- We propose an Evolving Transformer Network based on Hybrid Dilation Convolution. Our approach adopts the vanilla transformer's encoder-decoder architecture, which is based on scaled dot-product attention. We develop a novel convolutional embedding layer that learns the dynamism and local correlations of traffic flow time series data by stacking dilation convolutions with different dilation rates.
- We conduct residual connections to the original transformer structure, connecting the attention scores of adjacent layers to fully capture the transferability of attention values between different layers, thereby better learning the evolution trend of attention patterns.
- We evaluate our model on two public datasets. The experimental results demonstrate that our model outperforms state-of-the-art baselines on three metrics: MAE, RMSE, and MAPE.

The rest of this paper is organized as follows. In Sect. 2, we introduce the related work of this article, including traditional traffic flow prediction methods and traffic flow prediction methods based on transformer networks. In Sect. 3, we introduce some basic symbols and problem definitions. In Sect. 4, we describe the specific implementation details of the traffic flow prediction method proposed in this paper. In Sect. 5, we evaluate the performance of the proposed method on two real datasets through experiments and ablation studies. Finally, we summarize the work of this paper and discuss future research directions.

2   Related Work

2.1   Traffic Flow Prediction

The traffic flow prediction can be seen as a mapping from historical time series traffic data to future time series traffic conditions. Early methods for traffic flow prediction were based on statistical theory, such as the Historical Average (HA) [15], which uses weighted calculations of traffic flow between adjacent time periods and historical periods as the prediction result. The ARIMA [12] captures linear relationships in time series data for traffic flow prediction. Statistical models are simple in algorithm and rely on statistical assumptions, but cannot capture the temporal characteristics and deeper feature information of traffic flow data.

The emergence of machine learning methods has enabled models to begin capturing non-linear relationships in data. The most representative of these is the traffic flow prediction model based on the KNN [8], which selects K nearest vectors from the historical database for statistical analysis to obtain prediction results. The SVR [6] requires the selection of an appropriate kernel function to train the support vector machine and predict traffic flow in the next period. However, machine learning methods are still unable to cope with increasingly large and complex data.

To support the prediction of today's large amounts of traffic flow data, researchers have begun to use deep learning methods to explore and mine deep temporal features and dynamic dependencies between data [16]. Most traffic flow prediction models are based on CNNs [13] and RNNs [19]. On one hand, due to the architectural characteristics of RNNs, their network depth can be the length of a time series. Many researchers use RNNs to construct dynamic time relationships. LSTM [30] solves the gradient vanishing problem brought by deep RNNs by adding forget gates, input gates, and output gates. SBU-LSTM [10] developed a bidirectional LSTM layer to capture forward and backward dependencies in time series data. LSTM-BILSTM [21] further improves prediction accuracy by combining the advantages of sequential data with the long-term dependencies of bidirectional LSTMs. GRU [9] simplifies the neural network structure by omitting gates with small contributions in LSTM, improving model learning efficiency. However, due to its recursive nature, RNNs models are always limited in solving global parallelization problems in sequences. On the other hand, early on, CNNs were applied to capture spatial dependencies in traffic flow data in grid road networks. Recent work has also applied CNNs to time series prediction. G-CNN [34] explored a feature extractor for high-dimensional multivariate time series. Some researchers have proposed stacking dilated convolutions, or combining them with causal convolutions, such as [3,4,11], they all demonstrate the applicability of convolutional networks to time series prediction problems. Inspired by their works, we developed a hybrid dilated convolution layer to extract dynamic relevance in time series.

2.2   Transformer Networks for Traffic Flow Prediction

The work [2] first used the attention mechanism in the encoder-decoder, applying it to the task of neural machine translation. Subsequently, the attention mechanism was widely used in time series prediction tasks [18,22,24]. The vanilla transformer [26] is a network architecture completely based on self-attention mechanisms. Due to the outstanding performance of transformers in the field of natural language processing, more and more researchers have begun to explore the feasibility of transformers in traffic flow prediction tasks. Traffic transformer [5] captures the continuity and periodicity of time series using the transformer framework. TERMCast [33] proposes a transformer-based urban traffic prediction architecture that extracts proximity, periodicity, and trend components from urban traffic sequences.

In addition, researchers have improved the original transformer from two aspects to achieve optimal prediction performance. The first is to improve several important modules in the transformer framework. For example, LogSparse [17] Transformer proposes a convolutional self-attention mechanism that better incorporates local environments into the attention mechanism. Informer [36] selects major queries based on query and key similarity to participate in attention score calculation, reducing computational complexity. Pyraformer [20] introduces a pyramid attention module to capture a wide range of time dependencies. Crossformer [35] captures cross-dimensional dependencies to achieve multivariate time series prediction. The second is to design a new transformer architecture. For example, an article [28] proposes a convolution-enhanced attention network that promotes information flow between tokens across layers. Autoformer [31] designs an autocorrelation mechanism that progressively decomposes complex time series to reduce complexity. Scaleformer [23] designs a new iterative scaling scheme that iteratively improves predicted time series at multiple scales. We design convolutional network modules and residual connections to improve the vanilla transformer architecture.

3   Preliminary

Relevant formal definitions are listed here.

- **Definition 1: Traffic Flow Tensor.** We define the traffic flow tensor of all nodes over the total T time slices as $\{X_1, \cdots, X_n, \cdots, X_N\} \in \mathbb{R}^{N \times T}$, where $X_n = \{x_1, \cdots, x_t, \cdots, x_T\} \in \mathbb{R}^T$ represents the historical time series of node n at the last T time steps, N represents the number of nodes in the road network.
- **Definition 2: Traffic Flow Prediction Problem.** The objective of traffic flow forecasting is to accurately predict future traffic flow values utilizing historical data obtained from N nodes. By fitting a complex function $\tilde{f}$, traffic values for the coming P time steps can be forecasted based on traffic data from N nodes over the previous T time steps. The function is defined as shown in Formula 1, where θ represents the learnable parameter that is shared among the time series of all N nodes within the model.

$$[x_{T+1}, \cdots, x_{T+p}, \cdots, x_{T+P}] = \tilde{f}([x_1, \cdots, x_t, \cdots, x_T; \theta]). \tag{1}$$

4   Methodology

Figure 1 illustrates the framework of HDCformer, which consists of a data embedding layer, a positional encoding layer, a stack of M identical encoder-decoder layers, and an output layer. HDCformer is an improved model based on the transformer network, where the modification specifically includes two aspects. On the one hand, hybrid dilated convolution is used to construct the data embedding layer, which captures the correlation of local time series. On the other hand, a residual connection is added between adjacent encoding layers. That enables the encoding layer to generate attention based on inherited information and learn the evolving trend of attention patterns.

4.1   Hybrid Dilated Convolution for Data Embedding

In addition to being influenced by historical ones, traffic flow is also heavily related to the temporal characteristics [17]. The trend brought by these temporal characteristics are reflected in the surrounding context. As shown in Fig. 2(a), points A and B have the same value which is just the median within a one-hour, but they have completely different fluctuation trends in subsequent time steps. In other words, the two points have different local temporal characteristics.

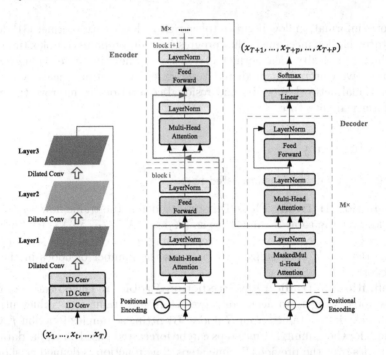

Fig. 1. The framework of HDCformer

For our model, it is necessary to capture such local relevance of time series. In the vanilla transformer network, the attention score is calculated on a point-by-point basis, which may lead to time steps with similar traffic flow data capturing more incorrect matching information. To address this issue, we propose a data embedding layer based on hybrid dilated convolution, which obtains richer local information with different dilation rates.

Dilated convolution, as the name suggests, involves injecting holes into standard convolution to increase the receptive field of the convolutional kernel [32]. The number of holes injected, i.e., the interval between kernels, is referred to as the dilation rate (denoted as r). In standard convolution, the dilation rate r is equal to 1. As can be seen from Fig. 2(b), for a 3×3 convolutional kernel, the setting $r = 2$ significantly increases the receptive field. However, when we stack multiple 3×3 kernels with $r = 2$, we find that our kernel is not continuous. This stacking method results in a loss of information continuity, which contradicts our original intention of learning time series correlations. A feasible solution [27] adopts different dilation rates are set for dilated convolutions at different layers to cover all holes, and achieves better prediction performance than traditional standard convolution.

The implementation of the data embedding layer is shown in Fig. 1. We combine hybrid dilated convolution with one-dimensional standard convolution. The one-dimensional standard convolution unit processes the input time series and

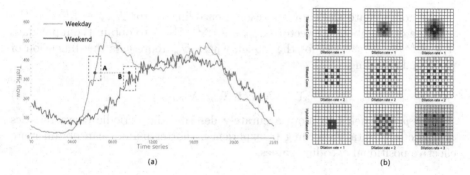

Fig. 2. (a) shows time series on PeMSD4 dataset, where two curves represent the traffic flow of a node on a weekday and a weekend respectively. Each row in (b) shows the pixels involved in the convolutional kernel calculation when the convolutional kernel size is 3×3 for standard convolution (dilation rate = 1), dilated convolution (all dilation rates = 2), and hybrid dilated convolution (dilation rates of 1, 2, and 3), respectively.

sequentially captures local context. By stacking one-dimensional convolution, the sequence features are expanded without altering the sequence length. Then, three layers of hybrid dilated convolution with different dilation rates are used to improve the local correlation of the time series. Assuming that the input traffic flow data is X_{input}, the mathematical expression of the convolution module is shown in Formula 2, where B represents the batch size, T_{in} represents the length of the input sequence, D_{in} represents the input feature dimension, $HDC(\cdot)$ represents the hybrid dilated convolution and D_{emb} represents the expanded feature dimension.

$$X_{input} \in \mathbb{R}^{B \times T_{in} \times D_{in}} \xrightarrow{HDC(\cdot)} X_{emb} \in \mathbb{R}^{B \times T_{in} \times D_{emb}}. \tag{2}$$

Furthermore, to prevent the front position from accessing future information, padding is adopted with a one-sided complement that has the same output sequence.

4.2 Positional Encoding

Due to the parallel nature of the framework, sine and cosine functions were introduced as position encoding in the vanilla transformer framework to mark the order of the input sequence. In text data, position encoding records the position information of words in sentences. Compared to text data, traffic flow data has obvious periodic trend [5]. Therefore, we need to set an appropriate period value in the positional encoding for time series data. The mathematical expression of position encoding is shown in Formula 3, where t represents the time step in the sequence and *period* is the pre-defined parameter.

$$\begin{cases} X_{pos}(2t) & = sin(\frac{2\pi t}{period}) \\ X_{pos}(2t+1) & = cos(\frac{2\pi t}{period}) \end{cases}. \tag{3}$$

We concatenate the above positional encoding vector $X_{pos} \in \mathbb{R}^{B \times T_{in} \times D_{pe}}$ with the data embedding vector $X_{emb} \in \mathbb{R}^{B \times T_{in} \times D_{emb}}$ to obtain the input data $\mathcal{X} \in \mathbb{R}^{B \times T_{in} \times (D_{pe} + D_{emb})}$ for the model, where D_{pe} represents the dimension of positional encoding.

$$\mathcal{X} = Concat(X_{pos}, X_{emb}). \tag{4}$$

The *period* helps to more accurately describe the periodic characteristics of traffic flow data. According to experience, shorter periods can obtain more effective positional encoding values.

4.3   Evolving Transformer

In the vanilla transformer network, the attention scores of each layer are learned separately and no interaction exists between layers. That makes it impossible to learn the evolution trend of attention patterns. Based on the encoder-decoder architecture using Scaled Dot-Product Attention [26] in the traditional transformer, we propose an evolution mechanism that enables stacked blocks to capture the dependency relationship between attention scores at different layers. Accordingly, predictive accuracy can be further improved.

The Evolving Mechanism. Inspired by the work [28], our Evolving Transformer adds residual connections between adjacent encoder blocks. Specifically, the attention score of the previous layer is combined with the output result of the previous block as the input of the current layer's attention mechanism. Then, the calculated attention score of the current layer is combined with the input of the current block and sent to the feedforward network. After layer normalization [1], the output of the current block is obtained. We use $\mathcal{X}_{res}^{i-1}$ to represent the computed result of the previous block after residual connection (before Feed Forward Layer), $\mathcal{X}_{out}^{i-1}$ to represent the output of the previous block, $\mathcal{X}_{in}^{i}$ to represent the input to the attention mechanism of the current block, and $\mathcal{X}_{out}^{i}$ to represent the output of the current block. Further, $Attention(\cdot)$ is used to represent the attention operation on $\mathcal{X}_{in}^{i}$ in the current block. In addition, symbols α and β are pre-defined hyperparameters ranging from 0 to 1 based on empirical values. The mathematical representation is as follows:

$$\begin{aligned}
\mathcal{X}_{in}^{i} &= \alpha \cdot \mathcal{X}_{res}^{i-1} + (1-\alpha) \cdot \mathcal{X}_{out}^{i-1}, \\
\mathcal{X}_{res}^{i} &= \beta \cdot \mathcal{X}_{in}^{i} + (1-\beta) \cdot Attention(\mathcal{X}_{in}^{i}), \\
\mathcal{X}_{out}^{i} &= LayerNorm(FeedForward(\mathcal{X}_{res}^{i})).
\end{aligned} \tag{5}$$

Multi-head Attention. We use the Scaled Dot-Product Attention model to calculate attention scores, which is a core part of the transformer architecture. First, the input data $\mathcal{X}_{in}^i$ is linearly transformed to obtain the initial representations of the three vectors $Q = W_q \mathcal{X}_{in}^i$, $K = W_k \mathcal{X}_{in}^i$, and $V = W_v \mathcal{X}_{in}^i$, which are then input into the model. Next, the dot product is calculated between Q and K to determine their relevance, and then the attention scores are calculated through softmax.

$$Attention(Q, K, V) = softmax(\frac{QK^T}{\sqrt{D_{pe} + D_{emb}}})V. \tag{6}$$

By using multi-head attention, the model can simultaneously focus on information from different representation subspaces at various positions. This is not possible with a single attention head, as averaging would inhibit it. We assume the multi-headed attention mechanism of the H-heads is defined as follows.

$$head_h = Attention(Q_h, K_h, V_h),$$
$$Q_h = QW_q^h, K_h = KW_k^h, V_h = VW_v^h, h = 1, \cdots, H. \tag{7}$$

Finally, the outputs of the H-heads are merged and then subjected to layer normalization to obtain the output of the attention layer, where W_q, W_k, W_v, W^O represent the weight matrices.

$$Attention(\mathcal{X}_{in}) = LayerNorm(Concat(head_1, \cdots, head_H)W^O). \tag{8}$$

Feed Forward Networks. In our encoder and decoder, each block contains not only an attention sublayer but also a fully connected feed forward network. Such network is applied after the attention layer and consists of two linear transformations and an activation function. We define a_r, W_r and b_r as learnable parameters, the activation function uses the LeakyReLU function, as follows:

$$FeedForward(\mathcal{X}_{res}) = max(a_r \mathcal{X}_{res}, \mathcal{X}_{res})W_r + b_r. \tag{9}$$

5 Evaluation

5.1 Dataset

The performance of HDCformer was validated on two real-world traffic flow datasets, PeMSD4 and PeMSD8. The datasets were collected from the California highway traffic flow data by the Caltrans Performance Measurement System (PeMS) [7], with data aggregated at 5-min intervals, i.e., 12 sample points per hour. Details of the two public datasets are given in Table 1.

Table 1. Details of the two public datasets.

Datasets	Nodes	Time Interval	Timesteps	Time Range
PeMSD4	307	5 min	16992	1/1/2018-2/28/2018
PeMSD8	170	5 min	17856	7/1/2016-8/31/2016

5.2 Baseline

We compared HDCformer with the following 7 representative and advanced baselines:

- **HA** [15]: History Average Model, which uses the average historical traffic flow of a road section within a certain time interval as the predicted value.
- **ARIMA** [12]: Autoregressive Integrated Moving Average Model, which treats the sequence as a random time series and approximates it using a mathematical model.
- **KNN** [8]: K-Nearest Neighbor Model, which finds neighbors in the historical database that match the current real-time observation data and uses a prediction algorithm to obtain the traffic prediction for the next moment.
- **SVR** [6]: Support Vector Regression Model, which is an application of support vector machine to regression problems.
- **LSTM** [30]: Long Short-Term Memory Model, which is a special type of RNN designed to solve the problem of gradient vanishing and gradient explosion during training of long sequences.
- **GRU** [9]: Gate Recurrent Unit Model, which is also a type of RNN that more efficiently solves the problem of long-term memory and gradient in backpropagation.
- **RPConvformer** [29]: A novel Transformer-based deep neural network for traffic flow prediction, which developed a fully convolutional embedding layer and used relative position encoding for linear mapping in multi-head attention.

5.3 Setting

Our HDCformer is implemented using Ubuntu 20.10, Python 3.7 and the deep learning framework TensorFlow 2.2.0. We conduct and evaluate all of our experiments on a server equipped with an 8-core Intel(R) Xeon(R) Platinum 8163 2.50GHz CPU and an NVIDIA Tesla T4 16GB GPU.

We split two datasets into training set, validation set, and test set in a ratio 6:2:2. We use the past day's historical data (288 timesteps) to predict the traffic flow data for the next hour. Further, the hyperparameters in the model are set as follows: the initial learning rate is set to 0.001 with Adam as the optimizer, the batchsize B is set to 32, the maximum epoch is 100, the hybrid dilated convolution layer has a convolution kernel of 7×7 with dilation rates of [1,2,5], and the number of encoders and decoders is set to 3 with 8 attention heads.

We use three commonly used metrics to assess the performance of HDCformer model: Mean Absolute Error (MAE), Root Mean Square Error (RMSE), and Mean Absolute Percentage Error (MAPE). The mathematical representations are as follows,

$$MAE = \frac{1}{N} \sum_{i=1}^{n} |y_i - \hat{y}_i|,$$

$$RMSE = \sqrt{\frac{1}{N} \sum_{i=1}^{n} (y_i - \hat{y}_i)^2}, \tag{10}$$

$$MAPE = \frac{1}{N} \sum_{i=1}^{n} \frac{|y_i - \hat{y}_i|}{y_i} \times 100\%$$

where $\hat{y}_i$ represents the the predicted value, y_i represents the ground truth, N represents the number of samples in the test set.

5.4   Performance Comparison

Table 2 shows the comparison results of HDCformer and 7 baseline methods for traffic flow prediction on two public datasets. The results in bold indicate the best, and the results underlined are the second best. As can be seen, our proposed method outperforms all other baselines on all three indicators, especially compared to the most important baseline RPConvformer, HDCformer improves the prediction accuracy on PEMSD4 and PEMSD8 datasets by an average of 8.12% and 3.00%, respectively. Based on the experimental results, we can draw the following conclusions:

(1) Classical machine learning methods such as KNN and SVR models do not fully utilize sequence information, ignore the relevance of local trends in traffic flow sequences, and are easily affected by local outliers, resulting in poor generalization ability of the model.
(2) The serial attribute of deep learning-based methods such as LSTM and GRU models leads to the continuous transmission and amplification of errors in the recursive process.
(3) The RPConvformer model, based on one-dimensional convolution for sequence embedding, has a receptive field limited by the size of the convolution kernel, and the local sequence features learned cannot well represent trend relevance.

In summary, HDCformer combines improved strategies of hybrid dilated convolutional networks and evolutionary mechanisms of residual connections with the transformer framework for traffic flow prediction. Experimental results validate the superiority of the model.

5.5   Ablation Experiments

In order to further study the effectiveness of the HDCformer model in traffic flow prediction tasks, we designed the following variants for the data embedding module based on hybrid dilated convolution and the evolved transformer network.

Table 2. Predictive performance on the PEMSD4 and PEMSD8 datasets.

Model	PeMSD4			PeMSD8		
	MAE	RMSE	MAPE(%)	MAE	RMSE	MAPE(%)
HA	47.17	70.14	22.98	28.46	36.3	25.92
ARIMA	64.34	84.20	36.93	30.00	38.22	27.76
KNN	52.86	72.25	26.10	22.49	29.85	18.65
SVR	53.81	71.48	29.02	21.54	27.55	19.50
LSTM	38.50	52.06	19.23	19.75	25.96	16.96
GRU	39.78	52.25	22.52	20.19	26.68	17.01
RPConvformer	35.8	47.5	17.51	16.15	21.08	11.02
HDCformer(ours)	**32.80**	**43.60**	**16.15**	**15.71**	**20.54**	**10.61**

- HDCformer(no-dilated-conv): This variant removes the dilated convolution in the data embedding layer.
- HDCformer(same-dilated-rate): This variant sets the dilation rate of the three layers of dilated convolution to r=2 uniformly to evaluate the impact of gridding effects on the model.
- HDCformer(no-skip-connection): This variant removes the residual connections added between adjacent encoder layers, i.e., it degrades to the original transformer's encoder stacking method.

The predictive performance of HDCformer and the above three variant models on the PEMSD4 and PEMSD8 datasets were compared, and the ablation study results are shown in Fig. 3. By analyzing the experimental results, we can draw the following conclusions:

(1) HDCformer has a significant improvement in predictive performance compared to HDCformer(no-dilated-conv), which indicates that using dilated convolution for data embedding is effective in capturing local correlations in sequences.
(2) The performance of HDCformer(same-dilated-rate) is worse than that of HDCformer, which indicates that the gridding effect of dilated convolution causes the model to learn incomplete local sequence features and obtain defective trend information.

(3) The performance of HDCformer(no-skip-connection) is worse than that of HDCformer because this variant ignores the inheritance of attention patterns between layers and the attention scores of each layer are calculated independently.

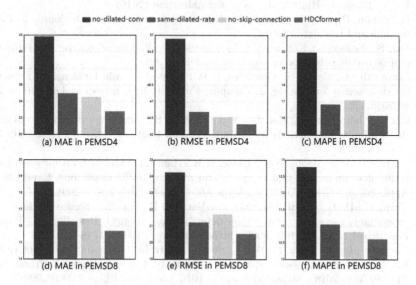

Fig. 3. Ablation study on the PEMSD4 and PEMSD8 datasets

6   Conclusion

In this paper, we propose An Evolving Transformer Network based on Hybrid Dilated Convolution for Traffic Flow Prediction. Specifically, we developed a data embedding layer based on hybrid dilated convolution by stacking dilated convolutions with different dilation rates to capture the local correlations in traffic flow time series and enable the model to learn the local trend of the sequence. We further connected the attention scores of adjacent layers in the original transformer to capture the evolution trend of attention patterns between different layers. Compared to the best baseline, our model improved by 8.12% and 3.00% on the two datasets respectively, demonstrating the superior performance of the HDCformer model. Ablation experiment results show that using a data embedding layer constructed with dilated convolution significantly improves the prediction accuracy of the model. Adding residual connections between adjacent attention modules also achieves the purpose of improving performance. As future work, we will further study the spatio-temporal correlation of traffic flow in road network structures, building on HDCformer and capturing the spatial dependence of traffic flows using, for example, spatial self-attention mechanisms and spatial graph modelling.

Acknowledgments. This work was supported by the Key-Area Research and Development Program of Guangzhou City (No. 202206030009).

References

1. Ba, J., Kiros, J., Hinton, G.: Layer normalization (2016)
2. Bahdanau, D., Cho, K., Bengio, Y.: Neural machine translation by jointly learning to align and translate (2014)
3. Bai, S., Kolter, J., Koltun, V.: An empirical evaluation of generic convolutional and recurrent networks for sequence modeling (2018)
4. Borovykh, A., Bohte, S., Oosterlee, C.W.: Dilated convolutional neural networks for time series forecasting. J. Comput. Finan. (2018). https://doi.org/10.21314/jcf.2019.358
5. Cai, L., Janowicz, K., Mai, G., Yan, B., Zhu, R.: Traffic transformer: capturing the continuity and periodicity of time series for traffic forecasting. Trans. GIS **24**, 736–755 (2020)
6. Castro-Neto, M., Jeong, Y.S., Jeong, M.K., Han, L.D.: Online-SVR for short-term traffic flow prediction under typical and atypical traffic conditions. Expert Syst. Appl. **36**(3), 6164–6173 (2008). https://doi.org/10.1016/j.eswa.2008.07.069
7. Chen, C., Petty, K., Skabardonis, A., Varaiya, P., Jia, Z.: Freeway performance measurement system: mining loop detector data. Transp. Res. Rec.: J. Transp. Res. Board **1748**, 96–102 (2007). https://doi.org/10.3141/1748-12
8. Cheng, S., Lu, F., Peng, P., Wu, S.: Short-term traffic forecasting: an adaptive ST-KNN model that considers spatial heterogeneity. Comput. Environ. Urban Syst. **71**, 186–198 (2018). https://doi.org/10.1016/j.compenvurbsys.2018.05.009
9. Chung, J., Gulcehre, C., Cho, K., Bengio, Y.: Empirical evaluation of gated recurrent neural networks on sequence modeling (2014)
10. Cui, Z., Ke, R., Wang, Y.: Deep bidirectional and unidirectional LSTM recurrent neural network for network-wide traffic speed prediction (2018)
11. Franceschi, J.Y., Dieuleveut, A., Jaggi, M.: Unsupervised scalable representation learning for multivariate time series (2019)
12. Isufi, E., Loukas, A., Simonetto, A., Leus, G.: Autoregressive moving average graph filtering. IEEE Trans. Sign. Proc. **65**(2), 274–288 (2016). https://doi.org/10.1109/tsp.2016.2614793
13. Jiang, W.: Internet traffic prediction with deep neural networks. Internet Technol. Lett. **5**(2), e314 (2021). https://doi.org/10.1002/itl2.314
14. Jiang, W., Luo, J.: Graph neural network for traffic forecasting: a survey. Expert Syst. Appl. **207**, 117921 (2022). https://doi.org/10.1016/j.eswa.2022.117921
15. Kaysi, I., Ben-Akiva, M., Koutsopoulos, H.: Integrated approach to vehicle routing and congestion prediction for real-time driver guidance (1993)
16. Lei, Y., et al.: The development of traffic flow prediction based on deep learning: a literature review. In: 2022 7th International Conference on Computer and Communication Systems (ICCCS) (2022). https://doi.org/10.1109/icccs55155.2022.9845878
17. Li, S., et al.: Enhancing the locality and breaking the memory bottleneck of transformer on time series forecasting (2019)
18. Liang, Y., Ke, S., Zhang, J., Yi, X., Zheng, Y.: GeoMAN: multi-level attention networks for geo-sensory time series prediction. In: Proceedings of the Twenty-Seventh International Joint Conference on Artificial Intelligence (2018). https://doi.org/10.24963/ijcai.2018/476

19. van Lint, J.W.C., Hoogendoorn, S.P., van Zuylen, H.J.: Freeway travel time prediction with state-space neural networks: modeling state-space dynamics with recurrent neural networks. Transp. Res. Rec.: J. Transp. Res. Board **1811**(1), 30–39 (2007). https://doi.org/10.3141/1811-04
20. Liu, S., et al.: Pyraformer: low-complexity pyramidal attention for long-range time series modeling and forecasting (2021)
21. Ma, C., Dai, G., Zhou, J.: Short-term traffic flow prediction for urban road sections based on time series analysis and LSTM_BILSTM method. IEEE Trans. Intell. Transp. Syst. **23**, 5615–5624 (2021). https://doi.org/10.1109/tits.2021.3055258
22. Qin, Y., Song, D., Chen, H., Cheng, W., Jiang, G., Cottrell, G.W.: A dual-stage attention-based recurrent neural network for time series prediction. In: Proceedings of the Twenty-Sixth International Joint Conference on Artificial Intelligence (2017). https://doi.org/10.24963/ijcai.2017/366
23. Shabani, A., Abdi, A., Meng, L., Sylvain, T.: Scaleformer: iterative multi-scale refining transformers for time series forecasting (2022)
24. Shih, S.Y., Sun, F.K., Lee, H.Y.: Temporal pattern attention for multivariate time series forecasting. Mach. Learn. **108**, 1421–1441 (2019). https://doi.org/10.1007/s10994-019-05815-0
25. Tedjopurnomo, D.A., Bao, Z., Zheng, B., Choudhury, F.M., Qin, A.K.: A survey on modern deep neural network for traffic prediction: trends, methods and challenges. IEEE Trans. Knowl. Data Eng. **34**(4), 1544–1561 (2022). https://doi.org/10.1109/TKDE.2020.3001195
26. Vaswani, A., et al.: Attention is all you need (2017)
27. Wang, P., et al.: Understanding convolution for semantic segmentation (2018)
28. Wang, Y., et al.: Convolution-enhanced evolving attention networks (2022)
29. Wen, Y., Xu, P., Li, Z., Xu, W., Wang, X.: RPConvformer: a novel transformer-based deep neural networks for traffic flow prediction (2023)
30. Williams, R., Hochreiter, S., Schmidhuber, J.: Long short-term memory. Neural Comput. **9**, 1735–1780 (1997)
31. Wu, H., Xu, J., Wang, J., Long, M.: Autoformer: decomposition transformers with auto-correlation for long-term series forecasting (2021)
32. Wu, Z., Pan, S., Long, G., Jiang, J., Zhang, C.: Graph WaveNet for deep spatial-temporal graph modeling. In: Proceedings of the Twenty-Eighth International Joint Conference on Artificial Intelligence (2019). https://doi.org/10.24963/ijcai.2019/264
33. Xue, H., Salim, F.D.: TERMCast: temporal relation modeling for effective urban flow forecasting. In: Karlapalem, K., et al. (eds.) Advances in Knowledge Discovery and Data Mining. Lecture Notes in Computer Science(), vol. 12712, pp. 741–753. Springer, Cham (2021). https://doi.org/10.1007/978-3-030-75762-5_58
34. Yi, S., Ju, J., Yoon, M.K., Choi, J.: Grouped convolutional neural networks for multivariate time series (2017)
35. Zhang, Y., Yan, J.: Crossformer: transformer utilizing cross-dimension dependency for multivariate time series forecasting (2022)
36. Zhou, H., et al.: Informer: beyond efficient transformer for long sequence time-series forecasting. In: Proceedings of the AAAI Conference on Artificial Intelligence, pp. 11106–11115 (2022). https://doi.org/10.1609/aaai.v35i12.17325

Prediction, Optimization
and Applications

DualDNSMiner: A Dual-Stack Resolver Discovery Method Based on Alias Resolution

Dingkang Han[1,2,3], Yujia Zhu[1,2,3], Liang Jiao[1,2,3], Dikai Mo[1,2,3], Yong Sun[1,2(✉)], Yuedong Zhang[4], and Qingyun Liu[1,2]

[1] Institute of Information Engineering, Chinese Academy of Sciences, Beijing, China
{handingkang,zhuyujia,modikai,sunyong,liuqingyun}@iie.ac.cn,
jiaol@cert.org.cn
[2] National Engineering Laboratory of Information Security Technologies,
Beijing, China
[3] School of Cyber Security, University of Chinese Academy of Sciences, Beijing,
China
[4] CNCERT, Beijing, China
zyd@cert.org.cn

Abstract. With the rapid development of IPv6 network applications, the transition to IPv6 dns has accelerated. In this process, dual-stack resolvers take on the crucial role that ensures the resolution of domains under hybrid network conditions. However, the lagging deployment of IPv6 defence measures may undermine the overall security of resolvers, making the discovery of dual-stack resolvers vital for DNS security analysis. Previous methods for discovering dual-stack resolvers are built on strong but impractical assumptions, ignoring resolvers with multiple alias IP addresses. In this article, we propose a new dual-stack resolvers discovery model based on alias resolution - DualDNSMiner. DualDNSMiner involves address alias resolution technology in order to recognize hosts with multiple alias addresses and identify dual-stack resolvers. Large-scale measurement experiments show that, DualDNSMiner can reliably discover over 80% more new dual-stack resolvers compared to previous judgment rules. In addition, we put forth a novel approach to validate the accuracy of our findings. The results demonstrate that the precision of DualDNSMiner can exceed over 90%. Finally, the results of DualDNS-Miner provide the first proof of the widespread use of alias addresses in DNS resolvers, which is crucial for analyzing the process of DNS's IPv6 evolution.

Keywords: DNS · IPv6 · dual-stack resolver · alias resolution

1 Introduction

With the rapid development of IPv6 networks, the adoption rate of IPv6 applications has been increasing year by year [2,3]. More and more users are now choosing to access websites and applications through IPv6 networks [14]. This

H. Gao et al. (Eds.): CollaborateCom 2023, LNICST 563, pp. 347–364, 2024.
https://doi.org/10.1007/978-3-031-54531-3_19

has resulted in a significant increase in the demand for IPv6 domain name resolution. This implies that, for a foreseeable amount of time, with the continued existence of IPv4 network applications, both IPv4 and IPv6 will have strong domain name resolution demands.

As the actual executor of domain name resolution, the Domain Name System (DNS) plays an important role in the transition from IPv4 to IPv6. DNS mainly consists of three components [23], namely: the client that sends requests, the authoritative name server that holds domain name records, and the resolver, which is the most important component in DNS resolution. The resolver can be divided into the forwarder, which forwards DNS requests, and the recursive resolver, which asks authoritative name servers directly. Due to the vital role played by recursive resolvers, various modifications have been proposed for recursive resolvers to handle the IPv4/IPv6 transition [4,5]. One of the proposed solutions is to modify existing IPv4 resolvers, so that they can also perform IPv6 resolution, which is referred to as **dual-stack resolvers** [12].

However, the interdependence between IPv4 and IPv6 is prone to unknown security issues. The lagging deployment of firewall, filtering, and intrusion detection systems for IPv6 provides an alternative path for application layer attacks [17]. Dual-stack resolvers could be at serious security risk from DDoS attacks because IPv6 protocol requires larger packets than IPv4 [16]. Whether an attack against the IPv6 address of a DNS server impacts an organization's corresponding service for IPv4 depends on whether it is dual-stacked. Therefore, discovering the deployment of dual-stack resolvers is a highly meaningful task for both network operators and researchers. By having a comprehensive understanding of the status of dual-stack resolver deployments, network security professionals can recognize potential risks.

To discover dual-stack resolvers, some previous work [1,7] based on the assumption that *dual-stack resolvers have a pair of {IPv4, IPv6} addresses* to discover dual-stack resolvers from the relationship between IPv4 and IPv6 resolvers. Obviously, this assumption holds true if there is only one IPv4 or IPv6 address pointing to the host. However, because some hosts have multiple network interfaces, there can be multiple different IPv4 or IPv6 addresses pointing to the same host. These addresses are called *alias addresses*. Some work has shown that alias addresses are abundant in networks, especially IPv6 addresses [20,24]. This means that some resolvers could have multiple pairs of {$IPv4, IPv6$} addresses at the same time, but will never be discovered by previous methods. This creates a challenge for the discovery of dual-stack resolvers.

In this paper, we focus on recursive resolvers and propose a new dual-stack resolver discovery algorithm, DualDNSMiner. Unlike previous work, DualDNS-Miner will map multiple IPv4 (IPv6) alias addresses to the same IPv4 (IPv6) host by means of alias resolution. This makes the address relationship will be transformed into a host relationship. Thus, the criterion for a dual-stack resolver in DualDNSMiner is that **the resolver with a pair of {$IPv4, IPv6$} hosts** is dual-stacked. Our work makes three main contributions:

1 This is the first application of alias resolution method to solve the problem of dual-stack resolver discovery. The proposed discovery algorithm can

increase the resolver discovery rate by **more than 80%** compared to previous methods with relatively low cost. It helps to advance the analysis of DNS deployments during the IPv6 transition process.

2 We present a novel method for verifying whether a resolver is dual-stacked. In comparison to previous works that relied on verifying through IPv4&IPv6 addresses pattern similarity, our method offers a more reliable and data-supported approach for verification. This will facilitate the validation of the effectiveness of future works for the dual-stack resolver discovery.

3 Through our global measurements from two vantage points in different countries, our data suggests that close to 50% of known dual-stack resolvers have alias addresses. Owning more addresses indicates that dual-stack resolvers have more selectable data paths than previously thought, which increases the risk of being vulnerable to application layer attacks.

In Sect. 2, we will introduce some related works on the dual-stack resolver and alias address. In Sect. 3, we will present our innovative method, and in Sect. 4, we will compare the performance of our method and previous methods in practical detection. Section 5 & 6 provide our future work outlook and conclusion, respectively.

2 Related Work

2.1 Dual-Stack Resolver Discovery

To our knowledge, we are first one to achieve targeted discovery for dual-stack resolvers by leveraging their characteristics. However, some studies have observed the existence of associations between IPv4-IPv6 addresses of resolvers through CNAME redirection [7]. Al-Dalky *et al.* [1] referred to these addresses that have mutual association as a resolver collaborative pool and regarded pools that have only one IPv4 and one IPv6 address as dual-stack resolvers. They named this pool behavior as multi-port behavior and interpreted it as either a single multi-port machine or load balancing across resolver fields.

Some works have also made their own contributions to the discovery of dual-stack machines. Geoff *et al.* have tested 45 million clients by deploying dual-stack authoritative name servers [19]. The results show that 18% of clients use resolvers that can handle both IPv4 and IPv6 requests. Beverly *et al.* [8] focus on using TCP options and timestamps to identify IPv4 and IPv6 dual-stack machines, but this method have limitations when applied to DNS recursive resolvers. This techniques require TCP, which is a backup transmission protocol for DNS and not all TCP implementations support TCP timestamp options. Notably, our technique requires minimal support from the target resolver. Moreover, this method is primarily designed to determine whether a pair of IPv4 and IPv6 addresses are pointing to the same host. For situations that involve a larger number of addresses, the required probing cost for this method will increase exponentially. Our new algorithm, on the other hand, will complete the discrimination task in a more lightweight manner.

2.2 Alias Address

Alias addresses refer to a group of different addresses that point to the same host. Generally, an IP address represents an interface, and a machine may have multiple interfaces configured, and thus multiple addresses for the same host can be derived based on the interface. There has been a considerable amount of previous works on identifying IPv4 alias addresses [6,20], and the work by Murdock et al. [24] is the first to demonstrate the widespread existence of IPv6 alias addresses. Their data indicates that alias addresses are distributed across a considerable number of ASs. Some of these ASs belong to large network service providers such as Google, Cloudflare, and Akamai which are also major public DNS service providers.

3 Methodology

Taking into consideration the widespread existence of alias addresses, we confidently posit that a dual-stack resolver does not necessarily have only one IPv6 and one IPv4 address. In other words, the address relationship of a dual-stack resolver may be 1-N or even M-N. Based on this assumption, we have designed a novel dual-stack resolver discovery model called **DualDNSMiner**. The model's structure is illustrated as Fig. 1.

DualDNSMinner principally comprises of two steps. The first stage involves identifying the relationship between IPv4&IPv6 resolvers, and extracting address clusters that fulfill the requirements for determining the dual-stack resolvers, as well as their inter-relationships. The second step involves performing alias resolution on IPv4 and IPv6 addresses separately. Consequently, the address-address relationships can be converted into host-host relationships. Finally, the 1-1 host-host relationship will be identified, which represents the dual-stack resolvers recognized by DualDNSMiner.

3.1 Active DNS Measurements

It is essential to know the IPv4/IPv6 addresses owned by the dual-stack resolver first and confirm their correlation, so as to further confirm the possibility that they belong to the same host. We thus speculate on the relationship between IPv4 and IPv6 resolvers through active DNS measurement [7].

In DualDNSMiner, a prober actively probes the resolvers issuing specially crafted queries for DNS records for which we are authoritative. In this way, we control both the DNS probes and the authority of the DNS records being probed, thereby permitting testing of open DNS recursive resolvers in our dataset. Our authoritative domains are served by a custom DNS server that is standards compliant [13]. Our authoritative server listens on both IPv4 and IPv6, but returns different results depending upon the incoming request. The server handles multiple domains that support either IPv4 or IPv6 requests, where the choice of domain impacts the IP protocol used by a recursive resolver. We initiate queries

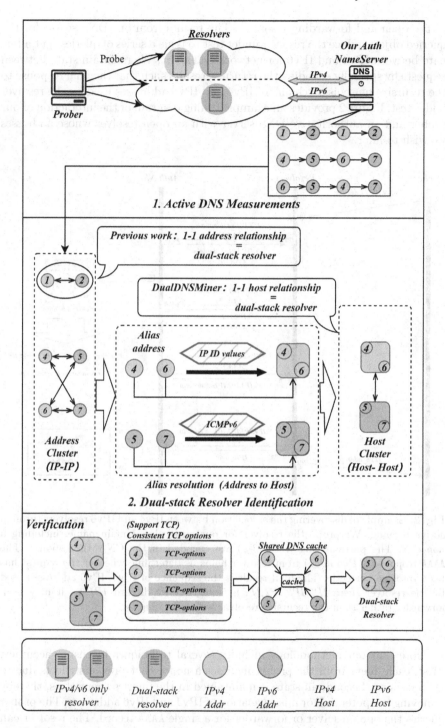

Fig. 1. The workflow of DualDNSMiner. The circle represents an address, and the rounded rectangle represents a machine with corresponding addresses.

to the open and forwarding resolvers. The results from our DNS server for the queried object induce the resolver under test to issue a series of queries that alternate between IPv4 and IPv6 for network transport. We maintain state between requests by specially encoding the returned results such that the final response to the recursive query is a "chain" of IPv4 and IPv6 addresses used by the resolver under test. Figure 2 provides an example timing diagram of the interaction of our prober and an authoritative DNS server with an open resolver whose addresses we wish to infer.

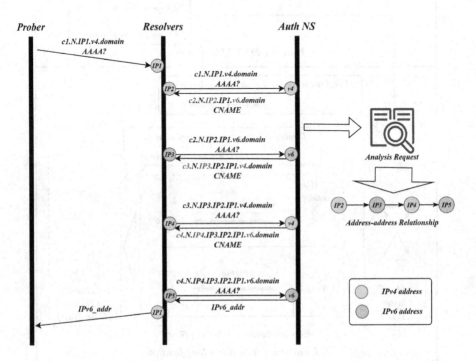

Fig. 2. Example of discovering the association between IPv4 and IPv6 resolvers through active probing. We probe the resolver for our particular domain name, including a nonce N. The participating IPs($IP2$-4) are encoded in the CNAME response. The AAAA response ($IPv6\_addr$) from resolver helps us determine whether the request has been resolved correctly. The final result is the sequence of IPv4, IPv6 addresses used by the resolver (here $IP2,IP3,IP4,IP5$). Note that we discard $IP1$, as it may be a forwarder rather than the recursive resolver we are looking for.

Note that our methodology includes several techniques to ensure accuracy. First, each query from the prober includes a nonce that prevents effects due to DNS caching. Second, all state is maintained in the queries themselves, thereby removing the potential for miscorrelation of IPv4 and IPv6 addresses. The prober queries the open resolver or forwarder for a single AAAA record. The resolver can only fetch this name using IPv4, but instead of returning the record's value, our server returns a canonical name (CNAME) alias. This CNAME encodes the IPv4 address which contacted our server; for example an IPv4 address 1.2.3.4 is encoded into the CNAME:

1-2-3-4.v6.domain.

This returned CNAME exists within the IPv6-only domain. The next CNAME redirects back to IPv4, encoding both IPs. After following another CNAME back to the IPv6 domain, our server finally returns a preset AAAA record. Note that while DNS authority servers may typically include multiple records in a single returned result, our server only returns one result at a time in order to force multiple lookups and infer the chain. The CNAME encoding scheme ensures that, even in the worst case ASCII IPv4 and IPv6 encoding expansion, the chains of length 4 are less than 512 bytes. As 512B is the limit for DNS over UDP, we ensure that the chains rely on neither truncation nor EDNS0 [26]. At the end of the domain name resolution, the authoritative DNS, notes the addresses contained in the requested domain (*IP2-IP4*), and notes the source address of the incoming query (*IP5*). The authoritative DNS then records this chain and returns the AAAA record that we set up in advance to allow the prober to check whether domain name resolution was successful or not.

As we will show in Sect. 4.2, many large-scale resolvers are actually clusters, not individual systems. A cluster might be behind a single publicly facing IP address with load distributed among multiple backend machines, or might encompass multiple publicly visible IP addresses. Thus, one can repeat the active DNS probes multiple times in order to gain a more complete picture of cluster structure when present. Since the DNS specification [13] requires that the recursive resolver process the entire CNAME chain, these four IP addresses should represent the same "system" responsible for completing the DNS resolution. The replies themselves have a 0 s TTL and the request contains a counter, thus a resolver should never cache the result.

Subsequently, DualDNSMiner merges the probing results (i.e. associations between addresses) to form a relational graph by merging same-IP nodes, as shown in Fig. 1. Strongly connected subgraphs are discovered from the relational graph in order to transform all the results into address clusters composed of different addresses. Since our objective is to discover dual-stack resolvers, DualDNSMiner will extracts address clusters satisfying specific conditions: **1) all addresses in the cluster belong to the same country; 2) all addresses in the cluster are managed by the same ISP.** Next, DualDNSMiner will perform alias resolution on these address clusters.

The active measurement forces the resolver to use IPv6 (instead of relying on a resolver's preference for IPv6 over IPv4). Since the measurements all occur within a short time window, this measurement is not affected by network changes. It also produces a set of up to four associations, allowing it to more effectively and precisely map the structure of a cluster resolver.

3.2 Dual-Stack Resolver Identification

This step is the core part of DualDNSMiner. Prior studies [1,7] regarded the addresses assigned to the same organization or company with 1-1 relationships as potential dual-stack resolvers, and attempted to evaluate their existence by assessing the similarity of address patterns between IPv4 and IPv6 addresses. Although this standard is simple, it has a flaw. As mentioned before, the relationships between v4-v6 resolvers discovered through active probing are address-address (or interface-interface) relationships that do not represent the host-host relationships. Due to the existence of alias addresses, different addresses can actually point to the same host, as Fig. 3 shows.

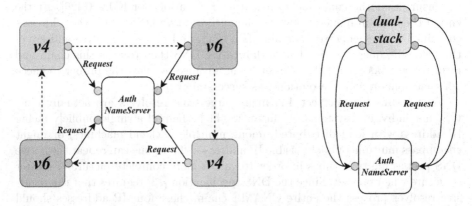

Fig. 3. The circle represents an address (interface), and the rounded rectangle represents a machine with corresponding interfaces. Active probing can reveal the relationship between dispersed address interfaces(left), but in reality, they may belong to the same dual-stack resolver(right).

Therefore, in order to determine whether a dual-stack resolver has these addresses, the addresses need to be took alias resolution. This will enable DualDNSMiner to convert the address-address relationships into host-host relationships. For any address cluster obtained in the first stage, DualDNSMiner employs different discrimination methods for the corresponding IPv4 and IPv6 addresses.

Alias Resolution for IPv4. The primary idea for alias resolution of IPv4 addresses utilizes IP identification (ID) values information within IPv4. Many routers generate IP ID values using a simple counter that is shared across interfaces on the router. If probe packets are simultaneously sent to two interface addresses of the same machine, it is possible to determine if they are generated by the same machine by inspecting the IP ID values in the response packets. This information can be used to confirm whether these IPv4 addresses are alias.

Ally [15], RadarGun [6], and MIDAR [20] all use this basic idea to detect aliases, but differ in how they detect shared counters. Since MIDAR is the first among the three to develop viable tools for conducting large-scale network topological analysis, we utilized MIDAR to perform alias resolution of IPv4 addresses within the address cluster.

Alias Resolution for IPv6. The protocol structure of IPv6 and IPv4 data packets is entirely dissimilar. The IPv6 protocol neither allows in-network packet fragmentation, nor the IPv6 header contains an identifier field similar to the IPv4. Thus, the method that relies on IP ID values cannot be applied to IPv6. Fortunately, the IPv6 protocol provides support for end-host fragmentation, and the end-host has the responsibility to maintain the PMTU status. If a prober tricks fragmentation for one address of a host, when the prober sends ICMPv6 Echo Requests of the same size to other addresses under the same host within a short time, those addresses will also respond to the fragmented packets. Building upon this concept, Beverly [9] *et al.* proposed to obtain the fragment identification of the interface by sending the ICMPv6 Packet Too Big message. Similarly, we have optimized the original probe steps to enable DualDNSMiner to handle large-scale IPv6 alias resolution tasks. Algorithm 1 represents our IPv6 alias resolution process.

Algorithm 1. isv6aliases(C): Determine whether the IPv6 addresses in the cluster C corresponds to the same machine

---

Require: Active IPv6 addresses in the cluster C
Ensure: Collection of addresses for the same machine M
1: **while** C is not null **do**
2:     $M+=1$
3:     sendTooBig(C_0)
4:     **if** IsFrag(C_0) **then**
5:         **for** $i = 1$ to $length(C)$ **do**
6:             sendEcho(C_i)
7:             **if** IsFrag(C_i) **then**
8:                 $\{IP_M\} \leftarrow C_i$
9:                 DELETE(C,C_i)
10:             **end if**
11:         **end for**
12:     **end if**
13:     DELETE(C,C_0)
14: **end while**
15: **return** $\{\{IP_M\},\{IP_{M+1}\},...\}$

Specifically, the IPv6 addresses in an address cluster will be treated as a single set. First, DualDNSMiner collects the status of all addresses in the set (whether they respond, whether they are fragmented, and the size of their PMTU) by sending ICMPv6 echo requests. Then it performs alias resolution in a loop. During each iteration, we send a Packet Too Big packet to the first address in the set and check if its response characteristics change (whether it responds, is fragmented, and the size of fragmentation). It sends echo request packets to other addresses and checks if their responses also change simultaneously. All IPv6 addresses that change simultaneously will be extracted as addresses of the same host and removed from the set. This process continues until the set is empty, completing the IPv6 alias resolution of the address cluster.

Identification. The host-to-host relationship is a crucial criterion for DualDNS-Miner to determine whether a set of addresses belongs to the same dual-stack resolver. After conducting alias resolution of the IPv4 and IPv6 addresses in different address clusters, DualDNSMiner will be able to group one or more addresses into a single host. This allows us to convert one or more IP nodes into a single host node in the original association graph obtained from active measurement. As a result, DualDNSMiner can obtain cooperative relationships between IPv4 and IPv6 hosts, yielding a cooperative association graph at the host level.

We believe that for a dual-stack resolver, it can only be abstracted as a $\{IPv4, IPv6\}$ host pair at the IP protocol level, and it cannot form multiple pairs (which means there are at least two different machines in it). Based on this concept, a dual-stack resolver's feature in the graph should exhibit **a stable association between an IPv4 host and an IPv6 host without a third one**. Therefore, DualDNSMiner searches for such host relationships to identify dual-stack resolvers and complete the discovery task. The addresses corresponding to the IPv4 and IPv6 hosts included in the relationship are the ones that point to the same dual-stack resolver.

4   Result

4.1   Data Sets

We first need to discover and collect the relationship between IPv4/IPv6 resolvers as our dataset by actively sending DNS query requests. In order to ensure the accuracy of the experiment, we rent two virtual private servers (VPS) in the America and China as our vantage points. All IPv4 open resolvers are tested by sending DNS query request packets to all globally reachable IPv4 addresses through these points. The observation time and collection results of each vantage point are shown in the Table 1.

Through active measurement experiments conducted across the entire IPv4 address space, we discover 77,709 unique recursive resolvers (addresses that send DNS requests to our authoritative servers) based on 895,702 open resolvers (addresses that could return DNS responses). Of these resolvers, 12,602 are IPv6 addresses and 65,107 are IPv4 addresses. After conducting strong connected subgraph detection, we identify 6,987 address clusters. By filtering the

Table 1. Configuration of the measurement and the result of the collected IPv4&IPv6 resolver address from name server's log. Note that the collected addresses all belong to recursive resolvers.

Vantage Point	Collection Period	IPv4	IPv6	Notes
Hong Kong, China	Apr. 19 to May. 27, 2023	64,421	12,059	10 repeated tests to global IPv4 open resolvers.
California, USA	Apr. 1 to 5, 2023	64,839	12,206	5 repeated tests to global IPv4 open resolvers.
Sum		65,107	12,602	Removing duplicate values from the results obtained at different vantage points

clusters according to the rule that all addresses in the cluster are located in the same country and managed by the same ISP, we narrow down the clusters to 2,184. All subsequent data analysis and DualDNSMiner's dual-stack resolver discovery results are based on these address clusters.

Based on the exploration results, we conduct comparative experiments to demonstrate the highlights of DualDNSMiner. In this section, we will introduce the experimental results and explain some of our findings.

4.2   Relationship Between IPv4-IPv6 Resolvers

1-1. The 1-1 IPv4-IPv6 relationship has always been considered as the primary feature of dual-stack resolvers. Our data reveals 741 address clusters that consisted of an IPv4 and IPv6 address. By comparing IPv4 and IPv6 address strings, we found that 279 address clusters had IPv6 addresses with the IPv4 address **directly** embedded in (e.g., 1.2.3.4 & abcd::1:2:3:4), while 84 IPv6 addresses with IPv4 **hex encoded** and embedded (e.g., 1.2.3.4 & abcd::0102:0304). This discovery led us to a conclusion similar to that of Al-Dalky's work [1], which is that there is a certain similarity between IPv4 and IPv6 addresses in the 1-1 relationship. This similarity may be due to special customization by network or resolver administrators to facilitate addressing.

1-N. The 1-N relationship is the primary focus of our DualDNSMiner. This relationship only requires alias resolution of N addresses to determine whether it is a dual-stack resolver. This is simpler than determining the M-N relationship (which is more likely to be caused by load balance) and is therefore more likely to discover new dual-stack resolvers. Our data reveals 938 address clusters that consisted of multiple addresses and are divided according to the IP protocol at a ratio of 1:N.

In addition, we also compare the distribution of addresses in each cluster. Out of the 938 address clusters, 644 are of the $1[IPv6]$-N$[IPv4]$ type, while 294 are of the $1[IPv4]$-N$[IPv6]$ type. Furthermore, the maximum N value in the former type is larger than that in the latter type (195 vs. 13). Obviously, compared with IPv6 resolvers, IPv4 resolvers are more concentrated and tend to choose the same IPv6 resolvers to complete domain name resolution tasks. It is more likely due to forwarding upstream by the resolver. For example, RFC3901 [11] provides a solution in which IPv4-only resolvers forward requests for IPv6-only domain names to dual-stack resolvers to complete the domain name resolution. Fortunately, only 47 address clusters had an N value greater than 10, which did not significantly affect the effectiveness of DualDNSMiner.

M-N. The association between IPv4 and IPv6 resolvers is extremely complex in some address clusters. Our data has revealed that 505 address clusters are composed of no less than one IPv4 and one IPv6 address, with the most common M-N combination being 2-2, as shown in the Table 2. The IPv4 and IPv6 addresses in these combinations exhibit similarity in address string patterns similar to the 1-1 relationship.

Table 2. The top 5 most numerous association and clusters with the most address in M-N

No.	$M - N$	Count	ISP	$M - N$
1	2-2	203	Chunghwa Telecom	317-623
2	3-2	47	Telmex Colombia	559-2
3	4-2	46	CAT Telecom	537-5
4	2-3	39	BIZNET NETWORKS	527-10
5	5-2	37	Chunghwa Telecom	109-398

Furthermore, we also have observed that there are some large address clusters, although they are highly unlikely to be dual-stack resolvers (as it is unusual to configure hundreds of IP addresses on a single machine). In these clusters, the proportion of IPv4 and IPv6 addresses is highly uneven. In the top five large clusters, three ones have over 50 IPv4 addresses for every IPv6 address. Such a large difference demonstrates the imbalance in DNS resolution. On the one hand, this may be due to IPv6 addresses pointing to resolver clusters much larger than those for IPv4. Thereby, the two are balanced in terms of hardware resources. On the other hand, it may be caused by defective IPv6 adaptation configurations.

4.3   Dual-Stack Resolver

Due to the current lack of publicly available datasets for dual-stack DNS resolvers, it is essential to employ appropriate verification methods to ascertain the accuracy of the results. Previous work [1,7] cannot prove whether the resolvers are dual-stacked by using the IPv4&IPv6 addresses pattern similarity method. To accurately discover dual-stack resolvers, we propose an active verification method by using the TCP options and cache sharing situations.

On one hand, the efficacy of TCP option-based techniques in detecting dual-stack servers has been demonstrated [8]. We believe that it can also accurately validate DualDNSMiner's dual-stack resolver discovery results. However, this method is only applicable to TCP, not to UDP, which is mainly used by DNS. This makes it impossible for us to accurately verify that resolvers are really dual-stack if they don't support the TCP protocol.

On the other hand, since dual-stack resolvers typically use a single component to simultaneously listen for requests on IPv4/IPv6 addresses, they could use the same cache to speed up resolution unless there is special customization [10]. Therefore, we can also verify whether it is a dual-stack resolver by whether the cache is shared between IPv4/IPv6 resolvers. For each pair of IPv4 and IPv6 addresses, both addresses are queried for the same qname, based on a hash of both addresses and the measurement timestamp:

h($ipv4$ipv6$timestamp).cachecheck.ourdomain.

This query is performed twice over IPv4, and twice over IPv6. All the four queries are 5 s apart. Based on the TTL values in the answers, we can determine whether the resolver is actually caching on any or both of the protocols, and whether that cache is shared. However, it should be pointed out that some works have shown that about 10% to 20% of resolvers will share the same cache server [21]. This means that this method has a certain percentage of false positives, so it cannot completely replace the TCP option-based method. Therefore, we only verify whether the parser that does not support TCP is dual-stack by judging whether IPv4/IPv6 share the cache.

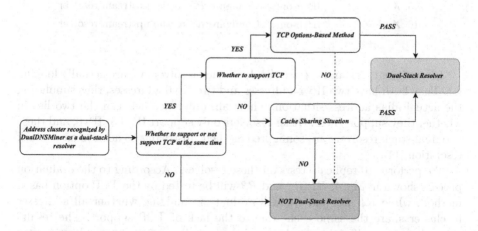

Fig. 4. The process of verifying whether the recognition result of DualDNSMiner is correct.

In summary, our verification method is as follows: First, we will check whether the resolvers (IPv4&IPv6) in a cluster support TCP consistently (all support or none). For clusters that all resolvers support TCP, verify whether they are dual-stack based on TCP options; and for clusters that none of the resolvers support TCP, verify whether they are dual-stack by checking whether resolvers in the cluster use the same cache; and for clusters that support inconsistent (Some resolvers are supported while others are not), which is obviously caused by different operating systems or different configurations of DNS services, so they can be considered as non-dual-stack. The entire verification process is shown in the Fig. 4.

Ground Truth Validation. Before verifying whether the result of DualDNS-Miner is correct, we need to test whether our verification method is reliable. We build 12 different resolvers as the ground truth in the docker environment using bind9 [25] and unbound [22]. The specifics of each resolver (use bind9) are shown in the Table 3. There are also 6 resolvers deployed with unbound using similar configurations. All resolvers enable caching and are built through the docker image of ubuntu [18].

Table 3. Configuration of our resolvers in docker.

ID	TCP Support	Type	Note
R1	✔	dual-stack	2 IPv4 & 2 IPv6 addresses
R2	✔	IPv4-only	Configure R1 as the upstream resolver
R3	✔	IPv6-only	Configure R1 as the upstream resolver
R4	✗	dual-stack	2 IPv4 & 2 IPv6 addresses
R5	✗	IPv4-only	Configure R4 as the upstream resolver
R6	✗	IPv6-only	Configure R4 as the upstream resolver

In particular, R1 and R4 are the dual-stack resolvers we are actually looking for. They both have two IPv4 addresses and two IPv6 addresses, thus simulating the actual alias address situation. The main difference between the two lies in whether they support TCP. Other resolvers only support IPv4 or IPv6, and these two dual-stack resolvers are configured as their upstreams to achieve cross-stack resolution [11].

We perform 10 replicate tests on these resolvers. According to the evaluation process shown in Fig. 4, R1, R2 and R3 will be tested by the TCP option-based method, while R4, R5 and R6 will evaluate by judging whether all addresses in cluster share the same cache due to the lack of TCP support. The results show that our verification method can successfully identify the address cluster (2 IPv4 + 2 IPv6) of R1 or R3 as the dual-stack resolver every time, while other resolvers be judged that their address cluster do not belong to one machine. This shows that the addresses of these resolvers do not belong to a dual-stack resolver, which also shows that our verification method is reliable.

However, it needs to be pointed out that although our verification method can accurately identify the dual-stack resolver, the TCP option-based method itself needs to send a large number of probe packets to confirm whether a pair of IPv4 and IPv6 addresses belong to the same host. As we will show later, this method is much less efficient for large-scale dual-stack resolver discovery than our DualDNSMiner. Therefore, we only use this method as the result verification. In fact, our results also show that DualDNSMiner can also quite accurately discover dual-stack resolvers.

Real-World Results. We compare the practical effectiveness of DualDNS-Miner with the 1-1 address relationship judgment rule used in previous works, and verify the results, which are shown in Table 5 in the Appendix A.

As shown in Table 5, DualDNSMiner further improves the discovery efficiency of dual-stack resolvers. Compared to previous methods, it can discover **over 80%** more possible dual-stack resolvers from 1-N and M-N address relationships. Moreover, the validation experiments indicate that DualDNSMiner also achieves a high accuracy rate (**over 90%**) for dual-stack resolver determination results. However, it is worth noting that DualDNSMiner and the new validation method are still unable to confirm some address clusters whether they are dual-stack resolvers. This is caused by the response or deployment characteristics of hosts in these clusters, such as the lack of TCP timestamp options or the lack of expected responses or changes after sending ICMPv6 Too Big packets.

We also analyze the distribution of IPv4 and IPv6 addresses in the 1,237 address clusters that are verified as dual-stack resolvers(**TCP option & share cache**), as shown in Table 4. A significant number of dual-stack resolvers with multiple IPv4/IPv6 addresses have been overlooked in previous work. Quite a few dual-stack resolvers have the same number of IPv4 and IPv6 addresses or more IPv4 addresses. We believe this is caused by all or some of the interfaces owned by the IPv4 resolver being assigned corresponding IPv6 addresses.

Table 4. Statistics on the address associations in different dual-stack resolvers.

No.	M − N	Count	No.	M − N	Count
1	1-1	735	6	1-3	39
2	2-1	134	7	3-2	30
3	1-2	127	8	3-1	24
4	2-2	49	9	2-3	23
5	3-3	47	10	4-2	19

Furthermore, in terms of discovery efficiency, the TCP option requires sending TCP packets to judge the **63,907** pairs of IPv4 and IPv6 address relationships in all address clusters. In comparison, in our experiments, DNSMiner only sent **49,823** packets to complete the alias resolution of the same address clusters. The discrimination process is based on the results of alias resolution, no request packets need to be sent. Therefore, DualDNSMiner can discover dual-stack resolvers from large-scale address relationships at a **lower cost**, improving actual discovery efficiency.

5   Future Work

DualDNSMiner has successfully excavated more dual-stack resolvers in DNS with traditional methods based on 1-1 addresses relationship, thereby advancing IPv6 DNS measurement efforts. However, due to a few addresses retaining their original response packet characteristics even after receiving a Too Big packet, DualDNSMiner cannot perform alias resolution on them. These addresses cannot be determined as a separate address or a host shared with other addresses. Consequently, a considerable portion of the address clusters in our experimental results remain *Unknown* (Table 5). We will endeavor to explore alternative methods to address this issue in our future work.

6   Conclusion

In this paper, our focus is on the recognition task of dual-stack DNS resolvers. Unlike previous works, we aim to discover dual-stack resolvers from the more complex relationship of IPv4-IPv6 name servers. We introduce a novel technology named DualDNSMiner, and apply it to practical measurements. This technique primarily utilizes alias resolution to transform address-address relationships obtained through active probing into host-host relationships, thus allowing the detection of dual-stack resolvers. We have also proposed a validation method to examine the accuracy of DualDNSMiner's results through data-driven means. The results indicate that compared with traditional dual-stack resolver discovery algorithms, DualDNSMiner can improve the discovery rate by over 80%, and the accuracy of DualDNSMiner's detection results exceeds 90%. Furthermore, DualDNSMiner's recognition results reveal that a considerable number of dual-stack resolvers have multiple IPv4 and IPv6 addresses. In the future, we will continue our research to find a more effective dual-stack DNS resolver discovery method.

Acknowledgment. This work is supported by the Strategic Priority Research Program of the Chinese Academy of Sciences with No. XDC02030400, the National Key Research and Development Program of China with No. 2021YFB3101001 and No. 2021YFB3101403.

A   Discovery and Verification Results

Table 5. Comparison of DualDNSMiner with previous methods, and verification of results.

Experiment	Method	1-1	1-1 Unknown	1-N	1-N Unknown	M-N	M-N Unknown	Not Dual
Comparison	Previous method [1,7]	741	0	✗	✗	✗	✗	1443
	DualDNSMiner	**741**	0	**411**	227	**218**	106	481
Verification	TCP Option [8]	646/741	89/741	332/411	19/411	141/218	12/218	131
	Share Cache(Not Support TCP)	89/89	0	18/19	0	11/12	0	2
	TCP Option & Share Cache	**735/741**	0	**350/411**	0	**152/218**	0	133

References

1. Al-Dalky, R., Schomp, K.: Characterization of collaborative resolution in recursive DNS resolvers. In: Beverly, R., Smaragdakis, G., Feldmann, A. (eds.) Passive and Active Measurement. Lecture Notes in Computer Science(), vol. 10771, pp. 146–157. Springer, Cham (2018). https://doi.org/10.1007/978-3-319-76481-8_11
2. APNIC: Ipv6 capable rate by country. https://stats.labs.apnic.net/ipv6/
3. APNIC: Use of ipv6 for world (XA). https://stats.labs.apnic.net/IPv6/XA
4. Bagnulo, M., García-Martínez, A., Van Beijnum, I.: The NAT64/DNS64 tool suite for IPv6 transition. IEEE Commun. Mag. **50**(7), 177–183 (2012)
5. Bagnulo, M., Sullivan, A., Matthews, P., Van Beijnum, I.: DNS64: DNS extensions for network address translation from IPv6 clients to ipv4 servers. Technical report (2011)
6. Bender, A., Sherwood, R., Spring, N.: Fixing ally's growing pains with velocity modeling. In: Proceedings of the 8th ACM SIGCOMM Conference On Internet Measurement, pp. 337–342 (2008)
7. Berger, A., Weaver, N., Beverly, R.: Internet nameserver IPv4 and IPv6 address relationships, pp. 91–104. Association for Computing Machinery (ACM), New York (2013). 10(2504730.2504745)
8. Beverly, R., Berger, A.: Server siblings: Identifying shared IPv4/IPv6 infrastructure via active fingerprinting. In: Mirkovic, J., Liu, Y. (eds.) Passive and Active Measurement. Lecture Notes in Computer Science(), vol. 8995, pp. 149–161. Springer, Cham (2015). https://doi.org/10.1007/978-3-319-15509-8_12
9. Beverly, R., Brinkmeyer, W., Luckie, M., Rohrer, J.P.: IPv6 alias resolution via induced fragmentation. In: Roughan, M., Chang, R. (eds.) Passive and Active Measurement. Lecture Notes in Computer Science, vol. 7799, pp. 155–165. Springer, Berlin, Heidelberg (2013). https://doi.org/10.1007/978-3-642-36516-4_16
10. CoreDNS.io: CoreDNS-cache. https://coredns.io/plugins/cache/
11. Durand, A., Ihren, J.: DNS IPv6 transport operational guidelines. Technical report (2004)
12. Durand, A., Droms, R., Lee, Y., Woodyatt, J.: Dual-stack lite broadband deployments following IPv4 exhaustion. RFC 6333 (2011). https://doi.org/10.17487/RFC6333, https://www.rfc-editor.org/info/rfc6333

13. Elz, R., Bush, R.: RFC2181: clarifications to the DNS specification (1997)
14. Google: IPv6. https://www.google.com/intl/en/ipv6/statistics.html
15. Gunes, M.H., Sarac, K.: Analytical IP alias resolution. In: 2006 IEEE International Conference on Communications, vol. 1, pp. 459–464. IEEE (2006)
16. Hendriks, L., Oliveira Schmidt, R.D., Rijswijk-Deij, R.V., Pras, A.: On the potential of IPv6 open resolvers for DDoS attacks. In: Kaafar, M., Uhlig, S., Amann, J. (eds.) Passive and Active Measurement. Lecture Notes in Computer Science(), vol. 10176, pp. 17–29. Springer, Cham (2017). https://doi.org/10.1007/978-3-319-54328-4_2
17. Hu, Q., Asghar, M.R., Brownlee, N.: Measuring IPv6 DNS reconnaissance attacks and preventing them using DNS guard. In: 2018 48th Annual IEEE/IFIP International Conference on Dependable Systems and Networks (DSN), pp. 350–361. IEEE (2018)
18. Hub, D.: ubuntu-official images. https://hub.docker.com/ubuntu
19. Huston, G.: IPv6 and the DNS. https://labs.apnic.net/?p=1343
20. Keys, K., Hyun, Y., Luckie, M., Claffy, K.: Internet-scale IPv4 alias resolution with MIDAR. IEEE/ACM Trans. Networking **21**(2), 383–399 (2012)
21. Klein, A., Shulman, H., Waidner, M.: Internet-wide study of DNS cache injections. In: IEEE INFOCOM 2017-IEEE Conference on Computer Communications, pp. 1–9. IEEE (2017)
22. Labs, N.: NLnet labs-unbound-about. https://nlnetlabs.nl/projects/unbound/about/
23. Mockapetris, P.V.: RFC1035: domain names-implementation and specification (1987)
24. Murdock, A., Li, F., Bramsen, P., Durumeric, Z., Paxson, V.: Target generation for internet-wide IPv6 scanning. In: Proceedings of the 2017 Internet Measurement Conference, pp. 242–253 (2017)
25. Okamoto, T., Tarao, M.: Implementation and evaluation of an immunity-enhancing module for ISC BIND9. Procedia Comput. Sci. **126**, 1405–1414 (2018)
26. Vixie, P.: Extension mechanisms for DNS (EDNS0). Technical report (1999)

DT-MUSA: Dual Transfer Driven Multi-source Domain Adaptation for WEEE Reverse Logistics Return Prediction

Ruiqi Liu[1,2], Min Gao[1,2]([✉]), Yujiang Wu[1,2], Jie Zeng[2], Jia Zhang[2],
and Jinyong Gao[3]

[1] Key Laboratory of Dependable Service Computing in Cyber Physical Society
(Chongqing University), Ministry of Education, Chongqing 401331, China
{liuruiqi,wuyujiang}@stu.cqu.edu.cn

[2] School of Big Data and Software Engineering, Chongqing University, Chongqing
401331, China
{gaomin,zengjie,jiazhang}@cqu.edu.cn

[3] Aibo Green Reverse Supply Chain Co., Ltd., Shenzhen 518000, China
gjy@boolv.com

Abstract. Reverse logistics (RL) return prediction for Waste Electrical and Electronic Equipment (WEEE) has gained attention due to its potential to improve operational efficiency in the recycling industry. However, in data-scarce regions, commonly used deep learning models perform poorly. Existing multi-source cross-domain transfer learning models can partially overcome data scarcity by using historical data from multiple sources. However, these models aggregate multi-source domain data into a single-source domain in transfer, ignoring the differences in time series features among source domains. Additionally, the lack of historical data in the target domain makes fine-tuning the prediction model inoperative. To address these issues, we propose Dual Transfer Driven Multi-Source domain Adaptation (DT-MUSA) for WEEE RL return prediction. DT-MUSA includes a dual transfer model that combines sample transfer and model transfer and a basic prediction model MUCAN (Multi-time Scale CNN-Attention Network). It employs a multi-task learning to aggregate predictors from multiple regions and avoids negative transfer learning. The dual transfer model enables fine-tuning of the base model MUCAN by generating long-term time series data through sample transfer. We applied DT-MUSA to real cases of an RL recycling company and conducted extensive experiments. The results show that DT-MUSA outperforms baseline prediction models significantly.

Keywords: waste electrical and electronic equipment · reverse logistics return predction · dual transfer learning · multi-task learning

© ICST Institute for Computer Sciences, Social Informatics and Telecommunications Engineering 2024
Published by Springer Nature Switzerland AG 2024. All Rights Reserved
H. Gao et al. (Eds.): CollaborateCom 2023, LNICST 563, pp. 365–384, 2024.
https://doi.org/10.1007/978-3-031-54531-3_20

1   Introduction

As reported by the United Nations University, only about 20% of the 44.7 million tons of WEEE generated worldwide each year undergo proper recycling and treatment [13,29]. If not properly treated promptly, the leaching of hazardous substances from a large volume of WEEE can pose significant risks to the environment and human health [7,30,32]. The use of RL return data prediction can enhance the efficiency of WEEE RL by supporting transportation scheduling, labor and material scheduling, and production planning for reverse recycling efforts [4,14,25]. Therefore, the RL return prediction of WEEE has received widespread attention [11,16].

[15,38] earlier investigated RL return prediction based on regression equations. A Bayesian-based prediction model developed by [34] assumed that RL flows obey a binomial probability distribution. [23] modeled RL return prediction by analytical moving averages, exponential smoothing, and causal analysis. These studies considered the time-series relationship of the data and achieved good results under certain applicable conditions. However, the models are extremely dependent on feature selection, and different modeling is required for different application scenarios, leading to difficulties in applying to complex scenarios. To be able to build an RL prediction model with generalization ability, [40] recently proposed a deep learning-based multi-time scale attention network (MULAN). By dividing the closeness window, period window, and trend window in the historical data as model inputs, this approach is able to capture various features at different time scales of the series. As a result, there is a significant improvement in the accuracy of the prediction. However, the prediction accuracy of MULAN is severely degraded in some scenarios lacking long-term history data (see Sect. 5.1), because historical data are scarce and trend window inputs are not available.

To improve model performance in historical data lacking scenarios, researchers proposed transfer learning that learns knowledge from selected sufficient data related to the target domain with sparse samples [5,12,26]. However, in RL prediction scenarios, the distribution of source and target domain data may differ significantly due to geographical and temporal differences, leading to severe negative transfer [28,39]. Many recent studies have tried to employ multi-source data adaptive transfer learning in the expectation that pre-trained networks can extract richer sets of common features in multiple source domains and overcome the differences in data distribution from source to target domains [6,10]. These methods can be used to predict RL return data in the data-lacking scenario, but there are still two challenges.

The first challenge is how to utilize multi-source data effectively to mitigate negative transfer. In a multi-source knowledge transfer learning task, the distribution of data in each source domain varies, and therefore, their contributions to the target domain task should be adjusted accordingly, so a key issue is how to adaptively aggregate the source domain predictors [3,33]. Traditional studies generally assign weights to source domains or select source domains subjectively and directly by domain similarity [1,9,17]. However, existing two-stage learning methods (involving domain selection and model transfer) lack adaptive algorithms capable of accurately quantifying the similarity between the source and target domains in relation to the assigned weights.

The second challenge is the lack of long-term time series data leading to suboptimal fine-tuning of model transfer, especially when the base prediction model for transfer needs to extract the features from multi-time scale windows. That is because trend data cannot be used in this case, and the multi-time window input structure does not have sufficient windows of data, leading to suboptimal fine-tuning of the model transfer eg. MULAN [40].

To this end, we propose Dual Transfer Driven Multi-source Domain Adaptation (DT-MUSA). In DT-MUSA, (1) we first propose a multi-source domain adaptation scheme based on multi-task learning to avoid the possible negative transfer effects caused by subjective source domain predictors aggregation. We compute the similarity between the data in the source and target domains and prioritize the source domains for labeling. After that, we use a multi-task learning strategy to perform association learning on the data from source domains and dynamically integrate the prediction loss of each source domain during pretraining. The model can adaptively aggregate the source domain predictors during multi-task association learning to minimize negative transfer by learning the mutual base model parameters in the shared layer of all tasks. (2) We propose a dual transfer model (model and sample transfer) and a base prediction model MUCAN (Multi-time Scale CNN-Attention Network) to tackle the suboptimal fine-tuning of the model transfer due to long-term time series data scarcity. First, we employ a sample transfer strategy to generate long-term time series data. Then, we build a specialized multi-scale time-series feature extraction network, referred to as MUCAN, which is built upon the convolutional attention module and utilizes a multi-time scale input window structure. This serves as the foundation for our dual transfer prediction model. Finally, we use the pretrained network of the source domain set for model transfer, initialize the shared layer parameters of MUCAN in the target domain, and then fine-tune the shared layer parameters of the model to better adapt to the data distribution present in the target domain.

In summary, our main contributions are as follows:

- We propose a novel approach to multi-source domain adaptation that utilizes multi-task learning to acquire mutual knowledge from various source domains. As far as we know, this is the first study to employ multi-task learning to mitigate possible negative transfer effects in the field of RL time series prediction.
- We propose a dual transfer model, where sample transfer is used to generate long-term time series of the target domain, and model transfer is utilized to effectively transfer mutual knowledge obtained from multiple source domains in multi-source domain adaptation. In addition, we propose a base prediction model MUCAN for model transfer, which relies on the convolutional attention module to obtain the degree of influence of different time-scale encodings on prediction and has better results than other network structures in encoding fusion.

- To evaluate the effectiveness of our model DT-MUSA, we apply it to a real-world case involving an enterprise specializing in RL returns. Through extensive experiments and ablation experiments, we analyze the benefits of utilizing multi-task learning for multi-source knowledge fusion and utilizing the dual transfer model.

2 Related Works

To overcome the distributional disparity between source and target domain data in transfer learning, and enhance the transfer effect. In the last decade, many research results on domain adaptation in transfer learning have been published. Shallow domain adaptation methods are typically used to establish a connection between the source and target domains by either learning invariant features or estimating the importance of instances from the source domain [20]. For example, [22] used a modified Transfer Naive Bayes (TNB) as a prediction model. They employed a similarity measure based on ranges to allocate weights to source domain instances, and subsequently trained the prediction model using these weighted instances. [24] proposed TCA+ to reduce the differences in the distribution of features that make the source and target domains.

With the rising prevalence of deep neural networks, there has been an increasing interest in investigating deep domain adaptation techniques. This type of method utilizes an adaptive module embedded in the deep architecture to minimize differences between the source and target domains. [19,35] proposed the DDC (Deep Domain Confusion) method and DAN (Deep Adaptation Network), respectively, which diminish the dissimilarity between source and target domains by introducing an adaptive adaptation layer or an additional domain confusion loss. Later, [21] extended DAN by proposing Joint Adaptation Network (JAN), which further considers the joint probability distribution of features and labels. [28] introduce a novel deep Transfer Learning based on Transformer (TLT) model that utilizes a recurrent fine-tuning transfer learning approach during the pre-training phase of knowledge transfer. The purpose is to prevent deep learning models from overfitting the source data and reduce domain gap between the source and target domains in transfer learning tasks.

Multi-source Domain Adaptation (MDA) is a powerful extension to Domain Adaptation (DA) that can collect labeled data from multiple sources with different distributions. With the success of DA methods and the widespread use of multi-source data, MDA has gained growing attention from both academia and industry. [17] proposed TPTL based on TCA+ to automatically select the two source items that have the closest match with the target domain distribution. After that, the two prediction models are constructed separately, and their predictions are combined to improve the prediction performance further. A Multi-Source Adaptive Network (MSAN) based on multiple GAN architectures [2] can effectively learn the bidirectional transfer between the source and target domains, thus reducing the distribution differences. A joint feature space is also introduced to guide the multi-level consistency constraint of all transformations to maintain consistent domain patterns during the adaptive process and simultaneously empower the recognition of unlabeled target samples. To address the cross-project defect prediction task, [1] proposed 3SW-MSTL, which did exploratory work in three directions, namely, the number of source domains, source domain instance weights, and multi-source data utilization scheme using conditional distribution information.

These ideas still have room for improvement in the RL return prediction task. When the data of the target domain is sparse, the data sparsity problem can be alleviated by using data from multiple source domains. However, the above model ignores mutual time series features among source domains in the design of multi-source domain predictors aggregation, which can be affected by negative transfer resulting in suboptimal performance. To this end, we propose DT-MUSA to solve the RL return prediction task. The model DT-MUSA will be introduced in the following section.

3   Methodology

3.1   Overview

Faced with the task of predicting RL return in the target domain, we are faced with the following challenges: (1) Difficulty in the aggregation of multi-source domain predictors leads to a negative transfer effect. Leveraging knowledge from multiple sources can improve prediction accuracy. However, minimizing knowledge conflicts and distribution differences between multiple source domains and the target domain presents a significant challenge in domain adaptation, which can adversely affect the transfer effect. What kind of source domain aggregation strategy can we adopt to avoid negative transfer effectively? (2) Long-term data scarcity leads to suboptimal fine-tuning of model transfer. The multi-time-window input structure is crucial to fully extract the regular features of the RL return time series. However, the data scarcity in the target domain leads to the lack of trend data input to the model, which makes the transfer ineffective. How can we improve the neural network structure or refine the model inputs to improve the model transfer effect?

To address the above challenges, we propose DT-MUSA as shown in Fig. 1, which consists of a multi-source domain adaptation module multi-task learning based, and a dual transfer module based on the feature extraction network MUCAN.

- Multi-source domain adaptation algorithm based on multi-task learning.
  - Possible ways to select the appropriate source domain for domain adaptation: The source domains are given priority by estimating the similarity between the data distribution of each source domain and that of the target domain. After that, the model is pre-trained on the source domains within the priority threshold to overcome the distribution differences between source and target domains.
  - Multi-task learning based multi-source predictor aggregation: Pre-training is performed in the source domain set using multi-task learning, with knowledge shared among source domains. The model adaptively

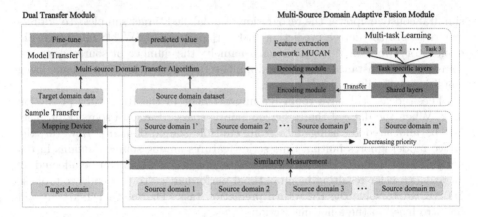

Fig. 1. Overall architecture of the DT-MUSA. Given m source domains with abundant historical data and current target domain historical data for prediction of future RL in the target domain, the DT-MUSA consists of a multi-source domain adaptation module based on multi-task learning and a dual transfer module based on feature extraction network MUCAN.

adjusts the weight distribution among the tasks to continuously learn the public knowledge, which is updated and retained within the shared layer to increase the amount of positive transfer knowledge.

– Dual transfer model based on feature extraction network MUCAN.
  • The base model MUCAN for transfer learning: A multi-scale time-series feature extraction network MUCAN is built specifically for RL regression prediction by combining a convolutional attention module and a multi-time scale window structure. MUCAN can accommodate the efficient transfer of source domain knowledge and the complete extraction of target domain features in model transfer.
  • Dual transfer algorithm combining sample transfer and model transfer: The data in the target domain are set as the direction of sample transfer, and the mapper is trained to fill the missing trend window data in the target domain. Model transfer with fine-tuned parameters is subsequently employed to complete the transfer of public knowledge and enhance the model's generalization ability.

3.2 Possible Ways to Select the Appropriate Source Domain for Domain Adaptation

The data features learned in the source domain can be effectively transferred to the target domain when the sufficient distributional similarity between the source and target domain data is satisfied. Otherwise, the source domain will transfer more knowledge carrying negative effects to the target domain, which will bring some adverse effects on transfer learning. Therefore, we introduce the domain similarity estimation algorithm to initially screen the source domains with high similarity to the target to avoid negative transfer.

We introduced the Jensen-Shannon (JS) divergence based on the Kullback-Leibler (KL) divergence as a measure of domain similarity estimation. The smaller the JS divergence of the source and target domains, the greater the similarity. The similarity is expressed as

$$KL\left(p||q\right) = \sum p \, log\frac{p}{q}, \tag{1}$$

$$JS(P_x||P_y) = \frac{1}{2}KL(P_x||\frac{P_x + P_y}{2}) + \frac{1}{2}KL(P_y||\frac{P_x + P_y}{2}). \tag{2}$$

After calculating the similarity between the distribution of the target domain P_y and that of the source domain P_x, we assign all source domains within the source domain set X priority rank $f_{x_i}(f_{x_i} \leq |X|, f_{x_i} \in Z^+)$. The higher the similarity between the source and the target domains, the smaller the value of the corresponding source domain priority rank, when $f_{x_i} = 1$ indicates that x_i is the source domain with the highest similarity. A reasonable parameter priority threshold β is also determined, i.e., the subsequent pre-training of the model is performed on the source domain $x_i(f_{x_i} \leq \beta, x_i \in X)$ only. We consider the data distribution of source domains with priority rank below the threshold to be highly similar to the target domain and use them as alternate source domains, thus enhancing the proportion of positive transfer in the transfer learning process.

3.3   Multi-task Learning Based Multi-source Predictor Aggregation

To make the model fully extract and aggregate the public knowledge of each source domain when pre-training in the source domain set, we define pre-training on different source domains as different tasks and use hard parameter sharing to associate these tasks. By sharing knowledge, model components complement each other and enhance the effectiveness of mining time series public features.

Figure 2 illustrates the architecture of the pre-training model utilizing multi-task learning. Based on MUCAN (we will cover this in detail in Sect. 3.4), we will slightly change the model structure by using multiple decoders in parallel to replace the original MLP network used for single-task decoding to obtain Muti-MUCAN. Each decoder acts as a private module for different pre-training tasks to independently decode the fusion codes extracted from the shared layer. In the face of multiple decoding outputs of multiple tasks, the output results of different tasks are calculated to obtain different *loss* magnitudes, and the task with larger *loss* may dominate the model optimization direction. To overcome this problem, we constitute the total *loss* by calculating the weighted *loss* of different tasks as follows:

$$L(t) = \sum_{i=1}^{\beta} w_i(t)L_i(t) \tag{3}$$

where t denotes the current training step number, and w_i denotes the weight of different task *losses*. For w_i, we are not sure that we can manually set the weights quite appropriately, so it is wiser to choose a method that can dynamically adjust

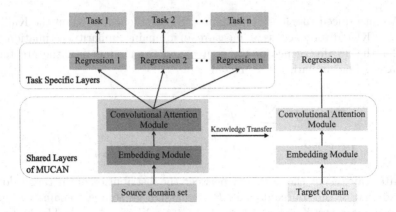

Fig. 2. A pre-trained model utilizing multi-task learning.

the weights according to the learning effect of different tasks. Dynamic Weight Average [18] reflects the learning difficulty by considering the rate of change of each task's *loss* and thus dynamically calculates the weights of the tasks.

$$w_i(t) := \frac{S \exp(r_i(t-1)/T)}{\sum_{i=1}^{\beta} \exp(r_i(t-1)/T)}, \quad r_i(t-1) = \frac{L_i(t-1)}{L_i(t-2)} \qquad (4)$$

$r_i(\cdot)$ denotes the relative rate of decline of *loss*, S is used to limit the range of variation of weights to satisfy $\sum_i w_i(t) = S$, and T denotes the degree of relaxation between individual tasks, if the larger the value, the more the weights of each task tend to be equal.

3.4   The Base Model MUCAN for Transfer Learning

To solve the prediction task for regions with sparse samples, we introduced a convolutional attention module based on the structure of multi-time scale window inputs [40] and built a feature extraction network MUCAN for the subsequent transfer task. The extraction of features at different time scales of the series is achieved to capture the dependence of WEEE at multiple time scales.

First, we label the closeness data window, period data window, and trend data window in the historical data as cw, pw, and tw, respectively, and the size of each window is c_{len}, p_{len}, and t_{len}. Based on the current time step s, the size of each window in the historical data is defined as follows.

- Closeness window: $cw = [s - c_{len}, s)$
- Period window: $pw = [s - 30 - \frac{p_{len}}{2}, s - 30 + \frac{p_{len}}{2})$
- Trend window: $tw = [s - 365 - \frac{t_{len}}{2}, s - 365 + \frac{t_{len}}{2})$

We extract cw, pw, and tw from the historical data as inputs to capture the temporal dependence of sequences at multiple time scales. Then the three input features are encoded by the corresponding LSTM modules to mine the correlation between the sequence adjacent data within each window to generate three coded sequences with the same dimension c^{enc}, p^{enc}, and t^{enc}. We use the convolutional attention module to weigh the three coded sequences for fusion to obtain the fusion coding m^{enc}. Finally, the fusion coding is decoded by a multilayer neural network as a regression layer to obtain the final prediction. The structure of our designed network model is shown in Fig. 3.

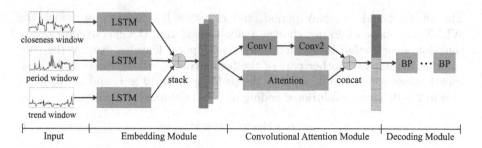

Fig. 3. Structure of feature extraction network MUCAN for model transfer.

The characteristics and design motivation of the MUCAN extraction layer are described as follows:

First is the LSTM-based coding module. Due to the unique gating unit and memory unit of LSTM, it avoids the gradient disappearance problem of RNN in the training process of long sequences and is good at extracting long-term time series features. We adopt LSTM as the encoding module for the input window to extract the characteristic laws of sequences in trend, period, and closeness, respectively. Our model encodes the window input data x at different time scales by LSTM to obtain dimensionally consistent encoding sequence x^{enc}.

$$x^{enc} = LSTM(x) \tag{5}$$

We generate 3 coding sequences: c^{enc}, p^{enc}, and t^{enc}, after inputting the window data cw, pw, and tw into their respective LSTM modules.

Second is the convolutional attention module. In exploring the three dependencies of sequences, we consider the mining of sequence trendiness and periodic regularity features to act as a supporting role. To focus the model's attention more on the closeness window encoding sequences c^{enc}, we use an additive attention mechanism [36] as part of the fusion encoding. Based on the prediction task of the time series, we define the encoding of the closeness window c^{enc} as a query vector q and set the key values $K = \{c^{enc}, p^{enc}, t^{enc}\}$. The scoring function for the additive attention mechanism is as follows:

$$s_i = s(k_i, q) = \varepsilon^T tanh(W_k k_i + W_q q) \tag{6}$$

where W_k, W_q, and ε are all learnable parameters. The attentional scoring s_i is obtained by this formula, which is subsequently softmax to obtain the attention distribution α_i. At this point we weight the coded input $V = [c^{enc}, p^{enc}, t^{enc}]$ with the attention distribution coefficients α_i to obtain the output m^{att}:

$$\alpha_i = softmax(s_i) = \frac{\exp(s_i)}{\sum_{j=1}^{len(K)} s_j} \tag{7}$$

$$m^{att} = \sum_{i=1}^{3} \alpha_i v_i \ , \ \ v_i \in V \tag{8}$$

The annual trend, monthly period, and closeness law features on which the WEEE data depend do not change easily. Considering the effectiveness of the convolution operation in extracting spatio-temporal features, we use the convolution module as another part of the fusion coding, where the convolutional kernel size of $conv1$ and $conv2$ is 3, the padding of $conv1$ is 1, and the padding of $conv2$ is 0. The convolutional coding m^{conv} is obtained as follows:

$$m^{conv} = conv1(conv2(stack(v_1, v_2, v_3)) \tag{9}$$

After deriving the attentional and convolutional encoding, the two are concatenated together to obtain the fusion encoding m^{enc}.

$$m^{enc} = concat(m^{att}, m^{conv}) \tag{10}$$

Finally, the decoding module. We use a multilayer neural network (MLP) to decode the fusion code m^{enc} and output the predicted values for the next t days. In addition, a dropout layer is added to the multilayer neural network to avoid the overfitting phenomenon.

3.5   Dual Transfer Algorithm Combining Sample Transfer and Model Transfer

Since the target domain with missing historical data generally only provides order data within the last three months, applying the model will result in missing trend window input tw for the feature extraction network MUCAN. This means that it will be difficult for MUCAN to model the trend, and the dependence of the series on the trend time scale will not be explored.

To solve this problem, we first select the source domain $x_1(f_{x_1} = 1)$ with the highest priority in the source domain set and define the trending data domains used in the source domain x and the target domain y as x^{tre} and y^{tre}, respectively. We learn the mapping rules from the sample data in the source domain x_1 to the sample data in the target domain y by training a mapper (see Fig. 4), and subsequently use x^{tre} as the input to the mapper to generate the missing trend data in the target domain y^{tre}. To simplify the complexity of the overall model, we use LSTM-MLP to learn the mapping rules for sample transfer.

After completing the trend window of the target domain, to minimize the loss of public knowledge in the transfer learning process between the source and target domains as much as possible, we set a lower learning rate for the part of the convolutional attention layer and the part of the LSTM layer in the

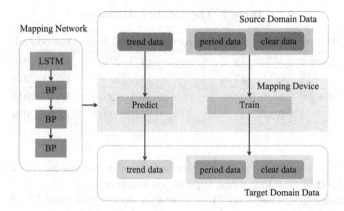

Fig. 4. Mapper structure for sample transfer.

network structure to achieve the effect of parameter fine-tuning while adapting the parameters of the regression layer to the distribution of the target domain data by retraining.

4 Experiment Setup

To assess the model performance, we conducted several experiments, including overall performance comparison, ablation experiments, and sensitivity analysis. In this section, we will provide details on the datasets utilized in the experiments, the selection of baseline methods, evaluation metrics, and other relevant experimental details.

4.1 Dataset

The commercial company Able Green provided the dataset used to test the model's predictive performance. From the company's WEEE recycling service order data for the last two years, two types of time-series data are available from 28 Chinese provinces: air conditioners (AC) and washing machines (WM). Some provinces are late to start recycling services and are missing long-term data, and our experiments will focus on predicting two types of data for AC and WM in such provinces. Detailed statistical data is shown in Table 1, where we distinguish the provinces with scarce data from those with sufficient data according to the earliest correct order time in each province and divide them into the training, validation, and test sets according to 7:1.5:1.5.

4.2 Baselines

- ARIMA [31]: A method combines an autoregressive (AR) model with a moving average (MA) model and a differential preprocessing step of the series to smooth the series.

Table 1. The statistics of datasets

Domain	Types	Provinces covered	Period begin	Period end
Source	AC	25	1/1/2018	12/31/2019
	WM	25	1/1/2018	12/31/2019
Target	AC	3	8/30/2019	12/31/2019
	WM	3	8/30/2019	12/31/2019

- LSTM [8]: A special type of RNN with special gated memory units that are good at extracting long-term time series features.
- Autoformer [37]: Based on Transformer, a model that enables efficient connection at the sequence level for better information aggregation.
- Informer [41]: Based on Transformer, a sparse attention mechanism is incorporated to reduce the network complexity.
- MULAN [40]: The model introduces multi-time scale windows and attention-based alignment fusion, which can capture the temporal dependence of sequences at multiple timescales.

4.3   Evaluation Metrics

To evaluate the performance of DT-MUSA and other models, we need to use appropriate evaluation metrics to measure the prediction accuracy of the corresponding algorithms. MAE and RMSE are the evaluation metrics employed in this study to assess the model's prediction performance. Lower values of these metrics indicate better performance by the model. The MAE and RMSE can be calculated as follows:

$$MAE = \frac{1}{t} \sum_{i=1}^{t} |pre_i - tru_i|, \tag{11}$$

$$RMSE = \sqrt{\frac{1}{t} \sum_{i=1}^{t} (pre_i - tru_i)^2} \tag{12}$$

where t denotes the step size that the model will predict, and pre_i and tru_i denote the predicted and true values of the day, respectively.

4.4   Experimental Details

By grid search, we set the three input window lengths c_{len}, p_{len}, and t_{len} of the feature extraction network MUCAN to 15, 10, and 20, respectively, and determined $\beta = 3$, $lr = 0.001$ and $epoch = 50$ rounds in the source domain and

$lr = 0.01$ and *epoch* $= 100$ rounds in the target domain. The best-performing model on the validation set was retained, and all RMSEs and MAEs were calculated on the test set. All experiments were performed in the PyTorch framework [27].

5 Results and Analyses

5.1 Predictive Performance Comparison

To demonstrate the superiority of DT-MUSA in solving the task of predicting RL return data in regions with sparse samples, we compare the results with other commonly used prediction models as shown in Table 2 and 3.

Table 2. Overal performance comparison (MAE) on the AC and WM datasets.

MAE	Jiangsu Province		Chongqing City		Peking City	
	AC	WM	AC	WM	AC	WM
ARIMA	25.659	16.888	1.360	4.103	0.652	1.032
LSTM	30.344	25.231	4.311	6.364	1.366	3.215
Informer	27.926	18.480	3.379	7.099	1.182	1.863
Autoformer	24.264	19.826	2.852	3.976	1.366	3.215
MULAN	20.386	<u>8.854</u>	1.838	3.637	1.508	1.505
MUCAN	<u>9.373</u>	12.586	<u>0.736</u>	<u>1.675</u>	<u>0.307</u>	<u>0.719</u>
MUCAN-sbs*	5.432	8.268	0.589	1.826	0.238	0.682
MUCAN-rt*	17.283	15.383	1.116	2.926	0.422	0.823
DT-MUSA*	**2.775**	**3.471**	**0.233**	**1.436**	**0.098**	**0.310**

Notes: The models with * in Tables 2 and 3 indicate the transfer learning models, while the rest indicate the non-transfer models. Bold in Table 2 indicates the minimum value of MAE obtained for all models involved in the comparison in the corresponding data set; the sliding line represents the minimum value of MAE obtained for the non-transfer learning models involved in the comparison.

Under the condition of no transfer, the models are highly susceptible to underfitting because the short-term data are difficult to meet the training requirements of most deep learning models. The comparison of the transfer-free methods in Tables 2 and 3 shows that various classical prediction models perform unsatisfactorily and are poorly adapted to the prediction task in regions with sparse samples. One of the statistical methods, ARIMA, achieves a relatively good result but is still objectively less than ideal. The feature extraction

Table 3. Overal performance comparison (RMSE) on the AC and WM datasets.

RMSE	Jiangsu Province		Chongqing City		Peking City	
	AC	WM	AC	WM	AC	WM
ARIMA	26.939	17.307	1.445	4.232	0.782	1.155
LSTM	27.753	21.755	3.571	2.939	1.573	3.879
Informer	30.278	20.288	2.962	3.092	1.279	2.379
Autoformer	28.738	20.896	3.725	5.527	0.942	2.072
MULAN	25.393	<u>11.665</u>	2.476	7.379	0.805	<u>0.644</u>
MUCAN	<u>10.981</u>	15.869	<u>0.861</u>	<u>2.333</u>	<u>0.356</u>	0.929
MUCAN-sbs*	8.327	9.236	0.627	1.923	0.188	0.572
MUCAN-rt*	20.238	13.378	1.630	4.132	0.283	0.592
DT-MUSA*	**4.801**	**4.610**	**0.327**	**1.553**	**0.112**	**0.418**

NotesNotes: Bold in Table 3 indicates the lowest RMSE value achieved across all models involved in the comparison in the corresponding data set; the sliding line represents the lowest value of RMSE obtained for the non-transfer learning models involved in the comparison.

network MUCAN achieves excellent results in the target domain by capturing the correlation patterns of the series on various time scales. However, due to the lack of sample data, the dependencies of sequences on various time scales cannot be explored more fully, resulting in the inability to predict some inflection points in the prediction task accurately.

When a large amount of source domain data is available for transfer, we compare DT-MUSA with some simple source domain selection strategies. As shown in Tables 2 and 3 for the comparison of transfer methods, DT-MUSA performs significantly better than single source domain transfer as well as random source domain transfer for the target domain prediction task. This demonstrates that a simple source domain selection strategy may introduce unsuitable source domain data, leading to negative transfer. Compared with MUCAN without transfer, DT-MUSA also has significant performance improvement. This proves that DT-MUSA not only overcomes the distribution difference between the source domain data and the target domain data to a certain extent but also solves the negative impact due to the missing data of the target domain. Overall, DT-MUSA performs adaptive aggregation of predictors from multiple source domains, effectively reducing negative transfer.

5.2 Strength and Weakness

Comparing the baselines in the table, our advantages are as follows:

- Pre-training in the source domain set by multi-task learning aggregates the common knowledge of multiple source domains to transfer to the target domain, which avoids negative transfer to a certain extent.

- For WEEE return data, we build a feature extraction network MUCAN based on the convolutional attention module, which fully explores the dependencies of sequences at multiple time scales and helps to obtain more accurate prediction results in transfer learning.
- Sample transfer is used to complement the trend window data input of MUCAN on the target domain to expand the range of explorable time-scale categories and enhance the effect of model transfer.

In terms of model shortcomings: our model initially screens the source domains by estimating the similarity between the data of each source domain as a whole and the data of the target domain and thus divides the priorities to initially screen the source domains in the expectation of reducing the data distribution differences from the source to the target domains. However, the instance adaptive approach has its limitations in the end, and the distribution differences between the source and target domains will not be completely eliminated. Suppose the deep feature adaptive approach is further explored, and the embedding of an adaptive module to encode the mapping of source domain data is considered. In that case, reducing the negative transfer phenomenon leads to an improvement in model prediction accuracy.

5.3 Ablation Experiments

In our experiments, (1) we introduced a model transfer approach to pre-train the model with shared parameters in the multi-source domain, followed by fine-tuning in the target domain; (2) we transferred data from the rich data domain to the poor data domain by mapping the model, which complements the trend window data input of MUCAN; (3) we built a feature extraction network MUCAN based on the Convolutional Attention Module for weighted fusing data from different time scales for decoding output. We designed the following ablation experiments to demonstrate the usefulness of each of the above three components.

- Validate the effect of fine-tuning.
  - DT-MUSA-ft: Remove the fine-tuning in the target domain, and apply the pre-trained model directly to the target domain.
- Validate the effect of sample transfer.
  - DT-MUSA-st: The closeness window data of the target domain is used to fill the trend window data of the target domain.
- Verify the effect of Convolutional Attention Module on data fusion at different time scales
  - DT-MUSA-at: Remove the Attention Module and use CNN-LSTM for training.
  - DT-MUSA-ac: Remove the Attention and CNN Modules, and use LSTM for training.

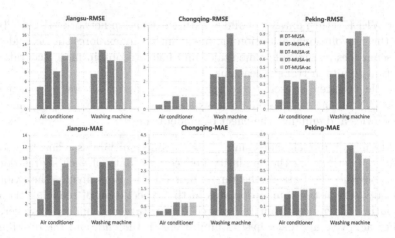

Fig. 5. The effect of each part on model performance.

From the experimental results in Fig. 5, it can be seen that these three components play an extremely important role in the excellent overall model results. (1) The model transfer based on the pre-training fine-tuning approach contributes significantly to the overall model performance. While the pre-training model is effective at extracting complex temporal feature information in data-rich domains, it can only provide a rough reflection of the trend characteristics of the data when carrying the public knowledge from the source domain. Without fine-tuning, it cannot make accurate predictions due to its neglect of the distributional differences between the target and source domain data. (2) Sample transfer based on a mapper trained on a rich set of samples is essential in this model. Previously, MULAN [40] has demonstrated that the window design based on trending scales can effectively improve prediction accuracy. Due to the lack of trend window data in the target domain, we complemented the trend window data input in the poor data domain by the LSTM-MLP based mapping model and achieved good results. (3) The embedding of the convolutional attention module is also shown to effectively improve the model's prediction performance, especially in scenarios with transfer learning, allowing the model to gain more room for improvement.

5.4 Model Sensitivity Analysis

The priority rank associated with the domain similarity size is introduced in the source domain set used for the model transfer. The model is pre-trained for multi-task association learning using only multiple source domains within the priority threshold β. Our model should be robust to moderate changes in β of the source domain set. To this end, we conducted sensitivity experiments to verify that the model performs consistently over various variations in the source domain set priority threshold parameter. When $\beta = 1$, the model degenerates to single source domain transfer, so we make β vary in the integer interval $[2 : 7]$ and compare the model predictions with the results of the transfer models ($\beta = 3$) in Sect. 5.1.

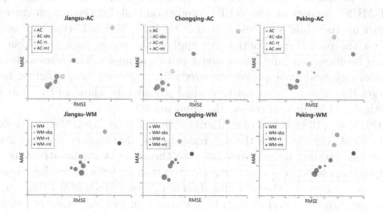

Fig. 6. The effect of changes in the source domain priority threshold β on model performance.

The comparison results are shown in Fig. 6, where (AC/WM)-sbs indicates the experimental results of the best single-source domain transfer on the air conditioner or washing machine dataset; (AC/WM)-rt indicates the random source domain transfer results; (AC/WM)-mt indicates the prediction results of MUCAN without transfer, and the bubble size of (AC/WM) type corresponds to the number of source domains used by DT-MUSA. It is easy to see that DT-MUSA effectively improves the accuracy of the RL prediction task, and the model's prediction performance fluctuates within an acceptable range. And the model generally outperforms other source domain adaptation strategies overall within a certain variation of the priority threshold β. This demonstrates that our model's performance is stable and less affected by variations in the priority threshold parameter.

6   Discussion and Conclusion

In this paper, we have extensively investigated the predictive effectiveness of various excellent models in the presence of sparse RL return data for WEEE. For multi-source domain adaptive models, we point out the challenges of their current application in practical scenarios: inefficient use of multi-source data in multi-source knowledge transfer learning tasks; lack of long-term time-series data leading to suboptimal fine-tuning of model transfer.

We thus propose DT-MUSA to address the above challenges. We first try to use multi-task learning in the pre-training of multiple source domains, which effectively resolves the knowledge conflicts among source domains and dramatically helps the fusion of source domain public knowledge. To overcome the adverse effects of long-term data scarcity, DT-MUSA performs model transfer from multiple source domains to target domains based on MUCAN neural networks and complements the input data of trend windows by training mappers.

DT-MUSA focuses on the WEEE prediction task for certain provinces with late start-up recycling services, where order information is typically only collected for the past three months. We applied the model to a real Able Green recycling business case and conducted a full experiment. The results show that the model significantly improves the prediction accuracy on prediction tasks in the target domain and is robust to critical parameters, showing that our model is practical and feasible in real-world applications.

In this study, the method of similarity estimation to screen the source domain cannot completely overcome the difference in the distribution of source and target domains. Adding an adaptive layer to the network model structure of the source and target domains may improve the transfer effect. Besides, there may be connections between the recycling data of different kinds of WEEE, and using these connections to build a multi-task learning model may achieve better prediction results.

Acknowledgments. This study was supported by the National Key Research and Development Program of China (2020YFB1712901) and the Science and Technology Research Project of Chongqing Education Commission (KJZD-K202204402).

References

1. Bai, J., Jia, J., Capretz, L.F.: A three-stage transfer learning framework for multi-source cross-project software defect prediction. Inf. Softw. Technol. **150**, 106985 (2022)
2. Chen, C., Xie, W., Wen, Y., Huang, Y., Ding, X.: Multiple-source domain adaptation with generative adversarial nets. Knowl.-Based Syst. **199**, 105962 (2020)
3. De Bois, M., El Yacoubi, M.A., Ammi, M.: Adversarial multi-source transfer learning in healthcare: application to glucose prediction for diabetic people. Comput. Methods Programs Biomed. **199**, 105874 (2021)
4. Dev, N.K., Shankar, R., Qaiser, F.H.: Industry 4.0 and circular economy: Operational excellence for sustainable reverse supply chain performance. Resour. Conserv. Recycl. **153**, 104583 (2020)
5. Ganin, Y., Ustinova, E., Ajakan, H., Germain, P., Larochelle, H., Laviolette, F., Marchand, M., Lempitsky, V.: Domain-adversarial training of neural networks. J. Mach. Learn. Res. **17**(1), 2030–2096 (2016)
6. Garg, S., Kumar, S., Muhuri, P.K.: A novel approach for covid-19 infection forecasting based on multi-source deep transfer learning. Comput. Biol. Med. **149**, 105915 (2022)
7. Govindan, K., Bouzon, M.: From a literature review to a multi-perspective framework for reverse logistics barriers and drivers. J. Clean. Prod. **187**, 318–337 (2018)
8. Graves, A.: Long short-term memory. Supervised sequence labelling with recurrent neural networks, pp. 37–45 (2012)
9. Gu, Q., Dai, Q., Yu, H., Ye, R.: Integrating multi-source transfer learning, active learning and metric learning paradigms for time series prediction. Appl. Soft Comput. **109**, 107583 (2021)

10. Gupta, P., Malhotra, P., Vig, L., Shroff, G.: Transfer learning for clinical time series analysis using recurrent neural networks. arXiv preprint arXiv:1807.01705 (2018)

11. Hasan, M.M., Nekmahmud, M., Yajuan, L., Patwary, M.A.: Green business value chain: a systematic review. Sustain. Prod. Consumption **20**, 326–339 (2019)

12. Huang, B., Xu, T., Li, J., Shen, Z., Chen, Y.: Transfer learning-based discriminative correlation filter for visual tracking. Pattern Recogn. **100**, 107157 (2020)

13. Ismail, H., Hanafiah, M.M.: Evaluation of e-waste management systems in malaysia using life cycle assessment and material flow analysis. J. Clean. Prod. **308**, 127358 (2021)

14. Jabbour, C.J.C., de Sousa Jabbour, A.B.L., Govindan, K., Teixeira, A.A., de Souza Freitas, W.R.: Environmental management and operational performance in automotive companies in brazil: the role of human resource management and lean manufacturing. J. Clean. Prod. **47**, 129–140 (2013)

15. Kelle, P., Silver, E.A.: Forecasting the returns of reusable containers. J. Oper. Manag. **8**(1), 17–35 (1989)

16. Kilic, H.S., Cebeci, U., Ayhan, M.B.: Reverse logistics system design for the waste of electrical and electronic equipment (WEEE) in turkey. Resour. Conserv. Recycl. **95**, 120–132 (2015)

17. Liu, C., Yang, D., Xia, X., Yan, M., Zhang, X.: A two-phase transfer learning model for cross-project defect prediction. Inf. Softw. Technol. **107**, 125–136 (2019)

18. Liu, S., Johns, E., Davison, A.J.: End-to-end multi-task learning with attention. In: Proceedings of the IEEE/CVF Conference on Computer Vision and Pattern Recognition, pp. 1871–1880 (2019)

19. Long, M., Cao, Y., Wang, J., Jordan, M.: Learning transferable features with deep adaptation networks. In: International Conference on Machine Learning, pp. 97–105. PMLR (2015)

20. Long, M., Cao, Z., Wang, J., Jordan, M.I.: Conditional adversarial domain adaptation. In: Advances in Neural Information Processing Systems, vol. 31 (2018)

21. Long, M., Zhu, H., Wang, J., Jordan, M.I.: Deep transfer learning with joint adaptation networks. In: International Conference on Machine Learning, pp. 2208–2217. PMLR (2017)

22. Ma, Y., Luo, G., Zeng, X., Chen, A.: Transfer learning for cross-company software defect prediction. Inf. Softw. Technol. **54**(3), 248–256 (2012)

23. Marx-Gomez, J., Rautenstrauch, C., Nürnberger, A., Kruse, R.: Neuro-fuzzy approach to forecast returns of scrapped products to recycling and remanufacturing. Knowl.-Based Syst. **15**(1–2), 119–128 (2002)

24. Nam, J., Pan, S.J., Kim, S.: Transfer defect learning. In: 2013 35th International Conference on Software Engineering (ICSE), pp. 382–391. IEEE (2013)

25. Ni, Z., Chan, H.K., Tan, Z.: Systematic literature review of reverse logistics for e-waste: overview, analysis, and future research agenda. Int. J. Logist. Res. Appl. **26**, 1–29 (2021)

26. Pan, S.J., Tsang, I.W., Kwok, J.T., Yang, Q.: Domain adaptation via transfer component analysis. IEEE Trans. Neural Networks **22**(2), 199–210 (2010)

27. Paszke, A., et al.: Pytorch: an imperative style, high-performance deep learning library. In: Advances in Neural Information Processing Systems, vol. 32 (2019)

28. Peng, L., et al.: TLT: recurrent fine-tuning transfer learning for water quality long-term prediction. Water Res. **225**, 119171 (2022)

29. Rocha, T.B., Penteado, C.S.G.: Life cycle assessment of a small WEEE reverse logistics system: Case study in the campinas area, brazil. J. Clean. Prod. **314**, 128092 (2021)

30. Sepúlveda, A., et al.: A review of the environmental fate and effects of hazardous substances released from electrical and electronic equipments during recycling: Examples from china and India. Environ. Impact Assess. Rev. **30**(1), 28–41 (2010)
31. Siami-Namini, S., Tavakoli, N., Namin, A.S.: A comparison of ARIMA and LSTM in forecasting time series. In: 2018 17th IEEE International Conference on Machine Learning and Applications (ICMLA), pp. 1394–1401. IEEE (2018)
32. Song, Q., Li, J.: A review on human health consequences of metals exposure to e-waste in china. Environ. Pollut. **196**, 450–461 (2015)
33. Sun, S., Shi, H., Wu, Y.: A survey of multi-source domain adaptation. Inf. Fusion **24**, 84–92 (2015)
34. Toktay, L.B., Wein, L.M., Zenios, S.A.: Inventory management of remanufacturable products. Manage. Sci. **46**(11), 1412–1426 (2000)
35. Tzeng, E., Hoffman, J., Zhang, N., Saenko, K., Darrell, T.: Deep domain confusion: maximizing for domain invariance. arXiv preprint arXiv:1412.3474 (2014)
36. Vaswani, A., et al.: Attention is all you need. In: Advances in Neural Information Processing Systems, vol. 30 (2017)
37. Wu, H., Xu, J., Wang, J., Long, M.: Autoformer: decomposition transformers with auto-correlation for long-term series forecasting. Adv. Neural. Inf. Process. Syst. **34**, 22419–22430 (2021)
38. Yang, Y., Williams, E.: Logistic model-based forecast of sales and generation of obsolete computers in the us. Technol. Forecast. Soc. Chang. **76**(8), 1105–1114 (2009)
39. Ye, R., Dai, Q.: A novel transfer learning framework for time series forecasting. Knowl.-Based Syst. **156**, 74–99 (2018)
40. Zhang, J., et al.: Multi-time scale attention network for WEEE reverse logistics return prediction. Expert Syst. Appl. **211**, 118610 (2023)
41. Zhou, H., et al.: Informer: Beyond efficient transformer for long sequence time-series forecasting. In: Proceedings of the AAAI Conference on Artificial Intelligence, vol. 35, pp. 11106–11115 (2021)

A Synchronous Parallel Method with Parameters Communication Prediction for Distributed Machine Learning

Yanguo Zeng[1], Meiting Xue[5(✉)], Peiran Xu[1], Yukun Shi[5],
Kaisheng Zeng[4,6], Jilin Zhang[1,2,3], and Lupeng Yue[1]

[1] School of Computer Science and Technology, Hangzhou Dianzi University,
Hangzhou 310018, China
{jilin.zhang,lupengyue}@hdu.edu.cn
[2] Key Laboratory for Modeling and Simulation of Complex Systems,
Ministry of Education, Hangzhou 310018, China
[3] Data Security Governance Zhejiang Engineering Research Center,
Hangzhou 310018, China
[4] National University of Defense Technology, Changsha, China
zks@nudt.edu.cn
[5] School of Cyberspace, HangZhou Dianzi University, Hangzhou, China
{munuan,202243270074}@hdu.edu.cn
[6] Department of Computer Science and Technology, Tsinghua University,
Beijing, China

Abstract. With the development of machine learning technology in various fields, such as medical care, smart manufacturing, etc., the data has exploded. It is a challenge to train a deep learning model for different application domains with large-scale data and limited resources of a single device. The distributed machine-learning technology, which uses a parameter server and multiple clients to train a model collaboratively, is an excellent method to solve this problem. However, it needs much communication between different devices with limited communication resources. The stale synchronous parallel method is a mainstream communication method to solve this problem, but it always leads to high synchronization delay and low computing efficiency as the inappropriate delay threshold value set by the user based on experience. This paper proposes a synchronous parallel method with parameters communication prediction for distributed machine learning. It predicts the optimal timing for synchronization, which can solve the problem of long synchronization waiting time caused by the inappropriate threshold settings in the stale synchronous parallel method. Moreover, it allows fast nodes to continue local training while performing global synchronization, which can improve the resource utilization of work nodes. Experimental results show that compared with the delayed synchronous parallel method, the training time and quality, and resource usage of our method are both significantly improved.

© ICST Institute for Computer Sciences, Social Informatics and Telecommunications Engineering 2024
Published by Springer Nature Switzerland AG 2024. All Rights Reserved
H. Gao et al. (Eds.): CollaborateCom 2023, LNICST 563, pp. 385–403, 2024.
https://doi.org/10.1007/978-3-031-54531-3_21

Keywords: Distributed Machine Learning · Synchronous Parallel · Communication Prediction · Collaborative Computing

1   Introduction

With the development of 5G, AI (artificial intelligence) technology, information technology, etc., intelligent collaborative computing is a good way to cope with the changing world. As AI technology is widely used in all walks of life, such as natural language processing [1], image classification [2], network traffic control [3], speech recognition [4], and other fields [5,6], the data has grown explosively, from the PB level to the EB level. It is a challenge to deal with such a huge amount of data with AI technology in a single device, as the limited resources of the single device. So, distributed machine learning technology, dealing with large-scale data with multiple devices, has become an inevitable trend and research hotspot.

The parameter server system is one popular distributed machine learning method to deal with large-scale data with AI technology. It trains a global model with the corporation of parameter server and worker nodes. Where the worker nodes use the subset of the data set to train the local models and update the local models to the parameter server, and the parameter server trains a global model by aggregating local models [7,8]. As deep learning models require multiple rounds of iterations to converge, they need to transport large-scale data, such as the parameters of the local model and global model, between servers and workers to complete the gradient descent method [9,10]. There is extensive communication between servers and workers. How to train a global model efficiently with low communication cost is an important problem for the parameter server system.

The bulk synchronous parallel method [11] is one of the mainstream parametric synchronization methods in the parameter server system. When the parameter server computes the global model by aggregating the local models, it needs to wait for all work nodes to upload the current version of the local models. The convergence time of model training depends on the slowest working node, which leads to low resource utilization and long training time [12]. In order to solve this problem, Dean et al. proposed the asynchronous parallel method [13], where each worker node is trained asynchronously and communicates with the parameter server to exchange models after completing a round of training without waiting for other worker nodes, which significantly utilizes the computation resources of worker nodes.

However, the uncontrollability of each node in the cluster in this method often leads to a significant difference in the number of iterations between fast and slow nodes, which finally makes the machine learning model converge poorly or even fail to converge. Combining the characteristics of the above two methods, Ho [14] et al. proposed the stale synchronous parallel method. It defines a delay parameter representing the maximum iteration difference between the working nodes to control the synchronization time of the work nodes. If the iteration difference between the work nodes is less than the delay parameter, the work nodes will use the asynchronous communication method. Otherwise, the work nodes will use the synchronous communication method, waiting until all working nodes have completed the current round of training and performing a global synchronization. That is, the setting of the delay parameter affects the performance of this method. However, the value of the delay parameter is hard to set, as it relies on expert experience. The synchronization delay with unreasonable delay parameters still leads to low computing performance.

In summary, the existing parameter communication methods of distributed machine learning still have some shortcomings: (1) the bulk synchronous parallel method cannot fully utilize the computational performance; (2) The asynchronous parallel method over-exploits the fault tolerance of machine learning, which may eventually lead to the non-convergence of the model; (3) The stale synchronous parallel model, in which most delay thresholds are set based on expert experience, needs to be better adapted to the cluster environment and wastes computational resources.

In order to solve these problems, this paper proposes a synchronous parallel method with parameters communication prediction for distributed machine learning, and we call this method the Prediction Synchronous Parallel (PSP) method in this paper. This method controls the synchronous time of work nodes by analyzing the last iteration of cluster training to predict the future cluster performance and set the optimal synchronization timing to reduce the synchronization delay. Furthermore, to further improve the utilization of cluster computing resources, the fast node still keeps training if it enters the synchronization barrier, and when it receives the latest global model parameters, it aggregates the incremental local model training at the synchronization barrier and uses the global model parameters as the initial model for a new round of training. The experiment results show that our method can effectively improve the computation performance and convergence performance and also improve the resource utilization compared with the bulk synchronous parallel method and asynchronous parallel method.

The rest of this paper is organized as follows. Firstly, related work is reviewed in Sect. 2. Then, this paper describes the prediction synchronous parallel method for distributed machine learning in Sect. 3. Experiments follow in Sect. 4. Finally, the conclusion is in Sect. 5.

2 Related Work

Many distributed machine learning systems have been proposed to deal with large-scale data with AI technology, such as Spark and Hadoop, which are implemented based on MapReduce schema. For these systems, the server must wait for all work nodes to update the local models before proceeding to global model aggregation in each iteration, which causes a significant delay. In order to solve these problems, the parameter server system has been proposed, such as Multiverso, Ray [15], etc., which can support bulk synchronous parallel method, asynchronous parallel method, and stale synchronous parallel method.

The bulk synchronous parallel method is one of the dominant communication methods for distributed machine learning, such as the spark-5 [16] and MLIB16 [17]. It requires that the performance of worker nodes is similar. Otherwise, the end-to-end training time of the deep learning model will be dragged down by the worst-performing worker node. Haozhao Wang [18,19] et al. have proved that the performance loss due to synchronous communication is vast, even in clusters with similar computational performance.

To solve the synchronization delay problem in the bulk synchronous parallel method, Dean [13] et al. proposed an asynchronous parallel method that can fully utilize the computational resources of the working nodes. For the asynchronous parallel method, the local model is sent to the server as long as the work node calculates it, and the server updates the global model according to the local model parameters rather than waiting for all other work nodes. Therefore, the cluster's performance can be fully utilized as the slow nodes do not slow down the fast nodes. Furthermore, the asynchronous parallel method has been widely used in Tensorflow [20]. The advantage of this method is that it can be much faster than the bulk synchronous parallel method in the clusters with heterogeneous computing performance of work nodes. However, as the server doesn't need to wait for the slowest work nodes if the parameters of the local model uploaded by the slowest work node lag far behind the local models of other work nodes, the accuracy of the global model will be reduced, or even not convergent [5].

In order to solve the above problems, the stale synchronous parallel method [14] has been proposed. It combines the advantages of the bulk synchronous parallel method and the asynchronous parallel method by introducing a delay threshold to limit the iteration difference between the fastest and slowest work node. Similar to the asynchronous parallel method, the delayed synchronous parallel method allows the work nodes not to be globally synchronized until the iteration interval between the fasted work node and the slowest work node reaches an obsolescence threshold. There are some distributed machine learning systems supporting the stale synchronous parallel method, such as Petuum [21] and Bosen [22].

The stale synchronous parallel method alleviates the delay problem of the bulk synchronous parallel method and the low accuracy caused by the slowest work node in the asynchronous parallel method. However, it still needs to solve the problem of low calculated performance or low convergence performance due to an unreasonable delay threshold. Where the value of the delay threshold is set by users, and it requires users to have knowledge of machine learning, distributed computing, architecture, etc. So it is hard to set a reasonable value for the delay threshold. In this paper, we propose a prediction synchronous parallel method for distributed machine learning to improve the calculated performance and convergence performance of model training.

3   Method

In this section, we first analyze the synchronization lag problem in detail in the stale synchronous parallel model and then propose the synchronous prediction by leveraging the continuity of cluster performance and parallelizing computation and synchronization. Finally, we prove that our proposed method is feasible from algorithm and theory.

3.1 Features of Synchronization

The main advantage of the stale synchronous parallel model is that it combines the characteristics of the global synchronous parallel method and the asynchronous parallel method, accelerating the computation of distributed machine learning models while ensuring convergence. However, there are still some problems in the previous section, not just the lag problem. This section discusses the design philosophy and algorithm implementation of the stale synchronous parallel model and points out the issues it faces when running on a real distributed machine learning cluster.

The utilization of computing resources in the stale synchronous parallel method is:

$$resource\_usage = \frac{\sum_{i=1}^{p} t_i}{p * \max(t_i)}, \tag{1}$$

where p represents the number of worker nodes and t_i represents the time spent on local computation in this round of synchronization. In the case of the global synchronous parallel model, $\max(t_i)$ represents the time spent on local model training by the worst-performing node. If the performance of all worker nodes is similar, higher utilization of computing resources can be achieved. In the case of the stale synchronous parallel model, $\max(t_i)$ represents the time taken by the last worker node to enter global synchronization. If a suitable stale threshold is set to make all worker nodes enter global synchronization at the same time, the stale synchronous parallel method can achieve higher utilization of computing resources. However, in practice, users often do not have a complete understanding of the performance of the cluster, so the stale threshold they set may not be able to achieve optimal utilization of computing resources. Additionally, the performance of each worker node in the cluster may change in real-time, so a fixed stale threshold may not be suitable for a real-world cluster environment.

We assume the ratio of the time required for one round of model training on these three worker nodes is 1 : 2 : 3, and then there are three worker nodes performing machine learning model training in a parameter server system.

As shown in Fig. 1, worker node 1 and worker node 2 have to wait for worker node 3 to complete local model training, as it has not yet finished, resulting in the stale synchronous parallel model degrading into the synchronous parallel model. In Fig. 2, worker node 1 enters the synchronization barrier after completing 6 local model training iterations when the stale threshold is reached. At this point, worker node 2 and 3 have also completed their local model training, and different from Fig. 1, worker nodes 1 and 2 do not have to stop local training and wait for worker node 3. Under ideal conditions, there is no synchronization stale, thus fully utilizing the cluster computing performance.

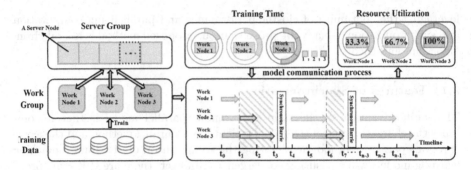

Fig. 1. The delayed synchronous parallel method communication process with a delay threshold of 1.

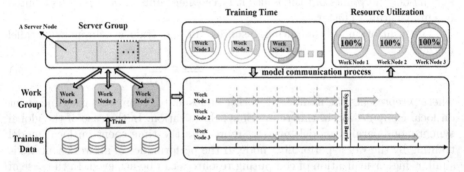

Fig. 2. The delayed synchronous parallel method communication process with a delay threshold of 5.

As shown in Figs. 1 and 2, the first problem is that the setting of the stale threshold in the stale synchronous parallel model will directly affect the efficiency of distributed machine learning model training. However, users often cannot set the appropriate stale threshold based on the performance of each worker node because they do not understand the cluster's performance.

The second problem is that external factors that may interfere with distributed machine learning model training were not taken into consideration. In real cluster environments, worker nodes typically perform tasks other than distributed machine learning model training. Therefore, the performance of each worker node is constantly changing, and a fixed stale threshold cannot adapt to the real distributed cluster environment.

As shown in Fig. 3, the initial time ratio required for one round of model iteration among worker node 1, worker node 2, and worker node 3 is 1:1:2. At this time, setting the stale threshold to 2 results in the minimum synchronization

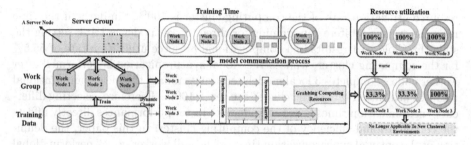

Fig. 3. The delayed synchronous parallel method under dynamic changes in the performance of the worker nodes.

delay. However, after two global synchronizations, other tasks on worker node 3 preempt computing resources, resulting in a performance decline. The originally designed stale threshold is no longer suitable for the new cluster environment.

In addition, when using the stale synchronization parallel model for distributed machine learning training in a real cluster environment, global synchronization of the worker nodes is unavoidable. When a fast node enters global synchronization, it will stop local training until every worker node in the cluster completes local model training before proceeding to the next round of training. Therefore, nodes that complete model training earlier are still held back by slower nodes, which affects the cluster's computational performance. To address this issue, this paper proposes a synchronous parallel method with parameters communication prediction, which uses the optimal synchronization time instead of a fixed stale threshold to solve the design problem of the stale synchronous parallel model. This method allows for simultaneous global synchronization and local computation, further improving the cluster's computing efficiency.

3.2 Synchronization Prediction

In the stale synchronous parallel method, setting the stale threshold to 0 transforms the stale synchronous parallel method into a synchronous parallel method, and setting the stale threshold to infinity transforms the stale synchronous parallel method into an asynchronous parallel method. The design of the stale threshold in the stale synchronous parallel model directly determines the global synchronization timing of nodes and directly determines the efficiency of the computing cluster. The following will use a typical scenario of distributed machine learning model training as an example to illustrate.

As shown in Fig. 1, if the time ratios required for one local model training for three worker nodes are 1:2:3, then setting the stale threshold to 1, in an ideal situation, worker node 1 has a computational resource utilization rate of only 33.3%, and worker node 2 has a utilization rate of only 66.7%. The overall computational resource utilization rate of the computing cluster is 66.7%. As shown in Fig. 2, if the stale threshold is set to 5, that is, worker node 1 enters the synchronization barrier after completing 6 local model training, then in an ideal situation, the resource utilization rate of the computing cluster is 100%. Similarly, if the time ratio for one model iteration training for three worker nodes is 1:1:3, setting the stale threshold to 1 results in a computational resource utilization rate of 55.5% for the computing cluster, while if the global synchronization is performed after worker node 1 completes 3 local model iteration training, the ideal computational resource utilization rate of the cluster can reach 100%. Therefore, selecting different synchronization times based on different cluster performances directly affects the computational efficiency of the computing cluster. In this paper, the definition of the optimal synchronization time is when all worker nodes perform global synchronization at that moment, achieving the highest computational resource utilization rate.

However, in a real computing cluster environment, users often do not have knowledge about the performance of each working node in the cluster, making it difficult to design a stale threshold that can achieve the optimal utilization of computing resources. Moreover, the computing performance of each working node may change unpredictably, and a fixed stale threshold may no longer be suitable for the real-time changes in the performance of each working node.

Most distributed computing clusters have performance that varies in real-time but also has continuity, meaning that the computing performance of various working nodes in the computing cluster will not change significantly in a short period of time. To address the above issues, the synchronous parallel method with parameters communication prediction replaces the stale threshold with the optimal synchronization time. Since the cluster's computing performance has continuity, the computing performance of each working node in the next synchronization can be predicted using the performance of each working node in the previous round of synchronization. If the time ratio of model training for the three working nodes in the previous round of synchronization was 1:2:3, the time ratio of model training for the three working nodes in the next round of synchronization is also approximately 1:2:3.

According to above analysis, assuming there are P working nodes in a cluster, and the parameter server obtains the training time $\{t_1, t_2, t_3, \ldots, t_P\}$ of each working node from the previous iteration, then the optimal synchronization time can be represented as the least common multiple of $\{t_1, t_2, t_3, \ldots, t_P\}$, show in Eq. (2), i.e., working node i enters global synchronization after T/t_i iterations,

$$gbc(t_1, t_2, t_3, \ldots, t_P). \tag{2}$$

As shown in Fig. 4, during the first global synchronization, the parameter server obtains the local model training time ratios of the three worker nodes, which are 1:2:3. Then, the parameter server calculates the optimal time for worker node 1 to perform global synchronization is after completing six iterations.

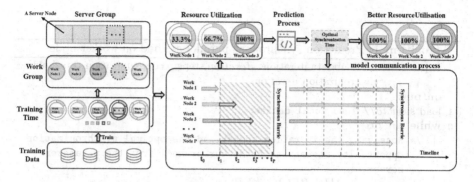

Fig. 4. The predictive synchronous parallel model communication process.

3.3 Implement

This section presents the implementation of the synchronous parallel method with parameters communication prediction. It is implemented under the parameter server system, where nodes are divided into working nodes and parameter servers. The algorithmic details of the working nodes and parameter servers are described in Algorithm 1 and Algorithm 2.

The specific execution process of Algorithm 1 is as follows:

(1) Load the sub-dataset on this worker node in line 1; (2) Line 2 - Line 9, the work node receives the iteration number of the current round of training from the parameter server and checks if the current iteration number is −1. If it is V1, end the model training. Otherwise, go to (3); (3) Receive the optimal synchronization time of this worker node. If the current iteration number has not reached the optimal synchronization time, continue to use the local dataset to compute the local model in line 10 - line 15. Otherwise, go to (4); (4) Calculate the average time consumption of one local model training on this worker node, and send the local model parameters and the average time consumption to the parameter server in line 16- line 19; (5) Use the local dataset to train the local model until receiving the new global model pushed by the parameter server in line 19 -line 26.

The specific execution process of Algorithm 2 is as follows:

(1) Initialize the iteration number and optimal synchronization time for the corresponding computing process in line 1 - line 2; (2) Receives the local model of the corresponding computing process through MPI communication and increment the iteration number of the corresponding computing process in line 3 - line 4; (3) If the optimal synchronization time is reached, enter global synchronization, wait for all work nodes to upload local models to the parameter server, calculate the optimal synchronization time based on the time required for each work node to perform one local model training, and wait for the parameter thread to aggregate the new global model parameters. Lastly, sends the new global model parameters and the optimal synchronization time to the corresponding computing process through MPI communication.

Algorithm 1: Prediction synchronous parallel method on worker node

---

Input : dataset subdata,iterations *iteration*,steps η,communication threshold τ,synchronization iterations i

output:

1 load *subdata*// load local dataset
2 **while** *ture* **do**

    /* Receiving the iteration number and the optimal synchronization opportunity iteration of the worker node from the parameter server.   */

3     $iternumber \leftarrow MPI\_RECV(ITER)$
4     $i \leftarrow MPI\_RECV(i)$

    /* If the iteration number of this iteration is -1, the model training is finished.   */

5   **if** $iternumber == -1$ **then**
6 | break
7   **end**
8     $start\_time = now$
9     $end\_iternumber = iternumber + i$

    /* The local model is used for model training before reaching the optimal synchronization opportunity.   */

10   **while** $iternumber < end\_iternumber$ **do**

      /* Calculating the parameter gradient of local model by back propagation method   */

11      $gradient \leftarrow ForwardBackward(parameters, subdata)$

      /* Updating local model parameters with gradient   */

12      $parameters \leftarrow Update(gradient, \eta, parameters)$
13      $iternumber + +$
14   **end**
15   $end\_time = now$

    /* Calculating the average time consumption of each round of model training.   */

16    $average\_time = (end\_time - start\_time)/i$
17    $MPI\_ISED(parameters)$ // Send local model
18    $MPI\_ISED(average\_time)$ // Send average time
19    $next\_flag = false$

    /* Continue to train the local model while waiting synchronously. */

20   **while** $!next\_flag$ **do**
21      $next\_flag \leftarrow MPI\_RECV(next\_flag)$
22      $gradient \leftarrow ForwardBackward(parameters, subdata)$
23      $parameters \leftarrow Update(gradient, \eta, parameters)$
24   **end**

    /* Receiving a new global model from the parameter server   */

25    $parameters \leftarrow MPI\_RECV(global\_parameters)$
26 **end**

Algorithm 2: Prediction synchronous parallel method on the server

---

Input : Calculation process number pid stale threshold s worker nodes p
output:
/* Initialize the iteration number and optimal synchronization
opportunity of the corresponding calculation process.   */
1 $iters\_pid \leftarrow 0$
2 $iters\_end\_pid \leftarrow iters\_pid + i\_pid$
/* Receiving a local model sent by a corresponding computing process
*/
3 $parameters\_pid \leftarrow MPI\_RECV(pid, parameters)$
4 $iters\_pid = isters\_pid + 1$
/* Judge whether the optimal synchronization opportunity is reached,
and if so, perform global synchronization.   */
5 **if** $iters\_pid = iters\_end\_pid$ **then**
   /* Global synchronization waiting for all working nodes to upload
      local models and average time consumption   */
6 | **for** $i = 1$ **to** p **do**
7 | | $wait(\&send)$
8 | **end**
9 | $next\_flag\_pid = true$
   /* Calculate that corresponding optimal synchronization
      opportunity   */
10 | $i\_pid \leftarrow Compute(time\_pid)$
   /* Sending the global synchronization end signal and the optimal
      synchronization opportunity to the corresponding computing
      thread.   */
11 | $MPI\_ISEND(pid, nex\_flag\_pid)$
12 | $MPI\_ISEND(pid, i\_pid)$
13 **end**

3.4 Theoretical Analysis

To ensure the correctness of using the implementation of the synchronous parallel method with parameters communication prediction for distributed machine learning, the following will theoretically prove that this method has the same correctness as the stale synchronous parallel model. We adopt the convergence of the method as the criterion for judging the correctness of distributed machine learning.

For the convenience of this chapter's proof, the following assumptions are made:

Assumption 1. The objective function F is continuously differentiable, and the gradient of the objective function is Lipschitz continuous [23], with a Lipschitz constant $L > 0$ as given in Eq. (3):

$$\|\nabla F(\omega) - \nabla F(\widetilde{\omega})\|_2 \leq L\|\omega - \widetilde{\omega}\|_2, \tag{3}$$

where ω represents the model parameters.

Assumption 2. The loss function has an upper bound, which means:

$$\|\nabla F(\omega)\| \leq K, \tag{4}$$

where K is a constant.

Assumption 3. The gradient in stochastic gradient descent is bounded, that is:

$$D(\omega\|\omega') = \frac{1}{2}\|\omega - \omega'\|^2 \leq F^2. \tag{5}$$

Most machine learning algorithms follow an iterative training pattern that involves an optimization process. The optimization function is represented by Eq. (6):

$$L = f(\omega) = f(I_{i=1}^N\{x_i, y_i\}, \omega). \tag{6}$$

Here, f is the loss function, x_i, y_i is a sample in the dataset, ω is the machine learning model parameter, and y_i is the expected output of the input data x_i. The loss function represents the difference between the actual output x_i and the expected output of the input. The machine learning program iterates using the dataset to minimize the loss function. We will now demonstrate that the efficient synchronous parallel model can ensure the final convergence of the model, using an optimization function shown in Eq. (7):

$$L = f(\omega) = \sum_{t=1}^T f_t(\omega_i). \tag{7}$$

where f_t is the loss function at the $t-th$ iteration and f is a convex function. The goal is to find the optimal solution ω^* of the machine learning model to minimize the loss function.

We introduce a regret value to represent the deviation between the currently trained model and the optimal solution, and its mathematical expression is shown in Eq. (8).

$$R[\omega] = \frac{1}{T}\sum_{t=1}^T f_t(\omega) - f(\omega^*). \tag{8}$$

If T tends to infinity, $R[\omega]$ tends to 0, it can be proven that the efficient synchronous parallel model can ultimately make the machine learning model converge. Based on Eq. (8), we can obtain Eq. (9):

$$R[\omega] = \frac{1}{T}\sum_{t=1}^{T} f_t(\omega) - f(\omega^*) \leq \frac{1}{T}\sum_{t=1}^{T}(\nabla f_t(\widetilde{\omega}), \widetilde{\omega} - \omega^*). \tag{9}$$

According to Ho [14], we can get the Eq. (10):

$$\frac{1}{T}\sum_{t=1}^{T}(\nabla f_t(\widetilde{\omega}_t)\widetilde{\omega}_t - \omega^*) \leq \sigma K^2\frac{1}{\sqrt{T}} + \frac{F^2}{\sigma}\frac{1}{\sqrt{T}} + \frac{1}{T}(\omega_t - \widetilde{\omega}_t, \widetilde{g}_t), \tag{10}$$

where $\sigma = \frac{F}{K\sqrt{2(\tau s+1)P}}$. When T tends to positive infinity, both $\sigma K^2\frac{1}{\sqrt{T}}$ and $\frac{F^2}{\sigma}\frac{1}{\sqrt{T}}$ tend to 0. Therefore, if we want to prove that the regret value $R[\omega]$ tends to 0 when T tends to positive infinity, we only need to prove that $\frac{1}{T}(\omega_t - \widetilde{\omega}_t, \widetilde{g}_t)$ tends to 0 when T tends to positive infinity.

$$\begin{aligned}
\frac{1}{T}(\omega_t - \widetilde{\omega}_t, \widetilde{g}_t) &= \frac{1}{T}\sum_{t=1}^{T}([\sum_{i\subseteq A_t} u_i - \sum_{i\subseteq B_t} u_i], \widetilde{g}_t) \\
&\leq \frac{1}{T}\sum_{t=1}^{T}[\sum_{i\subseteq A_t} \eta_i(\widetilde{g}_i, \widetilde{g}_t) - \sum_{i\subseteq B_t} \eta_i(\widetilde{g}_i, \widetilde{g}_t)] \\
&\leq \frac{1}{T}\sum_{t=1}^{T}[|A_t| + |B_t|]\eta_t K^2
\end{aligned} \tag{11}$$

Let the iteration difference between the fast node and the slow node be s, from which we can get $|A_t| + |B_t| \leq s$. Let the learning rate η_t of the t iteration be $\frac{\sigma}{\sqrt{T}}$. Therefore, Eq. (12) can be obtained based on Eq. (11):

$$\begin{aligned}
\frac{1}{T}\sum_{t=1}^{T}[|A_t| + |B_t|]\eta_t K^2 &\leq \frac{1}{T}\sum_{t=1}^{T} s\eta_t K^2 \\
&\leq \frac{1}{T}sK^2\sqrt{T} \\
&= sK^2\frac{1}{\sqrt{T}}
\end{aligned} \tag{12}$$

Therefore, we can get the Eq. (13):

$$R[\omega] \leq \frac{sK^2 + \sigma K^2 + \frac{K^2}{\sigma}}{\sqrt{T}} \tag{13}$$

where, as $sK^2 + \sigma K^2 + \frac{K^2}{\sigma}$ is a fixed value, when T tends to infinity, $\sqrt{T}$ tends to infinity and $\frac{sK^2+\sigma K^2+\frac{K^2}{\sigma}}{\sqrt{T}}$ tends to infinitesimal, that is, the regret value $R[\omega]$ tends to infinitesimal.

The Eq. (13) shows that when the number of training iterations of the distributed machine learning model tends to infinity, the gap between the model obtained by training calculation and the optimal model tends to zero. Overall, we prove that the efficient synchronous parallel model can ensure the final convergence of the model; that is, it proves the correctness of using this model for distributed machine learning training.

4   Experiments

4.1   Experimental Setup

Dataset. We use two widely used and publicly available datasets to validate the effectiveness of our approach: CIFAR-10 [24] and MNIST [25]. **1)** The CIFAR-10 consists of 60,000 samples, each of which is a 32×32 pixel colour image divided into three channels: R, G, and B. Among these 60,000 samples, five sets are reserved for training and one for testing. It is used for supervised learning. Each sample contains a label indicating the category of the object, with ten categories of images, including airplane, automobile, bird, cat, deer, dog, frog, horse, ship, and truck. **2)** The MNIST dataset is specifically designed for handwritten digit recognition. It consists of a training set with 60,000 samples and a separate test set containing 10,000 samples. Each sample in the MNIST dataset is a grayscale image of a handwritten digit, with a size of 28×28 pixels. The dataset is widely used as a benchmark for various machine learning algorithms and models.

Baselines. The baselines used in this study are the parameter communication methods currently mainstream in distributed machine learning, including the bulk synchronous parallel method [11], the asynchronous parallel method [13], and the stale synchronous parallel method [14]. The bulk synchronous parallel method, in which the server needs to wait for all work nodes to upload the current local models, performs global synchronization after each local model training iteration. For the asynchronous parallel method, each worker node is trained asynchronously and communicates with the parameter server. The stale synchronous parallel method only performs global synchronization when the iteration difference between fast and slow nodes reaches a delay threshold.

Metrics. We use three metrics to evaluate the models over the above-mentioned benchmarks: training time, training quality, and resource usage. The training time will be measured by the time spent per epoch, the training quality will be measured by the decrease of the loss function over time, and the computational resource utilization will be defined as the time spent on computation as a percentage of the total execution time, as shown in Eq. (14),

$$resource_{usage} = \frac{\sum_{i \subset workers} compute_{time_i}}{\sum_{i \subset workers} totall_{time_i}}. \tag{14}$$

Environments. The hardware environment used in this paper is a cluster of four servers, with one server as the parameter server and the other three servers as worker nodes. It has the following key components: 1) Parameter server: the CPU is an Intel Xeon processor (E7-4807) with 1.87 GHz, containing 12 physical cores in total; 2) Hyper-Threading: it has 24 logical cores, 32 GB of memory, and 256 GB of hard disk capacity; 3) Worker node: the CPU is AMD processor (Processor 6136) with 2.4 GHz. The nodes in the cluster are connected to each other via Gigabit Ethernet. In addition, a scenario with 3 and 6 clients is developed by using threads to simulate clients.

4.2 Experimental Results

Training Time

Tables 1 and 2 show the time required for different methods to achieve a given accuracy. We report the Prediction Synchronous Parallel method as the distributed machine learning communication method, the training time of the VGG-11 model on the CIFAR-10 dataset is reduced by up to 19.9%, and up to 55.8% reduction is achieved when training logistic regression on the MNIST dataset. This is because the Prediction Synchronous Method can predict the optimal synchronization time according to the history information, which can reduce the synchronization relay. So that, the method proposed in this paper is better suited for natural cluster environments where the performance varies in real-time.

Table 1. Training Time for VGG-11 model on CIFAR-10 using different methods with 75% accuracy

	Bulk synchronous parallel	Asynchronous parallel	Stale Synchronous Parallel	Predictive synchronous parallel
3 clients	4511 s	4230 s	4133 s	3756 s
6 clients	4225 s	3846 s	4033 s	3419 s

Table 2. Training Time for logistic regression on MNIST using different methods with 92% accuracy

	Bulk synchronous parallel	Asynchronous parallel	Stale Synchronous Parallel	Predictive synchronous parallel
3 clients	221 s	258	353 s	204 s
6 clients	208 s	231 s	445 s	197 s

Training Quality

According to Figs. 5 and 6, the method proposed in this paper has better convergence performance than other baselines. Although the asynchronous parallel method has a faster speedup, it excessively utilizes the limited fault tolerance of machine learning, resulting in inferior convergence performance compared to our method in this paper. Moreover, while ensuring model convergence, the Predictive Synchronous Parallel method proposed in this paper has better training speed than the bulk and stale synchronous parallel methods. Our method with the optimal synchronization time can reduce the synchronization delay in the bulk synchronous parallel method, solve the parameter stale problem in the asynchronous parallel method, and the unreasonable delay parameters in the stale synchronous parallel method. Therefore, regarding convergence performance, our method is superior to the other two methods, the final model converges, and the loss function of the Predicted Synchronous Parallel method is reduced by about 15% compared to the mainstream parametric communication method.

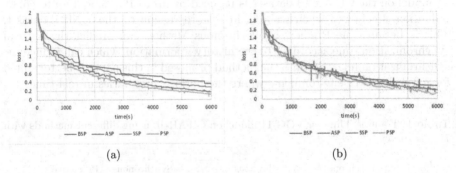

Fig. 5. Convergence performance of different methods trained with VGG-11 on CIFAR-10

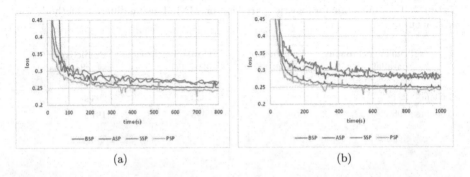

Fig. 6. Convergence performance of different methods trained with logistic regression on MNIST

Resource Usage

In Figs. 7 and 8, the utilization of network bandwidth is used as a metric to measure the utilization of computational resources. This is because computational tasks require data transmission and communication between different nodes. Our method exhibits a computational resource utilization rate second only to asynchronous parallel methods. This is because our method has lower synchronization latency compared to batch synchronous parallel methods and outdated synchronous parallel methods. In contrast, asynchronous parallel methods do not require global synchronization, resulting in higher computational resource utilization. Compared to mainstream parameter communication methods, our method improves computational resource utilization by 31%. As the number of worker nodes increases, the computational resource utilization rates of batch synchronous parallel methods, asynchronous parallel methods, sluggish synchronous parallel methods, and our method all exhibit varying degrees of decline. This is due to the increased number of worker nodes communicating with the parameter server in the cluster network, leading to network congestion. More resources are allocated to model transmission between worker nodes and the parameter server, ultimately resulting in a decrease in cluster computational resource utilization.

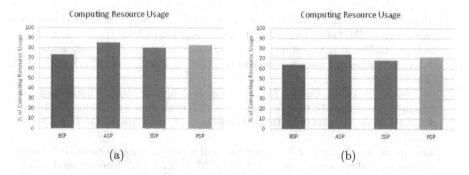

Fig. 7. Computational resource utilization of different models trained with CIFAR-10 using VGG-11 under three and six threads

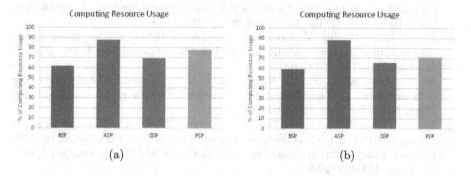

Fig. 8. Computational resource utilization of different models trained with MNIST

5 Summary

In this paper, we propose a synchronous parallel method with parameters communication prediction for distributed machine learning to solve the degraded resource utilization problem caused by the constant delay thresholds in the stale synchronous parallel method. It predicts the next round of training based on the previous round of training of each node in the cluster to select the optimal synchronization timing, thus reducing the synchronization waiting time. Moreover, the fast nodes in this method continue to train locally with local datasets instead of stopping training while waiting synchronously, which further increases the computational resource utilization of the cluster. The experiments show that the method proposed in this paper has good improvements in training time, training quality, and resource usage.

Acknowledgment. I would like to express my gratitude to all those who helped me during the writing of this work. This work is supported by the Key Technology Research and Development Program of China under Grant No. 2022YFB2901200.

References

1. Ahmad, F., et al.: A deep learning architecture for psychometric natural language processing. ACM Trans. Inf. Syst. (TOIS) **38**(1), 1–29 (2020)
2. Dabare, R., Wong, K.W., Shiratuddin, M.F., Koutsakis, P.: A fuzzy data augmentation technique to improve regularisation. Int. J. Intell. Syst. **37**(8), 4561–4585 (2022)
3. Liu, W.-X., Jinjie, L., Cai, J., Zhu, Y., Ling, S., Chen, Q.: DRL-PLink: deep reinforcement learning with private link approach for mix-flow scheduling in software-defined data-center networks. IEEE Trans. Netw. Serv. Manage. **19**(2), 1049–1064 (2021)
4. Kriman, S., et al.: QuartzNet: deep automatic speech recognition with 1d time-channel separable convolutions. In: ICASSP 2020–2020 IEEE International Conference on Acoustics, Speech and Signal Processing (ICASSP), pp. 6124–6128. IEEE (2020)
5. Wang, Y., Wang, K., Huang, H., Miyazaki, T., Guo, S.: Traffic and computation co-offloading with reinforcement learning in fog computing for industrial applications. IEEE Trans. Industr. Inf. **15**(2), 976–986 (2018)
6. Xu, C., Wang, K., Sun, Y., Guo, S., Zomaya, A.Y.: Redundancy avoidance for big data in data centers: a conventional neural network approach. IEEE Trans. Netw. Sci. Eng. **7**(1), 104–114 (2018)
7. Xu, C., Wang, K., Li, P., Xia, R., Guo, S., Guo, M.: Renewable energy-aware big data analytics in geo-distributed data centers with reinforcement learning. IEEE Trans. Netw. Sci. Eng. **7**(1), 205–215 (2018)
8. Jiang, Y., Zhu, Y., Lan, C., Yi, B., Cui, Y., Guo, C.: A unified architecture for accelerating distributed DNN training in heterogeneous GPU/CPU clusters. In: 14th USENIX Symposium on Operating Systems Design and Implementation (OSDI 2020), pp. 463–479 (2020)
9. Liang, X., et al.: Accelerating local SGD for non-IID data using variance reduction. Front. Comp. Sci. **17**(2), 172311 (2023)

10. Lin, G., et al.: Understanding adaptive gradient clipping in DP-SGD, empirically. Int. J. Intell. Syst. **37**(11), 9674–9700 (2022)
11. Gerbessiotis, A.V., Valiant, L.G.: Direct bulk-synchronous parallel algorithms. J. Parallel Distrib. Comput. **22**(2), 251–267 (1994)
12. Wang, Z., et al.: FSP: towards flexible synchronous parallel frameworks for distributed machine learning. IEEE Trans. Parallel Distrib. Syst. **34**(2), 687–703 (2022)
13. Dean, J., et al.: Large scale distributed deep networks. In: Advances in Neural Information Processing Systems, vol. 25 (2012)
14. Ho, Q., et al.: More effective distributed ml via a stale synchronous parallel parameter server. In: Advances in Neural Information Processing Systems, vol. 26 (2013)
15. Moritz, P., et al.: Ray: a distributed framework for emerging AI applications. In: 13th USENIX Symposium on Operating Systems Design and Implementation (OSDI 2018), pp. 561–577 (2018)
16. Zaharia, M., et al.: Resilient distributed datasets: a fault-tolerant abstraction for in-memory cluster computing. In: 9th USENIX Symposium on Networked Systems Design and Implementation (NSDI 2012), pp. 15–28 (2012)
17. Spark MLlib (2020). http://spark.apache.org/mllib/. Accessed Apr 2020
18. Wang, H., Guo, S., Li, R.: OSP: overlapping computation and communication in parameter server for fast machine learning. In: Proceedings of the 48th International Conference on Parallel Processing, pp. 1–10 (2019)
19. Wang, H., Zhihao, Q., Guo, S., Wang, N., Li, R., Zhuang, W.: LOSP: overlap synchronization parallel with local compensation for fast distributed training. IEEE J. Sel. Areas Commun. **39**(8), 2541–2557 (2021)
20. Abadi, M., et al.: TensorFlow: a system for large-scale machine learning. In: 12th USENIX Symposium on Operating Systems Design and Implementation (OSDI 2016), pp. 265–283 (2016)
21. Xing, E.P., et al.: Petuum: a new platform for distributed machine learning on big data. In: Proceedings of the 21th ACM SIGKDD International Conference on Knowledge Discovery and Data Mining, pp. 1335–1344 (2015)
22. Wei, J., et al.: Managed communication and consistency for fast data-parallel iterative analytics. In: Proceedings of the Sixth ACM Symposium on Cloud Computing, pp. 381–394 (2015)
23. Khalil, H.: Nonlinear Systems, 3rd edn. Pearson, Upper Saddle River (2001)
24. Abouelnaga, Y., Ali, O.S., Rady, H., Moustafa, M.: CIFAR-10: KNN-based ensemble of classifiers. In: 2016 International Conference on Computational Science and Computational Intelligence (CSCI), pp. 1192–1195. IEEE (2016)
25. MNIST (2020). http://yann.lecun.com/exdb/mnist. Accessed June 2020

Author Index

A

Angelis, Ioannis I-18
Antonopoulos, Christos I-3

B

Besimi, Adrian III-154
Bi, Zhongqin III-134
Blasi, Maximilian III-229

C

Cang, Li Shan II-265
Cao, Bin II-437
Cao, Cong II-205
Cao, Dun III-79
Cao, Wenwen II-414
Cao, Ya-Nan II-321
Chang, Jiayu II-131
Chen, Hui II-115
Chen, Juan II-173, II-375, III-100
Chen, Kaiwei II-79
Chen, Liang II-242, II-392
Chen, Mingcai II-20
Chen, Peng II-173, II-375, III-100, III-118
Chen, Shizhan II-281
Christopoulou, Eleni I-18
Cui, Bo I-207
Cui, Jiahe III-23
Cui, Jie II-414

D

Dagiuklas, Tasos III-41
Deng, Shaojiang II-495
Di, Qianhui II-514
Ding, Weilong III-329
Ding, Xu I-187, I-365, I-385
Ding, Yong I-167, I-243, II-301, II-321
Du, Miao I-54
Duan, Liang II-458
Duan, Yutang III-134

F

Faliagka, Evanthia I-3
Fan, Guodong II-281
Fan, Jing II-437
Fan, Yuqi I-187
Fan, Zhicheng II-20
Fang, Cheng I-54
Feng, Beibei II-341
Feng, Lin III-308
Feng, Shilong I-385, III-273
Feng, Xiangyang III-291
Feng, Zhiyong II-281, III-208
Fichtner, Myriel III-249
Fu, Jianhui II-205

G

Gan, Yanglan III-291
Gao, Chongming III-191
Gao, Jinyong III-365
Gao, Min III-191, III-365
Guo, Linxin III-191
Guo, Meng II-474
Guo, Ming II-20
Guo, Zhenwei II-321

H

Han, Dingkang III-347
Han, Jianghong III-308
Hao, Junfeng III-100
He, Hongshun II-474
He, Hongxia II-173, II-375
He, Yunxiang III-23
Henrich, Dominik III-249
Hu, Bowen II-96
Hu, Haize I-284, I-303, I-343
Hu, Qinglei III-23
Hu, Zekun I-128
Huang, Jie I-225
Huang, Jihai III-329
Huang, Kaizhu III-3
Huang, Xingru II-96

Huang, Yakun   II-474
Huang, Yi   III-3

I

Idoje, Godwin   III-41
Iqbal, Muddesar   II-265, III-41

J

Jablonski, Stefan   III-249
Jelić, Slobodan   I-38
Ji, Rui   I-385, III-273
Jian, Wenxin   I-93
Jiang, Qinkai   II-437
Jiang, Xinghong   I-93
Jiang, Yujie   III-173
Jiao, Liang   III-347
Jin, Yi   I-265
Jin, Zhifeng   I-187
Ju, Zixuan   I-225

K

Keramidas, Giorgos   I-3
Knežević, Milica   I-38
Kraft, Robin   III-229
Kuang, Li   I-265, II-131

L

Lei, Nanfang   III-79
Li, Baoke   II-205
Li, Bing   I-54
Li, Dongyu   III-23
Li, Fan   I-77
Li, Jiaxin   II-39
Li, Min   II-281
Li, Mingchu   I-421, II-3
Li, Peihao   I-225
Li, Peisong   III-3
Li, Qi   I-323
Li, Shuai   I-421, II-3
Li, Wenwei   II-474
Li, Xi   II-173, II-375
Li, Xiang   II-341
Li, Yang   II-96, II-414, II-474
Li, Yantao   II-495
Li, Yin   I-77, III-118
Li, Yixuan   II-96
Li, Youhuizi   II-514
Li, Yu   II-514
Li, Zhehao   I-365, III-273

Liang, Hai   I-167, I-243, II-321
Liang, Qingmi   I-265
Liang, Tian   II-131
Liang, Tingting   II-514
Liang, Weiyou   I-167
Liao, Jie   II-392
Liu, Donghua   III-208
Liu, Feng   I-365
Liu, Jianxun   I-284, I-303, I-323, I-343
Liu, Jinyuan   I-243
Liu, Lingmeng   II-79
Liu, Peiyu   II-39
Liu, Qingyun   III-347
Liu, Ruiqi   III-365
Liu, Xiangzheng   I-284
Liu, Xu   I-207
Liu, Yanbing   II-205
Liu, Yi   I-284
Liu, Yilin   II-301
Liu, Yumeng   II-223
Long, Teng   I-303
Lu, Tong   II-458
Luo, Huaxiu   II-495
Lyu, Zengwei   III-308

M

Ma, Jingrun   II-341
Ma, Yong   I-77, I-93, II-79
Mei, Tianyu   I-207
Mihaljević, Miodrag J.   I-38
Mo, Dikai   III-347

N

Nanos, Nikolaos   I-3
Ni, Mingjian   II-96
Niu, Xianhua   III-100

O

Oikonomou, Konstantinos   I-18
Ouyang, Zhaobin   III-118
Ouyang, Zhenchao   III-23

P

Peng, Chao   III-208
Peng, Qinglan   I-77, II-79, III-118
Peng, Xincai   II-265
Peng, Yang   I-225
Pryss, Rüdiger   III-229

Q

Qi, Chufeng   I-149
Qi, Wanying   I-421, II-3
Qi, Zhiwei   II-458
Qian, Shuwei   II-20
Qiao, Xiuquan   II-474
Qin, Huafeng   II-495
Qiu, Houming   II-357

R

Reichert, Manfred   III-229
Ren, YongJian   III-59
Riedelbauch, Dominik   III-249

S

Schickler, Marc   III-229
Selimi, Mennan   III-154
Ševerdija, Domagoj   I-38
Shan, Meijing   III-134
Shao, Shiyun   II-79
Sheng, Yu   I-265
Sherratt, Robert Simon   III-79
Shi, Lei   I-187, I-365, I-385, III-273
Shi, Yukun   III-385
Shkurti, Lamir   III-154
Shu, Xinyue   I-111
Song, Qihong   I-343
Song, Weijian   II-173, II-375
Song, Yi   II-115
Song, Yulun   II-96
Spournias, Alexandros   I-3
Su, Jiajun   II-79
Su, Majing   II-205
Sucker, Sascha   III-249
Sun, Haifeng   I-403
Sun, Maoxiang   III-329
Sun, Yong   III-347

T

Tchernykh, Andrei   III-3
Todorović, Milan   I-38
Tsipis, Athanasios   I-18
Tu, Jiaxue   I-77

V

Voros, Nikolaos   I-3

W

Wan, Jian   II-151
Wan, Zihang   II-223

Wang, Bin   II-39
Wang, Bo   II-115
Wang, Chongjun   II-20
Wang, Chunyu   II-189
Wang, Fan   II-39
Wang, Gongju   II-96
Wang, Hongan   II-223
Wang, Huiyong   I-167, II-301
Wang, Jiaxing   II-437
Wang, Jin   III-79
Wang, Peng   II-57
Wang, Pengwei   I-128
Wang, Quanda   II-96
Wang, Shiqi   III-191
Wang, Shunli   II-189
Wang, Xi   II-341
Wang, Xiaowen   I-225
Wang, Xin   III-59
Wang, Xinheng   III-3
Wang, Xu   III-118
Wang, Yang   III-100
Wang, Yongjie   II-57
Wang, Yujue   I-167, I-243, II-301, II-321
Wei, Zhen   III-273
Wei, Zhenchun   III-308
Wen, Baodong   I-243
Wu, Hongyue   II-281
Wu, Quanwang   I-111
Wu, Ruoting   II-242, II-392
Wu, Shouyi   II-474
Wu, Yujiang   III-365

X

Xi, Qinghui   II-173, II-375
Xia, Yunni   I-77, I-93, II-79, II-375, III-100, III-118
Xiao, Wang   III-208
Xiao, Wanzhi   II-131
Xiao, Ziren   III-3
Xie, Qi   I-265
Xie, Qilin   I-93
Xie, Yibin   I-365
Xing, Weiwei   I-149
Xiong, Jiasi   III-79
Xiong, Xinli   II-57
Xu, Chaonong   III-173
Xu, Fuyong   II-39
Xu, Jie   II-151
Xu, Juan   I-385
Xu, Junyi   III-308

Xu, Lei III-100
Xu, Peiran III-385
Xu, Xiaolin II-341
Xue, Meiting III-385
Xue, Xiao II-281, III-208

Y

Yan, Cairong III-291
Yan, Long II-96
Yan, Xiangpei III-208
Yang, Changsong I-167, I-243, II-301,
    II-321
Yang, Ke II-115
Yang, Peng I-54
Yang, Yuling II-205
Yao, Qian II-57
Yao, Xinwei I-149
Yi, Chen II-301
Yi, Meng I-54
Yin, Yuyu II-514
Yu, Qi III-329
Yuan, Fangfang II-205
Yuan, Xiaohui III-308
Yue, Kun II-458
Yue, Lupeng III-385

Z

Zang, Tianning II-341
Zeng, Jie III-365
Zeng, Kaisheng III-385
Zeng, Yan III-59

Zeng, Yanguo III-385
Zhan, Baotong I-385
Zhang, Beibei III-59
Zhang, Changjie III-23
Zhang, Daqing I-403
Zhang, Jia III-365
Zhang, Jilin III-59, III-385
Zhang, Jun I-187, II-189
Zhang, Lihua II-189
Zhang, Lu II-281
Zhang, Qingliang I-111
Zhang, Qingyang II-414
Zhang, Shuai II-265
Zhang, Weina III-134
Zhang, Xiangping I-303, I-323
Zhang, Xin II-151
Zhang, Yiwei III-291
Zhang, Yuanqing II-514
Zhang, Yuedong III-347
Zhang, Yuxin II-242, II-392
Zhang, Zhaohui I-128
Zhao, Han II-79
Zhao, Peihai I-128
Zhao, Yijing II-223
Zheng, Haibin I-243
Zheng, Hui III-59
Zhong, Hong II-414
Zhou, Mingyao III-59
Zhou, Sirui I-225
Zhu, Dongge I-77
Zhu, Kun II-357
Zhu, Yujia III-347

Printed in the United States
by Baker & Taylor Publisher Services